FROMMER'S

BUDGET TRAVEL GUIDE

IRELAND '92-'93
ON $40 A DAY

by Susan Poole

PRENTICE HALL TRAVEL

NEW YORK • LONDON • TORONTO • SYDNEY • TOKYO • SINGAPORE

FROMMER BOOKS

Published by Prentice Hall Travel
A division of Simon & Schuster Inc.
15 Columbus Circle
New York, NY 10023

ISBN 0-13-335233-1
ISSN 0276-9026

Design by Robert Bull Design
Maps by Geografix Inc.

PRENTICE
HALL
PRESS

Manufactured in the United States of America

FROMMER'S IRELAND '92–'93 ON $40 A DAY
Editor-in-Chief: Marilyn Wood
Senior Editors: Judith de Rubini, Amit Shah
Editors: Alice Fellows, Paige Hughes, Ted Stavrou, Lisa Renaud
Assistant Editors: Sara Hinsey, Peter Katucki
Contributing Editor: Lara Himes
Managing Editor: Leanne Coupe

CONTENTS

LIST OF MAPS

INVITATION TO THE READERS

In researching this book, I have come across many wonderful establishments, the best of which I have included here. I am sure that many of you will also come across appealing hotels, inns, restaurants, guesthouses, shops, and attractions. Please don't keep them to yourself. Share your experiences, especially if you want to comment on places that have been included in this edition that have changed for the worse. You can address your letters to:

Susan Poole
c/o Prentice Hall Travel
15 Columbus Circle
New York, NY 10023

A DISCLAIMER

Readers are advised that prices fluctuate in the course of time and travel information changes under the impact of the varied and volatile factors that affect the travel industry. Neither the author nor the publisher can be held responsible for the experiences of readers while traveling. Readers are invited to write to the publisher with ideas, comments, and suggestions for future editions.

SAFETY ADVISORY

Whenever you're traveling in an unfamiliar city or country, stay alert. Be aware of your immediate surroundings. Wear a moneybelt and keep a close eye on your possessions. Be particularly careful with cameras, purses, and wallets, all favorite targets of thieves and pickpockets.

TELEPHONE CHANGE

All telephone numbers in Ireland were in process of change at presstime. Dial 190 or 191 in Ireland if you have trouble reaching any of the telephone numbers in this book.

CHAPTER 1
GETTING TO KNOW IRELAND

You know about Ireland, of course—it's that lovely isle created when "a little bit of heaven dropped from out the sky one day." Skeptical? Well, look around for the most hard-nosed skeptic you know who's been to Ireland and then get set to listen to hours of rapturous memories!

Ireland has that effect on people. For me, it began back in 1973 when I first encountered the incredible beauty of this small country's landscape and learned with amazement that the magnificent sum of $2.40 would make me an instant member of warm Irish families who were eager to share their fireside, friends, favorite pub, innumerable cups of tea, and the most enormous breakfasts I'd ever seen. I stayed 3 weeks that year, and haven't missed going back for a part of every year since. That's been possible for me—a confirmed budget traveler—because Ireland is still affordable. Prices have risen there as fast as they have everywhere else in the world, but Ireland is still one of the best travel buys I've come across.

But there's much more to it than that. There are some things that would be cheap at any price, and Ireland has more than its fair share of those commodities. Each visit has brought fresh discoveries and new friends. There are always new tales to bring home, more of the witty one-liners that spring so naturally to Irish lips, more memories of nights of unplanned music and song that somehow just happened, still more miles of unbelievably beautiful coastline or mountains or rolling green fields suddenly unfolding around corners I'd not turned before, new Irish names to add to my Christmas list. Perhaps even more important is the glow I bring back each year after spending a little time with people who have managed to hold on to basic values that in other parts of the world these days seem as elusive as a dream.

It's a formidable task to write about Ireland and the Irish. Back in 1842, William Makepeace Thackeray wrote an English friend: "I am beginning to find out now that a man ought to be forty years in this country instead of three months, and then he wouldn't be able to write about it!" Far be it from me even to attempt to outdo Thackeray—I can only try to tell you about the Ireland I have discovered in several years of exhaustive research, pass along the finds of other travelers who have been kind enough to write, and tell you how it's not only possible to visit Ireland on our $40 a day—it's the best way to go!

Before diving into a detailed discussion of what you can expect to find in Ireland, let's talk about what you won't find. First of all, you won't find the stereotyped "stage Irish" of so many comedy skits. Neither will you find a land peopled entirely by saints and scholars (although there's a supply of both). Nor a land ravaged by violence, as the news media would sometimes lead you to believe—sure, it does exist, but it doesn't pervade the country. And as the Irish are the first to point out, you won't find a telephone system that works with anything like the efficiency you're used to at home. This can drive you a little dotty if you're in a hurry, but can also lead to some pretty interesting telephone conversations with operators while you both wait to get your call through. One thing more: You won't find a people out to take you for every cent in your holiday purse—in my experience, the phrase "what the traffic will bear" just doesn't exist in Ireland.

Today, Ireland is a land still covered with small farms in unspoiled countryside, although it is shifting away from an economy wholly dependent on agriculture as more high-tech industries move in. It's a land of cities whose antiquities live quite comfortably, elbow-to-elbow, with modern luxury hotels and growing number of sophisticated cabarets and nightclubs. It's a land filled with social centers that go by the name of pubs. Whose Tidy Towns competition each year rates even the tiniest hamlet on its success—or lack of it—in the ongoing battle against litter. Where there's never sweltering heat or bone-chilling cold, and a rainy day really *is* a soft day.

Today's Ireland will take over your heart the minute you land and send you away looking back over your shoulder with a head full of plans to come right back.

It's only when you see the delicate play of light and shade on the mountains while driving from Glengarriff in County Cork to Kenmare in County Kerry, or ride through the lush greenness of County Waterford byways, or drink in the mystical moonscape of County Clare's Burren, or stand on the rocky Dingle Peninsula shore at Ventry where legend says the King of the World went down to defeat at the hands of Fionn MacCumhaill ("Finn MacCool") and his Fianna warrior band—it's only then that the face of Ireland comes truly alive. Around every bend, that luminous, ever-changing landscape cries out for the poet, and many a poet has answered its call.

An Irish friend once said to me, "Whenever I am with visitors, I always wish there were some way to show them all the nooks and crannies of Ireland as well as the highlights tourists usually see." What this book will do is point you to those highlights you just must not miss and throw in a nook or cranny wherever I have found one. It's a safe bet, however, that you'll come home with fond memories of more than a few special places you've found on your own—it's the unexpected that will charm you most.

1. GEOGRAPHY, HISTORY & POLITICS

GEOGRAPHY

Covering 32,524 square miles, Ireland stretches out 302 miles at its longest and 189 miles at its widest points. It's the "last parish before America," the most westerly island of Europe, and its bowl-shaped contours are formed by a great limestone plain surrounded by mountains (Kerry's Carrantuohill is the highest at 3,414 feet).

Its coastline is so indented by jagged peninsulas that the sea is never more than 70

IMPRESSIONS

There is no magic like that of Ireland.
There are no skies like Irish skies.
There is no air like Irish air . . .
The Irish climate will make the stiffest
and slowest mind flexible for life.
—GEORGE BERNARD SHAW

miles distant. That glorious coastline measures more than 3,000 miles and encircles 9,000 miles of meandering rivers (the 230-mile Shannon is the longest) and some 800 lakes, the largest of which is Lough Neagh (153 square miles).

THE REGIONS & COUNTIES

THE FOUR PROVINCES   From its early history, Ireland's 32 counties have been divided into four provinces (those "Four Green Fields" of song and story).

Ulster: To the north, Ulster is now divided into the six counties that form Northern Ireland (Derry, Antrim, Armagh, Down, Fermanagh, and Tyrone) and three that lie in the Republic (Donegal, Monaghan, and Cavan).
Leinster: In the east, Leinster is composed of the 12 counties of Dublin, Wicklow, Wexford, Kilkenny, Carlow, Kildare, Laois, Offaly, Westmeath, Longford, Meath, and Louth.
Munster: In the south, Munster consists of Counties Waterford, Cork, Kerry, Limerick, Clare, and Tipperary.
Connaught: This province, of Cromwell's slanderous "To hell or . . ." remark, is made up of Counties Roscommon, Leitrim, Sligo, Galway, and Mayo.

THE SIGHTSEEING REGIONS   The provinces, in turn, divide rather naturally into eight sightseeing regions, and you will find most Irish Tourist Board information and literature separate the counties into the following regional patterns:

East: Counties Dublin, Wicklow Louth, Kildare, and Meath.
Southeast: Counties Wexford, Waterford, Kilkenny, Carlow, and South Tipperary.
South and Southwest: Counties Cork and Kerry.
Shannonside: Counties Limerick, Clare, and North Tipperary.
West: Counties Galway and Mayo.
Northwest: Counties Sligo, Donegal, Leitrim, Cavan, and Monaghan.
Midlands: Counties Laois, Longford, Offaly, Roscommon, and Westmeath.
Northern Ireland: Counties Antrim, Armagh, Down, Fermanagh, Londonderry, and Tyrone.

FLORA & FAUNA

Back in Neolithic times large areas of the oak, ash, and rowan forests that covered much of Ireland's central limestone plain were cleared for cultivation or grazing, and as a result, the vast majority of trees today are imports. One of the positive things the English landowners of the past few centuries brought across the Irish Sea was a passion for planting exotic trees and gardens, which went a long way toward the re-greening of the countryside. Since the beginning of this century, reforestation efforts have concentrated on large plantings of conifers and other evergreens, many in more than 400 national forests and other wooded areas open to the public. In addition to the verdant forest areas, you'll find the lovely heathers of the bogs and the unique wildflower population of County Clare's Burren.

One of the everlasting joys of Ireland's environment for me, personally, is that I can walk through the woodlands, bogs, or Burren without watching for snakes with every step. The experts say that's because the country was cut off from mainland Europe during the retreat of the Ice Age before the serpents could make their way across, but any true Irishman will insist that the good St. Patrick is solely responsible for this blessing. As for other fauna, no life-threatening species roam the countryside, although fossils of several gigantic examples of same have been unearthed by archeologists. The quite harmless fox, hare, and stoat are about all you're likely to find around today.

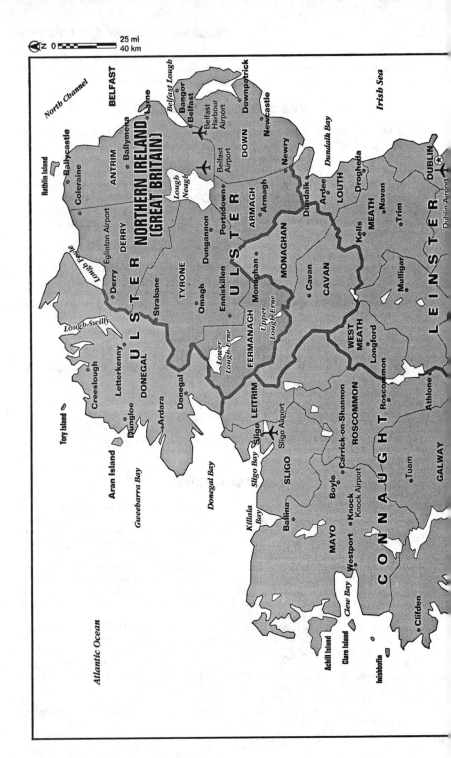

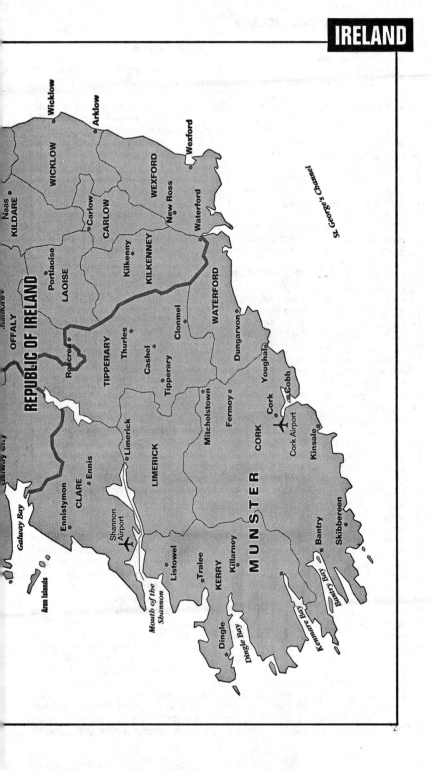

HISTORY

The landscape of Ireland is haunted by history; ghosts lurk along every road, around every bend. Stone Age Irish move eerily behind the mists of prehistory that cloak dolmens left in their wake. Visit the reconstructed crannog at Crag-gaunowen in County Clare and Bronze Age men and women almost materialize before your eyes. Iron Age forts make a quiet day ring with the sounds, just beyond your ears, of those who sheltered there. Great monastic crosses and ruined abbeys accent the strong influence of early Christians, while round towers tell of dangers faced from Viking raiders. Listen carefully in Dublin and Waterford and you may hear the echoing footsteps of Viking founders. Norman spirits inhabit ruined castles that squat along riverbanks, atop lofty cliffs, and in lonely fields. The multifaceted history that shaped the fascinating Irish char-acter we know today travels with you wherever you go.

IN THE BEGINNING Ireland took on its present shape when the world's last Ice Age retreated and left the country with multitudes of scooped-out lakes and tumbled moun-tains plus a land bridge that connected it to Great Britain. Sometime around 6000 B.C., Stone Age settlers crossed over that land bridge to Ireland. We don't know where they originally came from, only that they clustered around the seashore and along inland riverbanks, fashioning crude flint tools, and surviving by fishing and hunting.

Long after that land link to Britain disappeared and Ireland had become an island—about 2000 B.C.—new-comers brought with them cows and other domesticated animals. They also brought skills needed for clearing the land and planting crops, thus beginning Ireland's long tradition of farming and cattle raising. It was this Neolithic race who cremated their dead and created communal burial chambers beneath stone cairns or inside tunnel-filled earthen mounds. Newgrange, in County Meath, a full acre in size, is the best known of the surviving tumuli and the one most of us visit to give a tip of the hat to those long-ago Irish.

THE METAL WORKERS While farmers in Ireland were tending their fields, European tribes were beginning to work with metals, and their search for copper and gold eventually brought them to Ireland, with its rich deposits of both metals, around 3000 B.C. The Bronze Age had begun, and artisans, merchants, and peddlers traveled to this remote island. Those who came during this period were probably of Mediterranean origin, a short, dark people that the Romans knew as Iberni. They were called the Uib-Ernai in Ireland, where they were believed to be descendants of the fertility goddess Eire, whose name means "noble." The island country was soon known by that name, and today it is the oldest existing national name in the world.

As beautifully crafted as are the metal objects created by these early Irish settlers, they fade in significance when compared to the most important legacy they left us: a wealth of megalithic stone structures that still stand in solid, silent testimony to incredible scientific knowledge and engineering skill.

AND THEN CAME THE CELTS   Tall, fair-skinned, and red-haired, the Celts were fierce, warlike people who roamed the face of Europe before migrating to Ireland in the 4th century B.C. Their iron weapons and military prowess soon established them—and their language—as dominant in the land.

Some 100 tribes spread across the country, setting up small kingdoms under petty lords or chieftains, who in turn paid allegiance (at least in theory) to regional kings. In time a High King of Ireland sat at Tara. The five regional kingdoms were Ulster, Munster, Leinster, Meath, and Connaught, which became the four provinces of Ireland as we know it when the Kingdom of Meath merged with Leinster.

The countryside rang with the sounds of battle as petty king fought petty king, regional kings embarked on expansionary expeditions, and the High King of the moment never sat easy on his honorary throne. Peasants and bondsmen toiled for whichever chieftain was in power, and the free farmer anted up both tribute and loyalty, while craftily throwing up sturdy earthen ring forts (also called a "rath" or "lis") as protection against roaming marauders. Many of today's town names reflect their locations; for example, Lismore, in County Waterford, takes its name from just such a large lis on its outskirts.

Unity existed, if at all, in the strong bonds of common culture and tradition, held together by the common language. Petty kingdoms might be at war, but all paid strict obedience to the traditional laws of the Brehons (lawyers), who traveled freely from one kingdom to another. Learned men in all professions were honored throughout the land and established schools that set intricate graded scales of achievement. Traveling bards were much revered and richly rewarded, not only for their recitations of long, epic poems of past heroic deeds but also for new poems glorifying the exploits of whatever chieftain offered hospitality at the moment. Only slightly less homage was paid to the skilled artists and craftsmen who labored for each chieftain and often shared his table. All tribes regarded the Druids, who were in charge of the most sacred ceremonies, as wise men. It was this strange mixture of barbarous warring and highly developed culture that greeted the arrival of Christianity in the 5th century A.D.

The foregoing is the way archeologists and historians think Ireland evolved, based on their best research, carbon datings of artifacts, and educated guesses. For another version of the same story, see "Myth and Folklore" in Section 4 of this chapter.

SAINTS & SCHOLARS   In the mid-5th century A.D. a conquest of quite another nature took place. St. Patrick came to Ireland, traveled the land, and preached Christianity (see "Religion" in Section 4 below).

Irish ruler after Irish ruler listened to the missionary and adopted the new religion, although none went so far as to abandon such distinctly Celtic pastimes as intra-kingdom

DATELINE

of the Boyne begins a century of Catholic oppression under the Penal Laws.

- **1791**   United Irishmen founded by Wolfe Tone.
- **1798**   Insurrection led by Tone, Robert Emmet, and others squelched by English forces.
- **1800**   Act of Union hands direct rulership of Ireland to London Parliament.
- **1829**   Daniel O'Connell achieves Catholic Emancipation.
- **1846**   Potato famine causes widespread starvation; more than one million Irish emigrate.
- **1879**   Land League founded by Michael Davit to fight landlords and secure tenant landownership.
- **1905–08**   Sinn Fein political party evolves with Irish independence its primary goal.
- **1912**   Home Rule goes into effect, prompting formation of Ulster Volunteers by loyalists and the Irish Republican Army as a military adjunct of Sinn Fein.
- **1916**   The Easter Sunday uprising, led by Patrick Pearse, James Connolly, and others; their execution unites Irish public opinion be- *(continues)*

warfare and riotous revelry within the court. In homage to their new God (or maybe in penance for their more un-Christian practices?), kings and other large landowners granted lavish gifts of precious metals and land on which to build churches and monasteries that furthered St. Patrick's work.

With the coming of Christianity, Celtic culture took a giant step forward. Already deeply respectful of learning, hundreds of Irish entered the cloistered life. Within great monasteries, all the learning of the time was taught, both Celtic and Roman, and here philosophy, theology, and the known sciences were preserved as Europe entered its culturally deprived Dark Ages. Thousands of students fled the continent to Ireland during those centuries. Until the end of the 8th century, Ireland's Golden Age was the brightest beacon in the Western world.

Eventually, these monks and scholars carried this learning back to the cathedrals and royal courts of Europe, and helped establish the great universities.

VIKING INVADERS Viking raiders, Ireland's first invaders, came by sea in A.D. 795 to launch fierce, lightning-fast strikes along the coastline. Their superior mail battle dress and heavy arms made easy victims of even the battle-loving Irish, and as their raids moved farther and farther inland, the rich monastic settlements found an answer to the danger in building tall, round towers with one entrance high above the ground; there they stored their most precious treasures, pulling up long ladders to make access impossible. (I have, incidentally, run across more than one seanachie whose story is that Finn MacCool built the first of these and the doorway was simply put at his natural entry-level.)

As the years went by, raiders turned into settlers, establishing the first of a string of coastal cities—Dublin in 841, followed by Wexford, Waterford, Cork, and Limerick. Vestiges of city walls, gates, and fortifications remain to this day. Former raiders turned to trading and—in a pattern to be followed by subsequent "conquerors"—they were soon intermarrying with natives and becoming as Irish as the Irish themselves.

Not a few Irish chieftains, after disastrous defeats, began to take note of successful Viking battle methods and turn them back against the victors. But it wasn't until 1014 that Brian Boru, High King of Ireland at the time, engaged his enemies at Clontarf, just outside Dublin, and won a decisive victory. So intermixed had the two races become by that time that while a large part of the Viking forces consisted of "Irish" allies, Brian Boru's loyal "Norse" warriors were among the most valiant on the field!

THE NORMANS MOVE IN Brian Boru's death was followed by a century and a half of kingly tug-of-war to establish one central authority figure. It was one of those ambitious combatants who took the first step on Ireland's long path of involvement with the British. Dermot Mac-Murrough, King of Leinster, made the fatal mistake of stealing the beautiful wife of O'Rourke, the King of Breffni, who promptly stirred up Leinster's minor chieftains and hounded MacMurrough out of Leinster.

MacMurrough crossed the Irish Sea to Britain, which had been under the rule of Norman conquerors for a little over a century, and persuaded King Henry II to sponsor a volunteer army to help win back Dermot's lost throne. It landed in Waterford in 1169 under the command of the Earl of Pembroke, popularly known as Strongbow. By marrying MacMurrough's daughter in Reginald's Tower, the wily Norman became King of Leinster when his father-in-law died the very next year.

DATELINE

both the Republic and Northern Ireland to join with the other 11 EC members in creating the Single European Market in 1992.

Strongbow's military prowess quickly brought most of Leinster and Munster under his domination. He defeated Rory O'Connor, the last High King of Ireland, and appeared to be well on his way to achieving power to rival that of King Henry II.

Henry responded to this threat by hurrying to Ireland with a document from the pope giving him feudal lordship over all of Ireland, with the undisputed right to distribute all its lands to such nobles as professed loyalty to him. Armed with papal authority and masquerading as a religious reformer, Henry was able to win the support of most of the Irish bishops, and many Irish kings who, anxious to retain their territories even if it meant fealty to an English king, came to Dublin to pay obeisance. Still, many Normans did secure lands, acquiring title to more than half the country, but like the Vikings before them, they intermarried and were assimilated into the Irish culture to such an extent that laws were passed in Parliament banning their use of Irish dress, manners, and the native language.

This feudal relationship, though, flew squarely in the face of long-established Irish law—a fact that kept Anglo-Norman and Irish grumbling at each other for 350 years. The Irish chieftains and kings who refused to recognize English rights to their lands were never able to present a united front to oppose English claims, but the incessant skirmishing and fighting did eventually pen the English Crown forces into a heavily fortified area around Dublin known as "the Pale" and in a few other garrison towns around the country. Had a religious dimension not been thrown into the Irish stew, the Irish might eventually have wrested control of their ancient land from the English rulers, but King Henry VIII and the Reformation changed all that in the 16th century.

AN ENGLISH "KING OF IRELAND" & THE FLIGHT OF THE EARLS

Breaking with Rome, Henry VIII in 1541 proclaimed himself King of Ireland by right of conquest rather than by papal decree, dubbed all opposition "open rebellion," and set about driving rebel leaders from their lands, so that he might grant the properties to his loyal followers, be they English or Irish.

By the time Elizabeth became queen, the Reformation was firmly entrenched in England and the staunchly Catholic Irish found themselves fighting for their religion with even more fervor than they had fought for their lands. The great chieftains led uprising after uprising and in 1601 appealed to Spain for help to make a decisive stand at Kinsale, in County Cork. The Spanish arrived and joined Irish forces to occupy the town, which was quickly surrounded by English troops. From the north, however, Irish chieftains O'Neill and O'Donnell mounted an epic winter march to come upon the British from behind. Hopes were high for an Irish victory, but as luck would have it, a drunken Irish soldier wandered into English hands and spilled the whole plan, enabling the English to win the day and send the native chieftains into hiding. Their lands in Ulster were confiscated by the Crown and resettled by loyal—and Protestant—English and Scots. In 1608 the surviving Irish chieftains met in Rathmullen, County Donegal, and decided to set sail for the continent as a body, vowing to return to fight another day—a vow never fulfilled. That "Flight of the Earls" marked the end of any effective organized resistance to English rule for generations.

Organized or not, the ornery Irish continued to harass the British with bloody attacks, always followed by even bloodier reprisals. Finally, in 1641 they mounted a long-planned offensive to retake Ulster, and thus brought down on the land one of the bloodiest episodes in Irish history, one mirrored across its landscape even today.

TO HELL OR CONNAUGHT By 1649 Irish incursions into Ulster and the massacre of hundreds of its Protestant settlers had so ravaged the land that Puritan general Oliver Cromwell arrived in force to squelch the rebellious Irish once and for all. Driven by religious fervor as well as political motives, Cromwell embarked on a campaign of devastation kicked off by the brutal slaying of more than 30,000 Irish men, women, and children at Drogheda.

From there, his trail of blood and destruction led to Wexford and thence across the country, leaving in its wake thousands dead, churches and castles and homes demolished, forests burned, and a degree of horror greater than any the Irish had known. Irish who escaped with their lives were shipped in the hundreds to work as slave labor on English plantations in the Sugar Islands—banishment to a virtual "hell"—or were driven to the bleak, stone-strewn hills of Connaught.

To his loyal soldiers and their commanding officers, Cromwell awarded vast estates in the choice and fertile counties of the country. In the end, less than one-ninth of Irish soil remained in the hands of natives.

KING BILLY, THE TREATY OF LIMERICK & THE PENAL LAWS Irish spirits rose once more when a Catholic, James II, ascended to the English throne in 1688. When he was deposed by supporters of William of Orange, "King Billy," and fled to Ireland in 1689, they took up arms in his defense. Jacobite forces were resoundingly defeated in 1690 by an army led by King Billy himself in the Battle of the Boyne. In October of 1691 the Treaty of Limerick, which allegedly allowed the Irish to retain both their religion and their land, was signed. Parliament, however, had no intention of sanctioning any sort of threat to the Protestant Ascendancy, and refused to ratify the treaty, instituting instead a series of measures so oppressive they became known as the Penal Laws.

Under the Penal Laws, Catholics were stripped of all civil and political rights— they could neither vote nor hold office; enter any of the professions; educate their children; own a horse valued at more than £5; bear arms; or (the origin of Ireland's tiny farmlands of today) will their land to only one son, being required instead to divide it into smaller plots for all male heirs. Forced to work the estates of absentee English landlords, Irish farmers paid enormous rents for the privilege of throwing up rude huts and using a small plot of ground to raise the potatoes that kept their families from starving. This sorry state of affairs was to last a full century.

UNITED IRISHMEN, UNION, FAMINE & EMIGRATION In the time-honored pattern, Anglo-Irish Protestants gradually came to feel a stronger allegiance to Ireland than to England, and in the late 1700s Henry Grattan led a Protestant Patriot party in demanding greater independence. A token Irish Parliament sat in Dublin in 1782 but was controlled from London. Penal Laws were gradually relaxed and trade began to flourish. Dublin's streets blossomed with the Georgian mansions and gracious squares that are still its most distinctive features.

Like a little learning, a little independence turned out to be a dangerous thing. With a newly independent France as a model, a group of Irishmen led by Protestant Wolfe Tone formed the Society of United Irishmen in 1791 to work for the establishment of a totally independent Irish republic. Enlisting military aid from France, Tone led a full-fledged insurrection in 1798 that ended in disaster and gave British leaders the ammunition they needed to insist on ending any semblance of Irish parliamentary rule. Even so, it took considerable bribery, seats in the British Parliament, and threats to get the Dublin MPs to vote an end to their supposed legislative power. But in 1800 the Act of Union passed and Ireland became an extension of British soil. That should have put Ireland in her proper place—again— but in 1803 the Irish were at it once more, and with Robert Emmet urging them on, they launched yet another uprising. It was the same old story, however, and ended with Emmet gallantly declaring from the gallows, "When my country takes her place among the nations of the earth, then, and not till then, let my epitaph be written."

In the 1820s a young Catholic named Daniel O'Connell started to make noises about Catholic Emancipation—a total repeal of the Penal Laws and the restoration of all Catholic civil rights. Elected to Parliament in 1828, he accomplished that goal the following year and embarked on a campaign for repeal of the Act of Union, earning him the affectionate title of "The Liberator."

In 1846 tragedy struck, putting all these questions aside. A disastrous potato blight spread throughout the country, destroying the one basic Irish food crop. Until 1849 crop after crop failed, and a population of nearly nine million was reduced to a little over six million. Hundreds of thousands died of pure starvation—it became a common sight to see roadside ditches filled with bodies of famine victims who had been evicted from their wretched homes by landlords who continued to demand exorbitant rents from tenants who no longer had the means to pay them. Well over a million turned their backs on Ireland and set out for the United States and Canada on ships so overcrowded, filthy, and disease-infested that they were little more than floating coffins.

THE LAND LEAGUE, HOME RULE & SINN FEIN In 1879 Irish tenant farmers joined with Charles Stewart Parnell and Michael Davitt in forming a union known as the Land League. They enlisted farmers around the country to strike back at any landlord who evicted tenants by the simple, but deadly effective, method of "boycott" (called after the English Captain Boycott, against whom it was used for the first time). With their families shunned by an entire community and services of any kind cut off, landlords began to rethink their policies and to reduce rents to a fair level, grant some degree of guaranteed occupancy to tenants, and eventually to allow tenants to purchase their own acreage.

Far from being grateful for such small favors, the Irish continued to fan the flame of their inherited zeal for freedom from English rule. Parnell for years led an energetic campaign for Home Rule which would grant limited independence, but it wasn't until the eve of World War I that such a measure was adopted by the British. Even then, there was strong and vocal opposition by loyal Unionists in Ulster, Protestants all, who were determined to keep Ireland a part of Britain. Outnumbered by Catholics, they feared that Home Rule would become Rome Rule, and the Ulster Volunteers were formed to put up armed resistance against the equally determined Irish Republican Army, the military arm of Sinn Fein (Shin fain), a republican political party whose name means "ourselves alone." With the British army already firmly ensconced, the country fairly bristled with arms when everything was put on "hold" by the urgency of world conflict.

"A TERRIBLE BEAUTY IS BORN" To the astonishment of almost everyone— most of all, the Irish people—Easter Monday of 1916 put the whole question of Irish independence right back on a very hot front burner. Leading a scruffy, badly outfitted, and poorly armed little band of fewer than 200 patriots, Patrick Pearse and James Connolly marched up Dublin's O'Connell Street to the General Post Office and proceeded to occupy it in the name of a Provisional Government. Standing between the front pillars of the impressive building, Pearse read in stirring tones "The Proclamation of the Irish Republic to the People of Ireland." Behind him, his valiant little "army" prepared to dig in and hold their position as long as was humanly possible. Hopelessly small contingents were stationed at St. Stephen's Green and one or two other strategic points.

For six days following Pearse's proclamation, the post office stood embattled under the ancient symbol of Ireland (a golden harp on a pennant of brilliant green) and the Sinn Fein banner of green, white, and orange. The rebels numbered only about 1,000 all told, and their remarkable courage as they faced overwhelming British military might is the stuff of heroic legends—and indeed the very stuff of which Ireland's history is made!

It was a bloody, but unbowed, band that finally surrendered. Hundreds of these were to be imprisoned or exiled. Pearse, Connolly, and 14 others were executed by a firing squad. This act united Irish loyalties behind their new Republic as nothing else could have done. It was of that moment—as the executioners' gunsmoke cleared in Kilmainham Jail's yard—that Yeats's poem "Easter 1916" was to proclaim:

> *I write it out in a verse—*
> *MacDonagh and MacBride*
> *And Connolly and Pearse*
> *Now and in time to be,*

Wherever green is worn,
Are changed, changed utterly:
A terrible beauty is born.

In the years between 1916 and 1921 Britain tried every means at its disposal—including sending the ruthless Black and Tan mercenaries to terrorize the citizenry as well as rebels—to quell the rebellion, which continued to rumble even in defeat. In 1919, when Sinn Fein won a huge majority of parliamentary seats, they refused to go to London, and instead set up the National Parliament of Ireland in Dublin, which they christened the Dail (Dawl, meaning "meeting"). From then on, guerrilla warfare raged, replete with atrocities, ambush tactics, and assassinations on both sides. After 2 years of bitter bloodshed, a truce was finally called and negotiations began which ended in December 1921 with the signing of the Anglo-Irish Treaty that named 26 counties as the Irish Free State. Still within the British Empire, it was to be self-governing in the same manner as Canada and other British dominions. Six counties in Ulster would remain—as they wished—an integral part of Great Britain and be ruled from London.

A Free State under the treaty terms was not, however, what many Irish believed they had been fighting for, and civil war raged until 1923. Eamon de Valera, at the head of the I.R.A., stood solidly against William Cosgrave's pro-treaty forces in the conviction that only a united Ireland that included all 32 counties was acceptable. Cosgrave and the newly formed government felt that the treaty terms were preferable to continued war with Britain and that in time the six counties of Northern Ireland would join the other 26 by constitutional means. That question still throws its divisive shadow over Ireland today.

As it became clear that the Dublin government would endure, de Valera threw in the towel militarily and in 3 years' time had formed the Fianna Fail (*Fee-*na Foil) party. When that party took office in 1932 the oath of allegiance to the British Crown was finally abolished, and in 1948 Great Britain formally declared Ireland outside the Commonwealth when a coalition government headed by John A. Costello declared that "the description of the State shall be the Republic of Ireland."

ONWARD & UPWARD   Since the proud day it became truly independent, Ireland has set about catching up with the progress so long held at bay by the fight to become independent. Efforts to develop Irish industry resulted in state companies such as Bord na Mona building a thriving business from one of the country's greatest natural resources, peat (or turf). Aer Lingus, the national airline, was established, and the Shannon Free Airport Development Company has developed one of the world's leading airports, along with an industrial complex that attracts companies from all over the world. The Industrial Development Authority has assisted firms from the United States, Germany, Japan, Great Britain, and a score of other countries in setting up factories and processing plants (most of them remarkably clean industries) and providing employment opportunities for a new generation.

Along with all these developments, there have also been some interesting changes in demographics. In 1926, still feeling the decimation of its population by starvation and emigration that spanned a century following the famine of the 1840s, Ireland counted only 2.972 million inhabitants in its first official census. The vast majority lived in rural areas and looked to farming for a living.

A decline in population continued as recently as 1961, when the figures showed 2.818 million. Every census since then, however, has shown a slight increase, with a 2.2% jump in the short period of 1979–81. The 1981 report showed a population of 3.443 million and a shift in distribution. For example, Ireland now has one of Europe's youngest populations, with more than half under the age of 21, although the ranks of the young have been considerably thinned as severe economic conditions since 1986 sent Irish youth abroad in search of jobs. More and more, the Irish are moving to towns and cities—or, to be more precise, to the metropolitan suburbs, since most Irish still cling to the notion of a private house with its own garden. Back in 1966 urban and rural populations were just about even, but in 1981 some 1.915 million lived in urban areas compared to 1.529 million in rural localities.

Luckily for you and me, along with industry, successive Irish governments have recognized the potential for tourism in this gloriously beautiful land. Bord Failte (the "board of welcomes") has worked closely with hoteliers, bed-and-breakfast hostesses, restaurateurs, and entertainment facilities to see that we're well taken care of.

On the cultural scene, the lilting Gaelic language was reinstated as the official tongue, reclaiming an Irish identity nearly lost during long years of suppression. Called "Irish" to distinguish it from other forms of Gaelic, the language takes first place on street signs, city and town name signs, and Irish is used for governmental titles such as Taoiseach (Tee-shuck) for the prime minister or gardai (guard-ee) for police. Aer Lingus (Gaelic for "air fleet") welcomes you aboard in rhythmic Irish, and radio and television stations sign off in the native tongue. Though every schoolchild is required to study Irish in an attempt to revive its day-to-day use, English remains the first tongue of the vast majority. However, there are still some 40,000 Irish speakers who use English only occasionally. Most of them live in rural, poor, rather isolated locations in the west. These closely knit communities are called the Gaeltacht (Gwale-tack-ta), and receive government support. Donegal, Dingle, the Aran Islands, and Connemara form the larger part of the Gaeltacht.

POLITICS

On the political front, Ireland steadfastly held to neutrality during World War II, even in the face of tremendous pressure from both Britain and the United States. Nevertheless, hundreds of Irishmen volunteered in the armed forces of both countries. Since 1955 Ireland has been a member of the United Nations and has sent peace-keeping forces to Cyprus, the Congo, the Sinai Desert, and Lebanon. As long as Northern Ireland remains under British rule, however, no Irish government has authorized NATO membership, since NATO is pledged to guarantee the territorial integrity of its members. As a member of the European Community, Ireland shares in the joys and woes of that controversial alliance. With the rest of Europe, Ireland is busily gearing up for 1992, which will see the integration of all 12 countries of the European Community into a single European Market designed to simplify travel, trade, and—in due course—currency.

NORTHERN IRELAND The tangled threads of political events in Northern Ireland weave a pattern almost too complex to follow. It's always a temptation to oversimplify the underlying reasons for the tensions that have troubled the area since the 1921 treaty that set it apart from the rest of the country. While injustices of the past live on in the memories of a Catholic minority who support Irish nationalism, the Protestant majority, after generations, feel they are equally Irish and fear to be overwhelmed and to lose their privileged position. Certainly the history we have just gone through created an environment where violence has become an easy option to use in political disputes.

Nonetheless, most of the people in the two population segments live side-by-side, somewhat warily, but more interested in making a living and raising decent, law-abiding families than professing loyalty to extremists on either side. Americans all too often cut out of their Irish itinerary a corner of the country that has a unique dimension to add to any Irish visit. Travel north of the border presents few real

---

IMPRESSIONS

Irishness is not primarily a question of birth or blood or language: it is the condition of being involved in the Irish situation, and usually of being mauled by it.
—CONOR CRUISE O'BRIEN, *WRITERS AND POLITICS*, 1965

Ireland seems to me the right size for a country, the truly contemporary size, the size at which regionalism becomes nationhood.
—JAN MORRIS, *TRAVELS*, 1976

problems for the tourist, despite recent events, and I highly recommend that you read more about it in Chapter 19, "Getting to Know Northern Ireland," and in the subsequent chapters on that area.

2. THE PEOPLE

And what about the people? Well, if it's hard to find words for Ireland itself, it's nearly impossible to capture the personality of its people. There's a certain panache about the Irish. Flexible, warm-hearted, witty, sometimes devious, filled with curiosity about visitors, deeply religious at Sunday's mass but the very devil in the pub on Saturday night, great talkers and even greater listeners, sometimes argumentative to the point of combativeness—and with it all, friendly. That's the Irish, all right!

Ireland is where the word "friendly" probably originated. Where stopping to ask directions can land you in a family kitchen swapping tales over a "cuppa." Where the answer to every question is a short story. Where you may, as I once did, wind up as the Dublin house guest of an Irish lady you met quite casually over breakfast in a B&B in Kerry.

This is not to say, however, that the Irish are intrusive—yours will have to be the first conversational move. But ask the first question, make the first comment, and you're off and running, your American accent an open invitation for the inevitable "And where in America would you be from?" followed up by the equally inevitable "Well, now, and didn't my own uncle Pat [or brother Joe or great-aunt Mary] go out to Chicago [or New York or Savannah or wherever it is you hail from]."

All the foregoing takes place, of course, in English—but a most melodic, lilting rendition of the language: "Sure, the English gave us their language," say the Irish with a grin, "then we showed them how to use it." And they did, with writers like Jonathan Swift, Edmund Burke, Oscar Wilde, George Bernard Shaw, William Butler Yeats, James Joyce, and a host of others. But your average Irishman—or woman— embellishes everyday conversation with all the eloquence of colorful, image-making phrases that would make any writer weep with envy. And they string them together in yarns that may be wildly fanciful, but are never dull.

As for the celebrated Irish wit, it is consummately subtle rather than bombastic. Irish laughter creeps around words and phrases, then curls past curving lips to land in twinkling Irish eyes and a mischievous chuckle.

Tim Pat Coogan, in his excellent book *Ireland and the Arts,* suggests that the Irish have used their words and their wit as both a sly release from, and an effective weapon against, cruel oppression suffered over long centuries of invasion and foreign rule. There's truth in that, for in today's Ireland—as another Irish writer in an *Inside Ireland* article stated categorically—"Exaggeration and lighthearted blasphemy are national pastimes." And the paradoxical Irish nature led Chesterton to write: "All their wars are merry, and all their songs are sad."

3. ART, ARCHITECTURE & LITERATURE

ART Visual art, in its many forms, has been nurtured and has flourished in Ireland from the very beginning. Indeed, even such utilitarian structures as the prehistoric burial chamber at Newgrange were embellished with artistic spirals and mystical designs. During the great metal-working age, exquisite chalices, pins, brooches, necklaces, and combs were designed with an eye to beauty as well as utility. In the 8th and 9th centuries in Ireland's great monastic seats of learning, Celtic designs were used to adorn the pages of important historical and literary works. The height of their artistic achievement can be seen in the epic *Book of Kells.* That influence can still be

IMPRESSIONS

And to speake in generall of them all, this Nation is strong of bodie, and passing nimble, stout and haughty in heart, for wit quicke, martiall, prodigall, and carelesse of their lives . . . kind and curteous to strangers, constant in love, in enmitie implacable, light of beleefe, greedie of glory, impacient of abuse and injurie. If they bee bad you shall nowhere meete with worse: if they bee good, you can hardlie finde better.
—WILLIAM GOOD, in WILLIAM CAMDEN, *BRITAIN*, 1610

The Irish when good are perfect.
—LORD BYRON, Letter to Lady Melbourne, 1813

traced in the work of many artists and craftspeople of the 20th century. Irish art forms virtually disappeared during the centuries when the country was overrun by Viking and Norman forces.

With the arrival of the 18th century there was a resurgence of the arts in Ireland, but painters and sculptors turned to landscape and other European painting styles. The introduction of a wealthy landowning class had a tremendous effect, since many of its members had both the means and the leisure to indulge their artistic talents and to encourage native-born artists. Irish painters traveled to London and continental capitals, many subsidized by wealthy patrons.

By the late 19th century, leading Irish painters such as John Lavery and Jack B. Yeats (brother of W. B. Yeats, the poet) had embraced the impressionist school of painting. Artists Sean O'Sullivan, Sean Keating, and Maurice MacGonigal led the flight from impressionism into realism during the 1930s, and they were, in turn, displaced by Anne Madden and Louis LeBrocquy when they, along with a few others, introduced modernism to Ireland in the 1940s. More recently, expressionist Michael Kane and one or two other painters have added yet another dimension.

Today, Ireland has a large body of artists working in a wide range of media, bringing a new vibrancy to the visual arts scene with the addition of video and film to the traditional art forms of painting and sculpture. Oisin Kelly, Connor Fallon, John Behan, and Jim Connolly in the Republic, as well as Carolyn Mulholland and F. E. McWilliams in Northern Ireland, are leading contemporary sculptors. Among modern painters to look for are Pauline Bewick, James Scanlon, Camille Souter, Brian Burke, and Robert Ballagh in the Republic, and T. P. Flanagan, Gerard Dillon, and George Campbell in Northern Ireland.

Dublin's National Gallery and Municipal Gallery are important showcases, and Belfast has the Ulster Museum and Arts Council galleries. In both cities, there are a score of smaller private galleries. In Cork, there's the Crawford Gallery, and other major cities, such as Limerick and Waterford in the Republic and Derry in Northern Ireland, have frequent showings of contemporary and classical art. Be on the lookout, too, for the several excellent small private galleries like the Frank Lewis Gallery in Killarney and Raymond Klee's studio/gallery in Ballylickey, County Cork. Smaller towns often are venues for short-term exhibitions of Irish art, both contemporary and classical.

ARCHITECTURE Ireland's earliest settlers probably lived in wooden huts, traces of which have disappeared into the mists of time. Excavations have revealed, however, that some lived in *crannogs*, or lake dwellings on artificially created islands. Although there are no remains of actual Iron Age dwellings, great circular earthworks known as *lisses* or *raths* and stone enclosures known as *cahers* have been found to be homesteads as well as fortified centers. Prehistoric Dun Beg on the Dingle Peninsula and Dun Aengus on the Aran Islands are survivors of this period, and the reconstructed crannog at Craggaunowen, in County Clare, presents a vivid picture of the daily life of lake dwellers.

It was during the early Christian age (700–1150) that enduring structures such as *clochans*, the small stone beehive cells of ecclesiastics, appeared. The most impressive surviving examples are to be found on Skellig Michael, County Kerry, and near Slea Head on the Dingle Peninsula. They were soon followed by churches, round towers, and oratories. Outstanding examples of this type of architecture (sometimes called Hiberno-Romanesque because of the barrel-vaulted ceilings that introduced the arch to Irish architecture) are Cormac's chapel on the Rock of Cashel, St. Kevin's church at Glendalough, and the Gallarus Oratory on the Dingle peninsula. Most of Ireland's non-church-related residents lived in simple, one-room cabins with walls of clay or stone, thatched roofs, dirt floors, and few (if any) windows.

During the Anglo-Norman period (1170–1700), the castles that are so much a part of Ireland's landscape cropped up all over the land. Most are fortified dwellings consisting of simple square towers with slit windows, though some have curtain walls with corner towers enclosing a central courtyard. Bunratty, Dublin, and Carrickfergus castles are well-preserved remnants of the castle-building era. Stout town walls of stone were also constructed during this period, and traces remain in Waterford, Wexford, Drogheda, Clonmel, Limerick, and Derry, where city walls are still intact. The humble mud or stone cabin was expanded to more than one room, and sometimes to an upper floor. Villages sported simple public houses and shops grouped around a square, or "green," and many were planned by wealthy landowners as a convenient source of labor for their vast estates. Kilkenny's Rothe House, which dates from 1594, is an excellent example of a well-to-do merchant's home.

Between 1680 and 1684, Ireland's first significant public building, the Royal Hospital at Kilmainham in Dublin, was constructed.

The 18th century saw a great wave of building and ornamentation. Castletown House is an outstanding example of the classical style that began to appear. Also of interest are many fine examples of the Palladian style, led by Dublin's Parliament House (now the Bank of Ireland) in 1729, the Custom House, and the Four Courts. This is also the time when Dublin's renowned Georgian squares—St. Stephen's Green, Merrion Square, Fitzwilliam Square, Mountjoy Square, and Parnell Square— made their appearance. Cork (the Summerhill area, Camden Place, and the Ursuline Convent at Blackrock) and Limerick (the Custom House, the Town Hall, the crescent on O'Connell Street, Patrick Street, and St. John's Square) both have noteworthy examples of Georgian architecture. James Gandon (who designed the Custom House, Four Courts, and King's Inns) was one of Ireland's most prominent architects of this period. Others of importance were Francis Johnston (the General Post Office, St. George's Church, and the chapel in Dublin Castle), Richard Castle (Powerscourt, Leinster House, Russborough, and other fine private residences), and Francis Bindon, who collaborated with Castle on the design for Dublin's Rotunda Hospital.

By 1839 architecture had become so well established as a profession that the Royal Institute of Architects of Ireland was founded. The 1800s also saw a spate of church building, and for the first time, large-scale housing developments and industrial complexes were designed. In rural areas, improvements were made in the traditional cottage, as more windows made them brighter and slate or other materials created more durable roofs than thatch.

In Ireland, as in so many other parts of the world, 20th-century architecture has tended toward sameness, with modern bungalows springing up alongside the abandoned traditional cottage in the countryside, suburban housing estates built to standard specifications, and tall glass-and-steel structures dotting urban skylines. A distinctive modern Irish style has not yet crystallized, although architects such as Liam McCormick, in his church designs, have perhaps taken the first steps in that direction.

LITERATURE Literature in Ireland has a long and rich history. The written word in literary form dates all the way back to the 6th century, but long before monks began their laborious transcribing in Ireland's monasteries, a bardic oral storytelling tradition reached back into prehistory, with glorious tales of fierce battles, passionate love affairs, and heroic deeds, related in both prose and poetry. It was, in fact, from that treasure trove of oral literature that the monks drew their first recorded stories. *Tain Bo Cuailgne* (The Cattle Raid of Cooley), *Lebor na Huidre* (The Dun Cow), and *Lebor Laigen* (The Book of Leinster) preserve the exploits, triumphs, and

IMPRESSIONS

Talking of Ireland, he [Samuel Rogers] enumerated the long list of distinguished men whom she has poured into England. Believed the Irish to be beyond most other people in genius, but behind them in sense.
—THOMAS MOORE, *DIARY*, 1832

tragedies of such legendary figures as Finn MacCool and his Fiannan band, Cuchulain, Oisin, and the beautiful Deirdre. These were written in Irish, which continued to be the dominant language of Irish literature until the 17th century and was widely used right up to the beginning of the 19th century.

In the early 7th century, the epic *Cuirt an Mhean Oiche* (Midnight Court) was a masterful satire by Brian Merriman on the strong aversion to marriage held by Irish men, while the *Annals of the Four Masters*, written by Franciscans under the direction of layman Michael O'Clery and *Foras Feasa ar Eirinn* (History of Ireland) by Geoffrey Keating both dealt with Irish history. Also notable during this period were the works of Padraigin Haicead, Daibhidh O'Bruadair, Egan O'Rahilly, Michael Comyn, and, on a lighter note, the witty works of the blind poet Raftery and the roguish Owen Roe O'Sullivan.

By the end of the 17th century the Anglo-Irish literary movement was well launched, and during the 1700s such Irish writers as Oliver Goldsmith (*She Stoops to Conquer, The Vicar of Wakefield*) and Richard Brinsley Sheridan (*The School for Scandal, The Rivals*) penned English-style drawing-room comedies and English-manners novels. At the same time, Jonathan Swift—then dean of St. Patrick's Cathedral—was verbally flaying the English with his satires (*A Modest Proposal, A Tale of a Tub*, and *Gulliver's Travels*).

In the 1800s Maria Edgeworth (*Castle Rackrent*) joined the ranks of outstanding Anglo-Irish writers, as did Thomas Moore, Gerald Griffin, William Carleton, and James Clarence Mangan. The brilliant Oscar Wilde (*The Picture of Dorian Gray, The Importance of Being Earnest*), living and writing in London, suffered scandal, imprisonment, and poverty when his flamboyant life-style did him in. Toward the end of that century, dramatist George Bernard Shaw and novelist George Moore began brilliant careers that were to spill over into the next, as did poet William Butler Yeats and playwright John Millington Synge. On a smaller scale, two cousins living in West Cork, Edith Somerville and Violet Martin, were turning out comic sketches of Protestant life in rural Ireland and the notable "Big House" novel *The Real Charlotte*. Novelist Bram Stoker, on the other hand, loosed *Dracula* on the literary public.

The 20th century has brought with it a veritable explosion of literary talent in Ireland. Although three decades of the mid-1900s—1929 to 1959—were clouded by the oppressive Censorship Act that drove many Irish writers to foreign publishers, their vitality never flagged. Sean O'Casey's *Shadow of a Gunman, Juno and the Paycock*, and *The Plough and the Stars* put him in the forefront of Irish dramatists. Samuel Beckett, living in exile, was awarded the Nobel Prize, and Brendan Behan enjoyed an all-too-short burst of fame. James Joyce, who had to leave Dublin before he could write about it, is thought by many to be the greatest Irish writer of the 20th century.

As the last decade of this century begins, playwrights Hugh Leonard, Brian Friel, Bernard Farrell, Thomas Murphy, John B. Keane, and Frank McGuinness continue the tradition of drama excellence. Novelists and short story writers Ben Kiely, James Plunkett, Mary Lavin, John Banville, Francis Stuart, Edna O'Brien, John McGahern, Molly Keane, Dermot Bolger, and Maeve Beanchy add their names to the list of such 20th-century greats as Frank O'Connor, Kate O'Brien, Sean O'Faolain, Brian O'Nolan (who used the pen names Myles na gCopaleen and Flann O'Brien), and Elizabeth Bowen. Christy Brown's brilliant autobiographical novels portraying life in the Dublin slums as seen through the eyes of a severely handicapped boy (*Down All the Days* and *My Left Foot*) stand in a literary class of their own. W. B. Yeats and Patrick Kavanagh head the list of distinguished 20th-century poets, with Thomas

Kinsella, John Montague, and Seamus Heaney the most prominent of contemporary poets.

One last word: Your Irish reading should by no means be restricted to the authors listed here. There are scores of talented Irish writers hard at work—most to an extraordinarily high standard. So browse the bookshops, pick up any titles you find intriguing, and who knows—you may well discover the next "big name" on Ireland's literary scene.

4. RELIGION, MYTH & FOLKLORE

RELIGION   Religion has played an important role in Ireland from early times. Since St. Patrick introduced Christianity to the island, Ireland has been a predominantly Catholic nation. A little over three million Irish in the Republic are members of the Roman Catholic church, with a further 700,000 Catholics living in Northern Ireland. There are four Catholic dioceses, with the archbishop of Armagh serving as Primate of all Ireland.

Among Protestants, there are some 375,000 members of the Church of Ireland, and about 350,000 Presbyterians, mostly in Northern Ireland. Methodists, Quakers, and Lutherans are represented in much smaller numbers. Most of the country's Jewish population (about 2,000) live in Dublin or Belfast. There is also a small Islamic community, with its own mosque in Dublin.

MYTH & FOLKLORE   The early bards, and the *seanachies* (storytellers) who followed, tell of three distinct racial groups in Ireland's beginnings. There were the "men of the quiver" (the *Fir Bolg*), the "men of the territory" (the *Fir Domhnann*), and the "men of Gaul" (the *Fir Gaileoin*). In one of the oldest legends about the coming of the Celts, the bards explained that it was their iron-bladed spears (*laighens*) that gave Leinster its name. The stories speak of the brave deeds of Conaire Mor, King of Ireland in the 2nd century B.C. The hero we know as Finn MacCool was born as Fionn MacCumhail in a blaze of glorified chivalry and courage as gigantic as the fictitious man himself. His faithful Fianna warrior band matched their leader in feats of bravery and daring. There were tales of the Knights of the Red Branch in the north and of the Ulster hero, Cuchulain. Queen Maeve, who ruled Connaught, and the tragic Deirdre of the Sorrows were chief among the heroines who figured in song and story.

These tales are, of course, quite different from the beginnings of Ireland as explained by historians and scientists. But I can tell you that, to my Irish friends, those legendary heroes are as alive and well in their minds and hearts today as when the bards of old spun their tales. As for me, I tend to believe *both* versions—with just the slightest leaning toward Finn MacCool, Cuchulainn, and Queen Maeve.

There are many other intriguing legends: that of the magical *Tuatha de Danaan*, who some say became the "little people" of Ireland's fairy forts; the enchantment of the children of Lir, condemned to live as swans for centuries; Oisin's magical sojourn in the Land of Youth; and. . . . Well, they can—and do—fill volumes, and if you have any faith at all in the fanciful and mystical, you'll surely want to carry home with you at least one of the many books of these marvelous tales.

5. CULTURAL & SOCIAL LIFE

LANGUAGE   One of the first things you'll notice in Ireland is that each village, town, and city name is signposted in both its Anglicized spelling and the original Gaelic. The Irish language is not an easy one to manage, and since a fractured-Irish pronunciation is both awkward and embarrassing, I'll give you the correct pronunciation along with the original meaning of major place names. That way, when you're down in County Cork, you'll never once say "You-gal" for the town whose name is spelled Youghal and pronounced "Yawl."

All place names, of course, have some meaning, and in Ireland they often refer to a natural or artificial feature of the locality or to clans and leading families. Some of the Gaelic words used in place names that will tip you off as to the history, setting, or appearance of the village or town are given in the Glossary in the Appendix.

IRISH PUBS   A wise man once said that "a pub is the poor man's university." That it certainly is in Ireland, where—in city or country—the pub tends to be the hub of local social life. In rural areas the pub is often the only social center available. And it's an ongoing education as you encounter pubgoers from different walks of life and regions, each with an individual outlook on life, politics, religion, or any other subject, and each with a highly developed personal way with the words to expound on any of the above.

Pubs are, by and large, where you're most likely to find traditional music and song. "Singing pubs" bring in leading musical groups or give performing space to the local lads. It must be added that you're just as likely to find the familiar twang of country and western hits as the impassioned lyrics of Ireland's native music. Even if a pub is not known for music, however, the lyrical Irish spirit is frequently there. Especially toward the end of the evening, when a fiddle or tin whistle suddenly appears and song erupts—along with reams of poetry that can be from the classics or entirely spontaneous, depending on the clientele.

Pub decor ranges over a wide spectrum. In cities like Dublin and Belfast you can have a jar in an ornate, Victorian-style drinking establishment; a glitzed-up chrome-and-mirrored abyss of pseudo-sophistication; an old-time pub replete with time-worn wood, etched glass, and touches of brass; an elegant hotel bar that is considered a pub despite its fancy getup; or a bare-bones drinking place that depends on its colorful "regulars" for whatever decor might exist. Out in the country a pub might well be half of a grocery or hardware store; a traditional-style pub that's been dispensing drink and hospitality since the days of coaching inns; a cozy, wallpapered and carpeted appendage to a guesthouse or small hotel; or a large, barnlike room with linoleum on the floor and a telly behind the bar.

There are still pubs around with little blocked-off private rooms called "snugs" and lovely old etched-glass partitions along the bar to afford a bit of privacy. In some pubs the dart board stays busy; in others there's almost always a card game in progress; some keep the fireplace glowing. Most will have a main bar and an attached "lounge," which once was the only place you'd ever catch a female in what was exclusively a man's domain. Nowadays the lounges are filled with couples of all ages, as well as singles (even males who prefer not to elbow it at the bar).

Pub Etiquette: Pub etiquette is a delicate and complex matter, and your awareness of some of its intricacies can spell the difference between a night of unsurpassed conviviality and one of cool isolation that leaves you wondering where all that famed Irish-pub joviality is to be found. Novelist and radio newscaster David Hanly once laid down the one vital ground rule that should see you safely through those first few minutes when you enter what many Irishmen consider their own personal club. He was writing about Dublin pubs, but the rule applies across the board: "If you are to be accompanied on this jaunt, choose a partner who is loud neither in dress nor in voice. Dubliners abominate strange noises in their pubs, and high, demanding voices—no matter what the accent—carry deadly imperial echoes." Need I comment that his reference to "partner" was a typically Irish, backdoor, way of saying that you should tread softly?

So, keeping your voice and manners suitably moderated, order your brew (never a fancy mixed cocktail unless you're in one of those city hotel bars mentioned above) and gradually—oh, so gradually—drift into conversation by way of a question. You're on your own as far as the question is concerned; it doesn't really matter so long as you project a real need for assistance. Inquiries about the best place to eat, the best traditional music group around, etc., will do just fine and will open up a general conversation likely to run the length of the bar, with everyone anxious to lend a hand to a visiting Yank.

The times and economic pressures are slowly eroding one once-inviolate facet of Irish drinking etiquette, that of "buying the round." That ritual required each member in a drinking group to pick up the tab for a round of drinks for everybody. It was (still is in many places) as deadly a breach of manners to leave after you'd paid for your round as before your turn rolled around. Everybody drank until everybody had bought his round.

The only exception concerns women: In all my years of visiting Ireland, I've only insisted on buying my round once, and my male drinking companions were so uncomfortable with the whole thing that I've resolved to relax and go with local custom without the slightest twinge of guilt. As I said, however, what with the high price of the pint these days, round-buying is disappearing from the Irish pub scene. More often than not, today everyone buys his or her own.

About Prices: In some city bars you can pay as much as IR£1.65 ($2.90) for a pint of Guinness; in a country pub, about IR£1.45 ($2.55). A pint of lager (beer) will cost around IR£1.75 ($3.05), IR£1.55 ($2.70) in rural pubs. A "drop" of whisky will run a little less than a pint, and you should know that an Irish "drop" is a big one. Drinks in the lounge rather than at the bar sometimes cost around 2p more.

Pub Hours: In the Republic, pubs are open in the winter Monday through Saturday from 10am to 11pm, until 11:30pm in the summer months. On Sunday they're open year round from 12:30 to 2pm and 4 to 10pm.

Pubbing need not be limited to the evening hours. Perish the thought that you miss Irish pubs in the afternoon! Things are slower then, the publican is more relaxed, and the talk flows smoothly, sometimes playing hob with a big chunk of your afternoon. In rural pubs, this is when you're likely to encounter those craggy old-timers just itching for you to pose a question or otherwise open up a dialogue so that they can proffer their philosophy and local expertise without being bold. So my reason for discussing pubs right up front is that no matter what else you plan, a pub stop is the very best way to begin and/or end an evening.

One Last Word to the Women: You'll be very welcome in Irish pubs, whether you're on your own, with a group of females, or with a male escort. You may, however, be more comfortable in the lounge than at the bar (that varies from pub to pub, so try to size the place up when you first come in). Even being a nondrinker is no reason for missing out on pub sociability: all Irish pubs stock soft drinks (try the light, fizzy white lemonade) and nobody is going to look askance if you stick to those.

6. PERFORMING ARTS & EVENING ENTERTAINMENT

MUSICAL NIGHTS Since pre-Christian days the Irish have celebrated, mourned, exalted, damned, and lamented everything in their lives through music. Until the 1690s and Cromwell, songs and ballads were composed entirely in Irish; after that, the English language was enforced in an attempt to erase any remaining traces of nationalism. Even under the Penal Laws, however, the wily Irish praised their country in the guise of singing about their sweethearts: "Roisin Dubh," "Kathleen Huallachain," and "Grainne Uail" were, as every Irishman knew, odes to Ireland herself. Those traditional songs and airs are still played frequently today, and if you listen closely to modern Irish ballads, you'll notice that a good few still concern themselves with celebrating, mourning, exalting, etc., etc., some facet of Ireland or Irish life.

The tones that spring from the harp, uilleann (elbow) pipes (played sitting down; it was developed to get around English law, which forbade the playing of any instrument while standing in order to prevent the pipes from playing troops into battle), the bodhran (a sort of drum made of goatskin stretched tightly over a round wooden frame), the tin whistle, fiddle, and accordion mix in a unique harmony that can break your heart or send your spirits (and your feet!) soaring. We've heard them on this side of the Atlantic in recent years most often from groups such as the Chieftains, and they're to be found almost everywhere in Ireland itself.

The trick, of course, is to know where to look for them. A central organization whose sole purpose is the promotion of traditional music, song, and dance, is **Comhaltas Ceoltoiri Eireann** (Kool-tus Kool-tura Airan; universally known as "coalthus") based in the Dublin suburb of Monkstown, with branches in every county. It organizes traditional entertainment in hotels, pubs, and at local branch meetings, all of which are open to the public, and welcome visiting Americans.

At the Monkstown headquarters there are traditional music sessions on weekends all year round, with admission a mere IR£1.50 ($2.62). During summer months they organize other events, like the **Fonntrai** (folk-theater show featuring traditional music and dance), the **ceili** (kay-lee; traditional set dancing as done in Irish homes in years gone by), and the **cois teallaigh** (musicians, singers, and dancers talk about and demonstrate their various arts). Admissions range from IR£1.50 to IR£4 ($2.60 to $7), and scheduled nights vary. You can usually enjoy a preshow dinner of traditional, home-cooked recipes in their kitchen/restaurant by calling 01/800295 to book. Prices are moderate to cheap.

To learn what's on during your visit, both in Monkstown and around the country, contact Comhaltas Ceoltoiri Eireann, Belgrave Square, Monkstown, Co. Dublin (tel. 01/800295).

During the last weekend in August, look for the **All-Ireland Fleadh** (flah), a 3-day traditional music and song festival held each year in a different town. The **Fleadh Nua,** always held in Ennis, County Clare, on the last weekend in May, is another showcase for the best in traditional music.

No visit to the west of Ireland will be complete without taking in a performance of **Siamsa** (Sheem-sa) **Tire,** the national folk theater of Ireland. It's based in Tralee, but performs regularly during the summer months in Killarney and occasionally in other towns. Performers, through music and dance, demonstrate such traditional Irish folk ways as threshing and thatching the roof. Information on performance schedules and the low admission charges—around IR£4 ($7)—is available at most tourist offices (the Killarney office always has Siamsa information).

Another place to look for traditional Irish entertainment is **Seoda** (Sho-da), a dramatic and musical evening held in Galway's Gaelic theater, Taibhdhearc (Thive-yark), on selected evenings during the summer.

BANQUETS & CABARETS   A standout among nighttime activities is the **medieval banquets** held in Bunratty and Knappogue castles in County Clare and Dunguaire Castle in County Galway. Each begins with a meal that harks back to the days when these were residences as well as fortifications, and each ends with superb entertainment that includes music, dance, song, and a bit of pageantry. Prices—about IR£25.90 ($45.35) are well above "budget," but this is the one "Worth the Extra Money" you shouldn't miss.

For a different sort of musical evening that combines traditional and modern music, song, dance, and "stage Irish" comedy, look for the popular **cabaret shows** in leading city hotels. They're loads of fun, and many include a preshow dinner, although you can usually come for just the show if you prefer. A mark of the quality of these shows is the smattering of Irish you'll see in the audience (along with busloads of visiting tourists). Prices are about IR£23.90 ($41.85) for the dinner/show combination, IR£15.50 ($27.15) for the show and two drinks.

THEATER   Think of Ireland and one thinks immediately of the theater. Dublin's Abbey Theatre and the Gate Theatre should be high on every visitor's "don't miss" list, and prices are so affordable even those of us who keep a tight rein on the budget can work in at least one performance. Admission at the better-known theaters will run IR£7 to IR£10 ($12.25 to $17.50), and many smaller theaters charge even less.

There are good productions all around the country, some on a regular basis (like Cork's Opera House), others on a periodic basis. Look in local newspapers for productions, then go along, and for a pittance enjoy a night of good theater and—many times, though not always—a chat with the cast in the lobby after the show.

7. SPORTS & RECREATION

For the sports-minded, Ireland is veritably loaded with goodies!

GOLF   Golfers will be welcomed guests at more than 180 golf courses (over 50 are championship class) around the country, be they professionals or bumbling amateurs who just like to whack the ball around. Greens fees run around IR£5 to IR£20 ($8.75 to $35) per day. Courses range from 18-holers with such extras as a pro shop, resident pro to give instruction, and tea room to windswept greens overlooking the sea.

Caddies are not generally available (although they can be booked ahead at some of the larger courses), and don't look for a golfmobile—the closest you'll come to that is a lightweight pull cart. Some courses have clubs for rent at about IR£3 ($5.25) per round, but most do not, so you'll be well advised to bring your own.

The Best of Irish Golf and *Irish Golf Courses,* both available from tourist offices in Ireland, lists them all and gives specific information on what's available to visitors at each. For information on golfing holidays, see Section 6, "Alternative/Adventure Travel," in Chapter 2.

FISHING/WATER SPORTS   If there's such a thing as a fisherman's heaven, it must be the Emerald Isle! You can go **fishing** for such freshwater fish (coarse fishing) as bream, dace, pike, perch, and various hybrids in all those rivers, streams, and lakes, and/or stalk the famous Irish salmon from January 1 (later in some localities) to September 30 in coastal rivers, their stillwaters and headwaters. Sea trout and brown trout are among the other challenging game fish. Sea anglers will find plentiful supplies of bass, whiting, mullet, flounder, plaice, pollack, and coalfish to be had from shore casting on rocks, piers, beaches, and promontories.

Other water sports include **surfing, waterskiing,** and **boardsailing (windsurfing).** And of course there are all those lovely **beaches** for swimmers who don't demand summer temperatures much above 70° Fahrenheit. Personally, I find walking the sandy strands and deserted coves more fun than braving the waves—it's positively restorative to commune with sea and sun on long stretches when there's not another soul in sight. Seaside resorts can also be fun, from the lively, crowded Tramore in County Waterford to the quieter Kilkee in County Clare.

HORSERACING   As for spectator sports, Irish horseracing has got to be close to the top of the list. A day at a race meet is very like a day at a country fair, with bookmakers vying for punters (bettors) while shouting out odds that change momentarily, and punters shopping around to get their bets down when the odds are at their best. If your horse comes up a winner, you'll be paid from a big satchel at the bookmaker's stand at the odds in existence at the time you placed your bet (so timing can be important, and it pays to do a little shopping around). Irish horses, of course, are world famous, and it's a thrilling sight to see them round the last bend of a grass course against a backdrop of mountains or seashore or rolling green fields.

There are over 250 race meets each year at 28 courses around the country. The Curragh, County Kildare, is the venue for such classics as the **Irish Derby;** the best national hunt or jumping courses are Fairyhouse, for the **Irish Grand National,** Leopardstown, Punchestown, Navan, Gowran, and Galway. Probably the most popular of all with the Irish are the **Galway Races** in late July or early August, but there are also gala **raceweeks** in Killarney, Tralee, Tramore, and Listowel. Tourist board offices can furnish exact dates, and if you should happen on a meet somewhere else in the course of your travels, there goes another itinerary change (one of the happiest Irish times in my memory was an evening race meet at Clonmel in County Tipperary when my itinerary called for me to be en route to Killarney!).

GAELIC FOOTBALL & HURLING   In its present, organized form Gaelic football is only about a century old, but it must have roots way back in the days of fierce tribal rivalries before encroaching civilization shoved all that competitive spirit from battleground to football pitch. For sheer excitement nothing quite matches that of sharing the stands at Croke Park in Dublin with upward of 90,000 fans roaring support for their county teams in the All Ireland finals in early September.

Hurling is unique to Ireland, and I sometimes think it takes the Irish to figure out its two-level scoring. There are goals and points (depending on whether the little leather ball is hit past the goaltender and over the goal line or over the goaltender's head between the upright goalposts). And right there ends my personal knowledge of the game's scoring. My ignorance notwithstanding, I find a Sunday-afternoon match irresistible—the skill and speed of agile athletes wielding hurleys (wooden sticks not unlike our hockey sticks) are wondrous to behold!

STATE FORESTS Ireland's state forests—more than 300 of them—are for the most part small and undeveloped havens of nature trails, bird song, and tranquility. Many have picnic sites, inviting an outdoor lunch in a different woodland every day. You can do that—or just plot a peaceful half-hour break each day—with the help of *The Open Forest, A Guide to Areas Open to the Public,* a publication of **Coillte Teo, The Irish Forest Service,** Leeson Lane, Dublin 2 (tel. 01/615666). They can also, for a small charge, furnish a whole bevy of detailed pamphlets on individual state forests and parks.

You'll find the state forests well cared for and rubbish-free, and you'll be on your honor to help keep them that way.

8. FOOD & DRINK

FOOD For centuries, the Irish—sometimes by choice, sometimes from necessity—seemed to eat simply to exist, without much thought to anything beyond a basic diet of boiled potatoes and buttermilk.

Today's culinary scene is, however, a far cry from those early days of poverty and oppression. In recent years Irish chefs have traveled widely; imports of hitherto exotic fruits and vegetables have poured into the country; and the average Irish citizen has come to appreciate not only the excellent meats, vegetables, and fruits of the native soil, but those from abroad as well.

Meals and Dining Customs A skimpy **breakfast** of toast and coffee may be well and good for Americans, according to the Irish, but as for themselves, they'll stick with the hearty breakfast that will see them through whatever the morning hours may hold. Freshly squeezed orange juice, porridge or a cold cereal, one or two eggs, a rasher of bacon, a sausage or two, broiled tomato, black pudding, and brown bread and butter—now, *there's* a breakfast worthy of the name!

As an agricultural nation, the Irish have always had their heartiest meal (called **"dinner"**) at mid-day—workers in the fields needed sustenance to see them through the afternoon. In rural areas, it's still likely to be the largest meal of the day. In cities, however, it may be a salad plate or soup and a sandwich. The **evening meal ("tea")** is usually around 6pm, and depending on what you had for dinner, can be either the aforesaid salad plate, a grill of rashers, bacon, french fries, etc., or a complete main meal.

But as pennypinchers, our main interest is in satisfying each day's hunger on the budget we've set for ourselves. Believe me, you can do that and still eat *well!* So well, in fact, that I'll wager you'll be able to treat yourself to at least one pricey meal in the "Worth the Extra Money" restaurant of your choice. Remember, you're going to begin each day with a mammoth breakfast that will either carry you over all the way to dinner, or at the very least call for only a light mid-day repast. Remember, too, that if you're staying in B&Bs, it's probable that you'll be served tea and scones or cake along about 10 o'clock in the evening—and it won't cost you a cent!

The Cuisine Dairy products top the list of foods you should not miss: Never have I tasted butter or cream to compare with Ireland's. And if you're a cheese lover, you'll find some excellent cheddars. (I make it a practice to ask the locals about cheeses made in their locality, and I've struck real gold in Kerry's mountains as well as Waterford's fertile fields.) Smoked salmon is not only a delicacy, it's affordable in Ireland, and you can gorge yourself to your heart's content. Dublin Bay prawns are a "don't miss," as is plaice, a fish served all over the country. Small-town bakeries often have soda bread for sale fresh from the oven, as well as some cream-filled pastries that are as light as a feather.

At mealtime in Irish homes, starters can be barley, beef, or vegetable soup, shrimp cocktail, homemade pâté, or small portions of that wonderful smoked salmon. The main dish is likely to be local veal, beef, and lamb, or salmon (fresh and or smoked), prawns, plaice, and trout, accompanied by the old spud—roasted, baked, mashed, or in the form of french fries. Sweet lettuce, tomatoes, and cucumbers the size of our squash go into fresh salads, and vegetables both home-grown and from the gardens of Spain or Israel complete the heaping plates of "mains." Bread? It's that famous soda or brown bread, freshly baked and many times still warm, just waiting to be spread with golden butter. Desserts tend to be apple or rhubarb tart or sherry trifle, all topped with lashings of sweet, rich fresh cream. Tea, of course, comes in a bottomless pot. All fairly plain foods, all wholesome, and all in gigantic portions.

As for Irish restaurants, they've come a long way. Today's chefs are likely to have been trained in leading culinary schools on the continent or in one of Ireland's excellent hotel-training institutions. Menus are more varied than I ever thought I'd see in this land of plain-food eaters. International cuisine is available not only in Dublin, but in all the larger cities and many small villages tucked away beside the sea or in the basement of a mansion on the grounds of Bunratty Castle. French, Italian, Chinese, and even Russian restaurants are to be found, along with some very good places that serve wonderfully prepared native dishes.

It's even possible nowadays to get a decent cup of perked coffee in many restaurants, although I find the tea in Ireland is so much better that I seldom long for coffee. The tea you'll be served is downright habit forming, with a hearty, robust flavor that could make you foreswear coffee for all time.

If you should find yourself addicted, you'll be glad to know that it can grace your own breakfast table (or midnight tray) when you get back home. Richard Bewley and his wife, Jo, members of the famed Bewley's tea and coffee shops family in Dublin, now live in the U.S. and have established a mail-order business for Bewley's tea and other Irish products. Prices for the tea are quite reasonable, and there's no better memory-nudger than a steaming "cuppa" of the Bewley's brew. Contact Bewley Irish Imports, 1130 Greenhill Rd., West Chester, PA 19380 (tel. 215/696-2682).

DRINK   Ah, drink! The delight and the despair of the Irish! At least, that's the press they get. The truth of it is that they *do*, indeed, enjoy their drink, and Ireland surely has its fair share of dyed-in-the-wool alcoholics. On the other hand, it's tea you'll be offered most often.

Bottled Water and Soft Drinks   In the past few years, several brands of bottled **Irish spring water** have appeared on the market. Ballygowan leads the pack. Lightly carbonated, it comes plain and with a variety of flavors (my personal favorite is lime) and is a deliciously refreshing drink. Most pubs now stock Ballygowan, and it has proved to be very popular with locals, both young and old.

Other non-alcoholic drinks include most **sodas** you know at home (Coca-Cola, etc.), plus a fizzy white **lemonade** or orange drink that are both very popular.

Guinness, Whisky, and Wine   Order a pint in an Irish pub and what you'll get, unless you specify otherwise, is **Guinness,** the rich, dark Irish stout served with a white, creamy head that—if it's a properly pulled pint—will last right down to the last drop. The question of who pulls the best pint in Dublin, Killarney, Cork, etc., is a continually debated subject, and if your pint arrives just seconds after you order it, you may be very sure that *your* bartender is not among those in the running. There is a subtle, delicate art to drawing the stout, so be prepared to wait. Guinness is Ireland's oldest brewery, dating back to 1759, and is still brewed in its original location at St. James's Gate in Dublin, and available on draft or bottled in every pub worthy of the name in Ireland.

Irish whisky was first distilled in 1609 at the Bushmill's plant in County Antrim, as it is even today. "Black Bush" is the affectionate name for 12-year-old Bushmill's, while that matured for only 7 years goes by the name of the distillery.

Lager, or beers, popular in Ireland are Harp, Smithwick's, Carlsberg, and Murphy. **Dry cider** has enjoyed an upsurge in popularity in recent years, with Stag topping the list. Among **low-alcohol drinks,** the one most called for is a fruity wine called West Coast Cooler.

Until the last 10 years or so, sherry and port were about the only **wines** you were likely to encounter in Ireland. Not so these days. Most large supermarkets and all off-license shops now stock a respectable variety of wines from around the world. Spanish, Italian, and French wines are readily available, and show up regularly on Irish dinner tables. Most pubs also keep both red and white wine on hand.

9. RECOMMENDED BOOKS, FILMS & RECORDINGS

BOOKS I have tried to give some indication of the uniqueness of the Irish people and the country in which they live. But the characters of both are best illuminated by native writers, those luminary figures who have cast a glow across the world's literary scene for centuries. Their names are legion, and a complete listing would fill volumes. At the end of this section, however, you will find a short list that I hope will lend insight and color to your Irish experience.

I have always found that reading is a very personal choice, but I would like to share with you a few of the books that have been most meaningful to me as I have come to know Ireland and its people. Some of the titles listed below may not be readily available in the U.S. However, if you contact **Kennys Bookshop,** High Street, Galway, Ireland (tel. 091/61014 or 61021; fax 091/68544), they will mail both books and tapes if you send along a credit-card number. Many of the books are now out in paperback, so be sure to specify if that's what you prefer.

General Economic, Political, and Social History *The Oxford Illustrated History of Ireland,* edited by R. F. Foster (Oxford University Press), is a comprehensive history; each era is discussed by an authority on the period. Another solid introduction to Irish history, politics, and culture is Breandan oHeithir's *This Is Ireland* (The O'Brien Press, 1987). The author, a nephew of Liam O'Flaherty, the short-story writer, is an important journalist with incomparable knowledge of his native land.

The authoritative book on the great Irish famine of 1845–49 is Cecil Woodham-Smith's *The Great Hunger* (Hamish Hamilton, 1962), and *Paddy's Lament: Ireland 1846-1847, Prelude to Hatred,* by Thomas Gallagher (Harcourt Brace Jovanovich, 1982) is a vivid account of Irish families who fled to the United States and England during this period.

For a succinct and accurate description of the 1916 Rising and its aftermath, look for *The Troubles—the Struggle for Irish Freedom, 1912–1922,* by Ulick O'Connor (Mandarin Press). The best biography to date of the leader of that rising is undoubtedly *Patrick Pearse, The Triumph of Failure,* by Ruth Dudley Edwards (Poolbeg Press, 1990), and *The Big Fellow,* by Frank O'Connor (Poolbeg Press), has become a classic on the life of Michael Collins, a key figure in the fight for independence and in treaty negotiations.

The Arts In the early 1980s, Tim Pat Coogan edited a special issue of *Literary Review* under the title *Ireland and the Arts,* a comprehensive compilation of essays by leading authorities on just about everything that affects artistic sensibility—the *Book of Kells,* the Irish Renaissance of art (including the visual arts), novels, short stories, poetry, music, the theater, architecture, and crafts.

A *Short History of Irish Literature,* by Seamus Deane (Hutchinson, 1986), begins with the Gaelic background of Irish literature and goes on to talk about the Anglo-Irish tradition, the Celtic revival, modern fiction, poetry, drama, and contemporary writers up to 1980. Ulick O'Connor's *Celtic Dawn* is an immensely readable history of the Irish Literary Renaissance, and an ideal introduction to the subject.

Archeology   Dr. Peter Harbison is *the* authoritative voice on Ireland's archeological heritage, and his *Guide to the National Monuments in the Republic of Ireland* (Gill & Macmillan, 1975) is a "must" travel companion for anyone even slightly interested in traces of the past.

Fiction, Poetry, and Travel   There are, of course, the greats: Synge, O'Casey, Joyce, ad infinitum. For me, to capture the sheer poetry of the country, almost anything by Yeats can be recommended; the gutsy, gusty irreverence of Brendan Behan—I especially enjoyed *Brendan Behan's Island—an Irish Sketchbook* (Hutchinson, 1962)—brings a sense of poignant hilarity to the Irish scene that I've found nowhere else; James Plunket's *Strumpet City* (Hutchinson, 1978) paints a rich, full portrait of Dublin that encompasses that city's multilayered society in the years leading up to World War I; and John B. Keane's writings, be they essays, short stories, his one novel (*The Bodhrán Makers*), or plays, bare the soul of the Irish countryman in an honest and affectionate manner that lends understanding and depth to many an Irish encounter.

Further, I have a recommendation you won't find listed anywhere under Ireland's great writers, but which represents some of my most enjoyable and instructive Irish reading: Walter Macken's historical trilogy has quite literally brought the country's history alive for me. *Seek the Fair Land* is set in 1649, the Cromwell era; *The Silent People* tells of the famine years and British oppression; and *The Scorching Wind* is a tale of Ireland's Civil War. You'll find them in most Irish bookshops and at Shannon and Dublin airports, and I urge you to read any or all of them for the simple pleasure of a good story well told, as well as for a sort of "instant history" lesson.

Among other novels to seek out are: *Across the Bitter Sea,* by Eilis Dillon (Coronet), set in postfamine Ireland; *At Swim Two Birds,* by Flann O'Brien (Penguin Twentieth Century Classic), a classic of Irish fantasy and comedy that has become a cult book; *Without My Cloak,* by Kate O'Brien (Virago Press, 1986), one of Ireland's most important women novelists of this century, writing here about three generations of a Limerick family from the 1980s; and *Tarry Flynn,* by Patrick Kavanagh Proscenuim, 1977 (Penguin Modern Classics), an idyllic and beautifully evocative account of Irish life earlier this century.

The Penguin Book of Irish Short Stories, edited by Ben Kiely, is a comprehensive and delightful collection. Ben Kiely also edited what is one of the best and most lavishly illustrated introductions to the poet W. B. Yeats, *Yeats's Ireland, An Illustrated Anthology* (Arum Press, 1990). *The Faber Book of Irish Verse* has poet John Montague as its editor and traces Irish poetry from its very beginnings to the present day.

In the realm of travel, *The Pipes Are Calling—Our Jaunts Through Ireland,* by Niall and Christine Breen, is a relaxing ramble along the highways and byways as related in diary form; and *Off-Beat Ireland,* by Des Moore (Nomad Books), passes along some of the ghostly, bizarre, touching, and absolutely fascinating tales he picked up during more than 30 years of this distinguished journalist's travels around the country.

Autobiography and Folklore   Two classics of life on the Blasket Islands, both translated from the original Irish, are Maurice O'Sullivan's tales of life on the islands at the beginning of this century, *Twenty Years A-growing* (Oxford University Press, 1953; with an introductory note by E. M. Forster) and *The Islandman,* by Thomas O'Crohan (Oxford University Press; translated by Robin Flower).

Alice Taylor's *To School Through the Fields* (Dingle, 1990) is a delightful description of what it was like to grow up in the rural Ireland of the 1940s and '50s and a quick, easy read.

The Last of the Name: Memories of Donegal, by Charles McGlinchy (Blackstaff Press, 1989; with an introduction by Brian Friel and illustrations by Ciaran Hughes), is a truly extraordinary book that describes life in rural Ireland over the last two centuries and has a folk memory that goes back to 1703.

Ireland's folklore still has great meaning in the world of the '90s, and *Irish Sagas and Folk Tales,* by Eileen O'Faolain (Poolbeg Press, 1986), is easily the most comprehensive collection of important Irish myths and sagas to be found in one volume. Liam Mac Con Iomaire's *Ireland of the Proverb* (Masters Press, 1988) gives each proverb in Irish and English, with a full explanation of its origin, and Bill Doyle's photographs bring Ireland to vivid life.

Newsletters and Magazines *Inside Ireland* is a quarterly newsletter written especially for the likes of you and me who want to keep up with what's going on in Ireland. Its publisher, Dubliner Brenda Weir, is an expert on many far-ranging subjects. The newsletter is an eclectic collection of witty and informative tidbits, in-depth articles, humor, services such as restaurant and accommodation reviews, answers to subscribers' queries on costs of an Irish visit, advice on retiring to Ireland, and genealogy research. Subscribers enjoy such free fringe benefits as an annual shopping guide, accommodations directory, and a genealogy reference booklet. There are also supplements on real estate and annual features on Irish summer schools and Irish cookery, as well as special offers for certain Irish craft items. A valuable discount voucher for mail order or direct purchase also goes to all members. They also can arrange enrollment in summer-school sessions or short courses throughout the year with the Palladio Academy of Interior Design in Fitzwilliam Square in Dublin. You can get a sample copy by sending $3, or send $35 for a year's subscription, to *Inside Ireland,* P.O. Box 1886, Dublin 16 (tel. 01/931906).

The second publication that will keep your Irish memories fresh is *Ireland of the Welcomes,* a bimonthly magazine published by the Irish Tourist Board. Beautifully produced and illustrated, each issue has features by some of the country's leading writers, as well as those of other nationalities, but always on a subject intimately connected with Ireland. It's a grand way to transport yourself back to Ireland while sitting in America, and the cost is a mere $16 for a year's subscription, $28 for two years. Write to the Irish Tourist Board, Baggot Street Bridge, Dublin 2.

For Children Classical fantasy reigns in *The Hounds of the Morrigan,* by Pat O'Shea (Puffin Books, 1987), which is set in the west of Ireland. It has been translated into several languages, and the film rights have been sold to a major studio.

Tom McCaughren turns out entertaining and informative adventure tales for children, and *The Legend of the Corrib King* (Acorn Books, 1984) is one of his best.

The Viking Princess, by Michael Mullen (Poolbeg Press, 1988), will keep the kids' attention riveted until the very last page in this wonderful novel set in Viking Ireland.

FILMS & VIDEOTAPES Ireland made its mark in the film world in 1990 with the capture of no fewer than three Oscar awards for the film *My Left Foot,* a powerful and moving story of Christy Brown, the remarkable writer who grew up in the Dublin slums, so severely handicapped that he wrote the novel on which the film is based with one foot.

The Field, by John B. Keane, is based on one of this author's most famous plays, which depicts the vital role of landownership in Irish country life. Filmed in the west of Ireland during 1990, it features powerful performances from some of moviedom's greatest actors and promises to make a strong bid for still more Oscars in 1991.

Now available on videotape, the following are classics of Irish filmmakers or are based in Ireland:

Darby O'Gill and the Little People (1959), directed by Robert Stevenson, with Sean Connery and Janet Munro. One of Disney's best fantasies.

The Dead (1987) is John Huston's film based on a James Joyce story.

Juno and the Paycock (1929), Alfred Hitchcock's film of Sean O'Casey's play, with actors from the Abbey Theater.

Man of Aran (1934), Robert Flaherty's black-and-white documentary that preserves the hard, sometimes grim life of the Aran Islands.

Odd Man Out (1946), directed by Carol Reed, with James Mason and Robert Newton, is about a wounded gunman on the run during the Troubles.

The Quiet Man (1952), John Ford's rollicking classic of life in the west of Ireland and the return of a native son, with John Wayne and Maureen O'Hara—probably the best loved of all Irish films by Irish-Americans.

Ryan's Daughter (1970), a spectacularly beautiful film whose sometimes forgettable performances take a back seat to the dramatic backdrop of the Dingle Peninsula.

RECORDINGS   All the titles listed below are available on both cassette tapes and compact disks.

Ceol Tigh Neachtain, Music from Galway, by Tigh Neachtain. At the end of Ireland's presidency of the E.E.C. in early 1990, this is the tape presented by the Irish government to some 2,000 European delegates as the best example of traditional Irish music on tape.

Feadoga Stain, Traditional Irish Music on the Tin Whistle, the finest offering of one of the purest tin whistle players in Ireland.

Siul Uait (Take the Air), by Sean Ryan. A superb tape by the tin whistle player who is known as "the genius of Galway."

The Chieftains and James Galway in Ireland, a joining of forces by the country's most famous traditional group and James Galway—a magnificent tape.

Granuaile, an evocation of the Irish pirate queen, Grace O'Malley (1530–1603), with music by composer Shaun Davey, sung by Rita Connolly with Liam O'Flynn, uillean pipes, and chamber orchestra.

Omos Do Joe Cooley, a tribute to one of Ireland's finest fiddle players by Frankie Gavin and Paul Brock, worthy successors to the title.

Stony Steps, a beautiful tape of flute playing by Matt Molloy, a member of the Chieftains.

Mise Eire, by Sean O'Riada, the famous film score for the film of this name (which means "I am Ireland"), played by the Radio Telefis Eireann Symphony Orchestra and released to mark the 50th anniversary of the 1916 Rising—remarkable for its use of traditional music.

O'Riada Sa Gaiety le Sean O'Se agus Ceoltoiri Cuslann, by Sean O'Riada, a famous concert held in Dublin during the mid-1960s—the tape captures the excitement of truly great performances.

The Planxty Collection, an attractive collection of music and song by Planxty, a popular group during the '70s.

Two of the most popular balladeer groups in Ireland are The Dubliners and The Wolfe Tones, both of whom have recorded a number of good tapes featuring ballads from the past and the present—shop around for your favorite tunes.

PLANNING A TRIP TO IRELAND

This may well be the most important chapter of the book, since it is devoted to the things you must do ahead, such as arming yourself with the necessary documents and wardrobe, and knowing details about currency and the rate of exchange. Not the most exciting reading, perhaps, but certainly careful reading of this part of your "homework" can help make the difference in your getting the last bit of enjoyment from your trip.

1. INFORMATION, ENTRY REQUIREMENTS & MONEY

SOURCES OF INFORMATION The native hospitality of the Irish begins long before you embark on your visit—few countries send you off as well prepared as Ireland. The friendly folk at any branch of the Irish Tourist Board (ITB; Bord Failte, in Ireland) take their literal name, Board of Welcomes, quite seriously. It's an official government agency that somehow seems to escape the impersonal, don't-care attitude that so often pervades bureaucratic institutions. They'll supply you with literature to help with your initial planning, answer any questions that may come up, advise you on tracing your Irish ancestry, arrange for you to meet Irish families, and generally see to it that you're off to a good start.

The **Irish Tourist Board** office in the United States is at 757 Third Avenue, New York, NY 10017 (tel. 212/418-0800); in Toronto, 1160 Bloor Street East, Suite 934, Toronto, ONT, M4W 1BN (tel. 416/929-2777); in London, 150 New Bond Street, London W1Y OAQ (tel. 071/493-3201); in Sydney, MLC Center, 38th Level, Martin Place, Sydney NSW 2000 (tel. 02/232-7177). There are also offices in Paris, Frankfurt-am-Main, and Amsterdam, and another United States office is planned for Atlanta, Georgia.

Their informative publications include booklets about trip planning; accommodations (the Town & Country Association booklet has photos of individual homes); farm holidays (also illustrated with photos); self-catering accommodations (including photos); dining; special events; and historical sightseeing. And they can provide a good map showing scenic routes.

The board also issues information sheets that are concise, detailed reports on everything from sailing schools to hiking to museums to folk music.

ENTRY REQUIREMENTS A valid passport is all that U.S. citizens need to travel in Ireland. It is no longer necessary even to show proof of smallpox vaccination when returning to this country. If you're a British citizen, you can travel freely in Ireland without a passport, but I'd strongly advise bringing it along if you have one, since on some occasions it may be the only acceptable form of identification (for picking up money orders sent from abroad, etc.). If you're a citizen of any other country, be sure to check with the Irish Embassy in your area as to what additional documents you may need.

MONEY The 1970s saw two significant changes in Irish currency. First, in 1971 the country went on the decimal system; that is, the Irish pound was divided into 100 pence. Since the Irish pound at that time maintained parity with the pound sterling, English notes and coins were interchangeable with Irish money.

In 1979, however, the second currency change occurred when, as a member of the European Monetary System, the Irish government linked its monetary values to those of major EEC currencies and the Irish pound officially became the "punt." As a result, although English notes are now accepted on the same basis as any other foreign currency by many shops, restaurants, and hotels, life is simpler for the traveler if all transactions are in Irish punts (often still referred to as the "Irish pound").

The **Irish punt (IR£)** is divided into 100 **pence (p)**, and coins come in denominations of ½, 1, 2, 5, 10, 20, and 50 pence, and 1 punt. All banks make exchanges on the basis of daily quotations, and it is always wise to change your money at a bank or an American Express office. Some of the larger shops and hotels also work on daily quotations, but many more simply take a weekly average when figuring exchange rates, which can sometimes cost you more when changing notes.

At press time, IR£1 equals $1.75 U.S. ($1 U.S. equals 57p), and that is the rate of exchange used in calculating the dollar values cited in this book. Remember that this exchange rate fluctuates over time, so these dollar values are given only as a guide and will likely be different when you arrive in Ireland.

WHAT THINGS COST IN DUBLIN	U.S. $
Taxi from the airport to the city center	22.75
Tram (DART) discount day ticket inside the city	3.50
Local telephone call	.35
Per person sharing at the Leeson Court Hotel (deluxe)	55.15
Per person sharing with bath, at Kilronan House (moderate)	45.75
Per person sharing, without bath, at Harvey's (budget)	21.90
Brunch at Whelan's Pub (moderate)	7.00
Lunch for one at Le Coq Hardi (deluxe)	26.25
Lunch for one at the Aberdeen Room (moderate)	17.50
Lunch for one at Bewley's Cafe (budget)	8.75
Dinner for one, without wine, at The Lord Edward (deluxe)	35.00
Dinner for one, without wine, at the Aberdeen Room (moderate)	26.25
Dinner for one, without wine, at Gallagher's (budget)	12.25
Pint of beer (draft Guinness)	2.55
Coca-Cola	.75
Cup of coffee	.85
Roll of Kodacolor film, 36 exposures	8.75
Admission to see the Book of Kells	3.05
Movie ticket	7.00
Theater ticket	15.00

WHAT THINGS COST IN COUNTY KERRY & THE DINGLE PENINSULA U.S. $

Local telephone call	.35
Per person sharing at Doyles Townhouse (deluxe)	48.15
Per person sharing, with bath, at Cleevaun (moderate)	23.65
Per person sharing, without bath, at the Hibernian (budget)	17.50
Lunch for one at The Strawberry Tree (deluxe)	20.00
Lunch for one at the Armada Restaurant (moderate)	10.05
Lunch for one at The Laurels Pub (budget)	3.50
Dinner for one, without wine, at The Pygmalion Restaurant (deluxe)	35.00
Dinner for one, without wine, at Linden House (moderate)	19.95
Dinner for one, without wine, at The King's Inn (budget)	12.25
Pint of beer (draft lager)	2.35
Pot of tea with bread and butter	1.65
Roll of Kodacolor film, 36 exposures	8.75
Admission to Muckross House	3.50

In the last year or so, exchange rates of foreign currencies against the U.S. dollar have fluctuated more sharply than in the past, and you may want to consider this up-to-date recommendation by Deak International (formerly Deak-Perera), a leading currency-exchange company: If you know your travel dates several months in advance, keep a sharp eye on U.S./Irish exchange rates and purchase punts when the rate is favorable. While they don't advise converting more than one-third to one-half of your travel currency in advance, you can still realize a substantial increase in buying power if you take advantage of periods when the dollar is at its strongest.

For safety's sake, you'll want to carry most of your money in the form of **traveler's checks,** not in cash. Be sure to keep your traveler's checks separate from the record of their numbers so that any lost checks can be readily replaced. Bear in mind, too, that you'll get a better exchange rate with traveler's checks than with cash.

2. WHEN TO GO—CLIMATE, HOLIDAYS & EVENTS

CLIMATE Rave to the Irish about their glorious country and nine times out of ten the response will be "Sure, it's nice enough, if it only weren't for the weather." It's no use trying to convince them that the weather really isn't that bad—they're apparently born with an apology complex about their climate. The Atlantic brings the Gulf Stream's warming currents to Irish shores, creating a friendly climate that deals in moderation rather than extremes, seldom more than 65° Fahrenheit in July or August (occasionally "soaring" to 70°), and hardly ever lower than 40° in January or February.

The infamous Irish rainfall is heaviest and most frequent in the mountains of the west, and frequent enough in the rest of the country to keep at least 40 shades of green glowing. Showers come and go—sometimes several times in one day—but for the most part they consist of a misty sort of rain, one that adds an extra dimension to the landscape. If you want to see more sun than rain, you'll generally find it in May except in the midlands and southeast, where June is apt to be sunnier.

HOLIDAYS In the Republic, national holidays fall on: January 1 (New Year's Day), March 17 (St. Patrick's Day), Good Friday and Easter Monday, the first Monday in June, the first Monday in August, the last Monday in October, December 25 (Christmas Day), and December 26 (St. Stephen's Day). The whole country shuts down for these days. Northern Ireland observes the same holiday schedule, with the exception that the August bank holiday is replaced by the first Monday in September and the Battle of the Boyne is celebrated on July 12.

Also, some towns observe an "Early Closing Day," with shops closing at 1pm; since the day of the week varies from community to community, be sure to inquire if you have shopping to do.

EVENTS It may be a slight exaggeration to say that there's a "special event" of one sort or another every other day in Ireland, but it has been my experience that the simplest, most ordinary occurrence can take on a festive air if two or more natives are present.

If you're lucky enough to arrive in a small town or village when its own special festival (sometimes called a "pattern day") is in progress, you'll be in for a real treat. There is always at least one day, usually several, filled with the likes of fancy-dress parades, donkey races, traditional music and dance contests, and ending with a dance that draws locals from miles away. As far as I know, no one has compiled a list of these festivals and their dates, so you'll just have to be on the lookout for the homemade signs on the outskirts of town as you travel around. Also, if you pick up a current copy of *Old Moore's Almanac* at a news agent, you'll find a listing of most fairs, festivals, and pattern days for the year.

Especially from March through November, however, there are enough organized special events around the country to set you thinking about an extended visit. Any Irish Tourist Board office can furnish a complete current "Calendar of Events" to help you plan your travel dates around the ones that are most appealing. To avoid disappointment, be sure to check with the Irish Tourist Board or the Northern Ireland Tourist Board when planning to attend any special event.

IRELAND
CALENDAR OF EVENTS

FEBRUARY

☐ **Ulster Harp National steeplechase,** Downpatrick, Co. Down (the only place to see horseracing in Northern Ireland). Late February to early March.

MARCH

☐ **International Marching Band Competitions.** Colorful (and tuneful!) 1-day competitions held on successive days in Limerick and Galway. Mid-March.

✪ *ST. PATRICK'S WEEK (his day is the 17th). Celebrated throughout the country with parades, concerts, street performances, etc.* **Where:** *Throughout the country.* **When:** *March 12–19.* **How:** *Public events.*

APRIL

☐ **World Irish Dancing Championship,** Cork. Irish dancers from around the globe congregate for a week of elimination performances. Second week in April.
☐ **Circuit of Ireland Car Rally.** Thrilling road race around the country, with fierce competition between drivers from year to year. Mid-April.

MAY

⊙ *FLEADH NUA Festival featuring traditional Irish dance, music, and song. One of Ireland's most popular events, with music filling concert halls, hotel lounges, pubs, and the streets (be sure to book accommodations well in advance if you plan to attend this one).* **Where:** *Ennis, Co. Clare.* **When:** *Date varies from early to late May.* **How:** *Contact Comhaltas Cheoiltoire Eireann, 32 Belgrave Square, Monkstown, Co. Dublin (tel. 01/800-295) for information.*

☐ **Cork International Choral and Folk Dance Festival,** Cork. Prestigious gathering of dancers and singers from Europe, North America, and other parts of the world. First or second week in May.

☐ **Pan Celtic Week,** Killarney, Co. Kerry. Celts from Scotland, Wales, Cornwall, Brittany, Spain, and other parts of Europe celebrate their ancient heritage in a variety of cultural events. First or second week in May.

☐ **International Maytime Festival,** Dundalk, Co. Louth. A week-long celebration of the coming of summer. Last week in May, sometimes stretching into the first week of June.

JUNE

☐ **Writers' Week,** Listowel, Co. Kerry. Irish literature workshops, lectures, plays, etc., meant to inspire and assist beginning writers, but you don't have to be a writer to attend. Ireland's leading writers, playwrights, and poets are usually in attendance. Early June, although dates have varied from May to October in recent years.

☐ **Ballybunion International Bachelor Festival,** Ballybunion, Co. Kerry. Ireland's most eligible bachelors pay court to the swarms of maiden ladies who flock to West Kerry in search of a husband. Late June.

☐ **West Cork Festival,** Clonakilty, Co. Cork. Week-long festivities featuring the rugged people of West Cork making music, singing, dancing, and competing in a variety of sports events. Late June.

JULY

☐ **Cobh International Folk Dance Festival,** Cobh, Co. Cork. Celebrated its 30th year in 1991. Second week in July.

☐ **Galway Race Week,** Galway. Seven days of gala parties, exciting horseracing, and revelry in the streets (book a year ahead if you want to stay in Galway—otherwise you'll be bunking in the hinterlands and driving in each day). Late July.

☐ **Mary from Dungloe Festival,** Dungloe, Co. Donegal. Festive events of all descriptions—Mary is to Dungloe and County Donegal what Molly Malone is to Dublin. Last days of July into the first week of August.

AUGUST

⊙ *PUCK FAIR Much ado about goats, with one lucky ram reigning over one of the country's oldest festivals when the streets are filled with horses as traveling people and horse traders from all over Ireland deal and trade; 2 days of lively, sometimes riotous, fun.* **Where:** *Killorglin, Co. Kerry.* **When:** *Second week of August.* **How:** *Public events; book accommodations well in advance.*

☐ **Rose of Tralee Festival,** Tralee (with some events in Killarney), Co. Kerry. Much revelry as beauties from around the world with Irish connections, no matter how tenuous, parade and perform in search of the Rose title. Last week in August (sometimes held in early September).

☐ **Fleadh Cheoll.** A 3-day festival of traditional Irish music attracting an international crowd; there's no set venue, so check for the current location. Late August or early September.

SEPTEMBER

◐ *WATERFORD FESTIVAL OF INTERNATIONAL LIGHT OPERA*
Surprisingly professional performances, many times of little known operas.
Where: *Theatre Royal, Waterford.* **When:** *Mid-September.* **How:** *Call tel. 051-74402 for tickets and information.*

☐ **International Oyster Festival,** Galway. Unabashed tribute to gluttony, with all and sundry competing to see who can consume the most bivalves fresh from local waters—always washed down, of course, with many pints of Guinness. Last 2 days in September.

OCTOBER

☐ **Guinness Jazz Festival,** Cork. One of Cork City's best, drawing leading jazz musicians from around the world—the streets, concert halls, recital halls, and pubs are literally alive with this American art form. Last week in October.

◐ *WEXFORD OPERA FESTIVAL* *Eleven days of workshops, recitals, opera performances, and several "black tie" events.*
Where: *Theatre Royal, High Street, Wexford.* **When:** *End of October into first week of November.* **How:** *Call the Box Office, tel. 053-22144, for tickets and information.*

DUBLIN CALENDAR OF EVENTS

FEBRUARY

☐ **International Rugby Championship.** Home matches played at Lansdowne Road stadium. Early February (matches sometimes held in late January).
☐ **Dublin Film Festival.** Films of all description—commercial, artistic, documentary, etc.—compete, and Dublin is filled with the greats, near-greats, and would-be-greats of the film world. Last week of February into the first week of March.

MARCH

☐ **Irish Motor Show,** Royal Dublin Society grounds, Ballsbridge. First or second week in March.
☐ **Irish International Boat Show.** Draws an international crowd of seafarers. Late March.

◐ *ST. PATRICK'S DAY PARADE* *Dubliners and international visitors line the streets of the capital; it's on a much smaller scale than New York City's miles-long parade, but there's something very special about honoring the saint in the country that he made his own. March 17.*

MAY

☐ **Spring Show,** Royal Dublin Society grounds, Ballsbridge. Agricultural and industrial showcase with a "country fair" ambience; it's rather informal and lots of fun for youngsters as well as adults. 3 days in the second week in May.

JUNE

☐ **Festival of Music in Great Houses.** Recitals by world famous artists in lovely 18th-century mansions. Second week in June.

JULY

○ **KERRYGOLD DUBLIN HORSE SHOW** Deemed by some to be the social event of the year; there are gala parties and balls all over the city resplendent with horse people from around the world dressed to the nines (requires booking far in advance for accommodations in Dublin—as much as a year ahead). **Where:** the Royal Dublin Society, Ballsbridge **When:** Mid-July.

SEPTEMBER

☐ **All Ireland Hurling Finals,** Croke Park. One of Ireland's most popular sports events; tickets are next to impossible to obtain, but it's great fun to watch on the telly in a pub or with Irish friends at home. First week in September.

☐ **All Ireland Football Finals.** Same as above, featuring football instead of hurling. Mid-September.

○ **DUBLIN THEATER FESTIVAL** Two weeks of superb theater featuring Irish and international troupes. **Where:** Various venues. **When:** Last week in September through first week in October. **How:** Write to Dublin Theater Festival, 47 Nassau Street, Dublin 2, for information. Tickets are available at individual theaters.

3. HEALTH, INSURANCE & OTHER CONSIDERATIONS

HEALTH Medical facilities in Ireland are excellent! If you need a doctor, dentist, or hospital service, the first source of information should be your accommodations hostess or someone on the local scene. Failing that, the **Irish Medical Organization,** 10 Fitzwilliam Place, Dublin (tel. 01/767273), can put you in touch with local medical help.

If you take any form of medication, it's a good idea to bring along prescriptions from your doctor in case you need refills. It's also a good idea to carry a copy of your prescription for glasses or contact lenses.

INSURANCE Before leaving home, check to be sure that your property insurance is in good order, with premium payments up-to-date and full coverage for fire, theft, etc. It's a good idea, also, to have health and accident insurance when traveling. If your present policy does not provide coverage when you're out of the country, check with your insurance carrier about temporary medical coverage for the duration of your trip. Most travel agents can arrange this, along with travel-delay or cancellation and lost-luggage insurance.

When renting a car in Ireland, the small premiums for both collision damage and personal accident insurance are a good investment. Although your credit card company may offer such coverage when you use your card for car rentals, recently there have been a host of difficulties in settling claims through such companies—the premiums are a small price to pay for peace of mind.

MAKING ADVANCE RESERVATIONS Ireland is a country that invites a delightful, spur-of-the-moment travel plan. I am not, however, enamored of stumbling off a transatlantic plane, numb with jet lag and faced with the prospect of having to hunt for a room. Nor am I inclined to hop behind the wheel of a car and head off into the country before my body adjusts to the time change or my mind is clear enough to cope with left-side-of-the-road driving. Even less desirable would be arriving in the country and finding that there's no rental car available! Or plan on seeing a play at the Abbey Theater and find it booked out for the only night I'm in Dublin.

To put it succinctly, there are some advance reservations that are absolutely vital to a happy holiday, even for the most haphazard traveler. I suggest the following minimal advance bookings.

Accommodations: At the top of the list is your first night's accommodation. You can book that first night's stay through **Central Reservations Service,** Dublin Tourism, 14 Upper O'Connell Street, Dublin 1 (tel. 01/735209 or 735043; fax 786295), but only by charging to MasterCard or VISA 4 weeks in advance. Or you can write directly to one of the accommodations listed in this book. If you choose the latter, you'll save time by enclosing a deposit and an International Reply Coupon for postage. The same applies if you're especially anxious to stay at any particular accommodations and you're certain of the dates for each—during summer months you could be disappointed otherwise.

Car Rental: Then there's the matter of a car rental. Ireland is a small country, with most of its visitors descending during summer months, and there simply is not an inexhaustible supply of automobiles. Especially if you plan to come during the high season, it's absolutely essential to book your car as far in advance as possible. Reserve through travel agents or by writing the rental company direct at the addresses listed for each.

Special Events: As for special events, such as a castle banquet, hotel cabaret, or Dublin theater, Irish Tourist Board offices can make those bookings for you, but it's much more direct to write to each separately, enclose an International Reply Coupon for return postage and a deposit (or the full price), and ask for immediate confirmation. Tickets for major festivals—Dublin Theatre, Wexford Opera, and the Dublin Spring and Horse Shows—can be booked directly by using the addresses for each shown in this book.

4. WHAT TO PACK

One item is an absolute must for your Irish holiday. No matter what time of year you come or what you plan on doing, *bring a raincoat.* Ireland's capricious weather can, and often does, skip from a drizzly morning to a sparkling, sunny afternoon to showers in the evening. A lightweight raincoat comes in handy not only to keep dry but also for chilly days and evenings, and it's a useful substitute for a dressing gown on those trips down the hall to your B&B bathroom.

Ireland's weather can be cool, especially in the evenings, even in summer months, so you should bring along one or two lightweight sweaters or a shawl. Remember that unless you're steel-willed enough to resist those gorgeous Irish hand-knit sweaters, you'll no doubt acquire—and wear—one during your travels. Comfortable walking shoes are a must. It's advisable to stick in one more pair of shoes than you think you'll need—those unexpected showers can leave your feet pretty soggy, and it's well to have a spare pair.

Keep in mind that Ireland is basically a very casual country. However, the theater, a dinner cabaret, or a posh restaurant are definitely not places for jeans. For a woman, a dressy top with pants or a simple skirt will do for most occasions; for men a sports jacket and tie are appropriate. There are a few "Worth the Extra Money" restaurants where you'll be more comfortable with this type of attire.

One word of caution: If you plan to take in the swank Dublin Horse Show week or the Wexford Opera Festival, women will want to have along a cocktail dress and appropriate shoes for the round of parties and receptions that are so much a part of those scenes, and men will want to bring a dark suit for these occasions.

Ireland's department stores and pharmacies are well stocked with all the familiar brands of toiletries and cosmetics.

---

5. TIPS FOR THE DISABLED, SENIORS, SINGLES, FAMILIES & STUDENTS

FOR THE DISABLED Recognizing that all too often the wheelchair traveler, as well as his or her traveling companions, are excluded from guesthouse and other accommodations because of narrow doors, steps, and inaccessibility to toilets, the National Rehabilitation Board in Ireland has set about encouraging accommodation design to circumvent these problems. Although there is still a long way to go before these facilities will be available on a wide scale, the board can furnish an up-to-date list of hotels, guesthouses, and self-catering cottages that do provide accommodations designed for the comfort and convenience of the disabled. You may also see these properties identified in various brochures, listings, etc., through the use of the well-known international symbol of Access for the Disabled. In addition, the board has surveyed existing facilities and identified those most suitable for the wheelchair traveler and one helper, using a variation of the wheelchair access symbol.

A listing of public toilets in Ireland that are accessible for wheelchairs is also available from the board.

For these aids, plus answers to other queries you may have, contact the **National Rehabilitation Board,** 25 Clyde Road, Ballsbridge, Dublin 4 (tel. 01/684181).

Bord Failte also publishes an information sheet entitled "Accommodation for the Disabled," which is a partial listing of premises that have been inspected and approved by the National Rehabilitation Board.

FOR SENIOR CITIZENS The best news for those in the 65-and-over age group is that Ireland, more than any other country of my experience, hasn't the faintest notion about a generation gap! Age simply doesn't bar anyone from any social activity or outdoor recreation. You'll be very welcome to join in groups that vary from youngsters to teenagers to middle-agers to those of your own age bracket. Go along to a disco if it suits your fancy—the only limitation on your participation will be just how much gyrating on the dance floor you choose to do or not do.

Although relatively new to Ireland, **accommodation discounts** for those over 65 are becoming more and more frequent around the country. Usually labeled "Golden Years," "Autumn Gold," or the like, they apply almost exclusively to off- or low-season rates at the moment. However, senior citizen discounts are the coming thing, so be sure to inquire when booking, and if you're booking through an agent, stress that the discount should be requested since it's seldom offered voluntarily.

You will also find **senior-citizen discounts** identified for those hotels, guesthouses, and farmhouses listed in the illustrated **"Ireland Holidays"** booklet available from the Irish Tourist Board. These holiday offers cover the country, from the wilds of northern Donegal to Killarney to the outposts of West Cork to the cities of Cork and Dublin. Virtually every county is represented, and the senior-citizen discount, which runs around 10%, applies to special midweek and weekend rates that are substantially lower than per-day rates. This means that you can often afford accommodations that would otherwise be beyond your budget.

Few sightseeing attractions outside Dublin have senior-citizen prices as of this writing, but, again, it pays to inquire when you pay your admission fee.

FOR SINGLE TRAVELERS   Almost all of my traveling in Ireland is done alone, and I can tell you from firsthand experience that being a single traveler has never been a problem. On the social scene, there just aren't any places I hesitate to go on my own, and restaurants have yet to stick me next to the kitchen door or at the most undesirable table in the place. As for B&B or guesthouse hosts, they unfailingly go out of their way to make me feel at home, often taking great pains to see that I breakfast with compatible guests. If there is an evening entertainment on in the neighborhood, I am invariably asked to join the family or other guests when they set off. And in Irish pubs, I seldom sit alone for very long.

It is also true that in Ireland, as in most of the rest of the world, I frequently (but, I hasten to say, not *always*) pay a slightly higher per-person rate for accommodations than if I were one half of a couple—one of the realities of travel. The only tip I can offer in this regard is to look about for another single traveler and team up as roommates.

FOR FAMILIES   If ever a country were devised for memorable family holidays, it surely must be Ireland! The family unit is still very much the core of Irish life, and visiting families are welcomed with open arms. Your own young ones will not have been in a B&B very long before they are happily going along to play with the host family's brood, and teenagers will soon be out from underfoot as they set off with their local counterparts.

Most B&Bs, guesthouses, and hotels have baby-sitters on hand for the small fry when an adult night out is called for. And, contrary to many other cultures, the Irish don't frown on children in restaurants. Virtually every sightseeing attraction admits children at half price, and the vast majority have family prices as well. If you plan to take advantage of Bus Eireann's excellent day trips, be sure to ask about their special family discounts.

Look in "Ireland Holidays" for off- and low-season specials and family discounts.

Farmhouse Holidays: An increasingly popular family holiday with our readers is one spent in Irish farmhouses. Children and parents alike are utterly delighted to walk the fields with the farmer and, more often than not, lend a helping hand with farm chores. The one essential for a farmhouse holiday is a car, since almost all are off the beaten track and cannot be reached by public transportation.

Prices for farmhouse accommodations usually run one or two punts higher than town and country homes. They offer the budget-stretching partial-board weekly rates. The Irish Tourist Board can furnish a very complete, illustrated booklet, "Farm Holidays in Ireland," for a small charge. The Irish Farm Holidays Association (Failte Tuaithe) also has a publication (small charge) with pictures and a brief description of each member farmhouse. Standards are a little bit higher in association farmhouses, and they, too, will gladly book you. Reservations procedures for farmhouses are described in "Making Advance Reservations" above.

Self-Catering Holidays: On the budgetary front, self-catering facilities are excellent and widespread, and come in all guises, from inner-city town houses and flats to houses in small towns, country and seaside bungalows, thatched cottages, and chalets. In the off-season months, it's possible in some locations to rent for a few midweek days or weekends only, but most rental periods run from Saturday (beginning at 4pm) to the following Saturday (ending before noon). There are three price periods: April, May, June, September (midrange prices); July and August (peak prices); and all other months (lowest price). Rates can range from about IR£95 to IR£210 ($166.25 to $367) in the high season for a cottage that accommodates seven. More luxurious accommodations run more, but are still a very good buy.

Your basic rate will usually include all linens, and if not, they can almost always be rented for a small charge. Kitchens come fully equipped, and some premises even have central heating. In addition, you can expect extra charges for electricity, heating oil and cooking fuels, and, in some cases, television. Ask at the time you book for an estimate of these extras based on the length of your stay.

The **Irish Tourist Board** has compiled a listing of all approved self-catering accommodations, called "Self-Catering," available for a small charge. For Dublin flats, contact **Dublin Tourism,** 14 Upper O'Connell Street, Dublin 1 (tel. 01/747733).

Rent an Irish Cottage Ltd., Shannon Airport, Shannon, Co. Clare (tel. 061/61588), has rental cottages in the west of Ireland, arranged much as in a small Irish village, that combine the traditional hearth, half door, and raftered ceilings with modern conveniences like central heating, electric kitchens, and bathrooms with showers. They're located close to some of the country's most splendid scenic spots, never far from facilities for recreational activities like fishing, swimming, golfing, or pony trekking.

There are four types of cottage design, all hand-thatched, with accommodations for five to eight people. During peak season, weekly rentals range from IR£240 to IR£L340 ($420 to $595), but they descend to a low of IR£132 ($231) in some months, IR£85 ($148.75) on weekends.

The five locations are as follows:

Corofin, Co. Clare (close to lakes, castles, the Burren, and underground caves).

Puckane, Co. Tipperary (2 miles from the Shannon River in North Tipperary, with water sports, boating, and fishing nearby).

Kilfinane, Co. Limerick (27 miles from Limerick City near the Ballyhoura Mountains; horseback riding and fishing available).

Ballyvaughan, Co. Clare (close to the shores of beautiful Galway Bay; the ocean beach is just 3 miles away).

Carrigaholt, Co. Clare (set at the mouth of the Shannon, with historic ruins and majestic cliff scenery close by).

FOR STUDENTS   For students, Ireland has a lot going for it. First of all, with half its population aged 25 and under, Ireland is truly a haven for the young (Tir na nog, the ancient Celts called their version of heaven, and the Gaelic name translates to "land of youth"). Sports, music, dancing, and a host of other activities are geared for the young and available wherever you go in the country.

Not only are recreational and leisure pursuits at your fingertips in Ireland, but the ancient tradition and reverence for learning continue to this day, with all sorts of interesting educational experiences available (see "Educational/Study Travel" in Section 6, "Alternative/Adventure Travel," below).

International Student Identity Card (ISIC): This card opens doors to events and activities aimed only at students, as well as to substantial discounts on almost every facet of travel. You must, however, arm yourself with this valuable document before you leave home. The cost is $14, and you can obtain your card through the **Council on International Educational Exchange (CIEE),** 205 East 42nd Street, New York, NY 10017 (tel. 212/661-1414), or at any of the 30 Council Travel offices or 440 campus issuing offices across the country. With the card in hand, you'll be entitled to participate in all the listings below, as well as many, many more happenings you'll discover once you arrive on Irish soil.

Irish Student Travel Service (USIT). This is the student's best friend in Ireland. If you deplane at Shannon, your very first Irish stop should be the Limerick office at Central Buildings, O'Connell Street (tel. 061/45064 or 48925), open Monday through Friday from 10am to 2pm and 3:15 to 6pm, and from May to September also on Saturday from 10am to 1pm. The head office is in Dublin at 19 Aston Quay, Dublin 2 (tel. 01/778117 or 679-8833), open Monday through Friday from 9:30am to 5:30pm and on Saturday from 10am to 1pm. In Waterford you'll find USIT at 33 O'Connell Street (tel. 051/72601).

USIT will arrange cut-rate travel between Ireland and other European destinations, help you plan itineraries both inside the country and beyond, and advise you about accommodations, camping, summer jobs, and student bargains in every area you can think of.

Transportation Savings: One of USIT's most valuable services is the **Travelsave Stamp,** which, when affixed to your International Student Identity Card, entitles you to such benefits as a 50% discount on Dublin buses and trains, as well as 50% off all rail and bus travel throughout the country, and rail travel in Northern Ireland. In addition, students with a valid CIE stamp will be entitled to approximately one-third off round-trip weekend rail fares and 50% off the ferry service to the Aran Islands and B & I Ferry services.

With the International Student Identity Card in hand, you'll qualify for half-fare rates on all Bus Eireann routes around the country, an all-important moneysaver. In Dublin, you can purchase an **Educational Travel Concession Ticket** from Dublin Bus, 59 Upper O'Connell Street (tel. 720000), which permits unlimited travel on Dublin bus and train services at drastic discounts.

There are also excellent educational holiday programs available—see Section 6, "Alternative/Specialty Travel," below.

6. ALTERNATIVE/ADVENTURE TRAVEL

EDUCATIONAL/STUDY TRAVEL   Published by the Irish Tourist Board, **"Live and Learn,"** is a cornucopia of study possibilities in Ireland for all age groups, many of which include accommodations in Irish homes, weekend travel, and cultural events. Subjects are as varied as Irish literature, drama, music, archeology, crafts, and the Irish language. They also publish a **"Group Accommodations List"** of student residence halls, schools, and hotels that offer reduced rates to students. Bookings for every course should be made as far in advance as possible, so you should write for the booklet and make your decision early (see the ITB addresses listed in this chapter, or contact the Youth and Education Department, Irish Tourist Board, 757 Third Avenue, New York, NY 10017 (tel. 212/418-0800).

There are two excellent study programs in Ireland sponsored by U.S. organizations. The Council on International Educational Exchange (CIEE) offers **Encounter Ireland,** an Irish Studies summer course in association with Trinity College, Dublin, to any full-time student of an American college or university. For 4 weeks participants stay with an Irish family in Dublin and attend lectures, concerts, art exhibits, and other cultural events and visit the sightseeing highlights of the city and its environs. A fifth week is left free for you to travel around the country independently, using the rail pass that is included in the price. To qualify, you must submit an application form, two passport-type photos, and a reference from one of your professors. The price in 1991, including round-trip airfare from New York, was $2,950, and dates each year are late June to mid-August. For full details, an application, and a current price, contact CIEE, Encounter Ireland Program, 205 East 42nd Street, New York, NY 10017 (tel. 212/661-1414).

The second program, called **The Irish Way,** is sponsored by the Irish American Cultural Institute for 9th- through 12th-graders. Students spend 5 weeks in Ireland with time on two campuses: Gormanston College in County Meath, some 25 miles north of Dublin, and St. Brendan's College in Killarney, County Kerry. Studies range from mythology, history, and government to drama, literature, folk music, and balladry. There are interesting field trips, and for spare-time recreation there's an indoor swimming pool, tennis courts, and facilities for golf, handball, and soccer. Also included is a 1-week home stay, in which students live with Irish families, and a 5-night tour staying in hotels. The estimated cost for 1991 is $1,750, plus airfare, and some partial scholarships are available. The program begins in early July and runs into early August. For details, contact The Irish Way, Irish American Cultural Institute, 2115 Summit Avenue, College of St. Thomas, St. Paul, MN 55105 (tel. 612/647-5678).

There are also many other summer study programs available, and the comprehensive feature, **"Irish Summer Schools Directory,"** published as a supplement by *Inside Ireland* (see Section 9, "Recommended Books, Films, and Recordings," in Chapter 1), gives details on courses (both credit and noncredit), prices, accommodations (campus or home stays), extracurricular activities, etc.

GENEALOGICAL STUDY   If you're one of the more than 40 million Americans whose forebears were Irish, it's a good bet you'll want to look up your family while in Ireland. What with some 14 of our presidents claiming Irish ancestry, our White House having been designed by Irishman James Hoban, and one of our states (Pennsylvania) bearing the name of a Corkman (William Penn), you're in very good company indeed.

Tracking down your Irish roots may not prove to be such a simple matter. More than 1,000 basic family names were established in Ireland between the 12th and 19th centuries, each having several variations. Don't be discouraged, however: There are descendants of families described in a 1201 account of Cathal O'Conor's inauguration as King of Connaught still living on the same lands as their ancestors!

To find a particular branch of your family, you'll want to know all you possibly can about your family history before leaving home. Search any and all records (letters, Bibles, relatives' memories, etc.) for the mention of specific towns, villages, or counties from which your folks went out to America. The more you know about what they did, who they married, when they left home, and the like, the easier your job will be.

In Dublin, present yourself and your records to the **General Register Office of Births, Marriages, and Deaths** at Joyce House, 8/11 Lombard Street East, Dublin 2 (tel. 01/711000). Charges range from a low IR£5.50 ($9.63) for a Search Certificate, and IR£2 ($3.50) for each extra copy, when you go through the records yourself for a 5-year period in search of an individual. For 6 hours of unrestricted research, the charge is IR£12 ($21).

For genealogical and land-tenure records dating as far back as the 17th century, check with the **Public Record Office;** land transactions back to 1708 are recorded with the **Registry of Deeds,** on Henrietta Street. There is a wealth of all manner of family information at the **Genealogical Office** on Kildare Street, and the **National Library** on Kildare Street holds journals and directories relating to Irish families.

Once you have basic data, it's off to the locality of your ancestors, where **parochial registers** often hold exactly what you're looking for, and a talk with the parish priest may well send you off to shake the hand of a distant cousin or two still living in the neighborhood.

For roots in Northern Ireland, consult the **Public Record Office of Northern Ireland,** 66 Balmoral Avenue, Belfast, and the **Presbyterian Historical Society,** Church House, Fisherwick Place, Belfast.

No matter how you plan to go about your "roots" search, my best and strongest advice is to subscribe to *Inside Ireland* (see Section 9, "Recommended Books, Films, and Recordings," in Chapter 1) and receive their genealogical supplement with your very first issue. It's one of the most valuable aids available, and the helpful staff stands ready to help you reach Irish sources you might not otherwise find.

SPORTS HOLIDAYS Holiday facilities in Ireland include those featuring almost any sport you can imagine: golf, fishing, horseback riding, hunting, sailing, cycling— you name it and Ireland can probably provide it. You can devise your own schedule, take advantage of the many all-inclusive package plans, or join special-interest groups in highly organized tours.

If you are unable to obtain any of the information sheets mentioned below, write: Irish Tourist Board, Distribution Centre, P.O. Box 1083, Chancery Lane, Dublin 8, Ireland. They'll send you their "Publications Sales Order Form," which lists titles available and the small charge plus postage for each.

Camping If the great outdoors holds such appeal for you that tenting is the only way to go in your book, then the very first item in your backpack should be Bord Failte's **"Caravan & Camping Parks"** booklet. It's available for a small charge from the Irish Tourist Board, and it lists approved campgrounds, camping-equipment renters, and caravan renters (we know them as vans, recreational vehicles, or RVs).

To be approved, campgrounds must provide good toilet facilities, water-supply points, rubbish-disposal facilities, and properly spaced sites for tents and caravans. Many offer far more than these minimum requirements, with laundry and recreation facilities, a shop, or sometimes even a restaurant on the premises. Charges vary according to location and season, and can range from IR£5 to IR£8 ($8.85 to $14) per night for caravans or tents, with a small per-person additional charge.

Cycling   Cycling has always been a favorite sport, as well as pasttime, in Ireland, and there are excellent cycling holidays available, ranging from youth hostel (requires Youth Hostel membership) to farmhouse accommodations. Prices include bike rental, accommodation vouchers, and maps. For details, contact **The Bike Store,** 58 Lower Gardiner Street, Dublin 1 (tel. 01/725399 or 725931; fax 01/364763).

If you prefer to devise your own itinerary, there are more than 100 **Raleigh Rent-a-Bike dealers** around the country. Rates are IR£6 ($10.50) per day or IR£25 ($43.75) per week. You'll be asked for a deposit of IR£30 ($52.50) when you book. Booking is virtually a requirement if you plan a long bike trip during the months of July and August. Students can rent at a discount through USIT (see Section 5, "Tips for the Disabled, Seniors, Singles, Families, and Students," above). Note that unless you make special arrangements, bikes must be returned to the office from which they were rented.

The following Tourist Board information sheets will be particularly helpful in planning your cycling itinerary: no. 14A, "A Cycling Tour of Ireland"; no. 14B, "Cycling Dublin and Ireland East"; no. 14C, "Cycling the South East"; no. 14D, "Cycling Cork and Kerry"; no. 14E, "Cycling Shannonside"; no. 14F, "Cycling Donegal/Leitrim/Sligo"; no. 14G, "Cycling the Lakelands"; and no. 14H, "Cycling Ireland West."

Fishing   The Tourist Board also publishes a variety of booklets and information sheets on game angling for salmon, sea trout, brown trout, and some rainbow trout in rivers and lakes; sea angling, both inshore (small boat) and deep sea; coarse (freshwater) angling; and lists of approved deep-sea angling boat operators. Detailed information about seasons, as well as directories of all fisheries and facilities, licenses, etc., can be obtained through the **Central Fisheries Board,** Balnagowan, Mobhi Boreen, Dublin 9 (tel. 01/379206).

A IR£10 ($17.50) license, good for 21 days, is required for salmon and sea-trout fishing, and permits for freshwater fishing vary in cost from location to location. Licenses are available from the Central Fisheries Board and from selected tackle shops around the country. Deep-sea angling for shark, skate, dogfish, pollack, ling, and conger is yours at incredibly low cost, all around the coast—inquire locally for deep-sea charters.

For help in planning a fishing holiday, contact the **Angler's Information Service,** Irish Tourist Board, Baggot Street Bridge, Dublin 2 (tel. 01/765871). You may also want to send for one or all of the helpful information sheets (nos. 10A, 10B, and 10C) published by the Tourist Board for a nominal fee. Entitled "Sea Angling in Ireland," "Freshwater Coarse Angling," and "Game Fishing," they point you to the best fishing locations, boat rentals, fishing competitions, and bait stockers, and even provide angling maps.

Golf   Irish golfing holidays can be arranged to include accommodations, golf clinics, and special golfing weekends with groups and societies. For full particulars—or for help in setting up a golf holiday itinerary on your own—consult travel agents or the Irish Tourist Board (212/418-0800). A calendar of golf fixtures is published each year by the **Golfing Union of Ireland,** 81 Eglington Road, Dublin 4 (tel. 01/694111).

Published by the Irish Tourist Board, **"Irish Golfing Holidays,"** lists an extensive range of weekly and weekend golfing holiday package rates. For more details on golfing possibilities, contact any Tourist Office or the Golf Promotions Executive, Irish Tourist Board, Baggot Street Bridge, Dublin 2; or travel agents.

Hiking, Hill Walking, and Rock Climbing   If you are a hiker, you'll be drawn to off-the-main-thoroughfare spots of incredible beauty. The Irish Tourist Board issues an information sheet on "Hill Walking and Rock Climbing" (no. 26A) that highlights many of these spectacular climbs. Other Information sheets detail walks in Wicklow, Kerry, South Leinster, Kildare, Dingle, and Cavan.

Horseback Riding   There are equestrian holidays available based on trail riding, hunting, trekking, cross-country riding, and riding instruction for adults and children. A number of equestrian and accommodation centers offer week-long package rates, and you'll find them listed in Information Sheet 16B, available from the Irish Tourist Board.

Hunting and Shooting   The hunting season in Ireland runs from October to March. These hunts are only for the expert and experienced rider. While fox hunting is most popular, there are also stag hunts and harriers packs. A list of all hunts allowing visitor participation is given on Information Sheet 16D, available from the Tourist Board.

Participation in shoots for woodcock, snipe, golden plover, pheasant, mallard, wigeon, teal, and other duck is limited for visitors, and strictly controlled. Shooting without a guide is not condoned. For further details and a list of those shoots that do include visitors, send for Information Sheet 24.

Horses, guns, and cartridges are available through local clubs, to which you must pay a subscription fee.

Sailing   Ireland's long coastline, with its many indentations forming peaceful bays and harbors, has fostered generations of sailing folk. If skimming over the water under sail has great appeal, the Tourist Board's Information Sheet 28G lists outstanding sailing schools with approved training programs, or you can contact the Secretariat, **The Irish Association for Sail Training,** IFMI, Confederation House, Kildare Street, Dublin 2 (tel. 01/779801; fax 01/777823).

Other Sports   Surfing, board-sailing, and rowing are other sports holiday possibilities in Ireland, and information sheets are available on all from the Tourist Board.

HOSTELING   Although they're called *youth* hostels, you'll be welcomed if you're 6 or 60. In order to use them, you must have an **International Youth Hostel Card,** which must be purchased before you leave home. These are available from **American Youth Hostels, Inc.,** P.O. Box 37613, Washington, DC 20013 (tel. 202/783-6161), and cost $10 for those under 18, $15 for those 55 and over, and $25 for ages 18 to 54. This gives you a full 12-month membership. For another $10.95 (plus $2 postage and handling) you can purchase their *International Youth Hostel Handbook* (Vol. I, *Europe and the Mediterranean)* in which you'll find Irish hostels listed.

An Oige is the Irish Youth Hostel Association's official name, and it's a voluntary organization dedicated to helping residents and visitors take full advantage of Ireland's outdoor splendors and to providing hostel accommodations at minimum rates. It also puts together special package holidays available for 1, 2, 3, or 4 weeks. An example is the Rambler Hostelling Holiday, which includes 8 or 15 days unlimited travel on bus and rail, with overnight accommodation vouchers. There are also cycling holidays and combination cycling/rail holidays. For full details, contact **An Oige (Irish Youth Hostel Association),** 39 Mountjoy Square, Dublin 1 (tel. 01/363111 or 364750).

The **"An Oige—Irish Youth Hostel Handbook"** (small charge) details every one of the hostels throughout the Republic and Northern Ireland, along with loads of information, including international guest cards, advance bookings, and travel concessions available to hostel cardholders on certain ferry services.

An Oige youth hostels are situated in the most beautiful parts of the country—in mountains, on beaches, by lakes and rivers—and provide excellent venues for all sorts of activities. There are also well-located and convenient youth hostels in the major cities. The hostels vary in shape and size, from a large mansion in Killarney to a Norman castle in Kilkenny. Each hostel has self-catering facilities, a dining room, a common room, and separate sleeping and washing facilities for men and women. Many have resident house parents to help young hostellers during their stay.

Sheet bags (at a small charge), pillows, blankets, cooking utensils, and dishes are provided. All you'll need to bring is your own sleeping bag, cutlery, tea towel, and bath towel.

Overnight charges are based on age, season, and location, and begin at IR£3 ($5.25) for seniors (18 and over), IR£4 ($7) for under-18s. At the Dublin International Youth Hostel, rates range from IR£6.50 to IR£8 ($11.40 to $14), and breakfast is included in the rate.

If you arrive in Ireland without an International Youth Hostel Card but still want to go the hostel route, contact Paddy and Josephine Moloney, **Irish Budget Hostels,** Doolin Village, County Clare (tel. 065/74006). This is a chain of privately owned hostels for which you need no registration card, and there's no age limit. Facilities at each will vary, but all have both dormitory and private accommodations, hot showers, full kitchen facilities, blankets, and sleeping sheets on request. All have been approved by the Tourist Board. Rates range from IR£4.75 to IR£7.50 ($8.30 to $13.15).

CRUISE BOAT OR BARGE HOLIDAYS   Ireland's hundreds of miles of inland waterways offer one of the most peaceful travel experiences you could dream of. Cruising along the magnificent Shannon, or from Belturbet to Belleek by way of Lower and Upper Lough Erne and its connecting river, or on the Grand Canal from Dublin all the way to the Shannon or Barrow, invokes a tranquility that just doesn't exist behind the wheel of an automobile. Add to that the delight of a unique view of the Irish countryside and stopovers at waterside towns and villages, and you have the holiday of a lifetime.

You don't have to be a seasoned sailor to rent a cabin cruiser from one of the nine companies approved by the Irish Tourist Board. You'll be given free instruction on handling the craft, reading charts, etc., and I'm told most people are fully confident and ready to set sail after little more than an hour (if you're the least bit timid, however, your instructor will stay with you until your qualms have disappeared). It's a comfort, too, to know that, especially during peak holiday seasons, the waterways are constantly patrolled by professionals to keep an eye out for any holiday sailor who might get into difficulty. There's no license involved, but you must be over 21 years old and there must be one person other than the "captain" who understands the controls and charts.

Cruisers range in size from two to eight berths and are fully outfitted with all the comforts of home—full kitchen, showers, hot water, etc.

The Tourist Board can furnish a full list of companies that rent cabin cruisers. Booking is done directly with the firm of your choice. The costs for those listed below range from IR£175 to IR£950 ($306 to $1,662) per person per week, depending on the size of the cruiser and the season:

Carrick Craft, Carrick-on-Shannon, County Leitrim (tel. 078/20236).
Emerald Star Line, 47 Dawson Streets, Dublin 2 (tel. 01/798166 or 798162).
Athlone Cruisers Ltd., Shancurragh, Athlone, County Westmeath (tel. 0902/72892).
Shannon Castle Line, Ringsend, Dublin 4 (tel. 01/600964).

If a Shannon cruise is your idea of "Worth the Extra Money," you might consider the following. Surely one of the most relaxing and luxurious ways to enjoy Ireland's legendary landscape is from the deck of the 12-passenger **Shannon Princess** as it cruises the Shannon, stopping along the way to visit singing pubs, do some shopping, or take in a castle banquet. The elegantly appointed vessel has two suites, three twin-bedded staterooms, and two single staterooms, and meals on board fall into the gourmet class, accompanied by fine wines. Weekly departures are on Sunday from mid-April through October, and the itinerary is round-trip from Killaloe up the Shannon and 25-mile-long Lough Derg.

Fares included all meals, open bar, sightseeing, and round-trip transfers from Shannon, ranged from $1,500 to $1,800 per person (based on double occupancy), according to season; singles pay a supplement. Early booking is advised. Contact Mr. Ronnie Kearsley, Shannon River Floatels Limited, Killaloe, County Clare (tel. 061/376688; fax 061/76205).

HORSE-DRAWN CARAVANS   Ireland is one of the few places left in the world where you can pamper the gypsy in your soul. The gaily painted caravans are comfortably fitted out to accommodate up to four—in fact, you probably should have at least four in your party to travel this leisurely way.

You've never handled a horse? Well, unless you're just plain scared to death of the creatures, that's no problem at all. The caravan operator will give you a quick course in harnessing and unharnessing, as well as the care and upkeep of your animal companion. If you wish, he'll also take you for a test drive to be sure you and your horse are compatible. Farmers along your route are appointed to provide feed and give you a parking site for the night, and they'll be all too happy to help you with any questions that come up after you've hit the road.

Some roads are too steep or too heavily traveled to be suitable for your slow conveyance. So you'll be offered a choice of carefully selected routes to follow, with overnight stopping places clearly marked. At some you'll find showers, and almost all have sanitary facilities. You probably won't average more than about 9 or 10 miles a day, which allows plenty of time for chatting with the locals as you plod along, stopping for a pint in a friendly pub and just dreaming away the time. In fact, you won't know the meaning of the word "time" after a day or two of gypsying!

You'll have the option of eating in (you'll have cooking facilities, utensils, eating ware, and a sink) or a meal in the best local eatery. As a caravaner, you'll have an instant conversation opener, and you're more likely than not to be the last one out of restaurant or pub, with the talk still going strong.

What this idyllic journey will cost depends on the season. Charges for a four-berther range from IR£225 to IR£450 ($394 to $788) per week—cheap enough on a per-person basis! Add to that an average of about IR£6 ($10.50) per night for overnight stops.

The Tourist Board's Information Sheet no. 16C details the delights of traveling in a horse-drawn caravan, and the following are operators with whom you can book directly:

Slattery's Travel Agency, (ATTN: Mr. David Slattery), Slattery's Horse-Drawn Caravans, 1 Russell Street, Tralee, County Kerry (tel. 066/26277; fax 066/25981)—the Dingle Peninsula, North Kerry, and Killarney.
Dieter Clissmann Horse-Drawn Caravan Holidays, Carrigmore, County Wicklow (tel. 0404/8188)—the Wicklow mountains and coast.

PLANNING YOUR TRIP — ARRIVING IN IRELAND

Once you are well informed on all the subjects discussed in Chapter 2, it's time to get on with the actual planning. Your advance planning must, of course, begin with booking transportation and deciding just how you'll get around the country, since both require booking before you leave home (see Chapter 2). As is true for any holiday, however, you'll have a happier time in Ireland if you spend the necessary time and effort in setting up an itinerary (however tentative) based on your own special interests, deciding on money-saving accommodations and restaurants, and learning more about the practicalities of traveling around Ireland.

1. GETTING THERE

When it comes to the actual booking of your transportation, both price and convenience are factors to be taken into consideration. Your beginning point will help determine which mode of transportation you will use and which is the most convenient departure gateway. From the U.S., your only option is to come by air. From Britain, air, sea, and even bus (a combination of overland and sea travel) are all options. From Europe, you can choose between air and sea.

As for price, the smart budget traveler will do a *lot* of shopping around to get the best fare. It's a good idea to begin scanning newspapers as far in advance as possible before your departure date and to call all competing lines to inquire about any seasonal or promotional specials that may be offered for a limited time. It could well pay big dividends to change your travel dates by a few days or a week in order to take advantage of such savings.

My best advice is to work with a tried-and-true travel agent. If you don't know of one, ask around or look for the Certified Travel Counselor certification (it means that the agent has had specialized training and met rather high requirements). It will cost you no more, and will save a lot of time and mental strain. Having said that, I must add that you should be as well informed as possible before you sit down to talk to an agent—the more you know about what's available, the more intelligently you can assess what's best for the budget. If you're serious about this budget business, you'll get the best results by combining your own informed judgment with that of a good agent.

BY PLANE

FROM THE U.S. First of all, from New York to Shannon is a 5-hour flight, from Shannon back to the States takes 6 hours, and there's a 5-hour time difference, so you can count on having at least a touch of jet lag. Be sure to take that into account in your planning.

When you travel to Ireland is a very important money-saving factor. For example, travel from mid-September to mid-May eastbound, or mid-October to mid-June westbound, is considerably cheaper (it's called the "basic season" in airline jargon) than if you go during "peak season" (all other months). Specific dates for season changes can vary from one year to the next, so you should check with the airline before setting your departure date. You should be aware, too, of any restrictions concerning advance booking, stopovers, etc., that apply to some of the lower fares.

Aer Lingus and Delta serve Ireland from the U.S. **Aer Lingus,** Ireland's national airline, offers by far the most frequent flights, flying several nonstop flights from New York daily in peak season and one flight daily during the basic season. It also has direct flights from Boston and Chicago. During basic season, flights from these last three gateways are less frequent, so be sure to check before setting your dates. Contact: Aer Lingus, 122 East 42nd Street, New York, NY 10168 (tel. 212/557-1110, or toll free 800/223-6537); or 60 School Street, Boston, MA 02102.

Delta flies only to and from Atlanta, a gateway that may be more convenient for those coming from the Southeast and Southwest. During peak season, flights are daily except Monday; in the basic season, there are three flights per week. Contact: Delta Airlines, Hartsfield Airport, Atlanta, GA 30320 (tel. 404/765-2600, or toll free 800/241-4141).

If you really want to get a headstart on your Irish visit, then let me offer a very personal recommendation. As far as I'm concerned, *my* Irish arrival begins at Kennedy Airport in New York the minute I walk up to the Aer Lingus check-in counter and am greeted by a smile and a lilt straight from the "auld sod."

Fares: In these days of fierce airline competition and fares that change almost daily, you'll have to take the following figures as guidelines only. No matter what the figures, however, before you settle on a fare, remember to ask about any current specials or packages available—they can put considerably more money in your pocket to be spent on being there instead of getting there.

Because of those constant fluctuations, it's impossible to give you exact airfares. I can, however, tell you those quoted at presstime for New York–Shannon, and they serve as a pretty good basis for comparison between the different fare types. Departure from Chicago will run a little more. Flying on to Dublin, Cork, Galway, or Sligo rather than deplaning at Shannon will add extra dollars to your fare. Fares quoted below are sample round-trip costs between New York and Shannon. (Add an $18 departure tax to all fares. There are special conditions and restrictions connected with all fares except first class and executive class.

APEX: $428 to $529 in basic season, $816 in peak season. This one's good for 6 months only, and there's a 21-day advance-purchase requirement.

Economy Class: $1,266 in basic season, $1,438 in peak season. The ticket is good for 1 year, and there are no advance-purchase requirements.

First Class: $2,444 year round. Certainly not in the budget class, but it gives a good idea of the savings available by making another choice.

FROM THE U.K. Aer Lingus and Ryanair both offer air service to Dublin, Cork, and Galway from London and several other points in Britain, and both offer special reductions from time to time. For information, contact: **Aer Lingus** (tel. 212/557-1110, or toll free 800/223-6537 in the U.S.; 569-5555 in London; 041/248-4121 in Glasgow; 0345/010101 in Birmingham; and 01/733442 in Ireland), or **Ryanair** (tel. 0582/424211 in London; 061/998-5341 in Manchester; or 01/774422 in Ireland).

Scheduled service is also available to Belfast from numerous points in Britain by **British Airways** (tel. 01/897-4000 in London, 01/610666 in Ireland) and **British Midland Airways** (tel. 0332/810552 in Britain, 01/798733 in Ireland).

FROM THE CONTINENT Aer Lingus has direct flights from Amsterdam, Düsseldorf, Frankfurt, Hamburg, Moscow, Nice, Paris, and Rome.

BY SEA

FROM THE U.K. Ireland has excellent connections with the U.K. via the car-ferries listed below, and if you are not traveling by car, their offices can book your sea and overland transportation at the same time, at package rates. Ferry and overland transport can usually be arranged before you leave home through travel agents or the numbers listed for each line.

Sealink operates daily car-ferry service from Fishguard (Wales) to Rosslare, Holyhead to Dun Laoghaire (Dublin), and Stranraer to Larne (Northern Ireland). The one-way fare for passengers without cars traveling to Republic of Ireland ports was £20 ($37) sterling, and for a car with up to four passengers, £149 ($275.65) sterling. Round-trip specials are offered at certain times of the year, and all fares vary seasonally. A budget-stretching aid is their "Short Breaks" holiday program, which can save you a considerable amount if you're coming to Ireland for weekends or short stays of up to 5 days. Fares for the Northern Ireland service were £20 ($37) sterling for foot passengers, and drivers paid an additional £80 ($140) for the car.

In the U.S., you can get current Sealink sailing schedules and rate information by contacting: Sealink, c/o Britrail, 630 Third Avenue, New York, NY 10017 (tel. 212/575-2667; or 0233/47047 in Britain, 01/807777 in Ireland).

B&I Line sails between Holyhead and Dublin, and Pembroke and Rosslare, on a daily basis, with comparable fares and a whole slew of special offers. For current rates and schedules, contact: B&I Line, c/o Lynott Tours, 350 Fifth Avenue, Suite 2619, New York, NY 10118 (tel. 212/760-0101; fax 212/695-8347; 01/491-8682 in London; or 01/788077 in Ireland, fax 01/788490).

Belfast Car Ferries (tel. 051/922-6234 in Britain, or 0232/320364 in Northern Ireland) has service between Liverpool and Belfast. Call for current information.

FROM THE CONTINENT You can extend your Irish holiday into Europe on **Irish Ferries,** with frequent sailings all year from Rosslare (near Wexford) to Le Havre, Rosslare to Cherbourg, and from June 20 to August 30, Cork to Le Havre. One-way fares begin at IR£79 ($139) for a foot passenger in a six-berth cabin ($11 with a Eurail pass), IR£60 ($105) for a car and driver. Sailing time is 21 hours to Le Havre and 17 hours to Cherbourg. The line also has some terrific holiday package plans that can mean real savings for a European holiday. Packages change from year to year, but they offer very good value and are well worth looking into. (Ask for their "Ferrytours" booklet, which describes all current plans.)

Most travel agents can make ferry bookings for you before you leave home through Irish Ferries, Lynott Tours, 350 Fifth Avenue, New York, NY 10001 (tel. 212/760-0101); or Irish Ferries, 2-4 Merrion Row, Dublin 2 (tel. 01/610511).

BY BUS

There's good express coach service between London and several cities in Ireland, including Dublin, Cork, Waterford, Killarney, and Limerick. Round-trip tickets are good for 3 months and can have open return dates. "Superbus" bookings can be made at more than 3,000 **National Express** agents in the U.K. and at all National Coach stations. In Ireland, book through any **Bus Eireann** office.

PACKAGE TOURS

Dedicated budget watchers have long known that when it comes to travel, some of the best bargains going are chartered flights or tours (escorted or unescorted). Once upon a time that meant you were herded around with a group of other Americans, with little opportunity to break out on your own and freewheel it through a country. That is no longer true, and you can now realize enormous savings on airfare and accommodations and never see those other American faces except in the airplane going over and coming back. Not that I have anything against my countryfolk, you understand; it's just that I don't go to Ireland to be with Americans.

Aer Lingus offers a wide selection of such bargains. You can choose only the fly/drive combination and take care of your own accommodations; the fly/drive/farmhouse or B&B combination, which covers your room each night from a choice of over 800 accommodations; or one of the most popular, the Irish Heritage package that covers air and land arrangements plus the services of the Irish Genealogical Research Society. All can be tailored to your particular needs, time available, and budget. Book through Aer Lingus or travel agents.

Irish-owned **CIE Tours International,** 108 Ridgedale Avenue, Morristown, N.J. 07960 (tel. 201/242-3438 or toll free 800/243-8687) maintains offices in New Jersey, London, Paris, and Düsseldorf, with expert staffs who can help you decide among the many package tours offered by CIE, both escorted and unescorted. Their coach tours are among the best, with knowledgeable drivers and guides who add the sparkle of Irish wit to their expertise. Self-drive packages give you a car, accommodations listings, itinerary suggestions and maps, and reserved accommodations for your first night. After that, you're free to roam, staying as long as you wish at one destination before moving on.

When it comes to escorted tours, it's hard to beat the dollar-for-value tours offered by **Globus-Gateway,** a long-established tour company that operates excellent coach tours to Ireland from late-April through mid-October. The 8-day "Introduction to Ireland" tour circles the country from Dublin, and encompasses the Ring of Kerry, Killarney, Blarney Castle, Cork, Limerick, Tipperary, Galway, and Connemara. There are other sightseeing highlights, and optional activities include a medieval banquet, a jaunting-car ride in Killarney, and cabaret in Dublin. There's also a 13-day "Emerald Isle" tour, which includes all the above plus many other highlights and an extended itinerary. For full details of both tours, send for their "Europe and Britain" booklet: Globus-Gateway, 95-25 Queens Boulevard, Rego Park, NY 11374 (tel. 718/268-1700, or toll free 800/221-0090 in the eastern U.S. outside New York State), or 150 South Los Robles Avenue, Pasadena, CA 91101 (tel. 818/449-2019, or toll free 800/556-5454 outside California in the western U.S., Alaska, and Hawaii). Book tours through travel agents.

A good travel agent is an invaluable aid in finding just the right package tour, and one I can recommend is the **Grimes Travel Agency,** with offices at 250 West 57th Street, Suite 2511, New York, NY 10019 (tel. 212/307-7797), and 54 Mamaroneck Avenue, White Plains, NY 10601 (tel. 914/761-4550). Since 1921 this has been a family-owned and operated agency, with personalized service to clients around the country. There's a family member in each of the agency offices, and they're always available to find just the right package tour to suit your needs. They can plan individual, special-interest tours (golf, history, genealogical search, etc.) with an expertise acquired over the years. They also sponsor the Claddagh Club, which offers discounts on car rentals, specialized help in tracing family history, and many other benefits; there's a $25 membership fee, which is waived if you purchase a ticket through their offices.

2. GETTING AROUND

You'll find it easy to get around Ireland. If you're here for only a few days, you'll want to settle into one city (or B&B in the country) and take day trips only, perhaps using the excellent Bus Eireann coach tours to save the expense of renting a car. For longer visits, you have a multitude of choices via rail and bus travel with an unlimited-travel ticket, escorted coach tours, a rental car with unlimited mileage, canal and river cruising, a horse-drawn caravan, hiking, or cycling. There is also now a good network of local airports, with frequent commuter flights from Dublin.

BY BUS/TRAIN

You won't be long in the Republic before "bus and train" disappear from your vocabulary, to be supplanted by "Bus Eireann" and "Irish Rail" (officially it's "Iarnród Eireann"), collectively known as the Irish Transport System, which operates all bus and train services, as well as the Aran Islands ferry from Galway.

Somehow, that bald statement just doesn't convey the essence of these services. They are, quite literally, the lifeline of the country, transporting the Irish about their daily business or on pleasure jaunts, and getting visitors to and from just about anywhere in the country or cross-channel to the U.K. (see Section 1, above).

Of course, all those things are not all there is to public transportation. Rubbing elbows with the Irish on a bus or train journey is an added bonus, and I must confess that some of my most memorable Irish experiences (and eavesdropping) have come from bus or train trips. Like everything else in Ireland, this kind of travel is so informal you'll think you're riding along with friends and neighbors by the time you reach your destination.

BUS EIREANN Bus Eireann's home office is at the Central Bus Station (Busaras), Store Street, Dublin 1, and the central number for schedule and fare information is 01/302222 or 366111. Timetables and other travel information are available there, as well as at bus ticket offices and train depots around the country. In addition to regular commuter services, high-speed Expressway coaches operate between Dublin and all major points, with new coaches and up to three services a day each way.

Round-trip fares are only marginally more than one-way fares; Children under 15 go for half fare. Also, Bus Eireann constantly offers special fares (weekends, midweek, etc.). Whenever you travel, be sure to ask about the cheapest fare available at the time.

One of Bus Eireann's most popular offerings is its Breakaways program. and the cost was IR£28 ($49) per person per night, including round-trip coach fare and bed and breakfast—a real bargain for those traveling on a strict budget. Some 25 hotels nationwide provide accommodation.

IRISH RAIL Irish Rail's head office is at Dublin's Connolly Station, and the number to call for schedules and all passenger services is 01/366222.

Mainline passenger trains operate between Dublin and cities and towns throughout Ireland and to Belfast, and there are also commuter trains in the Dublin and Cork suburban areas. Services are fairly frequent and speedy (Galway, for instance, is just 3 hours from Dublin by train). Most long-distance trains have catering facilities, ranging from bar service and light refreshments to à la carte meals. Second-class travel is best for the budget, but you can go first class for a small supplement (best to book ahead for first class).

Irish Rail also operates many special trains: day trips in the summer, pilgrimage trains, and special excursions to sporting and entertainment events, many offering discounts to groups and families. Holiday packages vary from luxury weekends in Cork, Dublin, Killarney, and Galway to 3-day family breaks in several locations, with hotel or self-catering digs. For full details and current prices, contact: Irish Rail Travel Centre, 35 Lower Abbey Street, Dublin 1 (tel. 01/363333).

BUS/TRAIN PASSES The **Eurailpass** is a single convenient card that entitles you to unlimited rail travel throughout 17 European countries, including the Republic of Ireland (good on rail, Expressway coaches, and Irish Continental Lines ferries between Ireland and France), but not in the U.K. or Northern Ireland. It is available to any non-European resident, but must be purchased *before you leave home*, 21 days prior to departure. Eurailpasses are available through travel agents; both CIE Tours International (tel. 201/242-3438) and Lynott Tours (tel. 212/760-0101) offer the Eurailpass. The money-saving **Flexipass** at presstime cost $230 for a 15-day period with 5 days of travel; $398 for a 21-day period with 9 days of travel; $498 for a 1-month period with 14 days of travel. Those between the ages of 14 and 26 are eligible for the **Eurail Youthpass,** at considerable discount.

Bus Eireann sells you a money-saving **Rambler Pass** for unlimited travel on rail or bus. Prices for adults at presstime for bus or rail only were $107 for 8 days and $157 for 15 days, with a discount for children. A combination rail and bus Rambler Pass costs $139 for 8 days, $203 for 15 days. The **Overlander Pass** is valid on Irish Rail, Bus Eireann, Ulsterbus, and Northern Ireland Rail services, and costs $185 for 8 days, $315 for 15 days. Students are eligible for the **Youth Student Pass** at substantial discounts.

These passes are available from mainline railway stations and Bus Eireann ticket offices in Ireland, or you may purchase them through travel agents in the States or CIE Tours International (tel. 201/242-3438 or toll free 800/243-8687).

Northern Ireland Railways has a **Rail Runabout** pass good for 7 days of unlimited travel in Northern Ireland only, and available at most railway stations in the province.

LOCAL BUSES In Dublin (where its name changes to Dublin Bus), Cork, Limerick, Galway, Dundalk/Drogheda, and Waterford, Bus Eireann operates double-decker buses in the inner city and outlying areas, as well as frequent service into the respective cities from Shannon Airport (Limerick), Cork Airport, and Dublin Airport. Fares are computed on the distance you travel and are surprisingly low: airport buses average under IR£3 ($5.25). You won't pay as you board a local bus. Just get aboard and find a seat—the conductor will be along to collect your fare based on how far you're going. Those big double-deckers will usually accommodate everyone, so there's no need for the pushing, shoving, and elbowing we so often encounter at home—the Irish simply queue up politely and everyone boards in turn. Very civilized!

SIGHTSEEING TOURS Natives and visitors alike take Bus Eireann day trips to Ireland's most scenic spots at bargain prices, and for those addicted to escorted coach tours as a means of seeing a country with the least amount of personal planning, Bus Eireann provides some of the best. There are more than 60 day tours to more than 20 locations nationwide, and ticket offices, rail depots, and Tourist Offices can provide detailed brochures for each locality.

Bus Eireann also operates first-rate escorted coach tours, as well as self-drive, go-as-you-please tours using either hotel or B&B accommodations that represent exceptional value. (A 7-day escorted Irish Heritage tour loaded with cabaret, medieval banquet, and other bonuses, ranges from $769, depending on season). Some tours feature 2- and 3-night stopovers, a real boon to those who hate packing and unpacking every day.

BY CAR

CAR RENTALS The first thing you must know about renting a car in Ireland is that it's absolutely necessary to book ahead. That's especially true from the first of July through the end of September, but in this small country, a run on the stock available can also develop suddenly if there's a special event of some kind that draws lots of visitors. You must be between the ages of 23 and 70 (top age with some companies is 65, while others add a surcharge for insurance for those over the age of 70, so be sure to inquire when you book).

The rate you pay will depend on the size of the car and the season of the year. Seasonal dates may vary slightly from one company to another, but generally you'll find the highest charges from July through September, a more moderate rate in May, June, and October, and the lowest from November through April. Prices for the smaller stick-shift cars are the best value; larger vehicles can run as much as a third more.

The rates quoted will include third-party and passenger liability insurance, but unless you add on collision-damage insurance, you'll be responsible for the full cost of repairs should you be involved in an accident. I strongly advise you to take it—otherwise, you'll be required by most companies to make a refundable payment of as much as IR£150 ($262.50) or more if you are paying by cash. Some credit cards offer collision-damage insurance, but in recent years there have been serious difficulties in collecting on claims, and it's a much better idea to take the car-rental-company coverage. You may also be asked for a deposit at the time you book, but this is many times waived if you present a recognized credit card. Almost every company allows pickup at one airport and dropoff at another if you wish.

Discount Rates   Here's where this book can earn its cost many times over, for with it, you qualify for a 15% discount on some car rentals, which have escalated greatly in the past few years.

Jim Thornton is the genial and helpful general manager of **Johnson & Perrott Rent-a-Car Ltd.**, Emmet Place, Cork (tel. 021/273295, or toll free 800/223-6764 in the U.S.) a highly reliable company that has for years given readers of this book a 15% discount (and even better special rates may apply for rentals longer than 2 weeks) on basic car rentals if they mention it when booking and have it with them when they pick up the car. That's a nice saving, but even nicer is the fact that it will get you to one of the most efficient and helpful car-rental companies in Ireland.

To illustrate, let me tell you about my experience with J&P on my very first visit to Ireland back in 1973. I had requested a certain make of car, which wasn't available when I checked in with them at Shannon. However, Maureen, the woman behind the desk, assured me that one was due to be checked in later that afternoon and she'd be glad to drive me in to Limerick to my B&B for a bit of rest, then bring the car I wanted when it arrived. The trip included a running string of tips about where to go and what to do in the Shannonside area, as well as a lot of places around the country (that's how I first learned about Durty Nellie's), places I might otherwise have missed. In the late afternoon Maureen came with my car, followed by a second J&P car to deliver her back to Shannon so I wouldn't have to drive her myself. At the time I was overwhelmed by such consideration, but in the ensuing years I've become almost blasé about that kind of courtesy—it seems to come naturally to the entire staff. They've helped me plan itineraries and choose the best routes all over Ireland, all the while as gracious and friendly as if they weren't putting themselves out at all.

Johnson & Perrott have pickup points at all air- and seaports, and in Dublin, Cork, Galway, and Limerick, with desks at the Dublin, Cork, Sligo, and Shannon airports. In those cities, they'll even deliver the car to your accommodation at no extra charge. There's no dropoff charge either at Shannon, Dublin, Sligo, and Cork airports (or they'll arrange to pick the car up at your guesthouse in those cities). Like all car-hire firms, they charge more during the high season, but it's a remarkably short one—July 1 to September 15—and the same Ford Fiesta that goes for IR£181 ($316.75) per week during that period drops to IR£133 ($229.25) in other months. Both rates include unlimited mileage. There is also a special "Businessman's Discount" for people coming to Ireland on a regular basis for business purposes. Be sure to inquire when you book about any specials in effect at the time. When booking, enclose a minimum $60 deposit. You can book through travel agents or directly with J&P.

Jerry O'Riordan, with more than 25 years' experience in the car-rental business, is owner of Ireland's newest car-rental company, **MotorWorld Rent-a-Car**, Carrigrohane Road, Cork (tel. 021/542344). Jerry is committed to personal service and customer satisfaction, and gives our readers a 15% discount when they mention this book when making a reservation and have it with them when they pick up the car. There is an attractive special offer of a Nissan Micra Van for two people for only IR£98 ($171.50) in the off-season, IR£165 ($288.75) in peak season. Both prices include unlimited mileage and free pickup and dropoff privileges at Dublin, Shannon, and Cork airports, and all are subject to an extra 10% VAT (tax). In addition, there are up to 15 other new model cars in the 200-car fleet from which to choose, including automatics, minibuses, and four-wheel-drive vehicles. To book, write Motor World at the above address and enclose a $100 deposit.

A family-run business, begun back in 1971, **Dan Dooley Rent a Car**, Knocklong, County Limerick (tel. 062/53103, or toll free 800/331-9301 in the U.S.), gives our readers a special low guaranteed dollar rate if they mention this book when making a reservation and have it with them when they pick up the car. They have one of the largest fleets of rental cars in Ireland, with depots throughout the country. If your party is a large one, you will be glad to know they also offer nine-passenger minibuses. Timid drivers will find automatic-shift cars available. Rates range from

IR£15 ($26.25) per day (based on 1 week's hire) for a Ford Fiesta to IR£125 ($218.75) per day for a Mercedes. All rates include unlimited mileage.

Other Car-Hire Firms Other firms include **Murray's Europcar,** Baggot Street Bridge, Dublin 4 (tel. 01/681777), which operates a fleet of over 1,250 new model cars, and provides a highly personal service and customer attention. They have some 15 offices around the country: three in Dublin and one each in Cork, Shannon, Galway, Sligo, Knock, Wexford, Rosslare, Waterford, Killarney, Kenmare, and Kerry County Airport. Weekly rates range from IR£126 to IR£350 ($220.50 to $612.50), depending on season and car model. They also feature several specials that are real money savers. Their "Spring Sale" rate of only IR£112 ($196) per week is in effect from January 1 to May 31 each year, and there's a 10% discount for drivers over 55 years of age. For groups of up to nine traveling together, there are minibuses available. Murray's operates as official car-rental contractor to Aer Lingus and is the Irish agent for National Car Rental and Tilden, of Canada. Chauffeur-drive services are also available.

Both **Avis** and **Hertz** are represented in Ireland, each with offices around the country and free dropoff privileges from one office to the other. You can book through travel agents, but rates are considerably higher than those listed above.

DRIVING RULES & HINTS You probably don't need me to tell you that driving is on the *left* in Ireland, but I'll pass along a few tips garnered from my 17 or so years of driving on the "wrong" side of the road. First, before you even turn the ignition key, take time to check the rear-view and side mirrors to be sure they'll give you a clear view of the road behind. Go over the gear system to be sure you understand it (every rental car seems to have a different position for reverse!), then check the light dimmer and windshield wiper. Elementary details, to be sure, but while you're doing all this, you'll be adjusting to the transition from plane to Customs to car. If your arrival is an early-morning one, it's a good idea to stop for a nice hot cuppa in the airport to help that transition along. Remember, this is Ireland—you don't have to rush.

You'll be reminded of the drive-on-the-left edict by frequent signs between Shannon and Limerick and the Dublin Airport and that city. Still, the very first time you make a sharp turn, your inclination is going to be to head for the right-hand side of the road. Also, when you stop for gas or a meal, it's very, very easy to pull off on the right side (which is the wrong side in Ireland, of course). I make it a practice to stop the car headed in the direction in which I'll be going, which somehow makes it easier to pull off on the left side. No matter what precautions you take, however, you're bound to feel awkward the first day—and maybe the second. So try to set a little tape recorder up there in your head to play and replay "Drive left" until it becomes second nature.

Speed limits in towns and cities will be 30 or 40 miles per hour (they're prominently posted), and it's 55 m.p.h. on the open road. Mileage is signposted in both kilometers and miles (usually, *but not always,* if it's green and white, it's kilometers; black and white, miles). See "Metric System" in the Appendix for mileage and other conversions.

You'll learn a whole new automotive vocabulary: Your luggage will go into the *boot,* not the trunk; the hood is now the *bonnet;* the windshield becomes a *windscreen;* you'll park in a *car park,* not a parking lot; those are *lorries,* not trucks, you pass; and you're driving a *car-for-hire,* not a rental car, that runs on *petrol,* not gas. And those signs with bold Gaelic lettering reading GEILL SLI say "Give Way," and mean precisely that! Got it?

Now, about Irish roads—quite simply, *I* think they're wonderful! You may disagree. But I have an active dislike for huge, speedy double-lane highways (another new phrase, *dual carriageways*), and in spite of the fact that only about 5% of Ireland's roadways fall into that category, I grumble every time I see the bulldozers hard at it widening and straightening one of my beloved little country lanes. And they seem to be even harder at it with every visit. Of course, when you're trying to pass one of those gigantic lorries, the wider roads do come in handy. But if you take my heartfelt advice, most of the roads you travel will fall into the 95% that are small, sometimes bumpy, and 100-fold more interesting than the National Primary Routes—on those charming small roads, you're traveling right inside the landscape, not whizzing by it. One note of caution: U-turns can lead to disaster—no matter if you're driving on dual carriageways or country lanes.

There are some basic things you ought to know about those little roads. In early morning and evening you're sure to meet at least one farmer and his hard-working dog driving the cows to or from the fields—right down the middle of the road. Don't panic! Just stop like everybody else, relax, give the man a nod or a wave, and let the sea of cattle wash right around you.

Also, you're probably going to get lost at least once. That's because road signs sometimes mysteriously get turned around (leprechauns?), or you come to a junction with no signs. But let me tell you that getting lost in Ireland is a pleasant adventure. Stop at a pub to ask directions and you're in for some delightful conversation, especially if things are a little slow. The general discussion that erupts will enlighten you about all the alternative routes, and the advantages and disadvantages of each. When everyone has had his or her say (and not until then!), you'll be sent on your way with detailed instructions on where *not* to go as well as the right route. Many's the time a stern "You'll come to a crossroad with a church, but pay no mind to it and keep to the road straight ahead" has kept me from making a wrong turn.

If the whole thing gets too complicated, don't be surprised if someone hops eagerly into the car to show you the way, brushing aside his return with an easy "And wasn't I wanting to go to the next town, anyway." And he won't think a thing about hitching all the way back home, for he was raised in a tradition that says if you've a roof over your head, a fire at your hearth, and a potato in the pot, it's very close to a mortal sin not to share them all with a stranger in need. More than that, he'll welcome the chance of a bit of conversation with someone from other parts—and he'll take the time for both the help and the *crack* (that's Irish "crack," nothing more addictive than a good chat).

GAS   Gas (petrol) will cost anywhere from IR£3 ($5.25) a gallon up, and you'll find the cheapest prices at Jet stations. Those are Imperial gallons—larger by volume than ours—and in a small car, you'll cover remarkable distances on a tankful of gas. Increasingly, gas is sold by the liter, and the conversion chart in the Appendix will give you a quick comparison between liters, Imperial gallons, and those we're accustomed to at home.

MAPS   Your car-hire company will provide you with a map (not that it will keep you from getting lost), but many are not all that easy to follow. I highly recommend the **Holiday Maps** (regional, as well as for the entire country), which are much more detailed, have city maps (you'll need them), and give you a wealth of useful tourist information. They sell for about IR£3 ($5.25) and can be bought at most news agents. For quick itinerary planning, the mileage chart in the Appendix will be helpful.

TAPE TOURS   One last suggestion: **Comprehensive Communications, Inc. (CCI),** has put together three "Auto-Tape Tours of Ireland" which follow a circular route around the country, beginning at Shannon. Commentators are both American and Irish, and along with a very good narration on the localities you're passing through, they throw in bits of folklore and music and odd bits of information that add color to your trip. They come with a map, and the tapes are timed for your probable rate of speed, but make suggestions for deviating from the prescribed itinerary to explore a nook or cranny or two.

You don't have to buy all three if you're going to be in one section of the country only. Tape 1 takes you from Shannon to Sligo via Limerick, the cliffs of Moher, Galway, Yeats Country, and the prehistoric sites that dot this landscape. Tape 2 carries you on from Sligo through Dublin, Wicklow, Wexford, and Waterford to Cork. And Tape 3 completes the circle back to Shannon by way of West Cork's beautiful coastline and tiny villages, Kerry's mountains, Killarney, and Tralee. Actually, you'll enjoy your trip much more if you order these tapes ahead and listen to them before you leave for Ireland; when you return home, they're a lasting memento of your visit.

Order from CCI, P.O. Box 631, Goldens Bridge, NY 10583 (tel. 914/232-0322); each tape costs $11.95 plus $1 for postage and handling.

BY RV

In Ireland, RVs are known as *caravans,* and virtually all are drawn by a car. Rental rates at presstime ranged from IR£85 to IR£130 ($148.75 to $227.50) per week, depending on the size and season. In computing your costs, add the cost of a rental car (and you may have an additional cost for the fitting of a suitable hitch) and the IR£6 to IR£10 ($10.50 to $17.50) nightly site fee in caravan parks. For full details and booking, contact: **Irish Caravan Council Ltd.,** Caravan and Camping Holidays Ltd., 2 Offington Court, Sutton, Dublin 13 (tel. 01/323776; fax 01/324126).

BY AIR

Travel around the country by commuter plane can be a great convenience if your time in Ireland is extremely limited. **Aer Lingus** flies from Dublin to Cork, Farrenfore (Co. Kerry), Shannon, Galway, Knock, Sligo, and Derry. Thus in the course of 1 week you could spend a day or so in Yeats Country up Sligo way, another in Killarney, and add a day or so in Derry (Northern Ireland). It's not possible, however, to fly from one of these commuter airports directly to another—you must return to Dublin to connect to a flight to your next destination.

Aer Arann (tel. 091/55437) flies from Galway's Carnmore Airport to the Aran Islands from April through September. Call for current schedules and fares.

BY FERRY

There are three passenger-ferry routes to the Aran Islands off Ireland's northwest coast that run from June through September. From Galway, it's a 90-minute trip via the *Galway Bay,* which carries 250 passengers daily, with round-trip fares of IR£15 ($26.25) for adults and IR£6 ($10.50) for ages 5 to 17 (under 5, free). From Rossaveal (with coach service from Galway), the smaller *Aran Seabird* and *My Rose of Aran* make the trip year round in 40 to 60 minutes, with fares of IR£12 ($21) for adults, IR£6 ($10.50) for those under 14, and reductions for families, senior citizens, and students. In County Clare, the *Tranquility* operates from Doolin, also year round, at a cost of IR£10 ($17.50) and IR£5 ($8.75), with discounts for families and students.

The Killimer/Tarbert car-ferry is a great saver of driving time if you're heading from Killarney or other points south of the Shannon to Galway or other points north of the river and wish to bypass a stop in Limerick. The *Shannon Heather* and *Shannon Willow* sail every day of the year except Christmas Day, at one-way fares of IR£1 ($1.75) for foot passengers, IR£6 ($10.50) for car and passengers.

In the southeast, the *Dunbrody* car-ferry carries you from Ballyhack, in County Wexford, to Passage East, in County Waterford, both delightful waterfront villages off the beaten track, at one-way fares of IR£3.50 for car and passengers, no charge for those under 12, and an 80p ($1.40) charge for foot passengers.

HIKING, HITCHHIKING & CYCLING

Hiking, hitchhiking, and cycling are all quite acceptable and very popular ways to get around Ireland. My only caution would be against hitchhiking alone. If you team up with a companion, however, there is certainly no risk.

SUGGESTED ITINERARIES

Set itineraries present a very real danger in Ireland. They often get turned upside-down! You see, a 15-minute pub break in an afternoon drive can easily turn into a 2-day layover, all because your man behind the bar insists that you'll be very welcome at the evening's singsong with such conviction that it's suddenly very clear that the Blarney Stone can wait another day—which turns into yet another day when you fall in with such convivial company at the singsong that nothing will do but that you stay over for the next night! Now, don't misunderstand me: It's possible to "do" a very good, circular tour of Ireland in 2 weeks. But whether or not you get all the way around will depend entirely on how determined you are to stay on that schedule.

Bearing all that in mind, the recommended tours set out below can, perhaps, serve as a useful guide for the time you have to spend in Ireland. The longest takes you around the outer rim of Ireland's cuplike terrain (see the map in Chapter 1). This tour encompasses only the Republic: add another 3 to 5 days if you intend to visit Northern Ireland.

It's important to remember that although mileages may appear short, these are Irish miles—distances, road conditions, and the usual driving considerations have absolutely nothing to do with how long it takes you to cover them. There's an old Irish saying: "An Irish mile is long, but easy traveled." After one or two stops, you'll know the truth in that! Every pub or lunch or sightseeing stop will make it clearer, and you won't want to miss the photo "musts" that lurk around almost every bend.

The circular tour anticipates that you will move from place to place almost every night, but it is quite possible to select several major destinations along the route, settle in for a day or so and make longish day trips, returning to the same homey B&B in the evening.

Shorter, regional itineraries can be incorporated into the circular route or taken on their own, depending on the time you have to spend and your own inclinations. To help you make any such adjustments, you'll find full details for each region in the chapters that follow.

IF YOU HAVE 3 DAYS
THE SOUTHWEST

Day 1: From Cork (after you've visited some of the city's highlights), drive the 5 miles to Blarney Castle for the obligatory kiss of that magical stone, then back through Cork and south to the charming fishing town of Kinsale. Continue southwest through Timoleague, Clonakilty, Rosscarbery, Glandore, and Union Hall to the old town of Skibbereen. The route on through Ballydehob, Toormore, and Bantry into Glengarriff is one of the loveliest in the country. In Glengarriff, visit Garnish Island, then climb through rugged mountains via the Tunnel Road to Kenmare and on to Killarney for the night.

Day 2: Allow the entire day to drive the Ring of Kerry (110 miles), since you won't want to rush through some of Ireland's most spectacular sea and mountain landscape. From Killarney, head for Killorglin, Glenbeigh, Cahirciveen, Waterville, Derrynane, Castlecove, Sneem, and Kenmare before returning to Killarney for the night.

Day 3: See the Dingle Peninsula's very special charms. From Killarney, drive to Killorglin, then north to Castlemaine, west to Inch (where much of *Ryan's Daughter* was filmed), Annascaul, Dingle, Ventry, Slea Head, Dunquin, Ballyferriter, Murreagh, and back to Dingle. Cross Connor's Pass to the north side of the peninsula and Stradbally, Camp, and Tralee before heading back to Killarney. Alternatively, stay the night in one of the lovely B&Bs on the peninsula.

IF YOU HAVE 1 WEEK
THE WEST COAST

A good tour for those deplaning at Shannon.

Day 1: Stay in Limerick, visit Bunratty Folk Park, and take in a castle banquet in the evening (must be booked ahead).

Day 2: Drive to Ennis, then southwest to the picturesque seaside resort towns of Kilrush and Kilkee; north to Lahinch and skirt Liscannor Bay to the mystical Cliffs of Moher; on to Lisdoonvarna, through the bleakly beautiful Burren to Black Head, Ballyvaughan, Kinvara, and Clarinbridge into Galway, where you'll spend the night.

Day 3: Head for Connemara by way of Spiddal, Costello, Screeb, Derryrush, Carna, Toombeola, Ballynahinch, and Clifden. Head northward to Letterfrack and Leenane, where a turn to the southeast will take you through Maam, Cong (setting of *The Quiet Man*), Ballinrobe, Ballintubber (stop to see the abbey), and into Castlebar. Visit Clonalis House, and make Castlebar your overnight stop.

Day 4: Drive to Westport and visit impressive Westport House with its magnificent mansion and zoo park. Take the road to Newport and travel through Mulrany to the Curraun Peninsula, Achill Sound, and on to the breathtaking views of Achill Island (reached by a causeway). Allow time to drive as far out as Keel and Dooagh. Stay overnight on Achill or return to Westport.

Day 5: Turn inland through a changing landscape to Castlebar, Claremorris (Knock and its celebrated shrine are a short detour away), Ballyhaunis, Castlerea, and Roscommon (visit its famous abbey) to Athlone for the night.

Day 6: Heading south from Athlone, drive to Birr and stop to visit the gardens at Birr Castle. Farther south, Nenagh's fine castle dates from about 1200. Turn due west for Portroe and drive along the shores of Lough Derg to Killaloe. From here, it's a short drive, via O'Brien's Bridge and Ardnacrusha, into Limerick.

Day 7: Departure for home.

THE EAST COAST & LAKELAND

Day 1: Arrival in Dublin, settle in, and perhaps take in a cabaret in the evening.

Day 2: Drive south through Dun Laoghaire, Dalkey, and Killiney along the Vico Road, with its spectacular views of Dublin Bay, into the seaside resort of Bray (leave the main road to detour along the seafront). Then head on to Enniskerry beneath Sugarloaf Mountain. Visit nearby Powerscourt Estate and Gardens. Glendalough and its timeless ruins are next along the scenic mountain drive, then on to Rathdrum, Avoca, and Woodenbridge into Arklow. Proceed to County Wexford's Gorey, Enniscorthy (stop in the museum), and into Wexford town, where an overnight stop will give you time to walk its narrow streets and relive its gallant history.

Day 3: From Wexford, head southwest to Ballyhack to catch the ferry across Waterford Harbor to Passage East in County Waterford (if you're enamored of tiny seaside villages, make the short detour to Dunmore East). See Waterford's 1003 Reginald's Tower and remnants of its Viking-built city walls. Kilkenny is next, where you should stop to see Kilkenny Castle, Rothe House, and the Kilkenny Design Workshops. Then it's on through Tullamore (home of the famous Tullamore Dew) to Athlone, "capital" of the midlands. Make this your overnight stop.

Day 4: Drive northwest to Roscommon, look at Roscommon Abbey, then on to the market town of Longford, with its 19th-century cathedral. Head southeast to Edgeworthstown (where you may want to visit the museum dedicated to novelist Maria Edgeworth) and through the angling center of Castlepollard to see nearby Tullynally Castle. Lough Derravaragh, in the immediate vicinity, is the setting of the Irish legend of the Children of Lir. Detour to Fore to see its Benedictine abbey and ancient crosses, then back to Castlepollard and south to Mullingar to spend the night.

Day 5: From Mullingar, drive through Kinnegad to Trim, with its impressive Norman castle. Then head for Navan, where a short detour onto the Dublin road will bring you to the royal Hill of Tara before heading back to Navan and on to Donaghmore and Slane. Look for Bronze Age cemeteries at Brugh na Boinne and visit Mellifonte Abbey and Monasterboice; then go on north to Dunleer, Castlebellingham, and Dundalk. If there's time, drive a bit farther north to the rugged little Carlingford Peninsula, then back to Dundalk and along the coast through Clogher, Termonfeckin, Baltray, Drogheda, Balbriggan, Skerries, Rush, Swords, and Howth (where there are marvelous views of the bay) and on to Dublin by way of Sutton.

Day 6: Spend this day exploring Dublin.

Day 7: Departure for home.

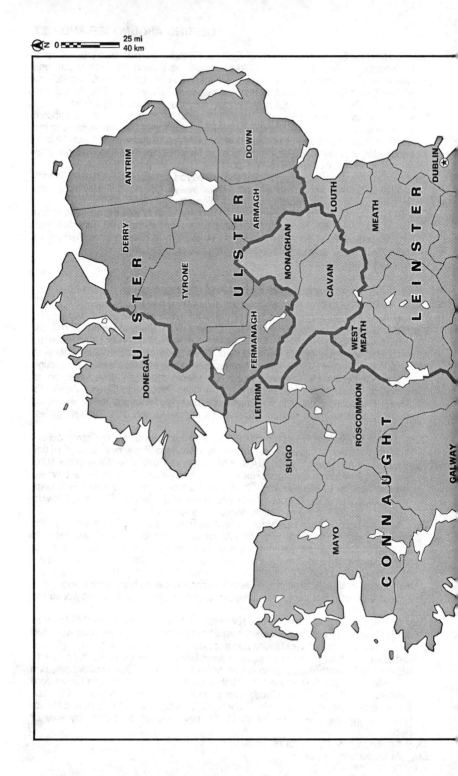

IF YOU HAVE 2 WEEKS — A CIRCULAR TOUR

The suggested starting point is Dublin. If you deplane at Shannon, however, you can simply begin with the Day 9 itinerary and follow the suggested route to the north or south, ending up again at Shannon for your flight home.

Days 1 and 2: *Dublin.* Allow your arrival day for settling into your Dublin digs and getting the feel of the city. Spend the second day exploring Dublin's fine historic buildings and Georgian squares, ending with a hotel cabaret or an evening's pub crawl.

Day 3: *Dublin to Waterford (or Tramore).* Get an early start and drive south to Enniskerry to visit the Powerscourt estate and gardens. Then on through Roundwood to Glendalough with its early-Christian ruins. Avoca is next, then south through Arklow to Enniscorthy, with time out to visit its small museum, and on straight through to Waterford—or detour over to historic Wexford before continuing on to Waterford. Stop for the night in the city itself, or drive on to the seaside resort of Tramore with its 3 miles of sandy beaches.

Day 4: *Waterford to Cork.* Drive south through the old market town of Dungarvan, then westward to Youghal. Stop at the clock tower in the middle of town to visit its interesting museum, allowing ample time for the walking tour described in a brochure available there, which will take you along some of Ireland's oldest surviving city walls. Then it's on to Cork, where you can play the famous Shandon Bells at St. Mary's, visit the city's many historic sites, enjoy an evening meal in one of its fine restaurants, and spend the night.

Day 5: *Cork to Killarney.* Stop by Blarney Castle to kiss the legendary stone, then head for Macroom, Ballingeary, and the Pass of Keimaneigh (you may want to make the short detour to Gougane Barra National Park). Go on to the lovely holiday resort of Glengarriff, then turn north through rugged mountain terrain to Kenmare and on to Killarney.

Days 6 and 7: *Killarney.* You'll want to spend 1 day visiting the famous lakes, islands, and ancient abbeys. The next day, Killarney is the ideal base from which to make either the 109-mile Ring of Kerry drive or a 93-mile circuit of the bewitching Dingle Peninsula.

Day 8: *Killarney to Limerick.* If you opted for the Ring of Kerry on Day 7, you can swing around Dingle en route to Limerick (but it makes for a long day of driving—Dingle is, in fact, a perfect place for one of those itinerary adjustments to allow for an overnight stop). Then back through Rathkeal, Newcastle West, and the beautiful village of Adare to Limerick (only 16 miles from Shannon Airport). Save this evening for the Bunratty or Knappogue Castle medieval banquet (which must be booked ahead).

Day 9: *Limerick to Galway.* Take time to explore Limerick's St. Mary's Cathedral before heading north; then add a few extra miles to take in the stunning Cliffs of Moher. Lisdoonvarna, the popular spa resort, is next, then the barren beauty of the Burren's limestone hills, Ballyvaughan, Clarinbridge, and Galway. Traditional music in a pub in Galway or nearby Salthill makes for a memorable evening.

Day 10: *Galway to Donegal.* A full day's drive will take you through Connemara to Moycullen, Oughterard, Recess, Clifden, Leenane, and along Clew Bay (with over 100 islands) into Westport. Not far away is Westport House, with its magnificent interior, beautiful gardens, and zoo park. Then head north through Castlebar, Pontoon, Ballina, and the seaside resort of Enniscrone. Then drive on to Sligo to see the 13th-century Franciscan friary and the county library museum or just walk the narrow old streets and soak up the atmosphere so dear to Yeats's heart. Finally, it's on to Bundoran, Ballyshannon, and Donegal.

Day 11: *Donegal.* Early in the day, explore Donegal town, with its Franciscan friary and castle. Then head off for a circular tour of County Donegal by driving west through Mountcharles, Killybegs, Ardara, Glenties, Maas, and Kincasslagh (Donegal tweed country). Push farther north through Annagry, Crolly, Bunbeg,

Bloody Foreland, Gortahork, and into Dunfanaghy, nestled at the foot of steep cliffs along the shores of Sheephaven Bay. Drive south to Letterkenny (and if you've an extra day, I strongly recommend the 120-mile loop around the Inishowen Peninsula to Buncrana, Malin Head, and Moville—the scenery is truly spectacular and well worth the drive), then through the picturesque Finn Valley back to Donegal town.

Day 12: *Donegal to Carrick-on-Shannon.* Make this a leisurely driving day, south through Ballyshannon and Bundoran, then southeast to Manorhamilton (look for the ruins of a 1638 castle brooding over the town). Continue south through Drumkeeran and along the shores of lovely Lough Allen (a good place for a picnic lunch) to Drumshabo and Leitrim and into Carrick-on-Shannon, with its fleet of cruise boats bobbing at the wharves.

Day 13: *Carrick-on-Shannon to Dublin.* Drive through lake country to Cavan town by way of Mohill, Carrigallen, Killeshandra, and Crossdoney, and on through Bailieborough and Carrickmacross to Drogheda. From Drogheda, visit the prehistoric tomb at Newgrange, then drive on through Slane into Navan. A further 6 miles will bring you to the Hill of Tara, home of ancient Irish high kings. From there, it's back to Dublin via historic Trim, Black Bull, Clonee, Blanchardstown, and the Phoenix Park.

Day 14: *Dublin.* A day for odds-and-ends and departure.

IF YOU HAVE 3 WEEKS

Days 1–11: Follow the 2-week itinerary above through Day 11.

Day 12: Head northwest from Donegal town for Ardara, Glenties, Maas, and Kinscasslagh, traditional home of the famous Donegal tweed. Continue north through Annagry, Crolly, Bunbeg, Bloody Foreland, and Gortahork to Dunfanaghy, on the shores of Sheephaven Bay.

Day 13: Take time to drive north around the wild and rugged Horn Head, then head south through Ards Forest Park and the Glenveagh National Park, where you'll want to spend an hour or two at the very least. Then it's on to Letterkenny for the night.

Day 14: Head north to the beautiful Inishowen Peninsula through Fahan, Buncrana, and Ballyliffin, to reach the village of Malin. Take the time to drive out to Malin Head, Ireland's northernmost point and a place of quite singular beauty. Then retrace your steps to Malin and turn south through Carndonagh, Moville, Carrowkeel, and Muff, to cross the Northern Ireland border and reach Londonderry for the night.

Day 15: Reserve at least half a day to explore Londonderry's ancient city walls, splendid Guildhall, and St. Columb's Cathedral before pushing on to Limavady and Coleraine to Portrush, a delightful Northern Ireland seaside resort filled with excellent accommodation possibilities.

Day 16: Follow the Antrim coast road for the short drive to that spectacular natural phenomenon, the Giant's Causeway—and if you're so inclined, take the even shorter detour (3 miles) to Bushmill's, home of the world's oldest brewery. Following the coast drive from the Giant's Causeway, pass through Ballycastle to picturesque Cushendall. Turn inland if you have time to visit Glengariff Forest Park. From Cushdall, you'll have the gentle hollows of the famed Antrim Glens on your right, with breathtaking sea views on your left. Pass through Larne to reach Carrickfergus, with its massive late 12th-century castle (there's a museum inside that's well worth a stop). A short drive will bring you to Belfast.

Days 17 and 18: Spend 2 days in Belfast, with day trips to the nearby Ulster Folk and Transport Museum, a fascinating step back into Ireland's past, and perhaps the Ards Peninsula.

Day 19: Drive from Belfast to Dublin, via Hillsboro, Newcastle (where "the Mountains of Mourne sweep down to the sea"), Dundalk, Drogheda with its ancient ruins, and Howth. Or from Dundalk, go through Slane to reach the Hill of Tara; then make the short drive to the prehistoric burial site at Newgrange before heading into Dublin.

Day 20: Dublin, with perhaps a play at the Abbey, a cabaret, or a pub crawl to end your last full day in Ireland.

Day 21: Pack and departure day.

THEMED ITINERARIES

As you can see from the itineraries above, this small island country presents an almost bewildering cornucopia of riches for the visitor. A much more manageable itinerary is one built around a special interest.

You might make your Irish visit a **literary pilgrimage,** beginning with several days in Dublin to visit the birthplaces and haunts of such writers as Jonathan Swift, Thomas Moore, George Bernard Shaw, Oscar Wilde, Brendan Behan, and of course, James Joyce (armed, in this case with the excellent *Ulysses Map of Dublin* available from the Dublin Tourist Office). From Dublin, head for Cork, whose streets and the people that walk them were recorded for all time by Frank O'Connor. A trip to Listowel, County Kerry, will take you into John B. Keane country, and a chance encounter with the man himself is always a possibility. North, then, to Sligo and Yeats country, where the poet left an indelible mark on this region he loved above all others in Ireland.

History and archeology buffs will find it difficult, indeed, to decide just which of Ireland's more than 120,000 national monuments and archeological sites to visit. They range from megalithic tombs of the Stone Age to city walls and fortifications built by Viking invaders to castles left by the Normans to relics of the long years of English landlordism to sites associated with Ireland's 20th-century struggle for independence. An authoritative guide to making those decisions is Dr. Peter Harbison's *Guide to the National Monuments;* and the booklet "Heritage: A Visitor's Guide," published by the Office of Public Works and available from the Irish Tourist Board and in bookshops, covers national monuments, national parks, waterways, and wildlife services.

Nature lovers might well plan an entire trip around the three **national parks**—Killarney in County Kerry, Glenveagh in County Donegal, and Connemara in County Galway—then add the Burren in County Clare, Glendalough in County Wicklow, and Gougane Barra Forest Park in County Cork. In addition to *Heritage: A Visitor's Guide,* mentioned above, "The Open Forest, A Guide to Areas Open to the Public," available from the Irish Forest Service (Leeson Lane, Dublin 2; tel. 01/615666), will present an embarrassment of natural-beauty treasures from which to choose.

Other themes that can easily fill a 2- or 3-week visit include the great houses of Ireland; abbeys, monasteries, and churches; offshore islands; traditional music, song, and dance; and theater. The Irish Tourist Board has a wealth of material on each to help in your planning.

3. WHERE TO STAY

Ireland has several categories of budget accommodations. If your notion of budget travel is camping, there are good campgrounds located in just about every scenic section of the country, and backpackers will find a marvelous supply of hostels at dirt-cheap rates. Next up on the cost scale come those wonderful Irish family B&Bs, no two of which are alike. Then there are the farmhouses, which range from modern bungalows to great Georgian mansions, all on working farms. If you lean toward the "small inn" type of home-away-from-home, there are the guesthouses, a little higher up the price range. And for families or small groups traveling together, self-catering cottages may prove to be the most economical way of all to enjoy an Irish visit. There's even a countrywide holiday program that includes some very nice hotels with special midweek and weekend package rates that can only be called budget.

BORD FAILTE–APPROVED ACCOMMODATIONS Wherever you see the

Bord Failte–approved sign, you'll find clean premises. The ever-vigilant Bord Failte staff keeps a sharp eye on accommodations they approve, with annual, unannounced inspections. Not only that, but each approved accommodation is required to register its rate for the year with the Bord and cannot charge more. Higher rates for holidays or special events must also be registered. Bord Failte also certifies that you'll get the exact accommodation you bargained for when you booked. If you run into what you think is a violation of these rules, you are expected to make your complaint known—first to the hostess, and failing satisfaction, to Bord Failte, Baggot Street Bridge, Dublin 2 (tel. 01/765871). If you think you've been overcharged, be sure to get a receipt to send on to Dublin. While there are some very good unapproved B&Bs in Ireland, it's a good rule of thumb to stick to approved places unless you have a recommendation from someone whose judgment you trust.

The Irish Tourist Board also offers a booking service, which frees you to move about as fancy dictates, secure in the knowledge that you have only to call the nearest ITB office when ready to move on. They'll happily telephone (you will be expected to pay telephone charges) ahead for your next night's lodgings. If you arrive in an Irish town with no place to lay your head that night, the local tourist office will perform the same service. However, during July and August some destinations may be booked almost solid, so if your trip falls in those months, it's a good idea to book ahead as far as possible.

Bord Failte is constantly coming up with off-season travel programs such as their "Springtime in Ireland" promotion that provides bargain airfare and accommodations, along with shopping discounts and several special activities. Then there's a "Christmas in Ireland" program most years, and the annual St. Patrick's Week celebrations. Details on money-saving features vary from year to year, so you should check with any Irish Tourist Board office or travel agents to see what's up when you plan to travel.

STAYING IN A B&B   One or two points will make your stay in any accommodation more enjoyable. First of all, when the Irish say "double room," they mean a room with a double bed; if a room has twin beds, it's called just that, a "twin-bedded" room. Note: In this book, I've used "double" to mean a room that will accommodate two people, so be sure to ask when you book.

Let me add here a word about central heating: Not all B&Bs have it, and you must remember that even where you do find it, Irish central heating is not as warm as that at home. Where it doesn't exist, there's almost always a small heater in your room to take the chill off. Your B&B hostess will gladly furnish a hot-water bottle to make your bed warm and toasty when you retire.

GUESTHOUSES   The Town & Country Homes Association publishes a "Guest Accommodation" booklet with pictures of all member homes. It's available for a small charge from any Irish Tourist Board office. The association's members can book you ahead to your next destination with any other member. I find standards exceptionally high in these homes, and have yet to find one I couldn't recommend, for both facilities and friendly hospitality.

Guesthouse rates range—depending on facilities, location, and season—from IR£23 to IR£47 ($40.25 to $82.25) per person, double occupancy. Not budget, but good value, all the same. The Irish Tourist Board includes all approved guesthouses in their "Guest Accommodations" booklet, available for a small charge, and their "Hotels and Guesthouses" booklet includes pictures.

4. ENJOYING IRELAND ON A BUDGET

Budgeting in Ireland, more than any other country I've encountered in my travels, turns out to be fun. It's all a matter of knowing what's available, what you are looking for, and how to go about finding it.

THE $40-A-DAY BUDGET

At the current conversion rate of U.S. dollars into Irish punts, the $40-a-day budget contemplates that you will spend a maximum of $21 for a place to sleep and your breakfast, around $6 for a pub lunch, and no more than $13 for your evening meal. The following sections point the way to coming in at that figure.

SAVING MONEY ON ACCOMMODATIONS

BEST BUDGET BETS   Hostels   If you are willing to purchase real savings at the expense of a private room, you'll sleep in comfort in dormitorylike space. More savings come from the fact that you can buy dinner makings at the local grocer's and prepare them in a communal kitchen. You'll meet fellow budgeteers from around the world, all eager to compare experiences and pass along budget tips.

   B&Bs and Farmhouses   For those whose budgets stretch to include a private room, Ireland's biggest bargain is its bed-and-breakfast homes (in town and country) and its farmhouses. Few such accommodations offer private baths, although the addition of private toilets and shower stalls in guest rooms, available on a first-come, first-served basis, is becoming more common. You'll be charged an extra IR£1 ($1.75) per night for a private bath.

   A budget-stretching device is to base yourself at one B&B for an entire week, taking advantage of the half-board rate which includes bed, breakfast, and the evening meal at a good reduction. If you book for a week in the southeast, you have a base for exploring the eastern and southeastern regions; then book for another week in the west.

   Self-Catering   Groups, especially families, can realize substantial savings by booking into self-catering accommodations.

   Single Travelers   Those traveling on their own can avoid the single supplement by inquiring at local tourist offices for other single travelers in the locality to share accommodations.

SEASONAL & OTHER DISCOUNTS   Virtually all of the **Ireland Holiday** discounts discussed in "Tips for the Disabled, Seniors, Singles, Families, and Students" in Chapter 2 apply to low-season months, as do most senior-citizen discounts. Through this program, guesthouses, B&Bs, and hotels in some of the most scenic locations in the country offer astonishingly low midweek and weekend specials.

   Family rates are sometimes available in summer months, so be sure to inquire. **Bus Eireann and Irish Rail package holidays** offer substantial discounts on accommodations (see Section 2, above).

SAVING MONEY ON MEALS

BEST BUDGET BETS   An Irish breakfast at your B&B will be very sustaining. Making your midday meal the main one of the day will provide you with as much to eat as most dinners, at several punts less cost.

   Pub Lunches   If you are not ready for a full midday meal, look for the nearest pub offering pub grub and relish a hearty soup and a sandwich or salad plate (at a "peanuts" price).

   Picnics   Even better, stop in a town or village, and at the local grocer's, pick up some fresh bread, a good Irish cheese, and a bottle of lager or stout, and head for the country to lunch under the trees or at the shore. You'll find picnic sites galore, many with tables and benches provided for your comfort.

   High Tea   Another option is to choose high tea instead of a dinner menu. "Tea" in Ireland was traditionally a mini-dinner that constituted a full meal, following an ample midday repast. Nowadays, however, the term is somewhat ambiguous. High tea (at about IR£4/$7) ranges from as much nourishment as can be comfortably handled to one consisting of one or two skimpy sandwiches and a sweet. While you can save as much as 50% of your dinner costs, you must know what "high tea" means to those offering it.

Tourist Menus The Irish Tourist Board has organized a Tourist Menu program with restaurants all around the country. Sometimes called "special value meals," these menus offer a three-course lunch or dinner at bargain prices. There are three price levels: for IR£6 ($10.50) you may be restricted to a limited choice of main-course meats; for IR£8.25 ($14.45) the selections will be more varied; for IR£12 ($21), a glass of wine comes with your dinner. The food is the same the restaurant serves on its pricier menu, and portions are never skimpy. You can identify those eateries serving these meals by a distinctive sign displaying a smiling Irish chef. However, you must be sure to ask specifically for the Tourist Menu or you may wind up being surprised when the check is presented. The Irish Tourist Board publishes a Touring Menu booklet, available for a small charge.

BUDGET RESTAURANTS Many budget restaurants, pubs, tea rooms, and department-store cafeterias serve very good food at budget prices. A good investment is the Irish Tourist Board's booklet "Dining in Ireland," available at a small charge, which gives details on eateries in all regions, including a brief description of the cuisine, hours, and prices.

GUESTHOUSE MEALS A happy way to dine inexpensively is to book for dinner with your B&B, farmhouse, or guesthouse hostess. You're almost certain to get a hearty meal based on local produce and meat. As a rule of thumb, the price of dinner will be about the same as your overnight B&B rate, but to be safe, ask the cost when you book for dinner.

SAVING MONEY ON SIGHTSEEING & ENTERTAINMENT

SPECIAL DISCOUNTS Most sightseeing attractions have **family discounts** for parents traveling with two or more children, and **group discounts** are available at a wide range of attractions for groups of 10 or more (see if you can join up with others to form a group). A good example is the admissions to the outstanding multimedia attraction, *The Dublin Experience*: IR£2.50 ($4.38) for adults, IR£1.50 ($2.65) for children, IR£5 ($8.75) for families, and IR£2 ($3.50) per person in a group. There are also **student discounts** to many attractions. If you fall into any of these categories, *be sure to ask* before paying admission charges.

Some few attractions sell **combination tickets,** such as the £1 ($1.75) saving when you pay IR£4 ($7) to see both *The Dublin Experience* and the *Book of Kells.*

OTHER MONEY-SAVING STRATEGIES Ireland's most striking sightseeing attraction is its **scenic beauty**—and it won't cost you one red cent to revel in it as you travel around the country! Furthermore, some of the most interesting **historic and prehistoric ruins**—castles, abbeys, monasteries, stone forts, etc.—sit quietly in lonely fields with not a ticket seller in sight. You won't pay, for example, to tramp down to the prehistoric cliffside Dunbeg Fort or explore the innards of the early-Christian Gallarus Oratory, both on County Kerry's Dingle Peninsula.

In Dublin, there are **free open-air concerts** during summer months at St. Stephen's Green, and in Cork, free concerts are held in Fitzgerald Park. Inquire at the Tourist Office in each city for exact days and hours.

SAVING MONEY ON SHOPPING

The one shopping absolute for me in Ireland is to buy it when I see it. There isn't a big difference in prices around the country as a rule, and I might never have been able to call some items my own had I waited to find a better price elsewhere, since I never came across them again.

BEST BUYS Most of Ireland's shopping bargains are variations of arts and crafts carried down from ages past, including Aran sweaters, Donegal tweeds, drawings in the Celtic style, and the incomparable Waterford crystal. One note about crystal: In recent years, master cutters trained at Waterford have left to found smaller factories around the country, and you can buy quite nice pieces of Tipperary or Galway crystal at prices substantially lower than you would pay for Waterford. As you travel around the country, be sure to look for other small factories, many of which are very good.

Aran Sweaters   At the top of most visitors' shopping lists is one of Ireland's famed Aran knit sweaters. Made in Ireland as far back as the 9th century, they originated with fishermen along the west coast (especially in the Aran Islands, hence the name), who valued their water resistance as well as their warmth. Today most of the heavy natural oil has been removed from the wool and they're much softer than they used to be.

Designs, however, have changed not one whit. And for good reason. Long ago, each stitch depicted a different part of Irish life: the cable stitch stood for the fisherman's strong rope (it's also supposed to bring good luck) and the trellis stitch represented familiar stone walls. Using a combination of many such symbolic stitches, fishing villages designed patterns unique to each community, making it possible to return any drowning victim to his hometown for burial. Interestingly, in the beginning the sweaters were knit by men—women were relegated to the spinning of the wool. The majority of Aran sweaters are knit in creamy, off-white bainin ("baw-neen") wool, but you'll also find them in soft browns or mottled grays that are undyed, just as they came from the sheep.

A word of caution: Not all the sweaters you see are handmade. More and more machine-knits are appearing in shops, and if price is the primary consideration or you prefer a lighter-weight garment, you may be just as happy with one of these. You should be able to tell the difference by the weight, but if you have any doubt, be sure to ask the salesperson.

You can expect to pay something like $60 to $95 for an adult hand-knit pullover, slightly more for cardigans, and anywhere from one-half to one-third less for children's sizes.

Books   What better memento to carry home from Ireland than a book! The bargain hunter will happily spend hours sifting through the wealth of used-book stalls and bookstore basements with their tables of reduced-price volumes. Dublin has lost a few of its oldest, most revered bookshops, which fell victim to increased taxes, rental costs, and traffic. You'll still, however, find one or two family-run shops along the Liffey quays, and both Greene's Bookshop on Clare Street and Parson's on Baggot Street are havens to which I could repair for weeks on end. In addition to these traditional shops, there are bright, new, and large bookshops galore. In Galway, Kenny's Bookshop is virtually a national treasure, and bookshops are tucked away in some amazing places.

Crafts   Back in the 12th century, a traveler to Ireland waxed lyrical about the country's fine craftsmen in these words: "Fine craftsmanship is all around you. . . . Look carefully at it, and you will penetrate to the very shrine of art. You will make out intricacies so delicate and subtle, so exact and compact, with colors so fresh and vivid that you might say all this was the work of an angel, not of a man."

There are more than 800 craftspeople working full time and over 1,000 part-time craft workers throughout Ireland. More than 44 craft guilds, associations, and organizations are affiliated with the Crafts Council of Ireland, which in turn is a member of the World Crafts Council and the Crafts Council of Europe. And there is now a minister for state responsible for crafts in the country.

Besides the skills I've already discussed above, beautiful woodwork, leathers, pottery, ceramics, artistic metalwork, and many, many others are produced, usually in small shops. The *Crafthunter's Pocket Guide*, from any tourist office (small charge), tells you exactly where to find those particular crafts in which you are interested.

Irish Lace   No purchase is more evocative of long-ago elegance than Ireland's handmade lace from Limerick or Carrickmacross. Supplies are becoming more limited each year as the younger generation become less willing to spend their days doing the exquisite, but tedious and time-consuming, handwork. You can, however, still purchase examples of both from the convents which have kept the art alive.

In Carrickmacross, County Monaghan (15 miles west of Dundalk, just off the road from Dublin to Belfast), it's Carrickmacross Lace Co-op (see Chapter 18), where a lovely collar and cuffs set will run about IR£40 ($70). In Limerick, a lace handkerchief will cost IR£50 ($87.50) and up at the Good Shepherd Convent on Clare Street (see Chapter 13).

Tweeds and Woolens For centuries lovely tweeds came from looms in Donegal homes. Today most of the weaving is done in small factories, concentrated in Donegal. You can watch a weaver at work if you call in at Donal Houlihan's Handcraft Shop in Glengarriff, County Cork, Magee's of Donegal in Donegal town, or at Avoca Handweavers in County Wicklow. All department stores carry woolens by the yard or made up into garments. Some of the best buys are to be found at Gillespi Brothers in the little County Donegal town of Mountcharles, Magee of Donegal, and Padraic O Maille's in Galway. The House of Ireland, in Dublin, has a stylish selection of woolen garments.

Waterford Crystal This famous crystal has been around for two centuries, and is both beautiful beyond words and expensive. However, you will pay much less for it here than at home. You can tour the factory in Waterford (see "Waterford— What to See and Do" Chapter 9) and buy its products there, as well as in many shops and department stores all around Ireland, or in the Shannon Duty-Free Shops.

Miscellaneous Among other things to look for: **Connemara marble** in anything from bookends to letter openers to ashtrays to jewelry; **Owen Irish Turf Crafts,** pressed and molded turf that comes in inexpensive pendants and paperweights and pricier wall plaques, all adorned with Celtic designs; the **Claddagh ring,** with its traditional folk design of two hands clasping a heart that wears a crown (it was originally the Claddagh, County Galway, wedding ring) in moderately priced silver versions as well as more costly gold; **records** of Irish traditional music groups; authentically dressed **character dolls** depicting such historical figures as Molly Malone, with her wheelbarrow of cockles and mussels; and the **Knockcroghery Dudeen,** an authentic replica of the clay pipes of Olde Ireland, now made by Anne Lally in her home, Mill House Pottery, Knockcroghery, County Roscommon, and sold in most good craft shops.

SALES/DISCOUNT SHOPPING About the only discount stores you'll find in Ireland are the **£1 Shops** scattered around the country in cities and towns, both large and small—if it's inexpensive souvenirs you're after, go in and take a look.

Dunnes' Stores is a good chain if you're in need of an extra piece of clothing. They're in most major cities and many of the larger towns, and they carry a good line of clothing at excellent prices.

Seasonal sales can be real money-savers. Large department stores in Dublin, Cork, and Limerick run spring and fall sales with reductions of up to 50%—and they often include Waterford crystal, Royal Tara china, and the like.

DUTY FREE—WORTH IT OR NOT? Back in the 1950s the world's first duty-free shop opened at Shannon Airport, and today it has grown into a supermarket offering an incredible array of international products plus a wide selection of the best of Irish-made goods. You'll save a bundle on Aynsley, Wedgwood, and Royal Worcester bone china from England, perfumes from France, cameras and Hummel porcelain figures from Germany, watches from Switzerland, and even cigarettes from the U.S. Prices on Irish goods, however, are not much better than those in Irish shops. Prices are marked in both Irish punts and U.S. dollars, and credit cards are accepted.

You can get your duty-free shopping off to a good start even before leaving home by ordering the very good catalog that illustrates a representative selection, with prices shown in U.S. dollars, plus shipping charges by surface or air. Send $2 to Shannon Mail Order Stores, Shannon International Free Airport, Ireland. If you order by mail (a time-saving device), you'll pay any Customs duty directly to your postman upon delivery.

RECOVERING VAT Recovering the Value-Added Tax (VAT) is a big break and can make a difference—as much as 10% to 23%—in the cost of your Irish purchases. When making your purchase, you must prove to the merchant that you are a nonresident of Ireland by showing your passport or other documentation (for example, a U.S. driver's license). You'll be issued an invoice which must be stamped by Irish Customs to prove that you did, indeed, take the merchandise out of the country, and is then returned to the vendor. One warning: You may be asked to produce the items you've bought as you're outward bound, so pack all your purchases in the same bag.

When you get the exemption is strictly up to the vendor. Some vendors will give the refund on the spot, but any shop that does so will be liable for the amount of the tax if you fail to return that stamped invoice. Many shops mail your refund after receiving the invoice; if you use credit cards instead of cash, of course, it's a simple matter to issue a credit to your account. You should be aware that any refund sent to you at home will be issued in Irish currency. An easy way to exchange your check is to send it to one of the following: **New York Foreign Exchange,** Public Relations Department, 26 Broadway, Suite 767, New York, NY 10004; **Ruesch International Monetary Services, Inc.,** 1140 19th Street NW, Washington, DC 20036; or any local branch of **Deak International** (formerly Deak-Perera). The U.S. equivalent of the punts, less a fee of around $2, will be mailed to you within a few days.

OTHER MONEY-SAVING STRATEGIES   First, **use credit cards.** Aside from the advantage pointed out above, and the obvious convenience of buying now and paying later, you'll usually save a dollar or two when you use American Express or VISA credit cards (the two most widely accepted, along with Diners Club and Access): Your billing will be at each company's exchange rate, which almost always averages several cents better per dollar than banks.

You won't be able to use credit cards in many small shops, but they're accepted in all major department stores and many souvenir shops, by car-rental companies, hotels, and some restaurants; and in all duty-free shops.

In addition to the excellent shopping guide available through the Tourist Board in Dublin, the newsletter *Inside Ireland* (see Section 9, "Recommended Books, Films, and Recordings," in Chapter 1) furnishes subscribers an excellent "Shopping and Touring Guide" that also includes cash vouchers for many of the shops listed.

SAVING MONEY ON TRANSPORTATION

As for transportation costs, there are several money-saving ways to get around. **Cycling** is one of the cheapest and most popular ways; shank's mare (**hiking**) is, it goes without saying, the least expensive; and **hitchhiking** is an accepted and time-honored mode of transportation (although it's prudent for female hitchhikers to travel in pairs).

Train   Take advantage of special **midweek, weekend, excursion, and package rates** offered by Irish Rail, and if your plans include Northern Ireland, opt for the **Overlander Pass.** If you plan to travel *only* by train, buy the "Rail Only" **Rambler Pass** (See Section 2, above).

Bus   See Section 2 of this chapter for money-saving **holiday packages** and **sightseeing day trips** offered by Bus Eireann. Invest in either the "Bus Only" or "Rail and Bus" **Rambler Pass** (also discussed in Section 2, above).

Car   See Section 2 of this chapter for three car-rental firms offering substantial discounts to our readers.

FAST FACTS   IRELAND

American Express   American Express International, Inc., Travel Service, has two offices in Ireland: 116 Grafton Street, Dublin 2 (tel. 01/772874); and c/o Hamilton Travel, 23 Waring Street, Belfast (tel. 0232/230321). Services at both offices include changing money, selling traveler's checks, accepting mail for clients, and operating a travel agency.

Business Hours   **Banks** close for the lunch hour all over the country, and are open Monday through Friday from 10am to 12:30pm and 1:30 to 3pm; they're closed Saturday, Sunday, and bank holidays. Some banks stay open until 5pm one day a week (in Dublin, it's Thursday, but days vary from location to location). **Airport banks** are open every day except Christmas from 7:30am to 11pm. **Shops** are open Monday through Saturday from 9am to 5:30pm (closed Sunday and holidays), and most large stores in Dublin have hours of 9am to 8pm one day a week (Thursday, as of this writing). Supermarkets and many small shops are open until 9pm on specified days of the week. Outside Dublin, most cities and towns have a midweek early-closing day (usually 1pm), which varies from town to town.

Cameras/Film   Film of most types is readily available in Ireland, even in small towns (usually at chemist shops outside large cities), and Dublin, Cork, and Limerick have good camera shops. You'll find film more costly than at home, however, and as a young American told me with great earnestness, "In Ireland, you're going to need about three times the film you thought you would—there's always another perfect shot around every bend in the road!" So keep that in mind and save money by coming prepared.

Climate   See Section 2, "When to Go," in Chapter 2.

Currency   See Section 1, "Information, Entry Requirements, and Money," in Chapter 2.

Customs   Citizens of non-EC countries may bring the following into Ireland: if you're over the age of 17, 200 cigarettes, 50 cigars, 9 ounces of tobacco, and 1 liter of distilled beverages and spirits exceeding 38.5 proof or 2 liters of other spirits; all ages may bring other dutiable goods valued at up to IR£32 ($56); and as much currency as you wish. (See "Drug and Firearms Laws," below, regarding those items.) On leaving, there are no restrictions on any Irish purchase you carry with you, but you may not take out of the country more than IR£100 ($175) in Irish currency (if you wind up with a surplus, be sure to have notes converted to traveler's checks—on which there is no restriction—at a bank prior to departure).

Upon reentering the U.S., you'll be allowed to bring back purchases valued up to $400 without paying Customs duties or filling out a declaration form. Anything in excess of that amount will be assessed a flat 10% on the next $1,000 and an average of 12% for all over $1,400. Antiques that are more than 100 years old come in duty free, but you must have an authentication of age from the dealer from whom you bought them to present to U.S. Customs. The detailed 15-page booklet "Know Before You Go" (Publication no. 512) is available without charge from the U.S. Customs Service, P.O. Box 7407, Washington, DC 20044.

Documents Required   See Section 1, "Information, Entry Requirements, and Money," in Chapter 2.

Driving Rules   See Section 2, "Getting Around," above.

Drug and Firearms Laws   There are strict laws prohibiting the importation of drugs and/or illegal handguns or other firearms, with stiff prison sentences the penalty. If you have a legitimate reason to bring any kind of firearm into Ireland, *be sure* you check with your nearest Irish consulate for regulations and that you comply with them to the letter. There are consulates in New York, Boston, Chicago, San Francisco, and Ottawa.

Electricity   Ireland's electricity is 220 volts AC, so if you must bring small appliances (like hairdryers), pack a voltage transformer and a variety of plug adapters. Electric shavers using 110 volts should present no problem, since there will be shaver points in virtually every accommodation.

Embassies and Consulates   In the Republic, the **U.S. Embassy** is in Dublin, at 42 Elgin Road (tel. 01/688777).

Emergencies   Dial **999** for fire, police, or an ambulance.

Etiquette   You will find the Irish, on all social levels, still observing old-world courtesies and niceties (God forbid that a lady, especially a *visiting* lady, should carry a heavy package when there's an able-bodied Irishman around!), and they are extremely appreciative of others who follow their example. A demanding tone of voice, breaking into a queue, or any other other form of "pushiness" is simply not acceptable. Such behavior may well go without comment (because of their own code of etiquette), but you may be very sure it does not go without notice. What is sure to bring beaming compliments is polite behavior on the part of American children, so a briefing to your young fry is definitely in order. Display old-fashioned good manners, and you won't go wrong. (See also "Irish Pubs" in Section 5, "Cultural and Social Life," of Chapter 1 for tips on pub etiquette.)

Hairdressers/Barbers There are branches of the excellent Peter Mark salons throughout the country, with Dublin addresses at 74 Grafton Street (tel. 714399) and 11a Upper O'Connell Street (tel. 745589), in addition to locations in several major shopping centers and outlying suburbs. Phone one of the numbers listed here for the location nearest you. They specialize in international standards of cutting and styling, as well as all regular salon services. Look for them also in Cork and Limerick.

Men will find barbershop prices moderate to inexpensive by American standards.

Hitchhiking See Section 2, "Getting Around," above.

Holidays See Section 2, "When to Go," in Chapter 2.

Information See Section 1, "Information, Entry Requirements, and Money," in Chapter 2.

Language See Section 5, "Cultural and Social Life," in Chapter 1.

Laundry There are few self-service laundries outside Dublin, so don't depend on popping into a launderette like the ones you have at home. Many B&B hostesses will be glad to do a washer load for you and hang your clothes in the fresh Irish air to dry while you're out sightseeing. Bear in mind, however, that this is *not* a part of her regular service, so *be sure* to ask nicely and be properly appreciative.

As for commercial laundries, there are few outside Dublin that can provide 1-day service, but local Tourist Offices can steer you to those that do.

Liquor Laws You must be 18 years or over to be served alcoholic beverages in Ireland. That does not exclude under-18s from pubs and lounges, only from being served the hard stuff. During summer months, pubs are open Monday through Saturday from 10:30am to 11:30pm, and on Sunday from 12:30 to 2pm and 4 to 11pm. In winter, the closing hour is 11pm. Hotels and guesthouses can serve alcoholic beverages at any time of day or night to resident guests only.

Mail In the Republic, airmail postage to the U.S. for letters is 50p (88¢) for the first 20 grams, 20p (35¢) for each additional gram. The less expensive, postpaid air letters (called Aerogrammes), available from all post offices, cost 42p (74¢) per letter, and you can save even more by asking for them in packs of five at IR£1.95 ($3.40). Postcards sent airmail to the U.S. require postage of 32p (56¢), and they may be purchased in packs of five for IR£1.30 ($2.30). Street mailboxes are painted green, and are either free-standing (usually at a street corner) or set into an outer wall.

General Delivery in Ireland is known as Poste Restante, and it is received at the General Post Office, O'Connell Street, Dublin, as well as local GPOs in other large cities around the country. Hours for pickup of mail in Dublin are Monday through Saturday from 10:30am to 8pm and on Sunday from 9am to 8pm; in other locations, it's Monday through Friday from 9am to 5:30pm, and some suboffices close at 1pm one day a week. Mail will be held a maximum of 1 month.

Maps See Section 2, "Getting Around," above.

Newspapers/Magazines National daily newspapers are the *Irish Times, Irish Independent, Evening Herald, Irish Press, Evening Press, Cork Examiner,* and *Evening Echo.* National Sunday editions are the *Sunday Independent, Sunday Press, Sunday Tribune, Sunday World,* and the Irish-language *Anola.* There are many good regional newspapers published on a weekly basis—check news agents in each locality.

Passports See Section 1, "Information, Entry Requirements, and Money," in Chapter 2.

Pets Ireland is a small country highly dependent on agriculture, and its island location provides good protection from disease for its beef and dairy industries. Disease brought in from abroad could, however, very quickly play havoc with both. For that reason, all dogs and cats brought into Ireland from any country except the U.K., the Channel Islands, and the Isle of Man, must be kept in quarantine in a government-operated kennel for a period of 6 months, at the owner's expense. All other animals are prohibited by anti-rabies laws.

Police   Dial 999. Garda Siochana, "protector of the peace," is the Gaelic name for the Irish police force, and they're familiarly known as Garda (if there's just one), and Gardai ("*Gard*-ee," collectively). Except for special detachments, they're unarmed, and they wear dark-blue uniforms.

Radio/TV   RTE (Radio Telefis Eireann) is the national broadcasting authority in the Republic. It controls three radio stations: RTE 1 (which has outstanding programming that includes short stories, plays, musical programs, and thought-provoking chat shows, as well as excellent news coverage and interviews of prominent persons from government, entertainment, and the arts); RTE 2 (with less weighty news and interview programming and lots of music of all sorts—rock and roll, country and western, jazz, and some classical); and Radio na Gaeltachta (with all programs broadcast in the Irish language). Independent regional broadcast stations with limited reception areas have also blossomed in recent years.

RTE also controls two television stations: RTE 1 and Network 2, both of which offer mixed programming of news, drama, musical entertainment, and the popular "Late Late Show" on Friday night during the winter months. BBC and ITN television programs are also received in Ireland, as is BBC radio 1, 2, and 3.

Rest Rooms   Even the smallest Irish town usually has public rest rooms (which are clean and safe to use), as do most hotels, department stores, pubs, restaurants, and theaters—gas (petrol) stations do not. A helpful tip: Some public toilets are not as well equipped as they might be, and it's a good idea to carry paper tissues in your handbag for emergencies. Rest rooms are usually marked with the Gaelic *Mna* (women) and *Fir* (men).

Safety   Your worst safety hazard in Ireland is likely to be on the roads—from driving on the left! Re-read carefully the driving hints in Section 2 of this chapter.

Ireland enjoys a relatively low crime rate, and there is very little physical violence. I must, however, add a cautionary note about hitchhiking or wandering around city streets in the wee hours on your own. You are advised, in either case, to team up with someone. In larger cities, such as Dublin and Limerick, you should be careful to carry your wallet or handbag in a manner not conducive to pickpockets or purse snatchers. Whenever you are traveling in an unfamiliar city or country, it is your responsibility to stay alert and be aware of your immediate surroundings.

Dublin has been the victim of waves of car thieves in recent years, so be sure you leave nothing in your parked car, even in guesthouse or hotel car parks.

Taxes   VAT (Value-Added Tax) applies to virtually every phase of your Irish expenses, with the exception of B&B accommodations. The percentage varies with the category—hotels and guesthouses, restaurants, petrol, shop goods, etc. See Section 4, "Enjoying Ireland on a Budget," above, for details on recovering VAT paid on goods you are taking out of the country.

Taxis   You'll find taxi ranks at bus and railway stations, airports, ferry ports, major hotels, and along the main street of some cities. Don't expect to be able to hail them on the street! The telephone directory will list numbers to call under the heading "Taxi-cab Ranks and Shelters." In rural areas, if there is taxi service available, everybody knows the number!

Telegrams   No Western Union—telegrams are sent through the post office, and even if regular postal services are not available on weekends, there is usually telegraph service for several hours on Saturday and Sunday (call the local telephone operator for specific information).

Telephones   Well, they're better than they used to be—but still a far cry from the service you're probably accustomed to at home. It can be an adventure to make a call in Ireland, and I must confess to a certain amount of enjoyment if it happens to entail a bit of conversation with the helpful (and witty) operators. Although they are fast being replaced by newer models, you will run into older coinboxes that use only 2p and 5p coins, and operate on a Button A and Button B basis (you deposit your coins and dial, then push Button A when your party answers—Button B is for coin return). Newer pay phones, which accept 5p, 10p, 20p, and 50p coins, are simpler to use and have instructions printed right on the telephone. Local calls cost 20p (35¢), and you should have an ample supply of change if you're making a toll call.

Time   A good part of the charm of the Irish is their almost total disregard for time. Be that as it may, Ireland's official time is Greenwich mean time in winter and Greenwich summer time (daylight savings) from mid-March to October. There is a five-hour difference with U.S. Eastern Standard Time. Summer days are brilliantly light (or mistily light, depending on the whimsical showers) until 10:30 or 11pm, while in winter darkness descends as early as 4pm.

Tipping There really is no hard-and-fast rule for tipping in Ireland—the tradition of no tipping at all still clings to some rural areas and in some social situations (such as pubs, where you never tip the man behind the stick), but in most cases the waitress, taxi driver, or anyone else rendering a service will accept your tip with courteous appreciation.

As a general rule, you'd want to tip porters carrying bags, waitresses, parking-lot attendants, hairdressers, and barbers. Many restaurants include a service charge on the bill, in which case it is usually printed on the menu and you need not tip additionally. If there is no service-charge information either on the menu or your bill, be sure to ask before you leave a tip. As for the amount you tip, observe the 10% to 15% rule, with one exception—your minimum tip should be 50p, whether or not a percentage of the bill amounts to that much. Actually, whether you tip or not, it's the sincere "thank you" that the Irish value most.

If you stay in a guesthouse or lodge, a small service tip will be welcomed. In B&Bs, tipping is not really called for unless someone has been especially helpful (but *never* your host).

Tourist Offices See Section 1, "Information, Entry Requirements, and Money," in Chapter 2, and also chapters on individual cities.

The **Irish Tourist Board** headquarters are at Baggot Street Bridge, Dublin 2 (tel. 01/765871). Regional offices in major towns are open year round, and they are supplemented by more than 50 others that are open only during summer months. These are easily spotted if you look for the green **"i"** sign that is posted in such diverse locations as a pub or grocer's out in the boondocks or along the Quay in Waterford or in the handsome modern quarters at 14 Upper O'Connell Street in Dublin. Wherever you find that sign, rest assured that there are friendly, knowledge-able people who seem to exist for no other reason than to point you to the accommodations, restaurants, sightseeing attractions, local pubs, or sporting events that will make your holiday a pleasant one.

Hours vary according to location and season, but you can count on year-round offices being staffed Monday through Friday from 10am to 5pm during the winter months, with weekend and longer evening hours during the summer season.

Visas See Section 1, "Information, Entry Requirements, and Money," in Chapter 2.

Water No problems with Ireland's drinking water, and the beaches are remarkably pollution free—many were awarded the European Clean Water flag.

Weather Forecast The weather in Ireland is fickle, and must give forecast-ers fits. You can, however, get their best judgment and a report on weather conditions at the moment for the Greater Dublin Area by calling 01/1199. There are four other regional meteorological service telephones—check telephone directories for the number locally.

CHAPTER 4

SETTLING INTO DUBLIN

1. **FROM A BUDGET TRAVELER'S POINT OF VIEW**
- **WHAT'S SPECIAL ABOUT DUBLIN**
2. **ORIENTATION**
3. **GETTING AROUND**
- **FAST FACTS: DUBLIN**
4. **WHERE TO STAY**
5. **WHERE TO EAT**

It's ancient name was Baile Atha Cliath ("the town of the ford of the hurdles"), the hurdles referring to the frail wicker bridge that once spanned the river just where Father Matthew Bridge stands today. Norsemen called it Dubh-Linn ("black pool") when they founded the present city on the banks of the Liffey in 840. And a modern writer has called it "the most instantly talkative city in Europe."

Although Dublin was founded as a trading port by the Danes in 840, the *Irish Annals* relate that in 988 the Viking settlement was handed over to the High King of Ireland. This occasion was celebrated in 1988 when the city put on a year-long festival to commemorate its millennium.

Dublin is one of Europe's loveliest capital cities, with proud old Georgian buildings, elegantly groomed squares of greenery (Fitzwilliam, Parnell, Merrion, etc.), and acres of shaded space in St. Stephen's Green and the Phoenix Park. Its heart beats to the rhythm of the Liffey, and its horizons extend to craggy Howth Head to the north, the softly curving shores of Dublin Bay to the east, and the slopes of the Dublin Mountains to the south. This sheltered setting along a natural transportation route has been the focal point of a long, rich, and complex history that has left a mark on the face of its landscape as well as its people. Indeed, Dubliners are convinced that their city is not only the centerpiece of Ireland's eastern region, but of the whole of Ireland as well.

1. FROM A BUDGET TRAVELER'S POINT OF VIEW

BUDGET BESTS

Accommodations   An Oige and other hostels, as well as self-catering facilities, are Dublin's best budget-stretchers (see Section 4, "Where to Stay," below).

Sightseeing   Bus Eireann coach tours of the city and day trips to surrounding areas are your best money-savers (see "Sightseeing Strategies" in Chapter 5). See, also, sights and events listed in "Special/Free Events" in Chapter 5.

Dublin has a wealth of free attractions (historic buildings like the Bank of Ireland, centers of natural beauty such as St. Stephen's Green and the Phoenix Park, and the National Gallery of Ireland, which charges only for the guided tour); see Chapter 5.

✓ **WHAT'S SPECIAL ABOUT DUBLIN**

Historic Buildings
☐ Dublin Castle, some parts of which date back to 1208, with the restored State Apartments, former residence of British viceroys.
☐ Bank of Ireland, former seat of the Irish Parliament.
☐ The Custom House, beautifully restored, 200-year-old building noted for its architectural detail.
☐ Kilmainham Gaol Historical Museum, in the prison that held political prisoners from 1796 to 1924, and scene of the execution of 15 rebel leaders that united the Irish in their fight for independence.
☐ Trinity College, which celebrates its 400th anniversary in 1992.

Churches
☐ St. Patrick's Cathedral, founded in 1190, whose most famous dean was Jonathan Swift, author of *Gulliver's Travels*.
☐ St. Michan's Church, 17th-century church whose vaults hold mummified bodies from centuries back.

Museums and Galleries
☐ National Museum of Ireland, holding national treasures dating as far back as the Iron Age, including the outstanding Tara Brooch and Ardagh Chalice.

☐ Irish Museum of Modern Art, in Royal Hospital Kilmainham.
☐ National Gallery, with collections of Irish and international painters.

Literary Landmarks
☐ Sites associated with such writers as James Joyce, George Bernard Shaw, Brendan Behan, and Cornelias Ryan.

Parks
☐ National Botanic Gardens, dating from 1795.
☐ Phoenix Park, 2,000 acres of natural beauty, site of residences of the Irish president and the American ambassador, and home of the Dublin Zoo.
☐ St. Stephen's Green, inner-city haven of natural beauty at the top of Grafton Street.

Cultural and Entertainment Venues
☐ The Abbey Theatre, the undisputed theatrical star in Dublin's crown, plus many other theaters large and small.
☐ Traditional music, most notably at Comhaltas Ceoltóirí Eireann at Monkstown, and the Abbey Tavern in Howth, but also featured in many Dublin pubs.

DISCOUNT OPPORTUNITIES

For Everyone Families will find a wide range of self-catering properties in Dublin at rates that—on a per-person basis—amount to an accommodations discount. Nearly all sightseeing attractions, such as the Dublin Zoo, have discounts for family groups.

Bus discounts are offered during certain hours on certain lines. One of the most useful is the shopping fare offered between 10am and 4:30pm within center-city boundaries. DART suburban rail discounts include commuter "Short Hop" tickets that range from IR£2 ($3.50) per day (with a family discount of IR£5/$8.75) to IR£10 ($17.50) per week. For details on commuter tickets and other discounts, call 01/63333.

For Students Read again Section 5 of Chapter 2 for details on obtaining the International Student Identity Card in advance of your departure for Ireland, then head for the Irish Student Travel Service (USIT), 19 Aston Quay, Dublin 2 (tel. 01/778117 or 679-8833), open Monday through Friday from 9:30am to 5:30pm and on Saturday from 10am to 1pm. Ask for the Travelsave Stamp for your International Student Identity Card, which gives you a 50% discount on Dublin buses and trains. Drastic discounts also come with the Educational Travel Concession Ticket, which covers unlimited travel on Dublin bus and train services; purchase it from Dublin Bus, 59 Upper O'Connell Street (tel. 734222).

Virtually all sightseeing attractions offer special student discounts, and some theaters have special student rates for plays, concerts, cultural events, and musical entertainments. Be sure to ask if you don't see these discounts posted or advertised.

For Seniors "Senior citizen" is defined by different age levels, and although you may not think of yourself as falling into that category, if you are over the age of 55, you may well qualify for the senior discount at some places. Many Dublin sightseeing attractions have discounts for senior citizens, as do theater performances and other cultural events; always inquire if they are not listed. Some Dublin guesthouses offer attractive weekend and 3- or 6-day package rates during the low season, with discounts for seniors, so be sure to ask (also see Section 5 of Chapter 2).

WHAT'S WORTH THE EXTRA MONEY

Accommodations Time saved and convenience make a center-city location worth the extra cost, especially if your time in Dublin is limited.

Entertainment Dinner and cabaret at one of Dublin's top hotels will provide a memorable evening, well worth the extra dollars you spend. Theater and National Concert Hall performances are also not to be missed if you can manage the extra expense. The cost of a night of Irish traditional music at the Abbey Tavern in Howth or at Comhaltas Ceoltóirí Eireann in Monkstown is money well spent.

2. ORIENTATION

ARRIVING

BY AIR Just 7 miles north of the city center, **Dublin Airport** is in Collinstown. There is an ample supply of free luggage carts, so you won't need a porter. Should you land without a place to stay, help is at the Tourist Information Desk located in the Arrivals Terminal. It's open Monday through Saturday: October through May, from 8am to 6pm; June through August, from 8am to 10:30pm; and in September, from 8am to 8pm.

On the mezzanine there's an inexpensive cafeteria for hot or cold snacks, as well as a Grill Bar for more substantial fare: A light meal goes for about IR£5 ($8.75), and a four-course dinner for less than IR£10 ($17.50). You'll also find bars and snack bars in both the arrivals and departure halls.

The Bank of Ireland is on hand in both halls to change your money (closed only on Christmas Day). For those flying on to Britain or the Continent, there is a duty-free shop selling a full range of goods. Those headed to North America will be given a 45-minute shopping stopover at Shannon Airport to browse through its well-stocked duty-free shop. There is also an Aer Lingus booking office in the airport.

Getting Into Town Airport bus fares into the Central Bus Station will run IR£2.30 ($4.05) for adults, half that for children. A taxi into town will cost about IR£13 ($22.75).

BY TRAIN For rail information, call 01/787777 Monday through Saturday from 9am to 9pm and on Sunday from 10am to 7pm. The three major railway stations are **Connolly Station,** on Amiens Street near Busaras; **Heuston Station,** near the Guinness Brewery on St. John's Road; and **Pearse Station,** on Westland Row (serves suburban rail lines). Irish Rail trains meet all ferries arriving at Dun Laoghaire (pronounced "Dun Leary") and the 7-mile ride into Dublin can be included in the boat fare if it is specified on the boat ticket.

BY FERRY Bus Eireann supplies transport between Heuston Station and Dun Laoghaire Pier at a minimum fare of IR£1.40 ($2.45); between the B&I ferryport and

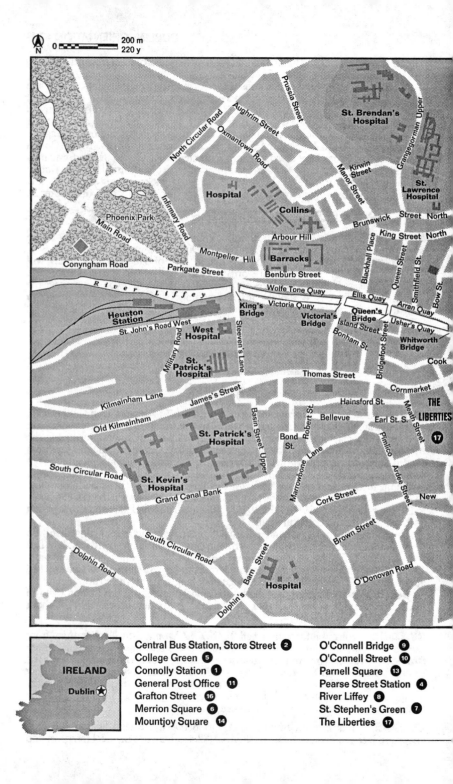

200 m
220 y

St. Brendan's Hospital

Grangegorman Upper

St. Lawrence Hospital

Street North

Kirwin Street

Manor Street

Prussia Street

Aughrim Street

Oxmantown Road

North Circular Road

Hospital

Collins

Brunswick

King Street North

Blackhall Place

Queen Street

Smithfield St.

Bow St.

Arbour Hill

Infirmary Road

Phoenix Park

Main Road

Conyngham Road

Montpelier Hill

Parkgate Street

Barracks

Benburb Street

Wolfe Tone Quay

Ellis Quay

River Liffey

Heuston Station

St. John's Road West

King's Bridge

Victoria Quay

Victoria's Bridge

Queen's Bridge

Island Street

Arran Quay

Usher's Quay

Whitworth Bridge

West Hospital

Steeven's Lane

Bonham St.

Bridgefoot Street

Cook

St. Patrick's Hospital

Military Road

Cornmarket

Thomas Street

THE LIBERTIES

Kilmainham Lane

James's Street

Hainsford St.

Meath Street

Old Kilmainham

Bellevue

Earl St. S.

17

St. Patrick's Hospital

Basin Street Upper

Bond St.

Robert St.

Marrowbone Lane

Pimlico

Ardee Street

South Circular Road

St. Kevin's Hospital

Grand Canal Bank

Cork Street

New

Dolphin Road

South Circular Road

Barn Street

Brown Street

Dolphin's

Hospital

O'Donovan Road

IRELAND

Dublin ★

Central Bus Station, Store Street ❷
College Green ❺
Connolly Station ❶
General Post Office ⓫
Grafton Street ⓰
Merrion Square ❻
Mountjoy Square ⓮

O'Connell Bridge ❾
O'Connell Street ❿
Parnell Square ⓭
Pearse Street Station ❹
River Liffey ❽
St. Stephen's Green ❼
The Liberties ⓱

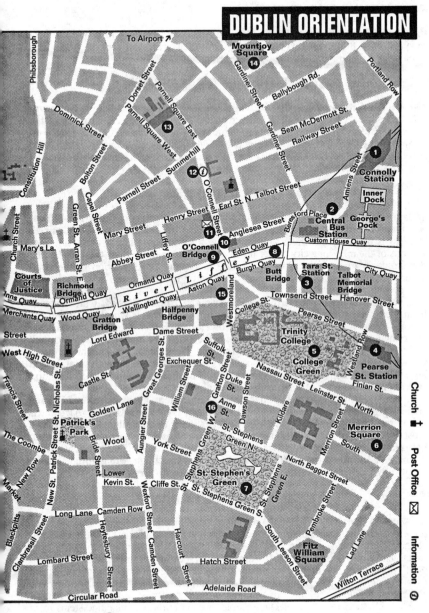

DUBLIN ORIENTATION

Church ✚   Post Office ⊠   Information ⊙

the Central Bus Station for 80p ($1.40); and between Heuston Station and the B&I ferry port for 80p ($1.40). There is also DART electrical rail service to the Dun Laoghaire Pier (fare determined by your destination).

TOURIST INFORMATION

The **Dublin City and County Tourism Visitor Center and Room Reservation Service,** 14 Upper O'Connell Street (tel. 01/747733), just across from the General Post Office, is open October to February, Monday through Friday from 9am to 5pm; and March to October, Monday through Saturday from 9am to 5pm; closed New Year's Day, St. Patrick's Day, Easter Monday, October Public Holiday, and St. Stephen's Day (Dec 26).

CITY LAYOUT

Today, as in its past, Dublin is delineated by the brown waters of the **River Liffey,** which flows from west to east, passing beneath some 10 bridges en route. **O'Connell Bridge** is probably the most important one for travelers, since it connects those sections of the mile-long city center north of the Liffey and south of the Liffey. Keep that firmly in mind, since Dubliners locate everything by its relation to the river. "North of" and "south of" are a part of the city's vocabulary you'll soon adopt as part of your own.

The main thoroughfare north of the river is **O'Connell Street,** which extends from the bridge to Parnell Square at its northern end. This is where you'll find the historic General Post Office and statues of Parnell, Father Matthew, and Daniel O'Connell. At the base of O'Connell's statue, look for the heroic "Victories," representing Fidelity, Eloquence, Courage, and Patriotism. The Dublin City and County Tourism Visitor Center is also on O'Connell Street, along with several good hotels, one large department store, and a jumble of smaller establishments, fast-food eateries, and a number of important office buildings.

To the south of O'Connell Bridge, the one-block-long **Westmoreland Street** gives onto the wide, statue-filled intersection known as **College Green,** that sprawls before the entrance to Trinity College. College Green, in turn, funnels into Dublin's most fashionable shopping thoroughfare, **Grafton Street,** so narrow that at certain hours it's blocked off for pedestrian traffic only. If you've walked that city-center mile, by the time you reach the southern end of Grafton, you'll sigh with gratitude for the beautifully landscaped, restful refuge of **St. Stephen's Green.**

NEIGHBORHOODS IN BRIEF

Medieval Dublin Little remains nowadays of medieval Dublin, but it is easy to trace its outlines and see how the modern city has grown around it. On the south bank of the Liffey, you'll see Christ Church Cathedral's square tower, which is almost the exact center of the original city. To the east, Grattan Bridge stands near the "black pool" that marked its eastern boundary. Little Ship Street follows the course of the River Poddle (now underground), once a city boundary on the south bank of the river, and the quays along the north bank marked another outpost of the ancient city.

The Liberties One of Dublin's oldest neighborhoods, its name stems from the fact that it was beyond the reach of official jurisdiction during medieval times. Located west of Upper Kevin Street, beginning at the Coombe (its main thoroughfare, named for the "coomb," or valley, of the Poddle River) and extending westward to rather indeterminate borders. Family roots of its residents go back for generations, and they have developed an accent and style all their own, instantly recognized by other Dubliners. Some of the city's most colorful characters have come from the Liberties, and many of the city's most important historic landmarks are nearby (St. Patrick's Cathedral, Christ Church Cathedral, and the Brazen Head public house, Dublin's oldest pub, scene of United Irishmen activity in the 18th century).

Southeast Dublin   Running from Grafton Street east to Upper Fitzwilliam Street, and from Clare Street to Lower Hatch Street, this area encompasses what can rightly be called the city center, holding Fitzwilliam and Merrion Georgian squares, St. Stephen's Green, Leinster House (seat of Dáil Eireann, the national parliament), Trinity College, the Bank of Ireland, the Mansion House of the Lord Mayor of Dublin, the National Museum, and many other points of interest.

Northeast Dublin   Extending roughly from the Custom House and Eden quays west to O'Connell Street and Parnell Square, then northeast along Denmark Street to Mountjoy Square, this area holds the General Post Office, the Abbey and Gate theaters, and the Municipal Gallery of Modern Art.

Northwest Dublin   Running west from Ormond Quay to Wolfe Tone Quay, and north as far as Bolton Street, Northwest Dublin is where you'll find the Four Courts, St. Michan's Church, the Botanic Gardens, and the Phoenix Park.

Dublin's Southern Suburbs   About 4km (2½ miles) southeast of the city center, **Ballsbridge,** is a pleasant residential area and also the setting for Lansdowne Road's internationally famous football stadium, the American Embassy, the Royal Dublin Society, and several posh hotels. **Other suburban areas** south of Dublin are Monkstown/Blackrock, Dun Laoghaire, Sandycove, Killiney, Dalkey, Stillorgan, Dundrum, Rathgar, and Templeogue.

Dublin's Northern Suburbs   In the northern reaches of the city's suburbs you'll find Clontarf, Sutton, Howth, Raheny, Drumcondra, Glasnevin, and Finglas.

3. GETTING AROUND

BY DART   The suburban electric train service that runs from Howth to Bray stops at some 25 stations en route. Operated by Irish Rail and called the Dublin Area Rapid Transit (DART), the service is fast and silent. Departures are every 5 minutes during peak hours, every 15 minutes at other times. Service begins at 7am and ends at about 11:30pm. Easy access to the city by DART makes staying at a resort like Howth, Dalkey, or even as far south as Bray, a feasible and money-saving option. Some 19 feeder bus lines link up with the rail system. Timetables can be obtained at most stations. For money-saving tips, see Section 1, "From a Budget Traveler's Point of View," above.

BY BUS   There is excellent bus service to all parts of Dublin and the outlying suburbs, making it easy to search out accommodations beyond the city center, where prices are considerably lower. Any bus marked "An Lar" (meaning "the center") will be headed for the city center. Buses run from 7am (10am on Sunday) to 11:30pm sharp. If you're planning a late night in the city, better plan on taking a taxi to any outlying accommodation. Many buses depart from Eden Quay Bridge, but you can check on your particular bus line by calling 01/720000 from 9am to 6pm or by picking up a copy of the Dublin District Bus and Rail Timetable from the Central Bus

IMPRESSIONS

The most hospitable city I ever passed through.
—MARY WOLLSTONECRAFT, *LETTERS,* 1796.

"Enjoy yourself now!" everybody says in Dublin, and they mean enjoy yourself notwithstanding.
—JAN MORRIS, *TRAVELS,* 1976

The most instantly talkative city in Europe.
—V.S. PRITCHETT, 1978

Station on Store Street or almost any news agent. Fares are determined according to distance, and children under 16 travel for half fare. For discount fares, see Section 1, "From a Budget Traveler's Point of View," above.

BY CAR Just one word about driving in Dublin: *Don't!* Public transportation is efficient and frequent, traffic can be heavy (especially in early-morning and late-afternoon hours), and Dublin's one-way streets can be so confusing that I urge you to drive directly to your accommodation, park the car, and leave it there until you're headed out of town! Parking can also present a real problem, since most spaces are metered for only 2 hours. All that is not to say, however, that it's impossible to drive around the city—but you'll come out better and save both time and nerves if you leave the driving to someone else.

Note: One bit of warning if you're driving in Dublin: Recently there has been a rash of rental-car break-ins, both on city streets and in guesthouse parking areas. The pattern has been for thieves to break the door lock to gain access. So you'd best leave all luggage, coats, cameras, purchases, etc., in your room and leave your locked car and trunk empty.

BY TAXI You should opt for at least one taxi ride just for the conversation—Dublin taxi drivers are both knowledgeable and entertaining. Taxis operate from ranks at all bus and rail stations, in the center of O'Connell Street, at College Green, at St. Stephen's Green, and at several leading hotels (listed in the telephone directory under "Taxi-cab Ranks"). Dublin is blessed with about 100 taxi companies, and you can telephone 783333 or 561111 for a taxi, but an extra service charge will be added to the fare. Minimum fare is IR£1.80 ($3.15) for the first mile (minimum charge of 75p/$1.30), plus 10p (18¢) for each additional 2/15 of a mile or 1.2 minutes of waiting time. All taxis are metered, with a charge of 40p (70¢) for each additional passenger and each piece of luggage, and 60p ($1.05) on bank holidays. Between the hours of 8pm and 8am there's an additional charge of 40p (70¢) per trip.

BY BICYCLE Inner-city traffic conditions make cycling a hazardous undertaking, and narrow streets with both-side parking often reduces traffic lanes in both city-center and suburban streets to a *very* narrow lane. If you're an expert cycler and stout of heart, you'll pay about IR£20 ($35) per week for bike rental and be required to pay a deposit of about IR£30 ($52.50). Bikes can be rented at The Bike Store, 58 Lower Gardiner Street (tel. 01/725399 or 725931).

ON FOOT Once you reach the city center, most places are going to be within easy walking distance, and there's no better walking city than Dublin.

FAST *FACTS* DUBLIN

American Express You'll find American Express International at 116 Grafton Street, Dublin 2 (tel. 01/772874). They provide travel-agency services, as well as currency exchange, accepting mail, etc.

Area Code The telephone prefix for Dublin is 01. *Note:* Dublin is experiencing major changes in telephone numbers, which will continue over the next year or two—if you experience difficulty in reaching any numbers listed in this guide, call Inquiries (tel. 191) for any changes that may have occurred. At the moment, all numbers that begin with 23, 24, 27, 28, 70, and 79 are being changed by adding the prefix of "6" (623, 624, etc.).

Baby-sitters Most B&B hostesses, and nearly all guesthouses and hotels, can obtain reliable baby-sitters if you give them sufficient notice. Best to inquire when you book.

Car Rentals See Section 2, "Getting Around," in Chapter 3.

Climate See Section 2, "When to Go," in Chapter 2.

Currency See Section 1, "Information, Entry Requirements, and Money," in Chapter 2.

Dentists and Doctors If you need a doctor, dentist, or hospital service, the first source of information should be your accommodations hostess or someone on the local scene. Failing that, the **Irish Medical Organization,** 10 Fitzwilliam Place, Dublin (tel. 01/767273), can put you in touch with the nearest medical help.

Drugstores   Drugstores are usually called "chemists" throughout Ireland, and in Dublin they're usually open Monday through Saturday from 9:30am to 6pm and on Sunday from 11am to 1pm. **O'Connell's Pharmacy** has three branches that observe late hours (8:30am to 10pm) 7 days a week: 55 O'Connell Street (tel. 01/730427); 310 Harolds Cross, Dublin 6 West (tel. 01/973877); and 85 Terenure Road North, Dublin 6 West (tel. 01/907179).

Embassies and Consulates   The **U.S. Embassy** is at 42 Elgin Road, Ballsbridge, Dublin 4 (tel. 01/688777).

Emergencies   Dial **999** for any kind of emergency assistance.

Eyeglasses   With full optical services, including contact lenses, **Donal MacNally Opticians** has seven branches in the Dublin metropolitan area. Head office is at 75 Grafton Street, Dublin 2 (tel. 01/715499, 715181, or 731303).

Hairdressers/Barbers   You'll find **Peter Mark Salons** at 74 Grafton Street, Dublin 2 (tel. 01/714399 or 714136); 11A Upper O'Connell Street, Dublin 1 (tel. 01/745589); and several shopping-center and suburban locations.

Holidays   See Section 2, "When to Go," in Chapter 2.

Hospitals   See "Dentists and Doctors," above.

Information   See Section 1, "Orientation," above.

Laundry/Dry Cleaning   For full laundry and dry-cleaning service, try **Prescotts Cleaners Ltd.,** 56 St. Brigids Road, Artane, Dublin 5 (tel. 01/311100). They have several branches, mostly in suburban areas, and will pick up and deliver. Also, many hotels and guesthouses will send out laundry and dry cleaning for you; B&B hostesses will sometimes share the family washer and dryer (but don't *depend* on that).

Libraries   Dublin has a wealth of libraries, with a combination of private, municipal, and national ownership. The National Library of Ireland, Marsh's Library, and the newly opened Space Age Institution are among the most interesting. See Chapter 5 for details, and ask at the Tourist Information Center for a complete list of Dublin libraries.

Lost Property   Bus and rail stations have lost-and-found departments if you have suffered a loss in transit. For all other losses, contact the police.

Luggage Storage/Lockers   There are luggage-storage facilities at the Central Bus Station on Store Street, and at Connolly Railway Station, and Heuston Railway Station. Also, some hostels will store luggage during the day.

Newspapers/Magazines   See "Fast Facts: Ireland" in Chapter 3.

Photographic Needs   For almost any photographic service, from new and used equipment to developing and jumbo-size printing, as well as good prices on film, try **Dublin Camera Exchange,** 98 Trinity Street, Dublin 2 (tel. 01/793410).

Police   Dial 999.

Post Office   The **General Post Office** on O'Connell Street is located across from the Dublin Tourist Center and is open Monday through Saturday from 8am to 8pm (to 7pm only for mailing or receiving parcels) and on Sunday and bank holidays from 10:30am to 6:30pm. General Delivery mail can be picked up at the Post Restante desk until 8pm.

Radio/TV   See "Fast Facts: Ireland" in Chapter 3.

Religious Services   The Tourist Board can furnish a list of Dublin churches and information telephone numbers for days and hours of services. Many of the world's religious orders—including Jewish, Islamic, and Jehovah's Witnesses—are represented in Dublin, in addition to the dominant Catholic orders and the leading Protestant order, the Church of Ireland.

Rest Rooms   The larger department stores and shopping centers all have public rest rooms, as do city-center hotels and pubs.

Safety   See "Fast Facts: Ireland" in Chapter 3.

Shoe Repairs   For shoe and luggage repair, try **Mister Minit IRE Ltd.,** Unit 123, St. Stephens Green South (tel. 01/781068).

Taxes   See "Fast Facts: Ireland" in Chapter 3.

Taxis See Section 3, "Getting Around," above.
Telegrams/Telex Telegraph service is available at the GPO, as well as at coin telephones.
Transit Information Phone 01/720000 for bus information.

4. WHERE TO STAY

You'll probably pay your highest accommodation rate in Dublin, which may not be as intimidating as it sounds, for "highest" can still keep you within the daily budget limit of this book. You should know in advance, however, that as distance from the city center increases, prices decrease.

Accommodations in Dublin and its immediate environs are so numerous that it's possible to stay in almost any section you like and in almost any price range you prefer. There are good hostels, bed-and-breakfast homes, guesthouses, self-catering flats, small intimate hotels, and large luxury hotels. In the city center, however, you're going to have to pay more, and places in this area are often heavily booked.

The alternative is to find a room in one of the outlying suburbs. You might consider Howth, Dalkey, Killiney, or Bray (in County Wicklow, but with rail service that makes it an easy commute) and spend mornings on the beach, afternoons or evenings in town. On the other hand, if you want to be able to stay out later than those last bus and train departures, you'll find it good value to avoid the taxi fares and pay more to stay right in the city.

Keep in mind that prices in Dublin often soar during holidays and special events such as Easter, the Spring Show in May, the Horse Show in August, All-Ireland Finals in September, and international rugby matches. It's best to plan your visit to Dublin to avoid those events unless you have a special interest in them. If you do plan to come during one of these periods, be sure to reserve well in advance.

In the recommendations below, you'll find a smattering of all the accommodations categories mentioned above, including some higher-priced guesthouses in the city proper that give readers of this book a substantial discount, along with some accommodations that fall into the "Worth the Extra Money" category. For your convenience, they are listed by price and by location.

Dublin is one place I advocate arriving with a firm reservation, but if you should arrive without one, contact the **Tourist Office Central Reservation Service,** 14 Upper O'Connell Street, Dublin 1 (tel. 01/735209), or arm yourself with their publication "Guest Accommodation" and start telephoning around.

DOUBLES FOR LESS THAN IR£14 [$25] PER PERSON

CITY CENTER

HARVEY'S, 11 Upper Gardiner St., Dublin 1. Tel. 01/748384. 5 rms (none with bath). **Bus:** Any city center bus to top of O'Connell Street and walk east.
$ Rates (including breakfast): IR£12.50 ($21.90) per person, sharing. No credit cards. **Parking:** Free.
Built in 1785, this four-story Georgian home is about half a mile from the city center. Eilish Flood is the personable hostess, very helpful to visitors. Her guesthouse is especially popular with young Americans. Comfortable modern furnishings are combined with some interesting antiques, and central heating has been installed; all rooms have sinks. Drivers have use of the private parking lot at no extra cost.

SOUTH OF THE CITY CENTER
Sandymount

DOLORES AND TONY MURPHY, 14 Castle Park, Sandymount, Dublin 4.
Tel. 01/698413. 3 rms (none with bath). **Bus:** 2 or 3. **DART:** Sandymount.
$ Rates (including breakfast): IR£11.50 ($20.13) per person, sharing. No credit
cards. **Closed:** Oct–Apr.

Dolores and Tony Murphy are the delightful hosts of this bed-and-breakfast off
Gilford Road. Their modern house is brightly decorated and guests are
welcome to enjoy the sun in the small garden out back. Rooms have built-in
wardrobes and sinks. The entire family seems dedicated to making guests feel at
home, and Dolores will be glad to prepare the evening meal if you give her sufficient
advance notice.

Ranelagh

ST. DUNSTAN'S, 25a Oakley Rd., Ranelagh, Dublin 6. Tel. 01/972286.
3 rms (none with bath). **Bus:** 11, 11A, 13, 48A, 62, or 86.
$ Rates (including breakfast): IR£12 ($21) per person, sharing. No credit cards.
Mrs. Bird's brick Edwardian home has been a favorite with readers for several years.
Set in a lovely residential area near Rathgar, the house is also within walking distance
of shopping and good restaurants. There's central heating, and the house is spotlessly
clean. The attractive bedrooms all include sinks.

Mount Merrion

SORBONNE, 54 Glen Abbey Rd., Mount Merrion, Co. Dublin. Tel.
01/882750. 4 rms (none with bath). TV **Bus:** 46A or 64A.
$ Rates (including breakfast): IR£12.50 ($21.90) per person, sharing. 20% reduc-
tion for children under 10. No credit cards. **Parking:** Available.
Mrs. Lily O'Shea is the popular hostess of this two-story home. Located just off the
N11 and Trees Road, Sorbonne is convenient to the University College Dublin (UCD)
campus, with off-street parking available. Each room has a sink, and Mrs. O'Shea can
provide high tea.

Dun Loaghaire

ANNESGROVE, 28 Rosmeen Gardens, Dun Laoghaire, Co. Dublin. Tel.
01/809801. 3 rms (none with bath). **Bus:** 7, 7A, or 8 from O'Connell Bridge.
DART: Dun Loaghaire.
$ Rates (including breakfast): IR£12.50 ($21.90) per person, sharing. 25% reduc-
tion for children. No credit cards. **Closed:** Mid–Dec to Jan.

Annesgrove is a pretty two-story home set in a cul-de-sac, close to train and bus
transportation, and a short walk from the car-ferry. Mrs. Anne D'Alton is the
gracious hostess, and she will provide an early breakfast for those with a
morning departure. All rooms have sinks.

CILL DARA, 5 Tivoli Rd., Dun Laoghaire, Co. Dublin. Tel. 01/807355. 3
rms (none with bath). **Bus:** 7, 7A, 8, or 46A.
$ Rates (including breakfast): IR£12.50 ($21.90) per person, sharing. 20% reduc-
tion for children. No credit cards. **Parking:** Available.
There is a warm, inviting atmosphere at Cill Dara, where Mrs. Mary Lehane will
happily provide an early-morning breakfast for ferrygoers. This is a modern house
opposite the golf course and a short walk from the beach and restaurants. It has three
comfortable double bedrooms with sinks, a TV lounge, and a walled garden for
relaxing in the sun. It is also convenient to bus and train service into the city center.
Parking facilities are available.

ROSMEEN HOUSE, 13 Rosmeen Gardens, Dun Laoghaire, Co. Dublin.
Tel. 01/807613. 6 rms (1 with bath). **Bus:** 7, 7A, or 8. **DART:** Dun Laoghaire.
$ Rates (including breakfast): IR£12.50 ($21.90) per person, sharing; IR£2 ($3.50)
additional for private bath. 20% reduction for children. No credit cards. **Parking:**
Available. **Closed:** Dec–Jan.

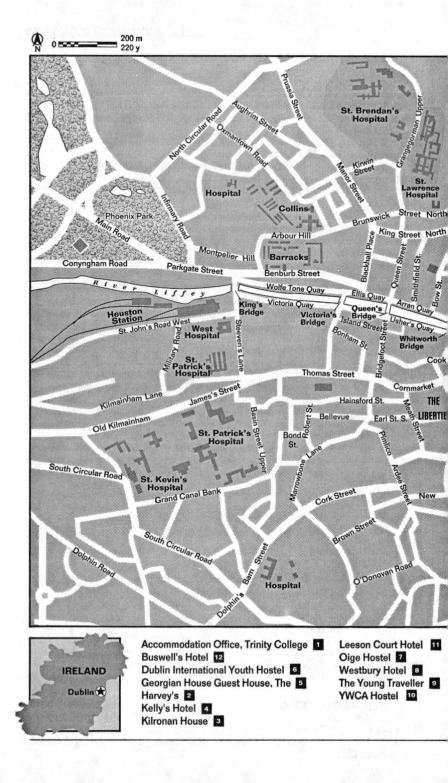

Accommodation Office, Trinity College	1	Leeson Court Hotel	11
Buswell's Hotel	12	Oige Hostel	7
Dublin International Youth Hostel	6	Westbury Hotel	8
Georgian House Guest House, The	5	The Young Traveller	9
Harvey's	2	YWCA Hostel	10
Kelly's Hotel	4		
Kilronan House	3		

IRELAND

Dublin

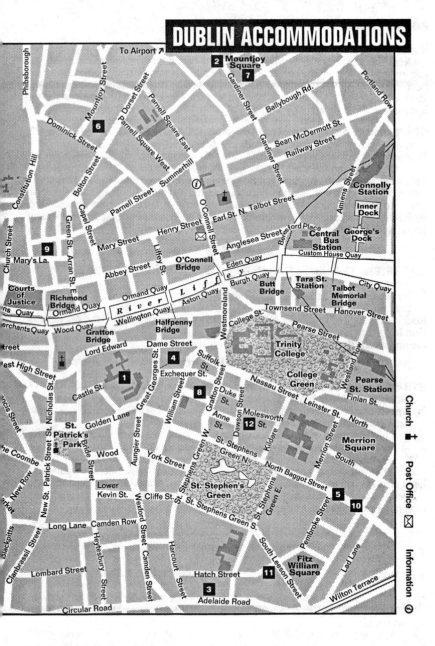

DUBLIN ACCOMMODATIONS

To Airport ↗

Mountjoy Square
2 **7**

Phibsborough

Portland Row

Mountjoy Street

Dorset Street

Parnell Square East

Gardiner Street

Ballybough Rd.

Dominick Street

6

Parnell Square West

Sean McDermott St.

Gardiner Street

Railway Street

Constitution Hill

Bolton Street

Capel Street

Green St.

Arran St. E

Parnell Street

Summerhill

Connolly Station

Amiens Street

Church Street

Dominick Street

ⓘ

O'Connell Street

Earl St. N. Talbot Street

Inner Dock

Henry Street

Mary Street

Anglesea Street

Central Bus Station

George's Dock

Beresford Place

9

Mary's La.

Abbey Street

Liffey St.

O'Connell Bridge

Eden Quay

Custom House Quay

Courts of Justice

Richmond Bridge

Ormand Quay

River L i f f e y

Burgh Quay

Tara St. Station

City Quay

ns Quay

Ormand Quay

Aston Quay

Westmoreland

Butt Bridge

Talbot Memorial Bridge

Hanover Street

erchants Quay

Wood Quay

Wellington Quay

Halfpenny Bridge

College St.

Townsend Street

treet

Gratton Bridge

Lord Edward

Dame Street

Pearse Street

est High Street

1

Castle St.

Great Georges St.

4

Suffolk St.

Exchequer St.

Trinity College

College Green

Pearse St. Station

Westland Row

ncls Street

Golden Lane

William Street

8

Grafton St.

Duke St.

Nassau Street

Leinster St.

Finian St.

North

St. Patrick's Park

St. Nicholas St.

arde Street

Aungier Street

Anne St.

Dawson Street

Molesworth **12** St.

Kildare

Merrion Square

he Coombe

Wood

York Street

St. Stephens Green W

St. Stephens Green N.

North Baggot Street

South

New Row

New St.

Patrick Street

Lower Kevin St.

Cliffe St.

St. Stephen's Green

St. Stephens Green E.

Merrion Street

5

10

Blackpitts

Camden Row

Wexford Street

St. Stephens Green S.

Pembroke Street

Lad Lane

rket

Long Lane

Heytesbury Street

Camden Street

Harcourt Street

South Leeson Street

Fitz William Square

11

Clambrassil Street

Lombard Street

Hatch Street

Adelaide Road

3

Circular Road

Wilton Terrace

Church ∎✝ Post Office ⊠ Information ⊙

Rosmeen House and its hostess, Mrs. Joan Murphy, have long been popular with readers. This Mediterranean-style villa sits in its own grounds (with private parking), just minutes away from the car-ferry and train, and bus transportation into town. Five bedrooms have sinks, but only one has a private bath. There is central heating, as well as electric blankets on all beds, and Mrs. Murphy is happy to supply an early breakfast if you have an early sailing.

SCARSDALE, 4 Tivoli Rd., Dun Laoghaire, Co. Dublin. Tel. 01/806258. 3 rms (1 with shower). **Bus:** 7, 7A, 8, or 46A.

$ Rates (including breakfast): IR£12 ($21) per person, sharing. 25% reduction for children. Evening meal IR£10 ($17.50). No credit cards.

This modern house in central Dun Loaghaire is nicely decorated and all bedrooms have clock-radios as well as sinks. Meals are served in a pleasant dining room looking out onto the garden, where Mrs. Doris Pittman, the hostess, grows flowers and vegetables. She'll furnish the evening meal with adequate notice, and give an early breakfast for ferry passengers.

Dalkey

ROCKVIEW, Coliemore Rd., Dalkey, Co. Dublin. Tel. 01/858205. 4 rms (none with bath). **Bus:** 8. **DART:** Dalkey.

$ Rates (including breakfast): IR£12 ($21) per person, sharing. 25% reduction for children. No credit cards.

Rockview is located in a quiet residential section on the coast, with the car-ferry at Dun Laoghaire just 2 miles away. All bedrooms have sinks. Mrs. Seaver doesn't serve evening meals, but there are good restaurants nearby.

Bray, Co. Wicklow

STRAND HOUSE, Seafront, Bray, Co. Wicklow. Tel. 01/868920. 5 rms (1 with bath). **DART:** Bray.

$ Rates (including breakfast): IR£11 ($19.25) without bath, IR£14 ($24.50) with bath. No credit cards. **Parking:** Available.

This two-story Neo-Georgian house faces the sea from its grounds (with convenient off-street parking). Mrs. Maeve O'Loughlin's home is nicely decorated throughout. The bedrooms all have sinks. She furnishes tourist literature for guests and is quite knowledgeable about local restaurants and sightseeing highlights in Dublin, as well as in County Wicklow. Breakfast comes atop linen tablecloths, with a selection of dishes and perfect butter curls, all of which reflect her long hotel experience.

NORTH OF THE CITY CENTER

Glasnevin

HILLCREST, 13 Marlborough Rd., Glasnevin, Dublin 7. Tel. 01/385340. 6 rms (3 with shower). **Bus:** 11, 13, 19, 19A, 34, or 34A.

$ Rates (including breakfast): IR£13 ($22.75) per person, sharing, without shower, IR£14 ($24.50) per person with shower and toilet. No credit cards. **Parking:** Available.

Hillcrest is within walking distance of the Phoenix Park, with parking and good bus service to the city center. Mrs. Mary Murphy has won high praise from readers for her hospitality over the years. Three rooms come complete with shower and toilet, and the other three have sinks.

Clontarf

AISLING, 19/20 St. Lawrence Rd., Clontarf, Dublin 3. Tel. 01/339097 or 338400. 9 rms (7 with bath, 1 with shower). **Bus:** 30 or 44A.

$ **Rates** (including breakfast): IR£12.50 ($21.88) per person, sharing; IR£2 ($3.50) per person additional for private facilities. 10% reduction for children. No credit cards. **Parking:** Available.

Joe and Mary Mooney are the hosts at Aisling. Their home, located on a quiet street just off the Clontarf–Howth road, is furnished with antiques such as the grandfather clock in the entrance hall, and the Waterford glass chandelier that lights the dining room. Breakfast comes on china and linen tablecloths, with Galway crystal stemware and sterling flatware. The bedrooms are spacious and attractively decorated, and there are tea and coffee makers in the lounge. There's central heating and a private parking area.

MRS. BRIDGET GEARY, 69 Hampton Court, Clontarf, Dublin 3. Tel. 01/331199. 3 rms (1 with shower/bath and toilet). **Bus:** 44A. **Closed:** Nov–Feb.
$ **Rates** (including breakfast): IR£12.50 ($21.90) per person, sharing; IR£2.50 ($4.38) per person additional for private bath. 20% reduction for children. No credit cards.

Mrs. Geary's home is a modern bungalow convenient to the airport, car-ferry, and transport into town via either bus or train. Clontarf Castle, which serves good, moderately priced meals, is a mere 10-minute walk away. Mrs. Geary's hospitality and graciousness have earned her a loyal following with our readers—as one reader wrote, "It was just like being home and the meals were fantastic."

MRS. EILEEN KELLY, 17 Seacourt, St. Gabriel's Rd., Clontarf, Dublin 3. Tel. 01/332547. 3 rms (2 with bath). **Bus:** 30 or 44A.
$ **Rates** (including breakfast): IR£12 ($21) per person, sharing; IR£4 ($7) per person additional for private bath. No credit cards. **Closed:** Nov–Feb.

Mrs. Eileen Kelly is an outstanding hostess who welcomes guests into the family circle around a cozy open fire in the lounge. Her large bedrooms are tastefully furnished. All rooms have sinks, and the house is centrally heated and bus transportation to the city center is not far away.

SAN VISTA, 237 Clontarf Rd., Dublin 3. Tel. 01/339582. 3 rms (all with shower). **Bus:** 30 or 44A.
$ **Rates** (including breakfast): IR£12.50 ($21.90) per person, sharing. No credit cards.

Mrs. O'Connell is the lively hostess at this attractive house set on the seafront along Dublin Bay. She has been described by our readers as being "a good listener," and is always eager to share with her guests her extensive knowledge of places to go and things to see and do in Dublin.

WAVEMOUNT, 264 Clontarf Rd., Clontarf, Dublin 3. Tel. 01/331744. 3 rms (2 with shower). **Bus:** 30.
$ **Rates** (including breakfast): IR£12.50 ($21.90) per person, sharing; IR£1 ($1.75) per person additional for private facilities. 25% reduction for children. No credit cards. **Closed:** Nov–Jan.

Wavemount is a pretty, two-story home overlooking Dublin Bay. Maura O'Driscoll and her husband, Raymond, have earned glowing reports from readers over the years, and it's easy to see why. The house itself is spotless and shining, but even more impressive is the warmth with which this couple greet their guests. Breakfasts (featuring homemade bread) are generous, and presented in a bright front room with a bay window looking out to the sea. Mrs. O'Driscoll will also provide the evening meal with sufficient notice. One bedroom has a bay window and a marvelous sea view; all are centrally heated. There's a good restaurant next door, and Clontarf Castle is within walking distance, with moderately priced meals and entertainment during the summer.

DOUBLES FOR LESS THAN IR£29 ($51) PER PERSON

CITY CENTER

THE GEORGIAN HOUSE GUEST HOUSE, 20 Lower Baggot St., Dublin 2. Tel. 01/618832. Fax 01/618834. 26 rms (all with shower and toilet). TV
$ Rates (including breakfast): IR£23–IR£24.50 ($40.25–$42.90) per person, sharing. Children under 4 stay free in parents' room; discounts for ages 4–12 and 13–16. ACC, AE, BARC, MC, V. **Parking:** Available.

 This restored Georgian town house is located just off St. Stephen's Green in the heart of the city. Annette O'Sullivan is owner and hostess of the four-story house. The bedrooms all have radios; there's no elevator. The former garden is now an off-street parking area. The basement Ante Room Restaurant serves breakfast, as well as lunch and dinner at moderate prices (see Section 5, "Where to Eat," below).

KELLY'S HOTEL, 36/37 S. Great George's St., Dublin 2. Tel. 01/779277 or 779688. 24 rms (18 with bath).
$ Rates (including breakfast): IR£22 ($38.50) single without bath; IR£20 ($35) per person, sharing, with bath; IR£2 ($3.50) per person additional for private bath. ACC, AE, BARC, MC, V.

Kelly's Hotel is in one of the city's most convenient locations, west of Grafton Street in the city center, within walking distance of many attractions. This rather old-fashioned, upstairs hostelry is presided over by the friendly owners/operators, Paula and Tom Lynam. There is also a delightful old-style pub/bar with tall windows and leather seating, offering TV and bar food.

KILRONAN HOUSE, 70 Adelaide Rd., Dublin 2. Tel. 01/755266. 11 rms (all with bath/shower). TV **Bus:** 14, 15, 19, 20, or 46A.
$ Rates (including breakfast): IR£25–IR£27.50 ($43.75–$48.15) per person. 25% reduction for children. Ask for the 10% discount to readers of this book (who pay cash) when you reserve. ACC, BARC, MC, V.

Kilronan House, just a 5-minute walk from St. Stephen's Green, is a four-story town house. Mrs. Josephine Murray, its gracious owner/manager, has years of hotel experience, which is evident in the smooth running of her attractive home. Tea and cookies are served each evening in the lounge, which has a TV and is a gathering point for guests. Breakfasts are highlighted by homemade brown bread and Mrs. Murray's preserves. All guest rooms have a radio, hairdryer, and tea and coffee maker.

SOUTH OF THE CITY CENTER

Ballsbridge

ARIEL HOUSE, 50-52 Lansdowne Rd., Ballsbridge, Dublin 4. Tel. 01/685512. Fax 01/685845. 30 rms (all with bath) TV TEL **DART:** Lansdowne Road.
$ Rates: IR£25–IR£32.50 ($43.75–$56.90) per person room; IR£35 ($61.25) per person suite. IR£5 ($8.75) per person extra for full Irish breakfast, IR£3.50 ($6.15) for continental breakfast, IR£4.50 ($7.90) for afternoon tea. Ask for the 10% discount to our readers who pay cash and mention this book when reserving. MC, V.

⭐ This is one of Dublin's most popular guesthouses, largely because of Michael
O'Brien, its genial owner/manager. He worked in some of San Francisco's
leading hotels for several years, and his attitude toward his guests goes far
beyond mere hospitality. His long-time manageress, Marian Geary, reflects the
🅂 same caring attitude. Ariel House is only 5 minutes from the city center, and
there's a DART rail stop just a few steps from the house. Lansdowne Football
Stadium is next door, and within easy walking distance are the American Embassy,
the Royal Dublin Society, and Chester Beatty Library.

The two adjoining, century-old red-brick houses and the modern garden extension
combine the graciousness of age with modern comfort. Guest rooms in the main
house have high ceilings and modern furnishings, and are reached via a lovely old
staircase. The garden-extension rooms are ground level, with a ramp for wheelchairs.
Rooms have hairdryers and twin beds or one double and one single bed, and there are
two large family rooms. The pride of Ariel House, however, is the elegant Garden
Suite, a very large bed-sitting room furnished with antiques, with wall-to-wall picture
windows overlooking the garden; the spacious bathroom holds a luxurious Jacuzzi.

Breakfast, with a wide variety of choices, is served in a beautiful Victorian-style
conservatory or the adjacent room that opens into the conservatory.

ELVA, 5 Pembroke Park, Ballsbridge, Dublin 4. Tel. 01/602931. Fax
01/602417. 3 rms (all with bath). TV **Bus:** 7, 8, or 10.
$ Rates (including breakfast): IR£17.50 ($30.63) per person, sharing. No credit
cards. **Parking:** Available. **Closed:** Dec–Feb.

⭐ Convenient to the American Embassy, Royal Dublin Society grounds, and the
National Concert Hall, Elva is a lovely Victorian home presided over by Mrs.
Sheila Matthews. All bedrooms have hairdryers. There is private parking area
and good transportation into the city center (only a short ride away). Restaurants are
within easy walking distance.

**HADDINGTON LODGE, 49 Haddington Rd., Ballsbridge, Dublin 4. Tel.
01/600974** or 601637. 5 rms (all with bath). **Bus:** 6, 8, 10, or 45.
$ Rates (including breakfast): IR£17 ($29.75) per person, sharing. No credit cards.
Parking: Available. **Closed:** Mid-Dec to mid-Jan.

Mrs. Mary Egan is hostess of this restored Georgian house located close to the Royal
Dublin Society grounds and the American Embassy. Top hotels and restaurants are
nearby, and art galleries and city shopping are within easy reach. A private car park is
available.

MONTROSE HOUSE, 16 Pembroke Park, Dublin 4. Tel. 01/684286. 4
rms (none with bath). **Bus:** 10, 46A, or 64A.
$ Rates (including breakfast): IR£16.50 ($28.90). No credit cards.

⭐ Just off Herbert Park, not far from the American Embassy, Montrose House is
a two-story, red-brick house fronted by a flower garden. Inside, you'll find lots
of mahogany and antique furnishings, and the gracious hostess, Mrs. Catherine
Ryan. The pretty white-walled dining room looks out onto the garden through a bay
window. All four rooms are attractively done up and comfortable, with sinks, and
there's central heating.

**MOUNT HERBERT, 7 Herbert Rd., Ballsbridge, Dublin 4. Tel. 01/
684321.** Fax 01/607077. Telex 92173 MHGI. 120 rms (101 with bath). TV TEL
DART:
$ Rates (including breakfast): IR£18.50–IR£22.95 ($32.40–$40.15) per person
with bath, depending on season; IR£26.50 ($46.40) per person with bath, during
special events and holidays; IR£4 ($7) per person less without bath. ACC, AE, DC,
MC, V. **Parking:** Enclosed private car park.

⭐ Once the residence of Lord Robinson, the central portion of Mount Herbert is
a handsome three-story, slate-roofed white mansion with black trim. Today it is
joined by extensions to form a guesthouse run by the Loughran family, set back
from the road, with a walled parking lot protected by an excellent security system.
The full Irish breakfast is served in a pleasant window-walled dining room
overlooking the garden, and moderately priced lunches and dinners are available. In

addition to the large lounge, there's a small, cozy sitting room that sports a fire in cool weather. Bedrooms are nicely furnished and come with color TVs with in-house movies, hairdryers, and trouser presses. Services include wheelchair access to both bedroom and shower in two ground-floor rooms, baby-sitting, and theater and car-rental bookings. Facilities include a gymnasium, solarium, sauna, badminton court, and gift shop.

Monkstown

CHESTNUT LODGE, 2 Vesey Place, Monkstown, Co. Dublin. Tel. 01/ 807860. 4 rms (all with bath). TEL **Bus:** 7 or 8. **DART:** Monkstown.
$ Rates (including breakfast): £25 ($43.75) single; £20 ($35) per person double. 50% reduction for children; £15 ($26.25) deposit required when booking. No credit cards.

Personable Nancy Malone has four bright, cheerful, and unusually spacious rooms in this 1840 Regency residence that has been refurbished to provide modern conveniences while retaining its 19th-century character. The house is just off the main Dublin–Dun Laoghaire road, about 6 miles from the city center and only a short stroll from the seafront and restaurants. The ferryport is also quite convenient. Facing a lovely little wooded park, it is a haven of subdued elegance and charm, and Nancy is the epitome of Irish hospitality, with an astounding knowledge of Dublin and a keen sense of what it takes to make your stay a happy one. Guest rooms overlook either the park or the landscaped back garden. A highlight of breakfast is the buffet of museli, cereals, fresh-fruit compote, and yogurt that compliments your traditional breakfast. Chestnut Lodge is an ideal base for exploring Dublin, as well as Dalkey, Killiney, and County Wicklow.

Rathgar

ABRAE COURT GUESTHOUSE, 9 Zion Rd., Rathgar, Dublin 6. Tel. 01/979944. 14 rms (all with bath). **Bus:** 15A, 15B, 15, 47, or 47B.
$ Rates (including breakfast): IR£25 ($43.75) per person, sharing. 20% reduction for children. ACC, BARC, MC, V.
Mr. Neville Keegan's guesthouse is a lovely Victorian home in this residential section. Rooms all have tea and coffee facilities, and there's central heating. Mr. Keegan is a warm, gracious host. Of special interest to our Jewish readers is the fact that Abrae Court is close to the chief rabbinate's office and Terenure Synagogue.

ARUS MHUIRE, 8 Old Bridge Rd., Templeogue, Dublin 16. Tel. 01/ 944281. 9 rms (7 with bath). TV. **Parking:** Locked car park. **Bus:** 15B, 49, 65, or 65A.
$ Rates (including breakfast): IR£17 ($29.75) single without bath, IR£18 ($31.50) single with bath; IR£15 ($26.25) per person double sharing without bath, IR£16 ($28) per person double with bath. No credit cards. **Parking:** Available.
Mrs. Colette O'Brien's modern home is 4 miles from the city center, but four bus routes are nearby. There's a TV lounge for guests and a locked car park, very important in the Dublin area. Her bedrooms are comfortable and attractive, all with clock radio, hairdryer, and tea/coffee maker.

ST. AIDAN'S GUEST HOUSE, 32 Brighton Rd., Rathgar, Dublin 6. Tel. 01/906178 or 902011. 12 rms (5 with bath). TV **Bus:** 15A, 15B, 15C, or 47.
$ Rates (including breakfast): IR£23 ($40.25) single without bath, IR£25 ($43.75) single with bath; IR£38 ($66.50) double without bath, IR£40 ($70) double with bath. 20% reduction for children. No credit cards. **Parking:** Available.
St. Aidan's, a large modernized Victorian house run by Ann O'Dwyer, is located on a tree-lined street. The lovely drawing room, complete with TV, has a tea and coffee trolley for the use of guests at any time. The bedrooms are done up in Laura Ashley decorator fabrics, have sinks and hairdryers, and are centrally heated. One is a large

double bed-sitter with a bay window, and four are singles. Facilities include an ironing room, playroom for small children, and a car park. Dinner is offered for IR£13 ($22.75).

NORTH OF THE CITY CENTER

Glasnevin

IONA HOUSE, 5 Iona Park, Glasnevin, Dublin 9. Tel. 01/306855, 306217, or 306473. Fax 01/306732. 14 rms (12 with bath). TV TEL **Bus:** 11, 13, 19, 19A, 34, or 34A.

$ Rates: IR£23.75 ($41.55) per person sharing. 50% reduction for children; 10% discount to our readers paying cash who mention this book when reserving and have it with them when they check in. ACC, AE, DC, V.

 Located in a charming Victorian section, Iona House is a lovely old red-brick house built around the turn of the century. Karen and Jack Shouldice provide such extras as perked coffee and American-style bacon to make visiting Yanks feel at home. There's a lounge and a private garden, plus central heating. Guest rooms (which tend to be on the small side) are attractive and comfortable, with hairdryers and radios. Both German and French are spoken here. There is also a restaurant offering meals at good value.

HOSTELS, Y'S & DORMS

DUBLIN INTERNATIONAL YOUTH HOSTEL, Mountjoy St., Dublin 7. Tel. 01/301396. 400 beds. **Bus:** Most city center lines.

$ Rates (including breakfast): IR£6.50 ($11.40) per person. No credit cards.
A warm welcome, comfort, and modern convenience set in a beautiful old building are features at An Oige's newest Dublin city hostel, only a 5-minute walk from the city center, an excellent base for exploring the capital city. Facilities include hot showers, central heating, a restaurant in a converted chapel, bicycle rental, supervised car parks, and an information desk.

OIGE HOSTEL, 39 Mountjoy Sq. S., Dublin 1. Tel. 01/363111. 62 dorm beds. **Bus:** All O'Connell Street lines.

$ Rates: IR£4–IR£5.90 ($7–$10.33) per person, depending on your age and when you come. No credit cards. **Open:** July–Sept. only.

Located north of the Liffey in a Georgian house that dates from 1798, this Oige hostel accommodates 22 men and 40 women in dormitory rooms, with separate shared baths for each sex. There is a common room and a completely equipped communal kitchen for preparing your own meals. It's essential to book ahead, and you must claim your bed by 9pm the first night of your stay. Book directly with the warden.

THE YOUNG TRAVELLER, St. Mary's Place, Dublin 7. Tel. 01/305000 or 305319. 15 rms (with toilet and shower).

$ Rates (including breakfast): IR£8 ($14) per person. No credit cards.
This popular privately run hostel has a city-center location, north of the Liffey a 15-minute walk from O'Connell Street. There are 14 four-bedded rooms and one twin-bedded room. Comforters, towels, and soap are provided, and there's hot water 24 hours a day. Amenities include an attractive lounge, TV lounge, and launderette.

YWCA HOSTEL, 64 Lower Baggot St., Dublin 2. Tel. 01/766273 or 608452. 22 beds. **Bus:** 4 or 10.

$ Rates (including breakfast): IR£8 ($14) per person. No credit cards. **Open:** June–Aug.
Located three blocks from St. Stephen's Green, the hostel is open most of the year to college students and working women, but tourists are welcomed during June, July,

and August. Each room contains hot and cold water and accommodates either two or three. Although the door is locked at midnight, a key will be provided if you must be out later.

Sandymount

YWCA RADCLIFF HALL, St. John's Rd., Sandymount, Dublin 4. Tel. 01/694521. 40 rms (none with bath), 20 chalets (all with bath). **Bus:** 3, 6, 7A, 8, 18, or 52. **DART:** Sydney Parade.

$ Rates (including breakfast): IR£10 ($17.50) per person, single or double without bath in the main house; IR£12 ($21) per person for twin-bedded chalet with bath. Half-board (breakfast and dinner) IR£100 ($175) per person for full week. Rates do not include 10% service charge. No credit cards.

Just two blocks from the sea, this YWCA was formerly a convent, and the chapel as well as the well-tended 2½ acres of flower gardens, lawn, and fruit trees have all been retained. The high-ceilinged rooms in the main building and chalets in the rear are attractive and comfortable, and all chalets have twin beds and private bath. The decor is simple and you're required to make your own bed in the morning. The modern dining room opens onto a patio, where meals are sometimes served in summer. Radcliff Hall is popular among both tourists and conference groups, and it caters mainly to students during winter months. Facilities include a library, laundry room with irons, and a TV and recreation room. Advance booking with a IR£10 ($17.50) deposit is an absolute must, especially if you'd like a room with a private bath.

OTHER SUPER-BUDGET CHOICES

ACCOMMODATION OFFICE, TRINITY COLLEGE, Dublin 2. Tel. 01/ 772941 ext. 1177. Telex 93782. Fax 01/711267.

$ Rates: Negotiable.

★ Accommodations are sometimes available to organized groups and conferences.

LONG-TERM STAYS

SELF-CATERING If your stay in Dublin will be a week or longer, you'll save money by booking one of the city's many flats that are available on a self-catering basis. Minimum rental is usually 1 week, although some are available for 3-day periods. Be sure to inquire when booking. Inquire, too, about credit-card acceptance—many of these operators prefer to work on a cash basis—and don't depend on using that bit of plastic until you're *sure* it will be accepted.

SOUTH OF THE CITY CENTER

Ballsbridge

LANDSDOWNE VILLAGE, Two- and three-bedroom luxury town houses. TV TEL **DART:** Sandymount

$ Rates: Apr–May, IR£290–IR£325 ($507.50–$568.75) per week; June–Sept, IR£320–IR£360 ($560–$630) per week; Oct–Mar, IR£275–IR£310 ($481.25–$542.50) per week.

★ Located in the Ballsbridge area, only 3km (2 miles) from the city center and convenient to DART transportation, these homes are fully equipped (including linen), centrally heated, and come with TV and telephone, as well as a washer/dryer. Two-bedroom houses have one double bed, three singles, one bunk, and one cot.

Reservations: Contact Mrs. Jacinta Stacey, Trident Holiday Homes, Unit 2, Sandymount Village, Dublin 4 (tel. 01/683534 or 735043; fax 01/786275).

DR. MARY SMITH, 45 Ailesbury Rd., Dublin 4. Tel. 01/693883. Fax 01/786275. Two-bedroom flat.

$ Rates: Apr–June, Sept, and Dec, IR£200 ($350) per week; July–Aug, IR£300 ($525) per week; other months, IR£180 ($315) per week.

This is a charming garden-level flat in a quiet residential neighborhood that's only 3km (2 miles) from the city center and close to city transport and shopping. The recently decorated flat is spacious and well heated, and reflects loads of Dublin character. Sleeping accommodations consist of two singles and two bunks in two bedrooms. Tennis is available on the grounds by arrangement.

MRS. C. O'CONNER, 1 Herbert Park, Ballsbridge, Dublin 4. Tel. 01/ 683722. Three-bedroom luxury apartment. **DART:**
$ **Rates:** July–Aug, IR£300 ($486) per week; the rest of the year, IR£250 ($405) per week.

 Each of the three bedrooms has one double and one single bed, and the elegantly furnished living room has a balcony (lovely for long summer evenings). DART and bus transportation are close by.

Monkstown

MRS. EVELYN LYNCH, 38 Seapoint Ave., Monkstown, Co. Dublin. Tel. 01/807303. Two-bedroom basement flat. **DART:** Monkstown.
$ **Rates:** Apr–June and Sept, IR£125 ($218.75) per week, July–Aug, IR£155 ($271.25) per week; other months, negotiable.
Just 15 minutes from the city center, Mrs. Evelyn Lynch offers a basement flat in her large house overlooking Dublin Bay. In addition to a sitting room, kitchen, and bath, there are two bedrooms, with four single beds.

Killiney

MRS. BRIDGET AYLMER, Ayesha Castle, Killiney, Co. Dublin. Tel. 01/852323. Three-bedroom flat. **DART:** Killiney.
$ **Rates:** April–June and Sept, IR£200 ($350) per week; July–Aug, IR£225 ($393.75) per week; other months, negotiable.
Out in Killiney, only a short drive from the city center, you can rent the west wing of Ayesha Castle, an authentic castle from the Victorian era, situated on 4 acres of grounds overlooking Killiney Bay. There are three bedrooms, as well as a sitting room, a large dining room, a kitchen/breakfast room, and a utility room.

NORTH OF THE CITY CENTER

MRS. B. MCDONAGH, 59 St. Lawrence Rd., Clontarf, Dublin 3. Tel. 01/333597. Two-bedroom flatlet. **Bus:** 28, 29, 31, 32, or 54.
$ **Rates:** IR£10.50 per person per night. No credit cards. **Parking:** Off-street parking.
Mrs. McDonagh provides an attractive self-catering flatlet in this quiet residential location, with good transportation into the city center. It's furnished and decorated to a very high standard, and both bedrooms have complete private facilities. Daily rates make this a good budget accommodation even if you're staying in Dublin for only a few days.

WORTH THE EXTRA MONEY

Yes, this *is* a book about budget travel. And, yes, budget travel in Ireland is a fun way to go. But as I have also said earlier in this book, you will also find Irish friendliness and charm in large, luxury establishments. And which of us has not yearned, at one time or another, to indulge a penchant for—as the Irish would say—"upmarket" accommodations.

I am listing below those Dublin accommodations in which your "splurge" dollars will buy as good value in the upper range as your budget dollars will in the foregoing recommendations.

CITY CENTER

BUSWELL'S HOTEL, 25 Molesworth St., Dublin 2. Tel. 01/764013. Fax 01/762090. 67 rms (all with bath). TV TEL
$ **Rates:** IR£51 ($89.25) single; IR£40 ($70) per person double. Breakfast IR£6.50

($11.40) extra. Special winter weekend offers at considerable discounts. ACC, AE, BARC, DC, MC, V.

 Buswell's is a Dublin institution, and over the years has hosted such Irish notables as Sir Roger Casement and Eamon de Valera. Located just across from the Dail, it offers center-city convenience, superb accommodations, and a dining room/bar lunch/drinking clientele liberally sprinkled with politicians, leading Dublin business people, and colorful personalities. And small wonder, for since 1925 the hotel has been owned and operated by the Duff family with the sort of personal involvement that has led to possibly the lowest staff turnover in the city and an enviable guest list of "regulars" who return year after year. More and more conferences are being held here, also, with the addition of several attractive meeting rooms. As for guest rooms, few are a "standard" size and shape, and each is individually decorated—there are quaint, old-fashioned rooms up under the eaves and others that are brightly modern. All come equipped with tea and coffee makers, trouser presses, hairdryers, radio, and color TV.

Dining/Entertainment: Georgian elegance surrounds you in the Leinster Room Restaurant and the Georgian Bar, while the Tudor-style Molesworth Cellar Bar offers conviviality along with excellent lunch and evening snack selections.

LEESON COURT HOTEL, 26/27 Lower Leeson St., Dublin 2. Tel. 01/763380 or 789428. 20 rms (all with bath) TV TEL
$ Rates (including breakfast): IR£43 ($75.25) single; IR£31.50 ($55.15) per person sharing. ACC, AE, BARC, MC, V. **Parking:** Off-street parking in secure car park.
Centrally located, just 5 minutes from Grafton Street, Leeson Court has nicely furnished and decorated guest rooms, some with bath and shower, others with only shower. All have clock radios and tea/coffee-making facilities. The pleasant Darby O'Gill Restaurant serves very good, moderately priced meals, and there's a high degree of personal attention to guests.

WESTBURY HOTEL, Grafton St., Dublin 2. Tel. 01/791122. Fax 01/797078. 200 rms (all with bath). TV TEL
$ Rates: IR£110 ($192.50) single; IR£62.50 ($109.40) per person double. 15% service charge. Some weekend rates available in low season. **Parking:** Valet parking.

Tucked away just off Grafton Street right in the heart of the city center, the Westbury is not only one of Dublin's poshest hotels, but it's one of the city's most convenient, and without doubt one of its most beautiful. Its white marble entrance leads into a lower foyer carpeted in pale pink, and that same Navan/Youghal carpet leads up a sweeping staircase of cream marble and brass to the upper foyer, lobby, dining room, and other public spaces. Soft shades of peach, lots of marble, walnut panels, peach silk wall coverings, oil paintings, valuable artifacts, and wing-back Chinese Chippendale chairs mixed companionably with modern furniture are tastefully combined to create an atmosphere of spacious elegance. Guest rooms and suites all are furnished in mahogany and brass, and have canopies over the beds, marble bathrooms, built-in hairdryers, radios, and bathrobes for guests. They're also among the most spacious I've encountered in Ireland, and there are even some suites with Jacuzzis.

Dining/Entertainment: The upper-foyer Terrace provides soft music throughout the evening and for afternoon tea; the Russell Room's peach and mint-green decor is the setting for fine dining; the Seafood Restaurant Bar features shellfish from Dublin Bay; and the Polo Bar is hung wall to wall with hunting prints.

NORTH OF THE CITY CENTER

HOWTH LODGE HOTEL, Howth, Co. Dublin. Tel. 01/390288. Telex 93348. Fax 01/322268. 17 rms (all with bath). TV TEL **DART:** Howth.
$ Rates: IR£38 ($66.50) single; IR£24.50 ($42.90) per person double. Special "Weekend Break" rates available. Breakfast IR£5.50 ($9.65) extra. ACC, AE, BARC, DC, MC, V. **Parking:** Large car park on grounds.

This attractive family-owned and -operated hotel has a delightful old-world air, with turf fires in the lounge bar and an elegant restaurant serving fresh seafood dishes and charcoaled steaks that have earned it an enviable reputation with Dubliners. Best of all, perhaps, is its location facing the sea, with the lovely old fishing village of Howth only a 10-minute walk away. As convenient as it is scenic, Howth Lodge is easily reached by DART.

Most guest rooms have a view of the sea, and all have tea- and coffee-making facilities. A bonus here is the tray of brown bread or toast and marmalade that comes to your room in the morning if you request it at no charge. Owner Bernard Hanratty and his sons, Gerard and Karl, plan to keep the same warm, friendly ambience as they extend the hotel to include 20 spacious new bedrooms and a leisure center (including swimming pool), due for completion in mid-1991.

SOUTH OF THE CITY CENTER

Dalkey

DALKEY ISLAND HOTEL, Coliemor Harbour, Dalkey, Co. Dublin. Tel. 01/850377. Fax 01/850141. 20 rms (all with bath). TV TEL **Bus:** 8. **DART:** Dalkey.

$ Rates (including breakfast): IR£38–IR£50 ($66.50–$87.50) single; IR£45–IR£66 ($78.75–$115.50) double. 25% reduction for children; 12½% service charge. ACC, AE, BARC, DC, MC, V.

This charming hotel sits on the edge of Dublin Bay looking out to Dalkey Island (boats are available next door to take you out for an idyllic day on the scenic and uninhabited island). Ten of the guest rooms face the sea, with glassed-in terraces for all-weather comfort.

Dining/Entertainment: The Island Lounge features nightly entertainment in the summer and sea views all year long. The Lighthouse Rooftop Panoramic Restaurant specializes in fresh seafood dishes at moderate prices, and also has views of the sea. Both the lounge and restaurant are popular local gathering places.

Killiney

FITZPATRICK'S CASTLE HOTEL, Killiney, Co. Dublin. Tel. 01/851533; or 212/684-1820 in New York City, or toll free 800/221-1074 in the U.S. Telex 30353. Fax 01/850207. 90 rms; 7 suites (all with bath/shower). TV TEL **DART:** Killiney.

$ Rates: IR£53–IR£65 ($92.75–$113.75) single; IR£35–IR£45 ($61.25–$78.75) per person double. 12½% service charge. ACC, AE, BARC, DC, MC, V.

This is one of Dublin's finest luxury hotels, and is about a 20-minute drive on the N11 south from the city center to an ancient and charming village on the outskirts. Situated on 9 landscaped acres, it was built in 1740 as a manor house. It occupies the site of a much older building, whose huge 15th-century stone fireplace is now the dominant feature of the Dungeon Bar. Transformation of the house, with its three turreted towers and white battlements, was undertaken by Paddy Fitzpatrick. The entire Fitzpatrick family is now involved in running the place, which accounts for the graciousness and warmth that extends to every member of the staff.

The bedrooms facing the front have walk-on balconies set with a table and chairs, and those at the back boast lovely canopied beds. There are luxury suites, some with a magnificent view of Dublin Bay, others with a Jacuzzi. Adjoining the castle is a block of modern, luxury time-sharing holiday homes which are often available for weekly rentals, providing self-catering facilities in addition to all the amenities of the hotel (contact the hotel for rates and availability if you're interested).

Dining/Entertainment: The popular Dungeon Bar is a gathering place for Killiney locals (it also has nightly entertainment), and the dining room, Truffles, is a favorite of Dublin businesspeople for lunch and families in the evening.

Facilities: Indoor swimming pool, indoor squash courts, saunas, hairdressing salon, shop.

READERS RECOMMEND

Darran House, 7 Pembroke Road, Ballsbridge, Dublin 4 (tel. 01/606126). "Mr. William Lloyd's B&B accommodations are the ultimate in space, cleanliness, convenience, and location for getting about Dublin. He is the most delightful host we have encountered in 15 years of travel, and after our stay of 1 week, we felt like he is a part of our own family."—James Delaney, Guilford, Conn.

Eileen and Jim McNamee. 15 Shangaugh Grove, Shanhill, County Dublin (tel. 01/820370). "This a superb place to stay, with outstanding hospitality and a big, beautiful breakfast."—Marjorie Tannehill, Akron, Ohio.

Gresham House, 384 Clontarf Road, Dollymount, Dublin 3 (tel. 01/331784). "This is an attractive and comfortable three-story home overlooking a golf course and the beach, and Miriam McAllister is a helpful and gracious hostess. All nine bedrooms come with showers, and there's a family room and a private park."—Patricia Ryan, Boston, Mass.

Stephen's Hall, 14/17 Lower Leeson Street, Dublin 2 (tel. 01/610585; fax 01/610606). "This is an all-suite accommodation right by St. Stephen's Green. It's pricey, well above our budget, but we felt that for our short stay in Dublin the money was well spent because of the convenience. We could walk to any place in the city center, and the bus transportation is excellent to those places outside walking distance."—David and Sara Luken, Greensboro, N.C.

Springvale, 69 Kincora Drive, Clontarf, Dublin 3 (tel. 01/333413). "Ms. Moira Kavanagh was the most helpful of all our B&B hostesses during our week's stay in Dublin, and the breakfast was the best—fresh fruit and many cereals to choose from, plus tea and cookies in the afternoon and evening. Springvale is on five bus lines, only 15 minutes away from town."—Carol Schrier-Polak, Falls Church, Va.

---

5. WHERE TO EAT

From picnics on St. Stephen's Green to pub grub, and Tourist Menu meals to elegant splurges, Dublin offers wide variety in cuisine as well as price. Cuisine categories include "Traditional," which I have used instead of the usual "American" to mean a rather general menu selection of steaks, chops, poultry, fish, etc., that may be prepared in a slightly different manner than "American" as you know it. The "Irish" heading means *traditional* Irish.

Let me suggest that you read through listings for those restaurants that appear to be above your budget in price—lunch can quite often be very good value and well within budget limits. Look also for "Tourist Menu" listings, since they give you a limited selection from the pricy menu at a bargain price. Both these money-stretching strategies will broaden your Dublin dining experience considerably.

A final tip: Pick up copies of the "Dining in Ireland" and "Tourist Menu" booklets published by the Irish Tourist Board and available for a small charge, and tuck them in your purse or pocket as ready references in every area of the city.

MEALS FOR LESS THAN IR£10 [$17.50]
SOUTH OF THE LIFFEY

BARRELS TRATTORIA & WINE BAR, 115 Grafton St. Tel. 801992.
   Cuisine: TRADITIONAL.
$ Prices: Appetizers IR£1.50–IR£4 ($2.65–$7); main courses IR£3–IR£8.50 ($5.25–$14.90); bar snacks IR£1.50–IR£3 ($1.75–$5.25); lunch IR£3–IR£6 ($5.25–$10.50); dinner IR£7–IR£9 ($12.25–$15.75). ACC, AE, MC, V.
   Open: Lunch daily noon–3pm; dinner daily 6–9:30pm; bar snacks daily 3–9:30pm.

This large, bustling publike eatery near College Green serves a wide selection of fish, pasta, veal, and steaks at surprisingly low prices. Bar snacks are especially good here (garlic bread, spareribs, mussels, etc.) and you can put together quite a satisfying light lunch or dinner from the bar.

BEWLEY'S CAFE, 78 Grafton St. Tel. 776761.
Cuisine: TRADITIONAL/PASTRIES.
$ Prices: Appetizers IR£1–IR£3 ($1.75–$5.25); three-course lunch IR£5 ($8.75). No credit cards.
Open: Breakfast daily 8:15am–6pm; lunch daily noon–3pm; coffee, tea, and snacks daily noon–6pm.

Here the quality of food is never in doubt—nor has it ever been in the chain's 145-year history. The devoutly Quaker Bewley family has, since 1972, shared ownership with all employees, which probably explains the courtesy and friendliness of the staff. The interior is much like old-time tea shops, with marble-top tables and lots of mahogany. In addition to lunch or a refreshing tea break, you can purchase teas, coffees, fresh-baked breads, and terrific pastries to take out.

This branch is between Nassau Street and St. Stephen's Green. Other locations are at 11/12 Westmoreland Street, 13 South Great George's Street, the ILAC shopping center north of the Liffey, and the Dundrum shopping center.

CASPER & GIUMBINI'S FOOD AND DRINK EMPORIUM, Wicklow St. Tel. 794347.
Cuisine: TRADITIONAL.
$ Prices: Appetizers IR£1.50–IR£4 ($2.65–$7); main courses IR£5–IR£9 ($8.75–$15.75); bar food IR£2–IR£4 ($3.50–$7); à la carte selections IR£4.50–IR£8 ($7.25–$12.75); Sun brunch IR£5.50 ($9.65). ACC, AE, DC, MC, V.
Open: Daily noon–midnight. **Closed:** Good Friday and Christmas Day.

Just off Grafton Street, across from Switzer department store's side entrance, this has been a gathering place for some of Dublin's younger executives, students, and office workers. Located in the basement of what was once the old Wicklow Hotel, it is replete with hand-carved mahogany, burnished brass, Tiffany lamps, and stained-glass windows on multilevel floors. This combination pub and restaurant is always lively with conversation, and there is a resident pianist at lunch and on weekends. At the handsome old bar (from the Wicklow), you can order any one of a dozen imported beers (including American brands) and soup, sandwiches, smoked salmon, bangers-and-mash, and other pub grub. Table service includes such items as seafood, chicken, veal, lamb, and steaks, as well as lighter fare like quiche, pizza, omelets, and hamburgers. Sunday brunch is a standout here, with two free drinks accompanying your selection of eggs Benedict; eggs with sausage, bacon, hash browns, black pudding, grilled tomatoes, and brown bread; smoked salmon and scrambled eggs with croissant; or steak and eggs with hash browns.

THE COFFEE DOCK GRILL, in Jurys Hotel, Ballsbridge. Tel. 605000.
Cuisine: TRADITIONAL/VEGETARIAN. **Bus:** 7, 7A, 8, 45, or 84.
$ Prices: Appetizers IR£1.50–IR£3.50 ($2.65–$6.15); main courses IR£4–IR£8 ($7–$14).
Open: Daily 6am–5am.

This is Dublin's only 23-hour restaurant—a handy place to know about at the end of a late evening or the early beginning of a day. It is also very much in the budget price range, with seafoods, salads, mixed grills, omelets, sandwiches, ravioli, and spaghetti available, along with snacks and sweets. There is also a good wine list.

GALLAGHER'S BOXTY HOUSE, 20 Temple Bar. Tel. 772762.
Cuisine: IRISH.
$ Prices: A la carte IR£5–IR£8 ($8.75–$14). No credit cards.
Open: Mon–Fri 7:30am–11pm, Sat–Sun. 12:30–11pm.

This truly traditional Irish restaurant one block south of the Liffey between Essex

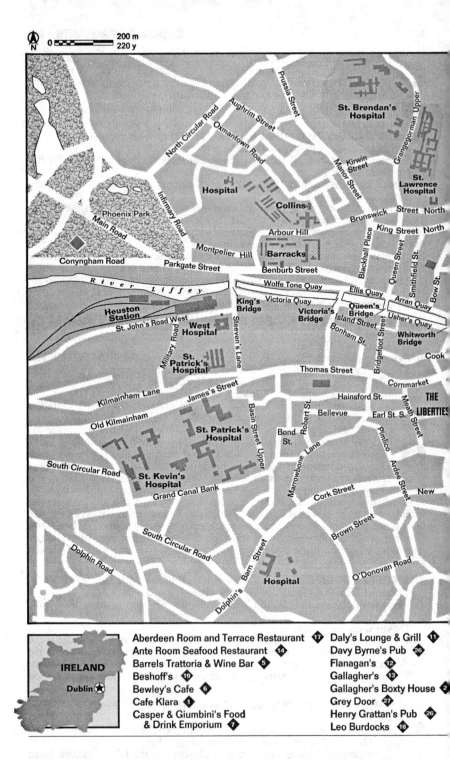

0 | 200 m
0 | 220 y

N

St. Brendan's
Hospital

Prussia Street

Aughrim Street

North Circular Road

Oxmantown Road

Infirmary Road

Kirwin
Street

Manor Street

Grangegorman Upper

St.
Lawrence
Hospital

Hospital

Collins

Street North

Brunswick

King Street North

Arbour Hill

Phoenix Park

Main Road

Montpelier Hill

Barracks

Blackhall Place

Queen Street

Smithfield St.

Bow St.

Conyngham Road

Parkgate Street

Benburb Street

Wolfe Tone Quay

Ellis Quay

Arran Quay

River Liffey

Victoria Quay

King's
Bridge

Queen's
Bridge

Usher's Quay

Heuston
Station

St. John's Road West

West
Hospital

Steeven's Lane

Victoria's
Bridge

Island Street

Bonham St.

Bridgefoot Street

Whitworth
Bridge

Military Road

St.
Patrick's
Hospital

Cook

Kilmainham Lane

James's Street

Thomas Street

Cornmarket

THE
LIBERTIES

Hainsford St.

Old Kilmainham

Basin Street Upper

Robert St.

Bellevue

Earl St. S.

Meath Street

South Circular Road

St. Patrick's
Hospital

Bond
St.

Marrowbone Lane

Pimlico

Ardee Street

St. Kevin's
Hospital

Grand Canal Bank

Cork Street

New

South Circular Road

Brown Street

O'Donovan Road

Dolphin Road

Barn Street

Dolphin's

Hospital

IRELAND

Dublin

Aberdeen Room and Terrace Restaurant ⑰
Ante Room Seafood Restaurant ⑭
Barrels Trattoria & Wine Bar ⑤
Beshoff's ⑲
Bewley's Cafe ⑥
Cafe Klara ①
Casper & Giumbini's Food
   & Drink Emporium ⑦

Daly's Lounge & Grill ⑪
Davy Byrne's Pub ㉖
Flanagan's ⑫
Gallagher's ⑬
Gallagher's Boxty House ②
Grey Door ㉗
Henry Grattan's Pub ㉖
Leo Burdocks ⑱

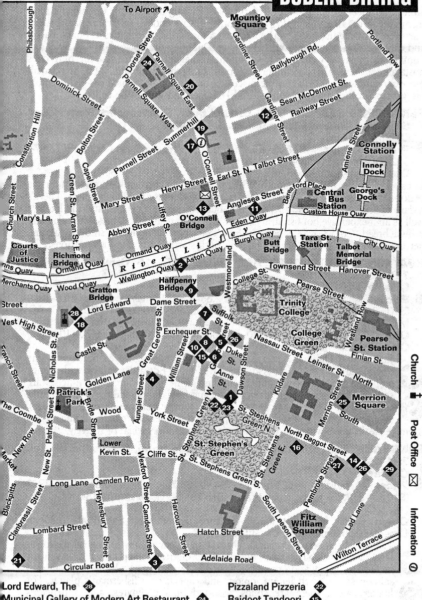

DUBLIN DINING

To Airport ↗

Mountjoy Square

Phibsborough

Dorset Street

Dominick Street

Parnell Square East

24

Parnell Square West

20

Gaardiner Street

Ballybough Rd.

Portland Row

Sean McDermott St.

Railway Street

12

Gardiner Street

Amiens Street

Connolly Station

Constitution Hill

Bolton Street

Parnell Street

Summerhill

19

17 i

O'Connell Street

Earl St. N. Talbot Street

Inner Dock

George's Dock

Church Street

Green St.

Arran St. E.

Capel Street

Mary Street

Henry Street

Anglesea Street

11

Beresford Place

Central Bus Station

Mary's La.

Abbey Street

Liffey St.

☒

O'Connell Bridge

13

Eden Quay

Custom House Quay

Courts of Justice

ns Quay

Richmond Bridge

Ormand Quay

Ormand Quay

River Liffey

Wellington Quay

2 Aston Quay

e y

Burgh Quay

Butt Bridge

Tara St. Station

City Quay

Talbot Memorial Bridge

Hanover Street

Merchants Quay

Wood Quay

Gratton Bridge

Halfpenny Bridge

9

Townsend Street

Street

28

Lord Edward

Dame Street

7

Suffolk St.

Pearse Street

Trinity College

Pearse St. Station

West High Street

18

Castle St.

Exchequer St.

8 5 26

10 15 6

Duke St.

College Green

Nassau Street

Leinster St.

Westland Row

Finian St.

Francis Street

Nicholas St.

Golden Lane

4

Aungier Street

Great Georges St.

William Street

G. Anne St.

Dawson Street

Kildare

Merrion Street

North

25

Merrion Square

Patrick's Park

Patrick St.

Bride Street

Wood

York Street

1

22 23

St. Stephens Green W.

St Stephens Green N.

South

The Coombe

New Row

New St.

Lower Kevin St.

Cliffe St.

St. Stephens Green S.

St. Stephen's Green

16

St Stephens Green E.

North Baggot Street

14 26

27

29

Market

Blackpitts

Clanbrassil Street

Long Lane

Camden Row

Heytesbury Street

Wexford Street

Camden Street

Harcourt Street

Pembroke Street

Lad Lane

Lombard Street

Fitz William Square

21

Circular Road

3

Adelaide Road

Hatch Street

South Leeson Street

Wilton Terrace

Church ⊪✝   Post Office ☒   Information ⊙

Lord Edward, The 28
Municipal Gallery of Modern Art Restaurant 24
National Gallery of Ireland Restaurant 25
Oisín's Irish Restaurant 3
Old Stand, The 21
Patrick Conway's 20
Patrick Guilbaud 29
Periwinkle Seafood Bar 8

Pizzaland Pizzeria 22
Rajdoot Tandoori 15
Rudyard's Restaurant and Wine Bar 9
Russell Room, The 10
Sandbank Restaurant 10
Shay Beano 4
Shelbourne Hotel 23
Unicorn Restaurant 16

Street and Fleet Street grew out of brothers Padraig and Ronan Gallagher's fond memories of the boxty pancakes their mother always cooked on Friday nights when they were growing up. Now, with its menu featuring such specialties as boxty, bacon and cabbage, and bread-and-butter pudding, Dubliners are flocking to Gallagher's in homage to those very dishes—it seems the Gallagher boys are not the only ones nostalgic for them. This is definitely a place to bring the entire family, but be warned: No reservations are taken, and the place can be packed—in which case, you simply hie yourself across the road to the Auld Dubliner and wait to be called.

PERIWINKLE SEAFOOD BAR, Ground floor, Powerscourt Town House Shopping Center, Clarendon St. Tel. 794203.
   Cuisine: SEAFOOD.
$ **Prices:** Appetizers IR£1.05–IR£4 ($1.85–$7); main courses IR£4–IR£7 ($7–$12.25). No credit cards.
   Open: Mon–Sat noon–5pm.
Located near Powerscourt's South William Street exit, Periwinkle's serves a terrific seafood chowder with brown bread and butter that acts as a good light lunch. There's a daily special (toasted crab toes in garlic butter, monkfish kebabs, and the like), as well as an inexpensive hot fish dish (such as cod provençal) that comes with salad and brown bread. Cold fish selections include crab, prawns, mussels, smoked salmon, herring, and fish pâté, and are available in both starter and main-dish portions.

RUDYARD'S RESTAURANT AND WINE BAR, 15 Crown Alley. Tel. 710846.
   Cuisine: VEGETARIAN/TRADITIONAL.
$ **Prices:** Appetizers IR£1.50–IR£3 ($2.65–$5.25); main courses IR£6–IR£9 ($10.50–$15.75); Tourist Menu IR£5.75–IR£7.90 ($10.05–$13.85). ACC, AE, MC, V.
   Open: Lunch Mon–Sat 12:30–2:30pm; dinner Mon–Sat 5:30–10:30pm.
   Closed: Public hols.
   Just behind Dublin's Central Bank, in the Temple Bar area between Dame Street and the Liffey, this is an attractive, rather Edwardian place, with plants, soft background music, and an upstairs wine bar where light lunches are served. There are good vegetarian, fish, and fowl dishes, and the menu features such inventive dishes as chicken biryani, a tasty concoction of fowl, spices, raisins, almonds, and rice. Also on hand, however, are standards such as an 8-ounce steak, rainbow trout, veal chops, and a seafood special of the day.

SANDBANK RESTAURANT, in the Westbury Hotel, Clarendon St. Tel. 791122.
   Cuisine: SEAFOOD/TRADITIONAL.
$ **Prices:** Appetizers IR£2.50–IR£5 ($4.40–$8.75); main courses IR£6–IR£7 ($10.50–$12.25); average dinner IR£9 ($15.75). Service charge of 15%. ACC, AE, DC, MC, V.
   Open: Lunch Mon–Sat 12:30–2:30pm; dinner Mon–Sat 6:30–10:30pm.
   Closed: Good Friday and Christmas Day.

   The Sandbank serves up terrific seafood in a cozy, pubby setting on the lower level of the Westbury Hotel, one block off Grafton Street. Lunch dishes might include fresh plaice on the bone with anchovy-and-garlic butter, oak-smoked salmon served with lemon, onion, and capers, or a fisherman's platter. For lighter eaters, there are soups, assorted hors d'oeuvres, and a delicious oak-smoked-salmon pâté.

NORTH OF THE LIFFEY

DALY'S LOUNGE AND GRILL, 10 Eden Quay. Tel. 725591.
   Cuisine: TRADITIONAL.
$ **Prices:** Appetizers IR£1.50–IR£3 ($2.65–$5.25); main courses IR£4–IR£7 ($7–$12.25). No credit cards.
   Open: Lunch Mon–Sat 12:30–2:30pm; dinner Mon–Sat 5:30–11pm.
Located right on the Liffey one block from O'Connell Bridge, the downstairs is an

old-time pub, often lively with the chatter of newspaper people. Upstairs, you'll find lunches that go a bit beyond the usual pub grub, with several hot dishes as well as cold salad plates. Evening meals are also good and inexpensive.

FLANAGAN'S, 61 Upper O'Connell St. Tel. 731388 or 731804.
  Cuisine: TRADITIONAL/VEGETARIAN. **Reservations:** Not taken.
  $ Prices: Appetizers IR£1.50–IR£3 ($2.65–$5.25); main courses IR£4.50–IR£10 ($7.90–$17.50); Tourist Menu (except Sat) IR£5.75 ($10.05). ACC, BARC, MC, V.
  Open: Daily noon–midnight. **Closed:** Good Friday, Dec 25–26.

This large, popular eatery three blocks north of O'Connell Bridge is roomy and pleasant, with high backs on booths to afford privacy, and a staff that's as friendly and efficient (even when the place is packed) as any I've encountered. The extensive à la carte menu includes steaks (most run about IR£7.95/$13.90), fish, chicken, pasta, vegetarian dishes, curries, and a children's menu. Wine is reasonably priced by the glass or bottle. Very good value for dollar here—families with small children are welcomed.

GALLAGHER'S, 83 Middle Abbey St. Tel. 729861.
  Cuisine: TRADITIONAL.
  $ Prices: Appetizers: IR£1–IR£3 ($1.75–$5.25); main courses IR£4.25–IR£8.55 ($7.45–$14.95). No credit cards.
  Open: Sun–Thurs noon–midnight, Fri–Sat noon–1am.

There's soft lighting, lots of dark wood, and red velvet booths in this pleasant restaurant one block north of O'Connell Bridge just off busy O'Connell Street. The à la carte menu includes fish, steaks, pork, chicken, lasagne, pizza, salads, and hamburgers. Good for families.

MEALS FOR LESS THAN IR£15 ($26.25)
SOUTH OF THE LIFFEY

ANTE ROOM SEAFOOD RESTAURANT, 20 Lower Baggot St. Tel. 604716.
  Cuisine: SEAFOOD/IRISH. **Reservations:** Recommended.
  $ Prices: Appetizers IR£1.50–IR£3 ($2.65–$5.25); main courses IR£7–IR£12 ($12.25–$21); fixed-price meal IR£9.90 ($17.35) at lunch, IR£12 ($21) at dinner; Tourist Menu IR£7.90 ($13.85). Service charge 10%. ACC, AE, DC, MC, V.
  Open: Lunch Mon–Fri 12:30–2:30pm; dinner Mon–Sat 6–10pm.
Located in the basement of the Georgian House guesthouse, the Ante Room is an intimate little place specializing in shellfish and seafood, as well as game in season. Traditional Irish dishes are also on the menu. This is a friendly, relaxed place, with moderate prices, and is very popular with Dubliners as well as visitors.

CAFE KLARA, 35 Dawson St. Tel. 778611.
  Cuisine: FRENCH.
  $ Prices: Appetizers IR£2–IR£4 ($3.50–$7); main courses IR£6–IR£12 ($10.50–$21). ACC, AE, V.
  Open: Daily noon–11pm.
This is Dublin's version of a Parisian-style brasserie. It's big, busy, and bustling, all with a huge dash of style, with mirrored wall panels and a separate fish bar. And you'll find all sorts of Dubliners on the scene, as much to see and be seen as to enjoy the French cuisine. While definitely not in the gourmet class, both classical and "moderne" dishes are of above-average standards, and prices are in the moderate range. Among starters, you might consider the cheese beignets, then move on to escalope of lamb as a main course. It's on Dawson Street between Nassau Street and St. Stephen's Green.

KILMARTIN'S WINE BAR, 19 Upper Baggot St. Tel. 686674.
  Cuisine: CONTINENTAL. **Bus:** 4 or 10.

$ Prices: Appetizers IR£2–IR£5 ($3.50–$8.75); main courses IR£8–IR£14 ($14–$24.50). Service charge 13%. ACC, AE, MC, V.
Open: Lunch Mon–Sat 12:30–2:30pm; dinner Mon–Fri 6pm–midnight, Sat 6–11pm; Sun 5–11pm. **Closed:** Good Friday, Christmas Eve, Christmas Day, New Year's Eve, New Year's Day.

Kilmartin's is a small, intimate restaurant located in a former bookmaker's shop on the fringe of Ballsbridge. Mementos of that work are displayed on exposed brick walls. The wine list here is excellent, and there's a good menu selection of lasagne, moussaka, fish, steak, veal, and chicken. Specialties include a crispy duck and wild smoked salmon.

NIEVE'S, 26 Castle St., Dalkey. Tel. 856156.

Cuisine: TRADITIONAL. **Reservations:** Recommended. **DART:** Dalkey.
$ Prices: Appetizers IR£2–IR£5 ($3.50–$8.75); main courses IR£8–IR£12 ($14–$21); fixed-price dinner IR£14.95 ($26.15); Tourist Menu IR£7.90–IR£12 ($13.85–$21). Service charge 10%. ACC, AE, V.
Open: Dinner only, daily 6:30pm–midnight.

This is an excellent choice for dinner if you're staying in or near Dalkey. It's a family-run restaurant with personal service, a cozy setting, and a resident pianist on weekends. The menu consists mainly of traditional Irish dishes, such as Irish stew and good beef, lamb, and chicken dishes. Seafood is also featured, and the restaurant has a good wine list.

RAJDOOT TANDOORI, 26/28 Clarendon St. Tel. 791122 ext. 132.

Cuisine: INDIAN/VEGETARIAN.
$ Prices: Appetizers IR£1.50–IR£5 ($2.65–$8.75); main courses IR£7–IR£10 ($12.25–$17.50); fixed-price meals IR£6.95 ($12.15) at lunch, IR£14.50 ($25.40) at dinner. Service charge 13%. ACC, AE, MC, V.
Open: Lunch Mon–Sat noon–2:30pm; dinner Mon–Sat 6:30–11:30pm.
Closed: Public hols.

Just off Grafton Street, between Wicklow Street and Chatham Street, in the Westbury Centre, this is one of Dublin's best Indian restaurants. Mr. Sarda, its owner, opened his first restaurant in London's Chelsea back in 1966. You enter the elegant restaurant beneath a glittering 200-year-old crystal chandelier from a maharajah's palace in India. Inside, subdued lighting, brass tables, statues, and Indian prints provide a proper setting for excellent northern Indian specialties. Tandoori dishes such as pigeon breast, lamb, and fish appear along with curries and kebabs. Nan, roti/shapat, paratha, and other Indian breads are also delicious.

UNICORN RESTAURANT, 11 Merrion Court. Tel. 762182 or 688552.

Cuisine: ITALIAN.
$ Prices: Appetizers IR£2–IR£4 ($3.50–$7); main courses IR£8–IR£12 ($14–$21). No credit cards.
Open: Lunch Mon–Fri noon–3pm, Sat noon–3:30pm; dinner Mon–Sat 6–10pm.
Closed: Bank hols.

A longtime favorite with Dubliners, the Unicorn is owned and operated by Mr. and Mrs. Renato Sidoli, who came to Dublin from Bardi, Italy, some 40 years ago. The Italian cuisine includes everything from traditional veal dishes to pastas and pizza. Italian wines are served (also on sale to take away), and there's marvelous espresso and cappuccino. This is a cozy place with white walls, booths, and tables. When the weather is fine, tables are set outside in the sun. It's just off Merrion Row, one block from St. Stephen's Green.

NORTH OF THE LIFFEY

ABERDEEN ROOM AND TERRACE RESTAURANT, in the Gresham Hotel, 23 Upper O'Connell St. Tel. 746881.

Cuisine: TRADITIONAL. **Reservations:** Recommended for dinner.

$ Prices: Appetizers IR£2–IR£4 ($3.50–$7); main courses IR£7–IR£16 ($12.25–$28); fixed-price meals IR£10 ($17.50) at lunch, IR£15 ($26.25) at dinner.
Open: Mon–Sat 7:15am–11:30pm, Sun 7:15am–10pm. **Closed:** Christmas Day.

The Gresham Hotel's dining facilities (located at the back of the lobby) reflect an understated elegance in a relaxing mixture of grays and pinks used throughout, with lighting that's bright and cheerful at lunch, romantic at dinner. The menu includes such standards as roast beef, lamb, chicken, and fish, and there's a good dessert trolley. Children and family groups are welcome, and service overall is both pleasant and efficient. It's four blocks north of O'Connell Bridge on the right side of O'Connell Street.

MEALS FOR LESS THAN IR£20 [$35]
SOUTH OF THE LIFFEY

BROPH'S, 16 Merrion Rd., Ballsbridge. Tel. 605288.
   Cuisine: FRENCH. **Reservations:** Recommended. **Bus:** 7, 7A, 8, 45, or 84.
$ Prices: Appetizers IR£2–IR£5 ($3.50–$8.75); main courses IR£11–IR£17 ($19.25–$29.75). Service charge 10%. ACC, AE, DC, MC, V.
   Open: Dinner only, Mon–Sat 7–11pm.

 Broph's is an intimate little upstairs restaurant where the atmosphere is rustic and informal. If you're a fish lover, be sure to ask about their fresh fish of the day; otherwise, choose from selections that might include beef filet with whole-grain mustard (or with red wine and ginger), pheasant with watercress in wine sauce, medallions of veal with kiwi fruit and green peppercorns, or breast of chicken with corn and basil. There is also a good wine list.

DOBBIN'S WINE BISTRO, 15 Stephen's Lane. Tel. 764679 or 764670.
   Cuisine: INTERNATIONAL. **Reservations:** Recommended.
$ Prices: Appetizers IR£2–IR£5 ($3.50–$8.75); main courses IR£10–IR£17 ($17.50–$29.75); fixed-price meal IR£13.50 ($23.65) at lunch, IR£18.50 ($32.40) at dinner. ACC, AE, DC, MC, V.
   Open: Lunch Mon–Fri 12:30–2:30pm; dinner Tues–Sat 8–11:30pm. **Closed:** Hols.

 On a small lane off Lower Mount Street, this is one of those delightful, intimate spots so friendly that you begin enjoying a meal even before you're seated, and the food is superb. The cuisine is best described as international, since in addition to succulent Irish lamb roasted with fresh herbs, you'll find Szechuan boned duckling, paupiettes of sole stuffed with fresh salmon and scallops, a lovely croustade of fresh seafood in sauce aux crevettes, and dishes of veal, pork, chicken, and steak. The wine list is one of Dublin's best. There is a nice selection of hors d'oeuvres (baked mushrooms in garlic butter, smoked salmon, fresh Dublin Bay prawns, etc.) and salads that will do quite nicely for a less expensive lunch.

LOCKS RESTAURANT, 1 Windsor Terrace, Portobello. Tel. 543391.
   Cuisine: FRENCH **Reservations:** Recommended. **Bus:** 10, 23, 25, 26, 51, or 51B.
$ Prices: Appetizers IR£3–IR£7 ($5.25–$12.25); main courses IR£10–IR£18 ($17.50–$31.50); fixed-price meals IR£12.50 ($21.90) at lunch, IR£18 ($31.50) at dinner. Service charge 10%. ACC, AE, DC, V.
   Open: Lunch Mon–Fri 12:30–2pm; dinner Mon–Sat 7:15–11pm. **Closed:** Bank hols, 1 week at Christmas.

Sitting on the banks of the Grand Canal not far from the city center is this delightful French provincial–style restaurant whose menu includes classic dishes as well as simpler choices. Only the freshest seasonal ingredients are used, and they come to table reflecting the touch of a master chef, both in taste (exquisite) and presentation (picture perfect). Among the fish dishes, you might choose filets of brill with a Noilly Prat and lettuce sauce, escalopes of wild salmon with a mint sauce, or the daily recommendation from the fish market. There's a lovely escalope of chicken with a tarragon-and-butter sauce, and grilled lamb cutlets are superb. Service is top-notch and friendly, and the informal decor and ambience add to the enjoyment of a meal here. Dress is informal. Highly Recommended.

OISÍN'S IRISH RESTAURANT, 31 Upper Camden St. Tel. 753433.
  Cuisine: IRISH/SEAFOOD. **Reservations:** Recommended.
$ **Prices:** Fixed-price dinner IR£18 ($31.50). Service charge 10%. ACC, AE, DC, MC, V.
  Open: Dinner only, Tues–Sat 6:30–11pm.

Just a 5-minute walk from St. Stephen's Green, at the intersection of Upper Camden Street and Harcourt Street (George Bernard Shaw once lived across the road), Oisín's is about as Irish as you can get. The ambience in this small upstairs restaurant is informal and relaxed, with paintings by contemporary Irish artists on the walls. The menu features traditional Irish dishes—the likes of corned beef and cabbage and Irish stew—and the menu is even printed in the Gaelic language (but, sure and you won't have any bother translating, what with owners Feargal and Angela O hUiginn and their friendly staff on hand). Fresh shellfish and lobster are also featured. For dessert, you might try Dublin Coddle (it was Swift's favorite dish and a specialty here), Bailey's Carraigeen, or homemade ice cream. The moderately priced wine list includes an international selection.

There's piano and guitar music nightly, and more often than not, spontaneous sing-alongs (the place is frequented by traditional Irish musicians, poets, and playwrights, along with a politician or two). Terrific food and a good night out just about sums up Oisín's! Highly recommended.

When dinner at Oisín's brings out all the Irish in you, just head for **An Beal Bocht,** a traditional Irish pub at 58 Charlemont Street (a short walk away) that's well known for its traditional music and impromptu seisuns.

THE RUSSELL ROOM, in the Westbury Hotel, Clarendon St., off Grafton Street. Tel. 791122.
  Cuisine: TRADITIONAL/VEGETARIAN. **Reservations:** Recommended.
$ **Prices:** Appetizers IR£3–IR£5 ($5.25–$8.75); main courses IR£9–IR£16 ($15.75–$28); fixed-price meal IR£16.50 ($28.90) at lunch, IR£18 ($31.50) at dinner. Service charge 15%. ACC, AE, DC, MC, V. **Parking:** IR£1.50 ($2.65) 7:30pm–midnight.
  Open: Lunch daily 12:30–2:30pm; dinner daily 7–10:30pm.

This hotel dining room is one of the most beautiful and relaxing restaurants in Dublin. Add to that the classic dishes that are superbly prepared from the finest seasonal ingredients and friendly and attentive service, and you have a real winner. The spacious Westbury Terrace Lounge just outside is a perfect place for predinner cocktails accompanied by pleasant piano music, and in the restaurant, soft shades of pink, green, and cream set the mood. Among standard favorites here are the crisp roast duckling with lemon, limes, and coriander; fresh sea trout filet with hazelnut-and-honey sauce; sliced beef filet with brandy, black peppercorns, and cream; and Irish salmon flavored with lemon balm, white wine, and cream. The wine list is extensive and moderate to expensive in price, coffee is freshly ground (both decaffeinated and regular), and there's a nice selection of teas.

SHAY BEANO, 37 Lower Stephen's St. Tel. 776384.
  Cuisine: FRENCH. **Reservations:** Recommended.
$ **Prices:** Fixed-price meal IR£12 ($21) at lunch; IR£20 ($35) at dinner. No credit cards.
  Open: Lunch Mon–Sat 12:30–2:30pm; dinner Mon–Sat 7–10:30pm.

Between Great George Street and Ship Street, in the vicinity of Dublin Castle, this is an intimate spot with wickerwork chairs, black Chinese-style screens, and sparkling linen. Owner Eamonn O Cathain tries to keep his small staff French, maintaining that the French are the most professional waiters and chefs. The menu changes daily (depending on the season and the chef's newest creation) and is limited to a choice from three starters, three main courses, and a wide selection of desserts. As for the wine list, it includes some 148 labels, with a concentration on reasonably priced Rhône Valley wines. The price is all-inclusive (excluding wine, but including very good coffee).

SPECIALTY DINING

FISH AND CHIPS

LEO BURDOCKS, 2 Werburgh St. Tel. 540306.
   Cuisine: FISH & CHIPS.
$ **Prices:** IR£2 ($3.50). No credit cards.
   Open: Mon and Wed–Sat 5:30–11pm. **Closed:** Hols.

You really shouldn't leave Dublin without calling here at least once. For three generations, Brian Burdock's family has been serving up what is probably the best fish and chips to be found in the country. Cabinet ministers, university students, poets, Americans who've had the word passed by locals, and almost every other type in Ireland can be found in the queue, patiently waiting for fish bought fresh that morning and those good Irish potatoes, both cooked in "drippings" (none of that modern cooking oil!). Great people-watching while you wait, and all that good eating costs a pittance for the priciest choice—ray and chips (whiting and chips are at the bottom of the range). It's in the Liberties/Christ Church Cathedral vicinity.

BESHOFF'S, 7 Upper O'Connell St. Tel. 743223.
   Cuisine: FISH & CHIPS.
$ **Prices:** IR£1.50–IR£3 ($2.65–$5.25); fixed-price lunch or dinner IR£2.20 ($3.85). No credit cards.
   Open: Mon–Thurs 11:30am–midnight, Fri–Sat 11:30am–1am, Sun 12:30pm–midnight.

This attractive Edwardian-style eatery two blocks north of O'Connell Bridge is a far cry from your everyday fish-and-chips stand. The tables are topped with marble and nicely spaced. There's a bright, cheerful look to the large, bustling room. There are several varieties of fish on order, which come in various combinations, and there's a wine license. It's self-service, and there's a children's menu.

There's also a Beshoff's at 14 Westmoreland Street south of the Liffey, with similar decor and hours.

PUB GRUB

The listings below barely scratch the surface of Dublin's pubs serving excellent and inexpensive meals during the lunch hours. You can pop into virtually any one of the scores of pubs offering pub grub and be assured of good quality *and* quantity. In fact, if you've foregone that gigantic Irish breakfast in your B&B, this could well be your main meal of the day at a tiny fraction of the cost of a full restaurant meal.

THE DUBLINER BAR, in Jurys Hotel, Ballsbridge. Tel. 605000.
   Cuisine: CARVERY. **Bus:** 7, 7A, 8, 45, or 84.
$ **Prices:** IR£4.95 ($8.65). Service charge 13%. ACC, AE, DC, MC, V.
   Open: Lunch only, Mon–Fri 12:15–2pm.

The Dubliner serves up a carvery lunch ample enough to be your main meal of the day. The chef carves from a joint of beef and you help yourself to as much as you want from a wide variety of salads. It's best to arrive early, as the place becomes packed with Dubliners.

THE LORD EDWARD, 23 Christchurch Place. Tel. ???.
   Cuisine: TRADITIONAL.
$ **Prices:** IR£4–IR£6 ($7–$10.50). ACC, AE, MC, V.
   Open: Lunch only, 12:30–2:30pm.

The Lord Edward, in the Liberties, near Christ Church Cathedral, has a genuine old-world atmosphere, complete with stone fireplaces, beamed ceiling, and white stucco walls in the ground-floor pub. Upstairs is one of the city's finest seafood restaurants (see "Worth the Extra Money," below), but the same high-quality food and excellent service come at modest prices in the pub during lunch hours. Choose from heaping plates of hot dishes (roasts, fish, chicken) or a nice selection of salad plates.

PADDY CULLEN'S, 14 Merrion Rd., Ballsbridge. Tel. 684492.
Cuisine: TRADITIONAL. **Bus:** 7, 7A, 8, 45, or 84.
$ Prices: IR£4 ($7). No credit cards.
Open: Lunch only, 12:30–2:30pm.
This is a character-filled, old-style pub presided over by the amiable Paddy himself, an ex-football player of some fame. Good pub grub and lots of locals to keep you company.

PATRICK CONWAY'S, 70 Parnell St. Tel. 732687.
Cuisine: TRADITIONAL.
$ Prices: IR£4–IR£6 ($7–$10.50). No credit cards.
Open: Lunch only, 12:30–2:30pm.
Dating from 1754, Patrick Conway's is just off O'Connell Street, opposite Rotunda Hospital and the Gate Theater. You'll often find theater people bending an elbow here before and after a show in the evening. At lunchtime, however, there's very good pub grub on offer (they are especially known for their hot apple tart). It's a large, rambling place, but do take notice of the huge circular bar just inside the entrance which encloses a carved wooden structure of Gothic proportions. For those visitors who need to know more about Dublin, just ask Frank, your host, who is a wealth of information.

THE OLD STAND, Exchequer St. Tel. 987123.
Cuisine: TRADITIONAL.
$ Prices: Lunch IR£5.50 ($9.65); dinner IR£5.50–IR£6.50 ($9.65–$11.40); Tourist Menu IR£5.75 ($10.05). No credit cards.
Open: Lunch 12:30–3:30pm; dinner 5–9:30pm.
A Dublin tradition, especially among sports figures. A century and a half ago this was a forge, but today you'll find outstanding figures of the sporting world gathered to enjoy "the crack" (talk) and exceptionally good pub grub. There's a daily special of soup, meat, vegetables, and tea or coffee, as well as omelets or salad plates, and hot platters of chicken, steak, or fish.
Note: This is one of the very few pubs serving meals during evening hours—a terrific budget-stretcher. It's just off Great George's Street.

THE STAG'S HEAD, 1 Dame Court. Tel. 679-3701.
Cuisine: TRADITIONAL.
$ Prices: IR£3–IR£5 ($5.25–$8.75). No credit cards.
Open: Lunch only, 12:15–2:15pm.
Built in 1770, the Stag's Head had its last "modernization" in 1895. There are wrought-iron chandeliers, stained-glass skylights, huge mirrors, gleaming wood, and of course, mounted stags' heads. Choose a light lunch of soup and toasted sandwiches or heaping hot platters of bacon, beef, or chicken plus two vegetables.
The pub is just off Exchequer Street (from Great George Street); or look for the mosaic depicting a stag's head imbedded in the sidewalk of Dame Street in the middle of the second block on the left side coming from College Green, then turn onto the small lane that leads to Dame Court—complicated, but worth the effort.

AFTERNOON TEA

Afternoon tea that goes beyond a mere "cuppa" is served in several of Dublin's leading hotels, and the ritual consists of a choice of specialty teas, pastries, scones or brown bread and butter, and cake. All are presented nicely, with soft piano music in the background in some hotels. Traditional hours are 3 to 4:30pm. The price varies very little from one establishment to another, ranging from IR£4 to IR£6 ($7 to $10.50). As we go to press, the following hotels serve afternoon tea, but it's a good idea to call for exact hours at the hotel of your choice. You might also inquire of any hotels in your immediate vicinity, since more and more hotels seem to be adopting this delightful custom.

BERKELEY COURT HOTEL, Landsdowne Rd. Tel. 601711.
In the Ballsbridge area. Tea is served in the comfortable lobby lounge.

GRESHAM HOTEL, 23 Upper O'Connell St. Tel. 746881.
Four blocks north of O'Connell Bridge. Tea is served in the relaxing lobby.

SHELBOURNE HOTEL, St. Stephen's Green. Tel. 766471.
On the north side of the Green. Tea is served in an elegant lounge just off the lobby, while a pianist plays.

WESTBURY HOTEL, Clarendon St. Tel. 791122.
Just off Grafton Street. Tea is served in the Terrace Lounge, and there's a pianist.

FAST-FOOD CHAINS

There are two **McDonald's** in central Dublin, at 9/10 Grafton Street and 62 Upper O'Connell Street. Same decor and menu you know from back home. Prices range from IR£2 to IR£4 ($3.50 to $7).

PIZZALAND PIZZERIA, 1 St. Stephen's Green N. Tel. 717175.
  Cuisine: PIZZA/PASTA.
$ Prices: IR£4–IR£8 ($7–$14); Tourist Menu IR£5.75–IR£7.90 ($10.05–$13.85). ACC, AE, MC, V.
  Open: Daily 9:30am–11:30pm. **Closed:** Good Friday, Christmas Eve, and Christmas Day.

Both traditional and deep-pan pizzas are served in this attractive eatery at the bottom of Grafton Street, and there's a good selection of pasta dishes, as well as a salad bar and some vegetarian menu selections. They serve a good breakfast for under IR£4 ($7), and wine is available by the glass.
North of the Liffey, its duplicate is at 4 North Earl Street (tel. 788944), everything the same.

SELF-SERVICE

MUNICIPAL GALLERY OF MODERN ART, Parnell Sq. Tel. 788238.
  Cuisine: TRADITIONAL.
$ Prices: Appetizers IR£1–IR£1.50 ($1.75–$2.65); main courses IR£3–IR£5 ($5.25–$8.75). No credit cards.
  Open: Tues–Sat 10am–5pm; Sun 12:30am–4:30pm.
This restaurant on the gallery's lower floor is a very good place to eat north of the Liffey. Choose from curries with rice, beef carbonnade with vegetables, a selection of salad plates, and desserts that include chocolate roulade, apple pie, and ice cream. There's also wine by the glass. On Sunday, the popular brunch is a fixed-price IR£6 ($10.50) for adults, IR£4 ($7) for children. The gallery is off Upper Dorset Street between Granby Row and Frederick Street.

NATIONAL GALLERY OF IRELAND, Merrion Sq. Tel. 615133.
  Cuisine: TRADITIONAL.
$ Prices: Appetizers IR£1.50–IR£3 ($2.65–$5.25); main courses IR£2–IR£5 ($3.50–$8.75). No credit cards.

Open: Mon–Wed and Fri–Sat 10am–6pm; Thurs 10am–9pm; Sun 2–5pm.

 You'll dine against a background of classical music, at prices that give "budget" a good name. In the Trinity College vicinity, south of Clare Street, it's self-service and offers as many as five fish selections, six meat or poultry dishes, and a couple of vegetarian choices.

BREAKFAST/BRUNCH

You can **breakfast** at budget prices at both McDonald's and Pizzaland Pizzeria (see "Fast-Food Chains," above). Hotel breakfasts run IR£6.50 ($1.40) up to IR£9 ($15.75)—a last resort for budget travelers!

Sunday brunch is served in many Dublin pubs, some of which throw in traditional and folk music, and in leading hotels. While the menu varies wildly (as well as widely!) from straight eggs, rashers, and sausages to smoked salmon and roast beef, one drink included, you can count on ample portions and a relaxed atmosphere.

DAVY BYRNE'S PUB, 21 Duke St., just off Grafton St. Tel. 775217.
Here you'll get a traditional Irish breakfast for IR£2.95 ($5.15), drinks extra. It's served Sunday from 12:30 to 2pm.

CASPER & GIUMBINIS, Wicklow St. Tel. 794347.
 Brunch costs IR£4.95 ($8.65), including two drinks, and is served Sunday from 12:30 to 3pm. See "Meals for Less Than IR£10," above, for a full description.

HENRY GRATTAN'S PUB, Lower Baggot St. Tel. 789083.
Brunch is a traditional Irish breakfast, served Sunday from noon to 3pm for IR£2.50 ($4.40), but drinks are extra. Lower Baggot Street is an extension of St. Stephen's Green North.

SHELBOURNE HOTEL, St. Stephen's Green N. Tel. 766471.
Reservations are essential for the traditional Irish breakfast served at brunch on Sunday from noon to 2:30pm. The price is IR£15 ($26.25) for adults; IR£7.50 ($13.10) for children, plus a service charge of 15%. The setting is elegant, ditto the service and food.

WHELAN'S PUB, Wexford St., just off Harcourt St. Tel. 780766.
The traditional Irish breakfast here costs IR£3 to IR£4 ($5.25 to $7), and drinks are extra. Sunday brunch is served from 12:30 to 2pm, with informal sessions of folk music.

LATE-NIGHT/24-HOUR

Both the **Coffee Dock Grill,** in Jurys Hotel, Ballsbridge (tel. 605000) (see "Meals for Less Than IR£10," above, for details), and **The Old Stand,** Exchequer Street (tel. 987123) (see "Pub Grub," above, for details), serve long or late hours.

PICNIC FARE & WHERE TO EAT IT

One of the best places to buy picnic fixings is **Bewley's Cafe,** 78 Grafton St. (tel. 776761) (see "Meals for Less Than IR£10," above). Or if burgers and chips appeal, stop in at **McDonald's,** 9/10 Grafton St. (tel. 778393).

Then hie yourself off to **St. Stephen's Green,** where you'll have your picnic along with half of Dublin's work force, who flock to the Green in fine weather (and sometimes in weather not so fine, such is their love of this oasis of greenery in the heart of the city). The **Phoenix Park** is another idyllic picnic spot, and if hunger pangs attack and you aren't prepared, head for the Dublin Zoo restaurant to pick up a sandwich to be eaten elsewhere on the park grounds.

WORTH THE EXTRA MONEY

THE GREY DOOR, 23 Upper Pembroke St. Tel. 766890.
Cuisine: SCANDINAVIAN/RUSSIAN. **Reservations:** Recommended.

$ Prices: Appetizers IR£4–IR£7 ($7–$12.25); main courses IR£10–IR£19 ($17.50–$33.25); fixed-price meal IR£13 ($22.75) at lunch, IR£22 ($38.50) at dinner. Service charge 13%. ACC, AE, DC, V.
Open: Lunch Mon–Fri 12:30–2:15pm; dinner Mon–Sat 7–11pm. **Closed:** Bank hols.

The Grey Door is an elegant restaurant that owner Barry Wyse and his partner, P. J. Daly, have created in the drawing room of a Dublin town house three blocks east of St. Stephen's Green, off Baggot Street. Service throughout is as elegant as the setting, and there's often a guitarist on hand softly strumming native folk music. Dishes such as blinis, borscht, pelmini, steak Rasputin, chicken Kiev, salmon Severnaya, and galupsti are all offered at the Grey Door. For those who might find the idea of a different type of cooking slightly daunting, be assured that once you have tasted the splendid dishes at this restaurant you'll be back.

On the ground floor, **Blushes** wine bar is a charming and informal bistro in a setting of arched alcoves and nicely spaced tables. Prices are a bit lower than upstairs, and Blushes has gained great favor with Dubliners for lunch or a pretheater light supper.

LE COQ HARDI, 35 Pembroke Rd., Ballsbridge. Tel. 689070.
Cuisine: FRENCH. **Reservations:** Essential.
Bus: 7, 7A, 8, 45, or 84.
$ Prices: Appetizers IR£4–IR£7 ($7–$12.25); main courses IR£18–IR£29 ($31.50–$50.75); fixed-price lunch IR£15 ($26.25). Service charge 13%. ACC, AE, DC, V.
Open: Lunch Mon–Fri 12:30–2:30pm; dinner Mon–Sat 7:30–10:45pm.
Closed: Bank hols, 1 week at Christmas, 2 weeks in Aug.

If it's sophisticated French cuisine you yearn for, this is Dublin's finest. Owner-chef John Howard features a blend of haute, bourgeois, and nouvelle cuisine. In the warm, inviting atmosphere of a Georgian house, surrounded by a decor of rosewood and brass, you can choose from such specialties as filet of spring lamb with fresh tomato and tarragon; milk-fed veal with sauce of wild mushrooms, apple brandy, and cream; and a good selection of seafood. The star of the menu is undoubtedly the Coq Hardi (what else!), a mouth-watering breast of chicken stuffed with mashed potatoes, mushrooms, and secret seasonings, wrapped in bacon, baked and flamed with Irish whiskey at your table. This sort of culinary expertise has won the restaurant several well-deserved awards. With seating for only 45, this is another place where advance booking is absolutely essential. Highest recommendation.

THE KING SITRIC, East Pier, Howth Harbour. Tel. 325235 or 326729.
Cuisine: SEAFOOD. **Reservations:** Recommended. **DART:** Howth.
$ Prices: Appetizers IR£3–IR£5 ($5.25–$8.75); main courses IR£10–IR£16.50 ($17.50–$28.88); fixed-price dinner IR£20 ($35). ACC, AE, DC, V.
Open: Dinner only, Mon–Sat 6:30–11pm. **Closed:** 10 days at Christmas, Easter.

Out in Howth, set right on the edge of Dublin Bay in the old harbormaster's house, this is one of the best seafood restaurants in the country. The owner/managers, Joan and Aidan McManus, personally oversee the entire operation, with Joan very much in evidence in the dining room, and Aidan (whose background includes extensive training on the Continent) negotiating seafood purchases directly from the trawlers that put into the harbor. The decor is Georgian, with antique chairs and sofas in the charming two-room lounge.

As for the menu, it all depends on the season. Your best bet is to ask the waiter about the day's catch, and from time to time you can expect to see dishes featuring salmon, bass, plaice, turbot, brill, scallops, prawns, and lobster (with more exotic fish depending on just what the trawlers have snared that day).

THE LORD EDWARD, 23 Christchurch Place. Tel. 542420.
Cuisine: SEAFOOD. **Reservations:** A "must."
$ Prices: Fixed-price dinner IR£20 ($35). ACC, AE, DC, MC, V.

Open: Lunch Tues–Fri 12:30–2:30pm; dinner Tues–Sat 6–10:45pm.

⭐

Ⓢ

The Lord Edward, in the Liberties, near Christ Church Cathedral, has already been recommended as an exceptionally good pub-grub source in Dublin. But for a memorable seafood lunch or dinner, make your way to the small upstairs restaurant, with a stop at the middle-floor bar where you imbibe before a glowing fireplace in a white stucco-walled room with a beamed ceiling. The cozy, bay-windowed dining room one floor above is a haven of soft lights, velvet chairs, and intimacy, with seating for only 36 diners. Relaxed elegance is the tone, with expert service and a menu that can offer as many as eight different prawn dishes and main courses you'll know are the freshest possible, since the knowledge-able and caring proprietors make shopping forays twice daily—once for lunch and again for dinner. There's a wide range of specialty coffees, including Calypso (with Tía María), Cossack (with vodka) and one of Dublin's best Irish coffees. There's an extensive à la carte menu if you don't go for the "best buy" fixed-price dinner. Highly recommended.

RESTAURANT NA MARA, Marine Rd., Dun Laoghaire. Tel. 806767 or 800509.
Cuisine: SEAFOOD/VEGETARIAN. **Reservations:** Recommended. **DART:** Dun Laoghaire.
$ **Prices:** Fixed-price meal IR£14 ($24.50) at lunch, IR£20 ($35) at dinner. Service charge 15%. ACC, AE, DC, V. **Parking:** Large car park.
Open: Lunch Tues–Sat 1–2:30pm; dinner Tues–Sat 7–10:30pm. **Closed:** 1 week at Easter, 1 week at Christmas.

The freshest of seafood is the specialty here. It's an attractive place with an interesting history that began as the result of a seafood festival a few years back when the Great Southern Hotel was requested to cater a seafood menu in the buffet room of the old railway station. The success of that short-term venture was such that the Great Southern set about a transformation of the Victorian-style room with its high, vaulted ceiling. Using the softness of salmon-pink walls, turf-brown carpeting, and candle-light, the managers have created a relaxing and inviting restaurant that serves mostly seasonal seafood dishes. The creative cooking turns out such specialties as the popular poached sole filets in white-wine sauce with prawns. Lobster comes in several guises, and the dessert in my own humble opinion is an elegant crêpe flambée that serves two. It's fully licensed, with an extensive wine list. About 90% of the business comes from locals who eat here regularly, so it's best to reserve. If you drive, know that there is ample parking.

THE PARK RESTAURANT, The Mews, 40 Main St., Blackrock, Co. Dublin. Tel. 886177.
Cuisine: FRENCH/CONTINENTAL. **Reservations:** Essential. **DART:** Blackrock.
$ **Prices:** Fixed-price meal IR£11 ($19.25) at lunch; IR£22.50 ($39.40) at dinner. ACC, AE, DC, MC, V.
Open: Lunch Tues–Fri 12:30–2:15pm; dinner Tues–Sat 7:30–11pm. **Closed:** Public hols and the day after.

Colin O'Daly is owner/chef of this attractive, relaxed eatery, and his culinary creations have won high praise from Dubliners as well as international visitors. What's more, although his dishes lean heavily toward those of France, the menu is in plain English, since Colin insists he wants diners to feel as though they are dining in his home and not have to struggle with menu translations. Among the outstanding offerings are pheasant, medallions of veal and beef, sole Véronique, brill with shellfish sauce, and venison. Vegetables are treated tenderly, and desserts are a delight to the eye as well as the palate.

RESTAURANT PATRICK GUILBAUD, 46 James Place, Lower Baggot St. Tel. 764192.
Cuisine: FRENCH/VEGETARIAN. **Reservations:** Essential.
$ **Prices:** Fixed-price meal IR£14.50 ($25.40) at lunch, IR£19.50 ($34.15) at dinner. Service charge 15%. ACC, AE, DC, MC, V.

Open: Lunch Mon–Fri 12:30–2pm; dinner Mon–Sat 7:30–10:15pm.
This lovely small restaurant (seating only 50) takes the very best of fresh Irish ingredients and combines them in dishes done in the French manner for a menu that is outstanding. A vegetarian dish or two always appears on the menu. Guilbaud's is extremely popular both at lunch and dinner with the business, financial, and society crowd in Dublin—and people-watching adds to the evening. It's in the Inchicore area, off Tyrconnell Road. Take a taxi.

READERS RECOMMEND

The Lane Gallery Restaurant, 55 Pembroke Lane (tel. 611829). *"We really enjoyed dining at the Lane Gallery. The food was excellent, and they had a reasonably priced fixed-price dinner, as well as an à la carte menu."*—Sharan Milford, Raleigh, N.C.

Ryan's Pub, 28 Parkgate Street. *"Ryan's is tops on our list of Irish pubs, but imagine our surprise when we discovered they have opened a tiny restaurant upstairs. We had a terrific meal in what was almost like a private club."*—Gerald White, San Francisco, Calif.

The Celtic Mews Restaurant, 109a Lower Baggot Street (tel. 760796). *"Our meal at the Celtic Mews was the highlight of our stay in Dublin—a real splurge, but worth every penny. We had a marvelous seafood appetizer and wonderful rack of Irish lamb."*—Sam Bianco, New York, N.Y.

The Olive Restaurant, 34 Glasthule Road, Dun Laoghaire (tel. 841024). *"This smart little bistro-style restaurant and wine bar was a real find. We had fish, and it was prepared to gourmet standards. One of our party had Irish stew, which he thought was superb, and their menu includes steaks and vegetarian dishes. Anyone going through or staying in Dun Laoghaire will dine well at the Olive without paying an arm and a leg—prices were at the low end of moderate."*—Sally Macken, Chicago, Ill.

CHAPTER 5

WHAT TO SEE & DO IN DUBLIN

- **DID YOU KNOW . . .?**
1. **ATTRACTIONS**
- **DUBLIN WALKING TOURS**
2. **SPECIAL & FREE EVENTS**
3. **SPORTS & RECREATION**
4. **SAVVY SHOPPING**
5. **EVENING ENTERTAINMENT**

Much of what you'll see in Dublin today consists of the lines and wrinkles, blemishes and beauty spots left on her face by a long, rich, and colorful history.

There were people living near the Liffey's hurdle bridge long before the Vikings arrived to found a proper town in 840. They came first as raiders, but gradually intermarried with the Irish and settled down to become traders and craftsmen.

When St. Patrick passed this way in 448, it is a fact that there were already several small churches, and possibly there was a monastery. But it was not until Viking King Olaf was baptized shortly before his death in 979 that Christianity gained any sort of foothold. His son, Sitric, founded Christ Church Cathedral in 1038, one of three medieval buildings that have survived through the centuries. St. Patrick's Cathedral, the second medieval structure to survive, dates back to 1191, and in 1204 King John authorized the building of Dublin Castle, the last of the city's medieval relics still standing.

There were few substantial changes in Dublin after that until the 17th century when Dublin's first notable public buildings were constructed. Those magnificent Georgian buildings began to appear in the 18th century with many examples of the Palladian style as well as Dublin's famous Georgian squares. The Victorian age in the mid-1800s left traces in railway stations, banks, pubs, markets, and hospitals, as well as some commercial buildings in the College Green vicinity. From 1916 to 1922 Dublin's face was scarred by the ravages of uprising, although careful rebuilding and restoration have erased most of the scars.

The 1960s brought the "office revolution" and the advent of characterless glass-and-concrete boxes to hail Ireland's new progressive era. Indeed, in a fit of "progressive" zeal, the grand old city came close to demolishing many of its finest legacies. Fortunately, concerned citizens halted the destruction at an early stage so that today's visitor may happily browse through the architectural treasures of the past along with the modern monstrosities.

In 1991, Dublin was the officially designated European City of Culture. The occasion was marked by the opening of a Writers Museum in Parnell Square the reopening of the Customs House after an extensive facelift; the launch of the *Book of Clashganna*, a 20th-century version of the *Book of Kells* that includes the work of leading contemporary Irish writers and artists; and a Festival of Literature in recognition of the 50th anniversary of James Joyce's death.

DID YOU KNOW...?

- Dublin's Whitefriar Street Carmelite Church contains the remains of that saint most revered by lovers around the globe, St. Valentine. February 14, the saint's feast day, was once believed to be the day on which birds mated and the day on which an unmarried girl should choose her sweetheart (origin, of course, of the Valentine card custom).
- More than 8,000 archaeological sites have been identified in county Kerry alone.
- There are more than 1,250 megalithic tombs in Ireland (Neolithic people)
- There are some 7,000 miles of stone walls on Innishmore in Aran Islands, itself 5 mi long, 2 mi wide.
- In the 6th century, Ireland's St. Brendan is supposed to have made an incredible voyage to Iceland and Newfoundland in a frail oak-and-hide boat, reaching the New World centuries before either the Vikings or Christopher Columbus.
- The Duke of Wellington was born at No. 24 Upper Merrion Street in Dublin in 1769.

SIGHTSEEING STRATEGIES

Time constraints and your own special interests will determine just *how* you spend the time you've allotted for the capital city. There are, however, sightseeing techniques that can help you cover the most territory in any time frame. Herewith, a few suggestions.

IF YOU HAVE 1 DAY Let Dublin Bus get you around hassle free via the "Dublin Heritage Trail" tour (see "Organized Tours," below, for details). Take the first departure (10am) and explore in depth those sightseeing attractions that appeal to you most; have lunch in one of the city's lively pubs; spend the afternoon in further exploration or call it a day in midafternoon and do a bit of browsing through Dublin's shops. Evening hours can be devoted to theater, cabaret, a traditional music session, or pub-hopping.

IF YOU HAVE 2 DAYS On your first day visit Dublin's outstanding attractions (see above). On your second day, reach back in time to Ireland's past and/or the scenic spots surrounding Dublin. Bus Eireann has a nice variety of all-day tours to points of interest within a short distance of the city. Each tour runs on specified days of the week, so your itinerary will be decided by just which day you can travel. Choose from the Boyne Valley tour, which includes such prehistoric relics as the Hill of Tara and Newgrange; the Avondale, Glendalough, and Wicklow Hills tour; or take one of the several half-day tours to outlying areas and spend the afternoon exploring city streets on foot. Use evening hours each day to enjoy theater, cabaret, traditional music sessions, or pub-hopping.

IF YOU HAVE 3 DAYS See the above suggestions for the first two days. On your third day, spend the morning in the Phoenix Park, with lunch at the zoo. In the afternoon, take in either *The Dublin Experience* or *The Viking Adventure* (see below for details)—both, if you're energetic and ambitious enough. Choose among the evening activities suggested above.

IF YOU HAVE 5 DAYS OR MORE With 5 days at your disposal, you can spread the suggestions above over a more leisurely time frame, adding to them more of Bus Eireann's half-day tours beyond city limits, the Dublin Literary Pub Crawl, or another of the organized walking tours of the city. You'll have time, too, for at least one lunchtime picnic on St. Stephen's Green, a barge cruise down the canal, and a visit to the Guinness Hop Shop. If you're staying in Dublin for *all* of your Irish visit, use 1 day for a Bus Eireann all-day excursion to Waterford and New Ross, Kilkenny, or the Carlingford Peninsula. Or invest in their "Days Away" round-trip ticket for a mere IR£5 ($8.75) that can give you a day on your own to any of the above-named cities, as well as Wexford, Cahir, and Cashel, and even points as far away as Cork and Limerick.

Be sure to save one evening for the Abbey Tavern out in Howth to take in their terrific Irish music show.

1. ATTRACTIONS

Before setting out to see Dublin, go by the **Tourist Office** at 14 Upper O'Connell Street and pick up a good map of the inner city, as well as informative literature on the major buildings, museums, etc., that you want to see. There's also an illustrated walking-tour guide titled "Tourist Trail" that follows a signposted route (allow about 3½ hours) and tells about the points of interest along the way. While you're there, take a look around the gift shop. It's one of the best you'll find anywhere in the country, with a wide selection of Irish crafts, souvenirs, books, and other items.

Dublin is one of the world's great walking cities, and you'll be well off exploring it on your own. If time is limited, however, one of the **organized sightseeing tours** (see below) will let you see more in less time than you would by shank's mare. It's also possible to engage a **personal tour guide,** one who can tailor a tour to your own special interests and share firsthand knowledge of Ireland's rich heritage. The Irish Tourist Board publishes a "Directory of Approved Guides," all of whom have passed a written and practical examination given by the Council for the Education, Recruitment and Training of personnel in the tourism industries. Some are multilingual, and languages represented include French, German, Italian, Spanish, and Dutch. For the guide directory and full details, contact the Tourism Services and Facilities Department, Board Failte Eireann, Baggot Street Bridge, Dublin 2 (tel. 01/765871).

THE TOP ATTRACTIONS

CHRIST CHURCH CATHEDRAL, Christ Church Place (off Lord Edward St.). Tel. 778099.

⭐ Christ Church is one of the oldest and most beautiful of Dublin's buildings. Founded by King Sitric in 1038, it was originally a wooden structure, but was rebuilt in stone after the Norman invasion in 1169. Strongbow, the Anglo-Norman leader who was instrumental in the rebuilding, lies here, and this is also where four Irish kings were knighted by Richard II in 1394 when they pledged allegiance to that monarch. In 1689 James II prayed here for divine protection before marching off to the Battle of the Boyne, and a victorious King William came back to offer thanks after that battle. There are lovely architectural details and stonework in the nave, transepts, choir, and chancel, and the crypt (the oldest section) is said to be one of the best of its kind in Europe. Tours are available on Sunday at 12:15 and 4:30pm.

Admission: Free.

Open: Daily 10am–5pm. **Bus:** 21A, 50, 50A, 78, 78A, or 78B.

ST. PATRICK'S CATHEDRAL, Patrick's Close. Tel. 754817.

⭐ Founded in 1190, St. Patrick's has, over its varied history, served purposes as disparate as a university (1320–1465) and a stable for the mounts of Cromwell's troops in the 17th century. Its best-known dean (1713–45) was Jonathan Swift, author of *Gulliver's Travels* and a host of other sharp-tongued attacks on the humbuggery of his times. His tomb is in the south aisle, and his beloved "Stella" (Esther Johnson in real life) lies nearby. It had fallen into near ruin by 1860, when a member of the Guinness family financed its restoration to its present magnificent state. All services are ecumenical, and all weekday choral services are also open to the public. Check with the Tourist Board for exact days and hours.

Admission: 70p ($1.23) contribution.

Open: Mon–Fri 8:30am–6:15pm; Sat 8:30am–5pm; Sun 8:30–9am and 10am–4:30pm. **Bus:** 50, 50A, 54, 54A, or 56A.

ST. MICHAN'S CHURCH, Church St.

⭐ North of the Liffey, the square tower of St. Michan's dates back to the 1096 Danish church that stood on this site. The present structure, however, is of 17th-century origin. Handel is said to have played its organ (perhaps when in Dublin to conduct the first performance of his *Messiah* in 1742). But most visitors are drawn by the perfectly preserved bodies that have lain in its vaults for centuries with no sign of decomposition. The Sheare Brothers, executed during the 1798 rebellion, rest here, and on my last visit it was a young Crusader and a 15th-century nun whose mummified bodies could be viewed. The rector of St. Michan's attended Robert Emmet in his last hours, and the patriot is reputed to be buried in the churchyard (Saul, the sexton, can fill you in on the story).

Admission: IR£1.20 ($2.10) adults; IR£1 ($1.75) students and seniors, 50p (88¢) children under 12.

Open: Mon–Fri 10am–12:45pm and 2–4:45pm; Sat 10am–12:45pm. **Closed:** Vaults closed Sun. **Bus:** 34 or 34A.

TRINITY COLLEGE AND THE *BOOK OF KELLS*, College Green. Tel. 772941.

⭐ Although founded by Elizabeth I in 1592, Trinity's oldest surviving buildings are the red-brick structures put up in the early 1700s. The striking West Front is worthy of note, as are the 1740 Printing House and the Dining Hall dating to 1760. It is, however, the Old Library that you should be sure not to miss, for it holds a priceless link with Ireland's antiquity, the magnificently illustrated *Book of Kells*. The book, which consists of the four gospels laboriously handwritten in Latin by monks and discovered in the monastery at Kells, has been bound in four separate volumes, two of which are displayed in glass cases. The lofty, vaulted Long Room, the exquisite beauty of the open pages, and marble busts of Ireland's famous figures all combine to create an awe-inspiring atmosphere you'll not soon forget. Pages are turned regularly to display different page spreads, and you may find yourself returning for a second look. Other illustrated manuscripts are on display, as well as an ancient harp said to have accompanied Brian Boru into battle.

Admission: IR£1.75 ($3.05) adults; IR£1.50 ($2.65) students and seniors, free for children; IR£3.50 ($6.10) for family ticket. *Note:* Combination tickets to see the *Book of Kells* and *The Dublin Experience* (see below) range from IR£4 ($7) to IR£8 ($14).

Open: Mon–Fri 9:30am–4:45pm, Sat 9:30am–12:45pm. **Bus:** All cross-city buses.

BANK OF IRELAND, College Green. Tel. 776801.

Just across College Green from Trinity, the Bank of Ireland building was once the seat of the Irish Parliament. This is where the hated Act of Union was passed in 1800. An ailing Henry Grattan, whose statue now stands across the way, donned his worn Volunteer uniform and rose in these halls to bid an eloquent farewell to the independent Parliament. Today you can visit the House of Lords simply by asking directions from any of the bank's uniformed attendants. Not so the House of Commons, however, for when the building was acquired by the bank, it was on the condition that the lower house be demolished to avoid any possible coup d'état.

IMPRESSIONS

This is the roiall City and seat of Ireland, a famous towne for Merchandize, the chiefe Court of Justice, in munition strong, in buildings gorgeous, in Citizens populous. . . . Seated it is in a right delectable and holesome place: for to the South yee have hils mounting up aloft, Westward an open champion ground, and on the East the sea at hand and in sight: The River Liffy running downe at North-East affordeth a safe roade and harbour for ships.
—WILLIAM CAMDEN, *BRITAIN*, 1610

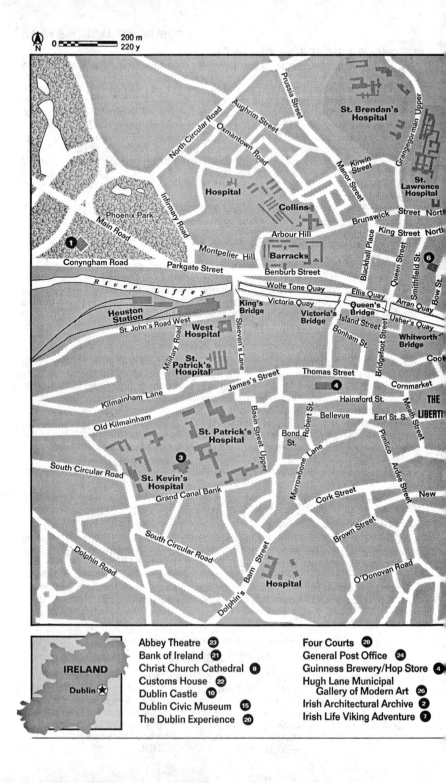

Map Scale: 0 — 200 m / 220 y

N (compass)

Streets and Places:

Prussia Street

St. Brendan's Hospital

Aughrim Street

Oxmantown Road

North Circular Road

Kirwin Street

Manor Street

Grangegorman Upper

St. Lawrence Hospital

Street North

Hospital

Collins

Brunswick

Arbour Hill

King Street North

Infirmary Road

Phoenix Park

Main Road

Montpelier Hill

Barracks

Blackhall Place

Queen Street

Smithfield St.

Bow St.

6

Conyngham Road

Parkgate Street

Benburb Street

River Liffey

Wolfe Tone Quay

Ellis Quay

Arran Quay

King's Bridge

Victoria Quay

Queen's Bridge

Usher's Quay

Whitworth Bridge

Heuston Station

St. John's Road West

West Hospital

Victoria's Bridge

Island Street

Bonham St.

Bridgefoot Street

Cook

Military Road

Steeven's Lane

St. Patrick's Hospital

James's Street

Thomas Street

4

Hainsford St.

Cornmarket

THE LIBERTI

Kilmainham Lane

Bellevue

Earl St. S.

Meath Street

Old Kilmainham

St. Patrick's Hospital

Basin Street Upper

Robert St.

Bond St.

Pimlico

Ardee Street

South Circular Road

3

Bellevue

St. Kevin's Hospital

Marrowbone Lane

New

Grand Canal Bank

Cork Street

South Circular Road

Brown Street

O'Donovan Road

Dolphin Road

Dolphin's Barn Street

Hospital

IRELAND

Dublin ⭐

Abbey Theatre ㉓
Bank of Ireland ㉑
Christ Church Cathedral ⑧
Customs House ㉒
Dublin Castle ⑩
Dublin Civic Museum ⑮
The Dublin Experience ⑳

Four Courts ㉘
General Post Office ㉔
Guinness Brewery/Hop Store ④
Hugh Lane Municipal
   Gallery of Modern Art ㉖
Irish Architectural Archive ②
Irish Life Viking Adventure ⑦

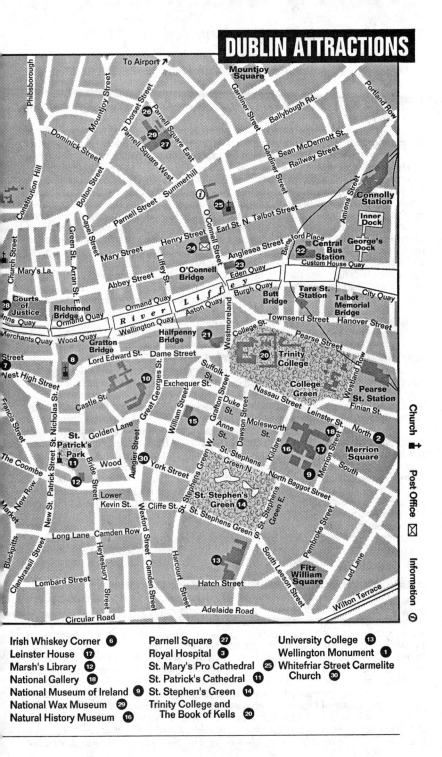

DUBLIN ATTRACTIONS

To Airport ↗
Mountjoy Square
Phibsborough
Portland Row
Gardiner Street
Ballybough Rd.
Dorset Street
Mountjoy Street
Parnell Square East
26
Dominick Street
Parnell Square West
29
Sean McDermott St.
Gardiner Street
27
Railway Street
Constitution Hill
Summerhill
Connolly Station
Bolton Street
Capel Street
Green St.
Parnell Street
25 ✝
Inner Dock
Arran St. E
O'Connell Street
Earl St. N. Talbot Street
Amiens Street
Church Street
Henry Street
George's Dock
Mary's La.
Mary Street
24 ✉
Anglesea Street
Beresford Place
22 Central Bus Station
Abbey Street
Liffey St.
O'Connell Bridge
Custom House Quay
Courts of Justice
28
Richmond Bridge
Ormand Quay
23
Eden Quay
Tara St. Station
City Quay
Inns Quay
Ormand Quay
River Liffey
Burgh Quay
Butt Bridge
Talbot Memorial Bridge
Merchants Quay
Wood Quay
Wellington Quay
Aston Quay
Townsend Street
Hanover Street
Street
Gratton Bridge
Halfpenny Bridge
21
Westmoreland
College St.
Pearse Street
7
8
Lord Edward St.
Dame Street
20 Trinity College
Pearse St. Station
West High Street
St. Nicholas St.
Castle St.
10
Exchequer St.
Suffolk St.
College Green
Nassau Street
Leinster St.
North
Finian St.
Francis Street
Golden Lane
Great Georges St.
William Street
Grafton Street
Duke St.
Anne St.
Molesworth St.
18
2
St. Patrick's Park
15
Dawson Street
Kildare
16
17
Merrion Square
11
Wood
30 York Street
St. Stephens Green W.
St. Stephens Green N.
9
South
The Coombe
New Row
St. Patrick Street
New St.
Bride Street
Aungier Street
Lower Kevin St.
Cliffe St.
St. Stephen's Green
14
St. Stephens Green S.
North Baggot Street
St. Stephens Green E.
Pembroke Street
Lad Lane
12
Market
Blackpits
Clanbrassil Street
Long Lane
Camden Row
Heytesbury Street
Wexford Street
Camden Street
Harcourt Street
13
Hatch Street
South Leeson Street
Fitz William Square
Wilton Terrace
Lombard Street
Circular Road
Adelaide Road

Church ✝   Post Office ✉   Information ⓘ

Irish Whiskey Corner **6**
Leinster House **17**
Marsh's Library **12**
National Gallery **18**
National Museum of Ireland **9**
National Wax Museum **29**
Natural History Museum **16**

Parnell Square **27**
Royal Hospital **3**
St. Mary's Pro Cathedral **25**
St. Patrick's Cathedral **11**
St. Stephen's Green **14**
Trinity College and The Book of Kells **20**

University College **13**
Wellington Monument **1**
Whitefriar Street Carmelite Church **30**

Admission: Free.
Open: Mon–Fri 10am–3pm. Guided tours Tues at 10:30am, 11:30am, and 1:45pm.

NATIONAL MUSEUM OF IRELAND, Kildare St. (at Merrion Row). Tel. 618811.

⭐ The museum holds collections of archeology, fine arts, and history. A major renovation program is nearing completion in the Kildare Street building, and as we go to press a number of the refurbished exhibition rooms have been opened to the public. Situated on the ground floor, the Treasury is the highlight of the archeological collections. This special exhibition traces the development of Irish art from the Iron Age to the 15th century and includes the Tara Brooch, the Ardagh Chalice, and the Cross of Cong, as well as a 20-minute audiovisual presentation. An exhibit of prehistoric Irish gold (the largest display of gold in a European museum) opened in 1991. A display of artifacts from the Dublin Viking Age excavations is also on view. Adjoining the main hall is a large room that holds a comprehensive study of the Uprising of 1916. The second-floor gallery holds cases of Irish silver, coins, glass, and lace. Also on the second floor, the Music Room features traditional instruments such as the Irish harp and the uileann pipes. A second building, entered from Merrion Street, holds natural-history exhibits and will be of special interest to youngsters. A third, on Merrion Row (entrance near Shelbourne Hotel), is devoted to the geology of Ireland.
Admission: Free, except for special exhibits.
Open: Tues–Sat 10am–5pm, Sun 2–5pm. **Bus:** 7, 7A, 8, 10, 11, or 13.

NATIONAL GALLERY, Merrion Sq. W. Tel. 615133.

Conveniently located just around the corner from the National Museum, and a mere block away from the National History Museum (setting up a great "museum crawl" for the energetic!), the National Gallery's collections include impressive works by Dutch masters, as well as 10 major landscape paintings and portraits by Gainsborough, and canvases by Rubens, Rembrandt, El Greco, Monet, Cézanne, and Degas. John Butler Yeats, perhaps Ireland's greatest modern portrait painter, is well represented, as are leading 18th- and 19th-century Irish artists. Portraits of Irish historical figures over the past 3 centuries are hung in the National Portrait Gallery. The collection includes 2,500 paintings, pieces of sculpture, and objets d'art. The young George Bernard Shaw spent much time browsing through the National Gallery and felt such a debt of gratitude for the education it afforded him that he bequeathed it a substantial monetary sum. There is also a very good restaurant with low prices and a souvenir bookshop.
Admission: Free.
Open: Mon–Wed and Fri–Sat 10am–6pm, Thurs 10am–9pm, Sun 2–5pm. Tours given Sat at 3pm, and Sun at 2:30, 3:15, and 4pm. **Closed:** Good Friday, Christmas Eve, and Christmas Day. **Bus:** 7, 7A, or 8.

KILMAINHAM GAOL HISTORICAL MUSEUM. Tel. 535984.

⭐ Within these walls political prisoners languished, and were tortured and killed, from 1796 until 1924 when the late President Eamon de Valera left as its final prisoner. Its rolls held such names as the Sheares Brothers; Robert Emmet, who went from here to his death, proclaiming, "When my country takes her place among the nations of the earth, then, and not till then, let my epitaph be written!"; Charles Parnell, who directed Land League boycott strategy from within Kilmainham's walls; the Invincibles of 1883, five of whom lie buried here where they were hanged; scores of Volunteers who rose up in rebellion during Easter Week of 1916; and Eamon de Valera, who was imprisoned twice—once in 1916 and again in 1921 when he opposed the Treaty of Union. It was, however, James Connolly and the 14 who were executed with him at Kilmainham Gaol in May 1916 whose sacrifice for Irish independence so fired their countrymen that the national will was united and, in the words of Yeats, "a terrible beauty" was born. The old gaol lay abandoned from the time of De Valera's exit until 1960, when a group of dedicated volunteers determined to restore it as a national shrine to Ireland's fight for freedom. Fittingly, it was President de Valera who opened the museum at Easter 1966. To walk along its corridors, through the exercise yard, or into the Main Compound is a moving experience that lingers hauntingly in the memory.

Admission: IR£1.50 ($2.65) adults, IR£1 ($1.75) seniors, 60p ($1.05) for students and children.

Open: Tours given June–Sept, Wed and Sun 11am–6pm; to arrange a tour on other days, phone 01/535984. **Bus:** 21, 78, 78A, 78B, or 79 at O'Connell Bridge.

DUBLIN CASTLE, Castle St. Tel. 777129.

West of Dame Street, just off Lord Edward Street, this is the site of an earlier Danish fortress. The only remaining portions of the castle built between 1208 and 1220 are a bit of a curtain wall and two towers. You can get a pretty good idea of the original outline, however, from the **Upper Castle Yard.** The **Record (or Wardrobe) Tower,** with its 16-foot-thick walls, is the most outstanding relic of the 13th-century Anglo-Norman fortress. Dating from the 15th century, **Bermingham Tower** was the state prison when Red Hugh O'Donnell was kept there in the 16th century. The **Church of the Most Holy Trinity** was formerly the Chapel Royal. British viceroys resided in the opulent **State Apartments,** which were converted into a Red Cross hospital during World War I. It was from these apartments that the prisoner James Connolly, patriot leader of the 1916 Uprising, was taken by stretcher to Kilmainham Jail to be executed, thus arousing international outrage and hastening the goal for which he gave his life. They have now been restored to their former elegance, and today every president of Ireland is inaugurated in these splendid quarters.

Be sure to stop a moment at the **memorial** outside the main gate honoring those Irish killed here during Easter Week of 1916—it stands on the spot where heads of Irish kings once were displayed publicly on high spikes.

Admission: Small charge for tour.

Open: Tours given Mon–Fri 10am–12:15pm and 2–5pm. Because the castle is sometimes closed to the public for official state functions, be sure to check with the Tourist Office before going, to avoid disappointment.

GENERAL POST OFFICE, O'Connell St.

To touch more recent Irish history, take a look around the imposing General Post Office, built in 1818. The massive granite building with its six fluted columns is where Padraic Pearse in 1916 gathered his Volunteers, hoisted the Irish Tricolour, and from its portico proclaimed to the Irish people and the world that Ireland would henceforth be an independent Republic. From the nearby Liffey, an English gunboat shelled the building, starting a fire that gutted its interior, now completely restored. Its central hall holds a statue of Ireland's ancient mythical warrior hero Cuchulain, who tied himself upright to a stake in order to fight a superior force to the death. A memorial to the men who fought here, its marble base is inscribed with the words of Pearse's Proclamation.

Admission: Free.

Open: Mon–Sat 8am–8pm, Sun and bank hols 10:30am–6:30pm.

THE IRISH LIFE VIKING ADVENTURE, St. Audoen's, High St. Tel. 679-7099.

This extraordinary re-creation takes you back to Dublin's very beginning, when Viking raiders were the first of Ireland's many invaders who came to plunder and stayed to settle. There's a very good informative audiovisual presentation before you set off to explore the re-creation of everyday life in the Viking Dublin of 988. This exciting project came about when, a few years ago, the Dublin Corporation began excavations for a building at Wood Quay and uncovered well-preserved artifacts left by the Vikings more than 1,000 years ago. Many of those artifacts are now on view at the National Museum on Merrion Row. Here you'll see authentic reproductions of a Viking house in mid-construction (showing the building methods of the day), daily dress (even the fabrics have been faithfully reproduced), jewelry (which defined social status), carved bone and metal knives and other utensils, and trades people (builders, fishmongers, etc.) as authentically dressed actors go about their daily business in the manner of those long-ago settlers. It's a fascinating experience, made even more so because visitors are urged to interact with the actors. Questions are encouraged, and answers come couched in the vocabulary of Viking Dublin. Highly recommended.

Admission: IR£2.75 ($4.80) adults; IR£2.25 ($3.95) for students and senior citizens, IR£2 ($3.50) children.

Open: Tues–Sat 10am–4:30pm. **Bus:** 78, 78A, or 78B.

THE DUBLIN EXPERIENCE, Davis Theatre, University of Dublin, Trinity College. Tel. 772941 ext. 1177.

A somewhat different look at Dublin's past, *The Dublin Experience* is every bit as dramatic in its own way as the *Viking Irish Life Adventure*. It's a marvelous multimedia show that traces the history of the city from its earliest days and introduces visitors to the modern city and its people. Really a great way to begin your stay in Dublin, and one that will make each day you're there more meaningful.

Admission: IR£2.50 ($4.40) adults; £1.50 ($2.65) for senior citizens, those 18 and under, and students; IR£5 ($8.75) family ticket. If you have purchased a combination ticket at prices of IR£4 ($7), IR£3 ($5.25), IR£1.50 ($2.65), and IR£8 ($14); you can also take a look at the *Book of Kells* in the Long Room of the Old Library (see above).

Open: May–Sept, daily on the hour 10am–5pm.

MORE ATTRACTIONS

ST. STEPHEN'S GREEN, Grafton St.

⭐ St. Stephen's Green has been preserved as an open space for Dubliners since 1690. Over the years it has evolved into the beautifully planted park that today finds city residents and visitors alike strolling along its paths, enjoying a lunch break picnic style, or simply soaking up its rustic charm as the city's traffic swirls around the edges. Formal flowerbeds, the arched stone bridge crossing one end of the artificial lake, shaded pathways, and statuary placed in pockets of shrubbery make this a very special place.

Admission: Free.

Open: Mon–Sat 8am–dark; Sun 10am–dark.

LEINSTER HOUSE, Kildare St.

Leinster House, in the city center south of the Liffey, is the home of the Parliament (Dail Eireann, pronounced "Dawl") that came into being when Ireland's long struggle finally brought liberty. If you can wangle an invitation to a session of the Dail, don't miss the chance to see Ireland's governing body in action. Otherwise, the chambers are somewhat impressive, and well worth a visit for those interested in government.

Admission: Free.

Open: You'll have to be introduced by a member to gain admittance when the Dail is in session. Check with the Tourist Board for hours when the Dail is not meeting. **Bus:** Any city-center bus.

DUBLIN CIVIC MUSEUM, 58 S. William St. Tel. 794260.

There's a treasure trove of Dublin detail housed in the city's own museum— streets and buildings, traders, industry, transport, political history, and scores of maps and views of Dublin provide great browsing. Exhibits also include artifacts from the Viking Age, and there's a model of the Howth tram. Every few months, other exhibits are mounted on a temporary basis.

Admission: Free.

Open: Tues–Sat 10am–6pm, Sun 11am–2pm. **Bus:** 10, 11, or 13.

NATURAL HISTORY MUSEUM, Merrion St. Tel. 618811.

This marvelous zoological museum is a delight for young and old alike. Its ground-floor Irish Room collections illustrate the country's wildlife, both vertebrate and invertebrate. Mammals (red deer, badger, fox, etc.) occupy the center of the room; two whale skeletons (salvaged when the giants of the deep were stranded on the Irish coast) are suspended from the ceiling; there's a terrific display of Irish birds that features sea birds and kingfishers; and butterflies and other insects are on view at the rear of the room. On upper floors you'll find their World Collection, which includes impressive displays of Asian and African wildlife (the Indian elephant, giant panda, pygmy hippopotamus, etc.).

Admission: Free.
Open: Tues–Sat 10am–5pm, Sun 2–5pm. **Bus:** 7, 7A, or 8.

HUGH LANE MUNICIPAL GALLERY OF MODERN ART, Parnell Sq. Tel. 741903.

North of the Liffey, near the top of O'Connell Street, the gallery occupies a fine Georgian mansion that was once the residence of Lord Charlemont. A word of explanation is in order about the works you may find on view. Before his death by drowning on the *Lusitania* in 1915, and before Charlemont House was acquired as a permanent home for his paintings, Sir Hugh Lane lent his collection to the National Gallery in London. A codicil to his will, however, left the pictures to Dublin's Municipal Gallery, but the codicil lacked the two essential witnesses to his signature. After a long dispute, an agreement has now been reached to divide the 39 pictures into two groups, one to be housed in London, the other in Dublin, with exchanges to be made every 14 years.

Among those you're likely to find in residence are works by Manet, Corot, Monet, Daumier, and contemporary works by Irish artists. There's an excellent downstairs restaurant (see Section 5, "Where to Eat," in Chapter 4), and just across the way is the beautiful **Garden of Remembrance,** dedicated in 1966 to those who died in the 1916 fight for liberty.

Admission: Free.
Open: Tues–Sat 9:30am–6pm; Sun 10am–5pm. **Bus:** 11, 12, 13, 16, 16A, 22, or 22A.

ROYAL HOSPITAL, Kilmainham. Tel. 718666.

The Royal Hospital in Kilmainham was founded by the Duke of Ormond to create a hospice for retired soldiers and was built between 1680 and 1684. After a stint as Garda Headquarters, followed by extensive restoration, it now houses the **National Centre for Culture and the Arts.** There are frequent exhibitions (check local newspapers or telephone for showing hours) with a small admission fee. On Sunday, there's a guided tour, and on Tuesday admission is free except during July and August.

Admission: Varies with the event.
Open: July–Aug, Tues–Sun noon–5pm; Sept–June, Tues–Sat 2–5pm, Sun noon–5pm. **Bus:** 21A, 23, 78, 78A, 78B, 79, or 90.

CHESTER BEATTY LIBRARY AND GALLERY OF ORIENTAL ART, 20 Shewsbury Rd. Tel. 692386.

Sir Alfred Chester Beatty, an American mining millionaire who made his home in Dublin, bequeathed his extensive collections to the city. Highlights are the biblical papyri, Persian and Turkish paintings, Qur'ans, Japanese wood-block prints, and Chinese jade books.

Admission: Free.
Open: Tues–Fri 10am–5pm, Sat 2–5pm. Guided tours given Wed and Sat at 2:30pm. **Closed:** Tues following public hols. **Bus:** 5, 6, 7, 7A, 8, or 10.

MARSH'S LIBRARY, St. Patrick's Close. Tel. 543511.

This impressive library was built by Archbishop Narcissus Marsh in 1701, and was the very first public library in Ireland. It houses four main book collections of more than 25,000 volumes, and the archbishop's wide-ranging interests extended to theology (of course), medicine, ancient history, Syriac, Greek, and Latin and French literature. The notes he scribbled in many of the volumes are still legible, and there are some 250 volumes in manuscript. Since these priceless books cannot be checked out to the public, Marsh's Library really qualifies as a literary museum. In fact, to peruse any one, you'll be ushered into an elegant wired alcove not too unlike an upmarket cage.

Admission: Free, but a voluntary contribution is appreciated.

Open: Mon and Wed–Fri 10am–12:45pm, Sat 10:30am–12:45pm. Anyone involved in research can make application for other hours.

IRISH ARCHITECTURAL ARCHIVE, 63 Merrion Sq. Tel. 763430.

While neither a museum nor an art gallery, this archive will certainly intrigue anyone interested in Ireland's past. Since its establishment in 1976, the archive has become the central source of information on architecturally and historically significant Irish buildings from 1600 to the present. In addition to more than 30,000 pictures, the reference library holds a vast number of publications such as pamphlets, press cuttings, historical manuscripts, and engravings. While the emphasis is on architecture, as you would expect, all sorts of extraneous information can be gleaned from browsing through the box files of photos, many of which are fascinating shots of landscapes, period village street scenes, craftsmen such as thatchers and masons at work, a hunt meet at a country mansion, etc. Who knows, the cottage from which your ancestors left for America, long since demolished, may show up in one of these old pictures! Pamphlets from the past also make good reading, while giving unique insights into Ireland's social history.

Admission: Free.

Open: Tues–Fri 10am–1pm, Sat 2–5pm.

CUSTOMS HOUSE AND THE FOUR COURTS

Two of Dublin's more impressive sights are on the north bank of the Liffey, especially at night when floodlights illuminate the noble outlines of the 1791 Customs House on Customs House Quay and the dignified, domed Four Courts building on Inns Quay. Both were burned-out shells after the 1921 Troubles, but have been totally restored and are now in use for their original functions.

Admission: Free.

Open: Four Courts, Mon–Fri 9:30am–5pm (closed Aug–Sept and public hols); court sittings are Mon–Fri 11am–1pm and 2–4:45pm. As we go to press, opening hours for the Customs House have not been established, pending completion of current renovations. **Bus:** Any city-center bus to O'Connell Street.

WHITEFRIAR STREET CARMELITE CHURCH, 57 Aungier St. Tel. 758821.

If you've a romantic bone in your body, you may well want to drop in to pay your respects to that saint most revered by lovers around the globe, St. Valentine. The saint was martyred when he was beheaded about A.D. 269, but his remains were moved here from Rome in 1835, presented as a gift from Pope Gregory XVI to Fr. Spratt, prior of this church, in recognition of his holy work. February 14, the saint's feast day, was once believed to be the day on which birds mated and the day on which an unmarried girl should choose her sweetheart (the origin, of course, of the Valentine card custom). As for the church itself, it stands on the site of a 1539 Carmelite priory, although this structure dates back only to 1825. Look for the impressive, life-size oak figure of Our Lady of Dublin and ask about her rather checkered history.

Admission: Free.

Open: Mon, Wed–Thurs, and Sat 8am–6:30pm; Tues and Fri 8am–9pm; Sun 8am–7:30pm. **Bus:** 16, 16A, 19, 19A, 22, or 22A.

NATIONAL BOTANIC GARDENS, Botanic Rd., Glasnevin. Tel. 374388.

The gardens were founded in 1795 by the Royal Dublin Society to "increase and foster taste for practical and scientific botany." Spread over 50 acres of an estate that once was the home of the poet Thomas Tickell, they are now under the direction of the Department of Agriculture and Fisheries. In addition to exotic trees, shrubbery, and tropical plants, there is an economic garden (for economic and poisonous plants), a vegetable garden, and a lawn garden. Just inside the gates you'll find Thomas Moore's famous "Last Rose of Summer."

Admission: Free.

Open: Summer, Mon–Sat 11am–6pm; Sun 2–6pm; winter, Mon–Sat 9am–sunset, Sun 2pm–sunset. **Bus:** 13, 19, 34, or 34A.

ST. ANNE'S PARK ROSE GARDEN, Mount Prospect Ave., Clontarf.

This is one of the prettiest in the city, with climbers, floribunda, hybrid tea, and old garden roses in profusion. In April and May, daffodils are in full bloom.

Admission: Free.
Open: Daily dawn–dusk. **Bus:** 44A or 30.

COOL FOR KIDS

The younger set will find many engaging attractions in Dublin. There's special delight for children in the **Natural History Museum,** natural history exhibits in the **National Museum** (Merrion Street building), the *Irish Life Viking Adventure,* and **St. Stephen's Green** (see above for details). Those listed below will also keep them quite happy during their Dublin stay.

THE PHOENIX PARK AND DUBLIN ZOO, entrances from Parkgate St. and N. Circular Rd. Tel. 213021.

Northwest of the city center, with its main entrance on Parkgate Street, this is one of the world's most beautiful parks, and is always referred to by Dubliners as "The" Phoenix Park. Within its nearly 2,000 acres are the residence of Ireland's president, that of the American ambassador, the lovely **People's Gardens,** the **Zoological Gardens** and **Dublin Zoo,** and the **Phoenix Park Racecourse.** Its lofty trees shade all manner of humans during daylight hours and a free-roaming herd of deer after dark.

The zoo is especially noted for breeding lions and other large cats, having bred the first lion cubs in captivity in 1857. Its fame also rests on the picturesque landscaping and gardens surrounding two natural lakes (alive with pelicans, flamingos, and scores of ducks and geese) and the spacious outdoor enclosures that house all manner of animals and birds. Youngsters will delight in the small **Children's Zoo,** where they can take a pony ride, pet tame animals, and wish on the Wishing Seat. Treetops, the glass-enclosed fast-food restaurant, provides high-quality food at budget prices, and the Garden Café and Lakeside Ice Cream Parlour have outdoor umbrella-table service.

Admission: Park free; zoo, IR£3.30 ($5.80) adults, IR£1.60 ($2.80) children 3–14 and seniors, free for children under 3; IR£10.50 ($18.40) family ticket.
Open: Park, daily 24 hours; zoo, summer, Mon–Sat 9:30am–6pm, Sun 11am–6pm (varying hours during winter months, depending on daylight hours). **Bus:** 10, 25, 26, or 51.

NATIONAL WAX MUSEUM, Granby Row, Parnell Sq. Tel. 726340.

Grownups as well as children will be enchanted by the exhibits centered around the heroes and legends from Ireland's past. Life-size figures include Robert Emmet, Wolfe Tone, Parnell, the leaders of the heroic 1916 Uprising, and such literary luminaries as Joyce, Yeats, and their contemporaries. The crowning touch is an excellent educational narrative for each, activated by the push of a button.

As for the young fry, they'll want to head straight for the **Children's World of Fairytale and Fantasy,** a wonderland that will set their imaginations flying. There's even a **Kingdom of Fairytales,** where they'll set off on their own magical journey in search of the genie and his wondrous lamp. You may, however, want to think twice before letting their little feet wander into the **Chamber of Horrors,** where horrible screams and the clanking of chains can send the imagination veering off the happy track of fairytales and fantasy.

Admission: IR£2.50 ($4.40) adults, IR£1.50 ($2.65) children.
Open: Mon–Sat 10am–5:30pm, Sun 1–5:30pm. **Bus:** 11, 13, 16, 22, or 22A.

SPECIAL-INTEREST SIGHTSEEING

FOR THE LITERARY ENTHUSIAST

Ireland's greatest gift to the rest of the world may well be its writers, whose keen insights into human foibles are timeless and universal. From this sparsely populated little island have sprung some of civilization's greatest wordsmiths; and a good many of them were born, lived, or died in Dublin. While some of the landmarks connected with them have disappeared and others have changed, the following will surely bring you closer to those whose legacy of words has prodded the minds and hearts of many.

The house at 7 Hoey's Court where **Jonathan Swift** was born is now gone, but it stood very near St. Patrick's Cathedral, where he was dean for 32 years, and where he was laid to rest. Listen for his footsteps, too, at Trinity College, where he was a student. **Thomas Moore** also studied at Trinity, and you'll find his birthplace at 12 Aungier Street. Both **George Bernard Shaw** and **Oscar Wilde** began their tumultuous lives in Dublin in the year 1854, Wilde at 21 Westland Row and Shaw at 33 Synge Street. The birthplace of **W. B. Yeats** was 5 Sandymount Avenue, and 42 Fitzwilliam Square was his residence from 1928 to 1932.

James Joyce was born in Rathgar at 41 Brighton Square West, and from his self-imposed exile mapped the face of his native city in unremitting detail. The Martello Tower he occupied with **Oliver St. John Gogarty** in 1904 is now a Joyce museum (see section 1, "County Dublin," in Chapter 6). His devoted followers can trace the Dublin meanderings of his Leopold Bloom as unerringly as if Joyce had written a guidebook rather than his *Ulysses* masterpiece. This is such an intriguing pastime for visitors that the Tourist Board offers a *Ulysses Map of Dublin* of the book's 18 episodes for a small charge, and if you should be in Dublin on June 16, there are scores of events commemorating "Bloomsday."

Sean O'Casey was born in the Dublin slums in 1884. He became the Abbey Theatre's leading dramatist until he broke with them in 1928. He recorded his experiences in his 4-volume autobiography, which is a vivid and realistic chronicle of Dublin and Ireland in the first part of the century.

Brendan Behan captured the heart and soul of modern Dublin in words that his countryfolk sometimes agonized over but never denied. He was born in Dublin in 1921 and remained its irreverent, wayward son until the early end of his life in 1964, when the president of Ireland led a huge crowd to Glasnevin Cemetery for the interment. His spirit no doubt still roams the city streets, reveling in the things that have changed and those that have remained the same.

Novelist **Elizabeth Bowen** was born at 15 Herbert Place, off Lower Baggot Street, in 1899; **Cornelius Ryan,** author of outstanding World War II novels, first saw the light of day in 1920 at 33 Heytesbury Street, off the South Circular Road; and **Bram Stoker,** whose *Dracula* lives after him, was born at 15 Marino Crescent, Clontarf, in 1847.

One terrific way to see this "writers' city" as its writers have seen it is to join the **Dublin Literary Pub Crawl.** This, you understand, is no heavy academic exercise—rather, it's an evening of the sort of conviviality that sustained the likes of Beckett, Joyce, Behan, and Kavanagh, in pubs that sometimes figured in their written works. The spirit and the characters that inspired them are still very much in evidence, and you'll finish the evening with a new insight to your favorite Irish author's Dublin life after dark. From June through August, the tour begins at the Bailey pub on Duke Street every Tuesday, Wednesday, and Thursday at 7:30pm. It costs a mere £5 ($8.75), and you pay for your own drinks. You can book at the Tourist Office on O'Connell Street, or call 747733 or 540228.

DUBLIN'S ARCHITECTURE

Dublin is a fascinating mixture of architectural styles, and the following are a few buildings that are of particular interest. Most are described in detail above.

St. Patrick's Cathedral, Patrick's Close, built between 1220 and 1254; **St. Michan's Church,** Church Street, dating from 1095, rebuilt in 1685; the **General Post Office,** O'Connell Street, designed by Francis Johnston and completed in 1818; the **Custom House,** Custom House Quay, designed by James Gandon in 1781; **Dublin Castle,** Castle Street, parts of which date to 1204, others from the 1400s; **Trinity College,** College Green, founded in 1592, present buildings dating from 1755–59, with a cruciform complex centered around quadrangles and gardens, and

300-foot Palladian facade designed by Henry Keene and John Sanderford; **Leinster House,** Kildare Street, a 1745 mansion designed by Richard Castle for the Earl of Kildare; the **Bank of Ireland,** College Green, designed by Sir Edward Lovett Pearce in 1729 as the Parliament House; **Four Courts,** Inn Quay, designed by James Gandon in 1785, destroyed by fire in 1922, and rebuilt as a square central block with a circular hall, and a shallow dome; **Mansion House,** Dawson Street, the official residence of the Lord Mayor of Dublin, built in 1705; **Powerscourt House,** South William Street, a classic mansion of 1771, designed by Robert Mack, now housing a shopping center, but with many fine architectural details preserved; and **Merrion Square,** with its elegant Georgian mansions.

BREWERY TOURS

GUINNESS HOP STORE, James's Gate. Tel. 536700 ext. 5238.

⭐ A sightseeing attraction in a class by itself is the sprawling Guinness Brewery, set on 60 acres south of the Liffey. The largest brewery in Europe, Guinness exports more beer than any other company in the world. The rich, dark stout it has produced since 1759 is truly the "wine of Ireland," and you'll no doubt be a devout convert after your second pint (it's sometimes an acquired taste!). Because of an extensive modernization and reconstruction program, there are no tours of the plant at present, but you are invited to call by the Guinness Hop Store (it's clearly signposted and just around the corner from the brewery front gate). The historic four-story building—which, as its name suggests, was once the storehouse for the hops used in brewing Guinness—has been carefully refurbished and restored, and you'll see a film about the brewing process, sample a glass or two of the dark stuff in a traditional-style bar, and browse through the Brewery Museum, which includes interesting sections on coopering and transport. If you'd like a souvenir of your visit, there's a very good shop on the premises.

Admission: IR£1 ($1.75) adults, 50p (90¢) children.
Open: Mon–Fri 10am–4pm. **Closed:** Bank hols. **Bus:** 21A, 78, or 78A.

THE IRISH WHISKEY CORNER, Bow St. Tel. 725566.

⭐ The unique blend of barley, yeast, and water that is Irish whiskey was first (back in the 6th century) called *uisce beatha* ("*ish*-ke *ba*-ha"), which translates as "the water of life." When King Henry II's soldiers spread its fame to England, the name took on an anglicized sound, *fuisce,* before eventually evolving into "whiskey." From the beginning, nothing about this blend was usual, and today it is still unique, even in the spelling of its name. It is the only European whisk(e)y that is spelled with an "e"!

The Irish Whiskey Corner has been established by the Irish Distillers Group (which includes all seven of the great whiskey houses in Ireland) to present an all-encompassing picture of the history of Irish whiskey, as well as a demonstration of how it's made. The old warehouse that was once used to mature whiskey has been converted into an exhibition center where you can view a short film on whiskey's history, see a copper-pot still and distillery model and other implements of the trade, view the lifelike figure of a cooper fashioning the oak casks that are so important in its aging, and perhaps be chosen as one of four tasters to try various brands. To top things off, everyone gets a sample in the Ball of Malt bar.

Admission: Free.
Open: Check with the Tourist Board for exact hours of tours.

WALKING TOUR — OLD DUBLIN

Start: Capel Street Bridge.
Finish: River Liffey Quays.
Time: About 3 to 4 hours.
Best Times: Weekdays.
Worst Times: Sundays during church services or bank holidays.

If you'd like to wander Dublin's streets on your own, begin south of the Liffey at the Capel Street Bridge and walk east toward Dame Street. On your right is the Palace Street gate of:

1. **Dublin Castle.** Continuing east, turn right from Dame Street onto South Great George's Street, a broad and colorful shopping street. Look for the Victorian shopping arcade on the left, which has all the vigor and color of an old-time bazaar. At the end of the arcade is South William Street, where you will find the:

2. **Dublin Civic Museum.** Continue on Aungier Street (an extension of South Great George's Street) to Whitefriar Street, location of the:

3. **Whitefriar Street Carmelite Church.** Poet and songwriter Tom Moore was born at no. 12 on this street.

   Aungier Street now becomes Wexford Street. Turn right onto Lower Kevin Street, and cross Heytesbury Street onto Upper Kevin Street, where you will pass the Garda barracks before coming to:

4. **Marsh's Library.** Walk west to the intersection at The Coombe, which marks the beginning of the Liberties.

   Turn right into Patrick Street to reach:

5. **St. Patrick's Cathedral.** Continue uphill to Christchurch Place and:

6. **Christ Church Cathedral.** Walk west from Christchurch Place to High Street, where you can see a restoration of a portion of the ancient city wall and the only surviving city gate (down toward the river).

   A short walk south on High Street brings you to:

7. **Tailor's Hall,** which dates from 1796 and is Dublin's only surviving guild hall. Retrace your steps to Cornmarket Square and continue on Thomas Street, which holds:

8. **St. Catherine's Church,** on your left. This is where Robert Emmet, the patriot, was hanged in 1803; the church is open to the public.

   The continuation of Thomas Street is James's Street, home of the:

9. **Guinness Brewery.** James's Street forks to the right via Bow Lane to:

10. **St. Patrick's Hospital,** which was founded in 1764, funded by a bequest from Jonathan Swift, and is still in use as a psychiatric center.

    A sharp right turn brings you onto Steeven's Lane, heading back toward the river, where you will pass the striking:

11. **Heuston Station** rail depot en route to the river. When you reach the:

12. **Quays along the Liffey,** turn right to walk back to the city center along the quays, with a good view of the Four Courts on the north side of the Liffey.

WALKING TOUR — GEORGIAN DUBLIN

Start: College Green.
Finish: Fitzwilliam Square.
Time: 2 hours.
Best Times: Daylight hours.
Worst Times: Sunday, when shops are closed.

Begin your walking tour at the foot of Westmoreland Street at:

1. **College Green.** On the right is the Bank of Ireland, and just opposite is Trinity College. From College Green, walk south onto Grafton Street, now a pedestrian mall lined with fashionable shops. Look for Johnson's Court, a narrow lane on your right, which leads to:

2. **Powerscourt House Shopping Centre** (see Section 4, "Savvy Shopping," below). Returning to Grafton Street, walk south to:

3. **St. Stephen's Green.** The north side of the Green was once known as "Beaux Walk," and now houses some of Dublin's most prestigious clubs.

   Follow St. Stephen's Green North to Dawson Street, site of the:

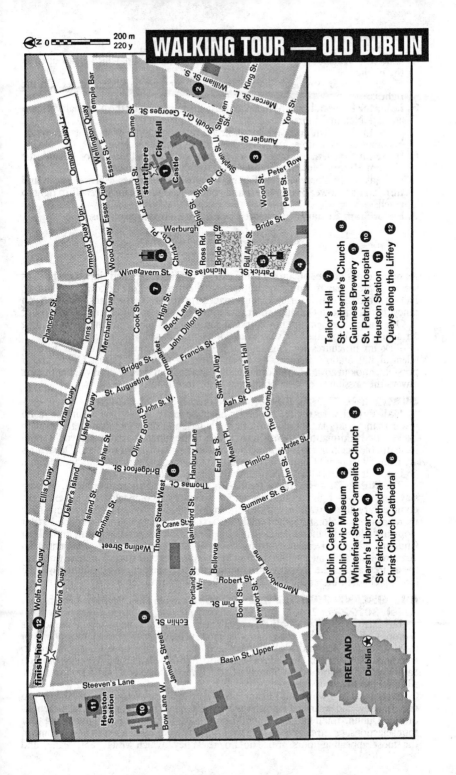

WALKING TOUR — OLD DUBLIN

200 m
220 y

IRELAND
Dublin

1 Dublin Castle
2 Dublin Civic Museum
3 Whitefriar Street Carmelite Church
4 Marsh's Library
5 St Patrick's Cathedral
6 Christ Church Cathedral
7 Tailor's Hall
8 St. Catherine's Church
9 Guinness Brewery
10 St Patrick's Hospital
11 Heuston Station
12 Quays along the Liffey

4. Mansion House, residence of the Lord Mayor of Dublin, which is not open to the public.

Return to St. Stephen's Green North and continue to Kildare Street. On the right is:

5. Leinster House, home of Ireland's parliament, flanked by the National Museum and the National Library.

From the north end of Kildare Street, turn right onto Nassau Street, which becomes Leinster Street and then Clare Street before reaching:

6. Merrion Square. Around the square, are the National Gallery of Ireland, the Natural History Museum, and the Irish Architectural Archive.

Walk south along Merrion Square West, which becomes Merrion Street, and turn left into Lower Baggot Street and continue to Fitzwilliam Street. Turn right to reach:

7. Fitzwilliam Square, surrounded by elegant Georgian mansions.

ORGANIZED TOURS
BUS TOURS

As pointed out above, organized tours can be terrific budget and time stretchers, as well as a great way to save shoe leather and the mental effort of advance planning. Dublin is blessed with an array of tours that can get you to virtually any attraction you fancy. If your time in Dublin is short, this is one of the best ways to make the most of it. One thing to remember, however: On Saturday and Sunday, many of the leading attractions are closed, so be sure to check when choosing your tour.

Pick up brochures for Dublin Bus (59 Upper O'Connell Street), Bus Eireann (Central Bus Station, Busaras, on Store Street) or from the Tourist Office, and if possible, book in advance. You can usually join a tour on the day of travel, but there is always the possibility of disappointment if the tour is fully booked.

DUBLIN BUS TOURS, 59 Upper O'Connell St. Tel. 734222.

Half-day city tours are a wonder of organization, giving you a glimpse of no fewer than 55 city landmarks, historic buildings, and other points of interest, with background information on every one. To add to the fun, if the day is fine, you'll travel in an double-deck, open-air bus (top deck enclosed in inclement weather). Departures are from 59 Upper O'Connell Street, April to October, daily at 10:15am and 2:15pm, and fares are IR£6 ($10.50) for adults, IR£3 ($5.25) for children.

The **Dublin Bus Heritage Trail Tour** is a sort of *semi*-organized tour. You can stay on the bus right around its entire itinerary, accompanied by an excellent commentary all the way, or you can opt to hop off at any of 10 top attractions for a more in-depth exploration, then catch the next bus to continue the tour. The 10 tour stops include such landmarks as Trinity College, St. Patrick's Cathedral, and Christ Church Cathedral. Departures from 59 Upper O'Connell Street are frequent from 10am to 4pm, and you can join the tour at any one of the 10 stops. Purchase tickets at the address above, the Tourist Office, or directly from the bus driver. Adults pay IR£5 ($8.75); children under 16, IR£2.50 ($4.40)—and your ticket is valid all day.

BUS EIREANN SIGHTSEEING TOURS, Central Bus Station (Busaras). Tel. 302222 or 74467.

Bus Eireann also has a **half-day city tour,** with admission to several attractions (Trinity College and the *Book of Kells,* etc.) included in the fare. Other points of interest include St. Patrick's Cathedral and the IDA Enterprise Centre, home to traditional Irish crafts. Departures March to mid-November are Monday through Saturday at 11:15am and on Sunday at 10:30am; fares are IR£7 ($12.25) for adults, IR£3.50 ($6.15) for children.

Even if you're driving, Bus Eireann's **full- and half-day excursions** can save you time, money, and wear and tear on the nervous system in exploring those attractions outside Dublin. You'll find full descriptions of most in Chapter 6, and in making your tour selections, *be sure to check that they run on the day you want to book.* Some of the most appealing tours are: The Boyne Valley, which visits Tara, Slane, and

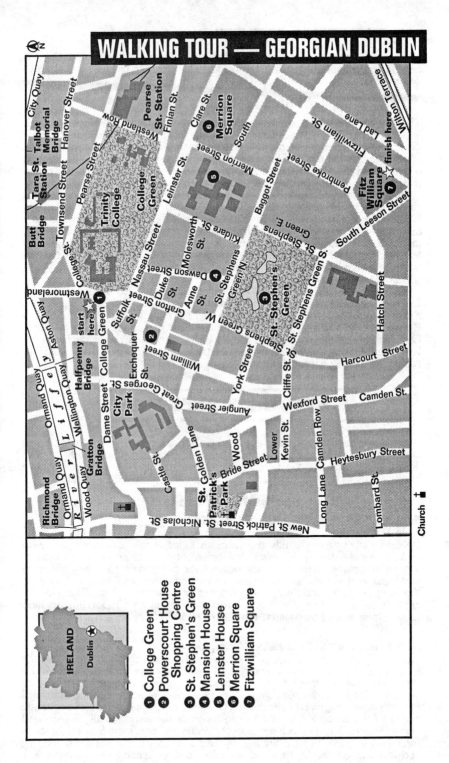

WALKING TOUR — GEORGIAN DUBLIN

IRELAND
Dublin

1 College Green
2 Powerscourt House Shopping Centre
3 St. Stephen's Green
4 Mansion House
5 Leinster House
6 Merrion Square
7 Fitzwilliam Square

Church

Newgrange; Avondale, Glendalough, and the Wicklow Hills; Powerscourt Gardens and Pine Forest; and Russborough House and Blessington Lakes. Days and hours of departure vary, and fares average IR£10 ($17.50) for adults, IR£5 ($8.75) for children.

GUIDED WALKING TOURS

The Tourist Office has an excellent guidebook for the signposted **۞ Heritage Trail** walking tour of Dublin, which features Georgian Dublin and major points of interest in the city center south of the Liffey. No matter what walking tour you follow, however, remember that Dublin is *not* laid out in simple grid style—it has evolved over the centuries into a patchwork of tiny lanes and streets that can change names three times in as many blocks.

Tour Guides Ireland (tel. 679-4291), an organization of expert and entertaining guides, gives you a choice of three marvelous guided walking tours: "The Literary Walk," "The Medieval Walk," and "The Georgian Walk." There are two walks daily during summer months, with a different tour in the morning and the afternoon, making it quite feasible to take in the two that interest you most in a single day if your feet hold out. You meet at Bewley's Museum in Bewley's Oriental Café, Grafton Street, and each tour lasts about 2 hours. The cost is IR£4 ($7) per person; IR£10 ($17.50) for families.

One of the best sightseeing buys in Dublin is a 2-hour guided walking tour of the Liberties, including visits to St. Patrick's Cathedral and Christ Church Cathedral, with a knowledgeable commentary all along the way. The tours are organized by **۞ Joe Byrne** (tel. 533407); and the assembly point is the main entrance to Christ Church Cathedral. In summer, tours depart daily at 10:30am and 2pm; during the winter, on Friday and Saturday at 10:30am and on Sunday at 2pm. The cost is IR£3 ($5.25) for adults, IR£1.50 ($2.65) for children.

2. SPECIAL & FREE EVENTS

If you arrive in Dublin during one of these special events, you're in for a real treat—the entire city enters into the spirit of the occasion. Check with the Irish Tourist Board about specific dates the year of your visit; accommodations should be booked as far as possible in advance and will probably cost you a little more.

SPECIAL EVENTS

SPRING SHOW, Ballsbridge. Tel. 680645.

In May of each year, the annual Spring Show action is concentrated in the Royal Dublin Society's show grounds in Ballsbridge. Billed as the "shop window of Irish agriculture and industry," it's a grand exhibition of both, with prizes for sheep, cattle, and pig champions; butter and cheese judgings; sheep-dog trials; pony shows; jumping competitions; and even fashion shows. For the young fry, there are Punch & Judy shows, magic shows, and a baby-sitting crèche to free parents for a ramble around the grounds. All in all, the atmosphere is that of a major country fair, and it draws farm families from around the country, as well as more than a few from across the Channel.

Admission: IR£4 ($7) per day.

KERRYGOLD DUBLIN HORSE SHOW, Dublin.

۞ The undisputed highlight of Ireland's social calendar each year comes with the Kerrygold Dublin Horse Show, usually in August (but be sure to check if this one is high on your list—it was moved up to July in 1990 to avoid conflict with another major European horse show). For one glorious week it draws a sophisticated international crowd, and the city dons its best duds to welcome them, with private and public parties scheduled around the goings-on at the showgrounds of the Royal Dublin Society. There's much pomp and splendor, and even more fun and frolic. As for the show itself, in what are acknowledged to be some of the finest jumping enclosures in the world, there are virtually nonstop jumping competitions. The

Kerrygold Nations Cup for the Aga Khan Trophy competition raises the excitement level on Friday, and the whole thing winds up with the Kerrygold International Grand Prix of Ireland on Saturday. Side events include a fashion competition for the best-dressed lady on Ladies Day, concerts by the army bands, a gorgeous floral display by the Royal Horticultural Society, and an exhibition of the prize-winning exhibits from the Royal Dublin Society's annual crafts competition. It's a great week to be in Dublin, and even 1 day at the showgrounds is bound to net you a score of new Irish friends. It is also probably the most heavily booked week for Dublin accommodations, so book as far in advance as possible.

Admission: IR£40 ($70) for all events, or a 1-day general admission ticket for about IR£8 ($14).

Contact: For a detailed program of events and ticket information, contact the Royal Dublin Society, P.O. Box 121, Ballsbridge, Dublin 4 (tel. 01/680645).

DUBLIN THEATRE FESTIVAL, Dublin.

✪ The Dublin Theatre Festival takes place during the last week of September and the first week of October. It's a unique theatrical celebration that incorporates all of Dublin's theaters and spreads onto the streets, university campuses, and community halls. Innovative Irish drama is offered, and major overseas theater and dance companies perform. Great Irish playwrights such as Behan, Leonard, Friel, and Murphy have been represented, and the festival has been the originator of classics like *Da, Philadelphia Here I Come!, The Importance of Being Earnest, Translations,* and *The Morning After Optimism,* which have gone on to grace the stages of the world. The festival specializes in presenting new Irish work, and the central weekend of the festival offers visitors to Dublin the opportunity to see nine new Irish plays over a period of 3 days. Other highlights are international theater and dance of the highest standards from countries such as Sweden, South Africa, the United States, Britain, France, Germany, and many others, representing all types of theater, from comedy to classics, experimental theater, mime, and musicals. A Festival Club, where the theater-goers mingle with actors, directors, and members of the international press, as well as workshops, exhibitions, and an international theater conference, all make this a very special celebration.

Admission: Varies with individual performances.

Contact: For schedules and ticket information, contact Dublin Theatre Festival, 47 Nassau Street, Dublin 2. It's a good idea to contact them well in advance.

FREE IN DUBLIN

In addition to the admission-free attractions listed in Section 1 of this chapter, Dublin frequently breaks out in special events for which there is no charge at all.

There is something going on in public spaces virtually every day of the week surrounding ✪ **St. Patrick's Day** (March 17). While the big parade on this day itself is not nearly as long or spectacular as many of those in the U.S., it's colorful and fun to watch. The Tourist Board can fill you in on specific happenings around the city during this holiday period.

All sorts of **street entertainment** liven up the city during summer months. Concentrated on the Grafton Street pedestrian mall during summer months are a gaggle of entertainers who run the gamut from folk and traditional music singers to mimes, rock singers, and jugglers. No charge, of course, but the odd coin dropped into the ever-present hat is much appreciated.

3. SPORTS & RECREATION

SPECTATOR SPORTS

Pick your sport, and Dublin probably can come up with an event. The following are highlights of spectator sports in Dublin, but if you have a special interest in a sport not listed (bowling, cricket, etc.), consult the Tourist Board's current "Calendar of Events in Ireland" to see if a tournament or match is on in the Dublin area during your visit.

✪ **GAELIC FOOTBALL**   Matches are regularly held in Croke Park, but the biggy of the year is the All Ireland Football Finals played in mid-September. As with the hurling finals, tickets are scarcer than hen's teeth unless you buy them months and months ahead. Still, it's great fun to share the entire city's excitement even if you can't make it into the park. For details, contact the Gaelic Athletic Association (tel. 01/363222).

HORSE RACING   There are four racecourses in the Dublin area, and meets are scheduled in at least one (sometimes more) during every month of the year. All can be reached by public transportation from the city, and if you insist on driving, be prepared for traffic congestion and a long hike from your parking space to the stands. Horse-racing events for the entire year are listed in the back of the "Calendar of Events in Ireland."

   The Curragh (tel. 045/41205), 30 miles west of Dublin in County Kildare, is the home of Ireland's classic races such as the Kerrygold International Grand Prix. Special buses and trains run from Busarus and Heuston Station on race days. Call for ticket information and race schedules.

   Leopardstown (tel. 893607) is on the outskirts of the city and can be reached via Bus no. 86. Phone for schedules and ticket information.

   Punchestown (tel. 045/97704) is 23 miles southwest of Dublin in County Kildare, and special buses run from Busaras on race days.

   Fairyhouse (tel. 01/256167) is some 16 miles to the north of the city in County Meath, and there are special race day buses from Busaras.

HURLING   The All Ireland Hurling Finals are held in Croke Park the first week in September. Tickets are sold out months in advance, but that doesn't dampen the enthusiasm of fans gathered around the telly in pubs all over the city. For details of this and all other hurling, soccer, and Gaelic football matches, call the Gaelic Athletic Association (GAA) (tel. 01/363222).

RUGBY   Ireland is regularly represented in international rugby finals, and all home matches for the International Rugby Championship are played at Lansdowne Road stadium, usually in late January or early February. Contact the Tourist Board or call the GAA (see above) for details.

RECREATION

If you'd rather participate than spectate, Dublin is a good venue for most forms of active recreation.

BEACHES   The following afford safe swimming and sandy beaches, and all can be reached by city bus: **Dollymount,** 3½ miles from Dublin; **Claremount,** 9 miles from the city; **Sutton,** 7 miles out; **Portmarnock** (one of the best), 9 miles from Dublin; **Donabate,** 13 miles away; and **Malahide,** 9 miles from Dublin.

BICYCLING   Cyclists should head first for the Tourist Office for a copy of Information Sheet no. 14B, "Cycling—Dublin and the Eastern Seaboard." It outlines cycling tours from Dublin, Dun Laoghaire, and Bray.

   Bikes can be rented from the **Bike Store,** 58 Lower Gardiner Street (tel. 725399 or 725931), which has a good selection of sports and mountain bikes in stock. Raleigh Rent-A-Bike is represented by **McDonald's Cycles Ltd.,** 38 Wexford Street (tel. 752586).

GOLF   There are some 35 golf courses in the Dublin area. Most are private, but nearly all will grant temporary membership to visitors. Those listed below are just a sampling of 18-hole courses; for a complete list, contact the Tourist Office: **Clontarf Golf Club,** 2½ miles from Dublin (tel. 311305); **Dun Laoghaire Golf Club,** 7 miles from Dublin (tel. 801055 or 805166); **Howth Golf Club,** 9 miles from the city (tel. 323055); and the **Royal Dublin Golf Club,** Dollymount, 3 miles from Dublin (tel. 337153).

HIKING/WALKING As I've said before, Dublin is truly a walker's city. Follow a specified route through its streets, on the lookout for sightseeing attractions, or simply pick a neighborhood and walk with no purpose other than pure enjoyment.

A lovely 3-mile walk along coastal roads is that **from Baldoyle to Portmarnock.** There are good Dublin Bay views all along the way, and you'll wind up at one of the Dublin area's best beaches. Take DART to Baldoyle and return to the city from Portmanock via bus no. 32.

Another bracing coastal walk is out in **Dalkey,** beginning at Bulloch harbor, continuing through the village and up Coliemore Road, past Coliemore harbor, stopping in a small seaside park for a breather, and then on to Vico Road, which is a marvelous vantage point for viewing Killiney Bay and Bray Head. It's about a 2-mile walk, and you can get to Bulloch harbor via bus no. 8 from the city center.

Dedicated hikers can tread in the footsteps of the ancient Irish if they walk **The Wicklow Way,** part of which traverses the same route as one of the five great roads radiating from the Hill of Tara. The Wicklow Way begins in Marlay Park, County Dublin, and extends about 132km (80 miles) to Clonegal, County Carlow. It can be done in shorter stages, however, and even one stage will be a memorable experience as you follow sheep trails and old bog roads. The route is set out in detail in the Tourist Board's Information Sheet no. 26B, and it is recommended also that you arm yourself with the Ordinance Survey Map, *Wicklow Way.*

HORSEBACK RIDING Equestrians who yearn to sit a horse in the Dublin area can contact **Ashtown Equestrian Centre,** Castleknock (tel. 383236); **Black Horse Riding School,** Castleknock (tel. 386021); or **Castleknock Equestrian Centre,** Dublin 15 (tel. 201104).

TENNIS You'll find public tennis courts at **Bushy Park,** Terenure (tel. 900320); **Herbert Park,** Ballsbridge (tel. 684364); **Mellowes Road Park,** Finglas; and **St. Anne's Estate,** Dollymount (tel. 313697).

4. SAVVY SHOPPING

THE SHOPPING SCENE

The Tourist Board issues an excellent free booklet called "Shopping in Dublin" to help you find anything you could possibly want to purchase in the city. It contains a very good center-city map, as well as a guide to sizes (many of which differ from those in America) and Customs regulations.

Gifts of any value can be mailed duty free to addresses outside Ireland.

VAT Return Be sure to save your receipts for the Value-Added Tax refund for all purchases you are taking out of the country (see "Saving Money on Shopping" in Section 4, "Enjoying Ireland on a Budget," in Chapter 3).

Main Shopping Areas Principal city-center shopping areas south of the Liffey are **Grafton Street and Wicklow Street;** north of the river, shopping is best on **O'Connell Street and Henry Street.**

Shopping Hours Unless otherwise stated, the shops listed below are open Monday through Saturday from 9am to 5pm; closed on Sunday.

SHOPPING CENTERS & DEPARTMENT STORES
South of the Liffey

POWERSCOURT TOWN HOUSE CENTRE, Clarendon St.

If you just can't get excited about shopping centers, wait till you see this one! It's set in a 1774 mansion built by Lord Powerscourt, and the house and courtyard have been expertly renovated to accommodate small shops, wine

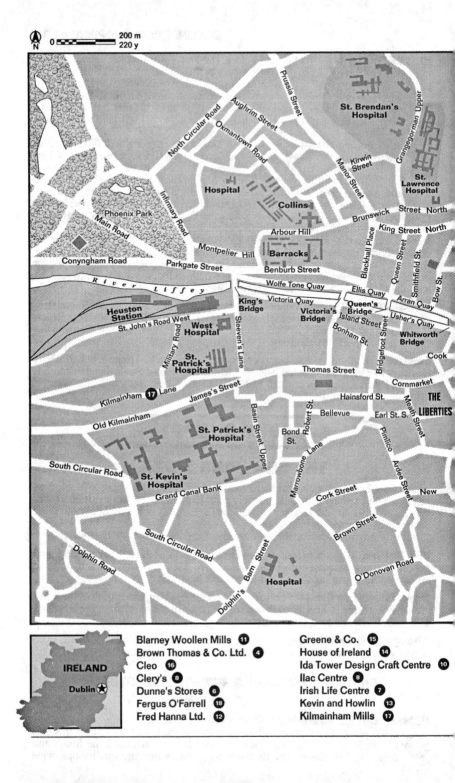

Blarney Woollen Mills	11	Greene & Co.	15
Brown Thomas & Co. Ltd.	4	House of Ireland	14
Cleo	16	Ida Tower Design Craft Centre	10
Clery's	8	Ilac Centre	8
Dunne's Stores	6	Irish Life Centre	7
Fergus O'Farrell	18	Kevin and Howlin	13
Fred Hanna Ltd.	12	Kilmainham Mills	17

IRELAND

Dublin ★

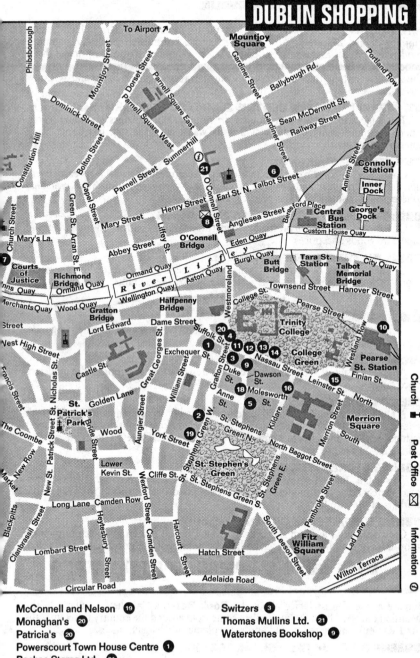

DUBLIN SHOPPING

McConnell and Nelson ⑲
Monaghan's ⑳
Patricia's ⑳
Powerscourt Town House Centre ①
Roches Stores Ltd. ㉑
Royal Hibernian Way ⑤
St. Stephen's Green Centre ②

Switzers ③
Thomas Mullins Ltd. ㉑
Waterstones Bookshop ⑨

Church ✚   Post Office ⊠   Information ⓘ

bars, and restaurants. Among the shops, there's an antiques gallery, high-fashion clothing shops, designer shoes and bags, and a hairdresser. Several restaurants, moderately priced, and a resident pianist in the central courtyard help make this a good place to begin your shopping, or just your browsing, for that matter. Look for the sign on Grafton Street at Johnson's Court between Chatham Street and Wicklow Streets.

ST. STEPHEN'S GREEN CENTRE, Grafton St. and St. Stephen's Green.
This huge, striking, and very modern structure is Dublin's largest shopping center. There are more than 100 shops within its walls, encompassing just about every category in existence.

SWITZERS, 92 Grafton St.
Considered by some to be Dublin's leading department store, Switzers carries very upmarket goods in a wide variety of clothing, housewares, furnishings, personal toiletries and cosmetics, linens, jewelry, gifts, etc.

BROWN THOMAS & CO. LTD., 15-20 Grafton St.
One of the city's most prestigious department stores, with both upmarket and moderate goods and prices.

ROYAL HIBERNIAN WAY, Dawson St.
On the site of the old Royal Hibernian Hotel, this shopping arcade holds some 30 shops, including high fashion, and a number of small restaurants.

North of the Liffey

ILAC CENTRE, Talbot St.
Good concentration of moderately priced shops, offering a wide variety of goods. Restaurants are in the moderate price range.

IRISH LIFE CENTRE, Moore St.
Another cluster of shops and restaurants offering goods and food in the moderate price range.

CLERY'S, O'Connell St.
A Dublin tradition, Clery's is the oldest and largest department store on the north side of the river. It's a complete department store, stocking everything from upmarket fashion, jewelry, and gifts to housewares and hardware. There's a good inexpensive restaurant on the premises.

ROCHES STORES LTD., 54/62 Henry St.
This is the Dublin branch of a department-store chain with good, middle-of-the-road merchandise and moderate prices. It's a good place to shop for fashionable clothing at sensible prices.

DUNNE'S STORES, ILAC Centre, Talbot St.
Crowded, busy, and not much charm, but Dunne's is a terrific place to pick up good buys in clothing, as well as the little necessities of life (toothpaste, hose, etc.).

BEST BUYS & WHERE TO FIND THEM
BOOKS

Inquire at the Tourist Office about the **Book Barrow Fair** held regularly in the Mansion House. About 30 booksellers come from around the country to set up stalls for 1 day only, many selling old and rare volumes for bargain prices.

GREENE & CO., 16 Clare St. Tel. 762554.
Book lovers can browse for hours through two floors of new and secondhand books, or the rows of trays out front on the sidewalk. The staff is both friendly and helpful, and they'll hunt down scarce or out-of-print books at no charge. They'll send a free mail-order catalog, and they accept most major credit cards.

FRED HANNA LTD., 27/29 Nassau St. Tel. 771255 or 771936.
They have good stocks of books of Irish interest here, as well as extensive stocks of

the newest publications and children's, secondhand, and antiquarian books. They'll mail overseas.

WATERSTONES BOOKSHOP, 7 Dawson St. Tel. 791415.

 A branch of the English chain, its stocks are extensive, and there are special reading areas. They have a good book-search service, as well as mail- and telephone-order departments. Late hours accommodate office workers and weary travelers: Monday through Friday from 8:30am to 9pm, on Saturday from 8:30am to 7pm, and on Sunday from noon to 7pm.

CRAFTS

IDA TOWER DESIGN CRAFT CENTRE, Pearse St. at Grand Canal Quay.

This is where you'll find all manner of craftspeople in more than 30 workshops. Good buys in traditional crafts: gold and silver jewelry, handmade pottery, designer hand-knits for ladies and children, pewter, and heraldic art. There's also a restaurant with lunch and snacks available every day except Saturday.

FASHION/FABRICS

BLARNEY WOOLLEN MILLS, 21/23 Nassau St. Tel. 710068.

This shop specializes in Irish sweaters, Pallas linen womenswear, and Donegal tweed suits and coats styled by leading Irish designers. They have a good selection of Waterford crystal and Belleek china, and will mail anywhere in the world.

CLEO, 18 Kildare St. Tel. 761421.

Around the corner from the Shelbourne Hotel, this shop specializes in designer woolens, as well as linens.

KEVIN AND HOWLIN, 31 Nassau St. Tel. 770257.

Tweed tailor-made jackets and suits for men are good value here, and last so long they're an investment rather than just a purchase. There's also a large range of ready-made men's clothing. It's located at the bottom of Dawson Street, facing Trinity College.

KILMAINHAM MILLS, Kilmainham Lane. Tel. 770051 or 773716.

Reputed to be the oldest working mill in the world, its products are exported to top designer houses in the U.S. and Europe. You can watch yarn being dyed and designs being laid out, and there's a shop featuring the finished goods.

MONAGHAN'S, Grafton Arcade. Tel. 770823.

 Monaghan's has my highest recommendation for Aran sweaters to fit all members of the family, as well as lambswool, cashmere, Shetland sweaters, and a good stock of menswear. They ship worldwide and offer a mail-order catalog. There's another branch at 4/5 Royal Hibernian Way.

GIFT/SPECIALTY STORES

FERGUS O'FARRELL, 62 Dawson St.

Some of the most unusual replicas of antique Irish jewelry, copper and wood handcrafts, and other top-quality items with historical emphasis can be found here.

HOUSE OF IRELAND, 37/38 Nassau St. Tel. 777473 or 777949. Fax 791023.

This shop is a standout for finding anything from Waterford crystal to Belleek, Wedgwood, Aynsley, and Royal Tara china to fine tweeds, special cashmeres, knitcrafts, linens, Celtic jewelry, pottery, blackthorn walking sticks, and a wide range of quality souvenir items. Of particular interest to Americans are the lovely miniature buildings in the Lilliput Lane Irish Heritage Collection. Chosen by owner Eileen Galligan, who delighted in their quaint view of an Ireland not altogether past, they are a perfect gift for the collector. Start a collection with the Kennedy Homestead, modeled on the Kennedy ancestral home where President Kennedy's great-grandfather was born in 1820. Typical of the many small country stores throughout Ireland, the O'Laceys shop miniature replicates one that would have sold everything from a garden spade to a hatpin. There's even a model of a stone-and-thatch cottage that would have been right at home in *The Quiet Man*. Outstanding service from a friendly staff. They will mail or ship overseas.

MCCONNELL AND NELSON, 38 Grafton St. Tel. 774344.

This is the best place to buy smoked Irish salmon to take home. Sean Nelson and his staff will seal it for travel, and prices are considerably below those at the airport duty-free shops.

PATRICIA'S, Grafton Arcade.

Run by Patricia York, a noted authority on heraldry, the shop has a good stock of heraldic items.

THOMAS MULLINS LTD., 36 Upper O'Connell St. Tel. 741133.

⭐ Standing beside the Gresham Hotel, this shop sells a long list of Irish-made goods—Waterford crystal, Belleek china, Royal Tara, Avoca hand-knits, Aran's Irish product lines, and many other select gift items.

RECORDS

WALTONS MUSICAL GALLERY, 2/5 N. Frederick St. Tel. 747805.

The best all-around music store in Dublin is at the top of O'Connell Street. The stock of Irish traditional records and sheet music is tremendous, and they sell a complete line of musical instruments.

READERS RECOMMEND

Patrick Flood, Gold and Silversmith, in the Powerscourt Town House Centre in downtown Dublin. "Patrick Flood does his own designing and crafting, and has reasonable prices on silver Claddagh rings and other fine jewelry."—N. Rounsefell and S. Gilmore, Baton Rouge, La.

5. EVENING ENTERTAINMENT

THE PERFORMING ARTS

MUSICAL CONCERTS

NATIONAL CONCERT HALL, Earlsfort Terrace. Tel. 711533.

⭐ A splendid auditorium that features first-rate musical events. The prestigious National Symphony Orchestra and the Irish Chamber Orchestra perform here regularly, and visiting artists run the gamut from harpists to jazz stars. During just 1 month, the productions here included a performance of *The Merry Widow*, a series of jazz concerts, the Dresden Philharmonic Orchestra, a Folk Aid Concert for

---

MAJOR CONCERT/PERFORMANCE HALLS

Abbey Theatre	Tel. 787222
Gate Theatre	Tel. 744045
National Concert Hall	Tel. 711533

Ireland, the Johann Strauss Orchestra of Vienna, a recital by an international opera singer, and about a dozen others! This is superb entertainment at bargain-basement prices. Check with the Concert Hall or the Tourist Office to see what's on during your visit.
Prices: Tickets IR£5–IR£8 ($8.75–$14).

THEATER

Tickets for all theaters can be purchased at box offices or through **Brown Thomas** (tel. 776861) and **Switzer's** (tel. 776821) department stores on Grafton Street.

ABBEY THEATRE, Lower Abbey St. Tel. 787222. Fax 01/729177.

This is the national repertory company, born in 1898 when Augusta Lady Gregory, W. B. Yeats, and Edward Martyn determined to perform Irish plays with Irish casts. It provided a voice for such passionate writers as Sean O'Casey and J. M. Synge, even when conservative Irish audiences rioted at the showing of Synge's *Playboy of the Western World.* Siobhan McKenna, Cyril Cusack, Sara Allgood, and Barry Fitzgerald are just a few of the stage talents who blossomed to stardom through their training at the Abbey. The original Abbey was quite small, and when it burned in 1951, members were pleased that the government would have to provide them with more spacious quarters. They did gain a modern, functional theater with the best in stage equipment—but it took 15 years for the government to get the job done. All the while the company performed in a variety theater to stay alive. The theater's emphasis is still on Irish playwrights (contemporary and classic) and Irish actors, with an occasional import. The Abbey stays booked year round, and to avoid disappointment you should contact them directly a minimum of 3 weeks in advance to book the performances you want to see.
Prices: Tickets IR£8–IR£10 ($14–$17.50).

PEACOCK THEATRE, Lower Abbey St. Tel. 787222.

Downstairs at the Abbey, this small theater hosts literary and poetry readings, experimental contemporary drama, and sometimes a retrospective of the classics.
Prices: Tickets IR£6–IR£8 ($10.50–$14).

THE GATE THEATRE, Parnell Sq. Tel. 744045.

Housed in a beautifully restored 18th-century European-style theater, its resident company stages established and modern classics, with a bias toward Irish plays and plays with a strong visual appeal. It's a small, intimate place, with only 370 seats.
Prices: Tickets IR£8–IR£10 ($14–$17.50). Free student tickets on a standby basis (for information, call 01/744368) and special group rates available.

THE PROJECT ARTS CENTRE, 39 E. Essex St. Tel. 712321.

Located in an interesting old Dublin neighborhood that was once known as "Smock Alley," this is an artists' cooperative where anything might happen, from poetry readings to rock music to the best of new Irish writing and productions of European theater classics. For the past 3 years the Project has won most of the principal Harveys (the Irish equivalent of the Oscars), including best actor, best music, best set design, and best costume design. Late-night Friday and Saturday shows in summer feature Irish and European left-wing cabaret artists. There is free admission to the gallery and other events such as contemporary music (most Saturday afternoons at 2:30pm).
Prices: Tickets about IR£6 ($10.50); 11:30pm late-night summer shows Fri–Sat IR£5 ($8.75); discounts for students, the unemployed, and senior citizens at 8pm shows.

THE GAIETY THEATRE, S. King St. Tel. 771717.

The Gaiety presents contemporary plays and features rollicking revues showcasing Ireland's beloved "house comedienne," Maureen Potter. There are pantomimes each Christmas, and frequent appearances of visiting artists.
Prices: Vary with the production, but tickets average about IR£6 ($10.50).

OLYMPIA THEATRE, Dame St. Tel. 778962.

This grand old ornate theater is very much in the music-hall style, and its program through the year can vary widely, from contemporary plays to musicals to opera.

Prices: Vary with the production.

EBLANA THEATRE, Store St. Tel. 746707.

 This intimate little theater is downstairs in Busaras (the Central Bus Station), and has made quite a name for itself in recent years for outstanding productions of contemporary plays.

Prices: Tickets about IR£5 ($8.75).

TRADITIONAL IRISH MUSIC & DANCE

To hear Irish music as it pours from the Irish heart in Ireland is something you almost always have to stumble onto when the music and song is totally unplanned. In Dublin, however, that same joyous or melancholy or rebellious spirit is yours to share out at Monkstown. **Comhaltas Ceoltoiri Eireann,** the organization dedicated to preserving Irish culture in all its forms, sponsors the functions listed below in its own headquarters building there, as well as some remarkable performing troupes of dancers, singers, and musicians who tour around the country during summer months. Keep an eye out for them as you travel, or inquire at local Tourist Offices. Admissions average about IR£4 ($7).

CULTURLANN NA HEIREANN, 32 Belgrave Sq., Monkstown. Tel. 80029.

 Some kind of traditional entertainment is on every night of the week, but to hear some of the best musicians in the country, go along on Friday, Saturday, or Sunday. Fiddlers fiddle, pipers pipe, whistle players whistle, dancers take to the floor, and singers lift their fine Irish voices in informal sessions that bear little resemblance to the staged performances mentioned above. Things get under way about 9pm and carry on until 12:30am.

Admission: IR£1.50 ($2.65).

THE PIPER'S CLUB, 32 Belgrave Sq., Monkstown. Tel. 800295.

The Piper's Club makes Saturday night special, when the members of this popular Dublin institution hold forth during those same hours. Other nights, there's ceili dancing that will get you out on the floor and stage shows featuring step dancers and traditional music. Call to find out what's on when you're there, then hightail it out to Monkstown. If you call 01/800295, you can book an inexpensive dinner of traditional, home-cooked Irish food in their kitchen/restaurant.

Admission: IR£4 ($7).

THE MERCHANT PUB, Bridge St. Tel. 793797.

There's traditional Irish music and ceili (set) dancing at 9:30pm every night except Friday.

HUGHES PUB, Chancery St. Tel. 726540.

Come along at 9:30pm Monday through Wednesday for set dancing.

SLATTERY'S, Capel St. Tel. 727971.

Monday through Thursday there's traditional music and set dancing at 9pm at this popular music pub north of the Liffey.

THE CABARET & DANCING SCENE

Cabaret is one of Dublin's most popular nighttime entertainments, and dancing comes as naturally to the Irish as breathing.

CABARET Cabaret in Dublin is served up with distinctly Irish seasonings: "Danny Boy" and "The Rose of Tralee" are favorites; there's an Irish comic telling Irish jokes; pretty, fresh-faced colleens dancing, singing, playing the harp, etc.; at least one Irish tenor or baritone; and usually one or more of those captivating Irish youngsters in traditional dress to step a lively jig or reel or hornpipe. They're loads of fun and the performances are usually well above average. Audiences are mostly visitors, but with more than a few Irish families in from the country. Most shows are held in hotels, and you can opt for dinner (featuring typical Irish specialties) and the show or the show alone. Prices vary slightly between venues and are shown in the listings below.

The most popular cabarets are those at **Jurys Hotel,** Ballsbridge (tel. 01/ 605000), IR£25.90 ($45.35) for dinner and show, IR£15.50 ($27.15) for show and two drinks; the ○ **Burlington Hotel,** Upper Leeson Street (tel. 605222), IR£25.95 ($45.40) and IR£15 ($26.25); and the **Braemor Rooms** at the Country Club, Churchtown (tel. 01/988664), IR£21 ($36.75) and IR£8.50 ($14.90). You must book ahead, which can be done directly with the hotels or through the Tourist Office.

Gray Line Tours Ireland, 3 Clanwilliam Terrace, Grand Canal Quay, Dublin 2, offers a **Nightlife Tour** that's a handy way to take in cabaret. Book through their desk at the Tourist Office, 14 O'Connell Street (tel. 744466, 787981, 612325, or 619666). They'll pick you up and deliver you back to your hotel. Prices run IR£15 to IR£30.90 ($26.25 to $54.10).

DANCE CLUBS Dancing is the national pastime among Ireland's youth. Although Dublin's discos and nightspots are constantly changing, you'll always find a cluster along Lower Leeson Street (sometimes called "The Strip"), with admission charges of about IR£5 ($8.75) weeknights and IR£8 ($14) weekends. Some are fully licensed, others sell wine only.

THE PUB SCENE

Dublin pubs are their own special kind of entertainment. It makes no difference if you wander into one known for its conversation (*crack*), its music, or its pint (actually, there probably isn't a pub in Dublin that won't tell you they "pull the best pint in the city"). My Irish friends agree that the best possible beginning and/or end to any Dublin evening is in one or more of the city's pubs.

If you're planning on one of the famous "pub crawls," however, better gear up your strongest will to move from one to another. Chances are very slim that you'll be able to walk out of the first one you enter, and very good that you'll settle in with the first pint as a newly appointed "regular," if only for that night.

With more than 1,000 pubs to choose from, every Dubliner you ask will come up with a different favorite (or list of favorites), and there probably won't be a clunker in the lot. The problem is to be selective, and in the section below I'll share with you the ones I've found most interesting. Whatever you do, however, don't confine yourself to my list. Pop into the nearest establishment anywhere in the city when you're overcome with a terrible thirst, and you'll likely come home raving about your own list of favorites.

And for nondrinkers, one last word: Irish pubs are centers of sociability, where you can chat the night away just as happily with nothing stronger than soda.

Pub hours are daily from 10:30am to 11:30pm in summer, to 11pm in winter.

SOUTH OF THE LIFFEY

THE STAG'S HEAD, Dame Court.

This is one much favored by the natives. Getting there is a bit complicated, but easy if you leave College Green on the left side of Dame Street and in the middle of the second block keep your eyes glued to the sidewalk, where you'll find a stag's head set in mosaic right in the pavement. It fronts a small alleyway on the left and at its end you emerge right at this beautiful old pub that has been here since 1770. Coming from Great George Street, turn onto Exchequer Street and keep your eyes peeled for Dame Court. An interesting mix of ages, occupations, and character types drink here in the evening; young executive types, tourists, etc., come for the excellent pub lunch (see Section 5, "Where to Eat," in Chapter 4).

THE OLD STAND, 37 Exchequer St. Tel. 770821.

Named for the "old stand" at Lansdowne Road rugby ground, it sometimes seems that half the rugby players (past and present) have congregated in this popular pub. Celebrated athletes like Moss Kene, Phil Orr, and Ollie Campbell are familiar faces here, and the talk centers around sports 90% of the time. The clientele is made up of all ages and occupations, and at around 5 in the afternoon you'll find some of Dublin's most attractive younger set relaxing after a day of toiling in an inner-city office. It's also popular for its excellent pub grub (see Section 5, "Where to Eat," in Chapter 4).

MCDAIDS, 3 Harry St. Tel. 678-4395.
If you're a Brendan Behan devotee, you'll know about this dark, high-ceilinged pub in which he claimed a corner for himself, his pint, and his typewriter. Patrick Kavanagh and Flann O'Brien are other literary lights who drank here, and the clientele is still very much concerned with the written word and those doing the writing.

NEARY'S, 1 Chatham St. Tel. 778596.
Neary's backs up to the Gaiety Theatre's stage door, and both patrons and the crack often center around things theatrical. You'll recognize Neary's by the two black sculptured bronze arms holding light globes at its entrance. Inside, the decor is Neo-Edwardian, with a pink marble bar, brass gas lamps, mirrored walls, and lots of mahogany.

DOHENY & NESBITT, 5 Lower Baggot St. Tel. 762945.
This old pub looks exactly like a Dublin pub *should*—a great old wooden front with polished brass proclaiming TEA AND WINE MERCHANT, high ceilings, mirrored partitions along the bar, iron-and-marble tables, and a snug. It has been here for more than 130 years, and no doubt has always enjoyed the popularity it does today, with Dubliners of every age and inclination claiming it as their "local," including the likes of journalists, politicians, artists, architects, etc. A great place for conversation and people-watching, equally good at the front bar or in the back room.

O'DONOGHUE'S, 15 Merrion Row. Tel. 614303.
Not strictly a "singing pub," but it's seldom without music of one sort or another, provided on a spontaneous basis by the bearded, bejeaned, and instrument-wielding horde who crowd in here to play traditional Irish music, blue grass, and country-and-western, on guitars, uilleann pipes, bones, spoons, etc. It's a lively, fun-filled gathering place if you don't mind the crush. Or you could take the advice of readers Ann and Brian O'Connell, who wrote me that they found Sunday after church (12:45 to 2pm) to be the most uncrowded hours, the time when they could relax and enjoy the conversation and music without someone's elbow in their faces.

TONER'S, 139 Lower Baggot St. Tel. 763090.
This venerable pub has been around more than a century and a half and is the hangout of art students and other cultural types. The long mahogany bar is set with partitions to provide a bit of privacy at the bar. W. B. Yeats drank here.

MULLIGAN'S, Poolbeg St. Tel. 739-1249.
Known to Dubliners as "Mulligan's in Poolbeg Street," this Dublin institution is located next door to the *Irish Press* offices ("within an ass's roar of the Liffey and the Port of Dublin," according to Dublin writer David Hanly). Since 1782 it has pulled pints for the likes of dockers, journalists, and in recent years, scores of students from nearby Trinity. Its front bar and four rooms still retain many of their original trappings, including 19th-century gas lights. As in the past, when the likes of James Joyce and other Dublin notables were regulars, there's the ring of clubby conversation, especially around 5 in the afternoon; then it settles down a bit as the evening progresses. Lots of newspaper types can be found hanging out among the students.

THE BRAZEN HEAD, 20 Lower Bridge St. Tel. 779549.
Licensed by Charles II in 1666, this is the oldest drinking place in Ireland. It is said to have got its name in memory of a curious redheaded beauty who stuck her head out a window during one of Dublin's public disturbances and promptly lost it to an English sword. Be that as it may, this ancient pub sits at what

used to be the only place you could cross the Liffey by bridge. It's tucked away at the back of a courtyard down an arched alleyway on the west side of Bridge Street, and the entrance is easily overlooked. Low ceilings, brass lanterns, and ancient, uneven wooden floors are the same as when patriots like Wolfe Tone and Daniel O'Connell came in to drink and when Robert Emmet lodged here while plotting his ill-fated uprising (his writing desk is pointed to with pride).

DAVY BYRNES, 21 Duke St. Tel. 711298.
James Joyce fans may want to look up the "moral pub" of *Ulysses* hero Leopold Bloom. It's been modernized into a tastefully sophisticated sort of cocktail lounge that one writer has called the closest thing Dublin has to a singles' bar. The 1890s wall murals are still here, and you can still get a very good pint, but there are now likely to be more orders for mixed drinks than for the old stuff.

THE NORSEMAN, 29 E. Essex St.
This is one of Dublin's oldest pubs. The old decor survives, but has been smartened up a bit to meet modern-day needs. It's situated just off Dame Street at the rear of the Olympia Theatre and not far from the Projects Arts Centre, which means you're likely to run into a gaggle of performers and theater-goers almost any evening. There are frequent ballad sessions, and the traditions of pub life mix companionably with Dublin's artistic traditions.

NORTH OF THE LIFFEY
RYAN'S, 28 Parkgate St.
This is one of Dublin's very special pubs over in the Phoenix Park area. It has been in the Ryan family since 1920 and is largely undiscovered by tourists. I've heard Dubliners claim that it's the finest pub in town, and they'll get no argument from me! It's a traditional place, with a marvelous old oak-and-mahogany central bar fixture that holds a double-faced mechanical clock. There is a superb collection of antique wall mirrors, and four antique brass lamp fittings mounted on the bar counter. The bar, incidentally, is partitioned with ornate dividers with beveled mirrors. Many heads of state and celebrities from the movie and theater worlds regularly pass through its doors. Great atmosphere, great staff, and a good place for a pub lunch.

KAVANAGH'S, 1 Prospect Sq., Glasnevin.
Next to what was once the main gate to Glasnevin Cemetery, this pub has been in existence for a century and a half, and proprietor John Kavanagh is the eighth generation of his family to run the business. His fund of stories is endless, many of which concern the gravediggers who worked next door and who popped over to bang stones against the pub's wall, whereupon drinks were passed through an opening and placed on the poor man's shovel so he could get on with his work in a livelier state. (You can still see marks from those bangings on the wall outside.) This is, as it has always been, a workingman's pub—sawdust on the floor, worn wooden booths and cubbyholes, a dart game or two, and the relaxed chatter of men who have finished an honest day's work.

PATRICK CONWAY'S, 70 Parnell St. Tel. 732687.
This pub is just across from the Gate Theatre and the Rotunda Maternity Hospital. You'll usually find a good mix of theater types and obstetricians welcoming friendly tourists, along with a good many Dublin regulars. Some of my best pub conversations have been at Conway's, and the pub lunches are terrific (see Section 5, "Where to Eat," in Chapter 4). This claims to be Dublin's second-oldest pub, dating from 1745, and while it has been modernized into comfort, there's still much of the traditional wood, brass, and convivial atmosphere. Take note of the back bar, a marvel of carved mahogany. For visitors who need more information, just ask Lorcan, your jovial host, or any of his friendly staff, all of whom know Dublin inside out.

BARRY FITZGERALD'S, 90-92 Marlborough St., and SEAN O'CASEY'S, 105 Marlborough St.

Frank Quinn, owner of the venerable Toner's, south of the Liffey, also has these two atmospheric pubs on the north side. Both are close to O'Connell Street and the Abbey Theatre, and both serve pub lunches and pretheater meals.

PUBS WITH MUSIC

Many Dublin pubs have sing-along nights from time to time, so check newspapers and "What's On in Dublin" (available from the Tourist Office) when you're there. Here are just a few:

THE ABBEY TAVERN, Howth. Tel. 322006.

This is probably the best ballad club in all of Ireland, some 9 miles north of Dublin on the peninsula that curves around to form the northern end of Dublin Bay. The village itself is a beauty, with cliff walks, narrow winding streets and pathways, gorgeous sea views, Howth Castle gardens with a collection of over 2,000 rhododendrons, and some very good seafood restaurants. Spend a day exploring this place—perhaps with a boat trip out to Ireland's Eye (an uninhabited island just offshore) thrown in—topped off with dinner and music at the Abbey. The cozy bar/restaurant is low-ceilinged and candlelit, and has a fireplace glowing on cool nights. Every night of the week the big hall out back is filled with music-loving souls coming to hear the Abbey Singers (instrumentalists as well as vocalists) and their host of ballads. The show is so popular that you must reserve at least a day ahead, more than that in summer months. They do hold back some seats which go on a first-come, first-served basis—but the lines are very long during July and August and you shouldn't count on getting in via this route. There's good bus and train service out to Howth—just be sure you leave the Abbey in time to catch the last one back to town. Show time is 8:30pm daily.

Admission: Small charge to the hall.

SLATTERY'S, Capel St. Tel. 775402.

North of the Liffey, in the city proper, Slattery's features traditional Irish music nightly during the summer and on Sunday from 12:30 to 2pm.

Admission: Small charge for the upstairs music lounge.

FOLEY'S LOUNGE BAR, Merrion Row.

South of the Liffey, you can find traditional music nightly and Sunday afternoon, plus jazz on Sunday night.

THE WEXFORD INN, 26 Wexford St. Tel. 751588.

Presided over by congenial host Oliver Barden, the Wexford Inn showcases the very best in popular Irish ballads, with the Wolfe Tones, the Furey Brothers, the Dubliners, Dublin City Ramblers, and Paddy Reilly all performing there regularly.

READERS RECOMMEND

The Purty Kitchen, Old Dunleary, Dun Laoghaire (tel. 843576). "We had two great nights of music in this terrific pub and restaurant. They feature traditional, as well as country-and-western and folk on different nights of the week. It's a lively place, great fun."—Paul and Caroline Hennessy, Boston, Mass.

CHAPTER 6

EXCURSIONS FROM DUBLIN

1. COUNTY DUBLIN
2. COUNTY LOUTH
3. COUNTY MEATH
4. COUNTY KILDARE
5. COUNTY WICKLOW

The five counties of Dublin, Louth, Meath, Kildare, and Wicklow make up Ireland's Eastern Region. Rich in antiquities and blessed with a plethora of scenic beauty, these five counties are a sightseer's dream come true. The Eastern Region has been at the center of so much Irish history and is literally so strewn with relics that it's hard to venture far without tripping over at least one.

To the north of Dublin, the Boyne Valley runs through northern County Dublin, and Counties Louth and Meath, holding the Royal Hill of Tara, the ancient burial mound at Newgrange, and monastic ruins at Mellifont and Monasterboise, as well as memories of the Battle of the Boyne which changed the course of Irish history. For lovers of the elegant, Malahide Castle, Newbridge House, and Trim Castle will be the drawing card. South of the city, for the literary-minded there are memories of James Joyce in southern County Dublin, the awesome beauty and mystery of Glendalough, the gardens at Powerscourt and Mount Usher, and the idyllic beauty of the Meeting of the Waters near Avoca. The great mansions of Russborough in County Wicklow and Castletown in County Kildare evoke the elegance of a bygone era. In this chapter, we'll take an in-depth look at each county of the Eastern Region.

SEEING THE EASTERN REGION

Whether you elect to make your base right in Dublin or opt for accommodations in a more relaxed country atmosphere, you'll be no more than an hour's drive from most of the sightseeing highlights of Counties Dublin, Wicklow, Louth, Kildare, and Meath.

For detailed information on sightseeing, accommodations, and any other subjects, contact the Dublin and **Dublin Regional Tourist Organization,** Tourist Office, St. Michael's Wharf, Dun Laoghaire (tel. 01/806984).

BY BUS & DART   The following attractions can be easily reached by bus or DART from Dublin (see individual listings for details): Malahide Castle, James Joyce Museum, Glendalough, Russborough House, Castletown House, and Mount Usher.

ORGANIZED TOURS   Many of the Eastern Region's attractions are reached via narrow and winding country roads, which can be a strain on drivers new to the country or this region. My best recommendation is to avail of **Bus Eireann's coach tours** that get you there and back in comfort and provide informative narrative all along the way. See "Organized Tours" in Section 1, "Attractions," in Chapter 5 for details.

DRIVING ITINERARIES   Each of these suggested itineraries can be covered in a full day of driving. However, be warned that for the first two, it will be a *long* day, and you may well want to take 2 days for each route.

North of Dublin   Leave Dublin on the main Navan road (N3) and watch for the unclassified road signposted **Tara** (about 24 miles from Dublin); leaving Tara, look for the small, unclassified road signposted **Trim** (4 miles), good for a lunch break and a tour of the castle. From Trim, head north on T26, continue through Navan on N51 (the main Navan–Drogheda road), and shortly after passing through Slane, watch for the unclassified road signposted **Newgrange** a few miles east of Slane. Rejoin T26 (N51) to Drogheda (9 miles), passing the obelisk marking the site of the **Battle of the Boyne.** From Drogheda, drive north on N1 and watch for the signposted unclassified road to **Monasterboice Abbey** (6 miles northwest of Drogheda). From Monasterboice, follow the unclassified road to reach T25 and another unclassified road signposted **Mellifont.** From Mellifont, rejoin T25 to reach Drogheda. From Drogheda, take N1 south past Balbriggan to L91A and turn left to Donabate and **Newbridge House.** Rejoin N1 to Swords, then turn left onto L143 to **Malahide.** Rejoin N1 back to Dublin (9 miles).

South of Dublin   The **James Joyce Museum** at Sandycove is best reached by DART from Dublin (see below).

From Dublin, take N11 to Bray and a few miles outside town turn right to Enniskerry; then take R755 to Roundwood and turn left on R764 to **Mount Usher.** Return to R755 via R763 and drive south to Laragh, turning left on R756 to **Glendalough.** From Glendalough, rejoin R755 and drive south to Rathdrum; **Avondale** is 1 mile south of Rathdrum. Return to Rathdrum and take R752 to Rathnew, then N11 back to Dublin (11 miles).

To visit **Castletown House and Russborough House,** leave Dublin via N6 to Lucan, then R403 to Celbridge (about 9 miles from Dublin) and look for the Castletown House signpost. From Celbridge, return to Lucan, then take L200 to Newcastle and turn east, cross over N7 to join N81, turn south and drive to Blessington. **Russborough House** is 2 miles from Blessington (signposted). Return to Dublin via N81.

1. COUNTY DUBLIN

The county of Dublin is blessed with a coastline sometimes soft and gentle, sometimes wild and rugged. The majestic crescent of Dublin Bay curves from Howth on its rocky perch in the north to Dalkey and its island at the southern tip. Its scenic fishing villages and pleasure-ridden seashore resorts north and south of the bay beckon invitingly to the visitor. Then there are the mountains that form a verdant, dramatic backdrop for bustling city, sleepy villages, and that enchanting seascape.

WHAT TO SEE & DO

Shades of James Joyce, King Billy, the High Kings of ancient Ireland, saints, and monks—they all roamed the hills and valleys of the North County Dublin, and their haunts are there for you to visit.

NORTH OF DUBLIN

MALAHIDE CASTLE, Malahide, Co. Dublin. Tel. 01/452655.
   This stately castellated residence was occupied until 1976 by the descendants of Lord Talbot de Malahide, its founder in 1185. One of the many historic happenings within its walls occurred on the morning in 1690 when some 14 Talbot cousins sat down to breakfast together before leaving to fight for King James in the Battle of the Boyne, a battle in which all lost their lives. Patrick Sarsfield and Oliver Plunkett were cousins of the Talbot family and visited the castle. Set in a 268-acre demesne whose

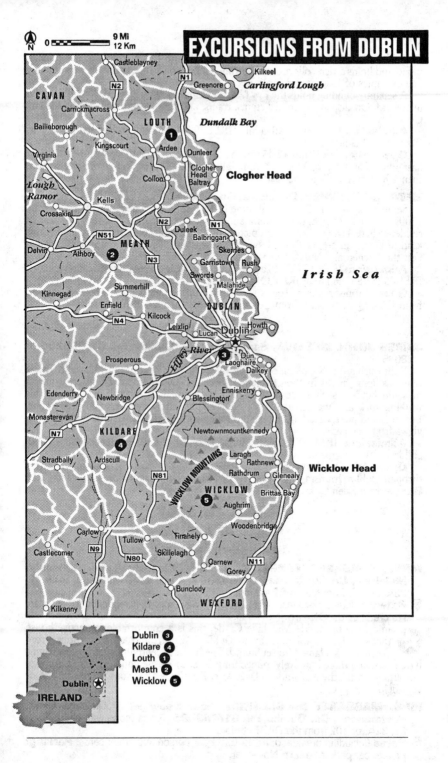

EXCURSIONS FROM DUBLIN

0 ——— 9 Mi
  ——— 12 Km

N

CAVAN

Castleblayney

N2

N1

Kilkeel

Greenore

Carlingford Lough

Carrickmacross

Bailieborough

LOUTH

Dundalk Bay

Virginia

Kingscourt

1

Ardee

Dunleer

Clogher
Head
Baltray

Clogher Head

*Lough
Ramor*

Kells

Collon

Crossakiel

Delvin

N51

MEATH

Duleek

Balbriggan

N1

Athboy

2

N3

Garristown

Skerries

Rush

Kinnegad

Summerhill

Swords

Malahide

Irish Sea

Enfield

Kilcock

DUBLIN

N4

Leixlip

Lucan

Howth

Dublin

Liffey River

Prosperous

Dún
Laoghaire

3

Dalkey

Edenderry

Newbridge

Enniskerry

Blessington

Monasterevan

N7

KILDARE

Newtownmountkennedy

Stradbally

Ardscull

4

Laragh
Rathnew

N81

Rathdrum

Glenealy

Wicklow Head

WICKLOW

Brittas Bay

5

Aughrim

Carlow

Finahely

Woodenbridge

Castlecomer

N9

Tullow

N80

Skillelagh

Carnew

Gorey

N11

Bunclody

Kilkenny

WEXFORD

Dublin **3**
Kildare **4**
Louth **1**
Meath **2**
Wicklow **5**

Dublin ⭐

IRELAND

formal gardens alone are worth a visit, the castle still retains traces of the original moat, and holds a rich collection of portraits of historical Irish figures as well as many fine examples of Irish period furniture.

A separate building holds the **Fry Model Railway Museum,** the first of its kind in Ireland. On display are model trains, trams, and railroad artifacts left by the late Cyril Fry.

Admission: IR£2.50 ($4.40) adults, IR£1.60 ($2.80) students and senior citizens, IR£1.15 ($2) children.

Open: Mon–Fri 10am–12:45pm and 2–5pm, Sat–Sun and public hols 2–5pm (last admission 4:45pm). **Bus:** 42 from Talbot Street. **Train:** From Connolly Station, then a half-mile walk to the castle.

NEWBRIDGE HOUSE, Donabate, Co. Dublin. Tel. 01/436534.

Set in a magnificent desmesne of some 120 acres, Newbridge House dates from the 1700s. Its great Red Drawing Room is just as it was when the Cobbe family was in residence here, giving you a perfect picture of how wealthy families entertained in this kind of Georgian home. To see how the "downstairs" staff kept the wheels turning, visit the kitchen and laundry, as well as the coach house and various workshops.

Admission: IR£2.10 ($3.70) adults, IR£1.60 ($2.80) senior citizens and students, IR£1.05 ($1.85) children; IR£6.30 ($11.05) family ticket.

Open: Mon–Fri 10am–1pm and 2–5pm, Sun and bank hols 2–6pm. **Bus:** 33B from Eden Quay. **Train:** From Connolly Station, then a half-hour walk.

SOUTH OF DUBLIN

JAMES JOYCE MUSEUM, Sandycove, Co. Dublin. Tel. 01/809265 or 808571.

Built during the Napoleonic Wars in the early 19th century, the Martello Tower that was home briefly in 1904 for James Joyce and Oliver St. John Gogarty is now a museum holding such Joyce memorabilia as personal letters and manuscripts, his walking stick and waistcoat, books, photographs, and other personal possessions. Lectures and poetry readings are held on the first floor, and there are marvelous sea views from the parapet.

Admission: IR£1.50 ($2.65) adults, IR£1.20 ($2.10) students, 80p ($1.40) children.

Open: Apr–Oct, Mon–Fri 10am–1pm and 2–5pm; Nov–Mar, by appointment through Dublin Tourism, 1 Clarinda Park North, Dun Laoghaire (tel. 01/808571). **Bus:** 8 from Eden Quay. **DART:**

WHERE TO STAY

NORTH OF DUBLIN

Bed-and-Breakfast

MRS. MARGARET FARRELLY, Lynfar, Kinsealy Lane, Kinsealy, Malahide, Co. Dublin. Tel. 01/463897. 4 rms (none with bath). **Bus:** 42, 32A, or 102 from the DART station.

$ Rates (including breakfast): IR£12 ($21) per person. 25% reduction for children. No credit cards. **Closed:** Nov–Jan.

In a location beside Malahide Castle, this is a comfortable, attractive house that's only 10 minutes from Dublin Airport and a short drive from Portmanock's famed Velvet Strand. The house is centrally heated, guest rooms have sinks, and there is a lovely lounge for guests. There are good, moderately priced restaurants in nearby Malahide village. Mrs. Farrelly is a gracious hostess and most very helpful to guests.

MRS. MARGARET M. GLENNON, Four Seasons, 1 Onward Walk, Portmanock, Co. Dublin. Tel. 01/463996. 3 rms (none with bath). **Bus:** 32, 32A, or 102 from the DART station.

$ Rates (including breakfast): IR£12 ($21) per person. No credit cards. **Parking:** Private car park. **Closed:** Nov–Mar.

Mrs. Glennon's modern two-story house is only 5km from Malahide, 15 minutes from Dublin Airport, and even closer to Portmarnock's splendid beach and an 18-hole golf course. Guest rooms are attractive as well as comfortable, all with sinks, and the house has central heating. With advance notice, you can have high tea for IR£6 ($10.50) or dinner for IR£10 ($17.50).

MRS. MARIE TONKIN, 29 Martello Court, Portmarnock, Co. Dublin. **Tel. 01/461500.** 3 rms (none with bath). **Bus:** 32, 32A, or 102 from the DART station.

$ Rates: IR£12 ($21) per person. No credit cards. **Closed:** Nov–Mar.

Mrs. Tonkin has won accolades from our readers, many of whom were referred to her by Mrs. Mary Geraghty (see below). Her warm, comfortable, and attractive home is convenient to nearby sightseeing, as well as a good base for exploring the Eastern Region north of Dublin.

MRS. MARY GERAGHTY, 57 Biscayne, Coast Rd., Malahide, Co. Dublin. **Tel. 01/451459.** 3 rms (none with bath). **Bus:** 42, 32A, or 102 from the DART station.

$ Rates (including breakfast): IR£12 ($21) per person. 25% reduction for children. No credit cards.

This semidetached end house has a lovely view overlooking the sea. A comfortable home, it's only a short drive from Dublin Airport, and convenient to Malahide Castle, golf and tennis clubs, Portmarnock's sandy strand, and several very good restaurants. Guest rooms, all with sinks, are attractive, and high tea is available in the evening.

A Guesthouse

SEA-VIEW GUESTHOUSE, Strand Rd., Portmarnock, Co. Dublin. Tel. **01/462242.** 9 rms (5 with shower). **Bus:** 32, 32A, or 102 from the DART station.

$ Rates (including a full Irish breakfast): IR£17 ($29.75) single; IR£32 ($56) double. 25% reduction for children. No credit cards. **Parking:** Private car park.

Maura and James Grogan's large, comfortable home is convenient to Dublin Airport and the B&I Ferry. The nine pretty bedrooms all have sinks and five have showers. They have a private car park and the house is centrally heated.

SOUTH OF DUBLIN

See Section 4, "Where to Stay," in Chapter 4 for accommodations in Dun Laoghaire.

WHERE TO EAT
NORTH OF DUBLIN

COUNTRY CLUB HOTEL, Portmarnock, Co. Dublin. Tel. 01/460611. **Cuisine:** STEAKS/SEAFOOD. **Bus:** 32 or 32A.

$ Prices: Main courses IR£6.50–IR£12 ($11.40–$21); Tourist Menu (Apr–Sept) IR£7.90 ($13.85). ACC, AE, MC, V.

Open: Lunch daily 12:30–2:30pm; dinner daily 6pm–midnight. **Closed:** Good Friday.

Gorgeous panoramic sea views add to any meal at this conservatory restaurant, as does the resident pianist. In addition to steaks and fresh seafood, vegetarian dishes are served in this attractive, relaxing setting.

OSCAR TAYLOR'S, in the Stuart Hotel, Coast Rd., Malahide, Co. Dublin. **Tel. 01/450399.** **Cuisine:** TRADITIONAL. **Bus:** 32, 32A, or 102 from the DART station.

$ Prices: Main courses IR£5–IR£9.50 ($8.75–$16.65); Tourist Menu IR£7.90 ($13.85). Service charge 10%. No credit cards.

Open: Bar snacks Mon–Sat 12:30–2pm; dinner Mon–Sat 5:30–11pm; Sun and public hols 12:30–10pm. **Closed:** Good Friday, Dec 24–27.

On the first floor of the Stuart Hotel, overlooking the sea, Oscar Taylor's is a local favorite for steaks (always cooked exactly to your request) and seafood. Grills and salads are also exceptional, and there are always vegetarian selections on the menu. It's an attractive place, with friendly and attentive service.

ROCHES BISTRO, 12 New St., Malahide, Co. Dublin. Tel. 01/452777.
  Cuisine: FRENCH. **Bus:** 32, 32A, or 102.
$ **Prices:** Main courses IR£10–IR£16 ($17.50–$28); Tourist Menu IR£12 ($21) at lunch (includes a glass of wine). ACC, AE, MC, V.
  Open: Lunch Mon–Sat noon–2:30pm; dinner Mon–Sat 7–10:30pm. **Closed:** Public hols.

This cozy little bistro serves only the freshest produce, beautifully prepared by the owner and his sister. Seafood stars on the menu, which also includes vegetarian dishes.

SOUTH OF DUBLIN

See Section 5, "Where to Eat," in Chapter 4 for a restaurant in Dalkey.

BARRELS TRATTORIA, upstairs at Goggins Pub, Monkstown, Co. Dublin. Tel. 01/801992.
  Cuisine: TRADITIONAL. **DART:** Monkstown.
$ **Prices:** Main courses IR£10–IR£13 ($17.50–$22.75). Service charge 10%. ACC, AE, MC, V.
  Open: Dinner only, Mon–Sat 6:30–11:30pm. **Closed:** Good Friday, Christmas Day.

The food is good, the atmosphere is lively, and on cool nights there's an open fire. The menu includes fish, steaks, pasta, veal, game, and vegetarian dishes (the vegetables are really fresh). Homemade desserts are scrumptious.

READERS RECOMMEND

Mullach Cottage, 4 Church Road, Malahide, Co. Dublin (tel. 451346). *"This is a terrific place to eat in Malahide. We especially liked the seafood mornay and the roast duckling with orange and kiwi sauce (which was nice and crispy, with a delicious sauce). The prices were really low for the quality of food: most main courses were about IR£7 to IR£8. The highest price on the menu was for a T-bone steak, IR£9.50. Really good value."*—Marjorie Lewis, Savannah, Ga.

---

2. COUNTY LOUTH

Together, Counties Louth and Meath hold enough historic sites to fill an entire book of their own—one the setting for Tara's home of Irish royalty, the other the scene of one of Cromwell's most devastating assaults on the Irish people.

County Louth also has restful open forest areas, which invite a picnic lunch or simply a walk in the woods away from the cares of civilization.

WHAT TO SEE & DO

MELLIFONT ABBEY ("The Big Monastery"), Co. Louth.
To walk in the footsteps of monks who founded Ireland's first Cistercian monastery here on the banks of the Mattock River back in 1142 is to drink in the peacefulness of a setting that invites meditation. The Chapter House and ruins of the cloister still remain from the structures built in the 13th century, but the foundations alone are left of the original building.
  Admission: Free.
  Open: Year round. **Directions:** Drive 6 miles west of Drogheda on a signposted unclassified road off T25.

MUIREDACH'S CROSS, Monasterboice, Co. Louth.

⭐ Standing a majestic 17 feet above this site, which once held a large monastic community and now consists of a small churchyard and round tower, this 10th-century cross is universally recognized as the finest example of the sculptured high crosses. The unknown master carver who created its many figures and ornamental designs used one piece of stone for this memorial to Muiredach, about whom we know only that he ordered the inscription on the shaft that asks for prayers on his behalf. Those dents in the base were left by immigrants who took chips of the cross with them as they crossed the seas to new homes.

Admission: Free.

Directions: Drive 6 miles northwest of Drogheda on a signposted unclassified road off N1.

TOWNLEY HALL (Halla de Túinlé), Open Forest, Co. Louth.

There are forest walks, nature trails, and picnic sites in this open forest, which lies just off the Boyne Valley Road to Navan and encompasses the Battle of the Boyne site. A lovely respite from the road.

Admission: Free.

Directions: Drive 6.5km (3½ miles) northwest of Drogheda on N51 (T26) and turn right at the signpost for 1.5km (1 mile).

WHERE TO STAY

AISLING HOUSE, Baltray, Drogheda, Co. Louth. Tel. 041/22376. 5 rms (3 with bath). TV

$ Rates: IR£11.50 ($20.15) per person without bath; IR£13 ($22.75) per person with bath. 20% reduction for children under 10. High tea, IR£10 ($17.50) extra; dinner, IR£10.50 ($18.40).

Convenient to Dublin (it's 2½ miles from Drogheda on the Bus Eireann Dublin–Drogheda route) and overlooking the Boyne River, this nice modern bungalow is the home of Mrs. Josephine McGinley. The house is centrally heated and just 100 yards from a good golf course and restaurant. There are five attractive bedrooms, three of which have private shower and they all have sinks and color TVs.

DELAMARE, Ballyoonan, Omeath, Co. Louth. Tel. 042/75101. 3 rms (2 with bath).

$ Rates (including breakfast): IR£12 ($21) per person. 50% reduction for children under 10. No credit cards. **Parking:** Private car park. **Closed:** Nov–Mar.

Mrs. Eileen McGeown is the charming hostess in this modern bungalow overlooking Carlingford Lough and the Mourne mountains in a lovely rural area. The house is set in beautiful surroundings and is very peaceful, and—a blessing for those who travel on their own—Mrs. McGeown warmly welcomes singles. It's 3 miles from Carlingford and 1km (half a mile) from Omeath on the Carlingford–Omeath road, opposite Calvary Shrine.

HARBOUR VILLA, Mornington Rd., Drogheda, Co. Louth. Tel. 041/ 37441. 4 rms (none with bath).

$ Rates (including breakfast): IR£16 ($28) single; IR£12 ($21) per person sharing. High tea IR£7 ($12.25) extra; IR£10 ($17.50) dinner. No credit cards. **Parking:** Private parking.

⭐ An ideal base for exploring the Eastern Region north of Dublin and convenient to Dublin Airport, Harbour Villa is a beautiful two-story home in its own grounds right on the River Boyne 1 mile from Drogheda, off the main Dublin road. There's a pretty sun lounge and private tennis courts. Mrs. Sheila Dwyer extends a warm welcome to Americans. One reader heaped laurels on the Dwyers and their home, saying they were "among the most interesting and helpful people that we met in a country full of exceptionally interesting and helpful people. They were available and concerned but our privacy was never endangered for one moment. Mrs. Dwyer's food (at breakfast and especially at high tea) was the best we were served in Ireland. The house is attractively furnished, immaculately clean, set in beautifully landscaped grounds on the tidal estuary of the Boyne." I couldn't have said it better!

WORTH THE EXTRA MONEY

BALLYMASCANLON HOUSE HOTEL, Dundalk, Co. Louth. Tel. 042/ 71124. Telex 43735 IMPH. 36 rms (all with bath). TEL TV

$ Rates (including VAT and 10% service charge): IR£35–IR£37 ($61.25–$64.75) single; IR£58–IR£62 ($101.50–$105) double. Many weekend and midweek breaks; special rates Jan–Mar and Oct–Dec. ACC, AE, MC, V.

✪ Set in 130 wooded acres and surrounded by green lawns, Ballymascanlon has twice won awards for its lovely gardens. The peaked-gabled old country mansion has high ceilings and spacious rooms in the original house, and there's a modern extension with more standardized guest rooms. All guest rooms are attractively decorated, with tea/coffee makers, and the garden supplies fresh vegetables for the dining room, which specializes in popular Irish dishes and international cuisine. Its location just about at the midway point on the main Dublin–Belfast road makes this a convenient stopping point.

Facilities: Sports center (including a heated indoor swimming pool, sauna, solarium, gym, children's playground, and squash and tennis courts); golf and the seaside nearby.

WHERE TO EAT

WALKERS HOTEL, West St., Drogheda. Tel. 041/31017 or 31018.

Cuisine: TRADITIONAL.

$ Prices: Main courses IR£7–IR£12 ($12.25–$21). ACC, AE, MC, V.

Open: Lunch daily 12:30–3pm; dinner daily 7–11pm.

This is a first-class hotel, and its restaurant, open daily, serves good meals at moderate prices, and the lower-priced Tourist Menu is available in the bar from noon to 8pm.

3. COUNTY MEATH

For centuries there was a "Royal Meath" province, which included Westmeath, ruled by pagan and early Christian kings. Traces of those ancient rulers, as well as the prehistoric Bronze Age, are scattered over the face of modern-day County Meath.

WHAT TO SEE & DO

HILL OF TARA, Co. Meath.

✪ From the time that pagans worshiped here, the Hill of Tara has figured in Irish history and legend. It was here that the High Kings were seated, and there's a rock that legend says roared when a new king was found to be acceptable—its silence spelled a candidate's doom. Burial mounds here go back some 4,000 years, and there are earthworks and low walls of earth left from a fortification of the Bronze Age. All else of Tara's regal trappings must be left to your imagination as you view this low

---

IMPRESSIONS

Ireland was contented when
All could use the sword and pen
And when Tara rose so high
That her turrets split the sky
And about her courts were seen
Liveried angels robed in green
Wearing, by St Patrick's bounty
Emeralds, big as half the county.

—W.S. LANDOR, "IRELAND NEVER WAS CONTENTED," 1853

hillside with the mind's eye and feel the mystical presence of pagan priests and ancient royalty. It's a magical place—the setting for many of Finn McCool's exploits, the home of Grainne when she deserted Finn and fled with Diarmaid, and the very center of religious and political power until the coming of Christianity—and your imagination is bound to take wings as you walk the grassy hills and see the gentle mounds that outline once-majestic palaces and banqueting halls.

Be sure to stop in the small shop at the foot of the Hill of Tara, either before or after you walk the slopes. They carry an array of inexpensive booklets about Tara's mystical past, and there are also smashing, one-of-a-kind, hand-knit mohair sweaters that are locally made and cheaper than comparable quality in Dublin shops, plus a small selection of other crafts, and a cozy tearoom.

Admission: Free.

Open: Summer, daily 10am–7pm; winter, daily 10am–dusk. **Bus:** 20, 40, or 43 from Dublin or Navan; it's 6 miles South of Navan, off N3.

NEWGRANGE, or BRUGH NA BOINNE (Palace of the Boyne). Tel. 041/24274.

Newgrange, along with the burial mounds of Nowth and Dowth, are the most striking of some 15 passage graves in this vicinity. Of those three, Newgrange is easily the most impressive. Even older than the burial mounds at Tara, Newgrange was probably built by the first settlers who came to Ireland from the Continent some 4,500 years ago. We know almost nothing about them, or what the ornamental spirals and other decorations at this impressive burial mound symbolized. We don't even know for whom the structure was built, whether holy men, chieftains, or kings. What we do know is that they were skilled builders, for the corbeled roof above the burial chamber has kept out the dampness of 40 centuries, and the 62-foot-long passage still serves quite well as an entry to the chamber, the stone at its entrance an enduring testament to prehistoric craftsmanship. Archeologists are constantly carrying out research at Newgrange in an effort to unravel such mysteries as the reason an opening above the doorway is so placed that the sun's rays reach the burial chamber only on the shortest day of the year, December 21, and then for exactly 17 minutes!

Admission: IR£2.50 ($4.40) adults, 90p ($1.60) students, children, and senior citizens.

Open: May–Sept, daily 10am–7pm; Oct–Apr, daily 10am–dusk. **Directions:** Drive 7 miles west of Drogheda, just off N51.

NEWGRANGE FARM, Slane, Co. Meath. Tel. 041/24119.

It's well worth your while to allow time to stop by this working farm, just 100 yards from the Tourist Offices and entrance to Newgrange. This is a traditional, 333-acre farm that grows barley, wheat, and other grains, but it is the farmyard, bustling with beef cows, bulls, heifers, goats, pigs, ponies, a horse, Hampshire Downs sheep (they're the ones that have a "teddy-bear" coat—children love them), rabbits, dogs, and poultry that are the main attraction for visitors. One of the farmers will lead you through this thriving menagerie, with a running commentary on just how the farm works. It's a delightful experience for all ages.

Admission: IR£3.75 ($6.55) adults, IR£1.50 ($2.65) students, 90p ($1.60) children.

Open: Apr–Sept, daily tours as requested.

TRIM CASTLE, Trim, Co. Meath.

Ireland's largest Anglo-Irish castle, built by Hugh de Lacy in 1172, is in this pretty little town. From its tall, gray central tower you can see across the river to ruins of town walls dating from the 14th century. The site of an abbey which once held a statue of the Virgin credited with miracles is marked by what is called locally the Yellow Steeple. The castle's drawbridge tower once hosted England's Prince Hal, and its grounds have yielded up a mass grave of skeletons minus their heads who may have been the unfortunate (and unsuccessful) defenders of the stronghold against the forces of Cromwell.

Admission: Free.

Open: Daily 10am–6pm. **Bus:** 44 or 45 from Dublin; it's 9 miles southwest of Navan on T26.

WHERE TO STAY

Close enough to Dublin for frequent trips into the city, and centrally located for exploring the northern part of the Eastern Region, County Meath is an ideal base for those who prefer accommodations outside the city.

BED & BREAKFAST

ARDILAUN, 41 Beach Park, Laytown, Co. Meath. Tel. 041/27033. 3 rms (one with bath).
$ Rates (including breakfast): IR£11.50 ($20.15) per person without bath; IR£1.50 ($2.65) per person extra with bath. 25% reduction for children under 10. No credit cards. **Parking:** Private car park. **Closed:** Nov–Mar.
Mrs. Peggy Downey is your hostess at her modern two-story home, set on its own grounds 5 miles south of Drogheda, just off N1 and convenient to Dublin Airport. All bedrooms have sinks, and the house is centrally heated. Guests are made very welcome and comfortable by the genial Mrs. Downey.

LATIMOR HOUSE, Old Castle Rd., Kells, Co. Meath. Tel. 046/40133. 5 rms (none with bath). **Bus:** 24, 43, or 91 from Dublin, or 23 from Drogheda.
$ Rates: IR£11.50 ($20.15) per person. No credit cards. **Parking:** Paved car park.
Mrs. Christina Woods, the lively proprietress, welcomes guests into her modern bungalow just outside the historic town of Kells (10 miles northwest of Navan on N3; 24 miles west of Drogheda) as though they were a part of her own family. Indeed, her seven grown children (always "coming and going," according to Mrs. Woods) join in the warm hospitality. The house is bright and cheerful, with a pretty living room, five attractive guest rooms, and central heat. Mrs. Woods will gladly furnish an evening meal if it's ordered in advance.

TARASIDE HOUSE, Growtown, Dunshaughlin, Co. Meath. Tel. 01/259721. 5 rms (two with shower).
$ Rates (including breakfast): IR£12 ($21) per person. 33⅓% reduction for children. No credit cards.
Mrs. Bridie McGowan's modern bungalow is located on N3, the main Dublin–Navan road, set on 2 acres of landscaped gardens. There is a good restaurant nearby and the house is centrally heated. There are five bedrooms, two of which have showers, and they all have sinks.

A FARMHOUSE

PAULINE AND PAUL MULLAN, Lennoxbrook, Kells, Co. Meath. Tel. 046/45902. 5 rms (none with bath).
$ Rates: IR£12 ($21) per person. 25% reduction for children. High tea IR£10 ($17.50) extra; dinner, IR£12 ($21). No credit cards.
This charming couple have opened up their rambling beef-and-sheep farm home 40 miles north of Dublin, 3 miles north of Kells on N3, to guests, and pretty little red-haired Louise seems to second the motion, eager to show off her sisters, Sally and baby Anna. The house has been Paul's family home for five generations, and there's an inviting, homey air about the place. Two of the five comfortable guest rooms have bay windows, and a real showplace is the upstairs bathroom that Pauline has given a quaint country look. Dinner, of home-grown meats, is available if you book before 3pm. Paul stocks a small trout stream right on the grounds, so you can fish for your dinner if you wish. Lennoxbrook is an ideal "home away from home" when touring this historic area.

WORTH THE EXTRA MONEY

WELLINGTON COURT HOTEL, Trim, Co. Meath. Tel. 046/31516. 18 rms (all with bath). TEL TV
$ **Rates** (including breakfast): IR£28 ($49) single; IR£35 ($61.25) double. ACC, AE, MC, V. **Parking:** Enclosed car park.

This small hotel in the town center, set behind stone walls that enclose a spacious courtyard, has a warm, inviting air, with an exceptionally friendly and helpful staff. The dining room and lounge are nicely laid out, and both bar food and full meals offer good value (see "Where to Eat," below). Guest rooms are spacious, attractively decorated, and have either a double bed or a double plus a single bed. There's a small, but well-equipped, Health Centre on the premises, and there's sometimes a disco on Friday or Saturday night.

WHERE TO EAT

MONAGHAN'S LOUNGE, Kells. Tel. 046/40100.
Cuisine: TRADITIONAL.
$ **Prices:** Main courses IR£10–IR£12 ($1.75–$21); average lunch IR£6 ($10.50); Tourist Menu (available year round). ACC, MC, V.
Open: Lunch 10:30am–2:30pm; dinner 5–11:30pm.
You can get just about anything from take-aways to steaks at this pub-cum-health-club in the town center. There's music on weekend nights during the summer. In addition to beef, pork, chicken, and seafood dishes, there are always vegetarian dishes on offer. The friendly, efficient staff include speakers of French, Spanish, and German.

WELLINGTON COURT HOTEL, Trim, Co. Meath. Tel. 046/31516.
Cuisine: TRADITIONAL/IRISH.
$ **Prices:** Main courses IR£8–IR£16 ($14–$28); fixed-price meal IR£10–IR£16 ($17.50–$28); bar lunch IR£3–IR£4 ($5.25–$7).
Open: Lunch daily 12:30–2:30pm; dinner daily 6:30–9:30pm. **Closed:** Good Friday, Christmas Day.

In this charming, small hotel dining room beef, pork, chicken, and fish are standards, and dishes such as pork en croûte are excellent, as is the roast lamb. Traditional Irish dishes, such as Irish stew or boiled ham, are also on offer. For dessert, try the apple tart. Portions are *huge,* but if you can save room, try the apple tart. The Tourist Menu is available May through September. Children are welcomed here, good news for harried parents.

4. COUNTY KILDARE

Kildare's flat fields and bogs have seen historic figures come and go, and today hold not only stables that have bred racehorses of international fame but also the world-famous Curragh racecourse, where modern-day sports-world history is written by home-grown champions of the sport.

WHAT TO SEE & DO

While a visit to most of Kildare's great stud farms can only be arranged by invitation, racing fans can see the stables' proud offspring in action when there's a scheduled meet. Equestrians can stop by a leading riding stable for a jog through the lush countryside, and sightseers will delight in Ireland's largest country house.

CASTLETOWN HOUSE, Celbridge, Co. Kildare. Tel. 01/288252 for information.

About 9 miles from Dublin on R403, this is Ireland's largest classical country home, and was designed in the Palladian style by the celebrated Italian architect Allessandro Galilei for the Speaker of the Irish House of Commons, William Connolly, in 1722. It's an imposing structure from the outside, approached via a long, tree-lined avenue. The interior, however, holds truly magnificent plasterwork, and there's a splendid Long Gallery painted in the Pompeian manner and lighted by Venetian chandeliers. Also of note are the Red Drawing Room and Print Room. There are frequent social and cultural functions in this elegant setting, drawing large numbers from Dublin, as well as the rest of the country.

Admission: IR£2.50 ($4.40) adults, IR£1 ($1.75) children; IR£6 ($10.50) family tickets.

Open: May–Oct, Mon–Fri 10am–5pm; Nov–Apr, Mon–Fri 2–5pm. **Closed:** Bank hols.

SPORTS

THE CURRAGH RACECOURSE, Co. Kildare. Tel. 045/41205.

⭐ The headquarters of Irish horseracing today is on that vast County Kildare plain known as The Curragh. Since ancient times, this has been a leading venue for the sport, and nearly all of Ireland's classic races are held here. If a meet is on during your visit, and if you're a fancier of horseflesh par excellence, you won't want to miss a visit to The Curragh.

Admission: Varies with the race.

Open: On scheduled dates throughout the year. **Bus and Train:** Special buses depart Busaras and there are trains from Heuston Station on race days; it's 7 miles northwest of Naas, just off N7.

FRENCHFURZE RIDING STABLES, Maddenstown, Co. Kildare. Tel. 045/41275.

When the time arrives that you long to sit on a horse instead of in a car, head for these prestigious riding stables east of The Curragh Racecourse. You'll ride some of the finest horses the county has to offer, and there are experts on hand to guide your selection of a mount.

Prices: Vary according to length of ride, instruction, and mount selected.

Open: Advance booking absolutely necessary.

CURRAGH GOLF COURSE, Co. Kildare. Tel. 045/41238.

Just east of the celebrated racecourse, this is an excellent 18-hole course, and very popular with the locals and Dubliners. If you want to get in a game, reserve your tee-off time well in advance.

WHERE TO STAY
BED & BREAKFAST

DARA LODGE, Curragh Racecourse, Pollardstown, Curragh, Co. Kildare. Tel. 045/21770. 7 rms (one with bath).

$ Rates (including breakfast): IR£12 ($21) per person without bath; IR£1.50 ($2.65) per person additional with bath. 20% discount for children under 10. High tea IR£6 ($10.50) extra; dinner IR£10 ($17.50). No credit cards. **Parking:** Private parking.

Overlooking the famous Curragh Racecourse, 3km (2 miles) from Newbridge, this strikingly modern house is presided over by Mrs. Joan McCann. She has seven attractive and comfortable guest rooms, and the house is centrally heated. She can also provide baby-sitting.

HILLVIEW HOUSE, Prosperous, Naas, Co. Kildare. Tel. 045/68252. 10 rms (6 with bath).

$ Rates (including breakfast): IR£17 ($29.75) single without bath; IR£12 ($21) per person sharing without bath; IR£2 ($3.50) per person extra with private bath. 25% reduction for children under 10. High tea IR£7.50 ($13.15) extra; dinner, IR£10 ($17.50). No credit cards. **Parking:** Large private car park.

Joe and Sheila O'Brien are the friendly hosts in this large, modern house 22 miles south of Dublin, a 10-minute drive from N7. There's a comfortable lounge and a relaxed atmosphere, and a fixed-price dinner is available for guests at 6 o'clock. The O'Briens can provide baby-sitting, and the house is centrally heated.

WORTH THE EXTRA MONEY

MOYGLARE MANOR COUNTRY HOUSE AND RESTAURANT, Maynooth, Co. Kildare. Tel. 01/286501, or toll free 800/223-6510 in the U.S. Fax 402/498-0574 in the U.S. Telex 4972677 UTELL. 16 rms, 1 suite (all with bath). TV TEL

$ **Rates** (including full Irish breakfast): IR£62.50 ($105.90) single; IR£47.50 ($79.63) per person sharing; IR£50 ($87.50) per person sharing suite. Fixed-price dinner IR£18.50 ($32.40) extra. ACC, AE, MC, V. **Parking:** Private parking.

Moyglare Manor is a gorgeous Georgian house set in a beautiful park 18 miles from Dublin, 1¼ miles west of Maynooth on N4; it's presided over by the gracious Norah Devlin. All the luxurious guest rooms are large and beautifully furnished, some with four-poster beds, and all have lovely views of the grounds and the woodlands beyond. As for the decor, one can only marvel at its elegance, with handsome antique pieces adding to the magnificence. Best of all, there's a warm, relaxed atmosphere and very personal service. There are four golf courses in a 10-mile radius, with tennis, horseback riding, and fox hunting available nearby. The family-run restaurant is known throughout Ireland for its fine cuisine (see "Where to Eat," below).

WHERE TO EAT

O'BRIEN'S HILLVIEW HOUSE, Prosperous, Naas, Co. Kildare. Tel. 045/68252.
Cuisine: TRADITIONAL. **Reservations:** Recommended.
$ **Prices:** High tea IR£7 ($12.25); fixed-price dinner IR£10 ($17.50); à la carte IR£11 ($19.25); Tourist Menu (May–Sept). No credit cards.
Open: Dinner only, daily 5:30–6:30pm. **Parking:** Large car park.

Good traditional dishes of beef, lamb, pork, chicken, and fish appear on the menu at this family-run eatery 22 miles south of Dublin, a 10-minute drive from N7. For a fuller description, see "Where to Stay," above.

WORTH THE EXTRA MONEY

CURRYHILLS HOUSE, Prosperous, Naas, Co. Kildare. Tel. 045/68150.
Cuisine: TRADITIONAL/IRISH. **Reservations:** Recommended.
$ **Prices:** Main courses IR£10.50–IR£12 ($18.40–$21) at lunch, IR£15–IR£19 ($26.25–$33.25) at dinner; Tourist Menu (year round 7–11pm). ACC, AE, MC, V.
Open: Lunch Mon–Sat 12:30–2pm; dinner Mon–Sat 7–11pm. **Closed:** Good Friday, Dec 24–31.

Set in a Georgian-style country house 35km (21 miles) from Dublin on N7, the dining room at Curryhills is the pride and joy of owner/managers Bridie and Bill Travers. Decor is Tudor, and the cuisine features gourmet dishes prepared from local, fresh ingredients. On Friday there's traditional Irish music, and on Saturday you're invited to an old-fashioned sing-along.

MOYGLARE MANOR COUNTRY HOUSE AND RESTAURANT, Maynooth, Co. Kildare. Tel. 01/286501.
Cuisine: INTERNATIONAL. **Reservations:** Essential.
$ **Prices:** Fixed-price meal IR£18.50 ($32.40). Service charge 12½%. ACC, AE, DC, V.
Open: Lunch Mon–Fri 12:30–2:15pm; dinner daily 7–9:30pm. **Closed:** Good Friday, Dec 23–26.

For a fuller description of this magnificent old Georgian mansion 1¼ miles west of Maynooth on N4, see "Where to Stay," above. The dining room is the epitome of elegance, with tall, draped windows, oil paintings, and the sheen of well-polished antique furniture. As for the menu, you might try the roast quail in burgundy sauce, pan-fried brill St. Germain, or simply a very good steak. Whatever your choice, the accompanying vegetables are sure to be fresh from the garden. Exceptionally good wine list.

TONGALEE HOUSE, Athy, Co. Kildare. Tel 0507/31473.
   Cuisine: INTERNATIONAL. **Reservations:** Recommended.
   $ Prices: Five-course fixed-price dinner IR£17.50–IR£18.50 ($30.65–$32.40). No credit cards.
   Open: Lunch Mon–Fri 12:45–2pm; dinner Mon–Sat 7:30–10:30pm; brunch Sun 12:30–2pm.

⭐ Marjorie and Mark Molloy fell in love with this lovely old country house 13 miles southwest of Naas on N78, and in 1990, after extensive renovations, they opened a restaurant that has already garnered accolades. The relaxing dining room, with its chocolate-colored walls, chintz curtains, and soft lighting is the perfect setting for a cuisine that can only be described as gourmet. Mark, in fact, has broad experience as a chef in London and in one of Dublin's most prestigious restaurants, and that experience and expertise show up on the menu. Worthy of note are the roast rack of lamb with a crépinette of vegetables and a shallot sauce, the escalope of salmon with mussels and tarragon sauce, and the breast of Barbarie duck with a brandade of duck leg. Desserts include thin apple tart with cinnamon cream and chocolate-and-almond Marjolaine (a creamy blend of chocolate, cream, and almonds). Highly recommended.

5. COUNTY WICKLOW

Wicklow glows with the greens and blues of a landscape often dubbed the "Garden of Ireland." The **County Wicklow Tourism Association,** in Market Square, Wicklow (tel. 0404/67904), can give you detailed information on the county's many attractions.

WHAT TO SEE & DO

POWERSCOURT ESTATE AND GARDENS, Enniskerry, Co. Wicklow. Tel. 01/867676.
   The O'Tooles, Lords of Glencullen, once occupied a castle on the site of Powerscourt House, an impressive 18th-century mansion of hewn granite that was gutted by fire in 1974 and is no longer open to the public. From its perch on high ground with a view of Great Sugarloaf Mountain, magnificent Japanese and Italian gardens slope downward, dotted with statuary and ornamental lakes. The 14,000-acre demesne, which straddles the River Dargle, holds rare shrubs, massive rhododendrons, and a deer park. Its most noted feature, however, is the Powerscourt Waterfall, which tumbles 400 feet from a clifftop and is the highest waterfall in Ireland and Great Britain—it's at its most magnificent after a rainy spell. Outside the fortified tower stand two cannon from the Spanish Armada. A tearoom and a giftshop featuring Irish goods are housed in the mansion's outbuildings.
   Admission: IR£2 ($3.50) adults, IR£1 ($1.75) children, with a small additional charge for the waterfall.
   Open: Mar–Oct, gardens daily 9am–5:30pm. Waterfall (reached by its own gate, 4 miles from Enniskerry), summer, daily 10:30am–7pm; winter, daily 10:30am–dusk.

GLENDALOUGH, Co. Wicklow. Tel. 01/818119.
⭐ "Valley of Two Lakes" is the literal translation of its name, and when St. Kevin came to this place of exquisite natural beauty, he found the solitude and spiritual atmosphere he was seeking. No visitor today can leave unaffected by that same peaceful atmosphere, which seems to cling to the hills and lakes and woods. For many years St. Kevin lived here as a hermit, sleeping sometimes in a tree, sometimes in a small cleft in the rocks. When his sanctity and wisdom began to draw

disciples to his side, a great school grew up that attracted thousands of students from all over Ireland, Great Britain, and the Continent. By the time of his death in 617 at an advanced age, the school had already become recognized as a great institution of learning.

Scattered around the shores of Glendalough's Upper and Lower Lake are ruins that trace the history of this mystical glen. There are relics of its great European influx, the Danish plunderers, the skirmishes between Wicklow chieftains, and Anglo-Norman invaders. On the south shore of the Upper Lake (and reached only by boat) stands the Church of the Rock (Tempall na Skellig), with St. Kevin's Bed (a tiny hollowed-out hole) to the east of the oratory and about 30 feet above the lake. The main group of ruins are just east of the Lower Lake and those farther east are near the mouth of the valley, where the monastic city developed long after St. Kevin's death.

Admission: Free.

Open: Mid-Apr to mid-June, Mon–Sat 10am–5pm; mid-June to mid-Sept, daily 10am–7pm; mid-Sept to mid-Oct, daily noon–5pm; Nov–Mar, Tues–Sat 10am–1pm, Sun 2–5pm. **Bus:** Two buses daily from Dublin year round, departing College of Surgeons, St. Stephen's Green, Dublin; it's 7 miles east of Wicklow on T7 via Rathdrum.

"MEETING OF THE WATERS," Co. Wicklow.

The spot at which the Avonmore River and Avonbeg River come together in an idyllic setting inspired Thomas Moore's tribute:

> *There is not in the wide world a valley so sweet*
> *As the vale in whose bosom the bright waters meet.*

There's a flagstone path from the road down to the riverbanks, leading to a clearing which holds a bust of the poet, and the tree stump on which he sat while composing his famous lines is marked with a plaque. It's about 4 miles south of Rathdrum.

AVONDALE HOUSE AND FOREST PARK, Co. Wicklow. Tel. 0404/46111.

Avondale House, 1 mile south of Rathdrum, dates from 1777 and is an integral part of Ireland's history. It witnessed the triumph and tragedy of Charles Stewart Parnell, one of the nation's greatest leaders. The main architectural features of the house have been preserved, and three of the rooms display Parnell memorabilia.

Admission: Free.

Open: Mon–Fri 10am–1pm and 2–6pm; May–Sept, Sat–Sun noon–6pm.

RUSSBOROUGH HOUSE, Blessington, Co. Wicklow. Tel. 045/65239.

Built between 1740 and 1750, Russborough House, about 26 miles south of Dublin on N11, was designed in the Palladian style by the noted architect Richard Castle for the first Earl of Milltown. The fine examples of Francini plasterwork are especially noteworthy. Main rooms are elegantly furnished, and the famous Beit art collection includes paintings by Rubens, Gainsborough, Vermeer, and many others. Lots of Irish silver, and interesting old Irish maps that date from 1592 to 1750.

Admission: IR£2.50 ($4.40) adults, IR£1.50 ($2.65) children 12 and over, 50p (90¢) children under 12.

Open: Mar–Oct, Mon–Sat 10:30am–6pm; Sun 11am–6pm.

MOUNT USHER GARDENS, Ashford, Co. Wicklow. Tel. 0404/40205.

This privately owned garden ranks among the leading—and loveliest—horticultural centers in Ireland. Its 20 acres of flowers, trees, shrubs, and lawns lie in the sheltered Vartry River Valley, and although it's not a true botanical garden, its plants come from many parts of the globe. Spindle trees from China, North American sweet gum and swamp cypress, the New Zealand ti tree, African broom, and Burmese juniper are among those represented in a harmony of color in a magnificent setting of superb landscaping. There's also a tea room at the entrance (serving coffee, sandwiches, snacks, and afternoon tea), as well as a shopping courtyard.

Admission: IR£2 ($3.50) adults, IR£1.50 ($2.65) senior citizens, students, and children.

Open: Mid-Mar to Oct, daily 11am–6pm.

AVOCA HANDWEAVERS, Avoka, Co. Wicklow. Tel. 0402/5105.

Not far from the junction of the two rivers, the little town of Avoca is where you'll find the oldest hand-weaving mill in Ireland. Save some time to stop by, where second- and third-generation weavers staff the mill that sits across a little bridge from the sales shop. The history of the mill is fascinating, as it went from near closing to its current humming state of good health. The patterns and weaves from this mill are marketed all over the world, and in the shop you'll find marvelous buys in bedspreads, cloaks, scarves, and a wide variety of other items, many fashioned by home workers from all over the country.

There's also another Avoca Handweavers shop on the Dublin road in Kilmacanogue, where tweeds are transformed into finished products right on the premises, and there's a very good shop at Bunratty in County Clare. But for my money, the original mill is a very special place to visit.

Admission: Free.
Open: Mon–Sat

ARKLOW POTTERY, South Quay, Arklow, Co. Wicklow. Tel. 0402/32401.

Beautifully situated overlooking the sea, Arklow is a seaside resort town, a fishing village, and home to these makers of fine earthenware, porcelain and bone-china tableware, tea sets, dinner sets, combination sets, and giftware, incorporating both modern and traditional designs. The retail shop attached to the factory carries a great selection of shapes and patterns.

Admission: Free.
Open: Daily 9:30am–1pm and 2–5pm. Call to book a guided factory tour June–Aug to watch the craftspeople at their trade.

SAVVY SHOPPING

CLARE SALLEY, Ashford, Co. Wicklow. Tel. 0404/46480.

The exquisite Carrickmacross lace of Ireland is fast disappearing, since few young women are willing to take up the painstaking skill. Clare, however, is a true artist, devoted to this particular form of art, specializing in the leaf, floral, shamrock, and harp designs. Her prices are remarkably low: about IR£65 ($113.75) for a shoulder bridal veil, IR£35 for a first communion veil, and much less for handkerchiefs, collars, cuffs, and mats. She does all the work herself, and will quote on special orders and look after mail orders promptly.

EVENING ENTERTAINMENT

TRADITIONAL IRISH MUSIC In the town of Wicklow, there are traditional Irish music sessions 1 night a week during the summer months at the **Boathouse.** Inquire at the Tourist Office for schedules.

WHERE TO STAY

BED & BREAKFAST

See Section 4, "Where to Stay," in Chapter 4 for an outstanding bed-and-breakfast choice in Bray, County Wicklow.

ABHAINN MOR HOUSE, Corballis, Rathdrum, Co. Wicklow. Tel. 0404/46330. 6 rms (4 with bath).

$ Rates (including breakfast): IR£18 ($31.50) single without bath; IR£12 ($21) per person sharing without bath; IR£1.50 ($2.65) per person additional with bath. 25% reduction for children under 10. Dinner IR£10.50 ($18.40) extra. No credit cards.
Parking: Private parking. **Closed:** Mid-Nov to Jan.

This very attractive, Georgian-style house on the Rathdrum–Avoca road is run by Mrs. Esther O'Brien and is convenient to Glendalough and a forest park. The house is centrally heated and there is a garden for guests to use. The six pretty bedrooms all have sinks.

THE ARBOURS, Avoca, Co. Wicklow. Tel. 0402/35294. 4 rms (none with bath).
$ Rates (including breakfast): IR£11 ($19.25) per person. Dinner IR£9 ($15.75) extra. No credit cards. **Closed:** Dec–Jan.

 Mrs. Maisie Caswell is the lovely and hospitable hostess of this modern bungalow set in a forest 6 miles from Arklow, with a beautiful view of the Avoca valley and river. Mrs. Caswell is well known for her good cooking, and dinner is available with advance notice.

ASHDENE, Knockanree Lower, Avoca, Co. Wicklow. Tel. 0402/5327. 5 rms (4 with bath).
$ Rates (including breakfast): IR£16.50 ($28.90) single without bath; IR£11.50 ($20.15) per person without bath; IR£1.50 ($2.65) per person additional with bath. 25% reduction for children under 10. High tea IR£8.50 ($14.90) extra; dinner, IR£10 ($17.50). Special weekend and midweek package rates available off-season. **Parking:** Private car park. **Closed:** Nov–Easter.
This modern, tastefully appointed house sits in a beautiful setting near the Avoca hand-weavers, and not far from Glendalough. Mrs. Jackie Burns has elicited many letters of praise from readers for her friendly and thoughtful manner with guests. The guest rooms are attractive as well as comfortable, and the house has central heating.

ESCOMBE COTTAGE, Lockstown, Valleymount, Blessington, Co. Wicklow. Tel. 045/67157. 6 rms (4 with bath).
$ Rates (including breakfast): IR£13 ($22.75) per person sharing. Five-course dinner IR£12 ($21) extra. No credit cards. **Closed:** Nov–Feb.
Mrs. Maura Byrne is the charming hostess of this modern bungalow overlooking Blessington lakes (ask for directions when booking). The house is centrally heated and dinner is available. The six bedrooms all have sinks.

SEA CREST HOUSE, Ashtown Lane, Wicklow, Co. Wicklow. Tel. 0404/67772. 6 rms (4 with bath).
$ Rates (including breakfast): IR£15.50 ($27.15) single without bath; IR£11.50 ($20.15) per person sharing without bath; IR£2 ($3.50) per person extra with private bath. 50% reduction for children under 10. High tea IR£6.50 ($11.40) extra; dinner, IR£1? ($21). **Parking:** Private parking. **Closed:** Christmas.
Mrs. Cora Crennan is the gracious hostess of this modern bungalow set on lovely grounds 1 mile from Wicklow on the Wicklow–Wexford road overlooking Wicklow Bay. The house is centrally heated and there is a garden which guests may use. All six attractive bedrooms have sinks.

SILVER SANDS, Dunbur Rd., Wicklow, Co. Wicklow. Tel. 0404/68243. 5 rms (3 with bath).
$ Rates (including breakfast): IR£11.50 ($20.15) per person without bath; IR£1.50 ($2.65) per person additional with bath. 50% reduction for children. IR£1 ($1.75) discount to our readers. High tea IR£8 ($14) extra; dinner, IR£10.50 ($18.40). No credit cards. **Parking:** Private car park.

 Mrs. Lyla Doyle's lovely bungalow looks out to the Irish Sea and the Sugarloaf mountains, with magnificent views and bracing cliff walks. Her home is nicely decorated, and guest rooms are quite attractive. There are sandy beaches, fishing, and golf nearby. Mrs. Doyle is very helpful to all her guests and extends a warm welcome to our readers. Driving through Wicklow town, take the Coast Road; the house is on the right about 500 yards from the monument.

THOMOND HOUSE, St. Patrick's Rd., Upper Wicklow, Co. Wicklow. Tel. 0404/67940. 5 rms (3 with bath).
$ Rates (including breakfast): IR£11.50 ($20.15) per person sharing without bath, IR£13.50 ($23.65) per person sharing with bath. 50% reduction for children. Dinner

IR£11.50 ($20.15) extra. No credit cards. **Parking:** Private car park. **Closed:** Nov–Feb.

 Mrs. Helen Gorman is the charming owner of Thomond House, which has splendid views of both the sea and the Wicklow Mountains. There's central heating and private parking. Wicklow is just half a mile away (St. Patrick's Road is just off the main Wicklow–Wexford road, about half a mile past the Catholic church). It's located 30 minutes from Glendalough and 45 minutes from Dublin, and Mrs. Gorman is very knowledgeable when it comes to exploring the area. She will also meet you at bus or train station if you call ahead.

A FARMHOUSE

BALLYGRIFFIN FARM, Arklow, Co. Wicklow. Tel. 0402/32251. 6 rms (4 with bath).

$ Rates (including breakfast): IR£12 ($21) per person sharing without bath; IR£13 ($22.75) per person sharing with bath. 33⅓% reduction for children. Dinner IR£9.50 ($16.65) extra. No credit cards. **Closed:** Nov–Mar.

David and Diana Lane will welcome you warmly to their large modern farmhouse. The dairy farm is set in the peaceful countryside 2 miles outside Arklow, off the Arklow–Wexford road (N11). The food is good, with home baking, and they have a wine license. The house is centrally heated, and there's a hard tennis court, basketball, games room, and a small library on the premises. Nearby are beautiful beaches and golf courses.

WORTH THE EXTRA MONEY

HUNTER'S HOTEL, Rathnew, Co. Wicklow. Tel. 0404/40106. 18 rms (10 with bath).

$ Rates (including breakfast): IR£28 ($49) per person without bath; IR£30 ($52.50) per person with bath. 25% reduction for children. Fixed-price meal IR£11 ($19.25) extra for lunch, IR£17 ($29.75) for dinner. AE, MC, V. **Parking:** Private car park.

Hunter's Hotel is a lovely old coaching inn situated 28 miles south of Dublin on the Coast Road (south of Greystones), on the banks of the River Vartry. Its beautifully landscaped gardens have won awards, and they're the perfect place to relax in the late afternoon or early evening. In fine weather, prelunch and predinner drinks, as well as afternoon tea, are served in these serene outdoor surroundings. The restaurant is superb (see "Where to Eat," below) and much patronized by locals and Dubliners. Mrs. Maureen Gelletlie is the fifth generation of her family to own and manage Hunter's, and she takes great pride in seeing to the personal comfort of all the guests. There are only 18 guest rooms, all charmingly decorated in country-house style.

THE OLD RECTORY COUNTRY HOUSE, Wicklow, Co. Wicklow. Tel. 0404/67048, or toll free 800/223-6510 in the U.S. 6 rms (all with bath). TV TEL

$ Rates (including breakfast): IR£35 ($61.25) per person. Fixed-price dinner IR£20 ($35) extra. ACC, AE, DC, V. **Parking:** Private parking. **Closed:** Mid-Oct to mid-Apr.

Linda and Paul Saunders welcome guests to their lovely 1870s Greek Revival–style rectory with a complimentary coffee tray with chocolates, tourist information, fresh flowers, and a welcome card. Set in landscaped grounds and gardens a mile off N11 on the Dublin side of Wicklow town, the Old Rectory features Victorian wood paneling, high ceilings, log fires in marble fireplaces, and individually decorated guest rooms with tea and coffee trays, radios, stationery, hairdryers, and assorted toiletries. Your full breakfast can be of the Irish, Scottish, or Swiss variety, and is accompanied by *The Irish Times*—it's even possible to have breakfast served in bed! Evening meals here have gained the Saunders an enviable reputation (see "Where to Eat," below). Dublin is only an hour's drive away, and County Wicklow's many sightseeing attractions are right at hand, including Glendalough, Avoca, and no fewer than five Heritage properties (stately homes, gardens, and museums). Golf and riding are nearby, and Leopardstown racecourse is only 25 miles away.

READERS RECOMMEND

Enniscree Lodge Inn and Restaurant, *Glencree Road, Enniskerry, County Wicklow (tel. 01/863542). "We discovered a wonderful country inn near Dublin in the Wicklow mountains. The inn is run by a brother and sister, who are friendly and helpful. We ate the best meal of our entire trip here, as we enjoyed the sunset from the dining room. It turned out to be a bit pricey, but you will find it worth the extra expense. Call for directions."* —John and Cathy Canzanella, New York, N.Y.

Rathsallagh House, *Dunlavin, County Wicklow (tel. 045/53112; fax 045/53343). "We found a pricey, but worth it, very special place not far from Dublin and close to many interesting sightseeing places. Joe and Kay O'Flynn are warm, welcoming hosts, and the house itself is beautiful. In short, the rooms, the food, and the service are simply superb. But one needs to reserve a long time ahead."* —Dr. Helga Winkler, Austria.

WHERE TO EAT

CHESTER BEATTY'S, Ashford, Co. Wicklow. Tel. 0404/40206.
   Cuisine: TRADITIONAL/IRISH.
$ Prices: Main courses IR£6–IR£10 ($10.50–$17.50); bar food IR£4–IR£6 ($7–$10.50). No credit cards.
   Open: Lunch Mon–Sat 12:45–2:45pm; dinner Mon–Sat 6–9:30pm, Sun 4:30–9:30pm.

The sign outside says HOME COOKING, but after a few meals here, I think it should be amended to read SUPERB HOME COOKING. This cozy bar/restaurant just north of Wicklow on N11 (the main Dublin road), in what was once a wayside inn, dishes up some of the best meals I've encountered in Ireland, and the decor is as inviting as the food if you're drawn to open fires, etched glass, and beamed ceilings. Very Irish, as is the clientele of locals mingling with passersby. Credit for the success of this popular place must go to the two Caprani brothers, Bobby and Paul, and their charming wives, Carol and Kitty. As for the food, chef Myles Moody uses only the freshest local produce to turn out traditional Irish dishes (such as Irish stew—not always easy to find) and mouth-watering fish, beef, chicken, and pork items. Plates come to table heaped high with huge portions, and homemade scones arrive piping hot and with plenty of butter, all served by a cheerful, friendly staff. This is a terrific meal break en route from Wicklow to Dublin, and if you happen by on a Friday or Saturday, you may be tempted to stop overnight for dinner and dancing in their adjacent nightclub. Very good value.

GRAND HOTEL, Wicklow, Co. Wicklow. Tel. 0404/67337.
   Cuisine: TRADITIONAL.
$ Prices: Main courses IR£10–IR£13 ($17.50–$22.75); fixed-price meal IR£9 ($15.75) at lunch, IR£16.50 ($28.90) at dinner. Service charge 13%. ACC, MC, V.
   Open: Lunch daily 12:30–2:30pm; dinner daily 5:30–9:30pm.
This lovely, moderately priced restaurant in the town center has glass walls that overlook the gardens. All three meals are served daily, good to know if you've missed your B&B morning meal because of an early start. The lower-priced Tourist Menu is also served year round.

THE COFFEE SHOP, Fitzwilliam Sq., Wicklow, Co. Wicklow. Tel. 0404/68194.
   Cuisine: DELICATESSEN.
$ Prices: Average lunch IR£6 ($10.50); Tourist Menu (available year round). No credit cards.
   Open: 9:30am–5:30pm.

This deli and restaurant in the center of town specializes in home-cooked lunches. Soups, breads, cakes, scones, salads, and meats are all delicious and modestly priced. They will also fix picnic meals of filled rolls and sandwiches—a very good idea in this scenic county. The special Tourist Menu is also available year round.

WORTH THE EXTRA MONEY

THE OLD RECTORY COUNTRY HOUSE, Wicklow, Co. Wicklow. Tel. 0404/67048.

Cuisine: SEAFOOD/VEGETARIAN. **Reservations:** Essential.
$ Prices: Fixed-price dinner IR£20 ($35). ACC, AE, MC, V.
Open: Dinner only, Sun–Thurs one seating at 7:30pm, Fri–Sat 7:30–9pm.

This 1870s Georgian-style rectory a mile off N11 on the Dublin end of Wicklow town has blossomed as one of County Wicklow's premier eateries under the loving guidance of Paul and Linda Saunders. Set in its own gardens, the house exudes tranquil elegance, with spacious public rooms, high ceilings, and cheerful log fires. Dinner is served by candlelight, with Linda in the kitchen and Paul attending to the very personal service in the lovely dining room. Fresh seafoods and local produce and meats are the basis of the gourmet menu, and there's a good wine list. Advance booking is absolutely essential.

HUNTER'S HOTEL, Rathnew, Co. Wicklow. Tel. 0404/40106.

Cuisine: TRADITIONAL. **Reservations:** Strongly recommended.
$ Prices: Fixed-price meal IR£11 ($19.25) at lunch, IR£17 ($29.75) at dinner. AE, MC, V. **Parking:** Private car park.
Open: Lunch daily 1–3pm; dinner daily 7:30–9:30pm. **Closed:** Christmas Day.

This charming country inn 28 miles south of Dublin on the Coast Road (south of Greystones) is a terrific place to stop in for lunch or afternoon tea if you're traveling (be sure to call ahead, however), and an even better overnight stop (see "Where to Stay," above) and one of their marvelous dinners. Vegetables come straight from the hotel's own garden, seafood is freshly caught, and roasts, steaks, and other meats are locally produced. Service is the pampering kind.

CHAPTER 7

COUNTY WEXFORD

1. WEXFORD
- **WHAT'S SPECIAL ABOUT COUNTY WEXFORD**

2. AROUND COUNTY WEXFORD

The "Sunny Southeast," they call it—there are more sunny days along this part of Ireland's coast than anywhere else in the country—and it encompasses Counties Wexford, Carlow, Kilkenny, Waterford, and South Tipperary. The Southeast is one of Ireland's most scenic regions, with lush greenery, good beaches, seascapes from cliff drives, wild mountain country, and some of the country's best fishing in rivers and coastal waters. Two American presidents, John F. Kennedy (County Wexford) and Ronald Reagan (South Tipperary), have family roots in this beautiful region. Since you'll encounter County Wexford first if you're coming from Dublin along the coast, we'll start there and move on to the other Southeast counties in following chapters.

Father Murphy, of legend and song, led a valiant band of rebels to Vinegar Hill near Enniscorthy in 1798, where for nearly a month the ill-fed and ill-armed patriots held out against the English king's forces. For Americans, there is a strong tie to their own history in the John F. Kennedy Arboretum out by New Ross, not far from the birthplace of his ancestors. Down on the Hook Peninsula, a light to guide sailing ships has burned continuously for more than 1,500 years, winking across the water to Crook Castle on the Waterford side and giving rise to Cromwell's declaration that he would sail up the river "by Hook or by Crook." Today's invaders are tourists such as you and I, who find the now-peaceful countryside a haven for sightseeing, sailing, fishing, and swimming.

1. WEXFORD

Wexford, 90 miles south of Dublin and 39 miles northeast of Waterford, is a small, prosperous town with industry, agriculture, and tourism happily blending into a relaxed atmosphere, and an annual opera festival that draws international artists.

Because of its shallow harbor, it was named Waesfjord (The Harbor of the Mud Flats) by the Vikings, but it was the legendary Fir Bolgs who christened the River Slaney after their leader Slaigne. Vikings came to build a town at the edge of a shallow harbor to use as a base for plundering excursions on land and at sea. And there they stayed until the first Norman forces to land in Ireland arrived on Wexford's coast in 1169 and settled in. And *they* stayed, in spite of uprisings followed by bloody massacres and a liberty-loving native populace that gave them little peace. Today, although very much in touch with the modern world, the town also displays with pride the many marks of its colorful past.

ORIENTATION

ARRIVING Car and passenger ferries from Fishguard, Wales, and Le Havre, France, dock at Rosslare Harbour, 13 miles to the southeast of Wexford town, and there's good bus and train service between Wexford and the port. Wexford can be reached by train from Dublin and by bus from most cities and towns around the country. For train information, call 01/735555; call Bus Eireann at 01/302222 or inquire at local bus stations around the country.

✓ WHAT'S SPECIAL ABOUT COUNTY WEXFORD

Historic Towns
- ☐ Wexford town, with narrow streets and lanes tracing its ancient Viking beginnings.
- ☐ New Ross, one of the county's oldest towns, with medieval buildings and narrow streets.
- ☐ Enniscorthy, setting for the annual Strawberry Fair, its skyline dominated by a huge Norman castle.
- ☐ Gorey, with many associations with 1798 rebellion.

Museums
- ☐ Enniscorthy County Museum, filled with relics of County Wexford's turbulent and agricultural past.
- ☐ Irish Agricultural Museum, at Johnstown Castle, an inside look at rural Irish life and work.
- ☐ Maritime Museum, at Kilmore Quay, housed in an old lightship.

Parks
- ☐ Irish National Heritage Park, where authentic reconstructions trace Ireland's past from prehistoric days through the arrival of the Normans.
- ☐ John F. Kennedy Arboretum, near New Ross, with more than 4,500 plants from around the world.

Wildlife Refuge
- ☐ Saltee Islands, home to thousands of birds of many species.

Beaches
- ☐ Courtown Harbour to Cahore, with wide, sandy strands lining the coast.
- ☐ Rosslare, a sea-and-sun resort popular with natives and visitors alike.

TOURIST INFORMATION The **Tourist Information Office** is at Crescent Quay (tel. 053/23111), and is open Monday through Saturday from 9am to 6pm (later in summer months). Current activities and a town map are available in the free booklet **"Welcome to Wexford,"** published by the Junior Chamber of Commerce from June to October and distributed by the Tourist Board, shops, and hotels.

CITY LAYOUT You can walk most of Wexford's streets in a half hour or so, which means it has never seen fit to install a public transportation system. The **railway station** is at the northern end of town on Redmond Place. **Main Street** is so narrow you can very nearly stand in the middle and touch shops on either side with outstretched arms. One block from the water, it runs parallel to the line of the quays. The **Bull Ring** is a wide intersection at the northern end of Main Street. The quay runs for six blocks along the water's edge, with an inset semicircular Crescent Quay near the center facing a statue of Commodore John Barry.

GETTING AROUND

BY TAXI Private for-hire cars are available in lieu of taxis. They meet most trains and buses, and can be called to pick up fares at hotels and guesthouses. There's no standard rate and no meter, so you should agree on a fare when you engage a car. The Tourist Board can furnish local telephone numbers.

BY CAR My best advice is to park the car and walk. Wexford's narrow streets can be tough going for most drivers, but there are public parking lots on the quays and just back of Main Street. All are prominently marked and charge a very small hourly fee.

FAST FACTS

The **telephone area code** is 053. In an **emergency,** dial 999 and tell the operator which emergency service you need to contact (police, ambulance, fire). The **General**

WEXFORD TOWN

IRELAND
Dublin ★
Wexford ●

ACCOMMODATION:
Westmount House 1

DINING:
The Bohemian Girl 2
The Granary
  Restaurant 1
Tim's Tavern 4
Wren's Nest 3

ATTRACTIONS:
Arts Centre, at Corn
  Market 4
Bull Ring 6
Commodore John
  Barry Statue 10
Main Street 7
Franciscan Friary 8
Railway Station 3
Selskar Abbey 2
Tom Moore's Tavern 5
Tourist Information
  Office 9
Westgate Tower 1

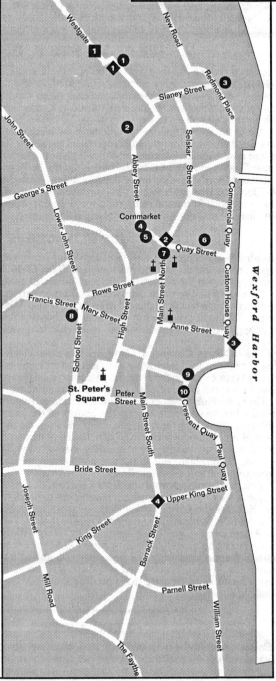

Church

Post Office is on Anne Street, and is open Monday through Saturday from 9am to 5:30pm. **Telegraph service** is available by dialing 196 (if you are dialing from a coin-box telephone with A and B buttons, dial 10 and tell the operator what you want). Most hotels in Wexford can provide **Telex** facilities.

WHAT TO SEE & DO

The very first thing you should do is stop in at the Tourist Office and pick up a copy of **"South Wexford."** It's a marvelous illustrated booklet that's one of a series by Pat Mackey, who knows the region like the back of his hand and will bring each town, village, and country lane vividly alive for you. It's available at a small charge. You can also get this and others in the series at the Waterford Tourist Office.

Ask at the Tourist Office about the time and place to join the free **walking tour** conducted every summer evening by members of the Old Wexford Society. It's a labor of love for the dedicated group, and they'll point out such places as the birthplace of Oscar Wilde's mother next to the Bull Ring, the house in Cornmarket where poet Thomas Moore's mother lived, the house on North Main Street where Robert McClure, the man who found the Northwest Passage, was born, and many other historical spots. At the end of the tour, you'll look at Wexford with a different vision. No charge, but a donation to the society is appreciated.

THE TOP ATTRACTIONS

No admission is charged to view most of Wexford town's attractions. At the northern edge of town near the rail and bus station, is **West Gate Tower,** the only surviving gateway of five in the old town walls. It is fairly well preserved.

Selskar Abbey, which dates from the 12th century, stands nearby on the site of an ancient pagan temple dedicated to Odin and a later Viking church. Henry II came here in 1172 to do penance for his murder of Thomas à Becket, and this is where the first Anglo-Irish treaty was signed when Wexford was surrendered to Robert Fitzstephen.

The ✪ **Arts Centre,** at Cornmarket, is the venue for concerts and dance and drama performances. Interesting historical and art exhibits are also housed here, and there's a coffee shop on the premises. Just down from the Arts Centre, **Tom Moore's Tavern** was the home of poet Thomas Moore's mother, a Wexford native.

Go by the **Bull Ring,** in the wide intersection at the north end of Main Street, and spend a few minutes reflecting on the bravery of the pikemen of the 1798 rebellion who are portrayed by the bronze statue there. Its name comes from the fact that the sport of bull-baiting was practiced here by the Norman aristocracy. Until Cromwell visited his wrath on the town in 1649, leaving only 200 survivors of the 2,000 populace, a great high cross stood here, and the valiant Irish knelt in prayer before it as Cromwell dealt out wholesale death.

Visit the **Commodore John Barry statue,** on Crescent Quay, presented to the people of Wexford by the American government to honor this native son who became the "Father of the American Navy." If you pass through Ballysampson, Tagoat (some 10 miles from Wexford), tip your hat to his birthplace. He is credited with founding the American navy after being appointed by George Washington in 1797.

An attraction unto itself, narrow little ✪ **Main Street** is always alive with the buzz of friendly commerce. It's pedestrianized, and an intriguing mix of traditional storefronts, boutiques, pubs, and gift shops. The house in which Cromwell stayed during his Wexford rampage stood on the present-day site of Woolworth & Co., 29 South Main Street.

IMPRESSIONS

Before dinner had a most delicious walk by myself along the banks of the river Slaney, which, for two or three miles out of the town, are full of beauty, and this sunny evening was quite worthy of them. It was likewise delightful to me to be alone in such a scene, for it is only alone I can enjoy Nature thoroughly.
—THOMAS MOORE, *DIARY*, 1835

The **Franciscan Friary,** on John Street, is built on the site of an earlier friary founded in 1230. It's noteworthy for its fine stucco work on the ceiling and for the reliquary of St. Adjutor, a young boy who was martyred in ancient Rome, and whose remains are encased in a wax figure.

NEARBY ATTRACTIONS

IRISH NATIONAL HERITAGE PARK, Ferrycarrig, Co. Wexford. Tel. 053/ 41733, 22211, or 23111.

⭐ Don't leave Wexford without a visit to this unique heritage park. Just 3 miles outside town, the park holds reconstructions of a campsite, farmstead, and portal dolmen from the Stone Age (7000–2000 B.C.); a cist burial and stone circle from the Bronze Age (2000–500 B.C.); an ogham stone, ringfort and souterrain, early Christian monastery, corn-drying kiln, horizontal water mill, Viking boathouse, and an artificial island habitat known as a crannog, all from the Celtic and early Christian ages (500 B.C.–A.D. 1169); and a Norman motte and bailey, the first Norman fortification in Ireland, and a round tower, from the Early Norman Period (A.D. 1169–1280). There's also a nature walk of real beauty. Work is still continuing on this fascinating look back into Ireland's past, and there may well be many other reconstructions by the time you visit.

Admission: IR£2 ($3.50) adults, IR£1 ($1.75) students; IR£5 ($8.75) family ticket.

Open: Apr–Oct, daily 10am–7pm. **Bus:** During summer months, special buses from Wexford town make regular trips to and from the park; check with the Tourist Board for fares and schedules; it's 3 miles northwest of Wexford town, just off N11 (well signposted).

IRISH AGRICULTURAL MUSEUM, Johnstown Castle, Co. Wexford. Tel. 053/42888.

Four miles southwest of Wexford town on the road to Murrintown, this interesting museum is in early 19th-century farm buildings on the grounds of Johnstown Castle. This major museum of agriculture and Irish rural life features displays on farming methods, life in the farmyard and the rural household (with a major collection of country furniture), and rural transport. There are also reconstructions of workshops of rural craftsmen. There's a tea room, as well as a bookshop and an Irish-made-souvenir shop (open June through August).

Admission: Free.

Open: June–Aug, Mon–Fri 9am–5pm, Sat–Sun 1–5pm; Sept–May, Mon–Fri 9am–12:30pm and 2–5pm.

SPECIAL EVENTS

I can't wish anything happier for you than that you should arrive in town in October for the ✪ **Wexford Opera Festival.** It's 18 days of music and revelry, with international and home-grown companies presenting both standard favorites and lesser-known operas, all with casts and orchestral support of the highest standards. Three are performed throughout each week, along with recitals, workshops, and a host of other related activities. The festival celebrated its 40th anniversary in 1991. For detailed information on scheduled performances and recitals, ticket prices, and booking, contact: Wexford Festival of Opera, Theatre Royal, Wexford (tel. 053/ 22144). Tickets vary from year to year, but run around IR£30 ($52.50) for Gala Night and weekends, and IR£24 ($44) for midweek performances.

SPORTS & RECREATION

Check with the Tourist Office for dates of race meets at the **Wexford Racecourse.** This is a horse-mad town, and meets here are attended by hours and hours of debate and sociability in Wexford pubs. Great fun!

Also see the Tourist Office staff for information on how you can participate in local **hunting, fishing, boating, and golfing.** There's a good **beach** at Rosslare, although the Irish Sea is not the warmest water you'll run across.

If you're a horseback rider, know that the **Shelmalier Riding Stables,** Forth Mountain, County Wexford (tel. 053/39251), has instruction for inexperienced or new riders, as well as pony trekking through forest and mountain country planned for every level of expertise, and a more exacting cross-country ride for experienced riders. A delightful offering is the periodic "pub ride" to imbibe a few jars in local establishments. The stables are 5 miles from Wexford town, and advance booking is essential. They are open daily.

SAVVY SHOPPING

BARKER'S, 36 S. Main St. Tel. 053/23159. Fax 053/23738.
Good gift selections, and they ship overseas. Stocks include a large selection of Waterford crystal, Royal Tara china, Belleek, Irish linen, bronze, and pottery. Open Monday through Saturday from 9am to 5:30pm.

THE BOOK CENTRE, 7 N. Main St. Tel. 053/23543.
Extensive stock of books on Irish topics, as well as a wide range of other fiction and nonfiction publications. It's open Monday through Saturday from 9am to 5:30pm.

JOYCES CHINA SHOP, 1 S. Main St. Tel. 053/22744.
An excellent place to shop for Waterford crystal, Belleek china, heraldic crests, and high-quality Irish souvenirs. Murt Joyce, who has visited the States and has a special fondness for Yanks, has a large stock of such items, competitive prices, and frequent specials on even the pricier merchandise. Open Monday through Saturday from 9am to 5:30pm.

MARTIN'S, 14 S. Main St. Tel. 053/22635.
Martin's will also ship gifts overseas. They carry good selections of Waterford and Tipperary crystal, Belleek, and Irish chinaware. Open Monday through Saturday from 9am to 5:30pm.

EVENING ENTERTAINMENT

Some say that it was shipwrecked Cornish sailors who first brought ✪ **mumming** to Wexford. No matter how it arrived, however, it has survived, albeit with a decidedly Irish accent, down through the centuries, and it is unique to this county. The medieval folkdance with sword play was based on the Miracle Play triumph of good over evil. Today's mummers portray Irish patriots like Wolfe Tone and Robert Emmet. The three or four groups are composed of Wexford natives who have inherited their place in the ritualistic performances from family members going back several generations. They don't follow a regular schedule, but the Tourist Office will usually be able to tell you when the next appearance is likely to occur in one of the local pubs. If you can track one down, don't miss it.

For other evening entertainment, check what's on at the Arts Centre.

The Pub Scene

Pubs and lounges are open Monday through Saturday from 10:30am to 11:30pm (to 11pm during the winter) and on Sunday from noon to 2pm and 4 to 10pm.

THE CAPE OF GOOD HOPE, N. Main St. Tel. 053/22949.
Stop in here where Con Macken (uncle of international horseshow jumping champion Eddie Macken) holds forth as publican, greengrocer, and undertaker. It may be the only place left in Ireland where you'll find all three occupations under the same roof.

THE CROWN BAR, Monck St.
This great old pub, in the same family since it was established as a stagecoach inn in 1841, has become internationally known through European television. Mrs. Annie Kelly is its present proprietor, and her sons, Paddy and Dick, are

usually on hand to show visitors around the Crown's unique collection of ancient weapons. The two small back lounges hold racks and cases filled with dueling pistols and flintlocks, pikes from the 1798 Vinegar Hill siege, brass blunderbusses, powder horns, and Michael Collins's revolver, among many other historical items. Lest you think this is a museum, let me hasten to assure you that it's one of the best drinking and talking pubs in these parts!

TIM'S TAVERN, 51 S. Main St. Tel. 053/23861.

There's always a good "crack" going here (see "Where to Eat," below), as well as sporadic singing nights. These folks are so good that they're sponsored by Guinness in the singing pub competitions during the Wexford Opera Festival, and you'll find them in fine voice almost any night of the week.

WHERE TO STAY

Wexford has few accommodations within the town limits. However, in addition to the following listings, many B&Bs and farmhouses are within easy driving distance of the town.

Note: Prices are usually higher during the Opera Festival in October.

IN TOWN

WESTMOUNT HOUSE, Westgate, Wexford. Tel. 053/24428 or 22167. 5 rms (1 with bath).

$ Rates (including breakfast): IR£11($19.25) per person without bath; IR£2.50 ($4.40) per person additional with bath. No credit cards. **Parking:** Private parking.

Mrs. D. Allen is the hostess at this comfortable home at the north end of town convenient to the rail and bus depot and a short walk into the town center.

NEARBY ACCOMMODATIONS

THE ANCHORAGE, Saunders Court, Ferrycarrig, Co. Wexford. Tel. 053/44902. 3 rms (none with bath).

$ Rates (including breakfast): IR£11.50 ($20.15) per person sharing. No credit cards. **Closed:** Dec–Feb.

Two miles from Wexford town, a short drive from Ferrycarrig bridge on N11 (signposted on your right coming from Wexford), the Anchorage is the lovely modern home of Mary and Paddy Hatton. Perched on a bluff overlooking the Slaney River estuary, its lounge has a panoramic river view, and two of the guest rooms look out on the river. There are two twin-bedded rooms, and another with one double and a single bed, all with sinks and nicely decorated by Mary. Incidentally, she graduated from the celebrated Ballymaloe Cookery School "with distinction"; her expertise shows up in the dinners at their nearby restaurant.

CLONARD HOUSE, Clonard Great, Wexford. Tel. 053/23141. 10 (all with bath).

$ Rates (including breakfast): IR£14 ($24.50) per person. 50% reduction for children. Five-course dinner IR£12 ($21) extra. No credit cards. **Closed:** Nov–Mar.

This lovely 1783 Georgian house 2 miles from Wexford, an eighth of a mile off the N25/R733 roundabout (signposted at the roundabout) was John Hayes's family home. Its 120 acres are still operated as a dairy farm, and his wife, Kathleen, and their four children now offer warm Irish hospitality to visitors. The bedrooms are unusually spacious, attractively decorated (some with four-poster beds), with bucolic farm views from every window (my favorite is the top-floor room under the eaves overlooking the century-old farmyard with its interesting outbuildings). Log fires and a piano make the lounge a friendly gathering place for guests, and Kathleen's evening meals are fast gaining a faithful following. Wine is available at the dinner hour.

ROCKCLIFFE, Coolballow, Wexford. Tel. 053/43130. 4 rms (2 with bath).
$ Rates (including breakfast): IR£11 ($19.25) per person. 20% reduction for children. No credit cards. **Parking:** Private parking. **Closed:** Nov–Easter.

Just 2 miles from town and about a half mile down the Johnstown Castle road (off the Wexford–Rosslare road), Mrs. Sarah Lee's attractive, modern home is set high on an acre of landscaped grounds that feature huge, colorful roses in summer months. The bedrooms are nicely furnished and attractively decorated, all with sinks, and the house is centrally heated. The Rosslare ferry is 10 miles away, and Mrs. Lee is happy to fix an early breakfast for departing guests. From Rosslare Harbour, take N25 and at the roundabout take the Wexford exit; it's signposted at the next left turn.

WORTH THE EXTRA MONEY

FERRYCARRIG HOTEL, Ferrycarrig Bridge (P.O. Box 11), Wexford, Co. Wexford. Tel. 053/22999. Fax 053/41982. 40 rms (all with bath). TV TEL
$ Rates (including breakfast): IR£37–IR£50 ($64.75–$87.50) single; IR£32–IR£45 ($56–$78.75) per person sharing. Children under 10 stay free in parents' room. Higher rates apply during the Opera Festival and in July and August; send IR£20 ($35) deposit when booking. Special weekend and package rates available. AE, DC, MC, V. **Parking:** Private car park. **Closed:** Christmas–Easter.

This hotel was described by one reviewer as "a modern lump of concrete," and I'd have to go along with that description except for several things that make it quite exceptional. First of all, it's situated 2 miles from Wexford town on N11 just across the Ferrycarrig Bridge (there's a large sign on the right almost immediately after crossing the bridge) on the Enniscorthy side of the Slaney Estuary, and although it's very close to a main thoroughfare, it's nestled on the riverbank, out of sight and sound of traffic, with green lawns that give it a true country setting. All the attractive rooms face the river with broad picture windows to take advantage of those river views. A wooded river walk from the hotel grounds leads (in about 3 minutes) to a ruined tower perched atop a craggy cliff at the northern edge of Ferricarrig Bridge, thought to be the first Anglo-Norman castle erected in Ireland. Just a short distance away on the south side of the river is the unique Wexford Heritage Park.

Best of all, I'd have to count personable Matt and Olive Britton, who run the hotel with the sort of hospitality you expect in Ireland. There's a cozy bar, and the Conservatory Restaurant (see "Where to Eat," below)—all in all, a good base for exploring County Wexford.

WEXFORD LODGE HOTEL, The Bridge, Wexford, Co. Wexford. Tel. 053/23611. 18 rms (all with bath).
$ Rates (including breakfast): IR£24–IR£26 ($42–$45.50) per person. ACC, AE, MC, V. **Parking:** Enclosed car park.

This small, two-story hotel sits directly across the bridge from Wexford town quays on R741 overlooks Wexford harbor, with good views of Wexford town across the water. Recently renovated by the Igoe family, its public rooms are attractive and inviting, and guest rooms are nicely done up, with glassed-in balconies for year-round comfort. Adjacent to the hotel is a heated swimming pool and sauna. The restaurant here has, in a very short time, established a name for excellent seafood at moderate prices.

WHITFORD HOUSE, New Line Rd., Wexford. Tel. 053/43845 or 43444. 27 rms (all with bath). TV TEL
$ Rates (including breakfast): IR£25 ($43.75) single; IR£24 ($42) per person double. MC, V. **Closed:** Dec 20–Jan 9.

Kay and Jim Whitty are the hospitable owners/managers here. The bedrooms in the two-story, white guesthouse are beautifully decorated, there's a large TV lounge, and meals in the dining room are exceptional. The attractive Fortside Lounge Bar is open for guests and the general public, with music 4 nights a week. Other facilities include a full-size, heated indoor swimming pool, all-weather tennis court, and children's playground. It's along the Duncannon road, 2 miles from Wexford, 100 yards from the Wexford–Duncannon roundabout.

READERS RECOMMEND

Ardruadh, Spawell Road, Wexford (tel. 053/23194). "This is a new facility in Wexford town recently opened by Peter and Nora Corish, who are former hotel operators. Both the house and grounds are gorgeous, a reflection of the fine taste of the Corishes."—William J. Trimble, Jr., Altoona, Penna.

WHERE TO EAT

THE BOHEMIAN GIRL, N. Main St., at Quay St. Tel. 053/24419.
Cuisine: PUB GRUB/TRADITIONAL/VEGETARIAN.
$ Prices: Lunch IR£4 ($7); dinner IR£8 ($14). Tourist Menu (available Mon–Sat). ACC, MC, V.
Open: Daily 10:30am–11:30pm.

This Tudor-style pub is a homey place, supervised by owner-chefs Kay and Seamus McMenamin, with a loyal local following and Bar Catering Competition Awards proudly displayed. Soups and brown bread are homemade, and on hand are pâté and smoked salmon and other seafood.

THE GRANARY RESTAURANT, West Gate. Tel. 053/23935.
Cuisine: SEAFOOD/TRADITIONAL.
$ Prices: Appetizers IR£2.50–IR£2.95 ($4.40–$5.15); main courses IR£6.25–IR£11.95 ($10.95–$20.90); lunch IR£1.15–IR£4.25 ($2–$7.45). ACC, V.
Open: Lunch Mon–Fri 12:30–2:30pm; dinner Mon–Sat 5:30–10:30pm.
Closed: Several days at Christmas.

This cozy, old-world-style restaurant has a warm, inviting ambience, with individual booths in the dining room and wooden beams in the cellar bar, where lunches are served. Paddy and Mary Hatton feature such specialties as Wexford mussels, monkfish and prawn provinçal, and sole on the bone. Steaks, duckling, venison (in season), lamb, and chicken are also featured, and there is always at least one vegetarian selection. The Granary is on the north end of town past the rail and bus depot, on N25, opposite the West Gate (a 5-minute walk from Main Street).

OAK TAVERN, Ferrycarrig Bridge. Tel. 053/24922.
Cuisine: SEAFOOD/STEAKS.
$ Prices: Appetizers IR£2–IR£4 ($3.50–$7); main courses IR£10–IR£14 ($17.50–$25). Service charge 10%. ACC, MC, V.
Open: Daily 10:30am–11:30pm.

On the south bank of Slaney River at Ferricarrig Bridge, about 2 miles from Wexford town, this old tavern dates back over a century and a half. It's in the two original front rooms, complete with open fire, piano, and lots of local faces, that you can indulge in in a bar lunch of soup, sandwiches, seafood snacks, or pâté for under IR£5 ($8.75). In fine weather, you can sit on an outdoor terrace fashioned from a part of the old bridge, right at the water's edge. Back of the bar is an intimate little restaurant that fits right in with the tavern. It's lined with windows to take advantage of the river view, and also has an open fire as well as lovely tapestry upholstered seating. Specialties include a huge (10-oz.) grilled salmon steak with parsley butter, river trout poached in tomato provençal concasse, and steaks.

TIM'S TAVERN, 51 S. Main St. at the corner of Upper King St. Tel. 053/23861.
Cuisine: PUB GRUB.
$ Prices: Lunch IR£5.50 ($9.65); dinner IR£9.50 ($16.65). No credit cards.
Open: Year round, Lunch Mon–Sat noon–2:30pm; July–Oct, dinner Mon–Sat 6–8pm.

Ken and Margaret Martin run this Tudor-style pub, which features exposed beams, whitewashed walls, and a thatch-roofed bar. All soups, meats, vegetables, and desserts are home-cooked, with portions more than ample. You can choose from a varied menu with everything from toasted sandwiches to open sandwiches of prawns, smoked or fresh salmon, or chicken to delicious salad plates of fresh or smoked salmon, prawns, or chicken. Evening meals include a 12-ounce sirloin steak, french fries, and vegetables, plus a good selection of salad plates. The food is exceptional, but even better is the clientele, many of whom lead off a singsong at the slightest provocation, and others (including Ken himself) who are only too eager to share their expertise at betting the horses at Wexford race meets or others around the country. This is a place you well could come to dinner and wind up staying until Ken sings out, "Time, gentlemen, please."

WREN'S NEST, Custom House Quay. Tel. 053/22359.
   Cuisine: PUB GRUB.
$ **Prices:** IR£1–IR£3 ($1.75–$5.25). No credit cards.
   Open: Hot foods, daily noon–3pm; snacks, daily noon–7pm.

This is one of the best places in Wexford for a good, inexpensive lunch. It's a good-looking bar whose backroom lounge features an attractive stone fireplace. The menu includes a hot-plate special, salads, the house pâté and brown bread (excellent), and sandwiches. It sits facing the harbor, a little north of the Crescent.

WORTH THE EXTRA MONEY

THE CONSERVATORY RESTAURANT, in the Ferrycarrig Hotel, Ferrycarrig Bridge, Wexford. Tel. 053/22999.
   Cuisine: SEAFOOD/TRADITIONAL.
$ **Prices:** Prix-fixe five-course dinner IR£20 ($35); lunch about IR£10 ($17.50). Service charge 10%. ACC, AE, MC, V.
   Open: Lunch Mon–Sat 12:30–2:30pm, Sun 12:45–2pm; dinner daily 7–9:30pm.

Since Matt and Olive Britton arrived to manage this first-class hotel in 1987, they have developed the pretty, greenery-filled Conservatory into a leading restaurant in the Wexford region. With marvelous views of the River Slaney just across the lawn, the room exudes a warm, inviting glow, and the menu is as inviting as the setting. There is a comfortable and spacious lounge in which to have a before-dinner drink and place your order from selections such as poached Atlantic sea-fresh filet of pink salmon with Dutch-Gewurtz hollandaise garni, sautéed suprême of chicken with orange and lakeshore whole-grain-whiskey mustard, and escalope of succulent veal au Cinzano bianco with saffron risotto. Desserts might include home-baked apple pie with that good fresh Irish cream, a crispy almond basket of assorted ice creams, or a selection of Irish farmhouse cheeses. The hotel is 2 miles north of Wexford on N11, just over the Ferrycarrig Bridge.

2. AROUND COUNTY WEXFORD

County Wexford entices you to ramble along a coast dotted with fine, sandy strands, or to wander from one historically significant point to the next. County Wexford is pure charm, from the solid stone ruins of Norman castles to whitewashed farmhouses overlooking rolling fields and wooded pastures to thatched cottages and fishing villages.

SEEING COUNTY WEXFORD While a car is essential to see many of County Wexford's attractions, those without wheels can plan day trips that rely solely on public transportation.
   By Bus Bus service is available to the following: Enniscorthy, from Wexford, Ferns, and Dublin; Ferns, from Wexford, Enniscorthy, and Dublin; Courtown Harbour, from Gorey and Wexford; New Ross, from Wexford, Waterford, and Dublin; Rosslare and Rosslare Harbour, from Wexford; and Kilmore Quay, from Wexford on specified days of the week. *Remember, however, that bus schedules*

must be carefully studied if you want to go and return in a single day—service can be infrequent to some points.

By Train   Trains reach Enniscorthy and Rosslare and Rosslare Harbour from Wexford and Dublin.

By Car   With a Wexford town base, all of County Wexford can easily be explored by car. The Tourist Board in Wexford town has an excellent (and free) magazine, entitled *Skylines,* that outlines 10 touring routes throughout the entire Southeast. Unless you wish to return to Wexford town each night, you can combine any or all of these excursions to make a circular tour of the county.

ENNISCORTHY

Using Wexford town as a base, drive 11 miles north on N11 to Enniscorthy, with its strong links to this region's history.

WHAT TO SEE & DO

Historic relics are displayed in the ✪ **Enniscorthy County Museum,** town center, Enniscorthy, County Wexford (tel. 054/35926), housed in a remarkably intact Norman castle built in the early 13th century. It is said that Spenser wrote some of his epic *Faerie Queen* while living here. Cromwell gave it a battering, and it was on its way to becoming just another ruin until it was reconstructed in 1900. Today its rooms hold items that figured in the lives of Irish country people in years past, as well as mementos of the tragic 1798 uprising and the 1916 rebellion, which had a happier outcome. There's a still in such good condition it could be put to work today turning out Ireland's brand of moonshine, poteen ("pot-*sheen*"). Other interesting items include the collection of rush lights that were the first torches in the country. There's a small admission charge, and it's open June to September, daily from 10am to 6pm; all other months, daily from 2 to 5:30pm.

At the eastern edge of town, **Vinegar Hill** provides superb views from its 390-foot summit, and you'll share them with the ghosts of valiant Wexford pikemen who made their last stand here in June 1798, led by the indomitable Father Murphy. There's a convenient car park, and no admission fee.

WHERE TO STAY

IVELLA, Rectory Rd., Enniscorthy, Co. Wexford. Tel. 054/33475. 3 rms (none with bath).

$ Rates (including breakfast): IR£10.50 ($18.40) per person. No credit cards.

✪ This modern house sits on a hillside abloom with colorful garden flowers. There are three attractive guest rooms, two with double and single beds to accommodate families, and one double room. Breakfast comes with home-made brown bread and jam, and Miss Ann Heffernan, who is as bright and ⑤ sparkling as her home, also serves guests fresh strawberries from her own garden, topped with generous dollops of fresh cream. Rectory Road is signposted on N11 as you enter town from Dublin.

BALLYORLEY HOUSE, Boolavogue, Co. Wexford. Tel. 054/66287. 3 rms (none with bath).

$ Rates (including breakfast): IR£12.50 ($21.90) per person. 50% reduction for children. No credit cards. **Closed:** Jan–Feb.

Mrs. Mary Gough presides over this lovely Georgian house 3 miles off the main Wexford–Dublin road (N11). Her four bedrooms are nicely decorated and very comfortable. With advance notice, she will also provide the evening meal.

WHERE TO EAT

THE ANTIQUE TAVERN, Enniscorthy, Co. Wexford. Tel. 054/33428.
   Cuisine: BAR FOOD.
$ Prices: Under IR£3 ($5.25) inclusive. No credit cards.
   Open: Lunch only, daily 12:30–2:30pm.

Proprietor Vincent Heffernan is proud of the fact that the Antique Tavern has won "best pub" awards in both County Wexford and the entire Leinster province. It certainly has served some of the best bar lunches I've had in Ireland—homemade soups with homemade brown bread and a vast and varied selection of sandwiches, washed down with either tea or coffee. On the northern outskirts of town on N11 (Gorey road), it's a cozy, friendly place, with all the atmosphere of an old Irish pub.

FERNS

Some 8 miles farther north on N11 is Ferns (21 miles north of Wexford town) and its impressive historical ruins. The little village of Ferns was once the capital of all Leinster, and relics of its long history invite a ramble. Look for impressive **Ferns Castle**, which dates from the 13th century, the 12th-century **Augustinian abbey** (now in ruins), and on a hill just outside the village, the 16th-century **St. Peter's Church.**

WHERE TO STAY & EAT

CLONE HOUSE, Ferns, Co. Wexford. Tel. 054/66113. 8 rms (3 with bath).
$ Rates (including breakfast): IR£15 ($26.25) single without bath; IR£12 ($21) per person sharing without bath; IR£2 ($3.50) per person extra with bath. 25% reduction for children. High tea IR£9 ($15.75) extra; dinner, IR£11 ($19.25). No credit cards. **Closed:** Nov–Feb.
Built in 1640, this delightful farmhouse is set in some 300 acres of farmland, and its pretty garden has won several National Garden awards, while the house has received the Best Farm House award. Mrs. Betty Breen and her whole family have been very popular with readers. The house is centrally heated, and electric blankets are supplied if needed. It's a working farm and excellent home-produced cuisine is guaranteed. A real convenience are the laundry facilities, available to any guest who may need them. The River Bann river runs through the farm, providing good trout fishing. It's 2 miles off N11 at Ferns Village, 5 miles from Enniscorthy, and 21 miles from Wexford.

GOREY

It was on Gorey Hill, at the western edge of Gorey, that those 1798 rebels pitched camp on their way to march on Arklow, and a granite Celtic cross near the hill commemorates their brave, albeit ill-fated, effort. In July and August, the **Funge Arts Centre,** on Rafter Street, hosts an arts festival that attracts participants from around the world.

WHERE TO STAY & EAT

WOODLANDS HOUSE, Killinierin, Gorey, Co. Wexford. Tel. 0402/7125. 5 rms (4 with bath).
$ Rates (including breakfast): IR£16 ($28) single without bath; IR£13 ($22.75) per person sharing without bath; IR£2 ($3.50) per person extra with bath. 25% reduction for children. Five-course dinner IR£12 ($21) extra. **Closed:** Dec–Feb.
Mrs. Phyllis O'Sullivan is the hostess of this large farmhouse, whose amenities include a playroom, pool table, and amusements. There are spacious, pleasant lawns and gardens surrounded by a forest which has beautiful walks. It is centrally heated, but there's a log fire in the TV lounge. Some bedrooms are traditionally furnished, as befits this 140-year-old Georgian house. Meals include fresh, home-grown ingredients and home-baking. It's a mile off the Gorey–Arklow road (N11) near the Wexford-Wicklow border, 28 miles north of Wexford.

Worth the Extra Money

MARLFIED COUNTRY HOUSE, Gorey, Co. Wexford. Tel. 055/21124. Fax 055/21572. 19 rms (all with bath).
$ Rates (including full Irish breakfast): IR£50–IR£125 ($87.50–$218.75) per person. ACC, AE, MC, V. **Closed:** 2 weeks in Jan.

⭐ Surrounded by some 35 acres of wooded countryside and landscaped gardens, 1¼ miles from Gorey on the Courtown road (R742), this stately Regency house was once the home of the Earl of Courtown, and is filled with antiques, gilt-framed mirrors, and crystal chandeliers. Log fires in the public rooms add a gracious note of warmth, and a lovely curved staircase sweeps up to elegantly furnished guest rooms. Mary and Ray Bowe, the owners who have brought the old home back to its former glory, go out of their way to see that guests are catered to.

Dining: Even if you are not staying at the hotel, you may want to have a memorable meal at the excellent restaurant. Mary Bowe is known for her expertise with seafoods, although any choice from the menu will consist of home-grown or locally produced ingredients prepared with a gourmet cook's touch. The restaurant is set in a Victorian-style conservatory, with sweeping views of the lawns and gardens. It's altogether charming and the epitome of luxury dining. A fixed-price lunch costs IR£14.50 ($25.40); a fixed-price dinner, IR£26 ($45.50). It's open for lunch daily from 1 to 2:30pm, and for dinner daily from 7:30 to 9:30pm; closed for 2 weeks in January.

COURTOWN HARBOUR

To reach one of the county's best beaches, take R742 from Gorey to Courtown Harbour, 24 miles north of Wexford.

This picturesque little fishing village is a popular family resort, with a fine, 2-mile-long sandy beach, amusements for the young fry, and golf for their elders.

Return to Wexford via R742 south, a delightful drive through small coastal villages.

WHERE TO STAY & EAT

COURTOWN HOTEL, Courtown Harbour, Co. Wexford. Tel. 055/25108. 21 rms (all with bath). TV TEL
$ Rates (including breakfast): IR£21–IR£31 ($36.75–$54.25) per person. ACC, AE, MC, V. **Closed:** Nov–Mar.
Set right in the center of this small seaside resort, the Courtown Hotel is an ideal stop if you fancy a dip in the Irish Sea. Guest rooms are plain but very comfortable, and the staff is friendly and efficient. There's an indoor pool for inclement weather, and frequent entertainment in the evening.

ROSSLARE & ROSSLARE HARBOUR

To reach Rosslare, 11 miles southeast of Wexford, a popular seaside resort with good beaches, or Rosslare Harbour, 5 miles farther south, ferry port for the U.K. and France, follow N25 south from Wexford town. The **Tourist Information Office** (tel. 053/33623) is set back from N25 (on your right coming from Wexford) between Rosslare and Rosslare Harbour, open March to September.

Main attractions here are the 6-mile-long beach that arcs along the coast at Rosslare and, of course, the ferry port at Rosslare Harbour.

To reach the Hook Peninsula from Rosslare Harbour, turn onto R736 from N25, then onto a signposted, unmarked road south to Churchtown. For Kilmore Quay and the Saltees, continue on R736 and turn south on R739. From Kilmore Quay, you can travel to New Ross by following R736 north until it joins N25.

WHERE TO STAY

GILNORE HOUSE, Brittas Tagoat, Rosslare Harbour, Co. Wexford. Tel. 053/31340. 5 rms (2 with bath).
$ Rates (including breakfast): IR£15 ($26.25) single; IR£11.50 ($20.15) per person sharing. 25% reduction for children. Dinner IR£10 ($17.50) extra. No credit cards.
The large, white house on the left-hand side of N25 (Wexford–Rosslare road), 12km (7¼ miles) from Wexford, 4km (2½ miles) from Rosslare Harbour, is built in the Georgian style and is the home of Noreen and Gilbert Monti. The attractive bedrooms are spacious and have built-in wardrobes. Both Mr. and Mrs. Monti take a keen interest in guests and are happy to furnish local information.

KILRANE HOUSE, Kilrane, Rosslare Harbour, Co. Wexford. Tel. 053/ 33135. 6 rms (4 with bath).
$ Rates: IR£18 ($31.50) single; IR£12 ($21) per person sharing. 50% reduction for children. Dinner IR£10 ($17.50) extra. ACC, MC, V.
This 19th-century house on the Wexford–Rosslare Harbour road (N25), half a mile from Rosslare Harbour, has one of the most elegant lounges I've come across in a B&B, with beautiful plasterwork and a decor of shades of rose. Siobhán Whitehead extends a special welcome to families. She has several large family rooms, and is happy to supply cots for the little ones. All rooms have tea/coffee makers.

MARIANELLA, Kilrane, Rosslare Harbour, Co. Wexford. Tel. 053/ 33139. 5 rms (2 with bath).
$ Rates: IR£15 ($26.25) single; IR£11 ($19.25) per person sharing. 50% reduction for children under 10. ACC, EURO, MC.

 Maeve and Dan O'Neill welcome guests to their pretty bungalow on the main Wexford–Rosslare road (N25), half a mile from Rosslare Harbour, which is screened from the busy highway by a high hedge. With flowers, a pond, and a fountain, the grounds are rather like a small private park. Guest rooms are nicely done up, all with tea/coffee makers; there's a pine-paneled dining room, and the lounge has a piano.

TUDOR LODGE, Hermitage, Drinagh, Wexford, Co. Wexford. Tel. 053/ 23582. 2 rms (all with bath).
$ Rates (including breakfast): IR£16.50 ($28.90) single without bath; IR£11.50 ($20.15) per person sharing without bath; IR£2 ($3.50) per person additional with bath. 20% reduction for children under 10. No credit cards. **Closed:** Nov–Apr.

 Built in the Tudor style, this lovely home is set in landscaped gardens surrounded by verdant countryside. Mrs. Patricia Kinsella takes a real interest in her guests. Bedrooms are especially spacious and beautifully decorated, and the dining room overlooks the garden. There's a tennis court right on the grounds. In consideration of nonsmokers, Mrs. Kinsella requests that smoking is in the lounge only, not in guest rooms. Tudor Lodge is signposted from N25, the Wexford–Rosslare road, 12km (7½ miles) from Wexford, 4km (2½ miles) from Rosslare Harbour.

A Farmhouse

O'LEARY'S FARM, Killilane, Kilrane, Co. Wexford. Tel. 053/33134. 10 rms (7 with bath).
$ Rates (including breakfast): IR£14 ($24.50) single without bath; IR£11 ($19.25) per person sharing without bath; IR£12.50 ($21.90) per person with bath. 25% reduction for children. High tea IR£5 ($8.75) extra; dinner, IR£9 ($15.75). No credit cards.

 Mrs. Kathleen O'Leary and her engaging offspring (along with a grandchild or two) make you feel part of the family. Their farmhouse, 3 miles from Rosslare Harbour, prominently signposted on N25, looks out to the sea across flatlands that focus the eye on ferry comings and goings at Rosslare Harbour. The farmhouse, which provides large family rooms as well as the usual doubles, features a glassed-in front porch that takes advantage of the seascape, while an open fire warms the lounge (there is also central heating). One of the O'Learys is always on hand to pick up and deliver guests to the ferryport with advance notice.

WHERE TO EAT

TUSKAR HOUSE HOTEL, Rosslare Harbour, Co. Wexford. Tel. 053/ 33363.
Cuisine: SEAFOOD/TRADITIONAL.
$ Prices: Appetizers IR£1.25–IR£2 ($2.20–$3.50); main courses IR£4.95–IR£6.95 ($8.65–$12.15); fixed-price dinner IR£14.95 ($26.15). Service charge 10%. ACC, AE, MC, V.
Open: Lunch daily 12:30–3pm; dinner daily 6:30–10:30pm.

The pleasant dining room in this seafront hotel in the town center, with a window-wall overlooking the sea, takes pride in the freshness of the seafood that comes to table. Menus are extensive and varied, and I'm especially fond of the way they do mussels in garlic sauce. Nonlovers of seafood will find a host of meat and fowl dishes, and service is especially friendly and accommodating.

NEW ROSS & FOULKSMILLS

Some 15 miles west of Wexford town (on L160, off N25), the farming area around Foulksmills is fertile ground for farmhouse devotees who long for a landscape of rolling pastures, tilled fields, and wooded countryside.

From Wexford town, take N25 to New Ross (21 miles northwest of Wexford) and watch for the signpost on your left just before you reach the town for the turn to the John F. Kennedy Arboretum. From New Ross, you can reach Kilmore Quay, the Saltees, and the Hook Peninsula by taking N25 east (toward Wexford), then turning southeast toward the coast on R736.

WHAT TO SEE & DO

In 1848, when Patrick Kennedy left Dunganstown (near New Ross) for America, it was to escape the ravages of a devastating famine. He left behind a five-room thatched home set among stone farm buildings. A little more than a century later, his great-grandson, John Fitzgerald Kennedy, held the high office of president of the United States and returned to his ancestral home. The little thatched cottage had been replaced, but the outbuildings remained as they had been in his great-grandfather's time. Mrs. Ryan, a Kennedy by birth, and her daughter greeted the president and showed him around the place. Today the Kennedy homestead, on a pleasant river road, is marked by a small plaque on an outside wall, and if you'd like to take a look (from the road, please—Mrs. Ryan does not open the house to the public), make the short detour en route from Wexford to New Ross.

JOHN F. KENNEDY ARBORETUM, New Ross, Co. Wexford. Tel. 051/ 88171.

A little over 7 miles from New Ross, this outstanding plant collection is the tribute paid to the young slain American president by the Irish government and United States citizens of Irish origin. It was officially opened by the late President Eamon de Valera in 1968 and covers some 623 acres, of which more than 300 are set aside for the plant collection. Already there are more than 4,500 species of shrubs, and the number is expected to reach 6,000. In the forest plots, there are trees from all five continents of the world. There are lovely shaded walks throughout, with shelters and convenient resting spots. If you follow the signposts to the top of Slieve Coillte, you'll be rewarded by a marvelous panorama of southern Wexford and the splendid estuary of the Rivers Barrow, Nore, and Suir. Be sure to stop by the reception center and see the explanatory display fashioned in beaten copper.

Admission: IR£1 ($1.75); IR£3 ($5.25) family groups.

Open: May–Aug, daily 10am–8pm; Apr and Sept, daily 10am–6:30pm; Oct–Mar, 10am–5pm.

THE *NEW ROSS GALLEY*, The Quay, New Ross, Co. Wexford. Tel. 051/21723.

Skipper Dick Fletcher conceived the idea of this cruising restaurant some 20 years ago, and now the *Galley* sets sail for lunches (2 hours), afternoon teas (2 hours), and dinners (3 hours). Whichever you select, you'll spend 2 to 3 relaxing hours in the comfortable, heated cruiser as you slide between the scenic banks of the River Barrow, Nore, or Suir. No canned music, no commentary—just the blissful comfort of good food, drink (the *Galley* is fully licensed), and conversation and if you're curious about the ancient stately homes, castles, abbeys, and wildlife you glimpse along the shore, read the menu pages that give details of the area. That menu features delicious specialties created from locally grown produce, meats, and fish. There's seating for just 70, and the skipper is usually aboard in the role of gracious host. This is definitely a don't-miss!

Fares: IR£10 ($17.50) for the lunch cruise, IR£4 ($7) for the afternoon-tea cruise, IR£14–IR£18 ($24.50–$31.50) for the dinner cruise; IR£3–IR£7 ($5.25–$12.25) for the cruise only. Reservations essential. Book through Wexford or Waterford tourist offices or the above telephone. No credit cards accepted. Hours: From Wexford quays: Lunch and tea, June–Aug daily at 12:30 and 3pm; April–May, Sept–Oct on demand. Dinner, Apr–Aug at 7pm, Sept at 6pm. From Waterford quays: June–Aug daily at 3pm (frequency and departure times flexible, check locally).

WHERE TO STAY

INISHROSS HOUSE, 96 Mary St., New Ross, Co. Wexford. Tel. 051/ 21335. 6 rms (none with bath).
$ Rates (including breakfast): IR£11 ($19.25) per person. 10% reduction for children. High tea IR£8 ($14) extra. No credit cards.
Mrs. Mary Doyle's six pretty bedrooms are nicely decorated and furnished, all with sinks. There's a TV lounge, private parking, and central heat. One reader had this to say: "The hosts were friendly and helpful, the rooms were very nice, and breakfasts were superb." Inishross House is in the town center, 200 yards from the bridge on N25.

KILLARNEY HOUSE, The Maudlins, New Ross, Co. Wexford. Tel. 051/ 21062. 4 rms (none with bath).
$ Rates (including breakfast): IR£13.50 ($23.65) single; IR£11 ($19.25) per person sharing. 50% reduction for children under 10. No credit cards. **Closed:** Oct–Apr.
Mrs. Noreen Fallon's home has two things to make it highly recommendable: Guest rooms on the ground floor (a boon for those troubled by stairs), and a breakfast menu with several selections. Then there's the peaceful country setting, 2km (1¼ miles) from New Ross. All four bedrooms in this modern bungalow are equipped with sinks and electric blankets; there's a TV lounge for guests, central heating, and ample parking.

ROSSVILLE HOUSE, Knockmullen, New Ross, Co. Wexford. Tel. 051/ 21798. 5 rms (4 with bath).
$ Rates (including breakfast): IR£11 ($19.25) per person sharing, IR£1 ($1.75) additional with bath. 20% reduction for children under 10. No credit cards. **Closed:** Oct–Mar.
⭐ Mrs. Ann Foley's modern, spacious home perches on a hill just outside New Ross on N25 (the New Ross–Rosslare road), with great views of the surrounding countryside. The attractive bedrooms all have picture windows that take advantage of those views, as does the TV lounge, which also has a fireplace to cozy up cool evenings. Mrs. Foley's hospitality is legendary, as attested to by her award as "National Housewife of the Year" and her willingness to provide an early breakfast for guests departing from Rosslare Harbour, some 45 minutes away.

Farmhouses

FARM HOUSE, Foulksmills, Co. Wexford. Tel. 051/63616. 10 rms (none with bath).
$ Rates (including breakfast): IR£13.50 ($23.65) single; IR£10.50 ($18.38) per person sharing; IR£30 ($52.50) per person for weekend. 20% reduction for children. High tea IR£7 ($12.25) extra; dinner, IR£9.50 ($16.65). No credit cards. **Closed:** Dec–Feb.
Mrs. Joan Crosbie's homey, rambling farmhouse, 14 miles west of Wexford (N25/L160), 18 miles northwest of Rosslare, and 7 miles west of the seaside, is of 17th-century vintage; the "newer" wing only goes back to the 18th century. This is the wing that houses the 10 comfortable guest rooms. There's central heating, but wood fires add a warmth of their own in both lounge and dining room. Mrs. Crosbie's sons, John and Jerry, are on hand to help manage the 150 acres, the large herd of

cattle, and a fair few thoroughbred horses. The horses can be rented by guests, and you don't have to miss a ride through this lovely countryside just because you've never sat on a horse, for John is happy to give lessons to beginners.

MILL HOUSE, Foulksmills, Co. Wexford. Tel. 051/63683. 5 rms (none with bath).

$ Rates (including breakfast): IR£14.50 ($25.40) single; IR£11.50 ($20.15) per person sharing. 50% reduction for children. Dinner IR£9 ($15.75) extra. No credit cards. **Closed:** Mid-Sept to Easter.

Ivy-covered walls are the first hint of the traditional graciousness and hospitality to be found in Mrs. Anne Redmond's lovely old Georgian-style home 14 miles west of Wexford (N25/L160), 18 miles northwest of Rosslare (N25), and 7 miles to the seaside. The bedrooms are all spacious, and furnished with many antique pieces. The water-powered mill that gives this place its name is a delight to adults and children alike, and Mrs. Redmond has set up croquet and swings for the young fry, as well as providing an appealing pony to ride. Children are especially welcome. It's that "family" feeling that makes Mill House so special—along with marvelous Irish breakfasts and evening meals that feature homemade cream soups and tons of fresh strawberries in season. Wooded walks are handy after one of those sumptuous meals, the Mullinderry River lures fishermen, and both golf and tennis facilities are close by.

READERS RECOMMEND

Carrignee House, Carrigbyrne, New Bawn, Co. Wexford (tel. 051/24310). *"This is a lovely guesthouse on N25, convenient to J. F. Kennedy Park, Wexford, and New Ross. Mrs. French is a lovely and well-informed hostess."*—Mary M. Wentz, Suffern, N.Y.

WHERE TO EAT

THE OLD RECTORY, Rosbercon, New Ross, Co. Wexford. Tel. 051/21719.

Cuisine: SEAFOOD/TRADITIONAL/SNACKS.

$ Prices: Appetizers IR£1.50–IR£3 ($2.65–$$5.25); main courses IR£8–IR£10 ($14–$17.50); Tourist Menu IR£5.75–IR£7.90 ($10.05–$13.85); snacks less than IR£5 ($8.75). ACC, DC, V.

Open: Lunch daily 12:30–2pm; dinner daily 6:30–9:45pm. **Closed:** 4 days at Christmas.

Set in scenic grounds overlooking the River Barrow just over the bridge from the town center, this old country house is tastefully decorated with antiques. Fish and other seafoods are fresh each day from local sources, meats are locally produced, and the garden furnishes all the herbs used in the kitchen. Roast lamb with homemade mint sauce is especially good here, as is grilled Dover sole when available. Homemade bread and pastries are also outstanding. There's wheelchair access, and they cater to children (up to 8pm) and nonsmokers.

KILMORE QUAY & THE SALTEES

From Wexford town, drive south on N25 (the Rosslare road) and turn right onto R739, running southwest and well signposted, which will take you into Kilmore Quay. From New Ross, head toward the coast on R736, pass through Wellington bridge and Bridgetown to R739, where a right turn will lead you to the picturesque village of Kilmore Quay. To return to Wexford, take R739 to N25 and turn north; to reach Rosslare (11 miles southeast of Wexford), a popular seaside resort with good beaches, or Rosslare Harbour (5 miles farther south), ferry port for the U.K. and France, turn south on N25.

WHAT TO SEE & DO

County Wexford has a very special sightseeing attraction in the **Saltee Islands,** 4 miles offshore from the pretty little fishing village of Kilmore Quay, 14 miles south of Wexford town, where local boatmen will take you out to the island after you've negotiated a fee (fishing trawlers will sometimes drop you off as they leave for the day's fishing and pick you up on the way home). A day on the Saltees can be soul-restoring even if you're not a birdwatcher, but if you qualify as the latter, you'll be treated to the sight of razorbills, kittiwakes, puffins, and thousands of gulls, along with hosts of seagoing species. It was in one of the Great Saltee's sea caves that the rebel leader of 1798, Begenal Havey, was captured and taken back to Wexford, where he was tortured and finally beheaded.

On your way to Kilmore Quay, you'll pass through **Kilmore Village,** a quaint little place with many traditional cottages crowned with roofs of thatch. Between the village and the quay, look for **Brandy Cross,** where you'll see a mound of little wooden crosses beside a certain bush. They've been put there by mourners on their way to the graveyard to bury a loved one—no one knows exactly why, but it's an ancient custom.

On the waterfront, have a look at the ✪ **Maritime Museum,** Kilmore Quay (tel. 053/29832 or 29714). This is the former lightship *Guillemot*, which has been converted into a maritime museum. It's well worth a visit to view the many seafaring items, pictures, and models of famous ships and items of local history. If you'd like to visit this community-run project outside normal hours, contact Ann Kelly (secretary) or Billy Roche (chairman), Kilmore Quay Maritime Society, at the above telephone numbers. There's a small admission fee, and it's open June to October, daily from 2 to 6pm; in November and February to May, daily from 2 to 5:30pm; and in December and January, only on Sunday from 2 to 5pm.

THE HOOK PENINSULA

For a drive down the Hook Peninsula, take R733 at the roundabout just outside Wexford town on N25 (the exit is well signposted for Arthurstown, Duncannon, and Ballyhack). From Rosslare Harbour, take N25, then R736; it will get you to Arthurstown and Duncannon, and signposts will direct you to such points as Fethard, Churchtown, and Ballyhack. (For directions from New Ross, see above.) If your ongoing route lies through Waterford, this is an off-the-beaten-track approach via the Ballyhack–Passage East ferry (see below).

WHAT TO SEE & DO

Before leaving Wexford, arm yourself with Pat Mackey's informative booklet "By Hook or By Crook" (available at the Tourist Office), and set off for a marvelous ramble through historic and quaint old villages. The ruins of the Knights Templars foundation still stand at **Templetown. Hook lighthouse** is the oldest in Europe, built over 7 centuries ago. Near **Fethard-on-Sea,** at the now-buried town of Bannow, the Normans first landed in Ireland.

At Ballyhack, catch the car-ferry over to Passage East on the County Waterford side for 10 minutes on the water to see these shores as they were seen by Viking and Norman invaders. The ferry runs continuously April to September, Monday through Saturday from 7:20am to 10pm and on Sunday from 9:30am to 10pm (the last departure is at 8pm during other months). One-way fare is IR£3 ($5.25); round-trip, IR£4.50 ($7.90).

WHERE TO EAT

THE NEPTUNE RESTAURANT, Ballyhack Harbour, Co. Wexford. Tel. 051/89284.
   Cuisine: SEAFOOD. **Reservations:** Recommended.
$ **Prices:** Fixed-price meal IR£7–IR£9 ($12.25–$15.75) at lunch, IR£10–IR£16 ($17.50–$28) at dinner; Tourist Menu (includes glass of wine) in evenings only, IR£12 ($21). ACC, AE, MC, V.

Open: Lunch Tues–Sat 12:30–3pm; dinner Tues–Sat 6–9:30pm. **Closed:** Oct 1–16 and Dec 23–Mar 17.

This attractive little restaurant sits next to a 15th-century tower house just across from the harbor, and the seafood comes right out of local waters. Most other meats come from local sources, and everything is prepared by the owner himself. Service is friendly, and prices are only a little higher than moderate. It only seats 30, so best call ahead to reserve.

CHAPTER 8

COUNTIES KILKENNY & CARLOW

1. COUNTY KILKENNY
- **WHAT'S SPECIAL ABOUT COUNTIES KILKENNY & CARLOW**

2. COUNTY CARLOW

I f you're pressed for time, you may want to head straight for Waterford, Cork, and points west, but Counties Kilkenny and Carlow are an enticing swing inland from the usual around-the-rim tour of Ireland, and each holds attractions well worth the detour.

1. COUNTY KILKENNY

County Kilkenny's lovely pastoral landscape is dotted with Norman castles and keeps, with the most splendid castle of all in Kilkenny town, whose streets are haunted by vivid memories of medieval merchants and witches.

SEEING COUNTY KILKENNY

By Bus Bus Eireann reaches Kilkenny town, as well as most small towns and villages throughout the county, from all major Irish cities. Bus schedules to smaller towns, however, tend to be sporadic and will require some careful study.

By Train There's train service from Dublin to Kilkenny town, but not to other destinations in the county.

By Car Kilkenny town is 73 miles southwest of Dublin, 27 northwest of New Ross, and 30 miles north of Waterford city. From a Kilkenny town base, follow R700 southeast to Bennetsbridge and Thomastown, then take N9 to nearby Jerpoint Abbey. If your next destination is Waterford City, follow N10 south until it becomes N9, which goes on into the city.

KILKENNY TOWN

The town of Kilkenny is virtually a sightseeing destination in itself—its narrow, winding streets and well-preserved structures make it perhaps the most perfect example in Ireland today of a medieval town, and Pat Mackey has produced a splendid little illustrated booklet entitled "A City and County Guide to Kilkenny" which outlines walking tours of the town, as well as suggested day trips in the surrounding area. It's available at the Tourist Office in Waterford.

Sometimes called the "Marble City" because of the fine limestone quarried hereabouts, its Irish name is Cill Chainnigh, or St. Canice's Church, after a little monastery established here by the good saint in the 6th century on the grounds of the present St. Canice's Cathedral (the round tower dates back to the original settlement). But it was the Normans, and later the Anglo-Normans, who built up the dignified town as a trading center that enjoyed the protection of royalty up until the mid-14th

✔

WHAT'S SPECIAL ABOUT
COUNTIES KILKENNY & CARLOW

Historic Towns
☐ Kilkenny town, on the banks of the Nore River, a flourishing civic, ecclesiastical, and governmental center for more than 1,000 years with its splendid medieval structures.
☐ Carlow town, on the Barrow River, dating back to pre-Norman days.

Castles
☐ Kilkenny Castle, a fully restored 13th-century structure, surrounded by formal gardens and parklands, housing a modern art gallery.
☐ Carlow Castle, now in ruins, shows the marks of siege during the Cromwellian years.

Historic Buildings
☐ Rothe House, restored residence of a Tudor merchant in Kilkenny town in 1594, a window into medieval life.
☐ The Shee Alms House in Kilkenny town dating from 1582.
☐ Kyteler's Inn, built in 1324 in Kilkenny town, once the home of a famous witch.

Ancient Monuments
☐ Brown's Hill Dolmen, near Carlow town, one of Europe's oldest field monuments, dating to 2000 B.C.

Ecclesiastical Sites
☐ The 13th-century St. Canices Cathedral, in Kilkenny town.
☐ The richly ornamented Roman Catholic Cathedral of the Assumption, in Carlow town, built in the late 1800s.
☐ Jerpoint Abbey, near Thomastown, County Kilkenny, is an impressive 12th-century monastic ruin.

Crafts
☐ The Kilkenny Design Centre, in Kilkenny town, holds workshops for ceramics, glassware, metals, textiles, and jewelry.
☐ Duiske Handcut Glass, headquartered in Graigmananagh, County Kilkenny, with its beautiful designs.
☐ Mosses Pottery, Bennetsbridge, County Kilkenny.

century. In 1366 the infamous "Statutes of Kilkenny" forbade any mingling of Anglo-Normans with the native Irish. By the time Oliver Cromwell arrived in 1649, the city's population was pretty well demoralized, making it an easy matter for him to seize the town, stable horses in the cathedral and smash its beautiful stained-glass windows, and slaughter many residents. Others he banished to Connaught so he could confiscate their property. Despite its turbulent history, Kilkenny has held on to a cultural tradition that makes it a natural site for one of the most respected crafts centers in Ireland today, the Kilkenny Design Workshops, housed in the one-time stables of Kilkenny Castle (more about that later).

The **Tourist Information Office,** on Rose Inn Street, Kilkenny town (tel. 056/21755), is open from February through November, with varying seasonal hours.

WHAT TO SEE & DO

KILKENNY CASTLE, The Parade, Kilkenny, Co. Kilkenny. Tel. 056/21450.

★ The impressive 13th-century Kilkenny Castle dominates the town and was once the seat of the Butler family. It was built in 1391, Cromwell made a mess of it during his stopover, it was restored and continued to be used as a residence until 1935, and in 1967 the Marquess of Ormonde gave it to the people of Kilkenny, who turned it over to the state 2 years later. Now fully restored and rich in artworks and elegant furnishings, it is open to the public for tours. Guides are well versed in

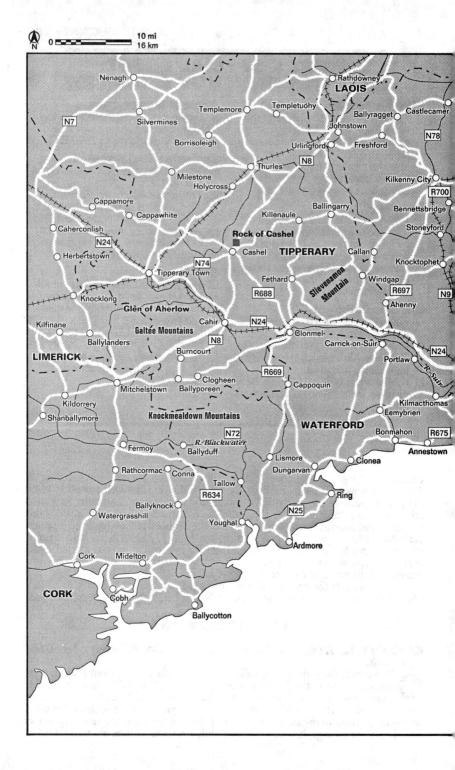

430

N9

Carlow Town

R726

Tullow

WICKLOW

Woodenbridge

Arklow

Leighlinbridge

Shillelagh

Old Leighlin

Gorey

Muine Bheag
(Bagenalstown)

Bunclody

R705

CARLOW

Borris

Ferns

N9

Graiguenamanagh

Thomastown

Enniscorthy

R729

St. Mullins

N11 *R. Slaney* Blackwater

Clonroche *R. Slaney*

N79 Oylgate

KILKENNY

New Ross **WEXFORD**

N25

John F.
Kennedy Park

Ferrycarrig Wexford Town
*Wexford
Harbour*

*St. George's
Channel*

Dunganstown

Mullinavat

Wellington Bridge

Rosslare

Cheekpoint Ballyhack

R733

*Rosslare
Harbor*

Waterford City Duncannon Duncormick

Passage East

R736

Tomhaggard Lady's Island

To Wales, France →

Tramore

Fethard-on-Sea

Fornlorn Pt. Kilmore Quay

Waterford Harbour

**Hook
Peninsula**

Saltee Islands

Celtic Sea

R. Barrow

R. Nore

IMPRESSIONS

That ancient and delightful City [Kilkenny] is not so remarkable for a splendid outside as for intrinsic Worth, the rich Marble that covers the Houses and even the streets not being distinguishable by the Eye from the vilest stone until by Tryall you have discover'd its Hardness and the Polish & Lustre it is capable of receiving.
—GEORGE BERKELEY, 1709

---

stories of the people who have lived here—ask about Black Tom; then get set to hear some rather outrageous tales.
Admission: IR£1.50 ($2.65).
Open: May–June, daily 10:30am–5:30pm; July–Sept, 10am–7pm.

ROTHE HOUSE, Parliament St., Kilkenny Town, Co. Kilkenny. Tel. 056/ 22893.
This home of a prosperous Tudor merchant, built in 1594 and now a museum and library, has been meticulously restored. You'll come away keenly aware of life in medieval Ireland's merchant class. Take time to examine the old pikes and other relics of local historical and cultural significance.
Admission: IR£1.50 ($2.65).
Open: Summer, Mon–Sat, 10:30am–12:30pm and 3–5pm, Sun 3–5pm; winter, Sun 3–5pm.

THE THOLSEL, High St., Kilkenny Town, Co. Kilkenny.
This 1761 toll house (exchange market) features a rather curious clock tower, and a front arcade that extends over the pavement. Inside are old records, charters, and the mayor's sword of 1609.
Admission: Free.
Open: Inquire at the Tourist Office, about 100 yards away.

SHEE'S ALMHOUSES, Rose Inn St., Kilkenny, Co. Kilkenny. Tel. 056/ 21755.
This interesting old building dates from 1594, so take time to look around when you drop in to the Tourist Information Office, which is housed here.
Admission: Free.
Open: Hours vary seasonally.

KYTELER'S INN, St. Kieran's St., Kilkenny Town, Co. Kilkenny. Tel. 056/21064 or 21888.
This historic building was once the home of Dame Alice Kyteler, a beautiful woman who grew rich by the successive deaths of her four husbands. When the Lord Justiciar of Ireland condemned her to death on charges of witchcraft, Dame Alice skipped town (nothing was ever heard of her again) and left her convicted accessories to go to the stake alone. Within the walls of this solid stone house had been found a vast array of herbs, ointments, and other makings of magic spells.
There are no magic potions in the food now, however—it's a pub/restaurant that is really a "don't miss" in Kilkenny town. Even if you don't make it for a meal, stop in for a drink and cast a leary eye at the "witchy" courtyard with its two wells that supplied Dame Alice with water to mix her deadly potions.
Admission: You pay only for food and drink.
Open: Daily 10:30am–11:30pm. **Closed:** Good Friday, Christmas Day.

ST. CANICE'S CATHEDRAL, off Dean St., Kilkenny Town, Co. Kilkenny.
This Church of Ireland cathedral, dating from the 13th century and thought to be on the site of a 6th-century church, is easily one of the most beautiful ecclesiastical buildings in Ireland. Cromwell's troops left it a roofless ruin in 1649, but careful repair and restoration has been carried out over the centuries, and it is notable today for its outstanding Early English windows, several stone tomb effigies, and many fine

medieval monuments. There's also a 100-foot-high round tower, whose conical cap has been replaced by a domed roof.

Admission: Free.

Open: Daily 9am–1pm and 2–6pm.

Savvy Shopping

THE BOOK CENTRE, 10 High St., Kilkenny, Co. Kilkenny. Tel. 056/ 63070.

★ This is one of three excellent bookshops (in Waterford and Wexford) that carry extensive stocks of books on Irish and general interest topics. Open Monday through Saturday from 9am to 5pm.

KILKENNY DESIGN CENTRE, Castle Yard, Kilkenny Town, Co. Kilkenny. Tel. 056/22118.

Created for the sole purpose of fostering good design in Irish industry, the centre is just across the street from the castle and occupies its former stables and coach houses. Its horseshoe archways and carriage-wheel windows are in quaint contrast to the highly contemporary display inside. The workshops, originally government sponsored, are now operated as a private company. First-rate designers and craftspeople are provided with equipment and work space to develop new designs for textiles, ceramics, glassware, jewelry, metals, and clothing for both sexes. The showroom where these designs are for sale is a good place to do at least part of your shopping. Open Monday through Saturday from 9am to 6pm.

ROBERTS' BOOKSHOP, St. Kieran's St., Kilkenny, Co. Kilkenny.

If you find yourself hooked on local history, head for Roberts' and browse through the excellent selection of books on the subject. Open Monday through Saturday from 9am to 5pm.

Pubs/Evening Entertainment

After-dark activities in Kilkenny town are centered around the bars and pubs, but those who indulge in lemonade or Ballygowan water are as welcome as those in search of a pint. Irish musical evenings are held in many local pubs, and details are available from the Tourist Office, as well as from almost any pub in town.

There are two exceptional pubs in Kilkenny town where you can put a terrible thirst to rest: **Tynan's,** John's Bridge (which has won the "Best Pub in Ireland" award for its combination of polished brass, gleaming wood, etched glass, and interesting clientele), and the much plainer **Marble City Bar,** High Street, a congenial spot since 1789 for the "meetin' o' the drinkers" that continues to thrive to this day.

WHERE TO STAY

In Town

ASHLEIGH, Waterford Rd., Kilkenny, Co. Kilkenny. Tel. 056/22809. 3 rms (2 with bath).

$ Rates (including breakfast): IR£11 ($19.25) per person without bath; IR£12.50 ($21.90) per person with bath. 50% reduction for children.

Set in lovely gardens on the Waterford road (N10), half a mile from the town center, Ashleigh is the domain of Mrs. Pauline Flannery. Her home is beautifully appointed, and she's well up on all that's going on in the area and anxious to be helpful to her guests.

BROOKFIELD, Bawn, Castlecomer Rd., Kilkenny, Co. Kilkenny. Tel. 056/65629. 4 rms (2 with bath).

$ Rates (including breakfast): IR£15.50 ($27.15) single without bath; IR£11

($19.25) per person sharing without bath; IR£1.50 ($2.65) per person additional with bath. 50% reduction for children.

⭐ Brookfield, 2km (1¼ miles) from the town center, the home of Mrs. Mary Trant, is a modern bungalow with central heating. One reader wrote, "Mrs. Trant is warm, friendly, and can't do enough for you. Her home is spotless, the rooms are very quiet, and she herself is a typical woman of Eire." That's an endorsement I am happy to echo!

HILLGROVE, Bennetsbridge Rd., Kilkenny, Co. Kilkenny. Tel. 056/ 22890. 4 rms (3 with bath).
$ Rates (including breakfast): IR£14.50 ($25.40) single without bath; IR£11 ($19.25) per person sharing without bath; IR£1.50 ($2.65) per person additional with bath. 50% reduction for children. No credit cards.
Mrs. Margaret Drennan is the delightful hostess of this country home, which is furnished with antiques and has an attractive garden that guests are free to use. Mrs. Drennan also has antiques for sale. Close at hand are fishing, golf, and horseback riding. Hillgrove is 3km (2 miles) from Kilkenny town center on the New Ross–Rosslare road (T20).

Nearby Accommodations

LUNAR LODGE, Baunlusk, Cuffes Grange, Kilkenny, Co. Kilkenny. Tel. 056/29925. 3 rms (all with bath).
$ Rates (including breakfast): IR£16 ($28) single; IR£13 ($22.75) per person sharing. No credit cards. **Parking:** Private parking. **Closed:** Oct–Apr.

⭐ Mrs. Milne, is the hostess of this bungalow 5km (3 miles) from Kilkenny town center, just off N76, and her rose garden is interesting as well as beautiful. There is an outside swimming pool and you can also have a game of croquet if you like. The three bedrooms are nicely decorated and comfortable, all with hair dryers, tea/coffee makers, and electric blankets.

READERS RECOMMEND

Tir Na Nog, Greenshill, Kilkenny, Co. Kilkenny (tel. 056/65250). *"Proprietors Mary and Eamonn offer guests a private sitting room with books and materials on local events and historical points of interest. Their five bedrooms all have private bathrooms and other little comforts usually not found in B&Bs. This is a very charming and comfortable place to stay, less than 5 minutes' walk from Kilkenny town center."*—Geraldine and Mark Bulwicz, Doylestown, Penna.

Blanchville House, Dunbell, Maddoxtown, Co. Kilkenny (tel. 056/27197). *"Monica Phelan and her family couldn't have been more gracious and welcoming. Their home, just 5 miles from Kilkenny, is a most impressive Georgian house with lovely accommodations. We enjoyed Blanchville House so much that we made a point to stay there again for our last night, and it was as if we had come home to friends."*—Sandra Grannis, Ridgefield, Conn.

Farmhouse Accommodation, Palmerstown, Tullaroan Road, Kilkenny, Co. Kilkenny (tel. 056/22313). *"Michael and Sheila Ryan's farmhouse is 1 mile from Kilkenny, and they are knowledgeable concerning the cultural, historic, and artistic offerings of the area. Michael is active in the musical life of Kilkenny. You're welcome to view their dairy and beef farm and enjoy their prize-winning gardens."*—Caroll Ann Bottino and Michael Lewis Sherdan, Lexington, Mass.

WHERE TO EAT

EDWARD LANGTON RESTAURANT AND BAR, 69 John St., Kilkenny, Co. Kilkenny. Tel. 056/65133 or 21728.
Cuisine: IRISH/TRADITIONAL/VEGETARIAN/BAR FOOD.
$ Prices: Main courses IR£5–IR£10 ($8.75–$7.50); Tourist Menu IR£5.75–IR£12 ($10.05–$21). ACC, AE, MC, V.
Open: Mon–Sat 10:30am–11pm, Sun 12:30–11pm. **Closed:** Good Friday, Dec 25–26.

It's no wonder that this bar and eatery has won national awards for several years running—the food here is not only superb but it's also great value-for-money. This restaurant is just the right place for vegetarians, although it offers all of the traditional choices as well. The old-style setting of the restaurant is perfectly delightful. Even if you don't plan to eat a meal here, at least nip in and have a pint—it's worth the trip.

KYTELER'S INN, Kieran St., Kilkenny, Co. Kilkenny. Tel. 056/21064.
Cuisine: IRISH/TRADITIONAL/VEGETARIAN.
$ Prices: Main courses IR£5–IR£12 ($10.50–$21); fixed-price Sun lunch IR£7 ($12.25); Tourist Menu IR£5.75–IR£12 ($10.05–$21). ACC, MC, V.
Open: Daily 10:30am–11:30pm. **Closed:** Good Friday, Christmas Day.
Kyteler's Inn is a sightseeing attraction as well as a pleasant bar-cum-restaurant. The menu features dishes based on local meats and vegetables, with a nice selection for seafood and meat lovers, as well as vegetarian dishes prepared from fresh local produce.

BENNETSBRIDGE & THOMASTOWN

The area around Bennetsbridge has attracted a host of craftspeople, and the Tourist Information Office in Kilkenny can furnish helpful lists and pamphlets to help you find them. One of the most interesting (and most popular with our readers over the years) is the ✪ **Nicholas Mosse Pottery,** Bennetsbridge, County Kilkenny (tel. 056/27126). About 4½ miles south of Kilkenny on R700, on the banks of the Nore, Nicholas Mosse has set up a workshop for his award-winning pottery. His mother runs the shop and a tiny museum of old Irish cottage pottery. She's so friendly that, to quote Nicholas, "Many's the visitor who gets a tour of the house and a cuppa." They're open in July and August only, Monday through Saturday from 10am to 6pm and on Sunday from 2 to 6pm, and it's well signposted on R700.

About 1½ miles southwest of Thomastown, look for ✪ **Jerpoint Abbey,** Thomastown, County Kilkenny. One of the finest monastic ruins in Ireland, this Cistercian abbey dates from 1158, and in 1540 it suffered the fate of many such institutions when the order was suppressed and its lands handed over to the Ormond family. There are interesting sculptures in the partially restored 15th-century cloisters. Other features of interest are the 15th- and 16th-century tombs of the Walsh and Butler families, and the square central tower with its distinctively Irish stepped battlements. The ruins are open for visitors June to September, daily from 10am to 1pm and 2 to 7pm; the rest of the year, by obtaining the key from the caretaker, Mrs. Wallace, in the adjoining house.

WHERE TO STAY

THE NORE VALLEY VILLA, Inistioge, Co. Kilkenny. Tel. 056/58418. 5 rms (3 with bath).
$ Rates (including breakfast): IR£15 ($26.25) single without bath; IR£10.50 ($18.40) per person sharing without bath; IR£2 ($3.50) per person additional with bath. 20% reduction for children. No credit cards. **Parking:** Private parking.
Closed: Dec–Feb.
Overlooking the River Nore outside Inistioge, 5 miles from Thomastown, on the Rosslare to Kilkenny–Athlone road, this Georgian villa is close to Woodstock Forest and makes an ideal base for day trips to historical sites nearby. In addition to sightseeing, you'll find golf, fishing, and hill-walking within easy reach, and not the least of its location charms is a local pub where "the crack is mighty." Leslie and Lucy Rothwell can steer you to all these and more attractions. The house is centrally heated.

Farmhouses

BRANDON VIEW HOUSE, Ballyogan, Graignamanagh, Co. Kilkenny. Tel. 0503/24191. 4 rms (1 with bath).
$ Rates (including breakfast): IR£11.50 ($20.15) per person without bath, IR£13 ($22.75) per person with bath. 20% reduction for children. Dinner IR£12 ($21)

extra. Special 3- and 7-night rates available. No credit cards. **Parking:** Private parking.

Mrs. Alice McCabe and her family will welcome you to their 18th-century farmhouse, set in scenic surroundings 8 miles from New Ross and 8 miles from Thomastown, well signposted on R705. In addition to the comfortable guest rooms, there's a restful sitting room with a log fire and a piano that has sparked many a sing-song session. Dinner is available and is made with fresh, organically grown fruits and vegetables from the kitchen garden. The house is centrally heated.

CULLINTRA HOUSE, The Rower, Inistioge, Co. Kilkenny. Tel. 051/23614. 4 rms (1 with bath), family suite (with shower).

$ Rates (including breakfast): IR£14 ($24.50) per person. Dinner IR£12 ($21) extra. IR£169 ($295.75) weekly B&B plus dinner. 10% reduction for children. Minimum stay 2 nights. No credit cards. **Parking:** Private parking.

Miss Patricia Cantlon is the gracious hostess at this 200-year-old farmhouse (6 miles from New Ross, 5 miles from Thomastown, on the Kilkenny road, R700) which is a member of the Hidden Ireland Country Homes Association. Actually, "gracious" aptly describes the overall ambience at Cullintra House, and it's not at all unusual for a house-party atmosphere to break out, complete with sing-songs and storytelling. The house is centrally heated, the food is delicious, and dinner is by candlelight before a log fire. There's also a large art studio/conservatory with free tea- and coffee-making facilities for guest use. There are four comfortable bedrooms, all with handbasins and hairdryers, and one three-room suite with private shower. Highly recommended.

Worth the Extra Money

MOUNT JULIET ESTATE, Thomastown, Co. Kilkenny. Tel. 056/24455. Fax 056/24522. Telex 80355. 32 rooms (all with bath), 1 suite. TV TEL

$ Rates (including full Irish breakfast): IR£90–IR£120 ($157.50–$210) single; IR£160–IR£250 ($280–$437.50) double; mini-suites and Presidential Suites available at higher rates. ACC, AE, MC, V.

Once the largest private estate in Ireland, Mount Juliet is a stately home set in some 1,411 acres of woodlands, pastures, and landscaped lawns, with two rivers passing through the grounds. It's 75 miles southwest of Dublin on N10, 11 miles southeast of Kilkenny on R700 (signposted in Thomastown center). Built in the 1760s, it has been developed as a fine stud farm and the house has been transformed into an elegant, self-contained resort.

From the moment you enter the house, and are greeted by Ted Richmond, the butler (known to all and sundry simply as "Richmond") and Warlock, the gentle resident Irish wolfhound, you have the feeling of being a guest in a magnificently appointed country home. Plasterwork, fireplaces, floor coverings, and the like have been painstakingly brought back to their former glory. The Tetrarch Bar (named for a famous racehorse), for example, proudly displays panels bearing details of the stud farm's racing triumphs from 1888 to 1902. Afternoon tea is served in the sedate drawing room. As for the guest rooms, each has a different character and each bears the name of someone associated with the house in the past. All are exceptionally spacious, beautifully appointed, and have spectacular views of the lush Kilkenny countryside.

Dining/Entertainment: Evening meals are taken in the Wedgwood blue-and-white Lady Helen McCalmont dining room. All three meals are served in the informal Old Kitchen restaurant that now shares the vaulted wine cellers with the cheerful Tap Room.

Services: Complimentary champagne, fruit basket, and chocolates.

Facilities: Indoor and outdoor tennis; badminton; squash; snooker; horseback riding and pony trekking, with some 16 miles of trails; fishing (they can even supply the equipment) for salmon and trout from the two rivers and three man-made lakes stocked with rainbow trout, scheduled for completion by presstime (salmon season runs from February to September, trout season from March through September); clay pigeon shooting year round (they can supply guns and cartridges); and pheasant shoots from November to January. From November to March, guests may join one of the several local fox hunts with which Mount Juliet is associated. A Jack Nicklaus-designed golf course will open in late 1991, and future plans include a leisure center with gymnasium, sauna, and Jacuzzi.

WHERE TO EAT

THE OLD KITCHEN, Mount Juliet, Thomastown, Co. Kilkenny. Tel. 056/24455.
   Cuisine: IRISH/TRADITIONAL/SEAFOOD. **Reservations:** Recommended.
$ **Prices:** Appetizers IR£2.50–IR£6.50 ($4.40–$11.40); main courses IR£7.55–IR£10.70 ($13.20–$18.75). ACC, AE, MC, V.
   Open: Lunch daily 12:30–2:30pm; dinner daily 6–9:30pm.

This delightful restaurant is located in the vaulted cellars of the luxurious Mount Juliet Estate just outside Thomastown (see above). It's a bright, cheerful place, with informality the keynote, and it's open to nonresidents at both lunch and dinner.

The menu features the freshest ingredients, many from local sources, and among the starters from the à la carte menu you'll find the likes of lamb kidneys in an Irish whiskey and mustard sauce or local Irish smoked salmon. Main dishes might include beefsteak, Guinness and mushroom pie; breast of chicken with garlic; and deep-fried Dublin Bay prawns.

Worth the Extra Money

LADY HELEN MCCALMONT RESTAURANT, Mount Juliet, Thomastown, Co. Kilkenny. Tel. 056/24455.
   Cuisine: IRISH/TRADITIONAL/SEAFOOD. **Reservations:** Recommended.
$ **Prices:** Five-course, fixed-price Tasting Menu IR£30 ($52.50); table d'hôte selections IR£25–IR£30 ($43.75–$52.50).
   Open: Dinner only, daily 7–9:30pm.

In this lovely blue-and-white dining room at Mount Juliet, nonresidents are booked for dinner only. Menus often include such items as oak-smoked cured ham on a bed of marinated baby white turnip with a cumin and balsamic-yogurt dressing; lightly grilled ocean prawn tails set on a thin slice of fresh wild river salmon with a light whole-grain mustard sauce; melon-and-ginger sorbet to refresh the palate between courses; breast of free range chicken filled with a mild fennel stuffing in a tomato and red-pepper sauce; and to finish off, a choice of an iced dessert of pistachio ice cream or lemon-and-strawberry sorbet in a strawberry sauce.

AROUND THE COUNTY

From Tinacashel crossroad (2 miles from the town of Urlingford, on N8 northwest of Kilkenny town) you can count no fewer than a dozen **Anglo-Norman castles.** In the town of Knocktopher (south of Kilkenny town on N10), the **Carmelite Priory** garden holds a flat-topped Mass Stone that was used during the long years when Catholics were forbidden to practice their religion. If you pass through **Castlecomer** (on N77 north of Kilkenny town), spare a thought to native son John Walker (uncle of New York's famous mayor, Jimmy Walker), who in 1899 invented the caterpillar track system that revolutionized so many phases of modern industry. And in Rathosheen townland (near the village of Johnstown, on N8, just north of Urlingford), tradition says the **Ring Fort** is the final resting place of Ireland's legendary hero, Oisin.

2. COUNTY CARLOW

Normans also left their stamp (and their castles) on the face of tiny County Carlow, no doubt drawn by land as fertile and productive as it is beautiful and rivers that teem with fish. Nor did they overlook its strategic location between Kilkenny and Dublin, which made it a frequent storm center in the ongoing struggle for power in Ireland.

Historic Carlow town, on the River Barrow, is a bright, pleasant place, with interesting walks through ancient streets and along the river. Its turbulent history includes the massacre of 600 insurgents in the 1798 rebellion (some 400 lie buried in the gravel pits on the Graiguecullen side of town, the site marked by a Celtic cross memorial).

If your touring takes you from Carlow to Stradbally via the N80, Windy Gap, the drive opens up some truly outstanding views.

SEEING COUNTY CARLOW

By Bus Bus Eireann reaches Carlow town, as well as most small towns and villages throughout the county, from all major Irish cities. Bus schedules to smaller towns, however, tend to be rather infrequent, so check carefully when planning day trips.

By Train There's train service from Dublin to Carlow town.

By Car Carlow town is some 52 miles southwest of Dublin on N9, and 36 miles directly north of New Ross, County Wexford, on R705 and N9. A short drive east of town on R726 will take you to the Brown's Hill Dolman. Return to town, then take N9 south to the picturesque village of Leighlinbridge on the River Barrow. Still heading south, take R705 to Bagenalstown, and stay on R705 south to Borris. Still farther south on R705 is Graiguenamanagh. If you're going on to County Kilkenny, turn west on R703 to reach Thomastown and nearby Jerpoint Abbey on N9. Return to Thomastown and follow R700 through Bennetsbridge to Kilkenny town.

CARLOW TOWN

In July and August, there's a **Tourist Information Office** (tel. 0503/31554) in the Town Hall in Carlow town, with varying hours.

WHAT TO SEE & DO

Near the Barrow bridge, in the grounds of the Corcoran's Mineral Water Factory, you'll find the ruins of imposing **Carlow Castle.** This was one of Cromwell's victims in 1650, but survived to be returned to the Earls of Thomond in the 1800s. Its final demise came about when a local doctor, who wanted to use it as a lunatic asylum, tried to thin its walls with explosives, rendering it so unsafe that it finally had to be demolished. The ruins are open Monday through Friday from 9am to 5pm, with permission of the factory staff; no admission charge.

The 1833 cruciform, Gothic-style **Cathedral of the Assumption,** off Tullow Street, holds a marble monument by the celebrated Irish sculptor Hogan to a Bishop Doyle, who wrote extensively about 19th-century politics, using a pen name to stay out of trouble. Its lantern tower is some 151 feet high, and there are magnificent stained-glass windows, designed by Harry Clarke. Open daily from 10am to 6pm, with no admission fee.

Housed in an old theater, the **Haymarket Museum,** adjacent to Town Hall (tel. 0503/31532), is an interesting little museum that features a reconstructed forge and kitchen, as well as tools and military and religious relics. There's no charge, and it's open in summer daily from 9am to 1pm and 2 to 5pm (closed the rest of the year).

Two miles east of Carlow on L726, **Browne's Hill** demesna holds an impressive dolmen—its capstone weighs 100 tons, the largest in Europe.

WHERE TO STAY

MEELTRANE HOUSE, Link Rd., Brownshill, Carlow, County Carlow. Tel. 0503/42473. 4 rms (1 with bath).

$ Rates (including breakfast): IR£12 ($21) per person without bath, IR£13 ($22.75) per person with bath. High tea IR£8 ($14) extra. No credit cards. **Closed:** Sept–May.

In the Brownshill section of Carlow town, 2km (1¼ miles) from the town center on

Link Road, Mrs. Mary Ruane's modern, two-story home features guest rooms that are spacious and well done up. Mrs. Ruane is a helpful and accommodating hostess.

THE SQUIRES, Link Rd., Brownshill, Carlow, Co. Carlow. Tel. 0503/ 43771. 5 rms (1 with bath).

$ Rates (including breakfast): IR£11 ($19.25) per person without bath, IR£12 ($21) per person with bath. 50% reduction for children. High tea IR£7 ($12.25) extra; dinner, IR£10 ($17.50). No credit cards.

This is the bright, modern home of Eva and Mike Byrne (he's Irish, she's English). There is little I can add to the testimonial of one of our readers, who wrote: "Eva is an animal lover and a marvelously friendly person who puts her guests at ease and will go out of her way to accommodate them. We found their home very attractive, and our breakfast was excellent." The Squires is 2 km (1¼ miles) from the town center.

WHERE TO EAT

THE BEAMS RESTAURANT, 59 Dublin St., Carlow, Co. Carlow. Tel. 0503/31824.
   Cuisine: SEAFOOD/CLASSICAL. **Reservations:** Recommended.
$ Prices: Five-course fixed-price dinner IR£17.50 ($30.65). DC, V.
   Open: Dinner only, Tues–Sat 7–9:30pm.

⭐ This lovely old coaching inn (with original old beams retained, hence the name) has been lovingly restored and now houses an excellent eatery presided over by Betty and Peter O'Gorman. It's an intimate sort of place, seating only 40, and the menu features a wide variety of fish and seafood dishes—wild salmon and trout, John Dory, and other unusual fish as they are available. There's also a very good selection of beef, veal, lamb, pork, and chicken dishes, and an extensive wine list.

LEIGHLINBRIDGE, BAGENALSTOWN, BORRIS & GRAIGUENAMANAGH

In Leighlinbridge, look for the ruins of 12th-century **Black Castle**. Bagenalstown is a lovely little canalside town with many fine public buildings, and Borris is a charming village in a wooded setting adjoining **Borris Castle**. In Graiguenamanagh, you can visit the showrooms of the **Duiske Handcut Glass factory** (tel. 0503/24174), open Monday through Friday from 8:30am to 5pm (closed 1 week at Christmas).

WHERE TO STAY

LORUN OLD RECTORY, Kilgreaney, Bagenalstown, Co. Carlow. Tel. 0503/75282. 4 rms (none with bath).
$ Rates (including breakfast): IR£18 ($31.50) single; IR£15 ($26.25) per person sharing. 20% reduction for children. Dinner IR£12 ($21) extra. No credit cards.
   Closed: Christmas.

 I can't imagine a more scenic place to stay than Bobbie and Don Smith's 150-year-old stone farmhouse, right in the middle of County Carlow's rich countryside, at the foot of the Blackstairs Mountains, a mere 15 miles from Kilkenny and midway between Bagenalstown and Borris on L18A. It's a good base for local sightseeing or crafts shopping, and croquet, tennis, and lawn games will help while away your leisure hours, with golf, swimming, tennis, and horseracing nearby. Furnishings include many antiques, home-grown fruits and vegetables grace the table, and there's central heating as well as electric blankets and open fires.

WHERE TO EAT

LORD BAGENAL INN, Leighlinbridge, Co. Carlow. Tel. 0503/21668.
   Cuisine: CLASSICAL/SEAFOOD.
$ Prices: Appetizers IR£2–IR£4 ($3.50–$7); main courses IR£8–IR£10 ($14–$17.50); fixed-price dinner IR£16 ($28). DC, V.

Open: Mon–Sat 12:30–10:30pm, Sun 12:30–9pm. **Closed:** Christmas Day.
Set on the banks of the River Barrow in the village of Leighlinbridge just off the Dublin–Carlow–Kilkenny road (it's signposted), the Lord Bagenal has a warm, inviting, old-world air. Locally grown vegetables and meats are used, and shellfish are kept in a tank to ensure freshness with each order. Roast duck, tournedos steak, escalopes of pork, and a wide variety of seafood and fish are menu stars.

CHAPTER 9

COUNTIES WATERFORD & SOUTH TIPPERARY

Say "Waterford" to most Americans and they'll promptly reply "crystal." And certainly a visit to the Waterford Crystal Factory is a highlight of any visit. But save time for a ramble through the rest of this beautiful and picturesque county. County Waterford is one of the most scenic counties in the Southeast, with a landscape that shades from a coastline of rugged headland cliffs and deep-cut bays ringed by sandy beaches, to the Comeragh mountains in the north and center and the Knockmealdown range farther south, to gentle hills and fertile valleys that separate the sea and mountains. Prehistoric dolmens, promontory forts, and passage graves in the area speak of the earliest settlers. Legends of valor and beautiful early Iron Age metalwork mirror the two sides of the battle-loving and artistic Celtic clan of the Deise.

Sharing County Waterford's mountain ranges is the southernmost portion of County Tipperary, making it impossible to consider one without including the other (North Tipperary can best be explored from the Shannonside region, as discussed in Chapter 13). Tipperary is Ireland's largest inland county, straddling the country from east to west. Along with that vast territory, South Tipperary holds a wealth of antiquities that also straddle much of Ireland's past.

1. WATERFORD

Just 40 miles from Wexford, Waterford is Ireland's fourth-largest city. Every phase of Irish history has left its traces here, and the harbor today is as alive with freighters along the broad River Suir as in the days when Viking longships plied its waters.

The most extensive remains of Viking walls in the country and massive Reginald's Tower (which has stood intact for 1,000 years) remind us of those fierce sea raiders. They came in 853 for a safe haven from which to launch their plundering forays, and stayed to become settlers and traders for more than 300 years. The Normans, who claimed the city in 1170, left a legacy of dozens of towers like the "Half-Moon" on Stephen Street. And the modern Waterford Crystal Factory, one of the city's most persistent claims to fame, is a descendant of the 1783 enterprise begun at the west end of the Quay by George and William Penrose.

☑

WHAT'S SPECIAL ABOUT COUNTIES WATERFORD & SOUTH TIPPERARY

Beaches
- ☐ Tramore, County Waterford, with a 3-mile-long sandy beach and amusement park.
- ☐ Clonea Strand, County Waterford, one of Ireland's cleanest.
- ☐ Ardmore, County Waterford, a small town of historical importance, with a wide, sandy beach.

Historic Towns
- ☐ Waterford, a small but important port city founded by Vikings, with many historic relics.
- ☐ Cashel, South Tipperary, seat of early kings of Munster, with the magnificent Rock of Cashel dominating the skyline.
- ☐ Ardmore, County Waterford, site of a 7th-century settlement by St. Declan, with ecclesiastical remains and a remarkably intact round tower.

Castles
- ☐ Cahir Castle, South Tipperary, a fully restored 15th-century stronghold on the site of a 10th-century residence of Brian Boru.

Scenic Drives
- ☐ The Comeragh Drive, a circular route just south of Waterford city, with good views of mountain peaks and pastures, waterfalls, and the coastline.
- ☐ Tramore–Dungarvan coastal drive, a 30-mile drive with spectacular views of cliffs and sandy beach coves.
- ☐ Nire Valley Drive, from Clonmel, South Tipperary, to Dungarvan, County Waterford, a pleasant rural drive.

For the Kids
- ☐ Tramore, with its large amusement park, and any of the beaches listed above.

Activities
- ☐ Fishing, with some of Ireland's finest salmon fishing in the Blackwater River at Cappoquin.

Special Events
- ☐ Waterford's International Festival of Light Opera in September, with musical ensembles from around the world.

The Irish call it Port Lairge ("Lairge's Landing Place"), and to the Vikings it was Vadrefjord. Always this city on the Suir has been the main seaport of the Southeast. Today it maintains a thriving shipping trade with the Continent and England. In 1210 King John of England dubbed it "a pearl of great price." Its walls withstood a siege by Oliver Cromwell in 1649, then fell to one of his generals the next year. James II was loyally received when he stopped in Waterford in 1690, en route to Kinsale after a crushing defeat at the Battle of the Boyne. Hot on his heels came the victorious King William III to receive the city's surrender on honorable terms.

The people of Waterford are an amiable blend of all who came over the centuries as settlers, conquerors, and/or artisans. As far back as 1586 it was written by one Richard Stanihurst, "The people are cheerful in their entertainment of strangers." And so you will find them today!

IMPRESSIONS

There lay the green shore of Ireland, like some coast of plenty. We could see towns, towers, churches, harvests; but the curse of eight hundred years we could not discern.
—RALPH WALDO EMERSON, *ENGLISH TRAITS*, 1856

ORIENTATION

ARRIVING   There is **bus** service from most major points in Ireland, **train** service from Dublin and Cork, and **air** service from Dublin, Cork, and London. For bus and train information, call 051/73401; for flight information, 051/75589.

TOURIST INFORMATION   The **Irish Tourist Office** is at 41 The Quay (tel. 051/75823), open from 9am to 6am every day during summer, closed on Sunday during winter. This is an office with an especially helpful staff and with facilities for booking accommodations, transportation, sightseeing—in short, as they say with pride, "anything that's bookable in Ireland."

CITY LAYOUT   As cities go, Waterford (103 miles southwest of Dublin, 40 miles west of Wexford, and 40 miles northeast of Cork city) is small, easy to find your way around in, with shank's mare the only vehicle you'll need for a good day's sightseeing. Its focal point is the broad quay that runs along the Suir's south bank and is named simply **The Quay**. Distinctive **Reginald's Tower** is at one end, the **Clock Tower** is at near center (an important landmark), and a bridge crossing the Suir is at the other. Narrow streets and lanes, as well as somewhat wider **Barronstrand Street,** lead off the Quay to the half dozen or so streets on which are concentrated a great many of Waterford's sightseeing attractions, restaurants, pubs, and a few first-rate accommodations. The Tourist Office can supply an excellent and easily followed street map.

GETTING AROUND

By Bus/Train   The bus and rail depot is at the northern end of the Suir Bridge. Bus Eireann has a good variety of day trips around the region. For bus and rail information, call 051/79000 Monday through Saturday from 9am to 5:30pm, 051/73408 at other times. There is city bus service, but routes are limited and service can be infrequent. City buses are not numbered, and most depart from the Clock Tower on the Quay—inquire of drivers for specific routes.

By Taxi   There is a taxi stand at the rail and bus station, and you can telephone 75222 for a cab to pick you up anywhere in the city.

On Foot   As noted above, Waterford is a walking town, and you'll seldom need to resort to other forms of transportation within the city.

By Car   It's fairly easy to drive around Waterford if you stick to the broad streets. Good parking is provided along the Quay for a small hourly charge, and at the top of Barronstrand Street (usually quite congested).

FAST FACTS

Waterford's **telephone area code** is 051. The **General Post Office** is on the Quay a few blocks from Reginald's Tower, open Monday through Friday from 9am to 6:30pm and on Saturday from 9am to 1pm (closed Sunday). The **Automobile Association** is on the Quay (tel. 051/73765). In an **emergency** (police, medical, fire), dial 999. There are two weekly Waterford **newspapers:** the *Munster Express,* and the *Waterford News & Star.*

WHAT TO SEE & DO

The very first thing you should do is drop by the Tourist Office on the Quay to pick up two booklets that will bring this historic old town's streets alive with the ghosts of Celts, Vikings, and Normans. **"Selected Walks Through Old Waterford"** will send you prowling down narrow lanes and through impressive buildings to see the likes of Christ Church Cathedral (first established in 1050 by the same Reginald of tower fame), the French Church ruins, town walls, towers, and castles. The second booklet, **"Reginald's Tower and the Story of Waterford,"** gives you a very complete (and entertaining) history of the massive tower that dates from 1003 and of Waterford from its very beginning. Both are written and illustrated by Pat Mackey, a former official of the Tourist Board who knows and loves Waterford and the Southeast Region.

Look for his "City and County Guide to Kilkenny" as well, and if you haven't yet been to Wexford, this is the time to get Pat's excellent and inexpensive South Wexford guide. Pat has also written a fascinating book that gives the flavor of Waterford in the 1930s, '40s, and '50s. Called *Talk of the Town*, it opens up a view of Pat's hometown that has long since vanished—"cockle women," pawnshops, pig buyers, and street characters.

The Tourist Board also has the helpful **Waterford County Guide** (for a small charge) and the free **Skylines** magazine with touring routes throughout the entire Southeast, as well as an excellent selection of maps and Irish publications. They will book you for a tour of the Waterford Crystal Factory (see below) and bring you up-to-date on what's going on in town during your stay and advise you on Bus Eireann day trips around the area. They can also book you for the 1½-hour guided walking tour that leaves from the Tourist Office daily during summer months at a cost of IR£2 ($3.50).

THE TOP ATTRACTIONS

REGINALD'S TOWER MUSEUM, The Quay, Waterford, Co. Waterford.

✪ At the end of the Quay, which turns into the Mall, Reginald's Tower stands sentinel as it has for 1,000 years, though today, as a museum, it guards gems from Waterford's historical treasures. When Reginald McIvor, the Danish ruler, built this stronghold, its 12-foot-thick walls stood right at the river's edge, and it was constructed so that entrance could only be gained from inside the city walls. In the centuries since, the tower has proved its worth as the strongest fortification on the River Suir, having resisted attack from all sides (even Cromwell failed to conquer it, although the bitterly cold winter may have had something to do with his unsuccessful siege). And it has witnessed events of major significance in Ireland's history, such as the marriage in 1170 of Strongbow to Eva, Irish King MacMurrough's daughter, which marked the beginning of England's entanglement with Irish affairs.

Today you enter the fascinating museum through what was once the tower's dungeon (wherein the Sitrics met their end and Reginald and O'Faolain were imprisoned). On the upper floors you'll find King John's mace and sword, along with many of the city's 30 royal charters. Interesting to Americans is the display on Timbertoes, the wooden bridge across the Suir (now replaced by a modern structure) that was the work of Boston architect Lemuel Cox in 1797. The following year, rebels who participated in the uprising of 1798 were hanged from its beams. There's also a bronze plate over which currency changed hands back in the 18th century—it's called simply the "Nail," and has entered our vocabulary through the expression "paying on the nail."

Admission: Small adult fee, free for children.

Open: Mid-Apr to Oct, Mon–Fri 11am–1pm and 2–7pm, Sat 11am–2pm; ask at the City Hall (on the Mall) about winter hours.

WATERFORD HERITAGE CENTRE, Greyfriars St., Waterford, Co. Waterford. Tel. 051/76123.

Just down the Quay from Reginald's Tower on Greyfriars side street, the Heritage Centre, new in 1990, focuses on the wealth of archeology in Waterford, with particular emphasis on the period A.D. 1000–1500. Among the more interesting exhibits are a model of medieval Waterford and a drawing of Viking Waterford just before the arrival of the Normans. There are fascinating explanations of the way in which archeologists work and the methods they employ to "dig up" Waterford's past, as well as a host of other interesting items. Well worth a visit.

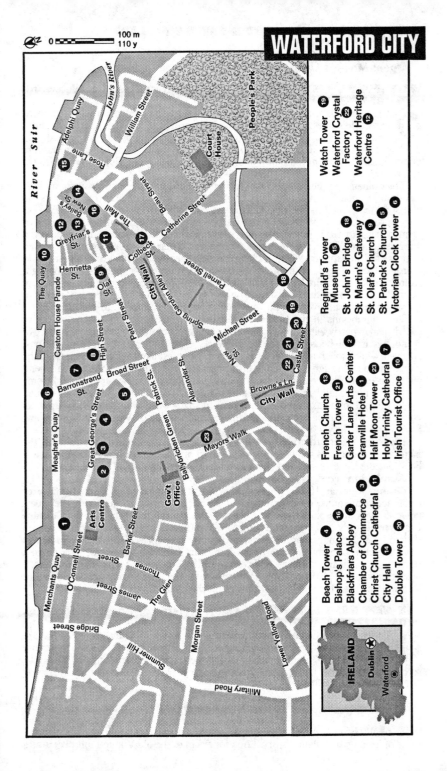

WATERFORD CITY

River Suir

Adelphi Quay
John's River
William Street
Rose Lane
The Mall
Beau Street
Catherine Street
People's Park
Court House
New St.
Bailey's New St.
Greyfriar's St.
The Quay
Henrietta St.
Custom House Parade
Olaf St.
City Wall
Colbeck St.
Parnell Street
High Street
Peter Street
Spring Garden Alley
Michael Street
New St.
Castle Street
Barronstrand St.
Broad Street
Patrick St.
Alexander St.
Browne's Ln.
City Wall
Meagher's Quay
Great George's Street
Ballybricken Green
Mayors Walk
Gov't Office
Arts Centre
Barker Street
Merchants Quay
O'Connell Street
Thomas Street
James Street
The Glen
Morgan Street
Summer Hill
Lower Yellow Road
Military Road
Bridge Street

Beach Tower 4
Bishop's Palace 16
Blackfriars Abbey 8
Chamber of Commerce 3
Christ Church Cathedral 11
City Hall 14
Double Tower 20

French Church 13
French Tower 21
Garter Lane Arts Center 2
Granville Hotel 1
Half Moon Tower 23
Holy Trinity Cathedral 7
Irish Tourist Office 10

Reginald's Tower Museum 15
St. John's Bridge 18
St. Martin's Gateway 9
St. Olaf's Church 5
St. Patrick's Church 6
Victorian Clock Tower

Watch Tower 19
Waterford Crystal Factory 22
Waterford Heritage Centre 12

IRELAND
Dublin
Waterford

0 — 100 m
110 y

Admission: 50p (90¢).
Open: Mon–Fri 11am–1pm and 2–7pm, Sat 11am–1pm.

WATERFORD CRYSTAL FACTORY, Kilbarry, Waterford, Co. Waterford. Tel. 051/73311.

⭐ You won't want to leave Waterford without a trip to the plant where some of the world's finest crystal is fashioned into works of art. Before we talk about what you'll see, let me warn you that, to avoid disappointment, you should book as far in advance as possible during the summer months. The half-hour tours are one of Ireland's most popular attractions and only small groups are allowed through at a time.

The brilliance of the crystal comes from the unique formula of ingredients, and the fastidious approach to the mixing of the "batch" (raw materials) accounts for its fire and sparkle, as well as for the difficulty in blowing. George and William Penrose began production of the crystal in modest premises on the Quay in 1783. Less than a century later, in 1851, horrendous taxes on raw materials closed its doors, but even after its demise, Waterford's reputation persisted. When the Irish government moved to revive the industry in 1947, it took 5 years to gather the necessary artisans and build a proper facility. Some 30 master glass blowers, cutters, and engravers were brought from Europe to train Irish apprentices, and in 1951 Waterford crystal was once more in production. Today there's a staff of hundreds, turning out 90,000 finished pieces of the beautiful crystal every week, of which about 60% is shipped to the U.S.

The tour begins in the blowing department, where teams of four to six work swiftly and expertly with molten glass as it emerges from the kiln, since in the space of 3 minutes it will become too hard to work. Once blown, the piece moves past checkers whose sole purpose is to spot even the slightest flaw—only two-thirds of the pieces make it through this minute inspection and go on to the cutting department, where cutters work in teams of six (four qualified cutters and two apprentices). Some 15% of the pieces fall by the wayside at this stage. The still-dull cut surfaces are dipped into a mixture of acids, followed by a bath in soapy water and a final rinse in white vinegar, by which time the characteristic fire and sparkle of Waterford crystal shine forth in all its glory.

For years, Waterford crystal was not available at its source. In 1986, however, the factory opened a sales showroom. Don't expect any discounts, however—prices will be about the same as you find them around the country.

Admission: Free.
Open: Tours at 10:15, 11, and 11:45am, and 1:45 and 2:30pm. Because of insurance regulations, no children under 10 are permitted on the tours; they may, however, wait in the showroom and watch a 20-minute film on the factory. **Closed:** Last week in July and the first 2 weeks in Aug (this can vary, so best check), but a skeleton staff continues working and a restricted tour is still available. **Reservations:** You can write directly to Waterford Glass Ltd., Kilbarry, Waterford, or arrange a booking through most Tourist Offices around the country. Many Waterford B&B hostesses will be glad to book for you when you make your accommodations reservation. **Bus:** From the Clock Tower on the Quay.

THE *NEW ROSS GALLEY,* The Quay, Waterford, Co. Waterford. Tel. 051/21723

⭐ The cost of the afternoon tea cruise is IR£4 ($7) and reservations are essential—book through the Tourist Office. From June to August the cruise departs daily at 3pm from the Quay (frequency and departure times are flexible, so check with Tourist Office. See "What to See and Do—Around County Wexford" in Chapter 8 for details.)

MORE ATTRACTIONS

Some of Waterford's most interesting sightseeing attractions are its extensive ruins, relics of its long, turbulent history. Look for traces of the old Viking-built **city walls** at the railway station, Mayor's Walk, and Castle Street. On Greyfriars Street, the ruins of the **French Church** are all that remain of the Franciscan foundation built in 1240 that once housed Huguenot refugees. And all along the Quay, shopfronts reflect the city's beginnings and evolution over the centuries.

ORGANIZED TOURS

From May to October, Waterford Tourist Service (tel. 051/73711 or 51043) conducts four **guided walking tours** daily. The 1-hour walk takes you to the most important historic buildings in the city and fills you in on the city's development since the Middle Ages. Tours leave from the reception desk of the Granville Hotel, The Quay, at 10am, noon, 2pm, and 4pm, and cost IR£2 ($3.50) per person. No need to book in advance—just show up at the appointed times.

NEARBY ATTRACTIONS

☼ The 9 miles from Waterford city to **Dunmore East** via R683/684 are picturesque, and when you reach the little town perched above its historic harbor (mail ships used to put in here, as did smugglers, pirates, and a variety of other characters), fine beaches, and sheltered coves, you'll be tempted to stay a day or two for the fishing, swimming, sailing, and/or the good crack with some of the friendliest Irish in the country. You might lunch at the Candlelight Inn, the Haven Hotel, or the Ocean Hotel, or if it's a pint you're after, look for the Strand Inn Pub, where there's a small stone fireplace in the front room and good conversation in all three rooms. The Butcher is a pub in an old butcher shop and attracts mostly a youngish crowd. Spend some time on foot exploring the winding streets and going down to the quay to examine fishing and leisure boats, and when you're ready to get on with your journey, head for the coast drive to Tramore (R685) that winds along the clifftops with glimpses of the sea.

SPECIAL EVENTS

☼ Wexford has its Opera Festival, but Waterford has the **International Festival of Light Opera,** a lighthearted gathering of amateur companies that converge on the city in September from Europe, the U.S., Great Britain, and all parts of Ireland. During each of the festival's 16 nights there are performances of such musicals as *Brigadoon* and *Showboat,* all of amazingly high standard, and things wind up with the presentation of a beautiful Waterford Glass trophy. Light opera, however, is not the only thing going on during this time. There are singing pub competitions (with all pubs granted an extension of hours up to 1am) and a host of auxiliary activities, with a special Festival Office set up to see that you get to the event of your choice.

Individual performances range from IR£2.50 to IR£6 ($4.40 to $10.50). For reservations, write: Booking Office, International Festival of Light Opera, Waterford.

SAVVY SHOPPING

THE BOOK CENTRE, 9 Michael St., Waterford, Co. Waterford. Tel. 051/73823. Fax 051/70769.

If you're looking for publications on subjects of Irish interest, history, contemporary fiction and nonfiction, poetry, travel—or just about anything else—chances are you'll find it in this bright, modern bookshop. Open Monday through Saturday from 9:30am to 5:30pm.

JOSEPH KNOX LTD., 3/4 Barronstrand St., Waterford, Co. Waterford. Tel. 051/75307. Fax 051/79058.

 This has long been one of Ireland's leading outlets for Waterford glass, fine bone china, and porcelain. They'll mail (a superb mail-order catalog is available on request), and they accept major credit cards. Open Monday through Saturday from 9:30am to 5:30pm.

THOMAS PHELAN, 14 George's St., Waterford, Co. Waterford. Tel. 051/74288.

Pipe smokers will love this old-fashioned shop. It's a relic of the days when gentlemen smokers were catered to by other gentlemen who loved the trade, and those behind the counter at Phelan's continue that tradition (catering just as happily to the odd lady pipe smoker like myself!). There's a good selection of pipes, as well as cigars, cigarettes, lighters, and tobacco. Open Monday through Saturday from 9:30am to 5:30pm.

TERESA CLEARY'S ART GALLERY, 56 O'Connell St., Waterford, Co. Waterford. Tel. 051/75022.

The specialty here is Irish landscape paintings, a nice souvenir to carry home. They also have a good stock of old Waterford prints. Open Monday through Friday from 10am to 4:30pm.

WOOL CRAFT, 11 Michael St., Waterford, Co. Waterford. Tel. 051/74082.

One of Ireland's leading suppliers of hand-knits and hand-loomed knitwear, this shop is loaded with Aran sweaters, along with a whole range of woolens. Best of all, prices average about 30% less than most other sweater shops, woolen mills, or department stores. Open Monday through Saturday from 9:30am to 5:30pm.

PUBS & EVENING ENTERTAINMENT

The Performing Arts

GARTER LANE THEATRE, 5 O'Connell St., Waterford, Co. Waterford. Tel. 051/55038.

New plays, old standbys, and musical performances appear at the Garter Lane, with local and imported acting ensembles. The box office or the Tourist Office can tell you what's doing when you're in Waterford.

Admission: Tickets IR£3–IR£7 ($5.25–$12.25).

THEATRE ROYAL, The Mall, Waterford, Co. Waterford. Tel. 051/74402.

This beautiful old theater is the venue of musicals and amateur drama productions these days, and it comes back into its past glory during the Light Opera Festival.

Admission: Varies with the production.

TRADITIONAL MUSIC SESSIONS On Saturday and Sunday nights there's traditional Irish music (and a good time!) at the **Munster Bar** behind Reginald's Tower on Bailey's New Street (tel. 051/74656). Call in around 9:30 or 10pm, when things should be just getting lively. Music is sometimes to be found in **Meade's Bar,** Ballycanvan, Halfway House (tel. 051/73187); **Mullane's,** 15 Newgate Street (tel. 051/73854); and **T&H Doolans,** 32 George's Street (tel. 051/72764); as well as other Waterford pubs, but seldom on a regular basis, so check with the Tourist Office and in local papers.

THE PUBS

THE MUNSTER BAR, Bailey's New St., Waterford, Co. Waterford. Tel. 051/74656.

✪ This is a cozy, wood-paneled, etched-glass haven of conviviality that began life as a coaching inn 200 years ago. In 1950 it was taken over by Pete Fitzgerald, and the small room known as Peter's Bar is a gathering place for some of Waterford's liveliest conversationalists. On cool evenings a coal fire reflects off wall sconces and chandeliers of "old" (pre-1851) Waterford glass. Peter's sons—Peter, Michael, and Tom—carry on their father's traditions of hospitality, and will see to it that you're not long a stranger. On Saturday and Sunday nights the large upstairs room rings to the strains of traditional music, and sing-songs erupt spontaneously.

What was probably the stables for the old Munster Inn has been converted into an extension of the original Munster. It can be mobbed at lunchtime (see "Where to Eat," below), and evening finds it filled again with convivial Waterford imbibers.

THE REGINALD BAR, The Mall, Waterford, Co. Waterford. Tel. 051/ 55087.

The Reginald Bar, directly behind Reginald's Tower, has its antiquity attested to by a plaque on the left-hand wall as you enter which bears the inscription BUILT CIRCA A.D. 850 BY SITRIC THE DANE. One of the original city walls, its arched stone alcoves once served the Vikings as "sally ports," through which small boats were launched to "sally forth" along the river that back then was just outside. For the most part, the Reginald is a pub for congenial mingling, but there's music from time to time, and on most Sunday afternoons between 12:30 and 2pm there are jazz sessions by very good local musicians. Visiting instrumentalists are welcome to the local group.

T. & H. DOOLAN'S, 32 George's St., Waterford, Co. Waterford. Tel. 051/72764.

You'll know T. & H. Doolan's by its Tudor-style front and frosted-glass door. Inside, there's a wonderfully eclectic collection of old farm implements, whiskey jars, stone crocks, mugs, copper jugs, and anything else the late Thomas Doolan took a fancy to hang from rough wooden beams or the whitewashed walls. He was, of course, the "T" of the proprietorship, and if anything went amiss, blame promptly fell on the "H" of that partnership—and thereby hangs a tale. H. Doolan, it turns out, was purely a figment of T. Doolan's imagination, who came into being when "Thomas" was too long, "T." and "Tom" too short, for the establishment's sign. The spirited characters of T. & H. still linger in this 150-year-old pub that was for many years a stagecoach stop.

THOMAS MAHER'S, O'Connell St., Waterford, Co. Waterford.

✪ Gentlemen, leave your ladies behind when you head for this pub. This one-of-a-kind old pub that dates back to 1886 is presided over by Thomas Maher, a small, white-haired, blue-eyed man who has been behind the bar some 60 years and knows his own mind when it comes to running his pub. "I don't want to see anyone too early, too late, or too long," he declares. He brooks no swearing, no singing—and no ladies. With those rules in force, you may well ask, who comes? Crowds of devoted "regulars," that's who comes, for behind a traditional storefront that has won many an award for its design there's an interior that has changed little, if at all, over the years. You may drink your pint in a glass stamped with a '20s or '30s date (since 1928, all pint glasses must bear a date stamp), and if there's no date at all, chances are it's one left from as far back as 1916. If you like, you can purchase spirits bottled by Mr. Maher himself. He and his pub are a Waterford institution. You'll find Thomas behind the bar Monday through Friday from noon to 2pm, 5 to 7pm, and 8:30 to 10pm.

WHERE TO STAY

IN TOWN

ANNVILL HOUSE, The Orchard, Kingsmeadow, Waterford, Co. Waterford. Tel. 051/73617. 5 rms (4 with bath). **Bus:** From the Clock Tower.

$ Rates (including breakfast): IR£15.50 ($27.15) single without bath; IR£12 ($21) per person sharing without bath; IR£1 ($1.75) per person additional with bath. 10% reduction for children. Dinner IR£9 ($15.75) extra. No credit cards.

Alice and Eammon O'Brien and their family welcome you to their modern two-story home and are happy to arrange tours and help with any other holiday plans. The guest rooms are bright, attractive, and comfortable, with built-in wardrobes and sinks. There's central heat and off-the-street parking. This is just off the Waterford–Cork road (N25), signposted at the Maxol Station just beyond the Tramore road turnoff as you approach the Waterford Crystal Factory.

DERRYNANE HOUSE, 19 The Mall, Waterford, Co. Waterford. Tel. 051/75179. 7 rms (1 with bath).
$ Rates (including breakfast): IR£12 ($21) per person without bath, IR£13 ($22.75) per person with bath. No credit cards. **Closed:** Dec–Feb.

Americans with a historic bent of mind will be drawn to this house. It was here that Thomas Francis Meagher was arrested by the British in 1848 and sent off to Tasmania. After escaping and making his way to America, he eventually rose to the rank of brigadier general in the Union's Fighting 69th Brigade during the Civil War. The four-story house is of Georgian style, with a wide, gracious entry hall. There's a large family room with its own bathroom, and six others have sinks and are served by two shower rooms and two bathrooms. Eilish O'Sullivan presides, and maintains a homey TV lounge for her guests.

MRS. MARY RYAN, 7 Cathedral Sq., Waterford, Co. Waterford. Tel. 051/76677. 5 rms (none with bath).
$ Rates (including breakfast): IR£11 ($19.25) per person. No credit cards. **Closed:** Dec–Feb.

Mrs. Ryan is located right in the heart of the city, facing Christ Church Cathedral and just one block up from the Quay. The old three-story house has been nicely renovated, and the bedrooms, all with sinks, afford views of either the cathedral and historic district or the hills across the River Suir. There's metered parking space on this quiet little street, and a great many places are within easy walking distance. You can catch a bus out to the Waterford Crystal Factory just a block away.

MAYORS WALK HOUSE, 12 Mayors Walk, Waterford, Co. Waterford. Tel. 051/55427. 4 rms (none with bath).
$ Rates (including breakfast): IR£12 ($21) per person. No credit cards. **Closed:** Nov–Mar.

Kay and John Ryder welcome you to their immaculate three-story home, and provide copious information on local attractions, restaurants, and shopping. There's a bath and shower on each floor, and rooms are pleasant, attractive, and comfortable. The location is ideal—a short walk from the town center, and convenient to bus transportation to the Waterford Crystal Factory. The rail and bus depot are also not too far away.

ROSELDA, Cork Rd. (N25), Waterford, Co. Waterford. Tel. 051/73922. 5 rms (none with bath). **Bus:** From the Clock Tower.
$ Rates (including breakfast): IR£11 ($19.25) per person. 10% reduction for children. Dinner IR£9.50 ($16.65) extra. No credit cards.

Mrs. Ann Walsh is an extremely helpful hostess, happy to arrange Waterford Crystal tours at the factory, just 3 minutes away. Husband Tommy worked as a cutter at Waterford Crystal for some 28 years and has a beautiful private collection, with many pieces of his own design. Rooms are attractive and comfortable, all with sinks, and the house is centrally heated.

SAINT MARTINS, 24 Decies Ave., Lismore Lawn, Waterford, Co. Waterford. Tel. 051/75713. 3 rms (none with bath). **Bus:** From the Clock Tower.
$ Rates (including breakfast): IR£11 ($19.25) per person. 20% reduction for children. High tea IR£7 ($12.25) extra; dinner IR£9.50 ($16.65). No credit cards.

I first learned of Mrs. Phyllis O'Reilly's home when a reader wrote to me. The modern, two-story home is only a few minutes away from the Waterford Crystal Factory, off the Waterford–Cork road (N25), and on a major bus route into the city center. The odd "cuppa" appears magically just when you are in need of it. Central heating keeps the premises as warm as its owners, and all rooms have sinks.

TALGINN, Ballynaneashagh, Cork Rd. (N25), Waterford, Co. Waterford. Tel. 051/73798. 4 rms (1 with bath). **Bus:** From the Clock Tower.

$ Rates (including breakfast): IR£14.50 ($25.40) single without bath; IR£11 ($19.25) per person sharing without bath; IR£1.50 ($2.65) per person additional with bath. No credit cards. **Closed:** Nov–Mar.

Mrs. Margaret Power is a warm hostess, and her immaculate modern home is 2km (1¼ miles) from the town center and a mere 3 minutes from the Waterford Crystal Factory (she's happy to book tours for guests). Guest rooms are attractive in decor and very comfortable, with ample bathrooms for those without private facilities. She also presents a breakfast menu that offers choices other than the traditional Irish spread.

Worth the Extra Money

DOOLEY'S HOTEL, 30 The Quay, Waterford, Co. Waterford. Tel. 051/73531. Fax 051/70262. 40 rms (all with bath) TV TEL

$ Rates: IR£38 ($66.50) single; IR£65 ($113.75) double. Service charge 10%. Children under 10 stay free in parents' room. AE, MC, V.

 Dooley's central location, friendly staff, and general character may well tempt you to go over budget bounds. This was a leading 19th-century coaching inn, and the grandniece of the Dooley family still books in whenever she's in Waterford, even though for more than 40 years the hotel has been owned and managed by Mrs. June Darrer and her family. The staff are longtimers who cater to guests as if the hotel were their own. The lobby and lounge bar (see "Where to Eat," below) are warm with rich reds and greens, stained glass, oil paintings, and leather circular booths. Guest rooms vary, according to whether they're in the older section, with its odd-shaped rooms (some small and cozy, others large and full of interesting nooks), or the newer wing, where rooms are more standard, although still furnished in the hotel's traditional style.

NEARBY ACCOMMODATIONS

BEECHMOUNT, R683/4, Dunmore East, Co. Waterford. Tel. 051/83293. 3 rms (none with bath).

$ Rates (including breakfast): IR£12 ($21) per person. 20% reduction for children. Dinner IR£11 ($19.25) extra. No credit cards. **Parking:** Available.

On the outskirts of Dunmore East (7 miles from Waterford city), Beechmount is a pretty country bungalow set on a hill overlooking the village and harbor, with a well-kept acre of lawn and garden. Mrs. Rita Power's bright and sparkling home is furnished with interesting antiques (you may want to take your impressive bedroom pieces home!); each guest room has a sink. The stone fireplace is a focal point in the lounge, whose windows look out to the garden. The two Power teenagers, William and Victoria, are great sailing and windsurfing fans and love to talk to guests about their favorite sports. There's central heating and a graveled car park.

DIAMOND HILL, Slieverue, Waterford. Tel. 051/32855 or 32254. 8 rms (5 with bath).

$ Rates (including breakfast): IR£13–IR£16 ($22.75–$28) per person. No credit cards. **Parking:** Private car park.

This pretty, modern house is set in lawns and gardens that have won the National Garden Award for guesthouses no fewer than four times. Its interior is as attractive as the exterior, with a nice lounge, beautifully decorated bedrooms featuring many built-ins, and central heating. Mary and John Malone have won many devoted fans among our readers. The hospitable Malones take a real interest in their guests, and in good weather set out chairs in the sunny gardens for a bit of outdoor relaxation. There is also a delightful craft shop displaying the best of Irish handcrafts at very reasonable prices. Diamond Hill is just off the Waterford–Rosslare road (N25) at Slieverue Junction, about 2 miles outside Waterford.

GLENCREE, The Sweep, Kilmeaden, Co. Waterford. Tel. 051/84240. 5 rms (3 with bath).
$ Rates (including breakfast): IR£16 ($28) single without bath; IR£12 ($21) per person sharing without bath; IR£1.50 ($2.65) per person additional with bath. 20% reduction for children. High tea IR£6 ($10.50) extra; dinner, IR£10 ($17.50). No credit cards. **Parking:** Available.
Readers have been lavish in their praise of Mrs. Rena Power and her family; typical comments are, "More than anything else, I was impressed by their hospitality," and "Of the many B&Bs in which we stayed, hers was the best." The attractive Power bungalow, in its scenic setting, is as warm as their welcome to guests, and guest rooms are bright, cheerful, and comfortable. They are happy to arrange Waterford Crystal Factory tours, as well as to advise on other local attractions and happenings, and there's ample private parking. Glencree is 9km (5½ miles) from Waterford, just off the Cord road (N25); it's signposted from the highway.

HALFWAY HOUSE, Passage East Rd., Ballymaclode, Waterford, Co. Waterford. Tel. 051/76055. 4 rms (2 with bath).
$ Rates (including breakfast): IR£17 ($29.75) single without bath; IR£12 ($21) per person sharing without bath; IR£2 ($3.50) per person additional with bath. 20% reduction for children. Dinner IR£12 ($21) extra. No credit cards.
Carol and Willie Kinsella's attractive two-story bungalow 3 miles from Waterford turns its back to the road, its front to gardens and rolling fields beyond. The bedrooms are nicely decorated, and the lounge and dining room are inviting public spaces. There's also a glassed-in back lounge that looks out to Willie's herb garden that sparks his many gourmet creations at the dinner table. Trained in Rockwell (Ireland), Lausanne (Switzerland), and London, Willie is the star of the kitchen here. His dinners feature the freshest local produce and seafood straight from the waters at Dunmore East. All include sherry before dinner.

SAN MICHELE, Newtown Park, Waterford, Co. Waterford. Tel. 051/73632. 3 rms (none with bath).
$ Rates (including breakfast): IR£11 ($19.25) per person. 25% reduction for children. No credit cards. **Closed:** Sept–May.
Mrs. Paula Heenan is the friendly lady who runs this clean, modern bungalow overlooking the River Suir 1 mile from Waterford just off the Passage East road. She is very helpful and will arrange tours of the Waterford Crystal Factory.

Farmhouses

ASHBOURNE HOUSE, Milepost, Slieverue, Waterford, Co. Waterford. Tel. 051/32037. 7 rms (6 with bath).
$ Rates (including breakfast): IR£12.50 ($21.90) per person. 25% reduction for children. High tea IR£6.50 ($11.40) extra; dinner, IR£10 ($17.50). No credit cards. **Closed:** Nov–Mar.
Mrs. Agnes Forrest is the gracious hostess of this lovely two-story, renovated farmhouse on 20 acres of mixed farming 2 miles northeast of Waterford just off N25, the Waterford–New Ross road (well signposted). Its scenic setting can be enjoyed from the garden, and both river and sea angling are close by, as is horse riding.

FOXMOUNT FARM, Dunmore East Rd., Waterford, Co. Waterford. Tel. 051/74308. 6 rms (none with bath).
$ Rates (including breakfast): IR£13 ($22.75) per person. 33% reduction for

children. Dinner IR£12 ($21) extra. No credit cards. **Closed:** Dec–Feb. **Parking:** Available.

⭐ This is another perennial favorite with readers. The 230-acre working farm is 4 miles out of town just off the Dunmore East road (well signposted). The elegant old home, dating from 1700, sits on a slight rise overlooking a verdant lawn edged with flowering shrubs, pastures, and tilled acres. Margaret and David Kent are always eager to accommodate their guests, whether by booking a glass-factory tour, explaining the history of the region, or simply showing them around the farm. Children delight in riding Nellie, the obliging resident donkey (there are also a horse and pony) and exploring the farmyard. Other amenities include table tennis and a tennis court.

The house is furnished with lovely antiques, and evening tea around a glowing fire in the drawing room is a special event. Meals are superb, featuring all fresh ingredients and home-baking, and you're welcome to bring your own wine. Let Margaret know by noon if you want the evening meal. There's central heat and plenty of parking.

MOAT FARMHOUSE, Faithlegg, Cheekpoint Rd., Waterford, Co. Waterford. Tel. 051/82166. 3 rms (none with bath).

$ Rates (including breakfast): IR£11 ($19.25) per person. 25% reduction for children. Dinner IR£12 ($21) extra. No credit cards. **Closed:** Nov–Mar.

The Gough family's home is a 16th-century farmhouse that has been in the family for generations, and the gardens surround the remains of 12th-century Faithlegg Castle, which was plundered by Cromwell in the 17th century. The whole family is hospitable, and the house is very comfortable. Meals are excellent, there is central heating, and the bedrooms are attractive, all with sinks. It's 5 miles from Waterford, 7 miles from Dunmore East, 1½ miles from Passage East, and 1½ miles from Cheekpoint.

Worth the Extra Money

WATERFORD CASTLE, The Island, Ballinakill, Waterford, Co. Waterford. Tel. 051/78203 or 80332. Fax 051/79316. 31 rms (all with bath). TV TEL

$ Rates: IR£80–IR£100 ($140–$175) single; IR£100–IR£135 ($175–$236.25) double; IR£220–IR£250 ($385–$437.50) suite. ACC, AE, MC, V.

⭐ I can't think of a better place to spend extra dollars than in this castle, whose setting and history push romance right to the brink of fantasy—it sits on its own wooded 311-acre island, which divides the River Suir at a point leading to Waterford city's deep-water port 1½ miles upstream. Its strategic location accounts for a long and colorful history, but it's the sheer beauty of that location that overwhelms when you board the small chain-link-driven car-ferry to cross some 300 yards of the Suir. The fine stone castle, a FitzGerald family stronghold from 1160 to 1958, is modest in size. The castle's Great Hall may be a bit on the small side, but it is impressive, with a large stone fireplace at one end. At the opposite end of the hall is one of the castle's original tapestries, depicting a hunting scene that looks as if it could have taken place right on the island.

Bedrooms are in the two Elizabethan-style wings (added in the 1800s) and all have views onto the Suir, woodlands, or the landscaped lawn out front. There's a magnificent oak-paneled dining room (once the ballroom), where superb meals are served with Waterford crystal glassware, and Wedgwood dinnerware bearing the FitzGerald crest on the table. On the castle grounds are lovely wooded walks, horseback riding, fishing, and hunting, with golf and tennis facilities near by, as well as the historic city of Waterford and the rugged Dunmore East coast to explore.

READERS RECOMMEND

Mall House, 20 The Mall, Waterford, County Waterford (tel. 051/76118). "By accident, we found ourselves on the Mall directly in front of Mall House, and when we knocked on the door, we were greeted by the most pleasant Mrs. McGoldrick. Our room was great, with *comfortable and warm beds, and she served breakfast in her beautiful dining room, furnished with lovely antiques and a chandelier that was so beautiful it had to be Waterford (I didn't ask). There was plenty of hot water, and central heating."*—Renée Steele, Newark, Del.

WHERE TO EAT

BARRETTS BISTRO, 3 Michael St., Waterford.
Cuisine: PASTA/SALADS/PIZZA.
$ Prices: IR£1–IR£5 ($1.75–$8.75). No credit cards.
Open: Daily noon–midnight.
This small, bright eatery has a traditional front and friendly, pleasant service. Pastas include excellent pizza and lasagne, and other specialties are barbecued ribs, seafood, and steaks. The homemade soups are outstanding (try the rich, creamy seafood bisque), and there's a full range of salads and sandwiches.

DOOLEY'S HOTEL, The Quay, Waterford. Tel. 051/73531.
Cuisine: BAR FOOD/TRADITIONAL.
$ Prices: Appetizers IR£1.50–IR£3 ($2.65–$5.25); main courses IR£4–IR£7 ($7–$12.25); bar snacks IR£1.50–IR£4 ($1.75–$7). Children's menu IR£3 ($5.25). ACC, AE, MC, V.
Open: Lunch daily 12:30–2:30pm; dinner daily 5:30–9:30pm.

There's good bar food in Dooley's cozy bar/lounge, as well as a three-course Business Person's Luncheon Special in the main dining room May through October. There are also excellent four-course lunches from the regular menu (seafood, beef, chicken, pork, lamb) in the pretty dining room, a good place for your main meal of the day, be it lunch or dinner.

GRANVILLE HOTEL, The Quay, Waterford. Tel. 051/55111.
Cuisine: BAR FOOD.
$ Prices: IR£2.50–IR£5 ($4.40–$8.75). ACC, AE, MC, V.
Open: Lunch only, daily 12:30–2:30pm.
Such specialties as smoked salmon and brown bread, along with several tasty hot dishes, salad plates, and snacks are available in the attractive ground-floor bar of the Granville.

MANOR COURT LODGE RESTAURANT, Manor Court, Cork Rd., Waterford. Tel. 051/78851.
Cuisine: SEAFOOD/TRADITIONAL.
$ Prices: Breakfast IR£4.50 ($7.90); fixed-price meal IR£6 ($10.50) at lunch, IR£12 ($21) at dinner. ACC, AE, DC, MC, V.
Open: Daily 8:15am–10pm. **Closed:** Good Friday, Christmas Day.
This was once the Gothic-style gate lodge to the Holy Ghost Friary, and its decor reflects its origin. Situated on N25 just before reaching the Waterford Crystal factory, it offers something to ward off hunger pangs almost any time of day. Breakfast, morning coffee, lunch, afternoon tea, and dinner are all tasty and attractively served. Oven-fresh scones are available with coffee and tea, and lunch might include lemon-baked chicken with crab. Among the dinner specialties are spiced silverside of beef, smoked haddock, and beef and seafood from local sources. There's also a good wine list with moderate prices.

THE MUNSTER, The Mall, Waterford. Tel. 051/74656.
Cuisine: PUB GRUB/TRADITIONAL.
$ Prices: IR£2.50–IR£4 ($4.40–$7). No credit cards.
Open: Lunch only, Mon–Sat 12:30–2:30pm.

The Munster serves a wide selection of budget-priced plates and half of Waterford's young working crowd at lunch. More than just pub grub, the heaping plates of roast beef, ham, or chicken with potato and two vegetables are ample enough to be the main meal of the day. If you're not that hungry, there's soup and sandwiches, cold salad plates, and something called a "blaa" (lettuce, meat, onion, and tomato on a small roll), found only in Waterford, that goes for about IR£1 ($1.75). With an entrance on the Mall, this is the "back room" of the Munster Bar on Bailey's New Street (see "Pubs and Evening Entertainment" in "What to See and Do," above).

THE OLDE STAND, 45 Michael St., Waterford. Tel. 051/79488.
   Cuisine: SEAFOOD/STEAKS/CARVERY.
$ **Prices:** Appetizers IR£1.50–IR£3 ($2.65–$5.25); main courses IR£6.95–IR£10.95 ($12.15–$19.15); fixed-price dinner IR£10.50 ($18.40); Tea-Time Special and Early Bird Menu (both three courses) IR£6.95 ($12.15); Carvery lunch under IR£5 ($8.75). ACC, EURO, MC, V.
   Open: Lunch Mon–Sat 12:30–2:30pm (bar carvery); Tea Time Special Mon–Sat 4:50–7:50pm; dinner Mon–Sat 5:30–10:15pm (Early Bird Menu 5:30–8pm).

This lovely authentic-looking Victorian-style pub and restaurant is the creation of Eamon Reid, who has combined lots of mahogany (the back bar came from an old church in England), deep shades of green, and a liberal dose of charm to come up with an ambience chock full of character. The downstairs bar is a cozy, intimate space, and the upstairs restaurant has two pleasant, relaxing rooms, with candles on the tables and a fireplace adding a cheery glow. As for the food, the lunchtime carvery features a roast joint (beef, lamb, pork) of the day, as well as homemade soups, salad plates, and a salad bar. From tea time on, the menu lists seafood (fresh from local waters), steaks from Ireland's Golden Vale, chicken, lamb, duck, and other local specialties. There's an excellent Irish cheese board that puts a perfect finish to your meal. As a crowning touch, the staff here are both friendly and efficient.

THE REGINALD BAR AND RESTAURANT, The Mall, Waterford. Tel. 051/55087.
   Cuisine: PUB GRUB/TRADITIONAL.
$ **Prices:** Appetizers IR£1.50–IR£3 ($2.65–$5.25); main courses IR£4–IR£7 ($7–$12.25); Tourist Menu IR£5.75–IR£7.90 ($10.05–$13.85) in the restaurant; IR£2.50–IR£4 ($4.40–$7) in the bar. ACC, AE, MC, V.
   Open: Bar, lunch daily 12:30–2:30pm; restaurant, Mon–Sat 10:30am–10:30pm, Sun noon–9:30pm. **Closed:** Good Friday, Christmas Day.
There's a choice at the Reginald—soup and sandwiches, salad plates, and hot dishes (meat plus two vegetables) in the bar, or full four- or five-course meals in the restaurant, with beef, lamb, chicken, fish, and some vegetarian dishes offering a wide variety.

T. & H. DOOLAN'S, 32 George's St., Waterford. Tel. 051/72764.
   Cuisine: BAR FOOD.
$ **Prices:** IR£1.50–IR£4 ($2.65–$7). No credit cards.
   Open: Lunch only, Mon–Sat 12:30–2:30pm.
This century-and-a-half-old pub, with much of its original decor and character still intact (see "Pubs and Evening Entertainment" in "What to See and Do," above), has a healthy local following for good pub lunches. Soup and sandwiches, salad plates, stews, and a variety of hot dishes are available.

WORTH THE EXTRA MONEY

WATERFORD CASTLE, The Island, Ballinskill, Co. Waterford. Tel. 051/78203.
   Cuisine: SEAFOOD/TRADITIONAL. **Reservations:** Recommended for dinner.
$ **Prices:** Fixed-price meal IR£16 ($28) at lunch, IR£29 ($50.75) at dinner.
   Open: Lunch daily 12:30–2:30pm; dinner daily 6–9:30pm.

Even if your plans don't include a stay at this lovely small castle set on its own wooded island (see "Where to Stay," above), a meal here will be a luxurious treat. The setting is idyllic, the dining room decor reflects the elegance of a bygone era, and the menu makes extensive use of fresh garden herbs and vegetables from the castle gardens and local suppliers. Vegetarians will usually find a savory vegetable terrine on offer, and other dishes might include veal with Calvados, duck with honey-and-ginger sauce, and fresh fish and shellfish from nearby waters.

2. AROUND COUNTY WATERFORD & SOUTH TIPPERARY

The delights of this part of the Southeast are legion. The coastal drive from Waterford to Dungarvan dips from clifftops to secluded bathing coves; Lismore's castle looms over a site once occupied by a great monastic community; the River Blackwater (Ireland's Rhine) at Cappoquin is a salmon fisherman's dream; Ardmore is a pleasant mixture of historic ruins and modern resort comforts; and South Tipperary contributes the great medieval leftovers of Cahir Castle and the Rock of Cashel.

In the sections that follow, you will find accommodations listed under the nearest town, but it's important to remember that wherever you base yourself, easy day trips will let you explore the entire region. I suggest that you select an accommodation that appeals to you, regardless of its proximity to any one sightseeing attraction, and return each night to the same bed, breakfast, and host family.

SEEING COUNTY WATERFORD & SOUTH TIPPERARY

By Bus/Train Bus Eireann serves most towns in County Waterford and South Tipperary, and there are several excellent sightseeing day trips by coach departing from Waterford (check with the bus depot or the Tourist Office for destinations and schedules). There's train service only to Waterford from Cork and Dublin. For bus and rail information, call 051/79000 Monday through Saturday from 9am to 5:30pm, 051/73408 at other times.

By Car The shortest route from Waterford to almost any of the destinations listed below is along Highway N25, which will carry you straight into Cork city, some 78 miles to the southwest. Scenic driving routes are listed under each heading below as a basic guide that can be as flexible as you wish.

A SUGGESTED ITINERARY FROM TRAMORE TO CASHEL VIA CAPPOQUIN

Tramore is 8 miles south of Waterford (via the Cork road, N25, to the well-marked turnoff onto R682) and 10 miles from Dunmore East on the coast road, R685. Dungarvan, 26 miles southwest of Tramore, is best reached via the breathtakingly scenic coastal drive, R675, which passes through the small resort of Annestown and tiny Bunmahon, once a busy copper-mining center. Rugged cliffs, tall rock "stacks" rising from the sea offshore, and small coves line the route all the way to Clonea, where the landscape flattens out. A short, well-marked, detour 3 miles northeast of Dungarvan will bring you to Clonea Strand and its broad, sandy, pollution-free beach. From Dungarvan, you can join the Cork road, N25, to reach Ardmore via a signposted turnoff 15 miles southwest of Dungarvan, or you can turn onto N72 for Cappoquin, 10 miles northwest of Dungarvan, saving Ardmore for a day trip. To reach Cappoquin from Ardmore, take R671 (signposted "Clashmore") through lush farmlands and wooded hills to its junction with N72 4 miles outside Cappoquin.

TRAMORE

Just 8 miles south of Waterford city, Tramore is a popular seaside resort with a 3-mile-long beach and a 50-acre amusement park (the kids will love it!). For the older generation, there's an 18-hole golf course; call the Tramore Golf Club (tel. 051/ 81247). That giant of a statue you'll notice looking down on the bay from Great Newtown Head is known hereabouts as the Metal Man, and legend has it that any unmarried female who hops three times around its base on one foot will hop down the aisle within the next 12 months.

From Tramore, the coast road continues climbing and dipping among spectacular views through picturesque little towns until you reach Dungarvan.

WHERE TO STAY

RUSHMERE HOUSE, Tramore, Co. Waterford. Tel. 051/81041. 6 rms (4 with bath).

$ Rates (including breakfast): IR£17.50 ($30.65) single without bath; IR£11.50 ($20.15) per person sharing without bath; IR£3 ($5.25) per person additional with bath. 25% reduction for children. No credit cards. **Closed:** Dec–Jan. **Parking:** Large public car park directly opposite.

Mrs. Rita McGivney is the friendly hostess of this century-old, three-story Georgian house, which is flanked by wide chimneys at each end and sits on a rise looking across Tramore Bay to Brownstown Head. It's 8 miles from Waterford on the main Waterford–Tramore road as you enter town. The six guest rooms (three are family-size, with a double and a single with bath) are spacious, with high ceilings and tall windows, and the house is centrally heated.

READERS RECOMMEND

Seaview Lodge, Seaview Park, Tramore, Co. Waterford (tel. 051/81122). "We found Seaview Lodge to be exceptional. Mrs. Darcy was a most gracious hostess and went out of her way to make us welcome and comfortable. Her home was lovely; and her meals deliciously prepared."—Christine Rychetsky, Westmont, Ill.

WHERE TO EAT

PINE ROOMS, Turkey Rd., Tramore, Co. Waterford. Tel. 051/81686.
Cuisine: SEAFOOD/TRADITIONAL.

$ Prices: Appetizers IR£2–IR£5 ($3.50–$8.75); main courses IR£7–IR£10 ($12.25–$17.50).
Open: Lunch summer months only, daily 12:30–2:30pm; dinner year round, daily 5:30–10:30pm. **Closed:** Sun–Tues in Jan, Feb, Christmas week.

This attractive restaurant is set in a former residence, with pine furniture and sanded floors. Try their "Molly Malone" cockles and mussels starter, then opt for a seafood dish or one of their excellent steaks (peppered, with garlic butter, is a good choice). Vegetables are especially nicely done. Service is both friendly and efficient. The restaurant is in the town center on the main Waterford–Tramore road, near the car park, promenade, and Tourist Office.

DUNGARVAN

Dungarvan is a bustling market town where the River Colligan empties into Dungarvan Bay to form a secure harbor. It was named for a 13th-century saint who founded a monastery here, but the town's importance as a port made it a military center during the Norman invasions. The town withstood several sieges during the wars of 1641, but finally surrendered to Cromwell in 1649. The church and castle were destroyed; the remains of the **castle**, built by King John in 1185, are down along the quays a short way from the bridge crossing the Colligan.

The remains of a 13th-century **Augustinian priory** are in Abbeyside (across the river from the town center), a square tower resting on groined arches, which now serves as a belfry for the adjacent church. There's an excellent small **museum** at the top of North Main Street, and the **Tourist Information Office** is just upstairs.

Golfers can arrange to play the 9-hole course nearby by calling the Dungarvan Golf Club (tel. 058/41605). For a day of deep-sea fishing in the Irish Sea, contact **Dungarvan Charter Angling**, Paddy O'Riordan, Kilossera, Dungarvan, Co. Waterford (tel. 058/43286). And from November through February, the Clonea Strand Hotel can arrange for visitors to join one of the **fox hunts** in this locality.

WHERE TO STAY

BALLYGUIRY FARM, Dungarvan, Co. Waterford. Tel. 058/41194. 6 rms (3 with bath).

$ Rates: IR£13 ($22.75) per person daily (including breakfast); IR£132 ($231) per person per week (including breakfast and dinner), 50% reduction for children. High tea IR£7 ($12.25) extra; dinner, IR£9.50 ($16.65). No credit cards. **Closed:** Nov–Mar.

This lovely Georgian house in the foothills of the Drum Hills 2½ miles south of Dungarvan, just off N25, the main Dungarvan–Youghal road (signposted), dates from the 1830s. Kathleen and Sean Kiely make guests feel right at home, as do their four charming children. They will even map out sightseeing itineraries on an ordnance survey map for your use on day trips. There's central heating, and the guest rooms are exceptionally pretty, with floral wallpaper, pastel bedspreads, and electric blankets for added comfort. Two family suites with private baths and are suitable for parents and up to three children. There's a playground, hard tennis court, and a pony for children to pet and ride. Dinner comes with farm-fresh ingredients.

Self-Catering

GOLD COAST HOLIDAY HOMES, Ballinacourty, Dungarvan, Co. Waterford. Tel. 058/42249 or 42416. Fax 058/42880. Telex 80283. 10 cottages. TV

$ Rates: IR£140–IR£385 ($245–$673.75) per week per cottage, depending on season. Oct–May, attractive midweek and weekend rates are available. Rates include all linens, with an extra charge for electricity. ACC, AE, MC, V.

Set in a semicircle right at the edge of Dungarvan Bay, 2 miles outside Dungarvan, just off R675, the Dungarvan–Tramore coast road (signposted), each attractive semidetached cottage has its own garden area, and there's an outstanding restaurant and lounge bar on the premises. The cottages are two-storied, are carpeted throughout, and have living/dining rooms with fireplaces, fully equipped kitchens, two bedrooms on the ground floor and one upstairs, and baths. Bedrooms have built-in wardrobes and dressing tables, and there's one double bed and four twins in each cottage. Six people can be accommodated comfortably, and there's plenty of room to install an extra cot in the spacious upstairs bedroom.

Worth the Extra Money

CLONEA STRAND HOTEL, Clonea Strand, Dungarvan, Co. Waterford. Tel. 058/41416 or 41277. Fax 058/42880. Telex 80283. 40 rms (all with bath). TV TEL

$ Rates (including breakfast): IR£40 ($70) single; IR£60 ($105) double. ACC, AE, MC, V.

Clonea Strand is one of County Waterford's widest beaches, as well as one of its cleanest, having earned both the EC Blue Flag symbol of a pollution-free beach and the Starfish award signifying that it has never been polluted. This hotel, which has recently completed a multi-million-pound renovation, sits right at the edge of the beach 9 miles north of Dungarvan, just off R675, the Dungarvan–Tramore coast road (well signposted), and the transformation brought about by its owners, Ann and John McGrath, moves it far up the ranks of Ireland's seafront resorts. They and their children are all involved in the day-to-day operation of the hotel, adding personal attention to its other attractions.

The three-story-high, skylighted atrium foyer features teak and soft rose-colored, velvet-covered seating, a decor repeated in the pretty, window-walled Ocean Lounge overlooking the sea. All guest rooms have magnificent sea views and are exceptionally spacious, with solid oak built-ins and one double and one single bed.

There's good sightseeing—Waterford, Tramore, Cork, Blarney, The Vee, Cahir, and Cashel are all an easy drive away. The hotel can also arrange golf, deep-sea fishing, and fox hunting.

Dining/Entertainment: The restaurant has gained an enviable reputation locally. There is a resident pianist in the Ocean Lounge in the evening, and separate facilities for disco.

Facilities: The leisure center features a 20-meter indoor swimming pool housed in a soaring, timber-lined hall made light and airy by the skylight roof, a fully equipped gymnasium, games rooms, saunas, a Jacuzzi pool, sunbed room, ten-pin bowling alley, and beauty salon, all under the direction of gymnast and nurse Claire Morrissey.

WHERE TO EAT

AN BIALANN, Grattan Sq., Dungarvan. Tel. 058/42825.
    Cuisine: TRADITIONAL/SALADS/SAVORIES/SANDWICHES.
$ Prices: Snacks, salads, savories IR£1–IR£3.60 ($1.75–$6.30). No credit cards.
    Open: Mon–Sat 9:30am–7pm (8:30pm in summer), Sun 11am–3pm.
This cozy little restaurant has an attractive traditional front and high-backed booths inside. Everything on the menu is fresh and home-cooked, and selections range from soup and sandwiches to salad plates, hot savories (try the curried chicken and savoury rice), spaghetti bolognese, pizza, quiche, and five-course complete meals. There's a children's menu, and beer, wine, and specialty coffees. Since service is continuous, this is a handy, relaxing stop any time of day.

THE COFFEE POT, Grattan Sq., Dungarvan.
    Cuisine: PASTRIES/SALADS/SNACKS.
$ Prices: IR£1–IR£3 ($1.75–$5.25). No credit cards.
    Open: Mon–Sat 9am–6pm.
The management of the Shamrock Restaurant also runs the Coffee Pot, on the Square upstairs with windows overlooking the busy scene below. Luscious homemade pastries, pâté, light salads, quiches, and freshly brewed coffee are all moderately priced.

MERRY'S RESTAURANT AND BAR, Lower Main St., Dungarvan. Tel. 058/41974 or 42818.
    Cuisine: SEAFOOD/TRADITIONAL/BAR FOOD/GAME. **Reservations:** Recommended for dinner, especially on weekends.
$ Prices: Appetizers IR£2–IR£4 ($3.50–$7); main courses IR£16–IR£8 ($10.50–$14); bar food IR£2–IR£4 ($3.50–$7). ACC, DC, MC, V.
    Open: Lunch daily 12:30–3pm; dinner daily 6–10pm. **Closed:** Good Friday, Christmas Day.
Mrs. Carmel Feeney has transformed a centuries-old wine merchant's premises into a warm, cozy bar with adjacent restaurant. There's bar food available for lunch and during the afternoon. The dinner menu of this relaxed, intimate place is extensive and innovative, including scallops cooked in Noilly Pratt, with leek, tomato, and basil; monkfish with a sweet-and-sour sauce; grilled sole on the bone; baked salmon in puff pastry and anchovy sauce; roast duckling with orange sauce; and pork steak marinated in whiskey and coriander and served in a whole-grain-mustard sauce. In season, there are also game dishes. Desserts include homemade cakes and pastries and a selection of Irish and continental cheeses.

THE MOORINGS, The Quay, Dungarvan. Tel. 058/41461.
    Cuisine: SEAFOOD/VEGETARIAN/TRADITIONAL/BAR FOOD.
$ Prices: Fixed-price dinner IR£11 ($17.50); bar food IR£1.50–IR£3 ($2.65–$5.25). No credit cards.
    Open: Mon–Sat noon–9:30pm.

Right beside King John's castle, the Moorings is a 200-year-old pub and restaurant where Nora and Pat Spratt serve home-cooked meals from fresh ingredients in both the bar and the restaurant. Seafood, as you can imagine, is featured, and vegetarians are catered to. From time to time there's traditional and folk music.

Even if you don't plan to eat here, you shouldn't miss this marvelous old-fashioned pub—stop in for a pint, if nothing else.

THE SEANACHIE RESTAURANT AND PUB, Pulla, Ring, Dungarvan, Co. Waterford. Tel. 058/46285.

Cuisine: SEAFOOD/TRADITIONAL/IRISH/BAR FOOD.

$ Prices: Appetizers IR£2–IR£3 ($3.50–$5.25); main courses IR£6–IR£8 ($10.50–$14); bar food IR£2–IR£4 ($3.50–$7). ACC, MC, V.

Open: Bar food daily 10:30am–midnight; dinner daily 7:30–11pm.

If it's tradition you're looking for as well as good food, keep a lookout for this thatched bar and restaurant a few miles outside Dungarvan just off N25, the main Dungarvan–Ardmore–Youghal road (well signposted). It began life as a public house back in 1847, at the peak of the Great Famine, and a mass grave from those pitiful times is just next to the parking lot. These—happier—days, however, there's pub food in the rustic bar (with soup and brown bread hearty enough to be a full meal), and a restaurant that features such delicacies as Helvick Head turbot, lobster, and Blackwater salmon. The Seanachie has won numerous national awards for its food and restoration of the premises. In peak season, traditional music and dancing in the courtyard on Sunday afternoons reminds us that this was once the scene of crossroads dancing, when rural Irish gathered to dance away the shadows of oppression.

THE SHAMROCK RESTAURANT, O'Connell St., Dungarvan. Tel. 058/42242.

Cuisine: TRADITIONAL.

$ Prices: Complete dinners IR£3–IR£8 ($5.25–$14); light meals IR£2–IR£3 ($3.50–$5.25); dessert and tea IR£1 ($1.75). No credit cards.

Open: Mon–Sat 9am–9pm.

The Shamrock is a cozy, attractive restaurant upstairs (past the square on the Cappoquin route) that serves all three meals at prices which can only be called "bargain." The extensive menu ranges from a T-bone steak with salad or vegetable or buttered trout with two vegetables to burgers, quiche Lorraine, and a variety of other light meals. There's a full wine license, and there's continuous service, making this a good place for an afternoon snack or one of the delicious and inexpensive desserts and tea.

ARDMORE

Set on Ardmore Bay, with a long, sandy beach, Ardmore is a very pretty little seaside village, the descendant of a 7th-century settlement founded by St. Declan. It has won Ireland's Tidy Town Award seven times, and has a fine group of ecclesiastical remains, including one of the most perfectly preserved round towers in Ireland. **St. Declan's Oratory** is a tiny early church, with a grave in one corner that tradition says is the final resting place of the good saint himself. The cathedral remains show traces of architectural designs ranging from the 10th to the 14th centuries, and its west gable is adorned on the outside with a remarkable group of round-headed panels filled with sculptured figures. The **round tower** soars 97 feet into the air, with its four stories clearly delineated by rings of projecting stones. Overlooking the sea, this cluster of ancient ruins is bound to set your imagination roaming.

WHERE TO STAY

BYRON LODGE, Ardmore, Co. Waterford. Tel. 024/94157. 6 rms (3 with bath).

$ Rates (including breakfast): IR£14 ($24.50) single without bath; IR£11.50 ($20.15) per person sharing without bath; IR£1 ($1.75) per person additional with bath. 20% reduction for children. High tea IR£6.50 ($11.40) extra; dinner, IR£10 ($17.50). No credit cards. **Closed:** Nov–Mar.

More than a century and a half old, Byron Lodge is a Georgian home with lovely views of Ardmore's beach and monastic ruins (it's signposted on Main Street in the town center). Guest rooms are exceptionally spacious, and both Geraldine Ann Casey and Mary Byran Casey are steeped in the area's history and sightseeing attractions, as well as being very active in Ardmore's Tidy Towns Committee.

MELROSE GUESTHOUSE, Ardmore, Co. Waterford. Tel. 024/94208. 6 rms (none with bath).

$ Rates (including breakfast): IR£11 ($19.25) per person. Dinner IR£8.50 ($14.90) extra. No credit cards. **Closed:** Oct–May.

This beautiful Tudor-style family home overlooking the pretty and historic little seaside village dates from the 1840s. Melrose is run by Anja and Herbert Muendler. Rooms, all with sinks, are all nicely done up, there's a comfortable lounge, and the large, secluded gardens are the setting for a garden-style café in summer months.

CAPPOQUIN

Ten miles from Dungarvan, the small town of Cappoquin sits in a sharp bend of the Blackwater River, whose waters yield up vast quantities of roach, dace, sea and brown trout, and salmon. Fishermen descend on Cappoquin in droves, year after year, to try their luck. However, even if you're not a fisherman, I'd like to tempt you to stop a while in this quiet spot and learn something of the inner workings and everyday life of an average Irish small town. This is a town I know well that I would like to share with you.

Let me suggest that you take time to meander (that's slower than stroll!) down the short Main Street, taking in some of the shopfronts that have not, as yet, been gussied up. Saunter on down to Mary Five's shop, with its wooden front adorned with a sign announcing that she has JEWELLERY, FISHING TACKLE & SOUVENIRS to sell inside. Mary is a charmer, but more than that, she carries in the small shop an amazing amount of Waterford crystal, Belleek, Royal Tara, watches, silverware—all at competitive prices. Stop in the Toby Jug for a pint and a chat with John Noonan and locals who happen to be in residence at the time.

If, by then, you've begun to feel the rhythm of this Irish town, it's time for a picnic. Still farther down Main Street, you'll come to Maurice Kellerher's Supermarket, which doesn't look a bit like the little greengrocer you'd imagine in a town like this, but resembles the ones you left at home. Pick up a bit of Irish cheese (cheddar from the West Waterford creamery, if you can get it) and fruit, and head back up Main Street and around the Allied Irish Bank corner (that's Cook Street, but nobody ever calls it that). Halfway down, you'll find Mrs. Barron's bakery, where you can pick up fresh-baked loaves of brown, soda, or white bread and mouth-watering pastries. There has been a member of the family baking here for more than 200 years, and believe me, they've learned all the secrets of the trade! Then stop by the Lonergan brothers' tailor shop (they may be the only tailors who still sit in the window on a platform to do their work) for a small jar of the honey they gather from their hives. Now take all your goodies out to Glenshelane Park, about a quarter mile outside town (signposted as GLENSHELANE RIVER WALK) on the Mount Mellary road. Known locally as "The Glen," it's a shaded spot on the banks of a tumbling stream that flows beneath a charming old stone bridge, and there's a picnic table where you can spread out your lunch. Now, if the peace of the ages doesn't descend on your head, there's no hope for you a'tall!

Award-winning poet Thomas McCarthy (look for his books *The Sorrow Garden* and *The First Convention*) was born and grew up here, although he now lives in Cork. Art still flourishes in the town, however—Cappoquin's present resident artist is **Noel O'Donoghue,** O'Donoghue Terrace, Cappoquin (tel. 058/54344 or 54317). His paintings of local scenery are beautifully done, reasonably priced, and a perfect souvenir of your visit to this part of the country. Best to call ahead to make an appointment to see the paintings.

Mount Mellary and the Nire Valley Drive

Four miles east of Cappoquin, in the foothills of the Knockmealdown Mountains, you'll find **Mount Mellary.** A monastic center for the Cistercian Order of the Strict Observance, it was built over a century ago when the monks were banished from France. There's an impressive stone church and a cluster of other large stone buildings. The monks have turned a bare mountainside into productive fields and pastures, rising at 2am to do all their own work and retiring at 8pm each evening. Until recently they observed a strict rule of silence, with only the guestmaster permitted to speak. Visitors are welcome here, and many Irish Catholics come to stay for several days in the peaceful retreat.

Then there's the **Nire Valley Drive** through the heart of the Comeragh Mountains among mountain peaks and pastures dotted with sheep and cattle. Turn off the Dungarvan–Cappoquin road onto the signposted Clonmel route (R671), which is well paved all the way. About halfway along the Nire Valley Drive you'll find **Paddy Melody's Pony Trekking Center,** Ballymacarbry, County Waterford (tel. 052/36147). Experienced rider or novice, you can explore this beautiful mountain country from horseback. Guide Ann McCarthy will see that you are seated correctly (even children are safe in her care); the horses are gentle and sure-footed; and there's a choice of paths from 5 to 12 miles, through wooded mountainsides, alongside rushing river waters and sparkling lakes. For those who absolutely refuse to sit a horse, there are jaunting cars. Several 3- and 4-day trekking holidays are available. Especially in July and August, it's advisable to phone ahead and book for these popular treks.

Paddy (or anyone at Melody's) can direct you to a mountainside shrine to Irish patriots and leaders who met in March of 1923 in what is now known as the **Knockanaffrin Republican Cottage** ("The Cottage in the Glen of the Secrets") to talk in well-guarded secrecy of plans to bring about an end to the bloody Civil War. In the simple whitewashed cottage, the ghosts of De Valera, Liam Lynch, and others rise up unbidden to remind you that it is in secluded locales such as this that so much of Irish history was forged.

From Ballymacarbry, the Nire Valley Drive continues to **Clonmel,** the South Tipperary county town (in Irish, Cluain Meala, "Meadow of Honey"), which was a garrison town on the River Suir and the home of Charles Bianconi, a poor Italian who built up the first public-transport system in Ireland with a coaching service based here. Today a thriving market town, Clonmel retains traces of the original town walls (you can't miss the impressive West Gate in the very center of the town). Just outside the West Gate, call at John and Carol Kinsella's Pub, an atmospheric spot for refreshment (sandwiches and soup as well as beverages).

Note: Cahir is only 10 miles to the west, and Cashel 15 miles northwest, and you can include either or both of these on a circular tour that will take you back to Cappoquin via The Vee and Lismore (see below).

WHERE TO STAY

HILL CREST, Powerstown Rd., Clonmel, Co. Tipperary. Tel. 052/21798. 4 rms (none with bath).

$ Rates (including breakfast): IR£10 ($17.50) per person. 33% reduction for children. No credit cards.

Mrs. O'Reilly and her husband will welcome you warmly to their comfortable modern home which is convenient to town and the bus and railway station. Located in a nice quiet area just off the Waterford road (N24), the house is centrally heated and there is a garden which guests can use. The four pretty bedrooms share a bathroom and two shower rooms; all have sinks.

RIVER VIEW HOUSE, Cook St., Cappoquin, Co. Waterford. Tel. 058/54073. 21 rms (1 with bath).

$ Rates (including breakfast): IR£10 ($17.50) per person; IR£100 ($175) per person per week with full board. Dinner IR£5 ($8.75) extra. 33% reduction for children. No credit cards. **Parking:** Enclosed car park. Recommended, as far in advance as possible.

This three-story rambling house built by the Sisters of Mercy as an orphanage in the late 19th century has blossomed as one of the most unusual lodgings in the country under the loving direction of Evelyn and John Flynn. On N72 as you enter town from Dungarvan, the house is fascinating, with multiple stairways and corridors, a private dining room in what was once the chapel, two lounges (color TV in one), and a games room with pool tables, table tennis, darts, and board games. My favorite rooms are the four on the top floor under the eaves, whose swing-out windows open up views of the town and the Blackwater River. Outside is a play area with swings, swing balls, pitch-'n-putt, croquet, and a merry-go-round. Children are very welcome here, and the Flynn family makes certain that no River View guest, young or old, is neglected. The house is centrally heated.

Evelyn is always up-to-date on what's going on—the best fishing holes (the Blackwater is one of Ireland's best fishing rivers), where entertainment may be found locally—and if you're planning a day trip, she'll gladly pack a lunch. John will see that you have bait and fishing equipment if you decide on the spur of the moment to test your skill. Evening meals are very good, and tea and homemade scones (no charge) are a regular feature in the evening.

Farmhouses

AGLISH HOUSE, Aglish, Cappoquin. Co. Waterford. Tel. 024/96191. 3 rms (2 with bath). TV
$ Rates (including breakfast): IR£13 ($22.75) per person; IR£25 ($43.75) per person for bed, breakfast, and dinner. 20% reduction for children. Dinner IR£12 ($21) extra. No credit cards.
Even the approach to Aglish House is scenic—down winding country roads lined with lush farmlands, handsome estate mansions, and wooded hills. (Take the Clashmore-Youghal exit from the roundabout on N25 in Dungarvan; Aglish House is signposted on the Clonmel–Youghal portion of this road.) From the 200-year-old farmhouse, views are of green fields and distant hills, and the large guest rooms (two will hold family groups of up to six people), with their floor-length windows, look out onto rural serenity. This is the working dairy farm of Tom and Terry Moore and their six children, and there's no warmer welcome in Ireland than you'll get from this lively, hospitable family. Lovely antique pieces are scattered among the furnishings, and Terry is happy to furnish a cot for young children. Terry is flexible about breakfast and dinner hours.

THE CASTLE, Millstreet, Cappagh. Co. Waterford. Tel. 058/68049. 5 rms (all with bath). Directions: 4 miles north of Dungarvan on the main Clonmel-Youghal road (R672), just 4 miles north of the Dungarvan-Cappoquin road (N72) and is well signposted.
$ Rates (including breakfast): IR£13 ($22.75) per person. 50% reduction for children. High tea IR£8 ($14) extra; dinner, IR£9 ($15.75). No credit cards.
Closed: Nov–Mar.
Incorporated into this attractive farmhouse are an arched stone doorway and a few stone walls of a 350-year-old Irish castle. Joan and Emmet Nugent and their four children reign in this pleasant kingdom. There's central heat and brightly furnished bedrooms, all with electric blankets. Meals are a special treat, with Joan's fresh home-baked brown bread, lamb and beef from the farm, salmon caught in local rivers, and vegetables straight from the farm fields. Guests are free to fish for trout right on the Nugents' land, and there's a pony for the young fry as well as a playground, tennis court, and a good library. No wonder at all that the Castle won the National Award of Excellence in 1989.

CLONANAV FARMHOUSE, Nire Valley, Ballymacarbry. Co. Waterford. Tel. 052/36141. 12 rms (6 with bath).
$ Rates: (including breakfast): IR£13 ($22.75) per person without bath, IR£15 ($26.25) per person with bath. 50% reduction for children. Dinner IR£10 ($17.50) extra. Package holiday rates available. No credit cards.

Eileen and Larry Ryan's deluxe farmhouse, well signposted 1½ miles from Ballymarbry on the Clonmel–Dungarvan road (T27), has one of the most peaceful, scenic settings around, with landscaped gardens and beautiful Nire Valley views. The house itself has nicely furnished, comfortable guest rooms, a cozy family room with a glowing fire, central heating, and an electric blanket on every bed. Meals are a delight in the spacious dining room, with prime Irish meats, fish, fruit, and vegetables and herbs fresh from their garden. It is, however, the Ryans themselves, and their seven children, who have won the most accolades. As one reader wrote, "Guests from England, Holland, Belgium, the U.S., and Ireland gathered around the fireplace each evening for conversation and refreshments, and Eileen was glad to help research genealogical records in the Waterford area. We loved staying here and hated to leave."

MULLINARINKA HOUSE, Clonmel, Co. Tipperary. Tel. 052/21374. 5 rms (none with bath).

$ Rates (including breakfast): IR£13 ($22.75) per person. 25% reduction for children. Dinner, IR£13 ($22.75) extra. No credit cards. **Closed:** Oct–Apr.

This lovely Georgian manor with its large, pretty gardens is the centerpiece of the Phelan family's 100-acre farm, situated at the foot of Slievenamon 4km (2½ miles) from the town center off the main Waterford road (N24), signposted from the highway (first turn opposite Showerings factory). The house is furnished with beautiful antiques and is centrally heated. The Phelans enjoy sharing their knowledge of this scenic and historic locality with their guests. Dinner is available with advance notice.

Worth the Extra Money

KNOCKLOFTY HOUSE HOTEL, Clonmel, Co. Tipperary. Tel. 052/38222. Fax 052/38289. 15 rms (all with bath).

$ Rates (including breakfast): IR£55–IR£65 ($96.25–$113.75) single; IR£45–IR£55 ($78.75–$96.25) per person sharing. 3-day and weekend rates available. ACC, MC, V.

About 4 miles from Clonmel on the scenic Ardfinnan road, Knocklofty is a beautifully situated Georgian stately home on a 105-acre estate. The estate has a long history, with strong connections to America, since it, along with vast landholdings in Counties Tipperary and Waterford, was presented to one Richard P. Hutchinson in the mid-1600s. A kinsman, Thomas Hutchinson, was the first governor of the Massachusetts Bay Colony, and Richard himself had sojourned in New England from 1633 to 1648. In 1783 his descendants became the Earls of Donoughmore, and Knocklofty House remained their family seat until the end of 1983. The beautiful galleried library dates from 1650, although the original house was considerably altered and refurbished in the mid-1700s, when a second floor was added, and somewhat later, the north and south wings.

Nowadays it is Joyce and Paddy O'Keeffe who extend the gracious hospitality that is a tradition at Knocklofty House. Widely traveled, they have brought their expertise to bear in creating luxurious bedrooms and suites. The dining room has gained renown as a first-class restaurant that draws bookings from far and near (see "Where to Eat," below).

The well-equipped recreation center transforms the estate into a virtual self-contained holiday resort. There's a gymnasium, a 50-foot indoor heated swimming pool, Jacuzzi, sunbed, tennis court, squash court, table tennis, clay pigeon trap, and equestrian center. Excellent salmon and trout fishing can be found in the River Suir that winds through the grounds, and nature woodlands invite leisurely walks. Within easy driving distance are the sightseeing attractions of Waterford city, Kilkenny, Ardmore, Cahir, and Cashel.

READERS RECOMMEND

Hanora's Cottage Guesthouse, Nire Valley, Ballymacarbry, Co. Waterford (tel. 052/36134). *"We stayed the night with Mary and Seamus Wall and had a wonderful dinner served in a charming dining room by a turf fire. Then we sat by the fire and spent the evening learning about hurling and other aspects of Irish life and sharing a bit of our heritage, both Irish and American. We will surely visit them again."* —Susan E. Hagemann, Conroe, Texas.

WHERE TO EAT

SADDLER'S TEA SHOP, The Square, Cappoquin, Co. Waterford. Tel. 058/54045.
  Cuisine: SALADS/SANDWICHES/HOT PLATES/PASTRIES.
  $ Prices: IR£1.25–IR£4 ($2.20–$7). No credit cards.
  Open: Daily 9am–6pm.
This bright, cozy place is very popular with locals, who drop in all during the day for tea and snacks. Its specialties are home-cooked meats and home-baking. Hot plates and cold salads are superb, as are the delicious scones and pastries (which are fresh from Barron's Bakery next door).

Worth the Extra Money

KNOCKLOFTY HOUSE, in the Knocklofty House Hotel, Clonmel, Co. Tipperary. Tel. 052/38222.
  Cuisine: FRENCH/TRADITIONAL. **Reservations:** Recommended.
  $ Prices: Fixed-price meal IR£12 ($21) for lunch, IR£18 ($31.50) for a five-course dinner.
  Open: Lunch daily 12:30–2:30pm; dinner daily 7–10:30pm (last orders at 9:30pm).
Superb dining may be had in Knocklofty's splendid dining room, paneled in mellow oak and overlooking lawns and gardens that slope down to the River Suir. The menu features traditional dishes that reflect a French flavor in preparation. While selections change according to availability of fresh ingredients, typical choices are noisettes of lamb provençal, loin of veal with lemon and ginger, and filet of mullet with a rosemary-butter sauce. Vegetables are always fresh and cooked to perfection, and vegetarians are catered to. There's a nice selection of wines at moderate prices. If you'd like a pre- or après-dinner drink, you'll be served in the balconied library where a pianist often entertains during the high season. Knocklofty is 4 miles from Clonmel on the scenic Ardnifanne road (signposted).

LISMORE

Lismore sits on the south bank of the Blackwater, with the majestic lines of a picture-perfect **castle** looming over town and river. King John had it built in 1185 on the site of St. Carthach's monastery of the 7th century. For centuries one of the most renowned of Ireland's distinguished learning institutions, it became the target for Viking raids, as well as Norman and English conquest, and was finally destroyed in 1173 by Raymond le Gros. It was here that Henry II came to accept homage from the Irish chieftains. There are those in Lismore who will tell you that the shades of murdered monks still roam the castle grounds in the dark of night. Sir Walter Raleigh is listed among the castle's former owners, as is Richard Boyle, the Earl of Cork. Since 1753, however, it has been the Irish seat of the dukes of Devonshire. Today it is certainly among the most impressive still-lived-in castles in the country. The people of Lismore recall with a special fondness the years that Fred Astaire's sister, Adele, lived here as Duchess of Devonshire and was well loved in the town. The public is not admitted to the castle, but from early May to early September the gardens are open daily from 1:45 to 4:45pm for a small admission charge.

Another Lismore link with history is the **Cathedral of St. Carthach.** Although it was rebuilt in 1633, there are 9th- and 11th-century grave slabs with inscriptions in Irish in the west wall of the nave. An altar tomb is dated 1557. About a mile east of the town on the "back road" to Cappoquin is the great **Lis,** or earthen ring fort, from which the town took its name—not really a sightseeing attraction, but a pretty impressive high conical mound.

For a quiet drink in an old-fashioned pub, stop in **Michael and Eileen O'Donnell's pub** on Bridge Street in Lismore. In the old tradition, there is a hardware shop on one side, a pub on the other—not too many left like that these days.

Golfers can arrange a round or two at the **Lismore Golf Club** (tel. 058/54026).

WHERE TO STAY

BEECHCROFT, Deerpark Rd., Lismore, Co. Waterford. Tel. 058/54273.
3 rms (2 with bath).
$ Rates (including breakfast): IR£10.50 ($18.40) per person without bath; IR£11.50 ($20.15) per person with bath. **Closed:** Nov–Mar.
June Powers is the hostess in this bright, modern bungalow on the edge of town. Guest rooms are nicely done up, with built-in wardrobes and comfortable furnishings. She also has a four-bedroom self-catering bungalow next door.

WHERE TO EAT

EAMMON'S PLACE, Main St., Lismore, Co. Waterford.
Cuisine: BAR FOOD.
$ Prices: IR£2–IR£4 ($3.50–$7). No credit cards.
Open: Mon–Fri noon–9pm.
This attractive little pub is a cozy place, with a corner fireplace and three-legged iron pot for turf and wood. Try Eammon Walsh's chicken-liver pâté on Joan's homemade brown bread—scrumptious! And if salmon is available, I guarantee you'll get portions so ample you'll be hard-pressed to finish the plate. There's a fixed-price meal which varies from roast beef to bacon and cabbage. You'll be missing some of the best home-cooking in Ireland if you don't stop in at least once.

A SCENIC DRIVE AROUND THE VEE

As you can see from the above, there are several scenic drives around the Cappoquin/Lismore area. One of the most breathtaking is that through a gap in the Knockmealdown Mountains known as the Vee. It's signposted from the outskirts of Lismore and climbs through mountainsides covered with heather to the V-shaped pass, with lay-bys that overlook sweeping views of Tipperary's Golden Vale, before descending to the little town of **Clogheen,** County Tipperary. Between the gap and Clogheen, keep a watch on the high side of the road for one of the most curious graves in the world, that of one **Samuel Grubb,** one-time owner of Castle Grace, who so loved his lands that he decreed he should be buried upright on the mountain slopes overlooking them. There's a small pathway leading up to the stone cairn that is his final resting place. About halfway over the Vee, you pass into South Tipperary.

CAHIR

✪ **Cahir Castle** (tel. 052/41011) stands on a rocky islet in the River Suir that has been the natural site of fortifications as far back as the 3rd century. Brian Boru maintained a residence here as High King of Ireland. The castle you see today on this ancient site was built by the Norman, de Berminghams, in the 13th century, and was held by the Anglo-Norman Butlers until 1599, when the Earl of Essex captured it after a short siege. In 1650 it was surrendered to Cromwell without a single shot, and within its walls the articles ending the long Cromwellian wars were signed in 1652. Butler descendants held the castle title until the last of them died in 1961. After years of neglect the state took over in 1964 and opened the castle to the public in 1971. Restored to near-original condition, Cahir Castle has figured in a number of films. With its residential apartments refurnished in authentic reproductions, it brings alive the life and times of all its centuries-old history.

Admission is IR£1 ($1.75) for adults, 70p ($1.25) for senior citizens, 40p (70¢) for children and students. It's open May to mid-June, daily from 10am to 6pm; mid-June to mid-Sept, daily from 10am to 7:30pm; mid-Sept to Apr, Tues–Sat varying hours. Guided tours are conducted by request during summer months, when there's a resident Tourist Office, and in winter there's an informative caretaker on hand.

Just across from the castle, the **Crock of Gold** craft and tea shop has an excellent selection of crafts and books of Irish interest, and tea comes in Royal Tara cups.

WHERE TO STAY

BANSHA HOUSE, Bansha, Tipperary, Co. Tipperary. Tel. 062/54194. 7 rms (none with bath).

$ Rates (including breakfast): IR£12 ($21) per person. 25% reduction for children. Dinner IR£10 ($17.50) extra. No credit cards. **Closed:** Dec–Feb.

Mrs. Mary Marnane is hostess of this lovely Georgian house with beautiful views of the Glen of Aherlow and the Galtee mountains 6km (3½ miles) from Tipperary town. The house is centrally heated and the food is delicious, cooked in traditional Irish style. All rooms have sinks.

CARRIGEEN CASTLE, Cork Rd., Cahir, Co. Tipperary. Tel. 052/41370. 5 rms (1 with bath).

$ Rates (including breakfast): IR£11 ($19.25) per person without bath, IR£13.50 ($23.65) per person with bath. No credit cards.

Peg and Sean Butler have turned Sean's ancestral home into a fitting representative of castle hospitality of old. The 1600 castle, on the Dublin–Cork road (N8) at the edge of town, has a colorful past, having twice been used as a prison for rebellious Irish, but since Sean's father regained possession in 1919, it has taken back its function as family home. Bedrooms have been fashioned from the original upstairs rooms—this may be the only B&B in Ireland in which you enter your bedroom through a centuries-old stone doorway. Peg is a thoughtful hostess, always ready with the extra cup of tea, as well as good advice about sightseeing in the area. Her young son, David, takes a special interest in greeting and assisting guests. There's a fire in the lounge on cool evenings. Bedrooms include three singles, one triple, and a twin-bedded and double-bedded unit with private bath.

CLONMORE, Cork–Galbally Rd., Tipperary, Co. Tipperary. Tel. 062/ 51637. 6 rms (4 with bath).

$ Rates (including breakfast): IR£15.50 ($27.15) single; IR£11.50 ($20.15) per person sharing. 20% reduction for children. No credit cards. **Closed:** Nov–Mar. **Parking:** Private parking.

Mrs. Mary Quinn's pretty bungalow sits in its own grounds, within sight of the Galtee mountains and a 5-minute walk from town. The house is centrally heated, and guest rooms are both attractive and comfortable.

WHERE TO EAT

THE GALTEE INN, The Square, Cahir, Co. Tipperary. Tel. 052/41247. **Cuisine:** TRADITIONAL/BAR FOOD.

$ Prices: Appetizers IR£2–IR£4 ($3.50–$7); main courses IR£5.95–IR£10.45 ($10.40–$18.30); bar food IR£2–IR£4 ($3.50–$7); Fixed-price lunch IR£3.75 ($6.56).

Open: Morning coffee Mon–Sat 10am–noon; bar lunches Mon–Sat 12:30–2:30pm; full à la carte menu Mon–Sat 12:30–10:30pm.

The Malone family (John, Alan, and Rosealeen) have created a bright, cheerful eatery as an adjunct for this popular pub. A skylight makes the place light and airy, and there's lots of brass and wood. In addition to full meals, morning coffee is served, and sandwiches are available all day, making this a good place to drop in for a snack, coffee, tea, Irish coffee, or a relaxing drink from the bar. Bar lunches include a full range of salad plates and hot dishes. There's also an à la carte menu available until 10:30pm, with a good selection of starters (featuring smoked salmon, homemade pâté, etc.) and main dishes that include steak in several guises, lamb cutlets, pork cutlets, chicken, and a homemade steak burger in thick mushroom sauce.

CASHEL

Soaring above the South Tipperary town of Cashel (Caiseal, or "Stone Fort") is Ireland's most majestic historical landmark, the lofty **Rock of Cashel** (tel. 062/61437). It stands 300 feet above the surrounding plains, and is an awe-inspiring presence. Its summit encompasses a full 2 acres; its view is measured in miles. Ancient Celts worshipped here, and Irish kings built palaces on the sacred site. In the 5th century the King of Munster erected a cashel, or stone fort, and it was there that St. Patrick came in the year 450 to preach to the current King of Munster, Aengus, using the humble shamrock as a symbol of the Christian trinity. Aengus (for Angus) saw the light and with his family accepted baptism. Murtough O'Brien presented the Cashel of the Kings to the church in 1101, and in 1127 Cormac MacCarthaigh (McCarthy), King of Desmond, built the little chapel that is his namesake, a miniature gem of Romanesque style. In the years that followed, construction was begun on a massive cathedral; King Henry II came to receive homage from such Irish princes as Donal O'Brien, King of Thomond; Edward the Bruce (Robert the Bruce's brother, who attempted to make himself king of all Ireland in 1315) held a Parliament here; the first Protestant service was held in the cathedral; it was burned in 1495, restored, and damaged again by Cromwell's ruthless troops; and in 1748 the archbishop of the day left it abandoned and unroofed because—or so the Irish say—his coach and four could not make it up the steep incline to its great west door.

The Rock's mystical sense of ages past and ages yet to come can only be experienced as you follow the guided tour, then leave it to wander on your own among the ancient stones and ruins, climb to the top of the cathedral tower, and gaze at the stone Cross of Cashel whose base may once have been a pre-Christian sacrificial altar.

Admission is IR£1.50 ($2.65) for adults, IR£1 ($1.75) for senior citizens, 60p ($1.05) for children and students. June to September, tours are conducted daily from 9am to 7:30pm; other months, daily from 10am to 4:30pm.

A stylized, modern **Visitors Center** opened late in 1990, right at the foot of the Rock of Cashel, and plans are for regular Irish entertainments, a tea room, and frequent exhibitions of Irish arts and crafts. Inquire locally about the current schedule during your visit.

NEARBY ATTRACTIONS   Holycross Abbey is 4 miles south of Thurles (pronounced "*Thur*-less") on the west bank of the River Suir, some 13 miles north of Cashel on R660. It was founded in 1168 and was a revered place of pilgrimage, because it held a particle of the True Cross preserved in a golden shrine set with precious stones that had been presented to King Murtagh O'Brien, grandson of Brian Boru, in 1110. The shrine is now in the Ursuline Convent in Blackrock, Cork, but the abbey still contains many interesting and religiously significant ruins, and Sunday pilgrimages still take place from May to September.

From Cashel, take R688 southeast, then turn onto R692 for a 20-minute drive to the little village of **Fethard,** where you'll find the **Fethard Folk and Transport Museum,** Cashel Road, Fethard (tel. 052/31516). It's in the Old Railway Goods Store, and holds a wonderful collection of rural antiques relating to farming, family life, and transport. Kids will love the Victorian china dolls and prams, mom will get a kick out of the 1880 sewing machine, and dad will smile at the old-time bicycles. The proprietors, Christopher and Margaret Mullins, live on the site and will open it at any time by request, but regular summer hours are Monday through Saturday from 10am to 6pm and on Sunday from 1:30 to 6pm; there's a small admission fee.

WHERE TO STAY

THORNBROOK HOUSE, Kilkenny Rd., Cashel, Co. Tipperary. Tel. 062/ 61480. 5 rms (3 with bath).
$ Rates (including breakfast): IR£16.50 ($28.90) single without bath; IR£11.50 ($20.15) per person sharing without bath; IR£2 ($3.50) per person additional with bath. 20% reduction for children. No credit cards. **Parking:** Private car park.
Closed: Christmas.
Mary and Willie Kennedy will welcome you warmly to their modern bungalow half a mile from Cashel on the Dualla–Kilkenny road. The house features antique furniture, peat fires, and a large lawn overlooking the Rock of Cashel. They'll help you plan sightseeing, golf, fishing, or horse riding.

Farmhouses

KILLORAN HOUSE, Temple Tuohy, Thurles, Co. Tipperary. Tel. 0504/ 45271. 4 rms (none with bath).
$ Rates (including breakfast): IR£11 ($19.25) per person. 20% reduction for children. High tea IR£7 ($12.25) extra; dinner, IR£10 ($17.50). No credit cards.
Off the beaten track, and truly one of Ireland's appealing nooks and crannies, Peg and Ned Cambie's large Georgian house dates from the 1600s. This is Ned's family home, and among its antique furnishings are two stately grandfather clocks crafted by his ancestors. The four large bedrooms are comfortably furnished, and have electric heaters. Log and peat fires glow in the drawing room. All meals feature farm-fresh ingredients.
   Killoran House sits in its own parklands, and just across the road is a round crenelated tower known as a "folly," which has an interesting history. Signposted on Dublin–Cork road via Kilkenny (N8), Killoran House is 5 miles from the highway turnoff, 9 miles east of Thurles and Templemore, and 3 miles east of Thurles and Templetuohy.

RAHARD LODGE, Kilkenny Rd. (N76), Cashel, Co. Tipperary. Tel. 062/ 61052. 6 rms (4 with bath).
$ Rates: IR£11.50 ($20.15) per person without bath; (including breakfast): IR£13.50 ($23.65) per person with bath. 20% reduction for children. Dinner IR£12 ($21) extra. No credit cards. **Closed:** Jan.
Mrs. Moira Foley runs this pretty, modern farmhouse overlooking the Rock of Cashel, on the outskirts of town. It's in a nice quiet area and has lovely gardens and lawns. The house is centrally heated as well as having an open fire, and electric blankets are available. Dinner can be arranged with advance notice.

READERS RECOMMEND

The Chestnuts, Dualla, Kilkenny Road (N76), Cashel, County Tipperary (tel. 062/61469). *"This modern farm bungalow is on 100 acres in a peaceful rural setting just 3 miles from the Rock of Cashel. The four guest rooms have electric blankets, and home-baking is a specialty. John and Phyllis O'Halloran gave us the warmest welcome we received in Ireland."*—Mary E. Baily, Alberta, Canada.

WHERE TO EAT

THE BISHOP'S BUTTERY, in the Cashel Palace Hotel, Main St., Cashel, Co. Tipperary. Tel. 062/61411.
Cuisine: TRADITIONAL/SALADS/SNACKS.
$ Prices: Appetizers IR£2–IR£4 ($3.50–$7); main courses IR£6–IR£10 ($10.50–$17.50); fixed-price meals IR£12 ($21) at lunch, IR£12 ($21) at dinner; snacks IR£1.50–IR£4 ($2.65–$7). ACC, AE, MC, V.
Open: Daily 10am–10pm.
Not for budgeteers is the Four Seasons Restaurant, the Cashel Palace's main dining room. This elegant, first-class hotel was erected in 1730 as a palace for the archbishop

of Cashel. The drawing room overlooks gardens and a breathtaking view of the Rock of Cashel. Down stone stairs, the flagstone cellar holds the Derby Bar and the Bishop's Buttery, where you can hoist a pint or order salad plates and hot dishes or a simple snack of homemade soup and hot scones before a gigantic stone fireplace.

CARRICK-ON-SUIR

Elsewhere in South Tipperary, visit Carrick-on-Suir, where the **Ormond Manor House** is believed to be the birthplace of Anne Boleyn, and the town is, for sure, that of the Clancy Brothers and cyclist Sean Kelly. **Tipperary Crystal,** Ballynoran, Carrick-on-Suir, County Tipperary (tel. 051/41188), is headquartered here, where skilled master craftsmen with Waterford Crystal training create the lovely pieces you'll find in their factory shop, located in a traditional thatch-roofed cottage.

CORK CITY

This grand old city that native son and actor Niall Tobin has described as "an intimate higgledy-piggledy assemblage of steps, slopes, steeples, and bridges" is, to quote one visitor, "strewn like a bouquet along the valley."

Limerick was, Dublin is, and Cork shall be
The finest city of the three.

So says "The Old Prophecy" as quoted by Dean Hole in 1859. Well, never mind about "shall be," any Corkman worth his salt will tell you that Cork is, and always has been, the finest city in Ireland! And with more than a little justification, I might add.

Suffice it to say that Cork is friendly, cosmopolitan without the pseudo-sophistication of some large cities, and fun to visit. Its great age (its charter was conferred in 1185) imbues Cork with an enormous pride. As a native once assured me with a perfectly straight face, "Sure, it's only an accident of geography that Dublin is the capital of Ireland." Not that anyone really cares if it is the capital: To be Cork is quite enough.

Its ancient Irish name is Corcaigh, or "Marshy Place." In this place of marshes, Druids once held their religious rites in the dense woods of the southern hills that rose above it. Celtic tribes built forts and fought battles over territorial rights in the hills to the north. And in the 7th century, St. Finbar came to establish a monastery on a small island in the swamp, asserting that there would be "an abundance of wisdom continually in Cork."

Attracted by the religious foundation's riches, the Vikings arrived in the 9th century to plunder, and then to settle in. Normans took over in the 12th century, fortified the city, and proceeded to build great churches and abbeys. But it was the advent of Oliver Cromwell, who captured Cork in December 1649, that settled the hash of natives in the district.

Unlike the Danes and Normans, who had assimilated happily with the resident populace, those who came after Cromwell held in contempt everything that was Irish and imposed harsh penalties on any who attempted to live with them amicably. No doubt it is from the strangling repression of this period that present-day Corkmen date their fierce sense of independence and abhorrence of injustice. Nor did being on the losing side ever lessen their fighting spirit. For a few centuries, in fact, they consistently allied themselves with defeat, standing behind the pretender to the throne Perkin Warbeck, Charles I, and James II.

That the blood has never stopped flowing hot in their veins at any hint of injustice is clear from the fact that when their Lord Mayor, Terence MacSwiney, died after a 74-day hunger strike, his comrades-in-arms locked the door of St. George's where the requiem mass was to be held, opened his coffin, clothed his body in his I.R.A. Commandant uniform, and inscribed on his coffin "Murdered by the Foreigners in

Brixton Prison, London, England, on October 25th, 1920, the Fourth Year of the Republic." Blissful in his ignorance, the archbishop conducted the mass never knowing the message of the Irish inscription.

For centuries all that history slogged through acres of marshland, right up until the end of the 1700s. Vessels sailed up Patrick Street as late as 1760 (it was paved in 1791), and in 1780 there was a canal down the center of the Grand Parade and a bridge where the Berwick Fountain now stands between Tuckey Street and Oliver Plunkett Street.

Today the citizens of Cork are reckoned to be among the ablest merchants and traders in Ireland. They are a lively, cultural bunch, much attuned to the arts, and quick to welcome strangers. Theater, traditional music, and one of Europe's best jazz festivals are highlights of each year, while street musicians carry on the tradition of ballad singers down through the ages and the old piper who once trod Winthrop Street wheezing out "An' de Vallee Lay Smilin' Afore Me."

1. ORIENTATION

ARRIVING

By Plane   There are regularly scheduled direct flights from Dublin, England, and the Continent, with connecting flights to other Irish destinations. For flight information, phone 021/313131.

By Bus/Train   There is direct bus service from Dublin and other major cities, and connecting service from virtually any point in the country, plus rail service from Dublin and Limerick. The bus station is one block down from St. Patrick's Bridge on Parnell Place, and the railway station is on Lower Glamire Road. For all bus and rail information, phone 021/504422.

By Ferry   Service to the Continent is provided by **Brittany Ferries,** 42 Grand Parade (tel. 021/277801), and **Irish Ferries,** 2-4 Merrion Row, Dublin 4 (tel. 01/610714). **Swansea Cork Ferries,** 55 Grand Parade (tel. 021/271166), has service to Great Britain.

TOURIST INFORMATION

The **Tourist Office** is centrally located at Tourist House, 42 Grand Parade (tel. 021/273251). It's open in July and August, Monday through Saturday from 9am to 7pm and on Sunday from 3 to 5pm; months, Monday through Friday from 9:30am to 5:30pm and on Saturday from 9:30am to 1pm.

CITY LAYOUT

Cork's city center is on an island in the River Lee, which can be confusing when you suddenly encounter the river you thought you'd just left behind. Some 16 bridges cross the Lee, and the city center's maze of one-way streets and narrow lanes can confound the best drivers in the world. My best advice to drivers is to get to your accommodation, park the car, and leave it there. Public transportation (via lovely double-decker buses and a good taxi service) is excellent and can take you virtually anywhere you wish to go. Besides, Cork is a great town for walking. Another bit of advice is to go by the Tourist Office and pick up one of their free city maps. It will save you a lot of grief in getting around Cork.

The **River Lee** cuts across the city from east to west, and the hills bound it on the north and south. Major points of reference are **St. Patrick's Street** (called simply

Patrick's Street) and the **Grand Parade.** Other main arteries are **Washington Street** (which becomes Western Road as it runs past University College and heads out toward Killarney); **South Mall,** from which you turn onto Anglesea Street en route to both Kinsale (and the airport) and Douglas Road; and **Glanmire Road,** leading out to Fota Park, Cobh, and the main Youghal–Waterford road, with a turnoff to the Dublin road. Just across **St. Patrick's Bridge** at the foot of Patrick Street, a hill so steep you'll swear your car is going front over back leads to the **Montenotte** section, where the cream of Cork's merchant crop built great Georgian houses on the hillside overlooking the river.

GETTING AROUND

By Bus Double-decker buses travel 14 routes crossing the city from north to south. Service is frequent, and most buses can be boarded on Patrick Street. From the Parnell Place bus station, there's local bus service to Blarney and Crosshaven. For detailed route information, call 021/503399 or 506066.

By Taxi Taxis are stationed at the rank in the center of Patrick Street as well as at bus and railway stations and the airport, or you can telephone 961311 or 502211. They're metered, with a minimum fare of IR£1.80 ($3.15).

On Foot While Cork is a large, spread-out city, it's still a delightful walking town. The trick is to take it by neighborhoods (the city center, Shandon, etc.), using city bus transportation or taxi to get you from one area to the other.

By Car As I said above, my best advice is to leave the car at your accommodation. One-way streets, sometimes quite narrow, can be a real problem. If you *must* drive, however, you should know that a disc parking system operates in the city center every day but Sunday, and you must find a news agent, shop, or office that sells the discs (they're long, printed slips of paper to be affixed to your window), which cost 20p (35¢) per hour. There are several good parking lots, and two multistory car parks, which are marked on the city map provided by the Tourist Office (where you can also pick up the useful "Parking in Cork" pamphlet).

FAST FACTS

Area Code The telephone prefix for Cork is 021.

Bookshops Both **Easons,** 113 Patrick Street (tel. 270477), and **Waterstone's,** 69 Patrick Street (tel. 276522), stock books of Irish interest, as well as a full line of current and classic fiction. Secondhand and rare books are stocked by **Lee Bookshop,** 10 Lavitt's Quay (tel. 272307).

Car Rentals The head office of **Johnson & Perrott Rent-a-Car** is on Emmet Place (tel. 273295) (see "Getting Around" in Chapter 3); **Great Island Car Rentals,** 47 MacCurtain Street (tel. 503536), is a reliable local car-rental firm; and most major car-rental companies have desks at Cork Airport.

Emergencies For police, fire, or an ambulance, dial 999.

Hospitals General medical services are offered at the **Cork Regional Hospital,** Wilton (tel. 546400), and specialized service at the **Cork Eye, Ear, and Throat Hospital,** Western Road (tel. 274162).

Libraries The Central Library is on the Grand Parade (tel. 277110).

Newspapers/Magazines Current goings-on in Cork are reported in *Where to Go in Cork,* published by the Junior Chamber of Commerce during summer months and available through the Tourist Office and most hotels. Also, check the *Cork Examiner.*

Photographic Needs With a friendly and efficient staff, **O'Leary's Camera World,** 90 Oliver Plunkett Street (tel. 273988), carries an extensive range of photographic supplies, including secondhand cameras, has a 1-day developing service, and has video equipment for sale or rental.

Police Dial 999.

Post Office The General Post Office is on Oliver Plunkett Street (tel. 272000), open Monday through Friday from 9am to 6pm.

Taxis See "Getting Around," above. Also, **A1 Cabs,** Lavitts Quay (tel. 272424), can arrange special tours.

Telegrams/Telex Both services are available at the General Post Office (see above).

2. WHERE TO STAY

Prices in Cork are often higher during holiday and special-events periods.

WESTERN ROAD AREA (INCLUDING UNIVERSITY AREA)

As its name implies, this area lies west of the city center. University College Cork is located here, and some parts of the area are also called Wilton. There's heavy truck traffic along this road, but those listed below are either on quiet side streets just off the Western Road or are set back from the street in their own grounds. This area is within walking distance of the city center (a rather long walk) and there's frequent bus service.

ANTOINE HOUSE, Western Rd., Cork, Co. Cork. Tel. 021/273494. 5 rms (all with bath). TV **Bus:** 5 or 8.
$ Rates (including breakfast): IR£14 ($24.50) per person. ACC, AE, DC, MC, V. **Parking:** Available.
This is an exceptionally nice accommodation, with well done up guest rooms, central heating, and private parking. Mrs. Joan Cross is helpful to guests in planning their time in and around Cork city.

ASHFORD HOUSE, Donovan's Rd., Cork, Co. Cork. Tel. 021/276324. 6 rms (none with bath). **Bus:** 8.
$ Rates (including breakfast): IR£9 ($15.75) per person. No credit cards. **Closed:** Dec–Feb.
Run by Mairead Smythe and her husband, Jack, this three-story house just off Western Road, across from the university, has guest rooms (all with sinks) that are spacious and comfortably furnished. The Smythes also are eager to recommend places of interest as well as restaurants and entertainment centers.

GARNISH HOUSE, 1 Aldergrove, Western Rd., Cork, Co. Cork. Tel. 021/275111. 6 rms (all with bath). TV **Bus:** 8.
$ Rates (including breakfast): IR£15 ($26.25) per person. ACC, AE, DC, MC, V. **Parking:** Private car park.
Hinse and Conor Luasa have won great praise for their beautiful Georgian home. Elegantly decorated, it's only about a 5-minute walk from the city center, and has a private parking area. Hinse has won compliments for her excellent breakfasts, and both she and Conor take a personal interest in their guests. This is a relaxing accommodation in a homey atmosphere.

KILLARNEY HOUSE, Western Rd., Cork, Co. Cork. Tel. 021/270179. 20 rms (all with bath). **Bus:** 5 or 8.
$ Rates (including breakfast): IR£18 ($31.50) single; IR£15 ($26.25) per person sharing. No credit cards. **Parking:** Available.
Mrs. Margaret O'Leary, a nurse for many years, now devotes her time and energies to the comfort of her guests. Home-cooking is a specialty, and coffee and biscuits appear every evening. She'll also furnish sandwiches upon request. The house is centrally heated, and there's a large car park.

MRS. RITA O'HERLIHY, 55 Wilton Gardens, Wilton, Cork, Co. Cork. Tel. 021/541705. 3 rms (2 with bath). **Bus:** 5 or 8.

CORK CITY ACCOMMODATIONS & DINING

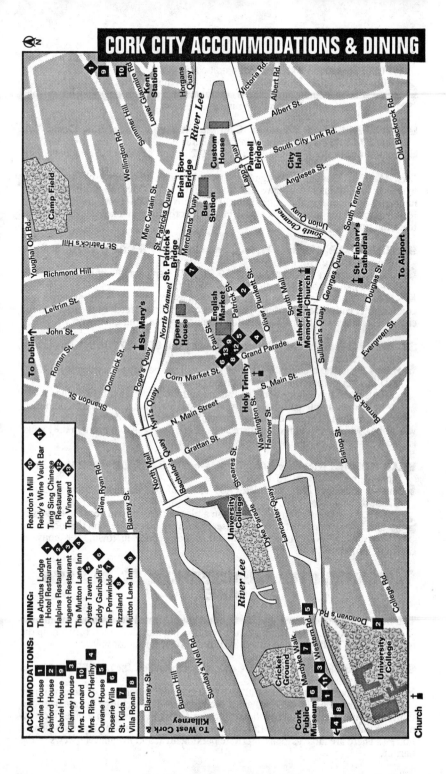

ACCOMMODATIONS:
Antoine House 1
Ashford House 2
Gabriel House 9
Killarney House 3
Mrs. Leonard 10
Mrs. Rita O'Herlihy 4
Ouvane House 5
Roserie Villa 6
St. Kilda 7
Villa Ronan 8

DINING:
The Arbutus Lodge Hotel Restaurant 1
Halpins Restaurant 2
Hugenot Restaurant 3
The Mutton Lane Inn 4
Oyster Tavern 5
Paddy Garibaldi's 6
The Periwinkle 7
Pizzaland 8
Mutton Lane Inn 9
Reardon's Mill 10
Reidy's Wine Vault Bar 11
Tung Sing Chinese Restaurant 12
The Vineyard 13

$ Rates (including breakfast): IR£11.50 ($20.15) per person without bath; IR£12.50 ($21.90) per person with bath. No credit cards.

⭐ Just off the Killarney road, near the university, this modern, two-story home has a warm, welcoming air. There is central heating, and good parking is available, as well as a garden for relaxing in nice weather.

OUVANE HOUSE, 2 Dunedin, Connaught Ave., Cork, Co. Cork. Tel. 021/271822. 6 rms (none with bath). **Bus:** 8.
$ Rates (including breakfast): IR£11 ($19.25) per person. 10% reduction for children. No credit cards.
Mrs. Maureen Vaughan makes guests very welcome, with a cuppa likely to appear whenever she thinks you have the need. The bedrooms, all with sinks, are unpretentious, comfortable, and homelike. There's central heat, and the lounge features a piano for guests' use. Ouvane House is at the top of Donovan's Road, across from the university.

ROSERIE VILLA, Mardyke Walk, Cork, Co. Cork. Tel. 021/272958. 7 rms (5 with bath). TV **Bus:** 5 or 8.
$ Rates (including breakfast): IR£11.50 ($20.15) per person without bath, IR£14 ($24.50) per person with bath. AE, DC, MC, V.
Mrs. Nora Murray is hostess here, and her guest rooms are both attractive and comfortable, with central heating. The villa is only a short stretch of the legs into the city center, and away from Western Road traffic, opposite the university.

ST. KILDA, Western Rd., Cork, Co. Cork. Tel. 021/273095. 6 rms (4 with shower). **Bus:** 5 or 8.
$ Rates (including breakfast): IR£10.50 ($18.40) per person without bath, IR£12.50 ($21.90) per person with bath. No credit cards.

⭐ This is the three-story home of Pauline and Pat Hickey. Set back behind a low wall, with ample parking out front, the old-style house has been completely refurbished. There's carpeting throughout, and the bedrooms have built-in wardrobes. Most are doubles, but there's one small, cozy single. A piano in the lounge is frequently the focal point for guests in the evening.

VILLA RONAN, Glasheen Rd., Cork, Co. Cork. Tel. 021/962459. 3 rms (none with bath). **Bus:** 10.
$ Rates (including breakfast): IR£11.50 ($10.15) per person. No credit cards.
Closed: Nov–Mar.

⭐ Mrs. M. Barrett's home is located on a pleasant, quiet road near the university and has a garden that guests can use. She is very hospitable, and the location is convenient to the university as well as bus service in town. The house is centrally heated.

MONTENOTTE (SUMMERHILL, ST. LUKE'S) AREA

The hilly section of Montenotte and Summerhill is located across from the railway station on the northeastern banks of the River Lee. For most locations, turn left up the hill at St. Luke's Church (also called St. Luke's cross, for crossroad).

GABRIEL HOUSE, Summerhill, Cork, Co. Cork. Tel. 021/500333. 22 rms (all with bath). TV TEL **Bus:** 12.
$ Rates (including breakfast): IR£16–IR£20 ($28–$35) per person, depending on season. Dinner IR£10 ($17.50) extra. No credit cards. **Parking:** Private car park.
Only a few minutes' walk from the city center, Gabriel House is in a quiet location near the railway station and St. Luke's Church. Mrs. Monica King is the hospitable hostess. There are large gardens, a private parking area, and magnificent views of the harbor.

MRS. LEONARD, 2 Ardskeagh Villas, Gardiner's Hill, St. Luke's, Co. Cork. Tel. 021/501800. 6 rms (none with bath). **Bus:** 12.
$ Rates (including breakfast): IR£11 ($19.25) per person. No credit cards. **Closed:** Oct–Mar.
Mrs. Leonard has an old-style home convenient to the railway station and within easy walking distance of the city center (although city bus lines are only half a block away). All rooms have sinks.

DOUGLAS AREA

Douglas is located southwest of the city center, a fair distance out, but with good bus service into town. It's clearly signposted from the South Ring Road as you leave the city.

FATIMA HOUSE, Grange Rd., Douglas, Cork, Co. Cork. Tel. 021/362536. 5 rms (2 with bath). **Bus:** 6 or 7.
$ Rates (including breakfast): IR£14 ($24.50) single without bath; IR£11 ($19.25) per person sharing without bath; IR£2 ($3.50) per person additional with bath. 40% reduction for children. No credit cards.
Fatima House, 4km (2½ miles) from the city center and convenient to the airport and Ringaskiddy ferry (signposted on the Airport–Kinsale road, R600), is presided over by Mrs. Elizabeth O'Shea. Mrs. O'Shea is especially fond of children and is quite willing to provide baby-sitting. Her bedrooms all are attractively furnished; there's central heating and good parking.

MISS JOAN MURPHY'S, 1 Palm Grove, Ashdale Park, S. Douglas Rd., Cork, Co. Cork. Tel. 021/362281. 3 rms (2 with bath). **Bus:** 6.
$ Rates (including breakfast): IR£12.50 ($21.90) per person. 25% reduction for children. No credit cards. **Closed:** Nov–Dec.
This attractive house is located in a quiet area off the Airport–Kinsale road (R600), with good restaurants in the immediate vicinity. Bedrooms are nicely appointed, and there's central heating and good parking.

SARTO, 2 Lislee Rd., Mayborough Estate, Rochestown Rd., Douglas, Cork, Co. Cork. Tel. 021/895579. 6 rms (4 with bath). **Bus:** 7.
$ Rates (including breakfast): IR£15.50 ($27.15) single without bath; IR£11.50 ($20.15) per person sharing without bath; IR£2.50 ($4.40) per person additional with bath. 10% reduction for children. High tea IR£10 ($17.50) extra; dinner, IR£12 ($21).
Mrs. Gretta Brien is the charming hostess here. Her guest rooms are attractive and comfortable, and the house is centrally heated. Mrs. Brien is always happy to share her knowledge of Cork and its surroundings with her guests. Sarto is 2 miles from the city center.

BLACKROCK AREA

Blackrock is a fair distance from the city center, on the southeastern side of the River Lee, and there's good bus service into the city.

BELROSE, 50 Maryville, Ballintemple, Cork, Co. Cork. Tel. 021/292219. 3 rms (none with bath). **Bus:** 2.
$ Rates (including breakfast): IR£15 ($26.25) single; IR£11 ($19.25) per person sharing. 10% reduction for children. No credit cards. **Closed:** Nov–Mar.
Mrs. O'Leary has a comfortable home in a quiet area about a mile from the city center. Two guest bathrooms serve the bedrooms, each of which has a sink, and the house is centrally heated. There's good parking, and Mrs. O'Leary will arrange baby-sitting.

SAN ANTONIO, 46 Maryville, Ballintemple, Cork, Co. Cork. Tel. 021/291849. 3 rms (none with bath). **Bus:** 2.

$ **Rates** (including breakfast): IR£15 ($26.25) single; IR£11 ($19.25) per person sharing. 10% reduction for children. No credit cards. **Closed:** Oct–May.

Mrs. Greta Murphy's home is not far from Blackrock Castle. There's a comfortable, "family" feeling about the place, and the bedrooms are attractive, all with sinks. There is also central heating and private parking.

KINSALE ROAD (AIRPORT)

You'll need a car for this area, about 5 miles out from the city center. All accommodations offer good value in rural surroundings close to the airport, a good base for exploring nearby Kinsale, as well as Cork city itself.

AU SOLEIL, Lisfehill, Cork Airport–Kinsale Rd., Ballinhassig, Co. Cork. Tel. 021/888208. 3 rms (none with bath).
$ **Rates** (including breakfast): IR£15 ($26.25) single; IR£11 ($19.25) per person sharing. 20% reduction for children. **Closed:** Oct–May.

This is a new bungalow with attractive guest bedrooms. Helen Deasy is a sister to Noreen Raftery, whose Shalom you'll find listed in the Western Region (County Mayo). Helen and husband Des will make you feel right at home. Au Soleil is 4 miles from Carrigaline, about 5 miles from Cork city via N71.

FUCHSIA, Adamstown, Ballinhassig, Co. Cork. Tel. 021/888198. 4 rms (3 with bath).
$ **Rates** (including breakfast): IR£11.50 ($20.15) per person without bath, IR£12.50 ($21.90) per person with bath. No credit cards. **Closed:** Nov–Feb.

Set in a terraced garden, Mrs. Kathleen O'Mahony's home overlooks hedgerows bordering green fields. It's 4 miles from Carrigaline, and about 5 miles from Cork city via N71. The house is centrally heated, and there are two twin- and two double-bedded rooms, all with feather comforters and sinks. The lounge, with a bay window affording splendid views, has tourist literature on this area. Both Mr. and Mrs. O'Mahony delight in recommending points of interest. Breakfast is served in a lovely conservatory, and features homemade jam and bread, as well as the delicious local sausage. The evening meal is available with advance notice.

BLARNEY

Blarney is some 4 miles northwest of Cork city and makes an ideal touring base. The Cork–Blarney road (N617) is well signposted from Cork city at the Patrick Street Bridge.

ASHLEE LODGE, Tower, Blarney, Co. Cork. Tel. 021/385346. 5 rms (4 with bath).
$ **Rates** (including breakfast): IR£12 ($21) per person without bath, IR£14 ($24.50) per person with bath. No credit cards. **Closed:** Nov–Mar. **Parking:** Private car park.
Mrs. A. Callaghan runs this outstanding guesthouse. About 4km (2½ miles) from the town center on the Blarney–Killarney road (R618), it is beautifully decorated, immaculate, and every possible convenience is thoughtfully anticipated and provided. There's private parking and lovely gardens to enjoy in fine weather.

THE GABLES, Stoneview, Blarney, Co. Cork. Tel. 021/385330. 3 rms (2 with bath).
$ **Rates** (including breakfast): IR£12 ($21) per person without bath, IR£14 ($24.50) per person with bath. 50% reduction for children. No credit cards. **Closed:** Nov–Feb.
The Lynch family will make you feel right at home at this lovely period house set in its own grounds 1½ miles from Blarney. It was once given to the parish priest by the owners of Blarney Castle. Guest rooms are attractive as well as comfortable, and home-baking is a specialty here. The Lynches will also help plan touring itineraries.

GLENVIEW HOUSE, Tower, Blarney, Co. Cork. Tel. 021/385370. 3 rms (none with bath).

$ Rates (including breakfast): IR£15 ($26.25) single; IR£11 ($19.25) per person sharing. 50% reduction for children. High tea IR£7.50 ($13.15) extra. No credit cards. **Closed:** Oct–Apr.

⭐ This two-story stone house has been charmingly renovated with due regard to retaining its original character. May and Finbarr O'Brien take a personal interest in all their guests, and Mr. O'Brien (this is his family home) is especially helpful to those tracing their Irish ancestors. Glenview is a short drive from the town center on the Blarney–Killarney road (R618).

KNOCKAWN WOOD, Curraleigh, Inniscarra, Blarney, Co. Cork. Tel. 021/870284. 4 rms (3 with bath).

$ Rates (including breakfast): IR£15 ($26.25) single supplement without bath; IR£11 ($19.25) per person sharing without bath; IR£2 ($3.50) per person additional with bath. 50% reduction for children.

Mrs. Ita O'Donovan's lovely modern home sits at the top of well-cared-for lawns, with tranquil rural views from all guest rooms. Mrs. O'Donovan's hospitality extends to providing tea and snacks, as well as an evening meal, even without advance notice. The house is centrally heated and the four attractive bedrooms all have electric blankets. Knockawn Wood is 6km (3½ miles) from Blarney, signposted on the Blarney–Killarney road (R618).

ST. ANTHONY'S, 3 Sunset Place, Killeens, Commons Rd., Blarney, Co. Cork. Tel. 021/385151. 6 rms (3 with bath).

$ Rates (including breakfast): IR£14 ($22.75) single without bath; IR£11 ($19.25) per person sharing without bath; IR£2 ($3.50) per person additional with bath. 10% reduction for children. No credit cards. **Closed:** Dec–Easter.

Mr. Pat O'Flynn is the charming host of this lovely bungalow 2 miles from Blarney and 3 miles from Cork. The house is centrally heated, and guest rooms are nicely done up. Mr. O'Flynn truly likes to make his guests feel that this is their "home away from home."

WOODVIEW HOUSE, Tweedmount, Blarney, Co. Cork. Tel. 021/385197. 8 rms (4 with bath).

$ Rates (including breakfast): IR£16 ($28) single without bath; IR£12 ($21) per person sharing without bath; IR£2 ($3.50) per person additional with bath. 20% reduction for children. Dinner IR£11 ($19.25) extra. **Closed:** Christmas.

⭐ Catherine and Billy Phelan operate this pretty guesthouse on the outskirts of Blarney on the main Cork–Blarney road (N617), and as one reader wrote, "Both are charming, intelligent, and provide the utmost of excellent company and conversation." Guest rooms are tastefully decorated, there's a bright, sunny lounge overlooking peaceful fields, and the house is centrally heated. A big bonus here is the excellent restaurant run by the Phelans in their attractive dining room (see Section 3, "Where to Eat," below), with a special reduced dinner price for residents.

FARMHOUSES

BIRCH HILL HOUSE, Grenagh, Blarney, Co. Cork Tel. 021/886106. 6 rms (none with bath).

$ Rates (including breakfast): IR£15 ($26.25) single; IR£12 ($21) per person sharing. 25% reduction for children. High tea IR£8 ($14) extra; dinner, IR£10 ($17.50). **Closed:** Dec–Mar.

Birch Hill House is a longtime favorite with readers. The lovely century-old Victorian home sits on a wooded bluff, part of a 105-acre farm half a mile off N20, 4 miles from Blarney (signposted from Blarney town center). Mrs. Dawson is the interesting hostess of this plant-filled home. Some of the guest rooms are quite large. All are nicely decorated and comfortably furnished, all with sinks. There are wood fires downstairs, electric heaters in guest rooms.

CALLAS FARM, Callas, Berrings, Blarney, Co. Cork. Tel. 021/332114. 5 rms (2 with bath).

$ Rates (including breakfast): IR£15 ($26.25) single; IR£12 ($21) per person sharing. 30% reduction for children. High tea IR£8 ($14) extra; dinner IR£10 ($17.50). **Closed:** Nov–Mar.

Bernadette and Eugene Murphy are hosts at this modern farmhouse that's signposted 2¾ miles from Blarney on the Blarney–Killarney road (R618). Its scenic setting and clean, airy, and pretty guest rooms make it a delightful retreat. The Murphys are delighted to help with sightseeing information, as well as show guests around the large dairy farm.

COBH

Some 15 miles southeast of Cork city, Cobh ("Cove") is an easy drive into town, and there's regular train service (approximately every half hour).

MISS MARY O'DRISCOLL, 1 Upper Park, Cobh, Co. Cork. Tel. 021/811506. 5 rms (none with bath). **Train:** Every half hour from Cork train station.

$ Rates (including breakfast): IR£15.50 ($27.15) single; IR£11.50 ($20.15) per person sharing. 25% reduction for children. No credit cards. **Closed:** Christmas.

This lovely Georgian home is set in a private residential park overlooking Cork Harbour. Bedrooms are nicely furnished, and the house is convenient to golf, tennis, a swimming pool, and swimming. Fota House is only 3 miles away. A good base for exploring Cork city and eastern County Cork.

CORK–YOUGHAL ROAD

Touring East Cork is a cinch from a base along N25, the main road from Cork to Youghal, with easy access to major sightseeing attractions.

CEDAR-VILLE, Carrigtwohill, Co. Cork. Tel. 021/883246. 5 rms (2 with bath).

$ Rates (including breakfast): IR£13 ($21.75) single without bath; IR£11 ($19.25) per person sharing without bath; IR£1.50 ($2.63) per person additional with bath. 50% reduction for children. High tea IR£6 ($10.50) extra; dinner, IR£10 ($17.50). No credit cards. **Closed:** Dec–Feb. **Parking:** Private car park.

Breda Hayes is the warm, bubbly hostess here, taking a keen interest in all her guests, and those lovely blooms that welcome you to the private car park out front are the handiwork of husband Dennis, a high school science teacher who must have been born with a green thumb. The house itself is spotless, and the five bedrooms are nicely decorated in soft pastels, all with sinks, as well as wide windows that look out to colorful flowers in front and back of the house. Meals here are superb, reflecting Breda's College of Catering training. Highly recommended. It's 10 miles east of Cork city, signposted on N25.

SOUTHEAST OF THE CITY

On the southern side of Cork Harbour, the coastal villages of Crosshaven and Myrtlesville—about 12 miles from Cork city, 8 miles from the airport, and 7 miles from Ringaskiddy—make idyllic sightseeing bases. Follow the signs for the ferryport of Ringaskiddy, then the signs on R613 and R612.

BUNNYCONNELAN, Myrtleville, Co. Cork. Tel. 021/831237. 12 rms (2 with bath).

$ Rates (including breakfast): IR£16 ($28) per person. Dinner IR£14 ($24.50) extra. No credit cards.

In the little village of Myrtleville, about 12 miles southwest of Cork city and 3 miles from Crosshaven (signposted on the Crosshaven road), a quite extraordinary guesthouse perches atop a high cliff overlooking the sea. Built as a holiday home for a British diplomat back in 1830, it was not given its unusual name until a

Scotsman bought it soon after World War II and christened it after his four daughters—Bunny, Connie, Nellie, and Ann. Now it's in the capable hands of Pat and Sheila O'Brien. The view is spectacular, with the Roches Point lighthouse blinking in the distance and award-winning gardens sloping down the cliffside. The ground-floor bar/lounge features stone fireplaces, a beamed ceiling, and the most eclectic collection of decorations you can imagine: bagpipes, barometers, a brass hunting horn, and tartan drapes. Outside, umbrella tables dot a flag-paved patio. On weekend nights this place is mobbed with people from Cork, often bringing their own music with them. The dining room is moderately priced and excellent (see Section 3, "Where to Eat," below). Pub grub is available in the bar during the day. Upstairs, there are a dozen simply furnished rooms, most with that smashing view. Advance reservations are absolutely essential in summer months.

WHISPERING PINES GUESTHOUSE, Crosshaven, Co. Cork. Tel. 021/ 831843 or 831448. 15 rms (all with bath). TEL

$ Rates (including breakfast): IR£17–IR£19 ($29.75–$33.25) per person, depending on season. Fishing and cycling packages available. ACC, AE, DC, MC, V.

⭐ Norma and Barry Twomey pride themselves on offering all the "traditional hospitality of a small inn" at this popular boating-resort village some 12 miles south of Cork city and 16 miles from the Blarney Stone (it's on the main road from Cork as you enter Crosshaven). The two-story ultramodern guesthouse certainly offers every convenience you can imagine, and it's just across the road from the Owenabee River and Crosshaven Harbour, with their pageantry of colorful sailboats. Guest rooms are beautifully decorated, and have built-in wardrobes and a view of the river. The dining room, with a fireplace for cool days, opens onto a patio, where breakfast is served in fine weather. In the lounge, large windows look out to the water, and a piano is on hand for guests (and Barry, when he can be prevailed upon to play). There are two deep-sea angling boats here which go out daily with anglers and return with fresh fish for the restaurant. You have a choice of 12 pubs in the village, an easy walk from Whispering Pines.

NORTHWEST OF THE CITY

The listing below is close to Cork city, yet in a scenic rural location. Take the Cork–Mallow road (N20) to the turnoff for the village.

EVERGREEN HOUSE, Rathpeacon, Co. Cork. Tel. 021/305715. 4 rms (all with bath).

$ Rates (including breakfast): IR£13 ($22.75) per person. No credit cards. **Closed:** Nov–Feb.

Noreen and Martin Curran are the very hospitable proprietors of this pleasant rural home 2 miles from Cork on the Mallow road (N20), near the Country Squire Restaurant on the right-hand side of the road. Guest rooms are nicely appointed, with bucolic views from each window, and the Currans greet guests with complimentary tea and scones. There are two excellent restaurants within walking distance, making a trip to town for a meal unnecessary.

HOSTELS

CORK INTERNATIONAL YOUTH HOSTEL, ½ Redclyffe, Western Rd., Cork, Co. Cork. Tel. 021/543289. 124 beds. **Bus:** 8.

$ Rates: IR£4.30 ($7.55) per person over 18, IR£3.50 ($6.15) per person under 18. Breakfast IR£1.50–IR£3.50 ($2.65–$6.15) extra; dinner, IR£4 ($7). No credit cards.

These hostel facilities are rated "superior," and with good reason. In addition to the excellent sleeping accommodations and showers, there's a TV room, a Bureau de Change, a hostel shop, and bicycle rental. Also, unlike many hostels, both breakfast and the evening meal are served at low rates. They also run a hostel bus to the ferryport at Ringaskiddy. Although run by An Oige, prior membership in the

International Youth Hostel Association is not required here. Advance booking during summer months is absolutely essential.

SHEILA'S CORK TOURIST HOSTEL, Belgrave Place, Wellington Rd., Cork, Co. Cork. Tel. 021/505562. 100 beds. **Bus:** 12.
$ Rates: IR£4.50 ($7.90) per person. No credit cards.

Sheila Maher has opened this fine hostel in a section of the city that is very convenient for budget travelers, two blocks from the railway station. The 100 beds are available in single, double, four-bedded, and six-bedded rooms. There are free hot showers, a large kitchen with a microwave, a sauna, TV and games room, laundrette, picnic garden, and off-street parking. There's no age limit or curfew, and you don't need prior hostel membership.

WORTH THE EXTRA MONEY

FITZPATRICK SILVER SPRINGS HOTEL, Lower Glanmire Rd. (N25), Tivoli, Cork, Co. Cork. Tel. 021/507533, 212/684-1820 in New York, or toll free 800/221-1074 in the U.S., 800/268-9051 in Canada. 110 rms and suites (all with bath). TV TEL
$ Rates: IR£55–IR£65 ($96–$113.75) single; IR£68–IR£84 ($119–$147) double—depending on season. ACC, AE, DC, MC, V.

This tall white hotel overlooks the River Lee in a beautiful setting of some 40 acres of wooded and landscaped grounds, and has long been a Cork city landmark. Since coming under the ownership of the Fitzpatrick family (see Fitzpatrick's Castle in Killiney, County Dublin, and the Shannon Shamrock, in Bunratty, Shannonside), it is fast taking its place as one of the city's leading hostelries.

Under a massive renovation program the 110 bedrooms have been decorated in cool pastels, with two double beds or one double and one twin bed in each. Most have lovely views of the Lee, the city, or the shady grounds from large picture windows. There are also elegant one- and two-bedroom suites.

Superb meals are served in the attractive River Room, and there's a more informal Waterfront Grill Room for less expensive dining. You can order afternoon tea in the spacious lobby lounge, something stronger from the lobby bar or the cozy downstairs Blarney Bar, both of which are favorite gathering places for Cork businesspeople as well as guests. After dark, repair to Fitzies downstairs nightclub.

In the leisure complex, there's an Olympic-size heated pool, sauna, steam room, Jacuzzi, sunbeds, snooker, two tennis courts, a squash court, and a gymnasium. There's a nine-hole golf course right on the grounds.

The Silver Springs is an ideal touring base, since the attractions of Cork city are just minutes away, and Fota House only a short drive, as are Blarney, Kinsale, and other County Cork sightseeing highlights.

READERS RECOMMEND

White Lodge, Airport Cross, Kinsale Road, Cork, County Cork (tel. 021/961267). "Mrs. Phyllis McIntosh and the White Lodge proved to be one of our most pleasant visits in Ireland. She's a genial hostess, and the accommodations were very comfortable, very clean, and very reasonable."—Mary Price, Houston Texas.

Victoria Lodge, Victoria Cross, Cork, County Cork (tel. 021/542233; fax 021/542572). "We were lucky to find this marvelous B&B in a former monastery. Set in its own grounds on the outskirts of Cork city, it has been renovated with 22 executive-style bedrooms, each with its own bath, orthopedic beds, telephone, TV, and tea maker. It's a lovely, unique atmosphere. There's good parking in the grounds. We could walk to the nearby Crow's Nest Pub, a good place for a pint or a light meal, which they serve all day."—J. O'Reardon, Long Island City, N.Y.

Christy's Hotel and Restaurant, Blarney, County Cork (tel. 021/385011; Telex 75589). "We stopped off to do some shopping at the Blarney Woollen Mills and decided to have a meal at Christy's, which is just next door. We fell in love with the hotel and booked in for several days of touring. Our rooms were really spacious, with a nice decor and private bath. Best of all, it was much less expensive than we expected for a hotel of these standards, and we took advantage of their special weekend rate, which includes breakfast and one dinner over a 2-day period."—C. Murray, White Plains, N.Y.

3. WHERE TO EAT

BEECHER'S INN, Faulkners Lane, Cork. Tel. 021/273144.
Cuisine: SEAFOOD/PUB GRUB.
$ Prices: Pub grub IR£1.50–IR£3 ($2.65–$5.25); hot and cold plates IR£2–IR£4 ($3.50–$7). No credit cards.
Open: Lunch only, Mon–Sat 12:30–2:30pm.

Pat O'Donovan is the genial proprieter, Ita Magee the manager, of Beecher's, which wears the soft patina of time. Cork regulars gather at lunchtime for hot plates and cold salads. Seafood is a specialty, and a lunch of smoked salmon and brown bread washed down with a rich, dark pint is memorable. Coffee and scones are served all day. It's tucked away on a narrow old lane (enter from Emmet Place or Patrick Street).

HALPINS RESTAURANT, 14/15 Cook St., Cork. Tel. 021/277853.
Cuisine: TRADITIONAL/VEGETARIAN.
$ Prices: Appetizers IR£1.50–IR£3.50 ($2.65–$6.15); main courses IR£5–IR£12 ($8.75–$21); breakfast IR£3 ($5.25); Tourist Menu IR£5.75–IR£7.90 ($10.05–$13.85). ACC, MC, V.
Open: Daily 9am–midnight.

David Halpin has used traditional materials of wood, slate, and stone to reconstruct this 300-year-old wax works into a very good eatery, with an extensive menu and moderate prices. There are, for example, some 36 main courses, which range from chicken Kiev to 10 kinds of steak, with a wide variety in between. They also serve burgers and other light selections—a very good, inexpensive meal can be put together from their appetizer list alone. It's also a good place for breakfast if that meal doesn't come with your room. This is a great favorite with locals, who find it good value. It's on a small street between Patrick Street and South Mall.

HUGUENOT RESTAURANT, Frenchchurch St., Cork. Tel. 021/273357.
Cuisine: FRENCH/SEAFOOD/SPECIAL DIETS.
$ Prices: Appetizers IR£3–IR£5 ($5.25–$8.75); main courses IR£11–IR£14 ($19.25–$24.50); light lunch IR£3–IR£5 ($5.25–$8.75). ACC, AE, DC, V.
Open: Lunch Mon–Sat 12:30–2:30pm; dinner Mon–Sat 6:30–10:30pm.
Closed: Bank hols, Christmas.

This charming little restaurant is fitted out in period style, with antique furniture (the bar is actually made from an old ornate, horse-drawn hearse), and its name honors Protestant refugees from France who came to Cork in the 17th and 18th centuries. At lunch, there are pleasant sidewalk tables in fine weather, with menu specials like quiche, lasagne, salads, and a daily chef's special. Dinner menus are likely to feature such mouth-watering selections as pheasant, lamb with wild mushroom duxelle baked in puff pastry with madeira-rosemary sauce, or suprême of chicken with asparagus and smoked-salmon sauce. Vegetarians and those with special diets are catered to with advance notice, and they are careful that none of their sauces or stocks contains flour. Wheelchair accessible.

LA PIZZA, 35 Patrick St., Cork. Tel. 021/277957.
Cuisine: PIZZA/PASTA/VEGETARIAN.
$ Prices: Pizza IR£3.95 ($6.90); three-course dinner IR£7.50 ($13.15); Tourist Menu IR£5.75–IR£7.90 ($10.05–$13.85). ACC, AE, DC, MC, V. **Open:** Mon–Sat 9:30am–11:30pm.

⭐ ⓢ As a rule, you won't find restaurant chains listed in my recommendations, to say nothing of those of the fast-food genre. In this case, however, La Pizza has proved over several years to be one of my favorite stopping places, be it for a late breakfast (which is served all day), a selection from the salad bar (which is one of the few not to suffer from that tired, wilted look), one of their excellent pizzas, or a full meal that won't break the bank. There's a wide variety of pizza toppings, and the price shown above includes a traditional pizza plus two extra toppings. There is also a delicious deep-pan pizza and lasagne and canneloni are among the pasta choices. Wine is available by the glass. Good value, and some of the most pleasant service in town.

MUTTON LANE INN, Mutton Lane, Cork. Tel. 021/273471.
Cuisine: PUB GRUB/IRISH.
$ **Prices:** IR£2–IR£6 ($3.50–$10.50). No credit cards.
Open: Lunch only, Mon–Sat 12:30–2:30pm.

This charming old pub (see Section 8, "Evening Entertainment," below, for a full description) has earned an enviable local name for its good food. Choose a snack, salad plate, one of their traditional Irish dishes, or full hot meal, and leave room for dessert. Everything is homemade, and portions are large. It's down one of the quaint little laneways leading off Patrick Street to the English Market.

OYSTER TAVERN, Market Lane, 56 St. Patrick's St., Cork. Tel. 021/272716.
Cuisine: STEAK/SEAFOOD/TRADITIONAL/VEGETARIAN.
$ **Prices:** Appetizers IR£1.50–IR£3 ($2.65–$5.25); main courses IR£5–IR£10 ($8.75–$10.75). ACC, AE, MC, V.
Open: Lunch Mon–Sat 12:30–2:30pm; dinner Mon–Sat 7–11pm.

⭐ This is one of my all-time favorite Cork eateries. An old-world sort of place, lots of wood, etched glass, old prints, and mirrors reflect the centuries since its coachhouse days in 1792. The bar section is worth stopping by even if you don't eat. It's a bit complicated to find, but well worth the effort (there's a sign on the sidewalk on Patrick Street, which points you to Market Lane, one of Cork's last remaining cobbled laneways, leading into the block-long, covered city market), and if you go for lunch, take time to visit the city market (sometimes called the English Market) just down the lane. The à la carte lunch menu features the steaks and fish for which this place is famous. Portions are so generous that this could be your main meal. It's a good idea to reserve ahead.

PADDY GARIBALDI'S, Carey's Lane, Cork. Tel. 021/277915.
Cuisine: PIZZA/TRADITIONAL.
$ **Prices:** Pizza IR£3.50–IR£6 ($6.30–$10.50); grills IR£5–IR£6 ($8.75–$10.50); pasta IR£6 ($10.50). ACC, AE, V.
Open: Mon–Sat 10am–midnight, Sun 5pm–midnight.

ⓢ This light, airy eatery has upstairs and downstairs dining rooms, and one of the friendliest staffs around. Pizzas are large (7 in.) and come with either french fries or a green salad; burgers are charcoal-grilled and served on toasted sesame-seed buns, with an accompanying salad, coleslaw, and french fries. Assorted salad platters are also available, and the garlic bread, Peggy Garibaldi's homemade apple pie, and Nora Garibaldi's homemade cheesecake are outstanding. The restaurant is on the pedestrian lane connecting Paul St. Shopping Centre with Patrick Street.

Much the same menu (with the addition of steaks and one or two seafood specialties) appears at Garibaldi's sister restaurant, **Chew-Chews** on Phoenix Street (tel. 272708), open Monday through Saturday from 11am to 11pm, on Sunday from 5 to 11pm.

REARDON'S MILL, 25 Washington St., Cork. Tel. 021/271969.
  Cuisine: CARVERY/PUB GRUB.
$ Prices: IR£1–IR£4 ($1.75–$7). No credit cards.
  Open: Mon–Sat 10:30am–3pm.

 Situated in the premises of an 1800s wine merchant's shop and warehouse, this rather rustic, traditional-style pub has a blackboard menu that extends from a full carvery (two or three roasts) to dishes such as lasagne to sandwiches to the salad bar.

REIDY'S WINE VAULT BAR, Western Rd., Cork. Tel. 021/275751.
  Cuisine: PUB GRUB/IRISH.
$ Prices: IR£1.50–IR£5 ($2.65–$8.75). ACC, AE, DC, MC, V.
  Open: Lunch only, Mon–Sat 12:30–2:30pm.

 Owner Dan Reidy has converted the early-1800s Reardon's Wine Warehouse, opposite Jury's Hotel, into a lovely traditional-style pub with smart touches of brass and etched glass. The conversion was done so expertly, and with such concern for authenticity, that the Reidy family won an award for their preservation of the building's frontage. The antique Victorian bar is backed by mahogany beveled mirrors. Along with the salads, sandwiches, and hot plates usually found on pub menus, Reidy's features Irish stew and smoked Irish wild salmon.

TUNG SING CHINESE RESTAURANT, 23A Patrick St., Cork. Tel. 021/274616 or 273793.
  Cuisine: CHINESE/VEGETARIAN.
$ Prices: Appetizers IR£1.50–IR£2 ($2.65–$3.50); main courses IR£4–IR£8 ($7–$14); Tourist Menu IR£5.75–IR£7.90 ($10.05–$13.85). ACC, AE, MC, V.
  Open: Mon–Sat 12:30pm–12:30am, Sun 1pm–midnight.
Excellent and inexpensive meals are offered here. Wine is also available in this nice upstairs room overlooking Patrick Street.

THE VINEYARD, Market Lane, Cork. Tel. 021/274793.
  Cuisine: PUB GRUB.
$ Prices: IR£2–IR£4 ($3.50–$7). No credit cards.
  Open: Lunch only, Mon–Sat 12:30–2:30pm.
For the full atmosphere of this great old pub, see Section 8, "Evening Entertainment," below. As for the food, they serve everything from soup and sandwiches to cold salad plates to hot dishes. It's on a tiny lane off Patrick Street leading to the English Market.

SPECIALTY DINING

SELF-SERVICE CAFETERIAS

THE PERIWINKLE, Queen's Oldcastle Shopping Centre, Cork. Tel. 021/271199.
  Cuisine: SEAFOOD/VEGETARIAN.
$ Prices: Appetizers IR£1–IR£1.50 ($1.75–$2.65); main courses IR£3–IR£8 ($5.25–$14). No credit cards.
  Open: 9:30am–5:30pm.

The specialty here is seafood, some of the freshest and best prepared you'll find in Cork. There's a good seafood salad, and I especially like the seafood chowder. The tuna fish pâté salad and seafood stuffed pancake are also very popular. There are always one or two nonseafood selections as well. It's self-service, and downstairs you eat at the blond-wood counters; upstairs, at tables overlooking the busy arcade. It's in the city center, at the top of Patrick Street.

PICNIC FARE & WHERE TO EAT IT

If you fancy a picnic on a nice sunny day, there are any number of take-away and fish-and-chips shops along **North Main Street,** and stalls in the **English Market** sell sausage rolls, boiled eggs, and other picnic makings.

With your picnic fare in hand, head for **Bishop Lucey Park** (that's the city park between Grand Parade and South Main Street) or **Fitzgeralds Park** off the Mardyke. Then relax and enjoy!

WORTH THE EXTRA MONEY

ARBUTUS LODGE HOTEL RESTAURANT, Montenotte, Cork. Tel. 021/ 501237.
   Cuisine: SEAFOOD/TRADITIONAL/IRISH/FRENCH.
$ Prices: Appetizers IR£3–IR£6 ($5.25–$10.50); main courses IR£8–IR£18 ($14–$26.25). ACC, AE, DC, MC, V.
   Open: Lunch daily 1–2pm; dinner daily 7–9:30pm.

This gourmet restaurant, over on the Montenotte section's lofty heights (on the eastern edge of town, uphill from the railway station, near St. Luke's Church), is known all over Ireland and the Continent for its legendary cuisine and exquisite service. The hotel was once an elegant Victorian town house, and the decor is that of subdued (not stuffy) formality. Large windows overlook the city below. Seafood, meats, and vegetables are the freshest—if your main course includes mushrooms, you may be sure they've been hand-gathered from the woods, not emptied from a can. If the restaurant prices are a bit steep for your budget, the Gallery Bar at the Arbutus serves smoked salmon and delicious soups for prices that average about IR£10 ($17.50). Best to reserve (a few days ahead for dinner) at both the Restaurant and Gallery Bar.

BUNNYCONNELAN, Myrtleville, Co. Cork. Tel. 021/831237.
   Cuisine: SEAFOOD/TRADITIONAL. **Reservations:** Essential.
$ Prices: Fixed-price dinner IR£14 ($24.50). No credit cards.
   Open: Summer, Wed–Sat 7:30–10pm, Sun 12:30–2pm; other months, Fri–Sat 7:30–10pm, Sun 12:30–2pm.

Bunnyconnelan, out in Myrtleville 12 miles from Cork city, 3 miles from Crosshaven (signposted on the Crosshaven road), (see Section 2, "Where to Stay," above), serves fresh seafood, expertly prepared, at moderate prices in a window-walled dining room overlooking the gardens and the sea. Steaks, lamb, chicken, and pork are also on the menu, and there's a good wine list. So good is the food here, that Cork city residents regularly book weeks ahead for Sheila O'Brien's home-style cooking.

WOODVIEW HOUSE, Tweedmount, Blarney, Co. Cork. Tel. 021/385197.
   Cuisine: FRENCH/SEAFOOD/TRADITIONAL. **Reservations:** Recommended.
$ Prices: Fixed-price dinner IR£17 ($29.75) for nonresidents, IR£11 ($19.25) for residents. ACC, MC, V.
   Open: Dinner only, Tues–Sat 7:30–9:30pm. **Closed:** Christmas week.

Billy and Catherine Phelan have won high praise from Cork's food critics for their restaurant in this pretty guesthouse on the outskirts of Blarney half a mile from the town center on the main Cork–Blarney road (N617) (see Section 2, "Where to Stay," above), and the consensus is that the short drive out to Blarney is well taken in order to enjoy one of chef Billy's specialties. Swiss trained, and daytime chef for a prestigious banking group in Cork city, Billy turns out such delicacies as medallions of pork Normandy, Irish salmon in chive sauce, baked plaice with stuffed crab, an excellent rack of lamb, and a "symphony of seafood" combination of shellfish and fish in a butter, wine, and cream sauce.

READERS RECOMMEND

Flemings Silver Grange House, *Tivoli, Cork, County Cork (tel. 021/821621 or 821178).* "There are several features we found most appealing about Flemings. First among them are the proprietors, Michael and Eileen Fleming. Michael was trained at the Ritz in London and he specializes in French classical cuisine complemented by upscale versions of the traditional County Cork fare. During dinner, he visits your table to ensure that the meal measures up to your expectations. What makes Flemings so special is the careful personal attention with which they cater to your needs, and that carries over to their comfortably furnished guest room en suite on the second floor. We felt right at home with them . . . Irish country house hospitality at its best."—John Pattan, Macon Ga.

Clifford's Restaurant, *18 Dyke Parade (Mardyke), Cork, County Cork (tel. 021/275333).* "We were lucky to be referred to this elegant gourmet restaurant by Cork friends. Michael Clifford was chef at Dublin's White's on the Green, and his expertise certainly shown through in our dinner. Everything was fresh, and we especially liked the chicken-and-mushroom roulade. Prices were surprisingly moderate for this quality."—Dave Malone, Kansas City, Kans.

4. WHAT TO SEE & DO

ATTRACTIONS IN TOWN

THE COAL QUAY & NEARBY ART GALLERIES I can't really say that the **Coal Quay** (pronounced "kay" in this instance) qualifies as a sightseeing attraction, but I do know that it's a place unique to Cork and one I drop by on every visit. You won't find it listed anywhere under that name—the signs say Corn Market Street—but no one in town will know what you're asking for unless you say "Coal Kay." It's located in the heart of the city, to the right (opposite the Grand Parade which curves off to the left) at the end of Patrick Street, and it's as grand a collection of hardy Irish country-women as you're likely to run across. From stalls, tables, carts, or cardboard boxes on the sidewalk, these shrewd, witty ladies hawk secondhand clothes, fresh vegetables, old shoes, old pieces of china, and anything else they happen to have handy and can exchange for a "lop" or two ("lop" being, of course, a coin). I won't guarantee that you'll catch every nuance of conversation carried on in a language that's peculiar to this bunch, but I will guarantee that you'll catch a glimpse of genuine Irish folk life.

Not far from the Coal Quay, the red-brick ✪ **Crawford Art Gallery,** on Emmet Place (tel. 274415), was built as the Custom House back in 1724 when ships unloaded at what is now the sidewalk on the King's Dock. There's something almost homey about the big, rambling halls and exhibition rooms, and I've never been inside without encountering at least one art student diligently studying the masters. There are paintings and sculptures by modern Irish artists and an interesting collection of classical casts from the Vatican Galleries presented to Cork in 1818. There's also an excellent restaurant, run by the prestigious Ballymaloe House, with moderately priced snacks and lunches daily from 10am to 5pm, and pretheater dinners from 6:30pm on Wednesday, Thursday, and Friday evenings.

On nearby Lavitt's Quay, the Cork Arts Society operates the **Lavitt's Quay Gallery,** with continual exhibitions of fine art, paintings, sculpture, ceramics, and batiks Tuesday through Saturday (closed for lunch from 2 to 3pm).

CHURCHES & CITY HALL On Church Street, just off Shandon Street, ✪ **St. Ann's Church** (usually referred to simply as Shandon) is perhaps the most beloved of the city's many churches. Shandon takes its name from the Irish *sean dun,* meaning "old fort." The Protestant church is distinguished architecturally only by its red-and-white "pepper pot" steeple which houses the bells. Its 170-foot height is crowned by an 11-foot 3-inch weathervane in the shape of a salmon (the symbol of

IMPRESSIONS

*Wher'er I wander,
And thus grow fonder,
Sweet Cork, of thee;
With the bells of Shandon
That sound so grand on
The pleasant waters
Of the river Lee.*
—FRANCIS SYLVSTER MAHONY (FATHER PROUT), "The Bells of Shandon," c. 1830s

---

wisdom), and the clocks set in its four sides are known affectionately as the "four-faced liar," since no two of them ever show the same time. Climb the steeple's winding stairs to see the famous bells, and for a small charge you can follow numbers on the bell strings that will send "The Bells of St. Mary's" pealing out over the city. Father Prout, incidentally, lies below in the small churchyard.

There are other interesting headstones in the churchyard cemetery, as well as a mass grave from famine times, and the narrow, winding surrounding streets hold some of Cork's oldest inhabited dwellings, most of which have seen decidedly better days. Also nearby is the old Butter Exchange, which flourished as a major source of salted butter for Britain, Europe, and the West Indies from 1770 until 1924. Today, it flourishes as the home of the **Shandon Craft Center** (free admission), where you can visit craft workshops and enjoy a sit-down and refreshments at the coffee shop.

Across the River Lee from Shandon, Cork's birthplace is three blocks past the South Main Street Bridge, where ✪ **St. Finn Barre's Cathedral,** on Bishop's Street, marks the spot on which the venerable saint founded his monastery in 650. As it grew in stature as a seat of learning, it became a mark of honor among Gaelic chieftains and Norman knights to be buried in its grounds. At the time of the Reformation, St. Finn Barre's became the seat of the bishopric of the Church of Ireland, as it is today. The French Gothic structure you see today was opened in 1870, and its great West Window is of particular note.

Across the west arm of the River Lee, the magnificent **City Hall** on Albert Quay opened in 1936 to replace the one burned in 1920 during the War of Independence. This is where President Kennedy came to address an admiring throng during his visit in the 1960s, and it is the setting for special events during some of Cork's festivals (see below).

MONUMENTS The impressive **statue** you see at the junction of Grand Parade and South Mall commemorates Irish rebels in the 1798 and 1867 risings. Depicted are the Main of Erin, surrounded by patriots Thomas Davis, Michael O'Dwyer, O'Neill-Crowley, and Wolfe Tone, who represent the four provinces of Ireland. Alongside the river, there's a **War Memorial** to Irishmen who lost their lives in the two world wars, and the uncarved granite stone nearby is the **Hiroshima Memorial.**

At the foot of Patrick Bridge, right in the center of Patrick Street, the **Father Matthew statue** depicts the much-loved Corkman who lived from 1790 to 1861, who became known as the "apostle of temperance" because of his lifelong war against Irish alcoholism.

PARKS The **Bishop Lucey Park,** across Grand Parade from the City Market, is named after a beloved bishop of Cork, and is also known as ✪ **City Park.** The archway at its entrance came from the 1850 Cornmarket. During excavation of the site, a section of the medieval city walls was unearthed and preserved in the park. Remains of medieval timber houses were also found. That sculptured fountain and its eight bronze swans represent the 800th anniversary of Cork's first charter, granted in 1185.

Running parallel to the Western Road is **The Mardyke,** a mile-long, tree-shaded walk named after an Amsterdam walk called the "Meer Dyke" and bordered by **Fitzgerald Park,** where you'll find lovely landscaping, interesting sculptures, and a small museum.

TWO CORKMEN OF NOTE One last Cork sight that is sure to bring a smile to your lips is located in front of the Cork County Council offices on the "Straight Road" (just ask anybody where it is), otherwise known as Carrigohane Road. Right in front of what is fondly called "the tallest building in Ireland" (it beats the height of Liberty Hall in Dublin by all of 6 inches!), stand two figures who could only be ✪ **Corkmen.** Heads upraised, hands in pockets, they gaze quizzically at this upstart of a building, trying to make sense of it. Ironically, these two, the work of the late Oisin Kelly, began life in Dublin, Cork's archrival. It was only when that city treated them shabbily (they were found lying in a Dublin scrap yard and rescued by the County Council) that they came "home" to the city by the Lee. The people of Cork have affectionately dubbed them "Chah and Mial" after two beloved radio and television characters from the city, and any mention of the sculpture brings a smile to the lips of the locals. If you're driving by, slow down for a tip of the hat to these two embodiments of the Cork spirit. Stop to snap a photo, surely one of your most unusual souvenirs of this spirited city.

ATTRACTIONS NEARBY

Blarney, 4 miles northwest of Cork city, has long been a favorite destination of American visitors, and to the southeast, Fota House, its Arboretum, and its Wildlife Park, are fast gaining like flavor. Either of these locations makes a good base if you prefer a quiet, rural setting that is close enough to explore the city without a city base (see Section 2, "Where to Stay," above).

IN BLARNEY

Although the Cork–Blarney road (N617) is at the moment a narrow, twisting country road, much roadwork is being done at present, so things should be better when you arrive. It's well signposted from Cork city at Patrick Street Bridge, and there's regular bus service to Blarney from Cork, departing the bus station on Parnell Place.

BLARNEY CASTLE, Blarney, Co. Cork. Tel. 021/385252.
✪ Now, about that magical stone. Back in the 1830s, Father Prout wrote of Blarney Castle: "There is a stone there/That whoever kisses/Oh! he never misses/To grow eloquent." All that blather about the stone started, it is said, when the first Queen Elizabeth tried to elicit the fealty of one Cormac MacCarthy, an Irish chieftain who was then Lord of Blarney. The silver-tongued MacCarthy smiled and flattered and nodded his head, all the while keeping firm hold on his own sovereignty until the Queen, in exasperation, is reputed to have exclaimed, "This is nothing but Blarney—what he says, he never means!" Which may be the first recorded instance of that lovely Irish talent for concealing a wily mind behind inoffensive words.
    Be that as it may, if you'd like to acquire a bit of Irish eloquence, be warned that kissing the stone involves climbing 120 steep steps, having a guard hold your feet as you lie on your back on the battlements, and bending far back until you can reach the magic rock—and by the time you've gone through all those contortions, you'll have *earned* a silver tongue! Magic aside, however, the old castle ruin is well worth the trip in its own right, and there's a lovely sense of tranquility about the grounds filled with ancient trees.
    Admission: IR£2.50 ($4.40) adults, IR£1.25 ($2.20) children.
    Open: May, Mon–Sat 9am–7pm; June–July Mon–Sat 9am–8:30pm; Aug, Mon–Sat 9am–7:30pm; Sept, Mon–Sat 9–6:30pm, Sun 9:30pm–sundown. **Closed:** Christmas Eve, Christmas Day. **Bus:** 154 from the bus station on Parnell Place.

BLARNEY CASTLE HOUSE, Blarney, Co. Cork. Tel. 021/385252.
    Some 200 yards from Blarney Castle, Blarney Castle House is a magnificent turreted Scottish baronial building, with fine gardens designed in the 18th century. Within those gardens, you'll find the Rock Close, a spot legend says was much favored by Druids long before the advent of garden designers. As for the house, it has been beautifully restored and refurbished.
    Admission: House, IR£2 ($3.50) adults, IR£1 ($1.75) children; gardens, free.

Open: House, June to mid-Sept, Mon–Sat, noon–5:30pm. Gardens, year round, daily, noon–5:30pm (sundown in winter).

BLARNEY WOOLLEN MILLS, Blarney, Co. Cork. Tel. 021/385280.

Dedicated shoppers may want to make the trek out from Cork for no other reason than to visit the Blarney Woollen Mills, but it also qualifies as a sort of Irish crafts sightseeing attraction. One of Ireland's oldest mills, it has been producing fine wools and cloths since 1741, and the present building dates back to 1824. There's a marvelous traditional pub inside, and a moderately priced self-service restaurant adjacent to the main building, making it an ideal place for a bit of browsing and a bit of refreshment. Shoppers, however, will find it hard to draw themselves away from the extensive stocks of lovely Blarney Castle knitwear, superb selection of Aran hand-knit sweaters, and literally hundreds of high-quality Irish gift items. There's a Bureau de Change and shipping service.

Admission: Free.
Open: Summer, daily 9am–10pm; winter, daily 9am–5:30pm.

FOTA ISLAND

Six miles east of Cork city on the main Cork–Cobh road, Fota Island is a 790-acre estate that was once the property of the Earls of Barrymore.

FOTA ISLAND HOUSE, ARBORETUM, AND WILDLIFE PARK, Fota Island, Carrogtwohill, Co. Cork. Tel. 021/812555.

This splendid Regency-style manor house was built in the 1820s, and its elegant rooms, with their exquisite woodwork and molded ceilings, hold an impressive collection of 18th- and 19th-century furnishings. Don't miss the outstanding Irish landscape paintings, said to be the most extensive collection in existence. Nor should you miss the magnificent gardens and world-renowned arboretum, begun back in the 1820s. A 70-acre wildlife park is set among woods and lagoons, a fitting setting for the zebras, cheetahs, kangaroos, etc., that now call this home. Teas are available in Fota House, and there's a coffee shop in the Wildlife Park.

Admission: House, IR£2 ($3.50) adults, IR£1 ($1.75) senior citizens, 50p (88¢) children; Wildlife Park, IR£2.10 ($3.70) adults, IR£1.60 ($2.80) students, IR£1 ($1.75) children, senior citizens, and disabled persons, free for children under 3. No dogs are allowed inside the park.
Open: House, Apr–Oct, Mon–Sat 11am–6pm, Sun 2–6pm; other months, Sun and public hols 2–6pm. Wildlife Park, Apr–Oct, Mon–Sat 10am–5:15pm, Sun 11am–5:15pm. **Train:** The Cork–Cobh train stops at the estate; call 021/503399 for times and fares.

TOURS

CITY WALKING TOURS One of Cork's chief charms is that it is so much a walking city, which is, of course, the best possible way to get around any city if you are to capture its true flavor and mingle with the people who give it life. My first recommendation is to go by the Tourist Office and pick up their ✪ *Tourist Trail* guide to a signposted walking tour of Cork. It details a comprehensive route (in two 1¼-hour parts) around the significant landmarks and tells you about each one. One route focuses on the city center (built up from 1750 on), the other on the old medieval city from south to north. It makes for a lovely day's ramble, with a stop whenever your fancy dictates for a jar, lunch, or whatever.

ORGANIZED TOURS From time to time there are also free evening **guided walking tours** departing from the Tourist Office 2 or 3 days a week during July and August. Inquire when you're there to see if they're on.

For more personalized guided tours, contact Valerie Fleury, **Discover Cork,** Belmount, Douglas Road, Cork, County Cork (tel. 021/293873; fax 021/508568).

CORK CITY ATTRACTIONS

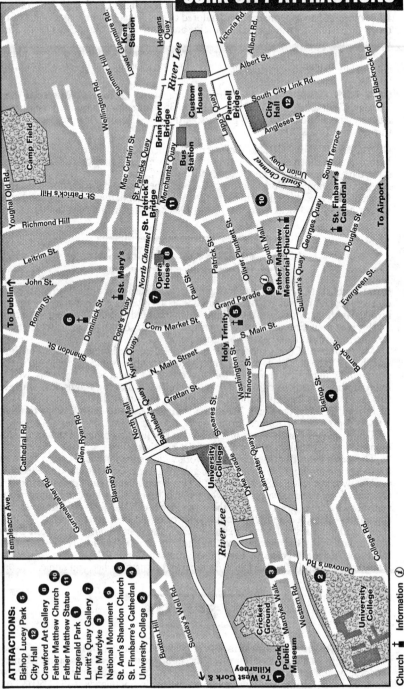

She can, upon request, put together half-day tours in and around Cork for groups of 10 or more. All are personalized and tailored to individual requirements. Some of the more interesting that go outside the city are those to Blarney, Cobh/Fota Park, Kinsale, and Killarney.

A sister company to Discover Cork, **Arrangements Unlimited** (same address and telephone number), can arrange entertainment, sporting and leisure activities, and dining.

CITY BUS TOUR There's a marvelous open-top ✪ **Tourist Bus tour** every Tuesday, Wednesday, and Thursday at 11am, 3pm, and 7pm from late June through August, with a fare of IR£4 ($7) per person, IR£10 ($17.50) for a family ticket. Book through the Tourist Office.

CORK HARBOUR TOURS During the summer months, there are regular 4-hour harbor cruises down the Lee. Hourly schedules vary, and they don't always run the same days every week, so check with the Tourist Office.

Also in summer, Cork Harbour Cruises operates a daily harbor tour from Kennedy Pier in Cobh, taking in harbor forts, Spike Island, the Naval Base, and other harbor highlights. Check with the Tourist Office for departure times and fares.

5. SPECIAL EVENTS

If you doubt that Cork is a party-loving town, just take a look at the festivals they put on every year. A festival in Cork, I might add, is a truly gala affair, with the entire city involved in the activities, and if you hit town in the middle of one, you're in for a treat. As this is written, firm dates are not available for 1992, but the Tourist Board should be able to furnish them before you leave home.

My favorite of Cork's special events is the ✪ **Jazz International Festival,** usually in October. This is a truly international event, as some of the world's most outstanding musicians show up for concerts held all around town, as well as impromptu jam sessions that break out in pubs, B&B drawing rooms, and wherever two jazz devotees happen to meet. It's a joyous, free-spirited time.

In April or May, the **Cork International Choral and Folk Dance Festival** attracts top-ranked performers from America, Great Britain, and the Continent. In 1990, a **Summer Festival** was inaugurated in late July and promises to be an annual event. Come September, it's the **Cork Folk Festival.**

The **Cork Film Festival** enjoyed a worldwide reputation for years as a showcase for independent filmmakers and was the gala of galas in Cork. It was cancelled for a year or two, but since 1986 it has been revived each year in late September or early October. Very good news for those of us who have always looked forward to the festival as a time of great gaiety in the city. Check with the Tourist Office to see if it stays alive—if so, it's well worth a day or two to join in the festivities.

As if all those festivals weren't enough, Cork also goes all out for the **Boat Show** in February, the **Summer Show** in June, the **Irish Assembly of Veteran/ Vintage Motor Cycles** in September, and the **Cork 20 International Car Rally** in October! Pretty hard to *miss* a party, no matter when you come.

6. SPORTS

The **Cork Greyhound Stadium,** out on Western Road (tel. 021/43013), is a good place to enjoy one of Ireland's favorite spectator sports. There's racing on Monday, Wednesday, and Saturday starting at 8pm. Other nights, there are trial heats which you can attend at no charge (but no betting); on race nights, admission is IR£1.50 ($2.65).

Golfers can rent clubs at the Cork Corporation–owned **Mahon Golf Course,** off Skehard Road, Blackrock, Cork, County Cork (tel. 021/362480). Drive out, or take bus no. 7 or 10 from Patrick Street. If you have your own clubs, there are 18-hole courses at the **Douglas Golf Club,** Carr's Hill, Douglas, and **Monkstown Golf Club,** Monkstown.

Tennis buffs will find six indoor courts and four floodlit courts at the **Tennis Village,** Model Farm Road, Cork, County Cork (tel. 021/342727). It's open 24 hours and has a bar and a restaurant on the premises.

7. SAVVY SHOPPING

Cork city is a major shopping center for the county, and the following are among its finest shops. There's a whole collection of boutiques, specialty shops, and bookshops along a quaintly cobbled square just off Patrick Street (on Patrick Street, turn right at a store named Moderne).

Shopping hours are Monday through Saturday from 10am to 6pm, and some shops observe one late night opening each week, usually Friday, remaining open until 9pm.

CASH'S OF CORK, Patrick and Caroline Sts., Cork. Tel. 021/276771.
This is perhaps Cork's leading department store, with everything from Waterford crystal, Belleek, Royal Tara, and Aran knits to the latest fashions for men and women.

CRAFTS OF IRELAND, 11 Winthrop St., Cork. Tel. 021/255864.
Turn left at Cash's department store to reach Cork's only "All Irish" shop, with its wide and wonderful range of Irish crafts.

EASON & SON LTD., 113 Patrick St., Cork. Tel. 021/270477.
Eason's stocks books of Irish interest, as well as a full line of current and classic fiction, and carries an extensive range of stationery, greeting cards, cassettes, magazines, and toys.

FITZGERALDS MENSWEAR SHOP, 24 Patrick St., Cork. Tel. 021/ 270095.
 This is Cork's only source of Burberry raincoats (with very competitive prices). It also stocks an excellent selection of Irish woolens, tweeds, and knits.

KELLY'S MUSIC SHOP, 15 Grand Parade, Cork. Tel. 021/272355.
There's not much in the way of Irish music that you won't find at Kelly's—records, tapes, books, and even musical instruments.

LEE BOOK STORE, 10 Lavitt's Quay, Cork. Tel. 021/272307.
 This marvelous book shop is browsing country par excellence, especially for out-of-print, secondhand books on Irish topics. Worth a walk over to the Quay, but be sure to allow a block of time—it won't be easy to leave!

MERCIER PRESS AND BOOKSHOPS, 4 Bridge St., Cork. Tel. 021/ 504022.
 A good many of the Irish books you browse through in bookshops around the country are published by this Cork publisher. Their inexpensive paperback editions are all by Irish writers on Irish subjects, fiction and nonfiction.

ROCHES STORES, Patrick St., Cork. Tel. 021/277727.
This upmarket department store also features giftware, travel goods, records, sports goods, and clothing.

WATERSTONE'S BOOKSELLERS, 69 Patrick St., Cork. Tel. 021/ 276622.
This large bookshop has extensive stocks of books on every conceivable subject, and they stay open until 9pm Monday through Friday, until 7pm on Saturday and Sunday.

MARKETS The ✪ **City Market,** sometimes called the English Market, is a block-long covered space between Patrick Street, Prince's Street, and Grand Parade. Its origins stretch back to the 1610 Charter of James I, although the present building was erected in 1782. It's a lively marketplace, with Cork housewives busily stall-hopping for the best buys on vegetables, fruits, meats, flowers, and occasionally secondhand clothes.

8. EVENING ENTERTAINMENT

THE PERFORMING ARTS

THEATER

CORK OPERA HOUSE, Emmet Place, Cork. Tel. 021/270022.
There is always something going on in this popular entertainment venue. It could be first-rate drama, a musical revue, comedy, concert, or an artist's recital—check with the Tourist Board or local newspapers for current schedules.
Prices: Tickets IR£6–IR£8 ($10.50–$14).

EVERYMAN PALACE THEATRE, Mac Curtain St., Cork. Tel. 021/ 501673.
In 1990 this outstanding playhouse moved from its 12-year home on Father Matthew Street to the Old Palace Theatre, built in 1897 beside the Metropole Hotel as a music hall and used in later years as a cinema. Its gilt-and-gingerbread decor is protected by a preservation order, as well it might be, since it is so steeped in the theatrical history of the city. Resident company productions of outstanding quality are presented regularly, and leading companies from Dublin, Belfast, Derry, Galway, Limerick, Great Britain, and America play here as well, and if the past is any indication, standards will be high. A nice feature is the intermission coffee service, and you'll still be able to hobnob with the actors after each production by dropping in at the Theatre Bar.
Prices: Tickets IR£6–IR£8 ($10.50–$14).

TRISKLE ARTS CENTRE, 15 Tobin St., Cork. Tel. 021/272022.
Located next to City Park, just off South Main Street, Triskle is host to a wide variety of talented artists and performers, many of them in the early stages of their careers. There are contemporary film exhibitions, literary readings, theatrical productions, and music sessions. There's an intimate little café that serves homemade food all day.
Prices: Tickets under IR£5 ($8.75).

IVERNIA THEATRE, Grand Parade, Cork. Tel. 021/273251.
Located in the rear of the Tourist Office, the Ivernia Theatre has performances several times a week during summer months. Occasionally there's lunchtime theater as well. Check with the Tourist Office, where you can buy tickets in advance, although they're also available at the door. Excellent entertainment at bargain prices.
Prices: Tickets under IR£5 ($8.75).

TRADITIONAL & CONTEMPORARY MUSIC

AN BODHRAN, 42 Oliver Plunkett St., Cork. Tel. 021/274544.

The traditional music sessions here are much more informal. The brick-walled century-and-a-half-old pub is a favorite with university students, most of whom take their traditional music quite seriously, while never losing that Irish twinkle of the eye. You'll usually find the ballads going Wednesday through Saturday nights, but you might drop in other nights to see what's doing. Open daily, regular pub hours.

AN PHOENIX, Union Sq., Cork. Tel. 021/964275.

You'll find bagpipes, bodrans, fiddles, and guitars holding forth with superb traditional Irish music 4 nights a week in this relaxed, friendly pub alongside City Hall. Open daily, regular pub hours.

DE LACY HOUSE, 74 Oliver Plunkett St., Cork.

There's traditional music here Wednesday through Sunday nights, and occasionally other forms of musical entertainment are offered on other nights. Open daily, regular pub hours.

REARDON'S MILL, 25 Washington St., Cork. Tel. 021/271969.

A variety of musical treats are offered at Reardon's Thursday through Sunday night. The music could be anything from traditional to country/western to jazz.

Admission: Cover charge IR£5 ($8.75).

THE PUB SCENE

There is, according to some Cork experts, a pub for every 200 residents. In a city populated by some 129,000 souls, that's a lot of pubs! You're just not likely to be seized by a terrible thirst without rescue close at hand, that's for certain. The pubs of Cork come in all sizes, styles, and decor, and I have no doubt you'll find your own "local" during your stay. The following few are some I've found appealing, with convivial conversation usually on tap along with libations.

AN BODHRAN, 42 Oliver Plunkett St., Cork. Tel. 021/274544.

A few years back, owner Daniel Teegan set about renovating this old pub, and wisely he gave a great deal of attention to its original character. It's a small, cozy place with brick walls, dim lights, low ceiling, lots of timbered beams, and a lively clientele. It's a student hangout, but you'll usually find a mix of older types as well. Traditional music is loved here with all the fervor of a truly Irish heart, as is stimulating conversation.

THE VINEYARD, Market Lane, Cork. Tel. 021/274793.

I first dropped into this old pub on the tiny lane off Patrick Street at the end of an exhausting afternoon of researching entries for this book. Things were pretty quiet except for a gaggle of Cork housewives, also exhausted from shopping, who had sensibly decided there was nothing for it but a "drop" before heading home to fix the dinner. It's an old, rambling place that dates back more than 2 centuries, but Liam Mackesy, the present owner, is the third generation of his family to run it. He has lightened it by installing a huge, high skylight in the center of the main bar. Rugby followers and players congregate in the Vineyard, where the *crack* (chat) leans a lot toward sports. Young, old, and in-between faces line up at the bar. It's a good pub in the evening, there's pub grub at lunch, and it can be a lifesaver in the late afternoon.

MUTTON LANE INN, Mutton Lane, Cork. Tel. 021/273471.

Down one of the quaint little laneways leading off Patrick Street to the English Market, the Mutton Lane was established way back in 1787, when whiskey was brewed in the kitchen. Today's owners, Vincent and Maeve McLaughlin, have made some renovations to the well-preserved old pub, and its interior these days is one of dark-stained timbers, soft lighting, and a noteworthy old pewter collection. They're also renowned locally for their excellent pub-grub lunches.

AN PHOENIX, Union Sq., Cork. Tel. 021/964275.

Located alongside City Hall, An Phoenix dates back to the early 1700s, when it set up shop in the premises of an old mill. With walls of old brick, pitch-pine verticals, exposed rafters, and redwood-and-pine seating, it's the perfect setting for the traditional music that holds sway 4 nights a week.

THE ROUNDY HOUSE, 1 Castle St., Cork. Tel. 021/277682.

At the top of the Coal Quay, the Roundy House dates back to 1858 and is one of the oldest in the city, with pictures from the past adorning its walls.

AROUND COUNTY CORK

The Southwest is composed of Counties Cork and Kerry and is worthy of as much exploration as your time will permit.

Scattered throughout the Southwest are quiet little villages peopled with strong characters and whimsical spirits. A Corkman is distinctive from other Irish, and a West Corkman is unique unto himself! A Kerryman combines wit, independence, and pride in a special blend like no other in the country.

SEEING COUNTY CORK

We'll start our exploration with County Cork, the largest county in Ireland (2,880 square miles). In the region we'll call East Cork, some 30 miles east of Cork city lies the picturesque harbor and town of Youghal. Heading west, historic Kinsale with its boat-filled harbor is 18 miles southwest of Cork city, and a scenic coastal drive takes you through the southern part of West Cork, meandering through small villages, out a long peninsula to Mizen Head, Ireland's southernmost point, and back inland to Bantry (57 miles southwest of Cork city), Glengarriff, and the Beara Peninsula. The northern part of West Cork holds the pleasant market town of Kanturk, from which easy day trips can be made to much of West Cork and County Kerry.

1. YOUGHAL & EAST CORK

YOUGHAL

Youghal (it means "yew wood" and is pronounced "yawl"), the picturesque fishing harbor and seaside resort, is 30 miles east of Cork city via N25. Founded by the Normans in the 13th century, it has distinctive American connections. Movie buffs will be interested to know that this is where *Moby Dick* was filmed back in 1954, and there are still tales told in the town about the movie folks and the giant white rubber whale that twice broke its moorings and drifted out to sea (local fishermen went to the rescue).

More important in the annals of history, however, is the fact that this is where Sir Walter Raleigh took his first puff on a pipe of American tobacco and put the first spud into Irish soil. So important do the Irish consider this latter event that they celebrate with a Walter Raleigh Potato Festival every year the last week of June and first week in July. If you should miss the festivities, you can still see Myrtle Grove, the Elizabethan house where he lived while in Youghal, although it's still a private residence and not open to the public.

✓ WHAT'S SPECIAL ABOUT COUNTY CORK

Historic Towns
- [ ] Youghal, Kinsale, and Bantry, which bring back the days of Irish rebellion and sailing glory, and are now the haunts of fishing boats as well as pleasure yachts from around the world.

Spectacular Scenery
- [ ] The Beara Peninsula, which County Cork shares with County Kerry, a marvel of mountainous and coastal beauty.
- [ ] Wooded Gougane Barra, a testament to man's reaching out to his God in a setting of mountains, forests, and river.

Historic Houses
- [ ] Bantry House, dating from the mid-1700s, holding a magnificent collection of art treasures and antiques from around the world.

Gardens
- [ ] Glengarriff, boasting exotic tropical plants both onshore and off, with Garinish Island a short boat ride from town.

WHAT TO SEE & DO

Your first order of business should be to go by the **Tourist Office,** located at the harbor in Market House, Market Square (tel. 024/92390), and pick up the **"Tourist Trail"** booklet. It features a signposted walking tour of the town. Highlights of the tour include the historic **Clock Tower,** right in the middle of town, erected in 1776 as a jail, which soon became so overcrowded with rebellious Irish that an entire new floor had to be added. Today it serves as an art gallery and museum, featuring the works of local artists, ancient town charters, and Sir Walter Raleigh memorabilia. A short distance away are fragments of the **old town walls,** constructed in 1275 and added to up to 1603. **Myrtle Grove** is at the top of Nelson Place, adjacent to **St. Mary's Collegiate Church,** built in the 13th century on the site of an 11th-century church that was destroyed by a mighty storm. Its neighbor, the **College of Youghal,** was founded in 1464.

Quaint, narrow ✪ **Main Street** is a microcosm of an ancient Irish town successfully melding into today's life-style, and **Market Square,** now a pedestrian plaza, is a focal point for locals and visitors alike. Across the square from Market House, the Water Gate is a reminder that this was once the shoreline of the harbor. Youghal's importance as a harbor over the centuries is best visualized from the water, and Bernard O'Keefe, 126 North Main Street (tel. 024/92820), conducts **harbor cruises** in summer months, as well as river cruises up the nearby Blackwater River, which empties into the sea just east of town. He can also arrange fishing trips.

Sightseeing aside, do stop by the ✪ **Moby Dick** pub on Market Square (tel. 024/92756), which dates back to 1798, for a pint and some conversation with the locals who frequent the place. If you're lucky, owners Paddy and Kevin Linehan will be on hand and you might prevail on them to break out the scrapbook that chronicles their many years as publicans, as well as souvenirs of the *Moby Dick* crew, who adopted the pub as its local during filming.

WHERE TO STAY

AVONMORE HOUSE, South Abbey, Youghal, Co. Cork. Tel. 024/92617. 8 rms (all with bath).

$ Rates (including breakfast): IR£11.50 ($20.15) per person. Dinner IR£10 ($17.50) extra. No credit cards.

Donal and Philomena (Phil) Brooks open their Georgian home to guests, with nicely done up guest rooms and superb meals. Donal is a retired forester and has a keen interest in traditional Irish music. Avonmore is conveniently located in the main residential section of Youghal and is only a short walk from the beach.

BROMLEY HOUSE, Killeagh, Youghal, Co. Cork. Tel. 024/95235. 4 rms (none with bath).
$ Rates (including breakfast): IR£14 ($24.50) single; IR£11 ($19.25) per person sharing. 50% reduction for children. Dinner IR£10 ($17.50) extra. No credit cards. **Closed:** Nov–Feb. **Parking:** Private car park.
The friendly Mrs. Eileen Fogarty gives a warm welcome to every new arrival at this modern, centrally heated bungalow 5km (3 miles) west of Youghal on N25. There's a TV lounge and open fires for cool evenings, and all guest rooms have sinks. Private parking space is a great boon to drivers.

WHERE TO EAT

AHERNE'S PUB AND SEAFOOD BAR, 163 N. Main St., Youghal. Tel. 024/92533 or 92424.
Cuisine: SEAFOOD/BAR FOOD/TRADITIONAL. **Reservations:** Recommended, especially for dinner.
$ Prices: Appetizers IR£2–IR£5 ($3.50–$8.75); main courses IR£6–IR£10 ($10.50–$17.50); bar food IR£2–IR£6 ($3.50–$10.50). ACC, AE, DC, MC, V.
Open: Lunch Tues–Sat 12:30–2:15pm; dinner Tues–Sat 6:30–9:30pm. **Closed:** Good Friday and 4 days at Christmas.
Aherne's serves bar food of such quality that it has won the National Bar Food award for several years. But pub grub is not its only distinction, for John and David Fitzgibbon have also installed an outstanding full restaurant and enhanced its decor with paintings, wood paneling, and soft lighting. Seafood dishes, such as mussels in garlic butter, take star billing, but beef, lamb, and chicken dishes are equally well prepared. Except for bar food, available all day, prices in this attractive eatery will run slightly above budget, but you'll count it money well spent.

EAST CORK

Although you'll seldom see the term "East Cork," it's a good term to define that part of County Cork that lies east and north of Cork city.

WHAT TO SEE & DO

About midway between Youghal and Cork city, the little seaside fishing village of **Ballycotton** (take R632 at Castlemartyr on N25) slopes down picturesque little streets to a sheltered harbor. Stop in at the bar of the 2-centuries-old Ballycotton Hotel—it's an authentic Irish country bar, run by the friendly O'Sullivan family, and its decor has been described by fellow American writer J. Herbert Silverman as "vintage country classic." Just 2 miles away at **Shanagarry** are the ruins of an ancient house that was once home to members of William Penn's family.

If your itinerary takes you directly from Cork to Killarney, you can join the scenic **Blackwater Valley Drive** by traveling N20 north to **Mallow** (a popular spa resort in the 18th century, whose riotous social activities are commemorated in the ballad "The Rakes of Mallow"), then N72 to Killarney. In the Tourist Office in either Cork or Youghal, pick up a copy of the *Blackwater Valley Drive* map and chart that will give details of the many historic relics along that route.

Incidentally, a few miles north of Mallow, on the main Cork–Limerick road

(N20), there are interesting and well-preserved ruins of 13th-century ✪ **Ballybeg Abbey** just outside the village of Buttevant on the Cork side. Buttevant itself was the model for "Mole" in Spenser's *Faeire Queene*, and it was the scene of the first-ever steeplechase (from the steeple of Buttevant Church of Ireland to that of Doneraile, a distance of about 4 miles), giving that name to one form of horseracing.

WHERE TO STAY

DANNAR HOUSE, Ballyhindon, Fermoy, Co. Cork. Tel. 025/31786. 4 rms (all with bath).

$ Rates (including breakfast): IR£12 ($21) per person sharing. IR£14 ($24.50) single; 10% reduction for children. High tea IR£8 ($14) extra; dinner, IR£10 ($17.50). No credit cards. **Closed:** Nov–Jan. **Parking:** Private car park.

Dannar House is a lovely modern bungalow, the home of Maureen and Dan Regan, who take a warm interest in their guests. The house is centrally heated, beds have electric blankets, there's ample private parking, and an open fire gives a nice glow to the lounge. It's about a mile from Fermoy, 50 yards off the Cork–Dublin road (N8), near the Moorpark Research Centre.

A Farmhouse

BEECHMOUNT FARM, Mallow, Co. Cork. Tel. 022/21764. 5 rms (none with bath).

$ Rates (including breakfast): IR£11.50 ($20.15) per person. High tea IR£8 ($14) extra. No credit cards. **Closed:** Oct–May.

This pretty Georgian house about a mile from Mallow dates back to the 17th century and is partially furnished with antique pieces. Mrs. Moira Fitzpatrick excels in the kitchen, and boasts that at Beechmount "you will never be cold or hungry." You'll want to sample her marvelous home-baking at afternoon tea. The 187 acres of green farm fields afford peaceful rural views, and the five simply furnished guest rooms feature sinks and electric blankets on all beds.

Self-Catering

KINOITH HOUSE COTTAGES, Shanagarry, Midleton, Co. Cork. Tel. 021/646785. 4 cottages. TV

$ Rates: IR£380–IR£420 ($665–$735) per week. ACC, AE, MC, V. **Closed:** Jan–Feb.

✪ You can relax into the peaceful Irish countryside in these very special holiday cottages, spend your days sightseeing in the area—Ballycotton and Shanagarry are both just a short drive away—and return at night for a meal that includes freshly baked bread, free-range eggs, and fresh vegetables and fruits you can buy from the farm. Kinoith House Cottages, 18 miles Southwest of Youghal (signposted from N25, the Youghal–Cork road), are in what were once the outbuildings of the 18th-century farmhouse known as Kinoith. Myrtle Allen's famed cookery school, the internationally known Ballymaloe House, is held here at Kinoith House under the tutelage of Darina Allen, her talented daughter-in-law. The proximity of Ballymaloe is a bonus for cottage renters, since one of Ireland's finest restaurants is right at hand for those times you'd really rather not cook.

From the graveled courtyard, where vivid blooms are bright splashes of color, stroll through the garden and out into the apple orchard. Inside each cottage are such modern conveniences as a dishwasher and TV (and you have the use of laundry facilities). There's the added, old-fashioned comfort of an open fire (the rent includes your firewood). The Pink Cottage and the White Cottage both sleep 8 to 10 people. The Barn sleeps 12, with two twin- or double-bedded rooms en suite and eight single rooms; and the Coach House sleeps eight. As you can see, on a per-person basis, these cottages are actually quite inexpensive. Early reservations are advised to avoid disappointment.

Worth the Extra Money

LONGUEVILLE HOUSE, Longueville, Mallow, Co. Cork. Tel. 022/47156
or 47306. Fax 022/47459. 16 rms (all with bath).
$ Rates IR£55–IR£65 ($96.25–$113.75) per person. Dinner (including breakfast):
IR£28 ($49) extra. ACC, AE, DC, MC, V. **Closed:** Mid-Dec to Feb.

⭐ Set in a 500-acre farmland estate 3 miles west of Mallow on the Mallow–
Killarney road (N72), Longueville House overlooks the Blackwater River
valley. Off in the distance are visible the ruins of 16th-century Dromaneen
Castle, ancestral home of owner Michael O'Callaghan, and on the front lawn, rows of
huge oaks are planted in the same formation as French and English troops at the Battle
of Waterloo. There's significance in both these views, for the castle was forfeit to
Cromwell in 1641 and the family heritage was reclaimed only in 1938 when Michael's
father purchased the land and castle.

The handsome 1720 Georgian mansion sports a wide entrance hall whose walls
are hung with O'Callaghan portraits, and a lounge with a carved fireplace and a
beautifully detailed stucco ceiling. The lounge bar is Victorian in style, with wine-red
upholstery, and in the gourmet restaurant (see "Where to Eat," below), portraits of
every Republic of Ireland president dub it the President's Room. There's trout and
salmon fishing in the Blackwater right on the estate, and free golf 3 miles away. A
decided bonus to those of a literary bent is the excellent library.

Note: Children are not encouraged as guests, since Longueville House is
essentially an adult retreat.

WHERE TO EAT

Worth the Extra Money

**BALLYMALOE HOUSE, Shanagarry, Midleton, Co. Cork. Tel. 021/
652531.**
Cuisine: IRISH/SEAFOOD. **Reservations:** Essential.
$ Prices: Fixed-price meal IR£24 ($42) at dinner, IR£14 ($24.50) at Sun lunch.
Service charge 10%. ACC, AE, DC, MC, V.
Open: Dinner daily 7–9:30pm; lunch Sun at 1pm. **Closed:** 3 days at Christmas.

⭐ Myrtle Allen's Ballymaloe House is internationally famous, and one of the
chief reasons for its excellence is the fact that the cuisine rests on strictly local
products. The nightly menu is quite small, but quality looms immense. The
simplest dishes have flavor you'd never expect to find outside the little auberges of
rural France. There's no predicting exactly what will be on the menu the evening you
dine here, but I know that every meal offers a choice of three soups, three or four fish
dishes, six main courses, and at least four desserts—all prepared with the flair of
traditional Irish recipes. I can only hope that Mrs. Allen's superb pâté is on the menu,
followed, perhaps, by watercress soup, escalopes of stuffed baby beef, and the savarin
au rhum as a topper.

LONGUEVILLE HOUSE, Longueville, Mallow, Co. Cork. Tel. 022/47156
or 47306.
Cuisine: TRADITIONAL/SEAFOOD. **Reservations:** Essential.
$ Prices: Fixed-price meal IR£15 ($26.25) at lunch, IR£24 ($42) at dinner. ACC, AE,
DC, MC, V.
Open: Lunch daily 12:45–2pm; dinner daily 7–9pm. **Closed:** Christmas to early
Mar.

⭐ The President's Room restaurant is one of the best in the country, and even if
you're only passing through this part of the Southern Region, you'll be in for a
very special treat if you phone ahead to book a meal here. Meals are served in
the stately Georgian dining room under the gaze of all of Ireland's presidents, beneath
an ornate plaster ceiling. In fine weather the Victorian conservatory, with its massed
greenery, white ironwork, and glorious views of the garden, is open to diners as well.

As for the food, it has won just about every award and international recognition going. Chef William O'Callaghan oversees the preparation of gourmet selections that utilize produce grown in the Longueville fields, local lamb, and fish fresh from waters that flow through the estate. Mallard and venison are featured in season, and the wine list includes wines produced from Michael's own vineyards (among the first—and only ones—in Ireland).

You'll find Longueville House 3 miles west of Mallow on the Mallow–Killarney road (N72).

2. KINSALE & WEST CORK

Between Cork and Killarney are several possible routes, each with its own special appeal. If time is all-important, you can take the Blackwater Valley Drive, or follow N22 through Macroom (the castle right off the town square belonged to the father of William Penn, founder of Pennsylvania), with a detour to Gougane Barra. My personal preference is the lengthy, meandering N71 that follows the coastline through West Cork, leading to Bantry and Glengarriff before turning northward to Killarney. You can also reach Bantry by diverting onto R586 at Bandon, which takes you through Dunmanway and Timoleague en route. An even better idea is to base yourself somewhere in this wondrous region and make day trips to explore it at your leisure.

KINSALE

A scenic 18 miles south of Cork city, the fishing and boating village of Kinsale has figured prominently in Ireland's history since it received its charter in 1333. Back in 1601 it was the scene of a decisive Irish defeat. When Don Juan d'Aguila arrived from Spain with a large force to assist the Irish rebels, it looked as though the Irish might prevail. Even though Mountjoy, the English general, threw some 12,000 soldiers into a siege of the town, his position seemed doomed when Irish chieftans O'Donnell and O'Neill massed their forces behind the English, leaving them surrounded. History might well have been dramatically changed had it not been for an Irish soldier (reportedly in his cups) who let slip vital information to Mountjoy, enabling him to successfully rout both Irish and Spanish.

WHAT TO SEE & DO

South of town, you can visit the remains of **King James Fort,** the very one that housed the Spanish in 1601.

In Summer Cove, on the east side of the bay, there's quite a lot left of **Charles Fort,** built by the English in 1677 and in constant use as late as the 1920s. It sits high on a clifftop, and the view of Kinsale Harbour is spectacular. Six miles south is the **Old Head of Kinsale,** where a 12th-century castle sits in ruins atop high cliffs overlooking the spot where the *Lusitania* lies in its deep-water grave, sent there (along with some 1,500 souls) in 1915 by a German submarine.

Other Kinsale tag ends of history to look for include the **town stocks** in **St. Multrose Church,** erected in the 12th century. A ruined 12th-century **Carmelite friary** and 15th-century **Desmond Castle** provide interesting poking around.

One bit of Kinsale miscellany: The town's womenfolk once wore the long, black, hooded cape that's known as the **Kinsale cloak**—you'll see it copied in rich fabrics to be used as an elegant evening cloak, but these days it's rare to see it on Kinsale streets.

PUBS If, by this time in your travels, you've become an Irish pub addict, there are two in Kinsale you won't want to miss. My personal favorite is the ✪ **Seanachie**

Pub on Market Street. If time permits, I'll warrant you won't be able to go along to the Seanachie just once—it's habit-forming! It's tucked away on a picture-postcard-pretty street, uses a second, phonetic spelling of its name (Shanakee), and is more than 200 years old. In the two small front rooms are original old stone walls, open fires, and a marvelous painting of the legendary Irish storytellers for whom the pub is named. Brothers Vincent and Gerard McCarthy, both musical, are genial hosts. A larger back room has been added, opening up equally old adjacent buildings, retaining stone walls, and restoring ceiling beams and crumbling fireplaces. During summer months there's music 7 nights a week—and that means traditional Irish music as well as the favorite sing-along ballads. Michael Buckley, the beloved All-Ireland accordion player, performs regularly, as do other local musicians. There's also dancing in the back room on weekends all through the summer, but absolutely nothing could draw yours truly from those front rooms where music and talk and the brown stuff flow easily until one of the McCarthys sings out "Time, gentlemen, please."

The second noteworthy pub is **The Spaniard,** an atmospheric converted stable where fishnets seem right at home in the horse-stall cubbyholes. This is where you'll find a crowd of international sportsmen, here for the world-famous shark fishing and a fair smattering of local characters. In summer months there's frequently live music in the evenings.

FISHING If you'd like to get in some fishing, arrangements can be made through the **Trident Angling Centre,** Trident Hotel, Kinsale (tel. 021/774099).

WHERE TO STAY

BLUE HAVEN HOTEL, 3 Pearse St., Kinsale, Co. Cork. Tel. 021/772209 or 772206. 10 rms (all with bath).
$ Rates (including breakfast): IR£22–IR£36 ($38.50–$63) per person. Special 2- and 3-day rates available. ACC, AE, DC, MC, V.

Right in the heart of town, Ann and Brian Cronin have created a haven of quiet, relaxed comfort in this small hotel. Guest rooms are nicely done up, the staff excells in friendliness and genuine helpfulness, and the Blue Haven is known far and wide for its superb seafood bar (see "Where to Eat," below). A little above the budget in rates, but well worth it. Advance booking is strongly advised in summer months.

HILLSIDE HOUSE, Camp Hill, Kinsale, Co. Cork. Tel. 021/772315. 6 rms (3 with bath).
$ Rates (including breakfast): IR£18.50 ($32.40) single without bath; IR£11 ($19.25) per person sharing without bath; IR£3 ($5.25) per person additional with bath. 20% reduction for children. Dinner IR£10 ($17.50) extra. No credit cards.
About a mile outside Kinsale, Mrs. Margaret Griffin's spacious modern bungalow has sea views and a pleasant garden. The house is centrally heated, and there's ample parking. This is an especially nice place to stay if you prefer the country but don't want to be too far from town.

THE LIGHTHOUSE, The Rock, Kinsale, Co. Cork. Tel. 021/772734. 5 rms (all with bath), 1 suite.
$ Rates (including breakfast): IR£19.50 ($34.15) single; IR£15.50 ($27.15) per person sharing. 20% reduction for children. Dinner IR£14 ($24.50) extra. ACC, MC. **Closed:** Dec–Feb.

Arthur and Ruthann Moran-Salinger are Americans who have settled in Kinsale. Their Tudor-style home is furnished with antiques collected from around the world. Ruthann, a professor of history, political science, and psychology, has put her Irish grandmother's treasures to practical use, using antique Irish table linens and lace-trimmed sheets and pillowcases in guestrooms. Irish porcelain and antique silver also appear at table, along with an excellent full Irish breakfast, one of Ruthann's specialties. Guest rooms are small and cozy, with canopied beds, and the one suite consists of a bedroom and a conservatory-style sitting room. Ruthann and Art are happy to share their knowledge of local places of interest and dining facilities. From the town center, the Lighthouse is just above St. Multose Church, around the corner from the Carmelite friary.

SIROCCA, Ballyregan, Kinsale, Co. Cork. Tel. 021/775129. 3 rms (none with bath).
$ Rates (including breakfast): IR£15.50 ($27.15) single; IR£11 ($19.25) per person sharing. 20% reduction for children. No credit cards. **Closed:** Oct–Apr.
Mrs. Sheila O'Regan is the charming hostess of this modern bungalow with magnificent views of the surrounding area and the garden, which guests can use. There are three attractive rooms, all with sinks, and the house is centrally heated. It's 5km (3 miles) north of Kinsale on the Innishannon road.

READERS RECOMMEND

The Old Presbytery, *Cork Street, Kinsale, County Cork (tel. 021/772027) "This high, narrow, Victorian house right in the middle of Kinsale is filled with antiques, and Ken and Cathleen Buggy are charming, hospitable hosts, very helpful to their guests."*—Iris Jones, Farmington Hills, Mich.

WHERE TO EAT

BLUE HAVEN HOTEL, 3 Pearse St., Kinsale. Tel. 021/772209 or 772206.
  Cuisine: SEAFOOD/TRADITIONAL/BAR FOOD.
$ Prices: Appetizers IR£2–IR£5 ($3.50–$8.75); main courses IR£6–IR£10 ($10.50–$17.50); bar food IR£3–IR£5 ($7.25–$10.50). Service charge 10%. ACC, AE, DC, MC, V.
  Open: Daily 10:30am–11:30pm. **Closed:** Christmas Day.
  Superior light lunches are served in the cozy Blue Haven Hotel's lounge bar. The hotel has won culinary awards for their seafood here, but the menu also includes lamb, corned beef, and sometimes very good lasagne. There's also a pricier and more extensive menu in the higher ranges listed above.

MAN FRIDAY, Scilly, Kinsale. Tel. 021/772260.
  Cuisine: SEAFOOD/INTERNATIONAL. **Reservations:** Recommended.
$ Prices: Appetizers IR£2–IR£6 ($3.50–$10.50); main courses IR£8–IR£12 ($14–$21). ACC, V.
  Open: Dinner only, Mon–Sat 7:30–10:30pm. **Closed:** Mon in winter, 2 weeks in Jan.
Overlooking the harbor on the outskirts of town, Man Friday is the sort of cozy eatery that invites you to relax from your first step inside. Among the outstanding dishes are baked black sole with a seafood stuffing, roast stuffed loin of lamb with mint-and-rosemary sauce, and Chinese beef, but anything you select will come to table at its very best, a fact testified to by the many awards given Man Friday over the past few years.

THE VINTAGE, Main St., Kinsale. Tel. 021/772502.
  Cuisine: GERMAN/IRISH/SEAFOOD. **Reservations:** Recommended.
$ Prices: Appetizers IR£2–IR£6 ($3.50–$10.50); main courses IR£8–IR£12 ($14–$21). Service charge 5%. ACC, AE, DC, MC, V.
  Open: Dinner only, Mon–Sat 7–10:30pm **Closed:** Mid-Jan to Feb.
This small restaurant is very cozy, very romantic, and totally delicious. There is an open fire in the dining room, 200-year-old beams, and original masts from sailing ships that came into Kinsale. Every evening in a minuscule kitchen master chef Michael Risse (formerly head chef at the Four Seasons Hotel in his native Hamburg), conjures up a menu remarkable for its freshness of ingredients and approach. As much as possible, Michael uses local foodstuffs—organically grown vegetables; free-range

geese, ducklings, and rabbits; eggs from free-range chickens; and seafood caught just offshore. His Kinsale hot smoked salmon steak and his sole Véronique (filets with white wine, cream, and grapes) are superb. There's an excellent wine list, and the Vintage is a member of the Kinsale Good Food Circle, as well as other prestigious professional organizations.

READERS RECOMMEND

Glebe House, *Ballinades, Bandon, County Cork (tel. 021/778294). "On our way from Cork to Bantry, we found this delightful country house and restaurant just 7 miles from Kinsale. A great meal, and we'd like to get back to stay overnight."* —Dee and Jack Lavelle, Pinehurst, N.C.

WEST CORK

Someone has written, "West Cork is bigger than Ireland." Well, an hour or two of gazing at its wild, unspoiled, and magnificent vistas of coastline, tiny villages, sheer cliffs, and miles and miles of emptiness will go a long way toward convincing you of the truth of that statement!

The ghosts of Ireland past who roam this ruggedly beautiful region include that of independence fighter Gen. **Michael Collins,** who was ambushed at a place called Beal na Blath in August 1922 (there's a memorial marking the spot on the Dunmanway–Crookstown road). And in Castlestownend, surely the shades of two Victorian novelists named Edith Somerville and Violet Martin Ross still haunt the hallways and grounds of their beloved Drishane House, where together they wrote gently humorous tales of their Irish neighbors. The entire English-speaking world has chuckled over the misadventures recounted in the television dramatization of their most famous work, *The Experiences of an Irish R.M.*

WHAT TO SEE & DO

En route to **Clonakilty,** birthplace of Michael Collins, stop by the **Timoleague Castle Gardens,** which date from the 1800s. Drive on to Clonakilty, where castles dot the shores of the bay and a regional museum displays minute books of the town corporation that date back to 1675, along with Michael Collins memorabilia and many other interesting relics. Stop for lunch or dinner or overnight at **Leap** (see below). In **Skibbereen,** visit the **West Cork Arts Centre** on North Street to see contemporary arts and crafts produced by artists and artisans from the Southwest. Detour south to visit **Baltimore,** with its ruined O'Driscoll castle brooding over the town from a high cliff and its tales of horror in 1631, when Algerian pirates massacred all but 200 of the inhabitants and carried off the survivors to a life of slavery in North Africa. Lovely **Sherkin Island,** with its ancient, ruined Franciscan abbey and peaceful, lonely coves, can be visited by passenger boat from Baltimore during the summer. Pass through villages like **Ballydehob,** and linger a while at the picturesque fishing village of **Schull** and stroll its waterfront. From Schull, travel the 18 miles to **Mizen Head** at land's end, through **Goleen,** with its sandy strand, **Crookhaven,** and around **Barley Cove.** Return to Schull along Dunmanus Bay on the other side of Mount Gabriel, which rises 1,339 feet.

WHERE TO STAY

ABBEY HEIGHTS, Skibbereen, Co. Cork. Tel. 028/21615. 4 rms (3 with bath).

$ Rates (including breakfast): IR£16 ($28) single without bath; IR£11 ($19.25) per person sharing without bath; IR£2 ($3.50) per person additional with bath. 33⅓% reduction for children. Dinner IR£10.50 ($18.40) extra. No credit cards. **Closed:** Oct–Easter.

The Glavin family will welcome you to their pretty bungalow, less than a mile from Skibbereen, with beautiful river views. The house is centrally heated and dinner is available with advance notice. It's 54 miles southwest of Cork city via N71, 21 miles southeast of Bantry, signposted from R556.

DUN MHUIRE, Kilbarry Rd., Dunmanway, Co. Cork. Tel. 023/45162. 5 rms (all with bath). TV
$ Rates (including breakfast): IR£15 ($26.25) per person. 50% reduction for children. ACC, MC, V.

Mrs. Carmel Hayes presides over this lovely, modern home and restaurant, centrally heated and set in nice, peaceful surroundings. The restaurant has won accolades from locals and visitors alike (see "Where to Eat," below). It's 37 miles west of Cork via N72 with signposted turnoffs, and 20 miles east of Bantry via R586.

LEAP INN, Leap, Co. Cork. Tel. 028/33307. 9 rms (5 with bath).
$ Rates (including breakfast): IR£12 ($21) per person (no extra charge for private bath). ACC, V.

In the little West Cork village of Leap (pronounced "Lep"), a night in this comfortable, old-fashioned hotel is like taking a giant step back to a time when friendliness and hospitality was the mark of all country inns. The same family has run this place since 1834, and today Brian and Ann Sheahan continue the traditions of innkeeping that have grown with the years. Public rooms include a bar (which serves pub grub all day), a lounge, and a dining room (see "Where to Eat," below). Upstairs, bedrooms are simply furnished, but very comfortable. The setting is idyllic, an ideal place for a quiet, relaxing stop. It's on the main Cork–Bantry road (N71), 50 miles southwest of Cork city, 43 miles southwest of Kinsale, and 15 miles southeast of Bantry.

SEA COURT, Butlerstown, Co. Cork. Tel. 023/40218, or 513/961-3537 in the U.S. 4 rms (all with bath).
$ Rates (including breakfast): IR£16 ($28) per person. Dinner IR£12.50 ($21.90) extra. No credit cards. **Closed:** Sept–Apr.

About an hour's drive southwest of Cork city and 16 miles southwest of Kinsale via Courtmacsherry, Sea Court is a Georgian country mansion that dates from 1760. Within easy driving distance of Kinsale, Bantry, and Killarney, the house sits in 10 acres of wooded grounds on the Seven Heads peninsula jutting out into the Atlantic, and beaches are only a short walk away. Americans David and Monica Elder bought this lovely place in 1983. The house has been designated a historic structure by the Irish government and is open to the public at large and to guests during the summer season. Rooms are spacious and well furnished, and some have ocean views. Breakfasts are sumptuous, and David will happily pass along the recipe for the scones of which he is so proud. He will also, with advance booking, provide a gourmet dinner by candlelight. Incidentally, Sea Court is available as a weekly or monthly rental in the off-season. Book through caretakers Donie and Kathleen McCarthy (tel. 023/40218).

A Farmhouse

FINDUS HOUSE, Ballyvoige, Kilnamartyra, Macroom, Co. Cork. Tel. 026/40023. 6 rms (3 with bath).
$ Rates (including breakfast): IR£16 ($28) single; IR£12 ($21) per person sharing. 50% reduction for children. Dinner IR£12 ($21) extra. ACC, AE, V. **Closed:** Nov–Apr.

Findus House is the family-run, working farm of Mary O'Sullivan and her lively family. Guest rooms are pleasant, and Mary has won much praise for her dinners; salmon dishes are her specialty, with wine and Irish coffee available at a small extra charge. The O'Sullivan children not only help at table and around the farm, but in the evenings they often join guests to entertain them with music, song, and dance. A delightful base for exploring this part of West Cork, Findus Farm is 24 miles west of Cork city, 30 miles south of Killarney, 3 miles south of the main Cork–Killarney road (N22), and 19 miles northeast of Gougane Barra.

Worth the Extra Money

ASSOLAS COUNTRY HOUSE, Kanturk, Co. Cork. Tel. 029/50015. 10 rms (all with bath).

$ Rates (including breakfast): IR£38–IR£65 ($66.50–$113.75) per person. ACC, AE, DC, MC, V. **Closed:** Nov–Feb.

 Set in beautifully landscaped grounds, this 17th-century Queen Anne-style house is surrounded by 100 acres of parkland, and its flower gardens have won the prestigious Ireland Garden Award. Towering old trees and green lawns lead down to the edge of the Blackwater River (where guests fish free). There are spacious public rooms and a large rumpus room with a stone fireplace. Upstairs, guest rooms come in a variety of sizes and shapes, all done up in country fabrics and colors. There's a comfortable, relaxed air about the place that's the direct result of Eleanor and Hugh Bourke's gracious hospitality. Dining is superb (the restaurant is recognized internationally; see "Where to Eat," below). In addition to fishing, guests have access to tennis, boating, and croquet. Assolas is 42 miles northwest of Cork city, signposted from the Cork–Killarney road (N72), approximately 3 miles from Kanturk town.

WHERE TO EAT

AN SUGAN, Wolfe Tone St., Clonakilty, Co. Cork. Tel. 023/33498.
Cuisine: BAR FOOD/SEAFOOD/VEGETARIAN/IRISH.
$ Prices: Bar food IR£1–IR£6 ($1.75–$10.50); Fixed-price meal IR£6 ($10.50) at lunch, IR£12 ($21) at dinner; Tourist Menu IR£5.75–IR£7.90 ($10.05–$13.85). ACC, MC, V.
Open: lunch daily 12:30–2:30pm; dinner daily 6–10pm; Bar food daily 12:30–10:30pm. **Closed:** Good Friday, Christmas Day.

 This old-style, homey pub and restaurant 33 miles southwest of Cork on N71 features a fascinating collection of bits and pieces of Irish life. It makes an ideal stop for bar food that's good enough and filling enough to serve as a main meal (I particularly like the Bantry Bay mussels). Upstairs, the restaurant has a lobster tank and serves lunch and dinner at the higher prices listed above.

DUN MHUIRE, Kilbarry Rd., Dunmanway, Co. Cork. Tel. 023/45162.
Cuisine: SEAFOOD/VEGETARIAN.
$ Prices: Fixed-price dinner IR£14 ($24.20). ACC, MC, V.
Open: Dinner only, Wed–Sat 7–11pm.
This family-run restaurant specializes in freshly cooked food, with a heavy emphasis on seafood. The service is friendly and efficient, and only the freshest produce is used. Dun Mhuire is 37 miles west of Cork via N72, with signposted turnoffs, and 20 miles east of Bantry via R586.

LEAP INN, Leap, Co. Cork. Tel. 028/33307.
Cuisine: BAR FOOD/SEAFOOD/TRADITIONAL.
$ Prices: Appetizers IR£1.50–IR£5 ($2.65–$8.75); main courses IR£4.50–IR£10 ($7.90–$17.50); bar food IR£1.50–IR£5 ($2.65–$8.75); fixed-price five-course dinner IR£12 ($21). No credit cards.
Open: Dinner daily 6:30–9:30pm; bar food daily 10am–7pm.

Excellent bar food is served here all day, making it an ideal lunch or snack stop. At dinnertime, the homey dining room in this little country inn is a relaxing venue for a meal of the freshest local produce and seafood just out of local waters. Leap Inn is on the main Cork–Bantry road (N71), 50 miles southwest of Cork city, 43 miles southwest of Kinsale, and 15 miles southeast of Bantry.

Worth the Extra Money

ASSOLAS COUNTRY HOUSE, Kanturk, Co. Cork. Tel. 029/50015.
Cuisine: SEAFOOD/VEGETARIAN/TRADITIONAL. **Reservations:** Essential.
$ Prices: Fixed-price dinner IR£20 ($35). Service charge 10%. ACC, AE, DC, MC, V.

Open: Mar–Nov, dinner only, daily 7–9pm.

The dining room at Assolas House (see "Where to Stay," above, for a full description) is a real gem, with Queen Anne period furnishings, Dresden china, mahogany tables, and a comfortable lounge for before- or after-dinner drinks. The pâté maison is homemade, and the menu always features home-grown fresh vegetables, and often offers salmon fresh from the Blackwater. The Irish coffee is excellent, and there's a good, extensive wine list. To all that, the Bourke family add friendly service that's of the same high standards as their meals. Assolas Country House is 42 miles northwest of Cork city, signposted from the Cork–Killarney road (N72), and approximately 3 miles east of Kanturk town.

3. BANTRY, GLENGARRIFF & THE BEARA PENINSULA

BANTRY

The little town of Bantry (named for an ancient Celtic chieftain) sits at the head of lovely Bantry Bay, surrounded by hills. The 21-mile-long inlet of the sea apparently had great appeal to the French, who twice (in 1689 and 1796) selected it for attempted naval invasions of Ireland. One relic of the ill-fated Wolfe Tone expedition, the French frigate *La Surveilante,* lies in a remarkably good state of preservation at the bottom of Bantry Bay, and work has begun to raise it from the deep and establish a 1796 Armada Exhibition Centre at Bantry House.

WHAT TO SEE & DO

You'll see fishing boats tied up right at the foot of the town, and if you elect to stay over here, your B&B hostess will be able to arrange a trip on the water with Ken Minehan. During the summer, 1½-hour **cruises on the bay** take you past Whiddy Island and its oil terminal and castle ruins. Sea-angling trips can also be arranged. For schedules and rates, contact Ken Minehan (tel. 027/50318).

BANTRY HOUSE, Bantry, Co. Cork. Tel. 027/50047.

Bantry House, on the southern outskirts of the town, sits in a magnificent demesne and is the ancestral home of the earls of Bantry. Beautifully landscaped lawns and gardens slope downward from the front of the Georgian mansion that looks out over the bay. Inside is an impressive collection of European antiques, paintings, sculptures, and other items that caught the fancy of globe-trotting earls over the centuries. A tea room and a craft shop are entered through a separate building.

Admission: IR£2 ($3.50) adults, IR£1 ($1.75) students and senior citizens, 50p (90¢) children (under 6, free). There's no charge to visit the grounds.

Nearby Attractions

There are lovely ○ **scenic drives and walks** around Bantry, one of the most spectacular being to the top of Seskin Mountain, where there's a lookout with incredible views of Bantry Bay. The antiquity of the region's settlement is attested to by many stone circles, standing stones, and cairns dating to the Bronze Age.

A beautiful spot, **Gougane Barra** (which means "St. Finbar's Cleft") is a still, dark, romantic lake a little northeast of the Pass of Keimaneigh 15 miles northeast of Bantry off T64 (also well signposted on the Macroom–Glengarriff road). The River Lee rises here, and all around are deeply wooded mountains. This is where St. Finbar founded a monastery, supposedly on the small island connected by a causeway which now holds a tiny chapel (nothing remains of the good saint's 6th-century community) and eight small circular cells, dating to the early 1700s, as well as a modern chapel. Its isolation and connection with St. Finbar made this a natural refuge for Irish worshippers during Penal Law days when they were forbidden to hold mass and turned to the out-of-doors for their services. Today Gougane Barra is a national forest park, and there are signposted walks and drives through the wooded hills. There's a small admission charge per car to enter the park.

Savvy Shopping

Philip J. Dix & Co. Ltd., on New Street (tel. 027/50112), has an exceptionally good range of Waterford crystal, Belleek, Donegal porcelain, Irish-made pewter, silver, and a host of other quality giftwear.

Between Bantry and Glengarriff, on the edge of the little town of Ballylickey, you'll see an unpretentious sign in a curve of the road reading ARTIST'S STUDIO, PAINTINGS OF IRISH SCENES. ✪ **Raymond Klee's studio** (tel. 027/50157) adjoins his home; the Welsh-born artist has lived and worked all over the world and has won coveted awards from the French Salon and the Fine Arts Guild (in England). His landscape canvases are remarkable in the way they capture the elusive colors and sweeping majesty of the Irish landscape. Sunsets over a dune-rimmed strand, storm skies that set fishermen scurrying to bring curraghs to safety ashore, and graceful configurations of sun-touched clouds are there to perpetuate your memories of those same scenes. Stone-enclosed fishing harbors and mountain stretches are other subjects, and hanging on the walls of his studio are portraits of that craggy Irish farmer and fisherman you were talking to just last night over a friendly pint. Prices are surprisingly low, and there are sizes small enough to wrap securely and take back home easily, as well as larger canvases that might well become the focal point of a Stateside room. Whether or not you buy a painting, stop by to see these marvelous works and chat with an interesting and talented artist.

Evening Entertainment

If you're in Bantry in the evening, there's usually ballad singing and dancing at **Crowley's Bar,** on the Square, in the summer, and the **Bantry Bay Hotel** has entertainment every night (special Irish nights during the summer).

WHERE TO STAY

SHANGRI-LA, Bantry, Co. Cork. Tel. 027/50244. Fax 027/51417. Telex 75513 AMSL. 6 rms (4 with bath).
$ Rates (including breakfast): IR£17 ($29.75) single without bath; IR£12 ($21) per person sharing without bath; IR£2.50 ($4.40) per person additional with bath. 20% reduction for children. Dinner IR£12 ($21) extra. **Closed:** Christmas. **Parking:** Private car park.

The Shangri-La is a modern bungalow perched on a hill on the western edge of town (signposted from N71, the Bantry–Glengarriff road) overlooking Bantry Bay. The glass-enclosed front porch affords gorgeous panoramic views of the bay, and chairs are often set out on the beautifully landscaped lawn for guests to savor spectacular sunsets. Guest rooms are comfortably furnished and each is decorated around a different color; all have tea/coffee makers and two have lovely semi-poster beds. The Muckly family know the area well and love helping their guests plan their time here. Angela is a former president of the Town & Country Homes Association and is keenly interested in tourism, providing a helpful printed guide to attractions in the area. She is also a superior cook and her evening meals are memorable, with wine available. For breakfast, she offers guests a choice of the traditional Irish menu or pancakes or crumpets and honey (a nice change). There's central heating and a private car park. They also have bicycles for rent.

Worth the Extra Money

BALLYLICKEY MANOR HOUSE AND GARDEN COTTAGES, Ballylickey, Bantry Bay, Co. Cork. Tel. 027/50071. Fax 027/50124. 11 suites, 6 cottages (all with bath).
$ Rates: IR£32 ($56) per person. Breakfast IR£6 ($10.50) extra. Weekly and 3-day half-board special rates. MC, V. **Closed:** Dec–Mar.

On the main Bantry–Glengarriff road (N71) overlooking Bantry Bay, this country manor is set in landscaped lawns and gardens. In the main house, four garden suites have been installed and decorated in country style. Each has a living room, bedroom, and bath, with fridge and tea-making facilities, and can accommodate up to three. Down by the swimming pool and outstanding restaurant (see "Where to Eat," below), cottages reflect a more rustic style, although all accommodations are the last word in luxury. Most luxurious of all, breakfast will be brought in from the restaurant if you just can't face the world without that morning meal. Cottage rooms may be booked as singles or as suites with connecting bedrooms, and though there's no separate living room, each is spacious enough to accommodate a table and chairs and provide comfortable seating.

Built by Lord Kenmare as a shooting lodge over 300 years ago, the beautifully restored home is centrally located for touring the Southwest of Ireland, there are two golf courses nearby, private salmon and trout fishing is available, and on the grounds there's an outdoor swimming pool.

SEA VIEW HOUSE HOTEL, Ballylickey, Bantry, Co. Cork. Tel. 027/ 50073 or 50462. 18 rms and suites (all with bath). TV TEL
$ Rates (including breakfast): IR£32–IR£40 ($56–$70) per person. Special reduction for children. ACC, AE, DC, MC, V. **Closed:** Mid-Nov to mid-Feb.

Set back from the road in spacious grounds, Sea View House is a sparkling white three-story house built back in 1888. The deft hand of Miss Kathleen O'Sullivan, owner and manager, can be seen in every room, where antiques are placed for convenient use. Every room is different in size and shape and is furnished in traditional style and fairly shouts "gracious" (tea/coffee makings are available upon request); all have hairdryers. There's a lovely cocktail bar and a library, and the dining room is the setting for exceptional meals (see "Where to Eat," below).

WESTLODGE HOTEL, Bantry, Co. Cork. Tel. 027/50360. Fax 027/50438.
90 rms. TV TEL
$ Rates: IR£26–IR£35 ($45.50–$61.25) single; IR£44–IR£55 ($77–$96.25) double—depending on season.
Set on a hillside on the outskirts of Bantry on the eastern edge of town, this modern hotel is surrounded by extensive landscaped grounds and wooded walks. There's a leisure center with heated pool, squash courts, sauna, gym, tennis, pitch and putt, and children's play area (during summer months, there are organized activities for children). The Saddlers Tavern Lounge offers regular entertainment during the summer season.

WHERE TO EAT

O'CONNOR'S SEAFOOD RESTAURANT, The Square, Bantry. Tel. 027/ 50221.
Cuisine: SEAFOOD/TRADITIONAL/BAR FOOD.
$ Prices: Appetizers IR£2–IR£6 ($3.50–$10.50); main courses IR£9–IR£15 ($15.75–$26.25); bar food IR£2–IR£6 ($3.50–$10.50). ACC, MC, V.
Open: Bar food daily noon–6pm; dinner daily 6–10:30pm. **Closed:** Sun–Mon Nov–Mar; Sun lunch Apr–Oct.

Matt and Ann O'Connor run this cozy pub and restaurant, and their seafood dishes are truly special (try the mussels Cordon Bleu). So keen are the O'Connors on freshness that they feature a live lobster and oyster tank. There are also good local lamb and steak for nonseafood lovers, and salads, sandwiches, shepherd's pie, and the like are on tap in the bar.

Worth the Extra Money

BALLYLICKEY MANOR HOUSE AND GARDEN COTTAGES, Ballylickey, Bantry Bay, Co. Cork. Tel. 027/50071. Fax 027/50124.
Cuisine: SEAFOOD/INTERNATIONAL. **Reservations:** Essential.

$ Prices: Fixed-price meal IR£12 ($21) at lunch, IR£20 ($35) at dinner. MC, V.
Open: Apr–Nov, lunch daily 12:30–2pm; dinner daily 7–9:30pm.

In the Bantry Bay area, one of the prettiest places to spend those above-budget dining dollars is the restaurant at this exceptional manor house. The dining-room decor is that of a garden room, with an open-flame hearth in the rear on which all main meals are cooked. Your meal gets off to a good start when your order is taken in the lounge before a cheerful open fire as you sip a before-dinner drink from the bar. As for the food, your biggest problem may be to choose among seafood, lamb, beef, and other main courses offered in tempting variations.

BLAIRS COVE RESTAURANT, Blairs Cove, Durrus, Co. Cork. Tel. 027/61127.

Cuisine: SEAFOOD/INTERNATIONAL. **Reservations:** Essential.
$ Prices: Fixed-price dinner IR£16–IR£21 ($28–$36.75); Sun lunch IR£12 ($21). Service charge 10%. ACC, AE, DC, MC, V.
Open: Lunch Sun 1–2pm; dinner Tues–Sat 7–9:30pm.

About 8 miles south of Bantry on Mizen Head Peninsula, Blairs Cove is the loving creation of Phillippe and Sabine De Mey, who have converted the stone stables of a 250-year-old mansion overlooking Dunmanus Bay in West Cork into a casually elegant restaurant. In summer, meals are served on the covered terrace overlooking the courtyard. Specialties are fresh seafood, lamb, and beef grilled over a big oak-log fire in the dining room, and there's an exceptionally good wine list. Candlelight and soft piano music complete the romantic setting.

SEA VIEW HOUSE HOTEL, Ballylickey, Bantry. Tel. 027/50073 or 50462.

Cuisine: SEAFOOD/TRADITIONAL. **Reservations:** Recommended.
$ Prices: Appetizers IR£1.50–IR£3.50 ($2.65–$6.15); main courses IR£7.50–IR£10.50 ($13.30–$17.50); fixed-price dinner IR£18.50 ($32.40). ACC, AE, DC, MC, V.
Open: Mid-Feb to mid-Nov, dinner only, daily 7–9:30pm.

Sea View is known for its excellent dining room, which has won several food awards. Seafood, as you might expect in this location, is fresh from local waters, and lamb, beef, veal, and the like are selected from local sources. Service here is both friendly and professional. This is one of the nicest dinner spots in the Bantry-Glengarriff area.

GLENGARRIFF

WHAT TO SEE & DO

Glengarriff is set in a beautiful, mountain-ringed cove on Bantry Bay, and you're not likely to get out of town without taking the boat trip out to **Garinish Island,** about a mile offshore—bold boatmen have been known to stop cars in midroad to hawk the trip. As in Killarney, however, I urge you to listen to their good-humored pitch and let yourself be hawked. The lovely little island is a riot of subtropical plants, and there's a landscaped Italian garden you shouldn't miss. George Bernard Shaw loved the place and wrote portions of *St. Joan* here. The cost is nominal, and both time and money are well spent.

Savvy Shopping

It's worth a stop at some of the **craft shops** you'll see lining the streets. I've found good values here over the years, but none as good as those at **Donal Houlihan's Handcraft Shop,** Glengarriff (tel. 027/63038). The shop is on the corner just across from the road that turns up a hill to go to Killarney. And in addition to the small showroom out front, there's a large store out back up a little hill that carries lovely knitwear, mohair, cashmere, and linen, as well as caps, gloves, and scarves. The most outstanding buys here, however, are the tweeds which Donal weaves in the shed back of the shop. You're welcome to step in to see the loom in action if your timing is right.

Not only are his tweeds beautiful blends of soft Irish colors, but prices are some of the best in the country.

WHERE TO STAY

SEA FRONT, Glengarriff, Co. Cork. Tel. 027/63079. 4 rms (none with bath).
$ Rates (including breakfast): IR£16 ($28) single; IR£11 ($19.25) per person sharing. 25% reduction for children. Dinner IR£11 ($19.25) extra. No credit cards. **Closed:** Nov–Mar.

As its name implies, Sea Front looks out over the harbor. Mrs. Ann Guerin knows the area well and is always happy to help her guests plan sightseeing, fishing, or other activities. Her centrally heated house is comfortably furnished, and has a nice decor; all guest rooms have sinks. She'll prepare an evening meal, given enough notice.

THE BEARA PENINSULA

The Beara Peninsula is a 30-mile-long, mountainous finger of land between Bantry Bay and the Kenmare River. Glengarriff lies at its head; the Cork-Kerry county border runs along the Caha mountain range, the northwest corner of the peninsula falling within County Kerry. The drive around the peninsula is a pleasant day trip and can easily be a 3- or 4-hour detour en route from Glengarriff to Killarney. I must warn you, however, you may well find this wild, sparsely populated spot so appealing that the only thing for it is to stop and linger at least 1 night.

WHAT TO SEE & DO

From Glengarriff, the road follows the shoreline of Bantry Bay, winding along the rocky coastal strip at the foot of the Caha Mountains. At Ardrigole Bridge, the spectacular **Healy Pass** crosses the mountains and is an alternative (and shorter) route to Kenmare and Killarney. Farther south along Bantry Bay, the long **Bere Island** lies just offshore, with regular ferry service from **Castletownbere.** If time permits, you may want to drive the 15 miles farther south to the cable car that connects **Dursey Island** with the mainland. The ruins of **Dunboy Castle** (destroyed in 1602) lie 2 miles outside Castletownbere, and the road continues south to Black Ball Head before turning to the northwest to reach Allihies through a gap in the hills. This was once a rich copper district, and the **sea views** are absolutely magnificent. From Allihies, the road leads north along the Kenmare River through rugged scenery to the little villages of Eyeries and Lauragh, the northern end of Healy Pass, and on to Kenmare and Killarney. **Antiquities** to look for along the way are the mass rock north of Allihies, the Ogham stone in Ballycrovane, near Eyeries, that is believed to be the tallest in western Europe, and the stone circle in Canfie on the Lauragh road.

WHERE TO STAY

Castletownbere

REALT-NA-MARA, Castletownbere, Co. Cork. Tel. 027/70101. 5 rms (3 with bath).
$ Rates (including breakfast): IR£10 ($17.50) per person without bath, IR£10.50 ($18.40) with bath. Dinner IR£10 ($17.50) extra. No credit cards.

This attractive modern home perches on the high side of the main road into Castletownbere, with a stone terrace overlooking Bantry Bay. Mrs. Mary Donovan opens spacious guest rooms, some of which have views of the bay, others overlooking the mountainside. There are two family rooms, central heating, and plenty of private parking space. Mrs. Donovan is a gracious hostess, her home is spotless, and when I visited, there were lambs sporting about on the front lawn.

SHANACLOON, Castletownbere, Co. Cork. Tel. 027/70050. 7 rms (none with bath).

$ Rates (including breakfast): IR£10 ($17.50) per person. No credit cards. **Closed:** Nov–Mar.

Overlooking Bantry Bay, Shanacloon is the home of Maureen O'Brien, who welcomes guests warmly. Her gracious home is nicely furnished, and an interesting feature is the dining-room sideboard in the shape of Johnston Castle. There's one large family room, and all have double beds and sinks. Central heating and plenty of private parking.

Bere Island

HARBOUR VIEW, Bere Island, Co. Cork. Tel. 027/75011. 4 rms (2 with bath). **Ferry:** From Castletownbere.

$ Rates (including breakfast): IR£15.50 ($27.15) single; IR£12.50 ($21.90) per person sharing. 30% reduction for children. Dinner IR£10 ($17.50) extra. **Closed:** Jan–Apr.

Mrs. Ann Sullivan's large, two-story house overlooks Berehaven Harbour, and it's near the Gleanns Sailing School. Fishing, golf, and mountain walks are other activities in the vicinity. Guest rooms are attractive and comfortably furnished, and there's central heating. Mrs. Sullivan is well known for her excellent evening meals, with the freshest of seafoods her specialty.

Adrigole

BAYVIEW FARMHOUSE, Faha, Adrigole, Bantry, Co. Cork. Tel. 027/60026. 5 rms (none with bath).

$ Rates (including breakfast): IR£14 ($24.50) single; IR£11 ($19.25) per person sharing. 25% reduction for children. Dinner IR£10 ($17.50) extra. No credit cards. **Closed:** Nov–Apr.

 This bright, cheerful home overlooking Bantry Bay—9 miles from Glengarriff, 2 miles from foot of Healy Pass—is presided over by Mrs. Sheila O'Sullivan. Rooms are spacious and well appointed, and there are ponies, donkeys, and traps (riding carts) for use by guests at no charge.

WHERE TO EAT

Castletownbere

OLD COTTAGE RESTAURANT, Castletownbere, Co. Cork. Tel. 027/70430.

Cuisine: SEAFOOD/CONTINENTAL/VEGETARIAN.

$ Prices: Appetizers IR£1–IR£3 ($1.75–$5.25); main courses IR£5–IR£8 ($8.75–$14). ACC, MC, V.

Open: Lunch by appointment only, 12:30–2pm; dinner daily 6–9pm. **Closed:** Tues in winter months.

 Vincent and Lidy van Nulck brought their young family to the Beara Peninsula from Amsterdam, and their handsome restaurant has drawn raves from a regular clientele as well as visiting tourists. Lunch, which must be booked, usually consists of soup, sandwiches, salads, and burgers. At dinner, however, chef Vincent uses fish and shellfish from nearby waters, as well as salmon, lobster, steak, lamb, and pork to create his dishes (black sole pan-fried on the bone is a standout). Wine is available by the glass or bottle.

Eyeries

AN CLOCHÁN RESTAURANTS AND CRAFTS, Eyeries Cross, Inches, Beara, Co. Cork. Tel. 027/74147.

Cuisine: SEAFOOD/IRISH/VEGETARIAN/SNACKS.

$ Prices: Snacks IR£1.20–IR£5 ($2.10–$8.75); fixed-price dinner IR£6–IR£8 ($10.50–$14). No credit cards.

Open: Snacks daily 10:30am–7pm; dinner Thurs–Sun 7–9pm.

Philip and Anne Nidecker-Pearce (he's English, she's French) came to Beara almost 8 years ago, and their bright, sunny café and craft shop is an ideal stop when touring the peninsula. The daytime menu covers everything from soup and sandwiches to pizzas, omelets, and salad plates. Everything is homemade (the soup is outstanding), and they keep a good range of Irish farmhouse cheeses on hand. Wine is available by the glass or bottle. Evening menus are likely to feature Irish whiskey steak, lamb chops provençal, and Atlantic salmon with hazelnuts, wine, and cream sauce. An unexpected culinary spot in this isolated setting!

KILLARNEY & COUNTY KERRY

Cross the Kerry border and Killarney is a testament to man's appreciation of nature's gifts; the Ring of Kerry is 112 miles of scenic splendor; and the Dingle Peninsula, with its ancient monuments and beehive huts, has a special "time standing still" charm. Your entire visit could well be spent within the confines of County Kerry and you'd still go home without seeing it all. No matter how much or how little you manage to get in, however, you'll come away convinced that it well earns its honorary title, the Kingdom of Kerry.

Before the advent of Christianity, the seat of the Celtic archdruid was just outside Killarney on the Hill of Aghadoe, sometimes called the Plain of the Two Beacons, as two huge fires would be lit at this great temple as a beacon to stone circles at Lissyvigeen and the Gap of Dunloe that they should all worship at the same time.

Killarney's ancient Irish name is Cill Airne ("Church of the Sloe"); it was aptly described by the poet Moore as "Heaven's Reflex"; and *Irish Echo* columnist Joe Murphy has written, "Assuredly, he or she who has not seen Kerry or Killarney knows not the beauty of nature." The sheer perfection of that beauty has defied the best efforts of many a writer, poet, and artist to capture its essence, and your first glimpse of the lakes in their magnificent setting is certain to leave you wonderstruck. Nor will that wonder be diminished by repeated viewings, for the mercurial nature of this splendid landscape colors its grandeur with whimsical, ever-shifting nuances of sun and cloud and mist.

SEEING COUNTY KERRY

The famed scenic drive known as the Ring of Kerry circles the broad Iveragh Peninsula. A good starting point is Kenmare, ending up at Killorglin, but you can just as easily travel in the opposite direction. To cover the 112 miles properly, you should allow an entire day, with plenty of time for stops along the way. The same applies to its neighbor to the north, the Dingle Peninsula, some 132 miles long. If 2 full days are out of the question, my recommendation goes to Dingle, which has a unique character that in some mystical way seems to touch the soul.

Three especially helpful publications to pick up from the Tourist Office in Killarney are the **"Killarney Area Guide"** (which includes the lakes area), the **"Ring of Kerry Area Guide,"** and the **"Dingle Peninsula Area Guide,"** all of which have excellent maps and detailed information on points of interest.

1. KILLARNEY

And what of Killarney town? Well, it was a quiet little country market town until a visiting Englishman named Arthur Young "discovered" it in the 18th century and told the rest of the world about this natural beauty spot. Since then, of course, the rest of the world has arrived on Killarney's doorstep in droves.

☑
WHAT'S SPECIAL ABOUT KILLARNEY & COUNTY KERRY

Natural Spectacles
☐ The Lakes of Killarney, the scenic network of Upper, Middle, and Lower Lakes that lie to the west of Killarney town.

Scenic Drives
☐ The Ring of Kerry, a 112-mile-long scenic panorama of mountains, lakes, cliffs, sandy beaches, and craggy offshore islands.
☐ The Dingle Peninsula, 132 miles along clifftops, dipping into inland valleys, with hundreds of prehistoric reminders of Kerry's ancient past.

Ancient Monuments
☐ Some 2,000 archeological sites identified on the Dingle Peninsula: stone beehive huts, Ogham stones, stone forts, and standing stones.

Beaches
☐ Inch Strand, on the Dingle Peninsula, a 1-mile stretch of wide, sandy beach, a setting in the movie *Ryan's Daughter.*
☐ Banna Strand, near Tralee, a magnificent beach that was the landing place of ill-fated Irish hero Roger Casement.

Right here, I'd like to dispel what seems to be a very popular myth about Killarney: If this is a "tourist trap," then the world could do with a few more like it! Sure, there are jarveys lined up ad infinitum, each hawking his own jaunting-car ride. But no matter which car you climb aboard, you can do so in the sure knowledge that fees are carefully controlled (so you won't be "ripped off") and you'll hear at least one good story (like the one about the lad who plunged into the Devil's Punchbowl and was never heard from until his poor mother got a postcard from Australia asking would she please send along his clothes). What I'm trying to get across is that you'll get your money's worth in Killarney.

ORIENTATION

ARRIVING Killarney is 190 miles southwest of Dublin, 54 miles northwest of Cork, 68 miles southwest of Limerick, 21 miles west of Kenmare, and 42 miles southeast of Dingle. There is bus service from most points in Ireland, and train service from Dublin, Limerick, and Cork. The bus and train station is off East Avenue (across from the Great Southern Hotel). For all bus and train information, call 064/31067.

DEPARTING For those heading north to Limerick or Galway, there is the quick inland route via Abbeyfeale and Newcastle West (N21), the long and lovely coastal drive along the Shannon estuary (N69), or a delightful ferry alternative that shortens both of these routes.

If, like me, you fancy a ferry ride any time one comes along, you can take the Shannon car-ferry from Tarbert over to Killimer in County Clare, about a 30-mile drive into Limerick. The crossing takes 20 minutes aboard the *Shannon Willow* or *Shannon Heather*, and from April through September there are 30 sailings per day, beginning at 7am and ending at 9:30pm (first sailing on Sunday at 9am), from October through March the last sailing is at 7:30pm. Departures from Tarbert, County Kerry, are on the half hour, and from Killimer, County Clare, on the hour; during peak holiday periods, there are half-hourly sailings from each side. For your car and all passengers, you'll pay IR£6 ($10.50) one way, IR£8.50 ($14.90) round-trip. Those on foot pay IR£1 ($1.75) one way, IR£1.50 ($2.65) round-trip.

TOURIST INFORMATION The **Tourist Office** is in the Town Hall on Main Street (tel. 064/31633), open July to September, Monday through Friday from 9am to

8pm and on Saturday from 10am to 1pm; other months, Monday through Friday from 9:15am to 5:30pm.

TOWN LAYOUT   Killarney is a small town, easy to find your way around. **Main Street** is its chief artery, and becomes **High Street** at its northern end. **New Street** runs to the west of Main Street, and **Plunkett Street** (which becomes College Street) runs east.

GETTING AROUND

By Bus   There's no local bus service, but Bus Eireann runs several good day trips to nearby locations, including the Ring of Kerry and the Dingle Peninsula.

By Taxi   Taxi ranks are at the railway station and in College Square, and taxis are unmetered. Phone 31331 for hire.

On Foot   It's easy walking in town, with many beauty spots within longish walking distance from the town center.

By Car   Killarney's streets are narrow and a little nervewracking when traffic is heavy, but there's a good network of wide major roads outside the city center. There's a large municipal parking lot (entrance from New Street) in the center of town back of the Town Hall, another on East Avenue (across from the railway station), and a third at the intersection of High Street and New Road.

FAST FACTS

Area Code   The telephone prefix for the area is 064.

Emergencies   Dial 999 and ask for the service you require (police, medical, fire).

Post Office   The General Post Office is on New Street, open Monday through Saturday from 9am to 5:30pm.

WHAT TO SEE & DO

The signposted **Killarney Tourist Trail** takes about 2 hours walking time at a leisurely pace. Also check with the Tourist Office for **conducted walking tours** of Killarney town.

A STROLL AROUND TOWN

True to its long ecclesiastical history, Killarney offers the visitor several sightseeing attractions of a religious nature. The **Franciscan friary** on College Street dates from 1860 and is notable for the fine stained-glass window above its main entrance. Opposite the friary, look for the **Memorial to the Four Kerry Poets** (Pierce Ferriter and Geoffrey O'Donoghue, from the 1600s, and Aodhgan O'Rahilly and Eoghan Ruadh O'Sullivan, from the 1700s). **St. Mary's Church** (Church of Ireland) at the foot of Main Street, built in Early English style, has a richly adorned interior. **St. Mary's Cathedral** (Catholic) on New Street is a splendid Gothic structure with interesting stained-glass windows and an awe-inspiring interior.

Just across the road from the cathedral, the wooded walks of **Knockreer Estate** offer a natural contrast to man's religious adoration and one more of Killarney's beauty spots in which to commune with nature. This is part of the large Killarney National Park, and a short walk will bring you to **Knockreer House,** which holds exhibits of the flora, fauna, and wildlife of this area. A longer walk takes you to the ruins of **Ross Castle** (about 1½ miles from the town center) on a long peninsula out into the Lower Lake. Built in the 14th century, it was a prominent fortification during the Cromwellian wars in the 1600s. The ruins can also be reached by car from the main Kenmare road, and you can actually begin your tour of the lakes here, where boats are for rent (see Section 2, below).

THE TOP ATTRACTION

MUCKROSS HOUSE, Killarney National Park, Killarney, Co. Kerry. Tel. 064/31440.

Surrounded by marvelously landscaped gardens 4 miles south of Killarney off N71, the Elizabethan-style Muckross House was built by Henry Arthur Herbert, a wealthy Kerry M.P., in 1843. Americans bought it in 1911, and in 1932 the entire estate was presented as a gift to the Irish people. The first two floors are furnished in the manner of the great houses of Ireland, while its upper floors hold some fascinating exhibits of maps, prints, and other documents, as well as a small wildlife and bird collection.

Housed in its basement is a marvelous folk museum and crafts shops that bring to vivid life the Kerry country life-style of a time long past. Exhibits include a country pub, printshop, dairy, carpentry shop, and weaving shop. You'll see craftspeople at work and you can purchase their products in the gift shop. There's a light, airy tea shop off the courtyard. Drivers will find ample parking space very near the house.

Admission: Park and gardens, free; house and museum, IR£2 ($3.50) adult, IR£1 ($1.75) children.

Open: July–Aug, daily 9am–7pm; other months, daily 9am–6pm.

MORE ATTRACTIONS NEARBY

Walkers will be able to reach the following on foot, and, of course, jaunting cars are available for nonwalkers.

Three miles outside Killarney on the main Kenmare road (N71), the ruins of **Muckross Abbey** are about a 10-minute walk from Muckross House. Dating from 1448, it occupied the site of an even earlier ecclesiastical establishment, and the ruins are in remarkably good condition.

About a mile beyond Muckross House, signposted from the main Kenmare road, the 60-foot-high **Torc Waterfall** sits in a beautiful wooded area and is reached by way of a scenic footpath that continues up the top of the falls, where there are magnificent views of the lakes.

In the opposite direction, 3 miles from the town center, the **Prince of Peace Church** is in Fossa, on the main Ring of Kerry road (R562). It was designed and built by men and women from the four provinces of Ireland, and its back wall is glass, bringing the wondrous beauty of mountains and lakes into focus as an integral part of religious worship. Catholics will find mass in this beautiful building a very special experience.

SPORTS & RECREATION

Check with the Tourist Office or the free *Weekly Killarney* to see if anything is on at Fitzgerald Stadium on Lewis Road, the venue for Sunday **hurling and Gaelic football matches.** Killarney **horseracing meets** occur in May and July, and it's worth juggling your schedule to catch them—the town assumes a "country fair" air.

You may go **swimming** in any of the lakes without charge, and you'll only need a license to go **fishing** for salmon—none needed to go after all those lovely brown trout. Donie Brosnan, at the Handy Store on Kenmare Place, is the man to fix you up with bait and up-to-the-minute information about the best fishing spots. There are excellent championship **golf courses** in and near Killarney (the Tourist Office can furnish a complete list), and most have clubs, caddies, and caddy-cars available at the clubhouse.

SAVVY SHOPPING
Crafts

JOHN J. MURPHY, Weaver, Currow Rd., Farranfore, Co. Kerry. Tel. 066/64659.

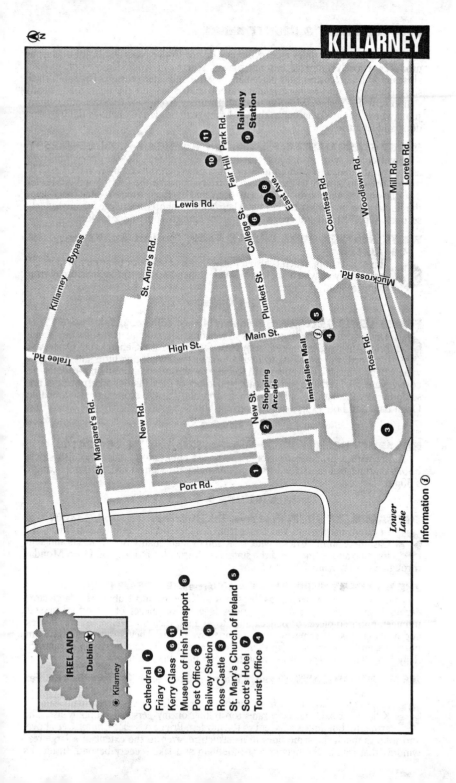

KILLARNEY

Railway Station

Park Rd.

Fair Hill

Lewis Rd.

College St.

St. Anne's Rd.

Plunkett St.

Main St.

High St.

New St.

Shopping Arcade

Innisfallen Mall

Port Rd.

Tralee Rd.

St. Margaret's Rd.

New Rd.

Killarney Bypass

Countess Rd.

Muckross Rd.

Woodlawn Rd.

Mill Rd.

Loreto Rd.

Ross Rd.

East Ave.

Lower Lake

Information *i*

IRELAND

Dublin

Killarney

Cathedral ❶
Friary ❿
Kerry Glass ❻ ⓫
Museum of Irish Transport ❽
Post Office ❷
Railway Station ❾
Ross Castle ❸
St. Mary's Church of Ireland ❺
Scott's Hotel ❼
Tourist Office ❹

Approximately 10 miles from Killarney on the Tralee road (N22), John Murphy produces a lovely range of woolen shawls, scarves in wool, lambswool, mohair, alpaca, and linen/cotton, and placemats in wool and linen/cotton. The small retail shop is an extension to his larger workshop and is just off the main road (clearly signposted). He's open Monday through Saturday from 9am to 6pm; other times, John (whose home is adjacent to the workshop) will be glad to open—simply go next door and ring the bell.

KERRY GLASS LIMITED, Fair Hill, Park Rd., Killarney. Tel. 064/32587.
Vivid colors swirl in the heart of lovely paperweights, bowls, plates, miniature animals and birds, vases, and a host of other objects produced by Kerry Glass. The main workshop is next to the Franciscan friary opposite the Great Southern Hotel. The glassmakers work right in the showroom, and it's fascinating to watch them shape the liquid glass and apply the colors. There's also a shop on College Street that sells seconds. Open Monday through Friday from 8am to 1pm and 2 to 4pm.

WHITE HEATHER HOME CRAFTS SHOP, Plunkett St., Killarney. Tel. 064/32160.
This small shop, which is also a florist, has a good stock of attractive craft gift items, many of which are locally made. Open Monday through Saturday from 10am to 5pm.

Art Gallery

FRANK LEWIS GALLERY, 6 Bridewell Lane, Killarney. Tel. 064/31108.
This excellent small gallery is a welcome addition to the Killarney scene. Bridewell Lane is entered from New Street near the General Post Office, and it's worth the walk just to take a look at this interesting little lane housing a variety of artisans. It's the only one in Killarney where all the more-than-a-century-old cottages are still lived in. Specialties are landscapes of the Killarney area, portraits, and sculptures by local artists, all of which are for sale. Tea and scones are also available. Open days and hours vary; call for current hours.

Books

KILLARNEY BOOKSHOP, 32 Main St., Killarney. Tel. 064/34108.
Along with a nice selection of Irish-interest publications, this shop also stocks books on the latest bestseller lists. Open Monday through Saturday from 9:30am to 5:30pm.

Clothing & Gifts

THE CASHMERE SHOP, East Ave. Rd., Killarney. Tel. 064/33306.
Located just around the curve from the Town Hall and Tourist Office, the Cashmere Shop carries a wide selection of high-quality tweed jackets and suits for men and women, and the staff is both friendly and helpful. Open Monday through Saturday from 10am to 5pm.

THE KILKENNY SHOP, Main St., Killarney. Tel. 064/31888.
Under the same ownership as the shops in Kilkenny and Dublin, this large store carries huge stocks of Irish-made goods (over 3,000 pieces of Waterford crystal, umpteen hundred pieces of Belleek and Royal Tara, Irish porcelain character figures, and a whole host of other items) at competitive prices. They'll ship and insure any purchase, and you can write for their extensive mail-order catalog. Open in summer, daily from 9am to 11pm; other months, daily from 9:30 to 6pm.

MACKEN OF IRELAND, Fossa, Killarney, Co. Kerry. Tel. 064/34766. Fax 064/34761.
Although a short drive from the town center (3 miles) out the main Ring of Killarney road, this shop rates top billing on my personal shopping list. The attractive building is adjacent to the modern Prince of Peace Church (see above) and follows much the same lines in its structure, even to the extent of a large rear window that frames the magnificent mountain and lake scenery beyond. Inside, its

shelves are brimming with what must be Killarney's largest stock of Aran knits, as well as a wide selection from such top Irish designers as Jimmy Hourihan, Henry White, and Brian Tucker. There's also an interesting line of women's clothes called Private Collection by a collective of leading designers around the country, and a wide range of tweed, cashmere, and mohair jackets. In the extensive gift department, Belleek, Tipperary Crystal, Cladagh jewelry, and Duiske hand-cut glass from County Kilkenny are just a few of the hundreds of Irish-made items. There's a bright, cheerful coffee shop with a terrace out back for fine weather dining.

SPECIAL EVENTS

Killarney is an ideal base from which to be a part of one of Ireland's major annual events, the **Rose of Tralee International Festival,** held in Tralee, just 20 miles to the north. For 6 days and nights in late August the competition is fierce to see which of the international beauties gathered in Tralee best fits the time-honored description "lovely and fair as the rose of the summer." The Rose of Tralee International Festival, however, is a far cry from other beauty pageants. This festival is one of lighthearted fun and frolic, with parades, pipe bands, street entertainment, inter-festival singing competitions for the **Folk Festival of Ireland** (which takes place at the same time!) and, finally, the crowning of the Rose.

There are usually several package deals that cover transportation and accommodations; details can be obtained from the General Secretary, Festival of Kerry Office, 5 Lower Castle Street, Tralee, County Kerry. If you're making your own arrangements, be sure to do it well in advance, whether you plan to stay in Tralee or in Killarney, 20 miles to the south.

In mid-August, Killorglin lets its hair down in 3 days of what many Irish call sheer madness disguised under the name of the ✪ **Puck Fair.** It has been held every year since 1613, and things get off to a right rowdy start when a tremendous male (or puck) goat is hauled up to a high platform in the square and crowned as King of the Fair. What follows is a sort of carnival/country fair/free-for-all, as most pubs stay open around the clock, and there's all sorts of street entertainment, and over on the green, some pretty serious horse and cattle trading. Just how all this began is a matter of dispute: Some say a goat bleated to alert a shepherd boy of approaching enemy forces and he, in turn, alerted the town about impending attack. Traditionally it is a gathering place for the country's traveling people, who come to drive some hard bargains in the horse-swapping business, catch up with travelers' gossip, and indulge in nonstop revelry.

For 1 week in mid-May, Celts from six countries converge on Killarney to celebrate and preserve their ancient ties during **Pan-Celtic Week.** There are interesting exhibits on display, and the week's schedule includes sports competitions, workshops, concerts, pipe-band competitions, informal seisiuns, dancing, and a marvelous Cornish Pen Gwyn torchlight procession led by a black-robed, jaw-snapping horse's skull, with musicians of all nationalities hypnotizing sidewalk spectators with ancient dance rhythms that inevitably draw them into the procession. Admission prices are minimal, and many events are free. Check with the Tourist Board for details.

EVENING ENTERTAINMENT

After dark, take your pick from singing pubs, traditional music sessions, cabaret, or theater performances.

SIAMSA TIRE, National Folk Theatre, Godfrey Place, Tralee, Co. Kerry. Tel. 066/23055, or 066/23049 (for credit cards).

✪ At the top of my own list of favorite nighttime entertainment in the Killarney area is at least one performance of Siamsa (pronounced *"Sheem*-sa"), the National Folk Theatre troupe that performs in their own Siamsa Tire (*"Tee*-ra") Theatre in nearby Tralee. "Merrymaking" is the English translation of the Gaelic *siamsa*, and this is as merry a show as you'll come across, as it depicts through music, song, dance, and mime Irish country life of the past. In a stage setting of thatched cottage and farmyard, expert performers go about the business of thatching, churning, milking, harvesting, and other routine tasks that were the foundation of everyday life on the farm. So professional is the performance that it will no doubt surprise you—as it did me—to know that the troupe operates on a very limited budget, with just a handful of full-time performers and that most of those skilled musicians, actors, singers, and dancers give hours and hours of their time to perfect the show and travel with it on a strictly voluntary basis.

Admission: IR£5 ($8.75) adults, IR£4 ($7) children and senior citizens; IR£15 ($26.25) family ticket (two adults and up to four children). There's a special bus and theater ticket for IR£7.50 ($13.15), available at Deros Tours, 22 Main Street, Killarney (tel. 064/31251).

HOTEL GLENEAGLE, Killarney, Co. Kerry. Tel. 064/31870.

There's something on every night at the Gleneagle, with the program changing every 2 nights or so. Cabaret, jazz, ballads, folk songs, traditional music, and stories as only the Irish can tell them are on tap, with top-flight entertainers like the Wolfe Tones, Susan McCann, and Joe Dolan frequently on the bill. There's dancing after the show until 1am, or you might want to opt for the Eagle's Nest, a disco that often features jazz sessions or pub theater (small admission charge). A resident pianist and guitarist hold sway in the Eagle's Whistle Lounge (no cover charge), and they'll have you singing your heart out in a true Irish sing-along.

Admission: IR£7 ($12.25); IR£14 ($24.50) family ticket (two adults and two children). **Bus:** Free shuttle-bus service to the hotel from Three Lakes Cinema between 8pm and 1am.

Traditional Music

Killarney has two singing pubs to tempt your vocal cords. There's ballad singing and general hilarity (which can get pretty hokey if the likes of "Dixie" breaks out) in the backroom of ✪ **The Laurels** pub on Main Street (tel. 064/31149), from May to October, and letters pour in from readers with enthusiastic endorsement of this liveliest of Killarney pubs. Go along about 9pm, when things are just tuning up. The larger and ever-so-slightly more subdued **Danny Mann** pub, on New Street, installs ballad groups every night right through the year, and in summer it's likely to be packed with Yanks rendering heartfelt versions of such stock Irish exports as "Danny Boy" and "When Irish Eyes Are Smiling." The action starts about 9:30pm.

The **Crock of Gold,** 19 High Street (tel. 064/32432), features music every night of the week and has proved very popular with our readers.

During summer months there's ceili dancing (you'll recognize the ancestor of our square dancing) Friday through Sunday at the **Ceili Club,** Scotts Hotel, East Avenue (tel. 064/31060), and traditional Irish music every night of the week in Scotts Pub.

The **Whitegates Hotel,** on Muckross Road (tel. 064/31164), has a traditional music seisiun and sing-along on Friday night and other entertainment on Saturday, as well as a sing-along session on Sunday at 12:30pm during the season.

WHERE TO STAY

When it comes to accommodations, Killarney has an abundance of high-quality, low-priced B&Bs and guesthouses, as well as some elegant luxury hotels whose prices are high but not exorbitant. Some of the "Out of Town" places are within reasonable walking distance of town, though not with heavy luggage.

IN TOWN

Bed-and-Breakfast

THE HIBERNIAN, 21 New St., Killarney, Co. Kerry. Tel. 064/31258. 5 rms (none with bath).

$ Rates (including breakfast): IR£10 ($17.50) per person. 33⅓% reduction for children. No credit cards. **Closed:** Nov–Feb.

The Hibernian is the home of Maura Brosnan and her charming family. Mrs. Brosnan is very happy to help you book tours by jaunting car, by coach, by boat, or even by bike. The house has three stories and the five guest rooms are comfortably and attractively furnished. Bathrooms are shared, but all rooms have sinks. There couldn't be a more convenient location.

KNOCKCULLEN, New Rd., Killarney, Co. Kerry. Tel. 064/33915. 3 rms (1 with bath).
$ Rates (including breakfast): IR£10.50 ($18.40) per person without bath, IR£12 ($21) per person with bath. No credit cards. **Closed:** Nov–Feb.
Knockcullen is the sparkling-clean, two-story home of Marie and Sean O'Brien, on a quiet, tree-lined street. The four guest rooms are all attractively furnished, and Marie's table is laden with fresh and healthy fare—she even caters to vegetarians at breakfast.

MYSTICAL ROSE, Woodlawn Rd., Killarney, Co. Kerry. Tel. 064/31453. 3 rms (none with bath).
$ Rates (including breakfast): IR£10 ($17.50) per person. 33⅓% reduction for children. No credit cards. **Closed:** Nov–Feb.
Mrs. O'Mahony is the friendly hostess of this bungalow with its beautiful rose garden (which guests are free to use). The house is located near the Killarney lake district and she will arrange tours for guests who want it. She has three nice, clean rooms and they all have sinks.

ST. ANTHONY'S VILLA, Cork Rd., Killarney, Co. Kerry. Tel. 064/31534. 3 rms (all with bath).
$ Rates (including breakfast): IR£12.50 ($21.90) per person. 25% reduction for children. No credit cards. **Closed:** Dec–Feb.
Mrs. Mary O'Connell is the friendly hostess of this attractive, modern bungalow that is convenient to town and the bus and railway station. She is very helpful and will arrange tours around Killarney for anyone who may want it.

WIND-WAY TOWN HOUSE, New Rd., Killarney, Co. Kerry. Tel. 064/32835. 4 rms (all with bath).
$ Rates (including breakfast): IR£12 ($21) per person. No credit cards. **Parking:** Private car park.
Bridie and Don Long are both enthusiastic about helping their guests get the fullest enjoyment from their Killarney stay. The house is in a quiet residential street a few minutes' walk of the town center and the Knockreer Estate portion of the national park. Its four guest rooms are nicely done up in bright colors, with a bit of decor whimsey in some. The Linden House restaurant (see "Where to Eat," below) is just across the road, a great convenience for the evening meal. There's central heat and a private car park.

Guesthouses

THE GARDENS, Countess Rd., Killarney, Co. Kerry. Tel. 064/31147. 21 rms (all with bath).
$ Rates: IR£20 ($35) single; IR£16 ($28) per person sharing. 25% reduction for children. No credit cards.

This charming place, owned and run by Mary and Tom O'Reilly, is set in private grounds very convenient to the railway station and the town center. In the main two-story building, 11 nicely appointed bedrooms are on the ground floor, motel style, and 10 are on the floor above. One measure of the O'Reillys consideration for their guests is the installation of a TV/reading lounge designated

"No Smoking" and a *separate*, similar lounge for smokers! There's central heat and good parking. I can't praise the O'Reillys highly enough. Their establishment is spotlessly clean, and their full Irish breakfast superb.

LINDEN HOUSE, New Rd., Killarney, Co. Kerry. Tel. 064/31379. 11 rms (all with bath).

$ Rates (including breakfast): IR£15 ($26.25) single; IR£13 ($22.75) per person sharing. 25% reduction for children. ACC, MC, V. **Closed:** Dec–Jan.

 Set on this quiet residential street, just one block down from Main Street, Linden House's location is ideal. The Knoblauch family have won special praise from our readers for the quality of their lodgings and the warmth of their hospitality. There's something of an old-world, small-inn air about the three-story stucco house, and bedrooms are exceptionally comfortable and attractively appointed. There's central heat and one of the best moderately priced restaurants in Killarney, with a large local following (see "Where to Eat," below). Popular with traveling Irish as well as tourists, Linden House is one place you must be certain to reserve ahead.

Small Hotels

Both the hotels below are located in the town center, and one offers a discount to our readers.

ARBUTUS HOTEL, College St., Killarney, Co. Kerry. Tel. 064/31037. 35 rms (all with bath).

$ Rates (including breakfast): High season, IR£27 ($47.25) single; IR£24 ($42) per person sharing. Low season, IR£23 ($40.25) single; IR£20 ($35) per person sharing. Reduced weekly rates available. ACC, DC, MC, V.

This three-story, distinctively Irish hotel has been owned and operated by the Buckley family for more than 65 years. There's an old-fashioned air about the place, enhanced by such touches as lots of etched and stained glass, a fireplace in the lounge, and an intimate lounge-bar presided over by the amiable Dennis, who has been here many years, as has his wife, Sheila. I'm particularly fond of the cozy dining room, and connecting to the Arbutus is a low-priced coffee shop called Pat's that offers very good value. Bedrooms are comfortably furnished, and this is a good place to settle if you plan to use Killarney as a base for as long as a week.

BELVEDERE HOTEL, New St., Killarney, Co. Kerry. Tel. 064/31133. 12 rms (all with bath). TV.

$ Rates (including breakfast): IR£21 ($36.75) single; IR£18 ($31.50) per person sharing. 10% discount to readers who have this book with them when checking in. ACC, AE, DC, MC, V.

Stephanie and John Lyne run this friendly small hotel just off Main Street. Frommer fans themselves, they offer a discount on room rates to readers of this book. Guest rooms are comfortably furnished, there's an old-style pub with snooker tables, and their Stephanie's Restaurant serves lunch and dinner at moderate prices.

A Hostel

THE FOUR WINDS INTERNATIONAL HOSTEL, 43 New St., Killarney, Co. Kerry. Tel. 064/33094. 100 beds.

$ Rates: IR£5.50 ($9.65) per person. 10% discount for readers of this book who bring it with them at check-in. Continental breakfast IR£2.50 ($4.40) extra. No credit cards.

The Four Winds is one of the nicer things to happen in Killarney in recent years. It provides comfortable, attractive, and inexpensive lodgings right in the center of town. There are sleeping accommodations for 80 in bunk-bedded dormitories, as well as four private rooms, plus a lounge, dining room, and kitchen. The building is centrally heated, and there are two open fireplaces for inner warmth. There's also a private garden for the exclusive use of guests. Guides and maps to local outdoor activities are provided, and they are agents for Raleigh Rent-a-Bike.

NEARBY ACCOMMODATIONS
Bed-and-Breakfast

ALPINE HEIGHTS, Gap of Dunloe, Killarney, Co. Kerry. Tel. 064/44284.
5 rms (none with bath).
$ Rates (including breakfast): IR£15 ($26.25) single; IR£11 ($19.25) per person sharing. 25% reduction for children. No credit cards. **Closed:** Nov–Mar.
This large, modern bungalow is the home of Teresa Ferris and her family, which includes five engaging children. Less than a half mile from the Gap of Dunloe (4½ miles from the town center on the Gap of Dunloe road), this pretty home, set behind white gateposts in a vibrantly green lawn, features guest rooms decorated in soft pastels (some with showers; all with sinks), built-in wardrobes, a bright, sunny dining room, central heating, and superb views of green fields and lofty mountains. The family-oriented Mrs. Ferris keeps a crib on hand for visiting youngsters. She is noted for her home-baking, and is happy to steer guests to nearby attractions such as Kate Kearney's Cottage, where there's traditional music and dancing.

COFFEY'S LOCH LEIN HOUSE, Fossa, Killarney, Co. Kerry. Tel. 064/ 31260. 10 rms (8 with bath).
$ Rates (including breakfast): IR£15 ($26.25) single without bath; IR£11 ($19.25) per person sharing without bath; IR£2 ($3.50) per person additional with bath. 25% reduction for children. No credit cards. **Closed:** Nov–Feb. **Parking:** Gravel car park.

This lovely modern, one-story guesthouse is the domain of the delightful Kathleen Coffey. Just 3 miles from Killarney, it's set in green lawns sloping down to the Lower Lake, and is approached via a country lane that's signposted on the main Ring of Kerry road (R562) just past the golf course (on your left as you approach from Killarney). The L-shaped guesthouse holds the exceptionally large and well furnished guest rooms. Natural-wool bedspreads were woven in Kerry mills. There's a TV lounge with a fireplace and a bright, window-walled dining room, as well as central heating.

As attractive and sparkling as is the house, it is outshone by Mrs. Coffey, a small, pixielike lady who is an accomplished conversationalist and storyteller. At least one of her five sons and five daughters is usually in attendance, as interested in guests' welfare as their mother. The family has been in this area for generations, giving the Coffeys a treasure trove of local legends they're only too happy to pass on to you—very special mementos of your Irish holiday.

MARIAN HOUSE, Woodlawn Rd., Killarney, Co. Kerry. Tel. 064/31275.
6 rms (none with bath).
$ Rates (including breakfast): IR£13.50 ($23.65) single; IR£10.50 ($18.40) per person sharing. 25% reduction for children. No credit cards.
Marian House sits just off the main Muckross road, less than half a mile from the town center, atop a small hill that looks out onto the mountains. It's a centrally heated, two-story house with six prettily decorated guest rooms, all with sinks. Mrs. Eileen Lucey is the hostess, always helpful to guests in planning their Killarney stay.

SHILLELAGH HOUSE, Knockasarnett, Aghadoe, Killarney, Co. Kerry. Tel. 064/31898 or 34030. 6 rms (4 with bath).
$ Rates (including breakfast): IR£15 ($26.25) single without bath; IR£11 ($19.25) per person sharing without bath; IR£1.50 ($2.65) per person additional with bath. 20% reduction for children. No credit cards. **Closed:** Nov–Feb.
Mrs. Mary O'Connor's modern two-story home is about 1½ miles from the town center in Aghadoe Heights, just off the main Ring of Kerry road (R562). The pretty guest rooms are comfortably furnished and have quilted headboards for the beds. There's a lounge with TV, and full Irish breakfasts are served in the bright dining room.

WHITE HOUSE, Lissivigeen Cross, Killarney, Co. Kerry. Tel. 064/ 32207. 6 rms (5 with bath).
$ Rates (including breakfast): IR£11 ($19.25) per person without bath, IR£12.50

($21.90) per person with bath. 50% reduction for children. No credit cards. **Closed:** Nov–Mar.

Mrs. Kathleen Doherty is the extremely helpful hostess of this luxurious, modern house half a mile from Killarney off the main Cork road (N22) with a beautiful view of the mountains. Its location is convenient to shopping, restaurants, etc. An evening meal is available with advance notice.

Farmhouses

CARRIGLEA HOUSE, Muckross Rd., Killarney, Co. Kerry. Tel. 064/ 31116. 9 rms (6 with bath).

$ Rates (including breakfast): IR£12 ($21) per person without bath, IR£13.50 ($23.65) per person with bath. No credit cards. **Closed:** Nov–Mar.

A beautiful 200-year-old country home, Carriglea sits a little over a mile from the town center on a rise overlooking the lakes. From the sweeping front lawn, approached by a tree-lined curving avenue, the view takes in the Lower Lake and Purple, Torc, and Mangerton Mountains. Marie and Michael Beasley own this working dairy farm and take great pleasure in helping guests plan their holiday time in Killarney. The lovely old centrally heated house has spacious rooms furnished with many antiques and tastefully decorated in restful colors. Particularly noteworthy is the dining room's chandelier of gold, blue, and pink porcelain. There are several additional guest rooms in the adjoining coachhouse. One large coachhouse room has a bay window overlooking the front lawn.

GAP VIEW FARM, Firies, Killarney, Co. Kerry. Tel. 066/64378. 6 rms (5 with bath).

$ Rates (including breakfast): IR£14 ($24.50) single without bath; IR£11 ($19.25) per person sharing without bath; IR£1.50 ($2.65) per person additional with bath. 33⅓% reduction for children. No credit cards. **Closed:** Nov–Apr.

Mrs. Kearney is the hostess of this large 18th-century farmhouse 8 miles from Killarney, off the Farranfore road (N22), with its lovely views of the Gap of Dunloe and the Kerry mountains. The house is centrally heated as well as having turf fires, and fresh farm foods are served at every meal. There is a garden that guests can use, and six lovely bedrooms, all with good views.

Hostels

AGHADOE HOUSE, Killarney International Youth Hostel, Killarney, Co. Kerry. Tel. 064/31240. Fax 064/34300. 220 beds.

$ Rates: IR£5 ($8.75) per person. No credit cards.

Killarney's An Oige youth hostel is one of the best in the country. An impressive 360-year-old brick mansion set in 75 wooded acres, it's about 2 miles from the town center (signposted on R562, the main Ring of Kerry road), with a courtesy bus from the railway station (phone the warden when you arrive or notify the hostel in advance). There's a TV room, self-catering kitchen and dining room, free hot showers, laundry facilities, rental bikes, and a small store. It's absolutely necessary to book in advance during July and August, and because many hostelers are hikers as well, the wardens here (Mr. and Mrs. Claffey) ask that you be reminded that the mountains in the area can be quite dangerous—if you intend hiking or climbing them, you should be sure to notify the Claffeys of your intended route. The Claffeys can arrange discount tours of the Ring of Kerry, as well as the lakes and several other areas.

FOSSA HOLIDAY HOSTEL, Fossa, Killarney, Co. Kerry. Tel. 064/31497. 60 beds.

$ Rates: IR£5 ($8.75) per person; IR£13 ($22.75) per person for bed, breakfast, and dinner.

The O'Halloran family run this bright, modern hostel 3 miles from Killarney on the main Ring of Kerry road (R562), just beyond and across the road from the Prince of Peace Church (look for the large Texaco sign). In addition to dormitories, there are family rooms, as well as a fully equipped kitchen, well-stocked shop, TV lounge, games room, laundry facilities, tennis court, and children's play area. A good, moderately priced restaurant, which also serves take-aways, is on the premises. They have bikes for rent and can help you arrange fishing or golf nearby. The O'Hallorans are always on hand to provide friendly assistance.

Self-Catering

KILLARNEY LAKELAND COTTAGES, Muckross, Killarney, Co. Kerry.
Tel. 064/31538. Fax 064/34113. Telex 73952. 19 cottages.
$ **Rates:** IR£125–IR£345 ($218.75–$603.75) per week. Special midweek and weekend rates available. ACC, MC, V.
These high-standard holiday cottages are about 3 miles from Killarney (signposted on Muckross road), just a short distance from the lakes, set in 12 acres of parkland adjoining the Killarney National Park. There are two cottage plans: The larger Dinis style sleeps up to eight; the Torc style sleeps up to six. Cottages are carpeted and kitchens are fully equipped. On the grounds are a tennis court, children's play equipment, a games room, food store, laundry service, bikes, fishing equipment, and TVs for rent. They'll be happy to send a fully illustrated brochure upon request.

READERS RECOMMEND

The Purple Heather, *Gap of Dunloe, Beaufort, Killarney, County Kerry (tel. 064/44266). "This is one of the most enjoyable B&Bs we stayed in on our trip to Ireland. Tim and Nora Moriarty have six lovely children, and four of them gave us a display of Irish dancing in full costume. Tim filled us in on the history of the Gap of Dunloe and the surrounding area, and Nora served us coffee and scones before we retired. We think they deserve full marks."* —David MacSweeney, Vienna, Va.

Muckross Lodge, *Muckross Road, Killarney, County Kerry (tel. 064/32660). "Mrs. Bernadette O'Sullivan is a truly delightful person, and her warmth and kindness make you feel so welcome. Her home is immaculate, tastefully decorated, and each room is en suite."* —Irene Klar, North Palm Beach, Fla.

Shraheen House, *Ballycasheen, Killarney, County Kerry (tel. 064/31286). "We loved this very attractive two-story house in a quiet area and surrounded by 2½ acres of lawn. Mrs. Maureen Fleming was the ideal hostess, and helped us with touring, as well as directing us to lovely forest walks. It's only 1 mile out of town on an extension of Woodlawn Road."* —Pat Higgins, Syracuse, N.Y.

The Wren's Nest, *Woodhaven, Woodlawn Road, Killarney, County Kerry (tel. 064/33580). "This lovely new home is only about a 15-minute walk from the town center, and we learned that Ann Wrenn's husband has actually dug the foundation and done all the masonry work himself. It sits in its own grounds in a peaceful setting, and our en suite room was immaculate. The Wrenns are friendly, warm, and helpful—reason enough for staying here."* —William Anthony, Giessen, West Germany.

Glenheather, *Caherslee, Tralee, County Kerry (tel. 066/21969). "Ann O'Connor is truly a perfect example of what I have always wished for when I imagined visiting Ireland and meeting its warm and wonderful people. In our 7-month sojourn in Europe we must have stayed in well over 100 accommodations, but there was nothing to equal Ann's home! We had a beautifully decorated bedroom, and our breakfast table was elegant, with linen napkins, beautiful china, a French coffee maker, and scrumptious food. We all felt like royalty!"* —Judy Wells, San Anselmo, Calif.

RECOMMENDATIONS IN BRIEF

Bed-and-Breakfast   The Silver Spruce, New Road, Killarney, County Kerry (tel. 064/31376), Mrs. Mary Sheehan; **St. Rita's Villa,** Mill Road, Killarney, County Kerry (tel. 064/31517), Mrs. Peggie Cronin.

Farmhouses   Mrs. Kathy Brosnan, Woodlawn Road, Killarney, County Kerry (tel. 064/32782); **Lois Na Manach Farmhouse,** Mill Road, Killarney, County Kerry (tel. 064/31283), Mrs. Noreen O'Sullivan; **Gorman's Farmhouse,** Tralee Road, Killarney, County Kerry (tel. 064/33149), Moira and Jim O'Gorman.

WHERE TO EAT

PUB GRUB

KIELY'S BAR AND RESTAURANT, College St., Killarney. Tel. 064/31656.
 Cuisine: CARVERY.
 $ Prices: Fixed-price lunch IR£3.25 ($5.70). ACC, AE, DC, MC, V.
 Open: Lunch only, daily noon–3pm. **Closed:** Good Friday, Christmas Day.
The carvery lunch in this large, attractive bar and restaurant could well be your main meal of the day, so ample are the portions. There are usually at least two roast joints on offer, with plenty of side vegetables and salads. Kiely's also serves an extensive menu at dinner (see below).

THE KING'S INN BAR, Main St., Killarney. Tel. 064/31479.
 Cuisine: BAR FOOD.
 $ Prices: IR£1.50–IR£4 ($2.65–$7). ACC, AE, MC, V.
 Open: Lunch daily 12:30–2:30pm.

The bar in this centrally located hotel (next door to the Tourist Office) is an attractive, cozy sort of place with a terrific bar-lunch menu that ranges from soup (I like the cockle-and-mussel soup) and sandwiches to piled-high hot dishes (such as homemade shepherd's pie and pan-fried rainbow trout) to smoked salmon salad. And if you want to go over budget, they'll do a sirloin steak for around IR£8.50 ($14.90). There's also a hot lunch-of-the-day special for just IR£4 ($7). They also offer good-value meals for dinner (see below).

THE LAURELS PUB, Main St., Killarney. Tel. 064/31149.
 Cuisine: BAR FOOD.
 $ Prices: IR£1.50–IR£3.50 ($2.65–$6.15). ACC, MC, V.
 Open: Lunch Mon–Sat 12:20–2:30pm.

There's terrific pub grub at the Laurels in old-style surroundings of low, beamed ceilings and rustic wooden tables. The food is good, the company congenial, and the *crack* (talk) stimulating. In addition to soup, sandwiches, and salad plates, there are hot specialties such as Irish lamb stew, Guinness beef stew, and stuffed roast pork. The Laurels also serves an excellent dinner menu in summer months only (see below).

RESTAURANTS IN TOWN

THE CARAGH RESTAURANT, 106 New St., Killarney. Tel. 064/31645.
 Cuisine: GRILLS/SEAFOOD/BURGERS/SNACKS.
 $ Prices: Lunch IR£3.50 ($6.15); dinner IR£7 ($12.25). No credit cards.
 Open: Daily 10am–midnight.
There's a large menu here with something to suit almost any taste. It's a handy place for good, inexpensive meals even at those awkward, in-between hours or in the late evening.

DINGLES RESTAURANT, 40 New St., Killarney. Tel. 064/31079.
 Cuisine: IRISH/TRADITIONAL/VEGETARIAN. **Reservations:** Recommended.
 $ Prices: Appetizers IR£1.50–IR£5 ($2.65–$8.75); main courses IR£7–IR£11 ($12.25–$19.25). ACC, AE, DC, MC, V.
 Open: Mar–Oct, dinner only, daily 6–10:30pm. **Closed:** Nov–Feb, and Thurs Mar–May and Oct.

Gerry and Marion Cunningham have created a traditional eatery in both decor and menu. It's a low-ceilinged, flagstoned place, with an open fire on cool evenings and a rustic look. The very freshest, most wholesome ingredients are used, and there is usually at least one vegetarian dish on the menu. Outstanding are the mussels in a sauce of garlic and herbs; smoked wild Killarney salmon; tender spring lamb chops; steak in a piquant sauce of green peppercorns, white wine, cream, and whiskey; and old-fashioned Irish stew.

FOLEY'S STEAK & SEAFOOD RESTAURANT, 23 High St., Killarney. Tel. 064/31217.
Cuisine: TRADITIONAL/SEAFOOD/VEGETARIAN/BAR FOOD. **Reservations:** Recommended in summer months.
$ **Prices:** Appetizers IR£1.50–IR£4 ($2.65–$7); main courses IR£8–IR£10 ($14–$17.50); breakfast IR£5 ($8.75). ACC, AE, DC, MC, V.
Open: Breakfast daily 8–10am; lunch/dinner daily noon–11pm; bar food daily noon–3pm.

Foley's was a coaching inn many years ago, and there's an old-style air about the front bar lounge, where a fireplace with turf fires adds to the coziness. The two pretty back dining rooms are more formal, decorated with soft shades of rose and green. Carol and Denis Hartnett are the family team responsible for turning out superb meals with the highest standards. Seafood, Kerry mountain lamb, and steaks are the specialties, and Carol (who does the cooking) uses only the freshest produce. Denis cuts all their steaks and buys only Kerry mountain lamb, using nothing but centerline cuts. Actually, this is a full-service eatery, serving all three meals, and there's a pianist on Friday, Saturday, and Sunday nights during the summer.

KIELY'S BAR AND RESTAURANT, College St., Killarney. Tel. 064/31656.
Cuisine: STEAKS/SEAFOOD/VEGETARIAN.
$ **Prices:** Appetizers IR£1.50–IR£3 ($2.65–$5.25); main courses IR£5–IR£7 ($8.75–$12.25); fixed-price four-course dinner IR£12 ($21). ACC, AE, DC, MC, V.
Open: Lunch daily noon–3pm; dinner daily 6–11pm. **Closed:** Good Friday, Christmas Day.
This is a large, attractive place, and the bargain here is the carvery lunch (see "Pub Grub," above). For dinner, there's an extensive menu that focuses on steaks and seafood.

THE KING'S INN BAR AND RESTAURANT, Main St., Killarney. Tel. 064/31479.
Cuisine: TRADITIONAL.
$ **Prices:** Fixed-price dinner special IR£7 ($12.25). ACC, AE, MC, V.
Open: Dinner only, daily 6–9pm.

This is one of Killarney's best centrally located places to eat, whether you drop in for the top-value bar lunch (see "Pub Grub," above) or take advantage of the "early-bird" dinner special. Typical of the menu selections are roast stuffed leg of lamb with mint sauce, medallions of pork with mild black-pepper sauce, and poached salmon with lobster-and-brandy sauce. If you can't make these early dinner hours, there's also a good à la carte menu on offer at moderate prices right up to 10pm.

THE LAURELS, Main St., Killarney. Tel. 064/31149.
Cuisine: IRISH/TRADITIONAL/SALADS.
$ **Prices:** Main courses IR£7–IR£10 ($12.25–$17.50); fixed-price traditional Irish dinner IR£11 ($19.25). ACC, V.
Open: Apr–Oct, dinner only, Mon–Sat 6–10pm.
This lovely wine bar and restaurant adjoins the main bar of the Laurels pub (see "Pub Grub," above) and is a continuation of its old-world style. Candlelit tables and linen tablecloths add a soft glow, and the reasonably priced menu includes such Irish specialties as Irish lamb stew, corned beef and cabbage, and traditional soups. Seafoods and steaks dominate the à la carte menu, where roast leg of lamb, pork, and beef dishes also make an appearance.

LINDEN HOUSE, New Rd., Killarney. Tel. 064/31379.
Cuisine: SEAFOOD/TRADITIONAL.
$ **Prices:** Fixed-price dinner IR£12 ($21). ACC, MC, V.
Open: Dinner only, Mon–Sat 6:30–9pm. **Closed:** Dec–Jan, and Mon to nonresidents.

One of the best places in town for a delicious, home-cooked evening meal is this guesthouse, described above in the "Where to Stay" section. Franz Knoblauch is German-born, Anne is Irish, and they have created a Bavarian-type dining room of exposed brick and wooden booths. It's a cozy place, very popular with locals, and the menu is good, solid family fare. Son Peter supervises the spotless kitchen and insists on the freshest ingredients. In July and August it's a good idea to book ahead—other months you'll usually have only a few minutes' wait at the most. There is also an à la carte menu available. Incidentally, residents are served a "House Special" menu at 6pm at the reduced price of IR£8 ($14).

SHEILA'S RESTAURANT, 75 High St., Killarney. Tel. 064/31270.
   Cuisine: SEAFOOD/TRADITIONAL/VEGETARIAN.
 $ Prices: Plate lunch IR£3.20 ($5.60); four-course lunch IR£6.50 ($11.40); four-course dinner IR£12.50 ($21.90). ACC, MC, V.
   Open: June–Sept, daily 9am–11pm. Oct–Jan, lunch daily noon–3pm; dinner daily 6–10pm.

Sheila's has a dark-green front and lots of light-blond wood inside. Good, inexpensive lunches (sandwiches, soups, quiches, and four-course hot meals) are served from noon to 3pm, four-course dinners of seafood, steaks, pork, chicken, and vegetarian dishes are served from 6 to 10pm, and there's an à la carte menu from 3pm on through the dinner hours. Wine is always available by the glass or bottle.

WORTH THE EXTRA MONEY

THE STRAWBERRY TREE, 24 Plunkett St., Killarney. Tel. 064/32688.
   Cuisine: IRISH/VEGETARIAN. **Reservations:** Strongly recommended.
 $ Prices: Appetizers IR£2–IR£6 ($3.50–$10.50); main courses IR£8–IR£12 ($14–$21). Service charge 10%. ACC, AE, DC, MC, V.
   Open: Morning coffee daily 11am–noon; lunch daily 12:30–3:30pm; dinner daily 6:30–10:30pm. **Closed:** Good Friday, Dec 25–26.

The Strawberry Tree exudes a warm, pubby feeling, and well it might, since for well over a century that's exactly what occupied these premises. The small bar up front is a perfect spot to have a before-dinner drink and study the menu. You do, in fact, place your order from this oasis of warmth before being seated in the small dining room in the back.

Owner Evan Doyle, who came to Killarney from a restaurant in Clifden, has produced an interesting menu using Irish fish, fowl, meats, and farm produce prepared with a slight French flavor. The menu changes monthly, and a typical starter is baked St. Killian (Irish farmhouse cream cheese baked in filo pastry accompanied by a raspberry sauce). Roast quail and chicken with pan-fried breast of woodpigeon with a sauce of strawberry vinegar and red currant is one of the more unusual main dishes, and there are several fresh fish dishes, meats, and vegetable purses (pastry filled with diced root vegetables served over three rices surrounding a mousse of three vegetables and accompanied by a sorrel sauce). A standout among desserts is the "chocolate box," a luscious creation of rich chocolate cake, ice cream, and fresh cream that comes in the form of a box of chocolates. Portions are ample but not overwhelming, and presentation is well nigh perfect. The restaurant is small (26 seats) and extremely popular, so book ahead.

IN NEARBY KILLORGLIN

Some 14 miles west of Killarney is the village of Killorglin with two restaurants worthy of mention.

NICK'S RESTAURANT, Lower Bridge St., Killorglin, Co. Kerry. Tel. 066/61233 or 61219.
   Cuisine: STEAKS/SEAFOOD/BAR FOOD.

$ Prices: Main courses IR£9–IR£12 ($15.75–$21); bar food IR£1.50–IR£4 ($2.65–$7). ACC, AE, MC, V.
Open: Morning coffee daily 10am–noon; bar lunch daily noon–5pm; dinner daily 6–10pm. **Closed:** Dec 24–Jan 2.

Nick and Ann Foley have converted what was once a butcher shop into a charming multilevel steak-and-seafood restaurant with exposed-stone walls, lots of dark wood, open fires, and comfortable seating. You'll be served only the best meats, since Nick is himself a master butcher. Prime beef comes in enormous steaks that actually *earn* the well-worn accolade "melt in your mouth." Lobsters, crayfish, and oysters reside in the restaurant's fish tank, and other fish dishes feature only same-day catches. The soups are thick and hearty, with the unmistakable taste of "homemade." Lunch salads of ham, beef, or seafood are featured on the special pub menu, and the dinner menu has 10 starters and a choice from more than a dozen main courses, followed by a mouth-watering dessert trolley. But if you should have a yen for a special dish not listed—and if the makings are available—the Foleys are quite happy to prepare it for you. There's an extensive wine list, with all the varieties imported directly from France. Music played on the grand piano can be enjoyed nightly.

THE OLD FORGE, Main St., Killorglin, Co. Kerry. Tel. 066/61231.
   Cuisine: BAR FOOD/TRADITIONAL.
$ Prices: Bar food IR£1.50–IR£4 ($2.65–$7); light meals IR£7 ($12.25). No credit cards.
   Open: Daily 12:30–9pm.
Named for the huge forge, complete with bellows and anvil, that separates the pub and lounge, this atmospheric pub and eatery serves home-cooked light meals of beef, seafood, pork, chicken, and the like, as well as soup, sandwiches, and salads. There's often traditional music in the lounge.

2. SEEING THE LAKES

A broad valley holds the three main lakes, with Lough Leane (the Lower Lake) closest to Killarney and separated from the Middle Lake by the Muckross Peninsula. It was on one of its 30 islands that dedicated monks faithfully recorded Irish history from the 11th to the 13th century in the *Annals of Innisfallen*. The Middle Lake covers 680 acres, holds four islands, and is connected to the small, narrow Upper Lake and its eight islands by a broad river called the Long Range. Each lake has several streams flowing into it, and the River Laune connects them to the Atlantic. Their waters hold the shimmering reflections of birch and oak and mountain ash and arbutus, while hovering over all are the peaks of some of Ireland's finest mountains: Macgillycuddy's Reeks, with Carrantuohill, the country's highest mountain at 3,414 feet; the Tomies; the Mangerton range; and Torc. As a Killarney jarvey once said to me, "'Tis a grand sight, one of God's blessings."

Killarney's wealth of natural beauties can be a bit overwhelming, but not to worry—the jarveys and boatmen and coach-tour people have it all worked out for you. Their routes will take you to the high points. Although it's perfectly possible to wander around on your own, this is one time I highly recommend that you plan the budget around at least one or two of the guided tours, whether by jaunting car, boat, or bus. Fares are reasonable, and the guides love the scenery and know the folklore of the places through which they escort you. After you've done that, I recommend that you go back on your own to linger and savor all that beauty. The two experiences make a soul-restoring combination.

BY JAUNTING CAR No need to stop by the Tourist Office to make arrangements—you'll be hassled by the long line of jaunting car drivers down the street, and my advice is to look them all over and pick the Irish face and twinkling eye that tickles your fancy most. In high season it's a good idea to reserve your seat the evening before you plan to go. Uniform rates and routes are set each year for the season.

If the budget can be stretched to include the ✪ **all-day trip,** you'll go home with glorious memories worth far more than the IR£20 ($35) fare. You can book in advance through Killarney Watercoach Cruises, 3 High Street, Killarney, County Kerry (tel. 064/31068). The day begins about 10am, when you hop into a jaunting car, tucking a woolly car rug around your knees if there's a chill in the air. Then it's off at a trot to Kate Kearney's Cottage (which is not the traditional thatched cottage you might expect from its name, but a gift shop, pub, restaurant, and snack bar) at the mouth of the Gap of Dunloe. Next comes a transfer to either a pony's back (for experienced riders only) or a pony trap to make the 6-mile trek through wild, silent walls of granite with still, mysterious lakes on either side. The legend says that the last snake in Ireland was drowned by the good St. Patrick in Black Lough—which explains, no doubt, why no fish have ever inhabited its depths. Lunch is a picnic at the end of the Gap (everyone brings his own) before meeting your boatman at the Upper Lake. The afternoon is a water tour of all three lakes, ending when your boat docks at Ross Castle, where your jaunting car waits to return you to town about 5:30pm. A lovely day, and unrivaled by any other in my own travel experience.

Half-day tours take you through the Killarney Estate along the lake shores to Muckross Abbey, home to Franciscan monks from 1448 until Cromwell ordered it burned in 1652. There's time to wander around Muckross House and its gardens, then on to view the lovely Torc waterfall before returning to town. The charge was IR£18 ($31.50). For the same fare, you can choose the heights of Aghadoe Hill for a breathtaking view of mountains, lakes, and the town below. A church and round tower date back to the 7th century. The return to town is by the way of the Lower Lake and Ross Castle. Various other routes are available at fares of IR£8 to IR£12 ($14 to $21).

BY BOAT   Killarney's boatmen are legendary for their skillful navigation of the lakes and their store of wondrous tales. Their numbers are diminishing, but arrangements can be made for a day on the lakes with a party of four at fares that are set each year for the season. If you want to do the rowing yourself, rowboats are available at Ross Castle and Muckross House, and bookings can be made through Torc Travel, College Street, Killarney, County Kerry (tel. 064/32911).

The watercoach ✪ **Lily of Killarney** leaves the Ross Castle slipway several times daily to cruise the Lower Lake, with shuttle-bus service to the departure point available from Dero's Tours, Main Street, Killarney, County Kerry (tel. 064/31251). The glass-enclosed cabin is completely heated, and there's a commentary on the history and legends of the lake as you pass Innisfallen Island, O'Sullivan's Cascade, Tomies Mountain, Darby's Garden, the old copper mines, Library Point, and many other points of interest. Fares were IR£4 ($7) for adults, half that for children, and IR£10 ($17.50) for a family with two children. To book, contact Killarney Watercoach Cruises Ltd., 3 High Street, Killarney, County Kerry (tel. 064/31068).

ON YOUR OWN   A delightful day can be spent **biking** along the Lower Lake and through the national park (entrance just off Muckross Road) or along the lakeside paths in Ross Castle Western Demesne. Cars are prohibited in both, and you'll feel very close to Nature as you wheel along wooded paths, with stops to contemplate the timeless waters of the lake. Bicycles may be rented from O'Callaghan's on College Street, O'Neill's on Plunkett Street, and O'Sullivan's on Pawn Officer Lane, off High Street.

If you're an experienced rider, know that **horseback-riding trips** are available from the Killarney Riding School in Ballydowney, Killarney, County Kerry (tel. 064/31686). They may also be rented at the Gap of Dunloe for the 2-hour ride to the top of the Gap and back, but as sure-footed as are these steeds, you want to be a good rider before attempting it. Those who prefer the exhilaration of **hiking** over the Gap should allow a minimum of 3 hours.

3. THE RING OF KERRY

Some of Kerry's most outstanding scenery lies along the 112 miles that are known far and wide as the Ring of Kerry. If you're coming to Killarney via West Cork and Glengarriff, you may well want to begin the Ring in Kenmare, ending in Killarney. From Killarney, the route lies through Killorglin and around the Iveragh Peninsula to Kenmare, then back over the mountains via a lovely scenic drive to complete the circle at Killarney.

SEEING THE RING OF KERRY

No matter how you approach this peninsula circle, it's a traveler's delight. The marvelous folder **"The Ring of Kerry Area Guide"** (mentioned in the introduction to this chapter and available from the Tourist Office) will make the trip even more meaningful. Again, however, from a Killarney base I strongly recommend that you stash the car and join one of the inexpensive bus tours, and as a reader of this book, you can take advantage of the discounts listed below.

DISCOUNT BUS TOURS   From Killarney, ✪ **Dero's Tours,** 22 Main Street, Killarney, County Kerry (tel. 064/31251), will give readers a 15% discount on some tours, 10% or 5% on others. Tours of the Ring run daily from Easter to October, and you'll be picked up at your accommodation in the morning and returned there in the evening. Be sure to mention this guidebook when you book the tour, and show it to the driver when he picks you up.

Barry O'Connor, of **O'Connor's Auto Tours,** Andross, Ross Road, Killarney, County Kerry (tel. 064/31052), will give readers of this book a 12½% discount on his minicoach tour priced at IR£12 ($21), bringing your cost down to IR£9 ($15.75).

OTHER BUS TOURS   Bus Eireann (tel. 064/31067) operates day tours for about IR£10 ($17.50) for adults, IR£5 ($8.75) for children.

BY CAR   If time permits, a leisurely drive around the Ring, with an overnight stop en route, is the ideal way to drink in and savor all the magnificent scenery you'll be passing through, and you'll find several recommended accommodations below.

With Killarney as a departure point, head for Killorglin via R562. A few miles to the north via N70 lies the little village of **Castlemaine,** home of Jack Duggan, "The Wild Colonial Boy." At Killorglin, take N70 southwest to **Glenbeigh,** along the north coast of the peninsula through some of the Ring's most spectacular scenery, with the peaks of the Dingle Peninsula visible across the water.

From Glenbeigh, continue along the southern banks of Dingle Bay to **Caherciveen,** where Valentia Island comes into view. Joined to the mainland by a causeway, the island's Irish name is Dairbhre ("Place of Oaks") and it is from a romanticized pronunciation of the Irish *Beal Inse* (the name of a nearby sound) that "Valentia" evolved—not from the Spanish.

IMPRESSIONS

The finest Sea I have seen is at Valentia (Ireland), without any wind and seemingly without a Wave, but with the momentum of the Atlantic behind it, it dashes up into foam—blue diamond it looked like—all along the rocks—like ghosts playing at Hide and Seek.
—ALFRED LORD TENNYSON, in Edward Fitzgerald, *SOME RECOLLECTIONS OF TENNYSON'S TALK,* c. 1852–3

Then it's on to **Waterville** (noted for its fine golf courses and a multitude of ancient ruins) and along the coast via the **Coomakista Pass,** which lifts you some 700 feet above sea level, with breathtaking views of the bay, the offshore **Skellig Islands,** and the coastline. It was on Skellig Michael, a massive rocky hulk that rises 700 feet above the sea, that a colony of early Christian monks built a retreat of stone beehive huts. From the villages of Ballinskelligs and Cahirciveen there are boat trips out to the ruins in good weather, and you reach them after a climb of 640 steps. The rocky islands that make up the Skelligs are also bird sanctuaries, and thousands of puffins and other seabirds are in residence.

Just beyond the pass lies **Caherdaniel,** and 1 mile away, on the Derrynane road, is **Derrynane House and National Park.** This is where the Great Liberator, Daniel O'Connell, lived for most of his political life, and the house is now maintained as a museum containing all sorts of O'Connell memorabilia. The national park covers some 320 acres and is worth a leisurely ramble to view some rather spectacular coastal scenery.

East of Cahirdaniel is **Castlecove,** another loitering spot. About 1½ miles north of the road stands **Straigue Fort,** one of the country's best-preserved stone forts, built during the Iron Age. The circular stone walls, 13 feet wide and 18 feet high, have held over the centuries without benefit of mortar, and along their interior are several flights of stairs of near perfect construction.

From Castlecove, the road turns inland through wild and gorgeous scenery before coming back to the coast at **Sneem.** This pretty little village is the last resting place of Fr. Michael Walsh, who was parish priest here for 38 years in the 1800s and is immortalized as "Father O'Flynn" in a well-known Irish ballad. Two miles to the south, **Parknasilla** is the site of the elegant Great Southern Hotel, whose rock gardens and colorful subtropical blooms are worth a stop.

From Sneem, travel east along the Kenmare River, looking across to the Caha and Slieve Miskish mountains on the opposite shore. From **Kenmare,** take the mountain road (N71) to Moll's Gap, Ladies' View, and back to Killarney.

WHERE TO STAY

KILLORGLIN

Worth the Extra Money

HOTEL ARD-NA-SIDHE, Caragh Lake, Killorglin, Co. Kerry. Tel. 066/ 69105 or 064/31900, or toll free 800/221-1074 in the U.S. Fax 064/32118. Telex 73833 DLOE El. 20 rms (all with bath). TEL

$ Rates (including full Irish breakfast, VAT, and service charge): IR£48–IR£59 ($84–$101.50) single; IR£78 ($136.50) double; IR£90 ($157.50) junior suite. ACC, AE, DC, MC, V. **Closed:** Oct–Apr.

★ This gem is a real find for those who value a scenic, tranquil holiday base. You may find it hard to believe that this grand red sandstone Victorian mansion was built more than a century and a half ago by one Lady O'Connell as a private guesthouse! The guesthouse combines traditional elegance with all the amenities of a modern luxury hotel.

The hotel's location is a bit isolated (17 miles from Killarney, on the edge of Caragh Lake; signposted from N70 between Killorglin and Glenbeigh), and I can only point out what the management itself tries to impress on prospective guests: Ard-na-Sidhe (which means "Height of the Fairies") is strictly for those who enjoy a quiet holiday—wooded walks, fishing (boats and guides are available), and reading are the main activities here. However, I should also add that Killarney is only 17 miles away, golf links are 3 miles away, and all the sporting and dining facilities of the Hotel Dunloe Castle and Hotel Europe (under the same ownership) are free to all guests here.

Spacious public rooms are decorated in soft tones of blues and browns, furnished with antiques, and feature open fireplaces. The dining room is an intimate and restful setting for fine dining. As for the bedrooms, no two are the same size or shape, most of those in the main house are furnished with antiques, and all have radios, hairdryers, and views either of the lake or the beautifully landscaped, award-winning gardens. A short distance from the main house, there's a modern block of more uniform rooms and suites.

GLENBEIGH

SEA VIEW FARM, Mountain Stage, Glenbeigh, Co. Kerry. Tel. 066/ 68109. 6 rms (1 family suite with bath).
$ Rates (including breakfast): IR£15 ($26.25) single; IR£11.50 ($20.15) per person sharing; special weekend rate IR£34 ($59.50) single, IR£30.50 ($53.40) per person sharing. 25% reduction for children. No credit cards. **Closed:** Nov–Apr.
Mrs. Ann Mather's home is an attractive, modern farmhouse 4½ miles southwest of Glenbeigh on the main Ring of Kerry road, with a beautiful view of Dingle Bay. There is a comfortable atmosphere here and the food is excellent.

WATERVILLE

SUNSET HOUSE, Waterville, Co. Kerry. Tel. 0667/4258. 6 rms (none with bath).
$ Rates (including breakfast): IR£11.50 ($20.15) per person. No credit cards. **Closed:** Dec–Jan.
Mrs. Fitzgerald is the hostess of this lovely house overlooking Dingle Bay and Ballinskellig Island. Guest rooms are attractive and comfortable, all with sinks, and there's a homey atmosphere.

LAKE RISE, Lake Rd., Waterville, Co. Kerry. Tel. 0667/4278. 4 rms (2 with bath).
$ Rates (including breakfast): IR£11.50 ($20.15) per person without baths, IR£13 ($22.75) per person with bath. 10% reduction for children. No credit cards.
Mrs. Breda McAuliffe's country home half a mile from the village center has gorgeous views of Waterville, and she gives a warm welcome, as well as real local expertise, to guests who come to fish, golf, explore archeological sites, or simply relax.

A Hostel

WATERVILLE LEISURE HOSTEL, Waterville, Co. Kerry. Tel. 0667/4400. 120 beds.
$ Rates: IR£4.50–IR£5 ($7.90–$8.75) per person. 25% reduction for children. No credit cards. **Open:** Apr–Sept, daily; Oct–Mar, weekends only.
Vincent Counihan has converted a big old stone building that once housed the first cable station linking Ireland to the U.S. and Europe into an outstanding privately owned hostel and outdoor adventure, sport, and leisure-training center. There are beds for 120, with bunk beds (continental quilts, pillows, and undersheet) in rooms for 2, 4, 6, 8, 10, and 12. Other facilities include shower rooms, washrooms, toilets, kitchen, dining room, laundry and drying room, two games rooms, a gym, and a TV lounge. Advance reservations are recommended.

SNEEM

AVONLEA HOUSE, Sportsfield Rd., Sneem, Co. Kerry. Tel. 064/45221. 5 rms (2 with toilet and bath, 3 with shower).
$ Rates (including breakfast): IR£13 ($22.75) single without bath; IR£10.50 ($18.40) per person sharing without bath; IR£1.50 ($2.65) per person additional extra with bath. 25% reduction for children. Dinner IR£10 ($17.50) extra. No credit cards. **Closed:** Dec–Feb.
Mrs. Maura Hussey's two-story home is on the outskirts of town, with nicely done up guest rooms. The food here is excellent, and there's a turf fire blazing in the residents' lounge most nights.

BANK HOUSE, North Sq., Sneem, Co. Kerry. Tel. 064/45226. 3 rms (all with bath).
$ Rates: IR£12 ($21) per person. No credit cards. **Closed:** Oct–Mar.

⭐ Margaret and Noel Harrington open their home—which one reader described as "clean, cute, and charming"—and welcome guests with a warmth that is exceptional, even for the Irish. Noel operates a shop of hand-knits and hand-loomed sweaters in the delightful village of Sneem, good browsing and shopping territory. Guest rooms are light and airy, and Margaret excels in home-baking and delicious snacks.

KENMARE

ARDMORE HOUSE, Killarney Rd., Kenmare, Co. Kerry. Tel. 064/41406. 6 rms (all with bath).

$ Rates (including breakfast): IR£15 ($26.25) single; IR£11.50 ($20.15) per person sharing. 50% reduction for children. Dinner IR£10 ($17.50) extra. V. **Closed:** Dec–Feb.

On the outskirts of Kenmare, in a quiet cul-de-sac just off the main Kenmare–Ring of Kerry road, Ardmore House is a modern one-story bungalow framed by a colorful rose garden. Toni and Tom Connor have six rooms with shower and toilet. Those on the front look out to the roses, and the back view is of peaceful green pastures, with mountains in the background. Central heat and plenty of parking space, and it's only about a 5-minute walk to the town center.

MARINO HOUSE, Reen, Kenmare, Co. Kerry. Tel. 064/41154 or 41501. 8 rms (1 with bath).

$ Rates (including breakfast): IR£11.50 ($20.15) per person (no extra charge for private bath). 20% reduction for children. Dinner IR£10 ($17.50) extra. No credit cards. **Closed:** Oct–Apr.

Marino House occupies a scenic site 2 miles from the town center on a small, wooded finger of land extending out into Kenmare Bay. There's an old-fashioned air about the place, yet there's total modern comfort inside—an irresistible combination. Run by Mrs. Edna O'Sullivan and her family, centrally heated Marino House features comfortable guest rooms and excellent meals, served in a dining room overlooking the green lawn. Much patronized by regulars, this place gets booked quickly from year to year, so best reserve as far in advance as possible.

Worth the Extra Money

PARK HOTEL, Kenmare, Co. Kerry. Tel. 064/41200. 17 rms, 31 suites (all with bath). TEL

$ Rates (including breakfast): From IR£90 ($157.50) single; from IR£200 ($350) double. ACC, MC, V. **Closed:** Jan–Mar.

Set in some 11 garden acres, the Park was originally built as an upmarket hostelry for railway passengers, but a few years ago it had reached a rather sad state of deterioration. That's when a new owner, Francis Brennan, took things in hand and restored it to a standard far higher than it had known even in its glory days. Its public rooms are furnished with lovely antiques, and down the wide corridors of the main hotel each of the spacious bedrooms is individually styled, while in a newer wing luxurious uniformity is maintained. Both the hotel and its dining room have won several international awards of distinction, including a Michelin star. In addition, golf, tennis, fishing, and croquet are available.

KILGARVAN

HAWTHORN FARM, Kilgarvan, Co. Kerry. Tel. 064/85326. 6 rms (3 with bath).

$ Rates (including breakfast): IR£15.50 ($27.15) single without bath; IR£12.50 ($21.90) per person sharing without bath; IR£1.50 ($2.65) per person additional with bath. 20% reduction for children. Dinner IR£11.50 ($20.15) extra. No credit cards. **Closed:** Nov–Mar.

This modern farmhouse is the domain of Kitty Dineen and her family. It's 5 miles east of Kilgarven and 2 miles off the Coolea road (R569), set some 1,500 feet high in a gorge in the red sandstone mountains that make this one of the most beautiful locations in the area. Kitty's table is widely known for its magnificent farm fare. Just wait until you taste her traditional Christmas cake (served year round), brown bread, scones, and Irish bacon and cabbage! And they arrive at a table laden with Irish linen, Irish china, and Irish silverware—more Irish than that it's hard to get! Located just 12 miles from the sea, Hawthorn Farm has central heating and plenty of parking space.

SILLERDANE LODGE, Coolnoohill, Kilgarvan, Co. Kerry. Tel. 064/ 85359. 6 rms (all with bath).
$ Rates (including breakfast): IR£15.50 ($27.15) single; IR£12.50 ($21.90) per person sharing. 25% reduction for children. Dinner IR£11.50 ($20.15) extra. No credit cards. **Closed:** 1 week in mid-Sept, Christmas Day.

Sillerdane Lodge offers a most unusual feature for an Irish B&B—a heated outdoor swimming pool! Set in a beautiful valley 13 miles east of Kenmare via R569, the pretty bungalow has more than just that to offer, however, and perhaps its most appealing feature is the gracious Mrs. Joan McCarthy. This lovely lady takes a personal interest in all her guests and her home reflects her concern for their comfort. The bright dining room has huge windows to take advantage of gorgeous views, and bedrooms have tea/coffee makers and are beautifully decorated and spotless, not surprising, since she is a talented interior decorator. There's central heating and plenty of parking space.

WHERE TO EAT

Most of the small hotels you'll pass in your trip around the Ring of Kerry serve up exceptional meals of fresh seafood and local Irish lamb, beef, or pork, and many also add vegetarian dishes to their menu. Unfortunately, space permits only the limited listing below.

KENMARE

THE PURPLE HEATHER BISTRO, Henry St., Kenmare. Tel. 064/41016.
Cuisine: SEAFOOD/TRADITIONAL/VEGETARIAN.
$ Prices: Cold and hot plates IR£4–IR£7 ($7–$12.25). No credit cards.
Open: Mon–Sat noon–6:30pm.

There's excellent bistro food here, in a setting best described as eccentric. Walls and ceiling are decorated with objects of wood and copper, with hanging wine bottles and an assortment of various other items. Lunch specialties include excellent omelets as well as salads and smoked salmon and mackerel, the latter two served with fresh brown bread.

Worth the Extra Money

LIME TREE RESTAURANT, Shelbourne St., Kenmare. Tel. 064/41225.
Cuisine: SEAFOOD/TRADITIONAL/VEGETARIAN.
$ Prices: Appetizers IR£2–IR£5 ($3.50–$8.75); main courses IR£9–IR£15 ($15.75–$26.25). No credit cards.
Open: Dinner only, Mon–Sat 5:30–9:30pm. **Closed:** Nov–Mar.
The owners of the Purple Heather also run this charming restaurant housed in an old stone schoolhouse. The Lime Tree is open in the evening only, and meals here are prepared with the same loving care as at the Purple Heather. Seafood figures prominently on the menu, and for a special treat, order the prawns, monkfish, and scallops in garlic butter or lobster from the seawater tank. Lamb, steak, chicken,

and veal are also available in tasty variations, and the desserts here are well nigh spectacular.

PARKNASILLA

Worth the Extra Money

PYGMALION RESTAURANT, in the Great Southern Hotel, Parknasilla.
Tel. 064/45122.
  Cuisine: FRENCH/VEGETARIAN. **Reservations:** Recommended.
$ **Prices:** Fixed-price meal IR£12 ($21) at lunch, IR£20 ($35) at dinner. ACC, AE, DC, MC, V.
  Open: Lunch daily 1–3pm; dinner daily 7–8:30pm. **Closed:** Nov–Mar.
In one of the most beautiful settings on the Ring, the Great Southern at Parknasilla, 2 miles south of Sneem, has won several international awards for the cuisine of its Pygmalion Restaurant. Examples from the menu include prawns with armagnac sauce, turtle soup, poached salmon with hollandaise sauce, and locally grown lamb and beef in a variety of preparations. The gracious decor and splendid service here make stretching the budget a real pleasure!

4. THE DINGLE PENINSULA & THE BLASKET ISLANDS

An entire book could be written about this varied region, with its magnificent scenery, relics of prehistory, and population of highly individualistic people. I'll hit the highlights, but take time to explore on your own—this is "nook and cranny" country!

The 30-mile-long Dingle Peninsula is the most westerly point of land in Europe, its offshore Blasket Islands the "last parish before New York." Its beginnings are shrouded in the mists of prehistory, which left its marks scattered over the face of the Slieve Mish mountains, along small coves and rocky cliffs, and in the legends that persist to this day. To date, no fewer than 2,000 archeological sites have been identified on the peninsula.

The peninsula's ancient Irish name is An Daingean ("The Fortress"), and the remains of seven earthen ring forts and two headland stone forts attest to the origin of that name. Its Glenagalt Valley translates as the "Valley of the Madmen," and is so called because as far back as the 12th century the mentally afflicted came to roam its wilds, drink the waters of Tobernagalt ("The Well of the Madmen"), and eat the watercress that grew along the stream, to return home sound in mind and body after a few months. Mystical? Oh, yes! I sometimes feel that the very essence of Celtic magic has been distilled into the soft air of the Dingle Peninsula.

The West Kerry Gaeltacht ("*Gail*-tuckt") is one of several areas around the country officially designated as Irish-speaking by the government in an effort to assure the survival of this ancient language. In summer months those interested in learning or improving their knowledge of Irish can arrange language courses with stays in Irish-speaking homes and many social activities based on traditional music and dance. For full details, contact **Comharchumann Forbartha Chorca Dhuibhne,** Ballyferriter, County Kerry (tel. 066/56100).

DINGLE TOWN

Dingle town is a bustling little market town, with a boat-building industry right in the middle of things, ideal for walking. In the old Spanish trading days this was the chief Kerry port, and in Elizabethan times it was a walled town. These days, fishing and tourism hold sway. There are several Irish goods shops, plenty of places to get a good meal, and enough music after dark to fill all your evenings.

GETTING THERE

Leaving Killarney, the route is well signposted all the way to Dingle town. Take the main Killorglin road (R562), and at Killorglin turn north on to N70 to Castlemaine, where R561 turns west, passing through Inch and Anascaul to reach Dingle town.

FAST FACTS

The **telephone area code** for Dingle is 066. The **Tourist Office** on Main Street (tel. 066/51188) is open only in summer; other months, make inquiries about Dingle and the peninsula at the Killarney Tourist Office.

WHAT TO SEE & DO

Dingle residents have always been known for their strong, individualistic character. In recent years they've been joined by ○ **Fungi the dolphin,** who has moved in and promptly become the beloved pet of the entire peninsula. The friendliest, most lovable dolphin in these waters, he has become Dingle town's No. 1 tourist attraction, cavorting through the waters of Dingle Bay, following the four boats that regularly ferry visitors out to his watery home, playing with scuba divers, and even, on one occasion, joyfully leaping right over a small boat. You can watch his antics from Hussey's Folly, an old Customs watchtower, or from the tiny sandy beach at Fladden. You'll find the four boats down by the harbor, and the fare for an on-the-water encounter with Fungi is IR£5 ($8.75).

There's an interesting **historical exhibition** of Dingle photos and memorabilia from the past at the Old Presbyter, Main Street, which is open without charge in summer months, Monday through Saturday from 10am to 6pm.

On the western edge of town, the ○ **Cearolann Craft Village** is a cluster of small cottages housing shops and workshops. Among the most interesting of the craftspeople who sell their wares here is silversmith Brian de Staic (tel. 066/51298). One very appealing item he fashions is an unusual silver necklace in the shape of an Ogham stone with your name inscribed in the strokes of that ancient language. He also has silver, gold, and enamel pendants of Fungi. The village also houses handcrafted leather goods, handmade uilleann pipes, knit goods, a cabinetmaker, and weavers.

On Dykegate Lane, ○ **An Café Liteartha** (tel. 066/51388) is a very special place that carries an impressive array of Irish-interest publications and records in the front shop section, with inexpensive food service in a back room. It's open year round, Monday through Saturday from 10am to 6pm and on Sunday from 11am to 6pm. For good buys in Waterford crystal, Aran sweaters, and other Irish goods, it's hard to beat **McKena's,** on Dykegate Street (tel. 066/51198), which gives a discount for payment in cash.

There's bar food during the day and music on summer nights at the **O Gairbhi pub** and **Garvey's Pub,** both on Strand Street, and at **Benner's Hotel** on Main Street. But for a night of traditional music and song that comes from true family tradition, look for the red-and-white pub on Bridge Street with the name **UaFlaibeartaig,** which translates to O'Flaherty's. The late father of the present O'Flaherty clan was recognized as one of the country's best traditional musicians, and now son Fergus and daughter Maire raise instruments and voice each night surrounded by locals and visitors who've come to hear the best. It's a warm, informal gathering in a setting that's as traditional as the music, with the haphazard collection of pictures, posters, and other assorted items that has accumulated here as in almost any country pub in Ireland.

WHERE TO STAY

DYKEGATE HOUSE, 8 Dykegate St., Dingle, Co. Kerry. Tel. 066/51549.
   5 rms (none with bath).

$ Rates (including breakfast): IR£11 ($19.25) per person. 50% reduction for children. No credit cards.

You'll get a very warm welcome from Mrs. Mary Leonard at Dykegate House. Conveniently located within walking distance of everything in town, the two-story house is rather plain but homey. Mrs. Leonard serves up one of the best breakfasts I've had in Ireland in a light and airy dining room. Guest rooms vary in size, but all have sinks and are comfortably furnished. This has been a favorite of readers for years, and after several personal stays, I heartily concur in their endorsements.

GREENMOUNT HOUSE, Gortanora, Dingle, Co. Kerry. Tel. 066/51414. 6 rms (5 with bath).

$ Rates (including breakfast): IR£11 ($19.95) per person without bath, IR£12.50 ($21.90) per person with bath. No credit cards. **Parking:** Available.

On the outskirts of Dingle town, this pretty, modern bungalow sits on a rise overlooking Dingle Bay. John and Mary Curran provide orthopedic beds with electric blankets, radios, tea/coffee makers, and hairdryers for their guests, the house is centrally heated, and there's private parking. At breakfast, there's a menu supplementing the traditional Irish breakfast.

MRS. BETTY HAND, Green St., Dingle, Co. Kerry. Tel. 066/51538. 5 rms (4 with bath).

$ Rates (including breakfast): IR£11 ($19.25) per person without bath, IR£12.50 ($21.90) per person extra with bath. 50% reduction for children.

Mrs. Betty Hand's large two-story home is also conveniently located in the heart of town and has nicely appointed guest rooms. The friendliness of the Hand family is legendary, and they are always delighted to have American guests. There's central heat and a garden where guests are welcome to sit on a sunny afternoon.

A Small Hotel

BENNER'S HOTEL, Main St., Dingle, Co. Kerry. Tel. 066/51638. Fax 066/51412. 25 rms (all with bath). TV TEL

$ Rates (including breakfast): IR£31–IR£40 ($54.25–$70) single; IR£27–IR£36 ($47.25–$63) per person sharing—depending on season. 33⅓% reduction for children (under 5 free). MC, V.

The interior of this 250-year-old coaching inn has been totally rebuilt to incorporate modern comfort and convenience. The result of that renovation, however, left it still loaded with much of its original character, with each room different, many Irish antique furnishings (two guest rooms have four-poster beds), and an over-all air of the graciousness of another era. The Garden Restaurant serves good, moderately priced meals; the Boston Bar serves bar lunches and is an atmospheric and convivial meeting place for locals as well as visitors; and Mrs. B's Lounge is a tribute to the Mrs. Benner, who ran the place for many years and whose portrait hangs over the fireplace.

Worth the Extra Money

DINGLE SKELLIG HOTEL, Dingle, Co. Kerry. Tel. 066/51144. 50 rms (all with bath). TV TEL

$ Rates: IR£38–IR£52 ($66.50–$91) single; IR£55–IR£84 ($96.25–$147) double—depending on season. Excellent Weekend Break rates available. **Closed:** Dec–Feb.

With one of the most dramatic locations on the Dingle Peninsula, the Skellig overlooks the harbor of Dingle Bay, and public rooms take full advantage of the view. The nicely furnished guest rooms all have private baths, satellite TVs, radios, and direct-dial telephones.

Dining: The restaurant, as you might expect, specializes in seafood from local waters and overlooks Dingle Bay.

Facilities: There's a leisure center with swimming pool, sauna, and sunbed, and other amenities include a children's playground, snooker room, jumbo chess (great fun), and tennis court. Guests are given reduced rates at the nearby golf course, and pony trekking and deep-sea fishing can be arranged.

DOYLE'S SEAFOOD BAR AND TOWNHOUSE, John St., Dingle, Co. Kerry. Tel. 066/51174. Fax 066/51816. 8 rms (all with bath). TV TEL
$ Rates (including breakfast): IR£32.50 ($56.90) single; IR£27.50 ($48.15) per person sharing. ACC, AE, DC, MC, V.

Settle in here and you're right in the heart of Dingle town. Over the past several years John and Stella Doyle have gained an international reputation for the quality of seafood served in their small, flagstone-paved restaurant in Dingle, a tribute to their single-mindedness in adhering to the highest standards in whatever they undertake. So it comes as no surprise that they have maintained that same high standard in renovating an adjacent 1830s house into eight attractive and comfortable bedrooms. Antique furnishings with a Victorian flavor add to their appeal, but comfort is not overlooked, with extra-large orthopedic beds. The two houses are interconnected, making access to the restaurant easy, while maintaining a high degree of privacy.

Nearby Accommodations

ALPENROSE HOUSE, Annascaul, Co. Kerry. Tel. 066/57105. 6 rms (all with bath).
$ Rates (including breakfast): IR£13.50–£14.50 ($23.65–$25.40) per person depending on season. No credit cards.

Mrs. Sheila Fitzgerald-O'Donnell is the hostess at this immaculate, modern, and very comfortable accommodation that resembles a small inn. In the center of Annascaul, 9 miles from Dingle town, it's a warm, clean, and cozy place to stay, both because the guest rooms meet a high standard of comfort and because of the personal warmth of Mrs. Fitzgerald-O'Donnell. During summer months she also operates an attached restaurant that dishes up good food at moderate prices.

CLEEVAUN, Lady's Cross, Miltown, Dingle, Co. Kerry. Tel. 066/51108. 5 rms (all with bath).
$ Rates (including breakfast): IR£16.50 ($28.90) single; IR£13.50 ($23.65) per person sharing. 25% reduction for children. No credit cards. **Closed:** Dec–Feb.

This modern bungalow's name, *Cliabhan* in Irish, means "cradle," and it's only about a 10-minute walk from Dingle town. Sean and Charlotte Cluskey have a seemingly inexhaustible knowledge of the Dingle Peninsula and a keen desire to share it with their guests. From the pleasant lounge and dining room, there are views of green pastures dotted with grazing sheep and a panorama that takes in Dingle Bay and Mount Brandon. There's an ancient Ogham stone in the field out back and a ring fort down in the pasture. The lounge and breakfast room decor makes use of pine wood and yellow walls, and guest rooms have an old-country pine theme, as well as orthopedic beds. Charlotte is one of the few Irish hostesses to serve percolated coffee to Americans who've overdosed on tea, and on arrival you'll be offered coffee (or tea) and homemade porter cake. The breakfast menu not only includes the traditional Irish breakfast, but adds choices of pancakes, cheese, and fruit.

READERS RECOMMEND

Four Winds, *Annascaul, Dingle, County Kerry (tel. 066/57168). "We really enjoyed staying with Mrs. O'Connor in this attractive, comfortable bed-and-breakfast just outside the village."*—Richard McGovern, Boston, Mass.

WHERE TO EAT

ARMADA RESTAURANT, Strand St., Dingle. Tel. 066/51505.
Cuisine: SEAFOOD/TRADITIONAL/VEGETARIAN.

$ Prices: Appetizers IR£1.50–IR£3 ($2.65–$5.25); main courses IR£6–IR£10 ($10.50–$17.50); fixed-price meal IR£5.75 ($10.05) at lunch, dinner IR£8.50 ($14.90) at dinner.
Open: July–Aug, lunch daily 12:30–2:15pm; dinner daily 6–9:30pm. Sept–Nov, lunch Tues–Sun 12:30–2:15pm; dinner Tues–Sun 6–9:30pm. **Closed:** Dec–Feb.

The Armada is a pleasant, moderately priced eatery run by Mark and Ann Kerry (Ann does the cooking), who also own the Star Bar on the ground floor. Meals in the upstairs restaurant feature seafood and local meats, and there's also a good vegetarian salad on the menu. The Special Tourist Menu is also offered.

BEGINISH RESTAURANT, Green St., Dingle. Tel. 066/51588.

Cuisine: SEAFOOD/VEGETARIAN. **Reservations:** Recommended.
$ Prices: Fixed-price dinner IR£15 ($26.25). ACC, AE, MC, V.
Open: Dinner only, Mon–Sat 6–9pm.

Mrs. Pat Moore runs this delightful small restaurant. She has managed to achieve a light and airy—and at the same time, cozy—look, and there's a lovely garden out back with tables for dining outside in fine weather. The food, with an emphasis on fresh seafood (what else, in Dingle!), is beautifully prepared and nicely served. *Note:* Pat also owns one of Dingle's best craft and gift shops, located just across the street, and gives excellent service to Americans.

BENNER'S HOTEL, Main St., Dingle. Tel. 066/51638.

Cuisine: SEAFOOD/TRADITIONAL.
$ Prices: Sun lunch IR£8.50 ($14.90). ACC, MC, V.
Open: Lunch Sun 12:30–2:30pm.

This attractive, old-style hotel serves all three meals daily in a nicely appointed dining room overlooking a walled garden. Prices are reasonable, and the well-rounded menu focuses on the best of local seafood and other products. It is the Sunday lunch, however, that offers the best value for dollar (dinners will run as high as IR£18/$31.50).

DOYLE'S SEAFOOD BAR, John St., Dingle. Tel. 066/51174.

Cuisine: SEAFOOD. **Reservations:** Recommended.
$ Prices: Appetizers IR£1.50–IR£3 ($2.65–$5.25); main courses IR£8–IR£10 ($14–$17.50). Service charge 10%. ACC, AE, DC, MC, V.
Open: Mid-Mar to mid-Nov, lunch Mon–Sat 12:30–2:15pm; dinner Mon–Sat 6–9pm.

John and Stella Doyle have created one of the best restaurants in Dingle, winner of Bord Failte's Award of Excellence year after year. The restaurant adjoins their luxury town house accommodations (see above), and the cozy old pub has rock walls, a flagstone floor, and a blackboard menu showing a selection of seafood from local fishing boats' same-day catch. You'll find John up front at the bar, while Stella reigns in the kitchen. In addition to lobster (a specialty of the house), salmon, oysters, and other shellfish, there's good homemade soup and Stella's freshly baked scones. If you haven't booked in advance you can expect a wait in this small, popular place (but that's no problem at all if you're ensconced at the friendly bar with other waitees). Don't plan to get there much after 7pm, however, to be sure of being seated.

THE HALF DOOR, John St., Dingle. Tel. 066/51600.

Cuisine: SEAFOOD/SALADS/SANDWICHES.
$ Prices: Appetizers IR£2.80–£5 ($4.90–$8.75); main courses IR£9–IR£12 ($15.75–$21); salad plates IR£5 ($8.75); sandwiches IR£3 ($5.25). ACC, AE, MC, V.
Open: Mid-Mar to mid-Nov, lunch daily 12:30–2pm; dinner daily 6–10pm.

Michael Casey, who prefers to be called "Mick," returned to Ireland after 22 years in Canada and took over this award-winning eatery, formerly under the direction of John and Celeste Slye. Seafood dishes are prepared with a marvelous simplicity that enhances their natural tastes. No need to worry about freshness—huge tanks hold several varieties of live seafood until they're ready to pop into the pot, and others come right from Dingle's fishing fleet to the kitchen. There's also an excellent wine list. At lunch, a bowl of terrific seafood chowder, followed by a salad plate or open salmon sandwich, is an inexpensive and satisfying meal.

THE DINGLE PENINSULA

If you have made the wise decision to base yourself locally, a good touring plan is to make a leisurely drive around the southern edge of the peninsula the first day, saving the Connor Pass and the northern shoreline for the next. For nondrivers, there are bus tours departing Dingle town, and you can get details from the Tourist Office. Pick up a copy of **"The Dingle Peninsula Guide"** from the Tourist Office before you set out. Walkers can also inquire about **The Dingle Way** walking track.

WHAT TO SEE & DO

Unfortunately, space will not permit a detailed description of the thousands of prehistoric relics around the Dingle Peninsula—that's best left to the guide named above. The peninsula also has some outstanding potteries and crafts shops, and interesting historical exhibitions.

FROM DINGLE TOWN TO SLEA HEAD Driving west from town, **Ventry Harbour** was, according to legend, the scene of a fierce battle between the King of the World, Daire Doon, and the King of Ireland, Fionn MacCumhaill.

Stop in at **Sheehy's Pottery,** Ventry (tel. 066/59962). Penny Sheehy is the potter, who specializes in unique ceramic Celtic murals and explanation plaques of old Celtic myths. She also has a nice range of unusual small kitchen utensils, mugs, ashtrays, etc., that fit easily into your suitcase. The old timber-ceilinged building is almost a sightseeing attraction in itself, and light meals of home-cooked food are served.

Still farther west, **Dunbeg Fort** perches on a high promontory, its landward side surrounded by earthen trenches, and its 22-foot-thick wall riddled with an elaborate souterrain (inner passage). Farther along, at the high cliffs of **✪ Slea Head** you get the most sweeping view of sheltered coves below and the Blasket Islands across the water.

THE BLASKET ISLANDS The Great Blasket is the largest of these seven offshore islands. It was once inhabited, but the last of its tiny population was moved to the mainland in 1953, when the fishing industry failed to provide a living wage and the government offered land grants for small farm holdings on the peninsula. Visitors from Springfield, Massachusetts, may feel a special bond to the people of the Blaskets, since many islanders who emigrated settled in that city. Boats go out from Dunquin Harbor on an intermittent basis during summer months, and a trip out to the island provides a break of sheer tranquility and scenic beauty that is exceptional even for Ireland.

As this is written, steps are being taken by the Irish Government to acquire title to the Great Blasket and maintain it as an official national historic park, preserving the ruined village intact and developing activities that reflect the island's culture and traditions.

THE REST OF THE PENINSULA Another of the very good potteries on the peninsula is **Dunquin Pottery,** on the road between Slea Head and Dunquin. Operated by local people—Maureen, Eiblin, Helena, and Sean Daly, who worked for founder Jean Oldfield for many years—the pottery turns out hand-thrown, ovenproof stoneware in shades of sand and browns and blues. The prices are reasonable, and the small café at the pottery serves Rambouts coffee, Irish porter cake, and other snacks.

On beyond Dunquin, in the center of Ballyferriter, stop at the old school that houses the **✪ Balliferriter Heritage Centre,** with "Treasures of the Dingle Peninsula." Ted Creedon, development officer of the exhibition, is usually on hand to expand on the story of Dingle's long history as illustrated by more than 200 photographs, artifacts, and text. You'll leave with more than a nodding acquaintance with the region's beehive huts, standing stones, mysterious graves, ring forts, and other relics. There's also a tea and coffee shop at the centre. It's open during summer months, Monday through Saturday from 10am to 6pm.

Also in Ballyferriter, the **West Kerry Co-op** has an excellent illustrated guidebook, which outlines a driving tour. The co-op can book you into local lodgings if you've fallen under Dingle's mystical spell and can't bear to leave just yet. The office is open Monday through Friday from 9am to 5:30pm. The story behind the co-op is an inspiring one, beginning in 1968 when young people were leaving in droves and there was great concern that the unique culture and heritage of the Gaelic-speaking region would wither and die. Much of the land had been untillable, but by banding together, 800 members of the farming community were able to import a special deep-plowing machine to break up the layer of iron that lay just inches beneath the surface of the land to turn it into productive acres. The co-op has now reclaimed more than 12,000 acres. They've also taken an active part in upgrading tourist facilities, as well as expanding the summer-school program that brings students to study Gaelic.

At Ballyferriter, internationally known Louis Mulcahy (tel. 066/56229) operates a ✪ **pottery studio/workshop,** where he trains local potters in the production of many unusual items made from clay and finished with glazes developed in the workshop. There are the standard dinner sets, mugs, pitchers, and the like, but in addition, giant jugs and vases, unusual lamp bases, and beautiful wall plaques are on display in the studio. Louis's distinctive designs set his work apart from any other. Visitors are welcome to visit the workshop and kiln, and prices are quite reasonable for the unusually high quality. Open 7 days a week.

One of the peninsula's most astonishing relics is ✪ **Gallarus Oratory,** just off the road from Ballydavid back to Dingle town. It's a marvelous specimen of early Christian architecture. Built in an inverted boat shape, it has remained completely watertight for more than 1,000 years, its stones perfectly fitted without benefit of any kind of mortar. In the same vicinity, look, also, for the **Alphabet Stone** in the churchyard of Cill Maolkeador, an ancient ruined church. The pillar is carved with both the Roman alphabet and Ogham strokes.

At **Brandon Creek** (the legendary starting point of St. Brendan's voyage to the New World), stop in at ✪ **An Bother** (it means "The Road," and it sits right at the roadside). It's a place to relax by the fire in the lounge or sit at the bar in the small front room, with the constant flow of Gaelic conversation lulling you into a sense of the timelessness that is Dingle. You'll meet mostly locals here, and they welcome visitors warmly, breaking into English often enough to keep you from feeling excluded.

To reach the northern shores of the peninsula, take the **Connor Pass** road from Dingle town over to ✪ **Castlegregory** with its views from the pass and along the coastal road.

In the little town of **Camp,** turn off the main road and drive up to ✪ **James Ashe's Pub.** This is the Irish pub you dreamed of before you came to Ireland — smoke-darkened wood, low ceilings, a peat fire glowing on the hearth, and Irish faces in the pub their families have frequented for generations. Margaret Ashe or her son, Thomas, will likely be behind the bar.

WHERE TO STAY
Bed-and-Breakfast and Guesthouses

AISLING, Castlegregory, Tralee, Co. Kerry. Tel. 066/39134. 5 rms (2 with bath).

$ Rates (including breakfast): IR£12 ($21) per person without bath, IR£13.50 ($23.65) per person with bath. 15% reduction for children. No credit cards. **Closed:** Nov–Apr.

This is one of the prettiest guesthouses on the Dingle Peninsula. The home of Mrs. Helen Healy, the two-story charmer is a mecca for visitors interested in Irish history and this unique region. Mrs. Healy is very helpful in directing her guests to good local eateries, craft workshops, etc. The house shines, with parquet floors, artistic arrangements of dried flowers, and examples of Irish pottery on display. The three upstairs bedrooms have sinks, but share two bathrooms with showers, while two downstairs rooms off a patio have private baths. At breakfast, Mrs. Healy's justly famed brown scones star. There are tennis courts next door and golf links overlooking Brandon Bay just 1 mile away.

COIS ABHANN, Emila, Ballyferriter, Dingle, Co. Kerry. Tel. 066/56201. 6 rms (all with bath).

$ Rates (including breakfast): IR£16 ($28) single; IR£12 ($21) per person sharing. 50% reduction for children. No credit cards. **Closed:** Oct–Feb.

In Ballyferriter, Miss Breda O'Sullivan's Cois Abhann (pronounced "Cush Owen"—it means by the side of the river) is a pretty, modern bungalow whose floor-to-ceiling windows frame magnificent mountain views. The six guest rooms are all done in pastel colors, and there's central heat and plenty of parking space.

DROM HOUSE, Coumgaugh, Dingle, Co. Kerry. Tel. 066/51134. 3 rms (all with bath).

$ Rates (including breakfast): IR£11 ($19.25) per person. 33⅓% reduction for children. High tea IR£11 ($19.25) extra; dinner, IR£12 ($21).

⭐ Rita and Gerald Brosnan, of Drom House (it means "hilly"), are both Dingle Peninsula natives. Rita was born in a house just up the road, and Gerald is manager of the West Kerry Co-op that has resurrected farming as a viable occupation hereabouts. Their hillside home sits amid sweeping mountain vistas 4½km (3 miles) from Dingle town, and the modern bungalow is nicely decorated throughout. There's a TV/video lounge, as well as a playground for children. Guest rooms come with clock radios and hairdryers.

MACGEARAILT'S BUNGALOW, Bothar Bui, Ballydavid, Dingle, Co. Kerry. Tel. 066/551421. 6 rms (all with bath).

$ Rates (including breakfast): IR£12 ($21) per person. 20% reduction for children. Dinner IR£12 ($21) extra. No credit cards. **Closed:** Oct–Easter.

There are views of lofty Mount Brandon from all six guest rooms at this bright, modern bungalow, home of Maura and Thomas MacGearailt, who delight in pointing out the splendors of the Dingle Peninsula. There's central heating and private parking.

SLEA HEAD HOUSE, Ventry, Tralee, Co. Kerry. Tel. 066/56234. 6 rms (none with bath).

$ Rates (including breakfast): IR£11 ($19.25) per person. No credit cards. **Closed:** Nov–Apr.

In a breathtakingly beautiful setting 11 miles from Dingle town, between Ventry and Dunquin, high on a hill overlooking Slea Head and the Blasket Islands, Slea Head House first opened as a guesthouse in the 1930s to provide lodgings for students of the Irish language. Over the years it created a tradition of warm, personal hospitality. Its present owner, Bonnie Reina, who left a successful newspaper and publishing career in Cape May, New Jersey, to move to Dingle, keeps that old tradition very much alive. Guest rooms are all different in size and shape, all are fitted out with plain but comfortable furnishings, and most have that smashing view.

A Small Hotel

OSTAN GRANVILLE, Ballyferriter, Dingle, Co. Kerry. Tel. 066/56116. 14 rms (all with bath).

$ Rates (including breakfast): Jan–Jun and Sept–Oct, IR£19.95 ($34.90) per person; July–Aug, IR£21.95 ($38.40) per person. **Closed:** Nov–Dec.

 This is a gem of an Irish country hotel, and in many respects it's more a bed-and-breakfast place than a hotel. That's because of the informality and personal service you'll receive from Billy and Breege Granville. *Ostan* is Irish for "hotel," but this 1838 Georgian house began life as a rectory, and then was used by the Royal Irish Constabulary as a barracks until the 1920s, when it burned. That's when the Granville family took it over, restored it, and opened its doors to the public. There's an old-fashioned, homey look to the place, and its bar looks out to Mount Brandon, Ballydavid Head, Smerwick Harbour, and the Three

Sisters—a wonderful place to bend an elbow before the fireplace while contemplating that sweeping view! Guest rooms are plain but comfortable, many furnished with antiques, and all have terrific views. A nice feature here is the attention given families with children; there's even a special tea each evening for the young fry, and baby-sitting is no problem at all. Meals are excellent and reasonably priced, with homemade soup and brown bread and fish straight from Dingle waters. There's central heat and plenty of parking.

Self-Catering

VENTRY HOLIDAY COTTAGES, c/o John P. Moore, Green St., Dingle, Co. Kerry Tel. 066/51588. 8 cottages.

$ Rates: IR£100–IR£345 ($175–$603.75) per week, depending on season.

Overlooking the picturesque little village of Ventry and its harbor, 4½ miles from Dingle town on the coast road to Slea Head, these charming cottages are traditional in design, yet equipped with fully fitted-out kitchens and other conveniences. Each features a large lounge/dining area, and there's a fireplace for cool days and nights. The three carpeted bedrooms will sleep six adults.

READERS RECOMMEND

Cois Corrigh, Emila, Ballyferriter, Tralee, County Kerry (tel. 066/56282). "Mrs. Breda Ferris welcomed us here with tea, muffins, and porter cake. Her house is immaculate and commands a lovely view of the meadows, mountains, and the sea. She was most helpful with directions, and when my husband injured his hand, she was so concerned, and applied first aid very professionally."—Marge Woodbury, Corning, N.Y.

Mrs. M. O'Mahoney, Reask View House, Reask, Ballyferriter, County Kerry (tel. 066/56126). "These are superb modern accommodations in a truly rustic area. Outstanding amenities of golf and food nearby."—G. W. Howard, Silver Springs, Md.

Goulane, Castlegregory, County Kerry (tel. 066/39147). "Mrs. Catherine Griffin's country farmhouse overlooks the bay, with a sandy beach. Our rooms were most comfortable. Mrs. Griffin is a delightful Irish mother of five and shared with us many wonderful stories of life in the country."—Tracy Shepard, Fort Lauderdale, Fla.

Grianan Allach, Kilcooley, Ballydavid, County Kerry (tel. 066/55157). "Mrs. Mary McHugh and her family are always happy to assist you in seeing the local sights. The meals served family style are a great example of Irish country cooking, and the rooms and facilities are modern and very comfortable."—W. V. Steele, New York, N.Y.

Accommodations in the Peninsula Area

ASHGROVE HOUSE, Ballybunion Rd., Listowel, Co. Kerry. Tel. 068/ 21268. 4 rms (all with bath).

$ Rates (including breakfast): IR£17.50 ($30.65) single; IR£12.50 ($21.90) per person sharing. 50% reduction for children. High tea IR£9.50 ($16.65) extra. **Closed:** Nov–Feb.

Tim and Nancy O'Neill will welcome you here. They're a charming couple, and their two teenagers, John and Carol, are very much a part of the hospitality they extend to guests. All four pretty guest rooms are on the ground floor. The dining room overlooks the garden where there's a pleasant patio, and out front, tea and scones are often served on the glassed-in sun porch. Ashgrove House is about half a mile outside town.

BURNTWOOD HOUSE, Listowel, Co. Kerry. Tel. 068/21516. 6 rms (4 with bath).

$ Rates (including breakfast): IR£13 ($22.75) per person without bath, IR£14 ($24.50) per person with bath; IR£14 ($24.50) per person without bath, IR£15 ($26.25) per person with bath, for events and hols. 20% reduction for children. Dinner IR£12 ($21) extra. No credit cards. **Closed:** Nov–Mar.

Mrs. Josephine Groarke is the pleasant hostess of this beautiful Georgian-style house set in very scenic countryside half a mile from town. The centrally heated house is comfortable and modernized, and the food is delicious. All six guest rooms are attractive, with country views.

CEOL NA H'ABHANN, Tralee Rd., Ballygrennan, Listowel, Co. Kerry. Tel. 068/21345. 4 rms (3 with bath).

$ Rates (including breakfast): IR£11.50 ($20.15) per person without bath, IR£13.50 ($23.65) per person with bath; IR£14.50 ($25.40) per person without bath, IR£16.50 ($28.90) per person with bath, during events and hols. No credit cards. **Closed:** Nov–Mar. **Parking:** Private car park.

Our readers have been profuse in their praise of this beautiful two-story, thatch-roofed home on a riverbank near a lovely wooded area about half a mile outside Listowel. Mrs. Kathleen Stack takes great pride in her beautifully furnished home, one of the very few thatch-roofed homes open to guests in Ireland. She offers tea and scones upon arrival, and breakfasts are served in the Georgian dining room, with fine linen, china, and silver. The house is centrally heated, and there's private parking. The famous Ballybunion golf course and beach are only 9 miles away.

CURRAHEEN HOUSE, Curraheen, Tralee, Co. Kerry. Tel. 066/21717. 5 rms (none with bath).

$ Rates (including breakfast): IR£14 ($24.50) single; IR£11 ($19.25) per person sharing. 25% reduction for children. High tea IR£8 ($14) extra; dinner, IR£10 ($17.50). No credit cards. **Closed:** Dec–Feb.

Mrs. Bridget Keane's traditional farmhouse is on the Tralee–Dingle road (R559), 4 miles from Tralee, overlooking Tralee Bay, with mountain views in the distance. The very embodiment of Irish hospitality, Mrs. Keane is known for her delicious high tea and dinner, often featuring salmon and fish fresh from local waters, as well as a lovely mixed grill. Those fantastic Dingle Peninsula sandy beaches are only 2 miles away, and golfing, pony trekking, and sea fishing are all available locally.

READERS RECOMMEND

Ballyseede Castle, *Tralee, County Kerry (tel. 066/25799; Telex 73050). "We loved this picturesque 15th-century castle just outside Tralee. It's surrounded by lovely farmland, and in addition to friendly hospitality and attractive accommodations, they throw in the story of the ghost that some guests swear they've seen roaming the halls—we were delighted!"*—Mr. and Mrs. John Duggan, New York, N.Y.

The Spinning Wheel, *Listowel, County Kerry (tel. 068/21128). "We discovered this delightful restaurant in Listowel. It's a spotlessly clean, friendly restaurant with excellent food and reasonable prices"*—Al and Eileen O'Sullivan, Long Beach, N.Y.

The Three Mermaids, *William Street, Listowel, County Kerry (tel. 068/21454 or 21784). "This is an excellent bar/restaurant, where we had a superb meal, one of us opting for fresh fish, the other for steak. We were also glad to see that they feature some vegetarian dishes. Good service, good food, reasonable prices."*—Josephine Dailey, Lynchburg, Va.

CHAPTER 13

SHANNONSIDE: COUNTIES CLARE, LIMERICK & NORTH TIPPERARY

1. COUNTY CLARE

• **WHAT'S SPECIAL ABOUT SHANNONSIDE**

2. COUNTY LIMERICK

3. NORTH COUNTY TIPPERARY

All too often, visitors rush through the Shannonside region, perhaps because so many deplane at Shannon and they're off and away without realizing that many of Ireland's treasures lie right at their point of entry. Yet it is quite possible, as I once did, to spend 2 full, happy weeks in Ireland and not go far beyond the boundaries of the area that has been dubbed Shannonside.

In County Clare you can span Ireland's history from Stone Age relics around Lough Gur to Craggaunowen's Bronze Age lake dwelling and 15th-century castle to mementos of the 1800s in the Clare Heritage Centre. Nature has turned up such wonders as the Aillwee Cave, the Cliffs of Moher, and the rocky expanse of the Burren. And the mighty River Shannon is ideal for fishing, boating, or just plain loafing. As far as entertainment goes, there's a choice of medieval banquets and the traditional music that lives so vigorously in generation after generation of County Clare fiddlers, whistle players, and pipers.

Limerick city is full of history, with fascinating sightseeing in and around town, and theater and good pubs after dark. Northern Tipperary's Holy Cross Abbey is an enduring tribute to the dedication and devotion of early Christians and in Roscrea there's a beautiful home built within ancient castle walls.

Any one of the accommodations listed in the three sections of this chapter will be convenient as a base for leisurely day trips to cover the entire region. With so many riches in such a small area, it would indeed be a pity to make the Shannonside region simply an overnight for first-day-in and last-day-out.

1. COUNTY CLARE

SHANNON AIRPORT Chances are your first and last glimpses of Ireland will be from a plane arriving at or departing from Shannon Airport, which is in County Clare, some 15 miles west of Limerick, with good bus service into town.

Flight Information For information on flight arrivals and departures, phone 061/61666 from 6am to 6:45pm in summer, 9:30am–5:30pm in winter. After hours, year round, dial 061/61582 or 61407.

Getting To and From the Airport Local **buses** will drop you off at Ennis Road guesthouses (ask the driver when you get on) or take you to the bus terminal or any of the stops along O'Connell Street. If you're going from Limerick to

WHAT'S SPECIAL ABOUT SHANNONSIDE

Beaches
- ☐ Lahinch, a wide sandy strand stretching for more than a mile along Liscannor Bay.
- ☐ Kilkee, a small, horseshoe-shaped beach backed by high cliffs, offering safe swimming with mostly calm waters.

Antiquities
- ☐ Craggaunowen, site of a 15th-century castle and reconstructed lake dwelling of the Bronze Age.
- ☐ Lough Gug, site of Stone Age dolmens, stone circles, pillar stones, and other relics.

Natural Wonders
- ☐ The Cliffs of Moher, 5 miles of majestic, undulating cliffs.

- ☐ The Burren, a vast, barren moonscape, carpeted with wildflowers found nowhere else in the world.
- ☐ Alwee Cave, a strange, spectacular underground landscape formed more than 1,000 years ago.

Entertainment
- ☐ Bunratty and Knappogue castles, with fun-filled medieval banquets and authentic period entertainment.
- ☐ Traditional music in West County Clare pubs in Doolin, Miltown Malbay, and Lisdoownvarna.
- ☐ Theater in Limerick city.

---

the airport, there's a Shannon Airport bus stop on Henry Street, you can flag the bus down on Ennis Road, or you can catch it at the main bus terminal on Parnell Street. One-way fare is IR£3 ($5.25).

The **taxi** fare to and from Limerick will run around IR£12 ($21).

Airport Services Shannon is much more than simply a passing-through sort of airport. There's a **Tourist Information Desk** to help you book accommodations (but don't arrive without them in July or August!), to assist you with itineraries, and to be as generally helpful as Tourist Offices all around the country. Here, too, you can book a medieval banquet (look for the Castle Tours desk).

Bus Eireann Tours also has a desk where you can find out about tours around the country and book those you fancy.

The airport's **other services** include a post office, a bank, VAT-refund desk, and scads of car-rental desks (again, please don't arrive in high season without having reserved a car in advance).

Where to Eat Budgeteers will find good, inexpensive food in the bright and attractive **Shannon Airport Grill.** It's self-service and offers a wide variety, from snacks to full meals, hot and cold. For a special meal at slightly higher prices, there's the buffet restaurant, the **Lindbergh Room,** named for the American aviator who had a hand in selecting Shannon as the site of this international airport. For bar snacks, drop in at the ground-floor **Burren Lounge and Bar.** All have hours coinciding with flight arrivals and departures.

WHAT TO SEE & DO

There are **Tourist Offices** on Clare Road, Ennis (tel. 065/28366), open year round, and at the Cliffs of Moher Visitor Centre, Liscannor (tel. 065/81171), open March through October.

THE TOP ATTRACTIONS

BUNRATTY CASTLE AND FOLK PARK, Shannon Airport Rd. (N18), Bunratty, Co. Clare. Tel. 061/61511.

★ You can drive or take a bus (the Shannon Airport bus makes a stop here) out to **Bunratty Castle.** Allow a full morning or afternoon for the excursion. The marvelously restored 15th-century castle was built for the O'Briens, earls of Thomond, and its restoration has included heavy carved-wood chests, woven tapestries, ornate wooden chairs, and pieces that look as though they have been here forever—furnishings so complete that the O'Briens who first lived here would feel right at home should their shades come back today. (That brings up a little aside: Officially, Bunratty has no ghosts, but if you should chance to encounter a sad lady dressed in pink, or a soldier wearing a torn tunic and holding an empty scabbard, look quickly before they vanish—the lady threw herself into the courtyard upon learning that her lover had been killed the night before their wedding day, and from time to time they're spotted wandering the castle, though never together. As I said, officially the story is not true, but unofficially, it is widely told.) Enter across a drawbridge into the vast, vaulted Great Hall, the center of castle life where the tradition of elaborate feasts is re-created these days with nightly medieval banquets (see "Evening Entertainment," below). Narrow, winding stone steps lead to upper floors where family life went on.

The authentic cluster of homes, shops, and workshops from early Irish life that make up the **Folk Park** on the castle grounds came about almost by accident. When a centuries-old farmhouse was moved from the Shannon Airport to make way for a longer runway, it became the nucleus of a collection of traditional buildings that include a blacksmith shop, a fisherman's cottage, a coastal cottage with thatch firmly tied against Atlantic gales, and several craft shops. Each is a "working" exhibit: A costumed "housewife" bakes brown bread in a covered iron pot on the hearth, weavers are at their looms, and the blacksmith is hard at work. At one end of the park, a typical village street has been reconstructed, complete with post office, draper, tea room, a tiny pub, and a reconstruction of Kearney's Hotel, a typical rural 19th-century hotel (its fully licensed bar is a great place to rest weary feet). This is a good place to pick up gifts, crafts, and souvenirs.

Admission: IR£5 ($8.75) adults, IR£2.50 ($4.40) children.

Open: Daily 9:30am–5:30pm. **Bus:** Limerick–Shannon Airport bus.

DURTY NELLY'S, Bunratty, Co. Clare. Tel. 061/364072.

★ While at Bunratty, day or night, you won't want to miss Durty Nelly's pub, even if you sip a nonalcoholic white lemonade. It's on a stone, arched bridge right at the entrance to Bunratty Castle grounds, and it served the soldiers of the garrison for centuries after it was built in 1620. Like the earls of Thomond in the castle, those soldiers would feel perfectly at home in today's Durty Nelly's. The wooden chairs and benches are the same, peat still burns in the fireplaces, and some of the hodgepodge hanging on the walls and from the rafters looks as though it was put there by one of the earl's protectors and hasn't been moved since. Even the pigeon cote has survived in one room of the loft. Durty Nelly's draws huge crowds: Tourists you'd surely expect, but amazingly, large numbers of locals come to the place. There's good pub grub (I never go past without stopping for a toasted corned beef and cheese sandwich or soup and brown bread), as well as two good eateries (see "Where to Eat," below). After about 9pm things get pretty lively with music and singing, and even those drinking in the outside patio join in.

Open: 12:30–2:30pm.

THE CRAGGAUNOWEN PROJECT, Quin, Co. Clare. Tel. 061/72178.

★ One of County Clare's most interesting sightseeing stops is the Craggaunowen (pronounced *"Crag*-an-owen") Project near Quin, 14 miles from Shannon Airport (signposted from Quin, north on R469). Craggaunowen Castle has an interesting display of medieval art objects, and in the lake a short walk away is a fascinating re-creation of a crannog, a Bronze Age lake dwelling. A cooking site of the Iron Age and a bowl dated to 148 B.C. can also be seen. The earthen ring fort on the grounds holds a reconstructed farmer's home of some 15 centuries ago, with fields of barleys and wheats of the types grown by prehistoric Celts.

For me—thrilled as I have been at Tim Severin's daring voyage across the Atlantic to retrace St. Brendan's legendary route of A.D. 700—a highlight here is the glass

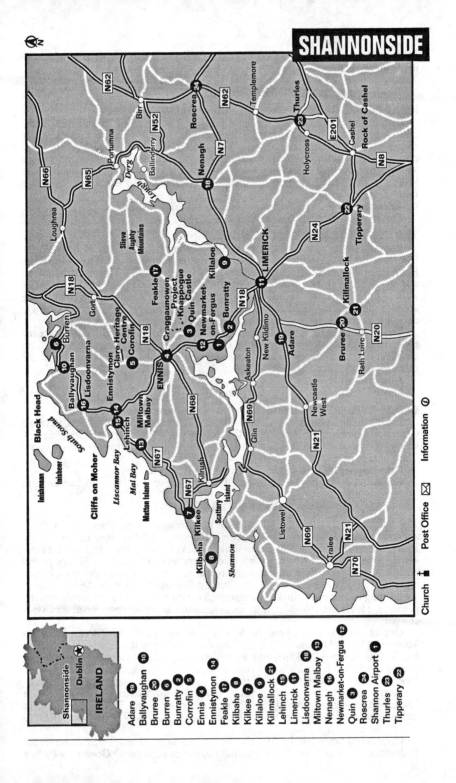

SHANNONSIDE

IRELAND

Shannonside
Dublin ⊛

Adare 19
Ballyvaughan 10
Bruree 20
Burren 6
Bunratty 2
Corrofin 5
Ennis 4
Ennistymon 14
Feakle 17
Kilbaha 8
Kilkee 7
Killaloe 9
Killmallock 21
Lehinch 15
Limerick 11
Lisdoonvarna 18
Miltown Malbay 16
Nenagh 16
Newmarket-on-Fergus 12
Quin 3
Roscrea 24
Shannon Airport 1
Thurles 23
Tipperary 22

Church ✝   Post Office ⊠   Information ⓘ

shelter which has been constructed to house the tiny leather *Brendan* in which he made the voyage.

Admission: IR£2.50 ($4.40) adults, IR£1.50 ($2.65) children.
Open: May–Sept, 10am–6pm; Oct–Apr, 9:30am–4:30pm.

KNAPPOGUE CASTLE, Quin, Co. Clare. Tel. 061/71103.

Knappogue Castle (of the medieval banquets) is furnished in authentic 15th-century pieces, somewhat more formally than Bunratty Castle. It's one of the many castles of the McNamara tribe, who held great power from the 5th to the 15th century. The beautifully restored courtyard has an excellent souvenir and crafts shop. Knappogue, about 12 miles from Shannon Airport (signposted from Quin, south on R469), is the setting for one of Castle Tours medieval banquets (see "Evening Entertainment," below).

Admission: IR£2 ($3.50) adults, IR£1.30 ($2.30) children.
Open: May–Oct, 9:30am–5:30pm.

THE CLIFFS OF MOHER, Co. Clare.

Ireland's spectacular coastline really outdoes itself at the Cliffs of Moher near Liscannor on R478. In Irish, they're named Ailltreacha Mothair ("The Cliffs of the Ruin"), and they stretch for 5 miles, rising at places to 700 feet. They're breathtaking and shouldn't be missed. There's an extensive car park, and you'll have a moderate walk to O'Brien's Tower, which affords the best view of the magnificent cliffs. There are also cliff walking trails, but you are warned by frequent signs to be extremely cautious, as there is some danger that the ground may give way near the edge.

The Visitors Centre at the Cliffs of Moher has a bright and cheerful self-service tea room offering inexpensive soups, sandwiches, and assorted snacks. There's also an excellent gift, literature, music, and souvenir shop, as well as exhibits of wildlife and other local attractions.

Admission: Free.
Open: Visitor Centre, Mar–Oct, daily 10am–6pm.

CLARE HERITAGE CENTRE, Corofin, Co. Clare. Tel. 065/27955.

If your family roots are in County Clare, you'll want to visit the Clare Heritage Centre at Corofin, near Ennis on R476, where you'll find a genealogical research service, thousands of family records, and interesting exhibits portraying life in County Clare in ages past.

Admission: IR£1.50 ($2.65) adults, IR£1 ($1.75) children.
Open: Mid-Mar to Oct, Mon–Sat 10:30am–12:30pm and 2–5pm, Sun 2–5pm.

MORE ATTRACTIONS

The northwestern hump of County Clare is a strange, barren moonscape with no apparent signs of life. This is **The Burren** (An Bhoireann, "The Stony District"—the Irish call it "The Berne"). Those who walk its rocky hills, however, find that far from being sterile, it holds a wealth of tiny wildflowers, some of which are unique to this area. It was also inhabited in prehistoric times, and there are many dolmens, cairns, and ring forts. In Kilfenora, stop by the **Burren Display Centre** (tel. 065/88030) to see an enlightening audiovisual presentation; a tea shop and craft shop are also on the premises. Hours are mid-March to October, from 10am to 6pm. Small admission charge.

One of the best ways to see the Burren is to join one of the **Burren Walking Tours** run by Collin Bunce (tel. 065/20885) from May 30 through September. The 8-mile walk begins at 10:30am, ends around 4:30pm, and costs a mere IR£4 ($7). You bring a picnic lunch, and it's important to wear comfortable, sturdy walking shoes. Pickup points vary with the day of the week, so be sure to check when you book.

In the midst of the Burren, you'll find **Aillwee Cave** (tel. 065/77036), a fascinating underground wonderland of magnificent stalactites. There's a tea room as well as craft shops on the premises. Admission is IR£2.70 ($4.75) for adults, IR£1.40 ($2.45) for children.

Doolin is a tiny coastal village that has gained international fame as a center for traditional Irish music. You'll find it in full sway most nights in **O'Connor's Pub,** a large, rustic place filled with musicians, singers, tellers of tales, students who may have hitchhiked across Europe to get here, and Yanks like us here to take it all in. There's regular **boat service to the Aran Islands** from here, only a 25-minute run, since Doolin is the closest point to the islands on the mainland. In fact, you'll sometimes meet Aran Islanders in O'Connor's of a Sunday night if the seas are calm. Boats leave from Doolin Pier daily, beginning at 10am during the summer, and the fare is IR£8 ($14).

The bustling market town of **Ennis** has many interesting historical buildings, and the Tourist Office (see above) can give you a walking-tour guide through the more historic sections. Headquarters for traditional music, song, and dance is **Cois No hAbhna** (pronounced "*Cush* Na *How*-na"), on Gort Road. The shop has a large selection of records, tapes, and books on Irish traditional music, and they maintain a good schedule of happenings during summer months.

The **Loop Head Peninsula** is a much-overlooked County Clare attraction. A delightful day is one spent driving to seaside **Kilkee** with its curved bay and strand, then down the long finger of land that is the West Clare Peninsula to its end, where the Loop Head lighthouse holds solitary vigil. The coastline is one of clifftops, inlets and coves, sandy beaches, and a softly wild, unspoiled landscape. Along the way there are the ruins of forts, castles, and churches, and should you stop for a pint in a country pub, there are legends to be heard, like that of Kilstiffin Bank, a shoal that lies beneath the Shannon's waters. It was once, so it is said hereabouts, a part of the mainland, but was swept into the Shannon during a fierce storm in the 9th century, carrying people and their homes to a watery grave. (According to the older residents of this area, when sailing ships used to drop anchor off the Kisstiffin Bank, they'd be visited during the night by a small man from beneath the water who would climb the anchor cable and ask them to take up the anchor, for it had gone down his chimney.)

In the little Shannonside village of **Kilbaha** (Cill Bheathach, or "Birch Church"), the Church of Moheen holds a small wooden structure that is one of Ireland's most unusual testaments to the devotion of the people to their faith. It's a tiny three-sided chapel on wheels known as the ✪ **Little Ark of Kilbaha** which, during the years when English-imposed law forbade any landlord to permit a Catholic mass to be held on his land, was hidden away during the week, but pulled down to the shore of Kilbaha Bay on Sunday and placed below the high-tide mark on land that belonged to no man. There mass was said in safety, reverence, and peace.

While you're in Kilbaha, look for sculptor **Jim Connolly's studio,** Kilkee, Kilrush, County Clare (tel. 065/58034). Jim lives and works in a thatched cottage, and his bronze sculptures are brilliant (the most noted is that of Eamon de Valera in Ennis). He's an interesting man to talk to, and while the bronzes may be too pricey and heavy to purchase, he does have a ceramics shop with creative, inexpensive souvenirs. You might phone before going, since he's often away.

The 13-mile drive north of Limerick city via R463 to the charming little Lough Derg harbor village of **Killaloe** is delightful, and **St. Flannan's Cathedral** (12th century) is worth visiting to see the ornately carved Irish Romanesque doorway and **Ogham stone** (which also has runic writings and a crude crucifix believed to be formed by a Viking who had converted to Christianity). Drive along the western shore of the lake to view magnificent scenery and ancient ruins on offshore islands. You're very welcome to fish or swim at no charge; coarse fishing is best at Plassy, and the Electricity Supply Board on O'Connell Street issues free fishing permits.

Ireland's largest inland marina is located at Killaloe, on **Lough Derg.** From May to September, the *Derg Princess,* a 48-seat enclosed river boat, has daily 1½-hour cruises past such historic spots as the site of Brian Boru's fort. Fares are IR£5 ($8.75) for adults, IR£3 ($5.25) for children, and IR£14 ($24.50) for a family ticket. For exact sailing times, contact Derg Line, Killaloe, County Clare (tel. 061/376364).

SAVVY SHOPPING

Antiques

MIKE MCGLYNN ANTIQUES, Bunratty, Co. Clare. Tel. 061/62011.
On the other side of Bunratty Castle, just beyond Fitzpatrick's Shannon Shamrock

Hotel, Mike McGlynn's has an interesting collection of antiques housed in an old-style thatched cottage. Mike and his brother have something to offer everyone from the dedicated antiques hunter to those of us who would simply like to bring back home an old souvenir. For me, it was an elegant teak walking stick which undoubtedly reached these shores by way of an Irish seafarer. For you, it might be a small piece of fine porcelain or some bit of ironwork. There are works of art, china, paintings, furniture, and a host of larger items. They'll gladly insure and ship any purchase too large to tote home. Open Monday through Saturday from 10am to 6pm.

Crafts

BALLYCASEY CRAFT COURTYARD, Shannon, Co. Clare.
This group of craft workshops is signposted on the Limerick–Shannon road, and it's a don't-miss for crafts hunters. Clustered around the farmyard of the 18th-century Ballycaseymore House, individual workshops are home to artisans, from weaver to potter to fashion designer to silversmith to a host of other arts and crafts. The Barn Restaurant serves fresh, appetizing light lunches, with wine available, at modest prices.

CRAFTS GALLERY/WORKSHOP, Doolin, Co. Clare. Tel. 065/74309.
Matthew O'Connell and Mary Gray own and operate this terrific crafts shop beside the church and cemetery in Doolin. Every item is Irish made: sweaters (both wool and mohair), classic fashions, ceramics, crystal, linens, lace, sculpture, leather bags, and even Christmas ornaments. Mary is a designer of contemporary and traditional gold and silver jewelry, much of it with themes drawn from the Burren. They are happy to mail goods anywhere in the world at cost. Open Monday through Saturday from 8:30am to 8pm and on Sunday from 8:30am to 6pm.

MANUS WALSH'S CRAFT WORKSHOP, Ballyvaughan, Co. Clare. Tel. 065/77029.
In Ballyvaughan, stop by this intriguing workshop and Gallery on the main Galway road. Manus's fascination with the Burren landscape is reflected in many of his paintings, and he also has a wide selection of enamelware of Celtic design, rings, necklaces, and wall hangings. Open Monday through Saturday from 10am to 5pm.

Fashions

BUNRATTY COTTAGE INTERNATIONAL FASHION SHOP, Bunratty, Co. Clare. Tel. 061/74321.
Bunratty Cottage, across from the castle, is where Irish designer Vonnie Reynolds displays her own designs as well as an exceptional stock of Irish woolens, tweeds, and gifts. Open Monday through Saturday from 10am to 6pm.

EVENING ENTERTAINMENT
Medieval Banquets

Right here, I have to confess that for years I resisted the lure of the medieval banquets in County Clare, convinced of two things: that I'd spend the evening in the company of other tourists when I had come to Ireland to enjoy the company of the Irish; and that the whole show would be too "cute" to be wholesome. My second confession is that I was wrong, and that I've seldom missed attending one each trip since friends dragged me along a few years back. True, your fellow diners will almost surely be other tourists (unless, that is, you come in the off-season, when the Irish come in droves), but the great thing is that it's that mischievous Irish sense of fun that prevails, no matter *who* is in attendance.

BUNRATTY CASTLE MEDIEVAL BANQUET, Bunratty, Co. Clare. Tel. 061/61444.

When you walk across the drawbridge into Bunratty Castle's Great Hall and are handed your first mug of hot mulled wine, the great good spirit of Irish fun takes over and Americans, French, German, Australians, Italians, and every other nationality represented lose their tourist trappings and become fellow conspirators in the evening's fantasy plot.

As for the show, of course it's hokey—it's meant to be! Blarney may have originated down there in County Cork, but there's lots of it afoot in Bunratty, as story follows story and song follows song, and the stuffiest, most "touristy" type turns mellow in the sometimes-hilarious struggle to get through a meal without benefit of cutlery. The talent on stage is first-rate, and I defy you to keep a dry eye as the golden notes of an Irish harp wash over you in a massive room brought suddenly to a complete hush.

A typical banquet menu will begin with a cup of broth, followed by spareribs, half a roast chicken (sometimes a hunk of well-done beef), salad, vegetables, homemade bread torn into ragged chunks, and a dessert just dripping with calories. To top it all off, you quaff a mug of mead (the traditional honey-based drink). You'll be given a knife, and after that it's you and your fingers, just as in the old days. Between each course, one little bit of stage business or another goes on, the most popular of which is the appointment of the evening's "Earl of Thomond" from among the guests, who reigns at the top of the long banquet table. His "duties" include banishing another one of the guests to the dungeon and addressing his assembled guests with as flowery a bit of oratory as he can manage. It's a memorable night—the earls of Thomond should have such a good time under their own roof!

Admission: IR£26 ($45.50).

Hours: Two banquets nightly, at 5:45 and 9pm. **Reservations:** You should reserve before leaving home if at all possible, either through a travel agent or by writing the Reservations Manager, Shannon Castle Tours, Shannon Airport, County Clare, Ireland. Should you arrive without a reservation, any Tourist Office will try to get you a seat, or you can give the reservations manager a call to ask about an opening (sometimes there are cancellations). Just don't miss it!

KNAPPOGUE CASTLE, Quin, Co. Clare. Tel. 061/71103.

This massive 1467 stronghold is some 19 miles from Limerick city, which means you must have a car, since it is not served by local buses. The banquet here differs from that at Bunratty in that the group is smaller and more intimate, and the entertainment tends to be somewhat less ribald, with sketches to bring to life myths and legends of Old Ireland and lots of song and dance. Many of my Irish friends prefer this to Bunratty (and there are usually a fair few Irish faces at the table), and in the best of all possible Irish holidays, you'd get to both.

Admission: IR£26 ($45.50).

Hours: May–Oct, two banquets nightly, at 5:45 and 9pm. **Reservations:** You should reserve before leaving home if at all possible, either through a travel agent or by writing the Reservations Manager, Shannon Castle Tours, Shannon Airport, County Clare, Ireland. Should you arrive without a reservation, any Tourist Office will try to get you a seat, or you can give the reservations manager a call to ask about an opening (sometimes there are cancellations).

SHANNON CEILI, Bunratty, Co. Clare. Tel. 061/61788.

While the banquets offer fun on a "lord and lady of the castle" level, over in the Bunratty Folk Park the merriment is more akin to that of the "downstairs" crew in those castles. There's traditional song and dance, as audience and performers engage in lively back-and-forth joshing. And the dishes that come to table are likely to include Irish stew, apple pie, and soda bread.

Admission: IR£21 ($36.75).

Hours: May–Sept.

Traditional Music

If there's one thing County Clare has, it's traditional music and good fiddlers, tin-whistle players, bodhran players, and pipers to play it. And their favorite venue by far is the local pub. Out at Bunratty, **Durty Nelly's** (tel. 061/364872) (see "The Top

Attractions," above) rings with music, some professional, some spontaneous, every night. The **Merriman Tavern,** in Scarriff (tel. 0619/21011), is an ancient place with a big ballad room that frequently hosts the likes of the Chieftains, with a small admission charge. The crowd in attendance is likely to include those cruising the Shannon who have pulled into Scarriff for the night, fishermen, and lots of locals.

On Friday nights, **Pat Donnlans,** in Kilkishen (tel. 065/72204), features music most nights. Other watering holes that regularly attract musicians are: **John Lynch's pub, Doonaha,** in Kilkee (tel. 065/57004); **Hassets,** in Quin (tel. 065/25683); **John Minogues,** in Tulla (tel. 065/25106); **Lena Hanrahan,** in Feakle (tel. 0619/24090); the **Smyth Village Hotel,** in Feakle (tel. 0619/24002); and **Kennedy's Pub,** in Puckane (tel. 067/24171). The ancient **Crabtree Tavern,** Ballycar, Sixmilebridge (tel. 061/71235), has ceili dancing and traditional music several nights a week during the summer. **Morrisey's Pub,** in Doonbeg (tel. 065/55012), has traditional music and sing-alongs on Saturday nights during the summer.

WHERE TO STAY

NEAR LIMERICK & SHANNON AIRPORT

✓ **GALLOWS VIEW, Bunratty East, Co. Clare. Tel. 061/72125.** 5 rms (4 with bath).
$ Rates (including breakfast): IR£15.50 ($27.15) single; IR£12.50 ($21.90) per person sharing. 20% reduction for children. No credit cards. **Closed:** Dec–Jan. **Parking:** Private car park.

Donal and Mary McKenna offer a rather special brand of hospitality at this pretty, two-story bungalow that's reached by a scenic country road that runs between Bunratty Castle and Durty Nelly's 1¼ miles from the castle. One nicely done up family room and a double are on the ground floor, a blessing for those who have trouble with stairs. Several of Mary's interesting antique pieces are scattered throughout the house, and there's an inviting air to the lounge and dining room. There's central heating.

HILL SERENE HOUSE, Carnakilla, Newmarket-on-Fergus, Co. Clare. Tel. 061/71294. 4 rms (none with bath).
$ Rates (including breakfast): IR£15 ($26.25) single; IR£12 ($21) per person sharing. No credit cards. **Closed:** Oct–Apr.
Perched on a hilltop just outside the village (from Limerick, turn right and look for the sign), this is a bright, modern bungalow. Carmel and Tim Murphy are the engaging couple who welcome guests, and their twin-bedded rooms are all attractively furnished, with sinks and shaving points.

SHANNONSIDE COUNTRY HOME, Newmarket-on-Fergus, Co. Clare. Tel. 061/364191. 8 rms (all with bath).
$ Rates (including breakfast): IR£16 ($28) single; IR£13 ($22.75) per person sharing. 50% reduction for children. High tea IR£6.50 ($11.40) extra; dinner, IR£10 ($17.50). No credit cards.
Mary and Noel Tobin's two-story home is a favorite not only of our readers, but of airline personnel flying into and out of Shannon. The large lounge sports a snooker table and chess board, as well as several musical instruments, which often leads to impromptu singing sessions—Noel plays the accordion, daughter Dee Dee plays the mandolin, and daughter Geraldine is a dancer, as well as an art student. Mary will provide breakfast for those with early airline departures.

To get here, from Limerick, turn right at the fourth traffic light after Bunratty Castle, then right at the next junction; from Shannon, turn left on the first turnoff after passing Shannon Industrial Estate (it's 2 miles from the airport).

Worth the Extra Money

FITZPATRICK'S SHANNON SHAMROCK HOTEL, Bunratty, Co. Clare. Tel. 061/361177. Fax 061/61252. Telex 72114. 100 rms (all with bath). TV TEL
$ Rates: IR£50–IR£60 ($87.50–$105) single; IR£64–IR£80 ($112–$140) double. Service charge 10%. ACC, AE, DC, MC, V.

⭐ Its location alone would justify the pricey rates at the Shannon Shamrock—5 miles from Shannon Airport, 9 miles from Limerick, and just next door to Bunratty Castle. The Folk Park, the medieval banquet, and Durty Nelly's are all just a short walk away, and there's courtesy bus service to the airport upon request, as well as to Limerick twice daily.

There's much more than location, however, to recommend this lovely hotel. It's a sister to Fitzpatrick's Castle Hotel in Killiney near Dublin and the Silver Springs in Cork, and while the three bear no outward resemblance, they are all looked over with the same personal care and attention by the Fitzpatrick family. The exceptionally efficient and friendly staffs reflect that same sort of personal concern.

The Shannon Shamrock, a low, rambling stone building, exudes low-key informality in a setting of pure luxury. The stone-floor lobby leads into a large lounge whose focal point is a huge stone fireplace (ablaze on cool evenings). Comfortable seating arranged for intimate groupings make this an inviting place to have morning coffee, afternoon tea, or late-night drinks. The pretty cocktail bar, with dark-blue velvet upholstering, skylights, and lots of dark wood and green plants, has music Wednesday through Sunday during summer months. Shades of soft green and rose dominate the dining room. There's an indoor heated swimming pool and a sauna on the premises and plenty of parking space. Decor and furnishings are outstanding in all guest rooms, but for a sumptuous break from the rigors of travel, treat yourself to a stay in one of the beautiful and spacious River Suites—velvet chair and sofa coverings, king-size beds, and windows with a view are featured in bed-sitting rooms for two and separate bedroom and bed-sitting room for four.

READERS RECOMMEND

Shannon View, *Bunratty West, County Clare (tel. 061/364056). "Mrs. E. Woulfe is a wonderful, hospitable hostess, with beautifully appointed and comfortable rooms. A perfect beginning or end for Shannon Airport travelers."*—Mr. and Mrs. W. Eich, Palo Alto, Calif. ✔

NEAR ENNIS

Ennis is a busy market town some 16 miles from Shannon Airport, 23 miles from Limerick on N18.

MASSABIELLE, off Quin Rd., Ennis, Co. Clare. Tel. 065/29363. 5 rms (4 with bath).

$ Rates (including breakfast): IR£15.50 ($27.15) single without bath; IR£11 ($19.25) per person sharing without bath; IR£1.50 ($2.65) per person additional with bath. 25% reduction for children. High tea IR£8.50 ($14.90) extra; dinner, IR£11 ($19.25). No credit cards. **Closed:** Nov–Mar.

⭐ Monica O'Loughlin, mother of seven engaging children, has one of the prettiest homes in this scenic area. The small lawn bordered by colorful flower beds gives some indication of the attractive interior. Monica has made extensive use of antiques and authentic reproductions in her furnishings, and her musical brood (among other instruments, they play the piano, viola, and tin whistle) echo their mother's warm hospitality. Among the five bedrooms, one family room will sleep three. Outside, there's a well-maintained tennis court. Massabielle is 2 miles from Ennis on the Quin road (from Limerick, turn right just past the West County Inn, then right at the next traffic light; it's signposted on the Quin road).

Worth the Extra Money

THE OLD GROUND HOTEL, O'Connell St., Ennis, Co. Clare. Tel. 065/ 28127. Fax 065/28112. Telex 71603. 60 rms (all with bath). TV TEL

$ Rates: IR£53–IR£63 ($92.75–$110.25) single; IR£70–IR£90 ($122.50–$157.50) double. 33⅓% reduction for children. ACC, AE, DC, MC, V.

This ivy-covered, two-story brick building is set behind an iron fence in spacious grounds right in the heart of Ennis, just 12 miles north of Shannon Airport. It's known for its happy blend of old-world elegance and charm with modern comfort and efficiency. Its interior is an intriguing mixture of contemporary and period decor and furnishings, with a luxurious restaurant in the traditional manner and open fires when there's a chill in the air. Guest rooms are furnished with the latest in guest conveniences. Some are decorated pretty much as standard hotel rooms are around the world, others have Victorian touches, and all have hand-woven Donegal bedspreads. The Celtic Bar is a relaxing meeting place for locals as well as guests. The Old Ground is a Trust House Forte property, assuring the highest standards in service as well as amenities. It's also a very convenient base for exploring the glories of Shannonside.

READERS RECOMMEND

Carberry, Kilrush Road, Ennis, County Clare (tel. 065/24046). "I highly recommend Mrs. Pauline Roberts, who provides a breakfast that can't be beat, and the rooms are immaculately clean and tastefully decorated."—Kate and Stan Katz, Albany, N.Y. [*Author's Note:* Another reader wrote to praise the good, firm mattresses at Carberry.]

KILKEE

Kilkee is a popular family seaside resort set on the shores of a beautiful horseshoe-shaped bay surrounded by high cliffs. It's some 35 miles southwest of Ennis, and the perfect base for exploring West Clare and getting in some safe swimming or other water sports.

ARAN HOUSE, West End, Kilkee, Co. Clare. Tel. 065/56170. 6 rms (1 with bath).

$ Rates (including breakfast): IR£16.50 ($28.90) single without bath; IR£11.50 ($20.15) per person sharing without bath; IR£2 ($3.50) per person additional with bath. 20% reduction for children. No credit cards. **Closed:** Nov–Easter.

Mrs. Mary Enright's Aran House sits near the end of the curved bay, with a view of the cliffs across the water. Mrs. Enright makes her guests feel right at home. Her buff-colored stucco house has twin bay windows in front and many antiques among its furnishings. There are six comfortable, homey guest rooms, and the two singles overlook a small garden and rocky cliffside.

HALPIN'S HOTEL, 2 Erin St., Kilkee, Co. Clare. Tel. 065/56032 or 56317. Fax 065/56317. 11 rms (7 with bath).

$ Rates: IR£15–IR£19 ($26.25–$33.25) per person, depending on season. ACC, AE, DC, MC, V.

Halpin's is a small, family-run hotel in this charming seaside resort. There are rooms both with and without private bath, the dining room serves good food at moderate prices, and there's entertainment in the bar during the summer season.

MILTOWN MALBAY

Miltown Malbay is about halfway between Lahinch and Kilkee on a scenic coastal road, N67. It is particularly noted for the large number of traditional Irish musicians and singing pubs in the area.

LEAGARD HOUSE, Miltown Malbay, Co. Clare. Tel. 065/84324. 6 rms (2 with bath).

$ Rates (including breakfast): IR£11 ($19.25) per person sharing without bath; IR£14 ($24.50) single without bath; IR£2 ($3.50) per person additional with bath. 33⅓% reduction for children. High tea IR£7 ($12.25) extra; dinner IR£10 ($17.50). No credit cards. **Closed:** Nov–Mar.

Leagard House is set in quiet, rural surroundings and is an interesting, rambling, one-story house that once was run as a nursing home by Ireland's President Hillary before he went into politics. Suzanne and John Hannon, the present owners, take a personal interest in all their guests, and John is happy to give advice on such important matters as getting to the right pub at the right time to hear some of County Clare's fine traditional musicians. Suzanne excels in the kitchen, and her meals have won such praise that they now accept dinner reservations for nonguests; there's also a wine license. The six guest rooms are all light and airy, and I especially was drawn to the two up front which open onto a small, glass-enclosed room. All look out on peaceful country scenes, and the dining room opens to a windowed porch.

ENNISTYMON

Some 16 miles northwest of Ennis on N85, Ennistymon ("Enn-iss-*teye*-mon") is a holiday center on the main Ennis–Lisdoonvarna road, just 2½ miles from Lahinch, with its beautiful sandy strand and excellent golf course.

MACMAHON'S PUB, Church St., Ennistymon, Co. Clare. Tel. 065/ 71078. 5 rms (none with bath).
$ Rates (including breakfast): IR£11.50 ($20.15) per person. Dinner IR£10 ($17.50) extra. No credit cards.
In Ennistymon, Tom and Mary McMahon have five homey guest rooms above this popular country-style pub. Mary is a cousin of a former Rhode Island governor, and Americans are given an especially warm welcome. Guest rooms are scattered about on several upstairs levels, and each has an individual size, shape, and character. Pub grub is available in the pub (along with good conversation with the locals who favor this place) at lunchtime.

TULLAMORE FARMHOUSE, Kilshanny, Ennistymon, Co. Clare. Tel. 065/ 71187. 4 rms (3 with bath).
$ Rates (including breakfast): IR£14 ($24.50) single without bath; IR£11 ($19.25) per person sharing without bath; IR£1 ($1.75) per person additional with bath. 20% reduction for children. High tea IR£8 ($14) extra; dinner, IR£10 ($17.50). No credit cards. **Closed:** Nov–Feb.
Mrs. Eileen Carroll is the charming hostess of this large house which is set in lovely countryside 6 miles from the Cliffs of Moher (signposted on the main Lahinch–Cliffs road). The house is centrally heated and there is a beautiful TV lounge with a view overlooking the hills. The food is excellent and there is a very relaxed atmosphere about the place.

LISDOONVARNA

One of Ireland's most popular holiday spots, Lisdoonvarna is 8 miles north of Ennistymon on N85, with a spa, therapeutic springs, and the sea just 5 miles away.

TESSIE'S FERNHILL FARMHOUSE, Doolin Rd., Lisdoonvarna, Co. Clare. Tel. 065/74040. 4 rms (3 with bath).
$ Rates (including breakfast): IR£15 ($26.25) single without bath; IR£12 ($21) per person sharing without bath; IR£1 ($1.75) per person additional with bath. 15% reduction for children. Dinner IR£12 ($21) extra. No credit cards. **Closed:** Dec–Feb. **Parking:** Paved car park.
★ This marvelous old (200 years at least, according to its owner, Tess Linnane), farmhouse, set on a hill overlooking fields and distant hills, 2 miles from Lisdoonvarna and 2 miles from Doolin, has twice won Best Farmhouse awards. There's a large front lounge with picture windows looking out to the fields, and one guest room on the ground floor is ideal for the handicapped. Upstairs bedrooms have kept the character of the house, some with wooden peaked or slanted ceilings. All are nicely furnished, and there's central heat.

READERS RECOMMEND

Ballinalacken Castle, *Lisdoonvarna, County Clare (tel. 065/74025). "This is a 19th-century house (bed-and-breakfast) with the castle right next door. We enjoyed the luxury of the huge double rooms. There is a bar and dining room downstairs and the owners even offer to bring* *drinks to your room. We enjoyed free baby-sitting services there as well. The bar manager will give you the key to the castle next door so you may explore on your own."*—K. O'Brien, Tujunga, Calif.

Lynch's Hotel, *The Square, Lisdoonvarna, County Clare (tel. 065/74010). "We loved this small, family-run hotel. It's very modern in outward appearance, but inside there's a very warm, homey atmosphere. Maureen Lynch and her family made us feel very much at home, and an added bonus was their family rate that saved us money."*—Sarah Caliri, Bogota, N.J.

DOOLIN

Doolin is a small, vibrant coastal village some 27 miles northwest of Ennis, and 5 miles southwest of Lisdoonvarna.

ARAN VIEW HOUSE HOTEL, Doolin, Co. Clare. Tel. 065/74061. 15 rms (all with bath).
$ **Rates** (including breakfast): IR£14–IR£18 ($24.50–$31.50) per person. 25% reduction for children. No credit cards. **Closed:** Dec–Apr.

A longtime favorite of our readers when it operated as a bed-and-breakfast accommodation, this large country home, built about 1736 high on a hill, is notable for its breathtaking sea views of the Aran Islands and the Cliffs of Moher. Owners Theresa and John Linnane extend an especially warm Irish welcome to guests. The window-walled lounge takes advantage of the magnificent views, and the cozy drawing room bar, with its crackling log fire, adds to the loveliness of this charming place. The rustic-style dining room, with its big bay window, is the perfect setting for an excellent Irish meal. Activities available to guests include fishing, golfing, horseback riding, walks on the Burren, boat rides to the Aran Islands, and, of course, musical nights in local pubs.

A Hostel

DOOLIN HOSTEL, Doolin Village, Co. Clare. Tel. 065/74006. 15 rms (double, single, and family rms). Bus: Service direct to the hostel from Galway and Limerick.
$ **Rates:** IR£5 ($8.75) per person. No credit cards.

Privately owned and run by Josephine and Paddy Moloney, with full Tourist Board approval, this is sometimes known as the "Old Farmhouse Hostel." It's located on the Moloney dairy farm and provides hot showers, central heating, full kitchen facilities, a dining room, a sitting room, laundry and drying room, bicycles for rent, and a hostel shop. The Moloneys also operate a bureau de change on the premises, and they provide farmhouse accommodations for nonhostelers. No registration card is required.

READERS RECOMMEND

Harbour View, *Doolin, County Clare (tel. 065/74154). "This is a first-rate accommodation. Mrs. Kathleen Cullinan's home is set on a hillside, with a magnificent view of the surrounding countryside. Mrs. Cullinan was very friendly and was helpful in recommending things to see and do in Doolin."*—G. Wazeter and S. Strazzella, Bayonne, N.J.

BALLYVAUGHAN

About 10 miles northeast of Lisdoonvarna via N67, Ballyvaughan is on an inlet of Galway Bay at the edge of the Burren.

HYLAND'S HOTEL, Ballyvaughan, Co. Clare. Tel. 065/77037 or 77015. Fax 065/77131. 12 rms (9 with bath).
$ **Rates:** IR£18–IR£23 ($31.50–$40.25), depending on season. ACC, AE, MC, V. **Closed:** Oct–Mar.

This small hotel is a real charmer. Dating back to the early 18th century, the two-story hotel is now in the hands of the eighth generation of the Hyland family, and the personal atmosphere is evident the minute you walk through the front door. The comfortable, attractive residents' lounge has a fireplace glowing with a turf fire, as does the public lounge on the premises, where local musicians gather nightly and in impromptu sessions uphold the County Clare tradition of good music and good spirits. Dunguaire Castle is just 15 miles away, and the hotel will arrange for you to attend the medieval banquet there if you wish. Bedrooms differ in size, but are quite nicely decorated.

FEAKLE

About 17 miles northwest of Killaloe via R461, Feakle is one of the Rent-A-Cottage holiday villages, a good spot for exploring the Lough Derg area.

SMYTH VILLAGE HOTEL, Feakle, Co. Clare. Tel. 0619/24002. 12 rms (all with bath).
$ **Rates** (including breakfast): IR£15 ($26.25) per person for first night, IR£11 ($19.25) per person for second and subsequent nights. 33⅓% discount for children. Dinner IR£10 ($17.50) extra. No credit cards. **Closed:** Oct–Mar.

WHERE TO EAT

PUB GRUB

BROGANS RESTAURANT AND BAR, 24 O'Connell St., Ennis, Co. Clare. Tel. 065/29859.
  Cuisine: BAR FOOD/GRILLS.
$ **Prices:** Fixed-price bar lunch and restaurant grills IR£3.50 ($6.15). No credit cards.
  Open: 10:30–4pm and 5–10:30pm.
Brogans serves bar food, as well as salads and hot or cold lunch plates and grills in the evening in the same price ranges. Soup and sandwiches are available in the bar continuously, beginning at 10:30am.

CRONIN'S BAR AND RESTAURANT, Newmarket-on-Fergus, Co. Clare. Tel. 061/71157.
  Cuisine: BAR FOOD.
$ **Prices:** IR£3–IR£5 ($5.25–$8.75). ACC, AE, DC, MC, V.
  Open: Daily 10:30am–10pm.

If a pricer meal in Cronin's lovely little restaurant (see below) is not on your agenda, stop in for an inexpensive meal in the bar and lounge. Homemade soups are excellent, and the menu includes sandwiches, salad plates, smoked salmon, seafood quiche, traditional Irish stew, sandwiches, and an Irish cheese platter.

DURTY NELLY'S, Bunratty, Co. Clare. Tel. 061/364861.
  Cuisine: BAR FOOD.
$ **Prices:** IR£3–IR£5 ($5.25–$8.75). ACC, AE, DC, MC.
  Open: Lunch only, 12:30–2:30pm.

Soup, sandwiches, salads, and hot dishes featuring roasts, seafood, or chicken are excellent value at this memorable pub next to Bunratty Castle (see "What to See and Do," above). It also houses the moderately priced Oyster Restaurant and pricier Loft Restaurant (see below).

RESTAURANTS

Doolin

BRUACH NA HAILLE, Doolin, Co. Clare. Tel. 065/74120.
  Cuisine: SEAFOOD/CONTINENTAL/VEGETARIAN.
$ **Prices:** Appetizers IR£2–IR£4 ($3.50–$7); main courses IR£6.50–IR£13.50 ($11.40–$23.65). No credit cards.
  Open: May–Oct, dinner only, 6–9:30pm.

⭐ 💲 In Doolin, alongside the Aille River you'll find this terrific little restaurant whose name means "Bank of the River." Helen and John Browne serve marvelous seafood and local dishes in a restored country house with flagstone floors and whitewashed walls. The menu features everything from soup and salads to fresh mackerel, salmon, and local shellfish, and a limited range of foreign specialties, with the emphasis on local seafood. Soups, desserts, and bread are all homemade. Wine is available by the glass.

New Limerick

CRONIN'S BAR AND RESTAURANT, Newmarket-on-Fergus, Co. Clare. Tel. 061/71157.
   Cuisine: PROVENCIAL FRENCH/VEGETARIAN/BAR FOOD. **Reservations:** Recommended.
💲 **Prices:** Dinner IR£16 ($28). ACC, AE, DC, MC, V.
   Open: Dinner only, Mon–Sat 6–10pm.

⭐ 💲 Right in the center of the village of Newmarket-on-Fergus, Pat and Teresa Cronin have created this combination of a lively public bar and an adjoining restaurant that is the epitome of intimacy and superb food. The bar food is excellent. The restaurant specializes in Irish harvests from land and sea, using only the freshest ingredients and injecting a bit of provincial French flavor in their preparation. You'll find such dishes as poached escalopes of salmon with leek sauce, Aran scallops in pastry with chive sauce, entrecôte Madagascar flambé, loin of lamb Athena, and breast of duckling in black-cherry sauce. There's also a very good wine list. Service is polished and professional, yet there's a relaxed atmosphere that, along with the food, makes this one of the most popular eateries in the area with locals as well as visitors. There's a public parking lot just down the street, important in this village of tiny streets.

DURTY NELLY'S OYSTER AND LOFT RESTAURANTS, Bunratty, Co. Clare. Tel. 061/364861.
   Cuisine: TRADITIONAL/SEAFOOD/VEGETARIAN.
💲 **Prices:** Oyster Restaurant, appetizers IR£2–IR£5 ($3.50–$8.75); main courses IR£8–IR£12 ($14–$17.50). Loft Restaurant, Appetizers IR£3–IR£5 ($5.25–$8.75); main courses IR£9–IR£14 ($15.75–$24.50). ACC, AE, DC, MC.
   Open: Oyster Restaurant, Daily 10:30am–10pm; Loft Restaurant, dinner only, Mon–Sat 6–10pm.

⭐ 💲 When Durty Nelly's set about adding on the downstairs Oyster Restaurant, I confess to serious misgivings, but I needn't have worried—you'd never know that the restaurant had not been there as long as the pub, so well does the design fit in with the original. As for the food, it's excellent, and I am especially fond of the fresh seafood (smoked trout, salmon, oysters, etc.). Steaks, pork, roast duckling, and chicken Kiev share the menu with the likes of traditional Irish stew and boiled ham and cabbage.

Upstairs, the Loft Restaurant, although rustic in decor, is that little bit more formal, intimate, and quieter. Specialties include veal escalopes stuffed with pork and herbs, scampi flambéed in brandy with a luscious cream-and-herb sauce, and chicken in a white-wine-and-ginger sauce.

Ennis

OLD GROUND HOTEL, O'Connell St., Ennis, Co. Clare. Tel. 065/28127.
   Cuisine: TRADITIONAL/CONTINENTAL/SEAFOOD.
💲 **Prices:** Fixed-price bar lunch IR£3.50 ($6.15); fixed-price restaurant meal IR£8 ($14) at lunch, IR£18 ($31.50) at dinner. ACC, AE, MC, V.
   Open: Lunch daily 12:30–2:30pm; dinner daily 6:30–10:30pm.

⭐ For a very special lunch or dinner in a setting of old-world charm, stop by the Old Ground. In its O'Brien Room restaurant, superb seafood, steaks, pork, chicken, and salads are given a continental touch in a setting of candlelit elegance. In the Poet's Corner Bar, there's an excellent buffet lunch featuring roasts and other hot dishes, as well as salads.

WORTH THE EXTRA MONEY

MACCLOSKEY'S AT BUNRATTY HOUSE, Bunratty, Co. Clare. Tel. 061/ 74082.
Cuisine: TRADITIONAL/CONTINENTAL. **Reservations:** Essential.
$ Prices: Fixed-price dinner IR£23 ($40.30), plus 10% service charge. AE, DC, V.
Open: Dinner only, Tues–Sat 6:30–10pm. **Closed:** Christmas–Feb.

Bunratty House (just back of the castle) is an elegant mansion that dates back more than a century and a half. Its living quarters have seen comings and goings that would probably fill a book, but it's a sure bet that its arched-ceiling cellar has never before seen the likes of MacCloskey's gourmet restaurant. Gerry and Marie MacCloskey left West Cork and their award-winning Courtyard restaurant in Schull to bring their expertise to Shannonside, and the result is one of Ireland's most beautiful restaurants. The low ceilings and 1½-foot-thick walls have been white-washed to a pristine white as a background for delicate shades of pink and rose, which are punctuated by the deep blue of tall candles at each table. The mansion's original wine cellar has been retained, and behind its ironwork gates rests an excellent selection of good wines.

Main courses of the fixed-price dinner change often to be sure that only the freshest produce, meats, and seafood are served. A typical five-course offering might include such starters as snails in garlic butter, a selection of melon with kiwi fruit, or smoked salmon; cream of lettuce soup or salad with Stilton cheese dressing; main courses of sea trout with hollandaise sauce, rod-caught salmon baked with herbs, leeks, and mushrooms, or black sole on the bone; fresh garden vegetables; and dessert of iced lemon-and-lime soufflé, rhubarb tart, or stuffed chocolate-covered pears.

READERS RECOMMEND

The Piper's Chair, Doolin, County Clare (tel. 065/74242). "Just next to O'Connor's Pub, the Piper's Chair serves fine food in a charming atmosphere, specializing in local seafood and using only the freshest ingredients. The O'Connors also provide B&B at really inexpensive rates."—Otis and Jane Maclay, Houston, Texas.

Kilkee

THE KRAZY KRAUTS, The Strand, Kilkee, Co. Clare. Tel. 065/56240.
Cuisine: SEAFOOD/SNACKS/LIGHT MEALS. **Reservations:** Recommended at dinner.
$ Prices: Snacks IR£2–IR£4 ($3.50–$7); fixed-price dinner IR£8 ($14). No credit cards.
Open: May–Sept, 9am–9pm. **Closed:** Oct–Apr.

Right on the Strand at Kilkee, Doris and Klaus Meya have opened this bright, cozy café. For now, it's open from May to September only, since the Meyas spend winters in their native Germany, but their plans are to become "Irish" year round as soon as possible. Their fully licensed place serves fresh and well-prepared light meals all day for exceptionally moderate prices. Don't miss the appealing little wine bar in the back with its tiny fireplace and paintings by local artists—wine specialties are German whites and French reds, and while you're there be sure to sample "Klaus's special" apéritif.

2. COUNTY LIMERICK

LIMERICK CITY

Limerick gets its name from the Irish *Luimneach,* meaning "Bare Spot," and centuries ago that's just what was here—a barren, hilly bit of land on an island. Today you'll find a well-laid-out city with row after row of Georgian-style houses. In the intervening years the site has been changed and molded by just about every group that has shaped the country's history. Because the island sat at the lowest ford of the Shannon, it is believed early Celts built an earthen fort at the island's highest point. Then came the Danes, in A.D. 831, to build a base from which to go aplundering. More than a century later Brian Boru sent them packing and installed the O'Briens as rulers. Next it was the Normans, with their stout city walls and castles. Portions of their walls remain to this day, as does King John's Castle. They were the first to bridge the Shannon (at the spot now crossed by the 1838 Thomond Bridge). Native Irish, of course, had no place in that Anglo-Norman stronghold, but were exiled to the south side of the river, where they eventually built their own walls and called their area Irish Town.

It was in 1691 that William III's siege of Limerick (which had once been abandoned as the city's stubbornly brave defenders prevented any breach of their walls) ended with the signing of a treaty of honorable and reasonable terms. You can see the stone on which it was signed at one end of Thomond Bridge, where it is enshrined as a memorial to a treaty whose terms were never carried out by the British. Even now Limerick is known as the "City of the Violated Treaty."

During the 18th century Limerick took on its present-day form, with stylish town houses going up along broad avenues extending far beyond the old boundaries of Irish Town and English Town. In the last few decades of this century, Limerick had declined into a dingy, somewhat gray city, with few outward charms. In the 1980s, however, the city began a restoration program that has put a bright new face on things, with even more improvements in the planning stage.

Limerick is 15 miles east of Shannon Airport, 123 miles southwest of Dublin, 23 miles southeast of Ennis, and 68 miles northeast of Killarney.

ORIENTATION

GETTING THERE There's direct train service from Cork, Dublin, and Killarney, with good bus connections from almost any destination in the country. By car, Limerick City can be reached via N7 from the east, N24 and N20 from the south, N18 from the north.

TOURIST INFORMATION You'll find the **Tourist Office** in a building on Arthur's Quay (tel. 061/317522). Behind the Tourist Office is a lovely riverside park, with a pathway joining the historic medieval quarter with the city center. The office is open Monday through Saturday from 9am to 7pm, with limited Sunday hours during the summer months. The Limerick Junior Chamber of Commerce publishes a Shannonside entertainment guide weekly during summer months, which is available at most hotels as well as at the Tourist Office.

CITY LAYOUT Limerick's main street is the three-quarters-of-a-mile-long **O'Connell Street,** which becomes **Patrick Street** at its northern end. The west-to-east road that leads to Shannon Airport is called **Ennis Road** west of the Shannon, **Sarsfield Street** at its western end in the city, and **William Street** at its eastern end. The major intersection of O'Connell and Sarsfield is the center of most of the city's business and shopping, and all city bus lines pass this junction.

ESSENTIALS The **telephone area code** for Limerick is 061.

GETTING AROUND

The **bus and railway station** is on Parnell Street on the southeast side of town, and the number to call for all bus and rail information is 061/42433.

Taxi ranks are at the railway station and at the corner of Thomas Street and Cecil Street, just off O'Connell Street. Call 48844 or 46230 for a taxi.

WHAT TO SEE & DO

The very first thing to do is to go by the **Tourist Office.** This is one of the best in the country, and they're prepared to book accommodations for you, steer you to eateries, help plan sightseeing excursions, tell you about craft shops in the area, alert you to any special events, festivals, or evening entertainment currently on, and send you away loaded down with maps and brochures to make your time in Shannonside a joy. There's also a very good selection of Irish publications for sale in the office.

Monday through Saturday they conduct **walking tours** of Old Limerick. Ask about the **Shannon Heritage Trail Explorer Ticket** that saves you money on sightseeing admissions.

For sightseeing out of town, pick up the Bus Eireann **day trips** folder from the Tourist Office. There are some 17 tours during the summer months, and they go as far afield as Connemara to the north and the Ring of Kerry to the south.

The Top Attractions

Among the points of interest in the city, **St. Mary's Cathedral** ranks near the top. In the oldest part of the city, it was built in 1172 by Donal Mor O'Brien, the then King of Munster, on the site of his palace. It holds some intriguing antiquities, and the view from its bell tower is especially fine. There's no charge, and in summer it's open daily from 9am to 1pm and 2:30 to 5:30pm (in winter, it's only open in the morning). From mid-June to mid-September, there's an excellent son-et-lumière (sound-and-light show) nightly inside the cathedral.

King John's Castle rises from the riverbank at one end of Thomond Bridge, and its 10-foot-thick walls include massive drum towers. The **Treaty Stone** is across the Shannon at the other end of the bridge.

The **Limerick Museum,** 1 St. John's Square (tel. 061/47826), exhibits artifacts from the Lough Gur area, as well as city charters, chains of office, the "nail" from the City Exchange on which merchants once struck their deals, currencies from periods in the city's history as far back as the Vikings, and a good deal more. It's free, and open Tuesday through Saturday from 10am to 1pm and 2:15 to 5pm. Another interesting collection of ancient Irish metalwork, medieval bronzes, and enamels is in the **Hunt Museum,** at the National Institute for Higher Education, Plassey House (tel. 061/61511).

Irish art from the 18th, 19th, and 20th centuries is exhibited at the **Limerick City Gallery of Art,** Percy Square (tel. 061/310633); hours vary, so check locally.

You're welcome to watch dedicated ladies making the famous ✪ **Limerick lace** at the Good Shepherd Convent, Clare Street (tel. 061/46676; it's out the Dublin road, across from the People's Park) Monday through Friday from 9:30am to 1pm and 2 to 5pm. Items ranging from lace handkerchiefs to bridal veils may be purchased.

Because it's painstakingly made on very fine Brussels net, few people are willing to devote time and care to such intricate work today. However, nine young women in Limerick, under the guidance of Fr. Joe Young from the Southill Parish, are working to keep the skill alive. If their enterprise thrives, they will be able to fill mail orders from the United States as well as meet future demands in Ireland. Contact **Traditional Handmade Limerick Lace,** Unit 8, Tait Business Centre, Dominick Street, Limerick; or in the U.S., Gerard South, c/o Sutton's Cache, 60 Kraft Avenue, Bronxville, NY 10708 (tel. 914/337-6077).

The Pub Scene

Sadly, a good many of the city's finest pubs have been modernized right out of their character, but ✪ **W. J. South's,** also known as the **Crescent Bar** (tel. 061/318850), on the Crescent (that's where Daniel O'Connell's statue commands the center of O'Connell Street), holds on to the trappings of age with a firm grip. There's a long white marble bar up front, divided by wood and etched-glass partitions. Faded tapestries hang on the wall, and behind the bar is an elaborate mahogany structure, its arched niches framing old bottles and backed by mirrors speckled with age. Just back of the small front bar, a larger room has walls devoted to a display of rugby photos (the Garyowen rugby team consider South's their "local"). The best pint in Limerick is said to be pulled here, and you'll hear a lot about sports. An attractive lounge bar has been added to the old pub; morning coffee is served, as well as good, traditional Irish food at pub-grub prices (see "Where to Eat," below).

The "aged" look at **Flannery's,** 20 Catherine Street, at the corner of Cecil Street (tel. 061/44450), comes from woodwork that once graced an old distillery, and according to Jerry Flannery, "there's still plenty of whiskey salted in it." The pub itself is only a little more than 50 years old, but it has the comfortable atmosphere of a country pub, with a small snug at one end, and in the evening a core of regulars ever ready to converse with the visiting Yank. Flannery's also serves good pub grub at lunch.

My personal favorite of all Limerick pubs is neither aged nor particularly atmospheric, but it's very, very Irish. ⚪ **Matt Fennessy's Pub,** New Street, Punches Cross (tel. 061/29038), is the epitome of a neighborhood local, filled with convivial souls, a good pint pulled, and in general just the sort of place to pass a pleasant evening. A bit out from the city center, but easily reached via either a longish walk or a short bus ride, New Street turns off O'Connell (it's the intersection with Dan Ryan's Garage on one corner, Punches Pub on the opposite). Inside, there's an old-fashioned bar, a lounge, and a snug affectionately dubbed "The Senate" by regulars, who often debate the affairs of the country. While there's no *scheduled* sing-along at Fennessy's, spontaneous sing-alongs often break out on weekend nights. The clientele is nearly all local, and they make Americans very welcome. Look for Mick Feerick behind the bar, one of Ireland's charmers. Incidentally, bar food is served from 12:30 to 2pm, should you find yourself in the neighborhood.

⚪ **Nancy Blake's (Mulcahy's Pub),** 19 Denmark Street (tel. 061/46327), is a cozy, old-style pub popular for pub lunches and traditional music on Tuesday nights.

EVENING ENTERTAINMENT

From the Tourist Office, pick up the **"What's On"** booklet, which lists current goings-on in Limerick and its environs, as well as a Calendar of Events.

The Performing Arts/Dancing

BELLTABLE ARTS CENTRE, 69 O'Connell St., Limerick. Tel. 061/ 319866.
The Belltable puts on very good concerts and plays at low to moderate prices. They have a very strong program of theater, visual arts, music, opera, and dance. In summer months, Irish theater is presented by Limerick's professional company, Island Theater Company. The centre also has a wine bar and restaurant on the premises.
   Admission: Tickets IR£5–IR£8 ($8.75–$14).

GLENTWORTH HOTEL, Glentworth St., Limerick. Tel. 061/43822.
You can sometimes trip the light fantastic in this hotel ballroom, combining it with a light supper if you wish.
   Admission: IR£4 ($7), IR£8 ($14) with supper.
   Open: Wed and Sun 9:30pm–12:30am. Days and hours can vary, so call ahead.

Traditional Music

NANCY BLAKE'S (MULCAHY'S PUB), 19 Denmark St., Limerick. Tel. 061/46327.
Ballads, reels, and jigs, offered Tuesday and Sunday at 9pm.

FOLEY'S BAR, Lower Shannon St., Limerick. Tel. 061/48783.
Monday, Tuesday, and Friday are devoted to traditional music, and on Sunday and Thursday there's a combination of ballads and traditional music, evenings at 9pm.

ROYAL GEORGE HOTEL, O'Connell St., Limerick. Tel. 061/44566.
The Glory Hole Pub in this popular hotel features traditional Irish music every night of the week at 9pm.

GLENTWORTH HOTEL, Glentworth St., Limerick. Tel. 061/43822.
Ballads hold forth here every Friday night at 9:30pm.

TWO MILE INN, Ennis Rd., Limerick. Tel. 061/53122.
Check Kitty O'Brien's Pub in this hotel on the main Limerick–Shannon Airport

road for traditional music, usually beginning at 9:30pm. From time to time, they also present cabaret on Saturday.

WHERE TO STAY

BOGSIDE HOUSE, Ennis Rd., Limerick, Co. Limerick. Tel. 061/52703. 5 rms (3 with bath).
$ Rates (including breakfast): IR£11 ($19.25) per person without bath, IR£13 ($22.75) per person with bath. No credit cards.

Opposite Dunne's Store on Ennis Road, this is the modern home of Carmel Beresford, and has been one of my most popular recommendations with readers. Airport and city buses stop just outside the door. The five guest rooms are spacious, the house is centrally heated, and there's good off-street parking. Carmel will gladly book banquets and help you arrange transport to them. She can also provide chauffeur-driven minibus packages for small touring or golfing groups of 8 to 10 people for 3, 4, or 7 days.

CLONEEN HOUSE, Ennis Rd., Limerick, Co. Limerick. Tel. 061/54461. 6 ✓ rms (4 with bath).
$ Rates (including breakfast): IR£14 ($24.50) single without bath; IR£12 ($21) per person sharing without bath; IR£4 ($7) per person additional with bath. ACC, AE, MC, V. **Parking:** Private car park.

Bridgit and Robert Power have made extensive renovations in this red-brick period home, only a 5-minute walk from the city center. The airport bus and city buses stop just outside the front gate, and there's ample parking in the rear. Guest rooms are most attractive, and the bay-windowed dining room overlooks a lovely rose garden.

CURRAGHGOWER, Ennis Rd., Limerick, Co. Limerick. Tel. 061/54716. 4 rms (none with bath).
$ Rates (including breakfast): IR£15 ($26.25) single; IR£11 ($19.25) per person sharing. 20% reduction for children. No credit cards.

Friendly Mrs. Power makes visitors feel right at home in her three-story brick home. There are four guest rooms, all with sinks, nicely decorated, and comfortably furnished, and you'll breakfast with a view of the pretty back garden. There's central heat and off-street parking.

DELLASTRADA HOUSE, 136 Upper Mayorstone Park, Ennis Rd., Limerick, Co. Limerick. Tel. 061/52300. 3 rms (none with bath).
$ Rates (including breakfast): IR£10 ($17.50) per person. 25% reduction for children. High tea IR£8 ($14) extra. No credit cards. **Closed:** Nov–Apr.
Mrs. Feeney is the friendly hostess of this semidetached two-story house set in a nice, quiet area. The house is centrally heated and dinner is available in the evening. All three bedrooms have sinks.

GLEN EAGLES, 12 Vereker Gardens, Ennis Rd., Limerick, Co. Limerick. Tel. 061/55521. 6 rms (2 with bath).
$ Rates (including breakfast): IR£15.50 ($27.15) single without bath; IR£11.50 ($20.15) per person sharing without bath; IR£2 ($3.50) per person additional with bath. 10% reduction for children. No credit cards. **Closed:** Dec–Feb.
Carole O'Toole is the sort of caring hostess who will pack you a lunch to take along on a day trip. The O'Tooles can also arrange for car hire and chauffeur-driven guided tours in the region. The two-story house is in a quiet cul-de-sac off Ennis Road and only minutes from the city center. It is centrally heated, and there's a TV lounge, a pretty garden, and off-street parking.

ST. ANTHONY'S, 8 Coolraine Terrace, Limerick, Co. Limerick. Tel. 061/52607. 3 rms (none with bath).
$ Rates (including breakfast): IR£11 ($19.25) per person. No credit cards.

The Misses Mary and Kathleen Collins are delightful sisters first brought to my attention by a reader who wrote that "they really put themselves out to make a tourist's stay pleasant." The two-story house is their family home. It's neat as a pin and has a warm, homey atmosphere. Meals are served in a dining room overlooking a garden, and breakfast comes with homemade apricot and other fruit jams. They also serve a lovely afternoon tea with home-baking. The guest rooms are comfortably furnished (one has three single beds) and have sinks and built-in wardrobes.

ST. MARTIN'S, 4 Clanmorris Gardens, Limerick, Co. Limerick. Tel. 061/55013. 3 rms (none with bath).

$ Rates (including breakfast): IR£12.50 ($21.90) single; IR£10 ($17.50) per person sharing. 10% reduction for children. No credit cards. **Closed:** Nov–Feb.

Mrs. Roche is a warm, friendly woman and her home is situated off the Ennis road, in a quiet area close to the city center. Her three bedrooms are nicely done up, and her breakfasts are delicious.

ST. MARY'S, Clancey's Strand, Limerick, Co. Limerick. Tel. 061/5519. 4 rms (none with bath).

$ Rates (including breakfast): IR£12 ($21) per person. No credit cards. **Closed:** Nov–Feb.

"Convenient" is one word for St. Mary's as the city center is only about 4 minutes away by foot. Mrs. Walsh's two-story home sits behind neat flowerbeds and rose trees, and there's a sun lounge for guest use. The four guest rooms have sinks and are comfortably furnished, and two connect to accommodate a family. There's a spacious dining room that also serves as a lounge, a small breakfast room, and off-street parking.

TREBOR, Ennis Rd., Limerick, Co. Limerick. Tel. 061/54632. 4 rms (3 with bath).

$ Rates (including breakfast): IR£13 ($22.75) single without bath; IR£11 ($19.25) per person sharing without bath; IR£1.50 ($2.65) per person additional with bath. 20% reduction for children. No credit cards. **Closed:** Christmas.

Mrs. Joan McSweeney's pretty home is only about a 5-minute walk from the city center. There's a TV lounge for guests, and the centrally heated house also has parking facilities.

A Hostel

AN OIGE HOSTEL, 1 Pery Sq., Limerick, Co. Limerick. Tel. 061/314672 or 312107. 70 beds.

$ Rates: IR£4.30–IR£5 ($7.55–$8.75) per person, depending on season; some reduction for under-18s. No credit cards.

The An Oige hostel in Limerick is a large old Georgian house. Right in the heart of the city center, it is located on a public park and has a fully equipped kitchen, dining room, common room, and showers. There are bicycles for rent, and meals can be provided on request. Advance booking is advisable during the summer months.

Worth the Extra Money

ROYAL GEORGE HOTEL, O'Connell St., Limerick, Co. Limerick. Tel. 061/44566. Fax 061/317171. Telex 70710. 58 rms (all with bath). TV TEL

$ Rates (including breakfast): IR£31–IR£37 ($54.25–$64.75) single; IR£26–IR£32 ($45.50–$56) per person sharing. ACC, AE, DC, MC, V.

You couldn't be in a more convenient location than this downtown hotel that has undergone considerable renovation and upgrading. Its pretty dining room is recommended separately (see "Where to Eat," below), and there's a nice lounge and pub, with entertainment in the summer months.

READERS RECOMMEND

Boylans, 22 Davis Street, Limerick, County Limerick (tel. 061/48916). "I spent 13 days in this bed-and-breakfast, which is less than 3 minutes from the rail and bus terminal. Mrs. Teresa

Boylan and family are the happiest and most accommodating people I have yet to meet, the rooms are immaculate, and the breakfast without comparison."—Evelyn Chorlton, Cambridge, Mass.

WHERE TO EAT

Pub Grub

Outstanding pub grub, with Irish specialties, salad plates, hot dishes, sandwiches, and soup is served at the following Limerick pubs between the hours of 12:30 and 2:30pm at a cost of IR£3 to IR£4 ($5.25 to $7):

Flannery's, 20 Catherine Street, Limerick (tel. 061/44450), at the corner of Cecil Street; **☼ W. J. South's,** also known as the **Crescent Bar,** on the Crescent (tel. 061/318850), which specializes in traditional Irish food; **Matt Fennessy's Pub,** New Street, Punches Cross (tel. 061/29038); and **Nancy Blake's (Mulcahy's Pub),** 19 Denmark Street (tel. 061/46327).

Restaurants

COFFEE DOCK RESTAURANT AND BAR, in Jurys Hotel, Ennis Rd., Limerick. Tel. 061/55266.
   Cuisine: BAR FOOD/TRADITIONAL.
$ **Prices:** Appetizers IR£2–IR£4 ($3.50–$7); main courses IR£6–IR£9 ($10.50–$15.75); bar food IR£3–IR£5 ($5.25–$8.75). ACC, AE, DC, MC, V.
   Open: Bar food Mon–Sat noon–2:30pm; Coffee Dock, dinner Mon–Sat 7–10:30pm.

 Jurys offers good value for money, with a wide range of cold meats and salads (with the chef's special dressing) served in the bar, and in the evening, heaping portions of beef, pork, chicken, and fish.

THE GRILL ROOM, in the Royal George Hotel, O'Connell St., Limerick. Tel. 061/44566.
   Cuisine: TRADITIONAL/SEAFOOD/VEGETARIAN.
$ **Prices:** Appetizers IR£2–IR£5 ($3.50–$8.75); main courses IR£6–IR£10.50 ($10.50–$18.40); Tourist Menu IR£5.75–IR£7.90 ($10.05–$13.85). ACC, AE, DC, MC, V.
   Open: Daily noon–10pm (Tourist Menu available Mon–Sat). **Closed:** Christmas Day.
The Grill Room in this centrally located hotel serves moderately priced meals in an attractive setting. Specialties include local beef, lamb, and pork, as well as the freshest of seafoods.

COUNTY LIMERICK

Whether you're driving or making use of Bus Eareann's excellent day trips by bus, there are several worthwhile attractions in County Limerick.

TOURIST INFORMATION Tourist Offices in County Limerick are located at **Lough Gur Stone Age Centre,** Bruff (tel. 061/85186), open May through September; and the **Thatched Cottage and Craft Shop,** Main Street, Adare (tel. 061/86255), open June to early September.

WHAT TO SEE & DO

Some 16 miles southeast of Limerick city via N20, with a turnoff onto the Killmallock road (R518), **☼ Lough Gur** is one of Ireland's most important archeological sites, and thousands of Stone Age relics have been found in and around it. The life-style of those long-ago Irishmen comes vividly alive in the **Stone Age Centre** at Lough Gur (tel. 061/85186). It's designed in the style of Neolithic period dwellings, and inside there are replicas of many of the artifacts discovered in this area, as well as models of burial chambers, stone circles, and dolmens. An audiovisual show tells you what we know of Stone and Bronze Age people and their habits, and, periodically, walking tours are conducted to some of the more important archeological sites. The centre is open mid-May through September, daily from 10am to 5:30pm, and there's a small admission charge.

The little town of **Dromcollogher,** 25 miles southwest of Limerick city (turn off N21 at Newcastle West onto R522), is where you can visit the **Irish Dresden Ltd.** plant and shop (tel. 063/9622), open Monday through Friday from 9am to 1pm and 2 to 5pm. Watch exquisite Dresden figurines being made; then browse through their showroom.

Virtually the entire little village of **Adare,** 10 miles southwest of Limerick city on N21, is a sightseeing attraction, with its pretty thatched cottages, monastic ruins, and a ruined Desmond castle. If your route between Limerick city and points southwest passes through this lovely place, I urge you to stop and ramble a bit.

WHERE TO STAY
Adare

ABBEY VILLA, Kildimo Rd., Adare, Co. Limerick. Tel. 61/86113. 6 rms (all with bath). TV

$ Rates (including breakfast): IR£16 ($28) single; IR£13.50 ($23.65) per person sharing. 33⅓% reduction for children. No credit cards.

Mrs. Mary Dundon's home is a modern bungalow in a scenic setting, and she is a member of the Town & Country Homes Association, keenly interested in all her guests. You'll find attractive guest rooms, central heat, and plenty of parking.

HILLCREST, Ballinvera, Croagh, Co. Limerick. Tel. 061/396534. 4 rms (3 with bath).

$ Rates (including breakfast): IR£15.50 ($27.15) single without bath; IR£11 ($19.25) per person sharing without bath; IR£1.50 ($2.65) per person additional with bath. 25% reduction for children. Dinner IR£10 ($17.50) extra. No credit cards.

Closed: Nov–Mar.

Some 3 miles outside the picture-pretty village of Adare on the main Limerick–Killarney road (N21), Jennie and Michael Power's home sits amid peaceful, bucolic beauty. The Powers are warm, hospitable hosts who take a keen interest in their visitors. With advance notice, Jennie will prepare an excellent dinner.

Worth the Extra Money

ADARE MANOR, Adare, Co. Limerick. Tel. 061/86566. 64 rms (all with bath). TV TEL

$ Rates: IR£130–IR£260 ($241.50–$455) per person, depending on season. ACC, AE, DC, MC, V.

This 18th-century manor, the former family seat of the earls of Dunraven, sits in an estate of some 840 acres of formal gardens and lush parklands on the outskirts of Adare. The manor house is a great combination of turrets, towers, and stonework, with 365 leaded-glass windows and 75 ornate fireplaces, an immense Gothic arched foyer, an elegant, rose-colored drawing room, cozy bar, and vaulted library walled by leather-bound books. Candlelight dinners are served in the formal dining room/conservatory, and there's entertainment in the basement Tack Room.

The guest rooms in the main house are reached by way of a magnificent staircase and are beautifully appointed, most furnished with period reproductions. In the river wing are 36 additional guest rooms. In addition to the exquisite formal gardens, there are wooded nature trails on the grounds, as well as a river well stocked with salmon and trout. A fitness center contains an indoor pool, and riding stables are close at hand. Due to open soon is an 18-hole Robert Trent Jones–designed golf course.

DUNRAVEN ARMS HOTEL, Adare, Co. Limerick. Tel. 061/86209. Fax 061/86541. 44 rms (all with bath). TV TEL
$ Rates: IR£39 ($68.25) single; IR£55 ($96.25) and up double. 50% discount for children. Service charge 12½%. Special weekend rates available. ACC, AE, DC, MC, V.

★ On the edge of what has been called Ireland's prettiest village, the Dunraven Arms is a traditional-style, two-story, yellow-colored hotel that has the look of an old-time inn. Indeed, that small inn-type hospitality greets you at the door and never diminishes throughout your stay. The spacious lounge bar overlooks the gardens and offers excellent bar lunches at budget rates, and the dining room features French cuisine, using fresh ingredients from local farms. Comfortable, traditional furnishings add a homey touch. Public rooms, guest rooms, and executive bedrooms are attractively done up in country prints. This is where Princess Grace and Prince Rainier stayed during their 1963 visit. Not only is this a great sightseeing base—only 10 miles from Limerick, 16 from Bunratty Castle, 25 from Shannon Airport, and about 60 from Killarney and Cork—but fishing, horseback riding, and golf are all close at hand.

Castleconnell

Castleconnell is a pleasant village some 8 miles north of Limerick city on the east bank of the Shannon River, via an unmarked road off R464 from Limerick city.

SPA HOUSE, Castleconnell, Co. Limerick. Tel. 061/377171. 5 rms (4 with bath).
$ Rates (including breakfast): IR£12.50 ($21.90) per person without bath, IR£14 ($24.50) per person with bath. 20% reduction for children. No credit cards. **Closed:** Oct–Mar.
This lovely 18th-century house is half a mile from the village of Castleconnell, about 7 miles from Limerick, on the banks of the Shannon, with its own historic spa well in the gardens. Mrs. Helen Wilson's five bedrooms are attractive and comfortable. There's central heat, plenty of parking, fishing, and marvelous scenic surroundings.

Killmallock

Killmallock is about 21 miles south of Limerick city on T50A, with several interesting ecclesiastical ruins in the vicinity.

ROSEVILLE, Kilbreedy East, Killmallock, Co. Limerick. Tel. 063/88009. 4 rms (none with bath).
$ Rates (including breakfast): IR£12 ($21) per person. 10% discount for children. No credit cards. **Closed:** Oct–May.

★ Sisters Ann and Maureen O'Shea's lovely farmhouse is 2½ miles from the village, just off N20, the main road to Cork, Tipperary, Dublin, and Lough Gur. Their comfortable, homey farmhouse won the Tourist Board's "Most Attractive and Well-Kept Farmhouse" award for several years. I've had nothing but praise from readers for the care and attention they give their guests. There's a lovely rose garden, for which the house is named, and the house has central heating.

Bruree

COOLEEN HOUSE, Bruree, Co. Limerick. Tel. 063/90584. 4 rms (none with bath).
$ Rates (including breakfast): IR£14 ($24.50) single; IR£11 ($19.25) per person sharing. 10% reduction for children. Dinner IR£11 ($19.25) extra. No credit cards. **Closed:** Nov–Apr.
This 300-year-old Georgian-style home is the happy domain of Mrs. Eileen McDonogh. Set on a working dairy farm overlooking the Maigue River half a mile off the main Limerick–Cork road (N20) and 4 miles west of Killmallock, the house is beautifully furnished. There's private fishing on the grounds for salmon and trout, and in the village of Bruree the De Valera museum was the late president's first shrine in the country. Guestrooms are attractive, there's central heat, and guests are welcome to relax in the garden.

READERS RECOMMEND

Mrs. Mary Harnett, *Duneeven Croagh, Rathkeale, County Limerick (tel. 069/64049). "Only a few miles outside Adare, we rented this farmhouse, which has four bedrooms and two baths, dining room, living room, lounge, and kitchen. It came complete with Mr. Harnett's cows and chickens. He was great with the children."* —Barbara Groogan, Milford, N.J.

Ardkeen, *Castlematrix, Rathkeale, County Limerick (tel. 069/64168). "Ardkeen is outstanding in every way. The welcome was warm, the rooms clean, neat, and tidy, the beds comfortable (fitted with electric mattress pads), the sanitary facilities fine. Breakfast was properly cooked and served in a friendly fashion. We were so impressed that we returned for another night a week later."* —Charles D. Fitzgerald, Hallstead, Penna.

Shemond House, *Killaloe Road, Clonlara, Limerick, County Limerick (tel. 061/343767). "Ray and Sheila Devine have the cleanest house I have ever been in. We were greeted with an invitation for tea and after 3 days we hated to leave."* —Mrs. H. Kemp, Ottawa, Canada.

WHERE TO EAT

DUNRAVEN ARMS HOTEL, Adare, Co. Limerick. Tel. 061/86209.
Cuisine: BAR FOOD/TRADITIONAL/CONTINENTAL.
$ **Prices:** Appetizers IR£3–IR£5 ($5.25–$8.75); main courses IR£9–IR£12 ($15.75–$21); bar food IR£3–IR£5 ($5.25–$8.75). ACC, AE, DC, MC, V.
Open: Lunch daily 12:30–2:15pm; dinner daily 7:30–9:30pm. **Closed:** Good Friday, Christmas Day.

You will find the Dunraven Arms bar lunches more than ample to serve as your main meal of the day, and the setting overlooks gardens to the side and back of the hotel. In the dining room, prices are higher and menu choices include such dishes as roast beef, eels in white wine sauce, duckling, and poached salmon.

3. NORTH COUNTY TIPPERARY

WHAT TO SEE & DO

Four miles south of Thurles (25 miles northeast of Tipperary town via R661), **Holy Cross Abbey** (tel. 0504/43241) was founded in 1180, and before it was restored in 1976, had lain roofless for more than 2 centuries. It is so named because a relic of the True Cross was enshrined there in 1180. Notice particularly the beautiful window tracery, especially in the east and west windows and those of the south transept. It's open to visitors daily from 10am to 6pm.

In Roscrea (21 miles north of Thurles via N62), a large Georgian residence, **Damer House,** was actually built within the curtain walls of Roscrea Castle. In the castle yard, the **☉ Roscrea Heritage Centre** displays local artifacts. There's a tourist-information service, as well as a genealogical service covering nearby parishes. It's open Monday through Friday from 10am to 5pm, and from June through September, also on Saturday from 11am to 5pm and on Sunday from 2pm to 5pm. Small admission charge.

The historic town of Nenagh, 25 miles northeast of Limerick city via N7, is the home of the **Nenagh District Heritage Centre** (tel. 067/32633). It's located in the former county gaol, and the governor's house, built in octagonal shape, houses a re-created shop, forge, schoolroom, and dairy. In the gatehouse, you can visit cells in which condemned persons awaited execution, as well as the execution room itself. There's a good pictoral exhibit on the history of the gaol and 19th-century crime and punishment. The centre also operates a genealogical service for those with North Tipperary family connections. It's open to the public April to November, Monday through Friday from 10am to 5pm, and on Saturday and Sunday from 2:30pm to 5pm, with a small admission charge.

WHERE TO STAY
NENAGH

Nenagh is 25 miles northeast of Limerick city via N7.

THE COUNTRY HOUSE, Thurles Rd., Kilkeary, Nenagh, Co. Tipperary. Tel. 067/31193. 6 rms (4 with bath).
$ Rates (including breakfast): IR£15 ($26.25) single; IR£12 ($21) per person sharing. 33⅓% reduction for children. Dinner IR£10 ($17.50) extra. No credit cards.

 This modern bungalow is the home of Joan and Matt Kennedy. The family lounge, which guests are invited to share for TV or just visiting, has a peat-burning fireplace, and the house is set in scenic rural surroundings 4 miles out from Nenagh on R498. Lough Derg is only about 20 minutes away. Guest rooms come with tea/coffee makers and hairdryers, and there's steam heat and good parking. An ideal location for exploring North Tipperary.

ROSCREA

Roscrea is 21 miles onrth of Thurles via N62.

CREGGANBELL, Birr Rd., Roscrea, Co. Tipperary. Tel. 0505/21421. 4 rms (all with shower).
$ Rates (including breakfast): IR£12 ($21) single; IR£10.50 ($18.40) per person sharing. 25% reduction for children. No credit cards.
Mrs. Mae Fallon has four guest rooms with sinks and private showers; all beds have electric blankets. This is a lovely modern bungalow on the outskirts of town via N62, with river fishing nearby. Centrally heated, and plenty of parking.

THURLES

Thurles, a prosperous market town, is some 25 miles northeast of Tipperary town via R661.

HAYES HOTEL, Liberty Sq., Thurles, Co. Tipperary. Tel. 0504/22122. 32 rms (all with bath). TV TEL.
$ Rates (including breakfast): IR£25 ($43.75) single; IR£46 ($80.50) double. ACC, MC, V.

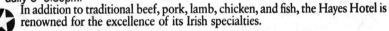 The Gaelic Athletic Association was founded in this historic hotel back in 1884. Today, there's every modern convenience, with comfortable, attractive guest rooms and an excellent restaurant (see "Where to Eat," below).

WHERE TO EAT

HAYES HOTEL RESTAURANT AND COFFEE SHOP, Liberty Sq., Thurles, Co. Tipperary. Tel. 504/22122.
Cuisine: IRISH/TRADITIONAL.
$ Prices: Coffee shop, IR£2–IR£8 ($3.50–$14). Restaurant, appetizers IR£1–IR£3 ($1.75–$5.25); main courses IR£5–IR£8 ($8.75–$14) at lunch, IR£6–IR£12 ($10.50–$21) at dinner. ACC, MC, V.
Open: Coffee shop, daily 9am–10pm. Restaurant, lunch daily noon–3pm; dinner daily 6–9:30pm.

In addition to traditional beef, pork, lamb, chicken, and fish, the Hayes Hotel is renowned for the excellence of its Irish specialties.

CHAPTER 14

GALWAY TOWN

1. ORIENTATION

2. WHERE TO STAY

3. WHERE TO EAT

4. WHAT TO SEE & DO

5. SPECIAL EVENTS

6. SPORTS & RECREATION

7. SAVVY SHOPPING

8. EVENING ENTERTAINMENT

9. EASY EXCURSIONS

Galway owes its existence to a tragedy: Breasail, an ancient Celtic chieftain was so overwhelmed by grief when his daughter drowned in the River Corrib that he established a permanent camp on the riverbank. Located at the only point at which the river could be forded, the camp had become a tiny fishing village by the time the Normans arrived. The newcomers set about trading, utilizing the fine harbor, and in time a medieval town with fine houses and shops grew up, around which they built stout stone walls. Trade soon flourished between Galway, Spain, and France. Early on, 14 of the most prosperous merchant families became known as the "Tribes of Galway," and in 1984 when the city celebrated the 500th anniversary of its charter there was a great "Gathering of the Tribes," with their descendants arriving from around the globe.

Today Galway is a prosperous commercial center, proud of its university and welcoming visitors with open arms. Traces of history abound: the Spanish Arch, a gateway of the old city walls; Lynch's Castle, a 14th-century town house; tiny cobblestone streets and lanes; and along the banks of the Corrib, the Long Walk, for centuries a much-loved waterside promenade.

1. ORIENTATION

Galway is 135 miles west of Dublin via N6, 65 miles northwest of Limerick via N18, and 86 miles southwest of Sligo via N17.

ARRIVING

By Train　There is train service between Galway and Dublin.

By Bus　There is direct bus service to Galway from Dublin, Cork, and Limerick, with connecting services from virtually anywhere in the country.

By Car　Major highways and dual carriageways lead into Galway from every direction except due west. See above for routes.

TOURIST INFORMATION

The **Tourist Office** is in a modern building called Aras Failte just off the Great Southern Hotel side of Eyre Square (tel. 091/63081). It's open from 9am to 6pm, and in July and August, hours are extended, with limited Sunday hours. During summer months an office is open on the Promenade in Salthill. They can book accommodations, excursions, ferry services, and arrange bicycle and car rentals. It's a busy office in July and August, so allow plenty of time if you need their help. You can, however, pick up helpful literature on Galway and the surrounding area, as well as a free **"Tourist Guide to Galway, Gateway to Connemara"** without a long wait.

During July and August, the Junior Chamber of Commerce publishes a weekly booklet, **"What's On in Galway and Salthill."** It is available from the Tourist Office and most hotels. Look also for the newspaper-type publication ***Western Tourism News,*** distributed free in the Tourist Office and many hotels.

TOWN LAYOUT

The **River Corrib** flows through the heart of Galway, with the main shopping and business districts centered between the river and **Eyre Square.** To the west, along the shores of Galway Bay, the popular seaside resort of **Salthill** holds a concentration of the best inexpensive accommodations in the area. There's good bus service between Eyre Square and Salthill, with stops along the main Galway–Salthill road. The **Claddagh** (An Cladach, "the seashore") district is just across the river from the **Spanish Arch,** although its jumble of thatched cottages and narrow lanes has long since been replaced by corporation houses laid out in neat rows. Only the lovely Claddagh ring (two hands clasping a heart surmounted by a crown) remains as the legacy of a people who once had their own manner of dress, dialect, customs—and even their own king—in this fishing village outside the walls of Old Galway.

GETTING AROUND

By Bus/Train   The bus and railway station is at the rear of the Great Southern Hotel on Eyre Square. Bus and rail information is available by calling 62141.

By Taxi   Taxis can be found at ranks around Eyre Square and the railway station, or call 63777.

By Car   Galway's streets are a mixture of narrow lanes and wide avenues. A network of clearly marked one-way streets makes driving in town relatively easy, and there are several well-placed car parks, a blessing for motorists, since on-the-street parking can be difficult to impossible.

FAST FACTS

Area Code   The telephone prefix for Galway is 091.

Currency Exchange   In addition to banks, Bureau de Change services are offered at the Tourist Office (Eyre Square and Salthill), the Imperial Hotel, Eyre Square, the Great Southern Hotel, Eyre Square, and the Browne Doorway, 17 Eyre Square.

Post Office   The General Post Office is on Eglinton Street, with hours Monday through Friday from 9am to 6pm.

2. WHERE TO STAY

There are very few inexpensive lodgings in Galway proper, so my best recommendation is to choose from the many superior accommodations listed in nearby Salthill.

IN TOWN

ADARE GUEST HOUSE, Fr. Griffin Place, Galway, Co. Galway. Tel. 091/62638 or 63963. 10 rms (6 with bath).

$ Rates (including breakfast): IR£12 ($21) per person without bath, IR£14 ($24.50) per person with bath. 25% reduction for children. No credit cards.

Padraic Conroy has taken over for his parents, Kay and Pat Conroy, who were for many years the hosts of Adare Guest House, halfway between the city center and Salthill. There's private parking out front, and in the lovely dining room you'll eat from Royal Tara china. The three-story centrally heated house has guest rooms with built-in sinks. Padraic continues his family's tradition of warm hospitality, and Kay and Pat have moved to a smaller bed-and-breakfast in Lower Salthill (see below).

READERS RECOMMEND

De Soto, *54 New Castle Road, Galway, County Galway (tel. 091/65064). "Dermot and Margaret Walsh own this new and very superior modern family home. There are six comfortable and sparkling bedrooms, TV in the lounge, central heat, and small favors over and above the usual, to say nothing of the marvelous Irish breakfast and private off-street parking. Located right in the city center."*—Bill and Mary Treacy, Fort Walton Beach, Fla.

IN SALTHILL

Salthill is little over a mile from Galway town center, and from May through October there's good bus service, with stops at major points. Lower Salthill is closer to the town center and Upper Salthill stretches out toward the Spiddal road. Both are within easy walking distance to Salthill attractions. There's only the one route, so if you're staying in Salthill, tell the driver the address of your accommodation and you'll be let off at the nearest point. Catch the Salthill bus at the bus station or at Eyre Square.

ALKENVER, 39 Whitestrand Park, Lower Salthill, Galway, Co. Galway. Tel. 091/68758. 4 rms (all with bath).
$ Rates (including breakfast): IR£13 ($22.75) per person. 25% reduction for children. No credit cards. **Closed:** Oct–Mar.

Mrs. Rushe and her family will welcome you warmly to their home, which is located in a quiet area and is convenient to Galway Bay and the city center. The house is centrally heated and there is an attractive TV lounge for guests. The comfortable bedrooms are all equipped with electric blankets.

GALWAY BAY VIEW, 2 Grattan Park, Lower Salthill, Galway, Co. Galway. Tel. 091/66466. 3 rms (all with bath). TV
$ Rates (including breakfast): IR£16 ($28) single; IR£14 ($24.50) per person sharing. No credit cards.

Kay and Pat Conroy are the hosts in this delightful small bed-and-breakfast overlooking Galway Bay. Guest rooms are attractive in decor and very comfortable, as well as coming complete with color TV.

GLENDAWN HOUSE, Upper Salthill, Galway, Co. Galway. Tel. 091/ 22872. 14 rms (10 with bath).
$ Rates (including breakfast): July–Aug, IR£14 ($24.50) per person without bath; Sept–June, IR£13 ($22.75) per person without bath; IR£2 ($3.50) per person additional with bath. 25% reduction for children. No credit cards.

Glendawn is right in the heart of Salthill, just off the coast road and adjacent to a bus stop. The guest rooms are nicely decorated and comfortably furnished. Run by Mrs. Eileen Jones, the low two-story building has an entrance hall paved with Connemara marble.

HIGH TIDE, 9 Grattan Park, Lower Salthill, Galway, Co. Galway. Tel. 091/64324. 5 rms (4 with bath).
$ Rates (including breakfast): IR£11.50 ($20.15) per person without bath, IR£13 ($22.75) per person with bath. 20% reduction for children. No credit cards. **Closed:** Nov–Mar.

Grattan Park is a short, quiet road that turns off the coastal road known as Grattan Road before it joins the Promenade. High Tide looks out to Galway Bay, with the hills of Clare in the distance across the water, and Mrs. Patricia Greaney is the hostess who makes her guests feel right at home. The guest rooms are all nicely decorated, and there's central heat and good parking.

INISHMORE HOUSE, 109 Fr. Griffin Rd., Lower Salthill, Galway, Co. Galway. Tel. 091/62639. 8 rms (5 with bath). TV
$ Rates (including breakfast): IR£15 ($26.25) single without bath; IR£11 ($19.25) per person sharing without bath; IR£1.50 ($2.65) per person additional with bath. 50% reduction for children. No credit cards. **Closed:** Christmas.

Joe and Kathleen Stephens are the friendly hosts of this large, attractive house. Each bedroom is nicely done up, and the house is centrally heated. Meals are delicious.

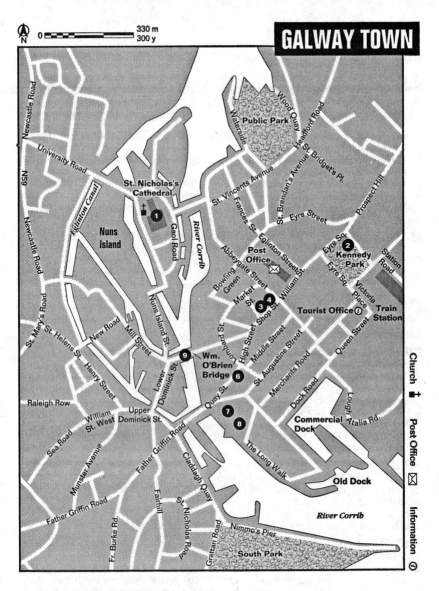

GALWAY TOWN

0 — 330 m / 300 y

N

Newcastle Road
University Road
N59
Newcastle Road
St. Mary's Road
St. Helens St.
Henry Street
Raleigh Row
Sea Road
William St. West
Munster Avenue
Father Griffin Road
Father Griffin Road
Fr. Burke Rd.
Fairhill
St. Nicholas Road
Grattan Road
Nimmo's Pier
South Park

Eglinton Canal
Nuns Island
St. Nicholas's Cathedral ✝ ❶
Gaol Road
River Corrib
Nuns Island St.
New Road
Mill Street
Lower Dominick St.
❾ **Wm. O'Brien Bridge** ❻
Upper Dominick St.
Quay St.
Father Griffin Road
Claddagh Quay
Raleigh Row

Waterside
Wood Quay
Public Park
St. Vincents Avenue
Frances St.
St. Brendan's Avenue
Headford Road
St. Bridget's Pl.
Eyre Street
Prospect Hill
Eyre Sq.
❷ **Kennedy Park**
Station Road
Eyre Sq.
Victoria Place
Train Station
Abbeygate Street
Post Office ✉
Market St.
Eglinton Street
William St.
Bowling Green
Lombard St.
High Street
Shop St.
❸ ❹
Middle Street
St. Augustine Street
Tourist Office ①
Merchants Road
Queen Street
Dock Road
Lough Atalia Rd.
Commercial Dock
The Long Walk
Old Dock
River Corrib

Church ✝
Post Office ✉
Information ①

IRELAND
● Galway Town
⭐ **Dublin**

Bank of Ireland ❷
Bridge Mills ❾
Eyre Square ❷
Galway City Museum ❼
High Street/Quay Street ❻
Lynch Memorial Window ❸
Lynch's Castle ❹
St. Nicholas Cathedral ❶
Spanish Arch ❽

KNOCKREA, Lower Salthill, Galway, Co. Galway. Tel. 091/21794. 9 rms (none with bath).
$ Rates (including breakfast): IR£12 ($21) per person. 10% reduction for children. No credit cards. **Closed:** Nov–Apr.
Knockrea sits in its own grounds and garden on a quiet street in northeastern Salthill. The attractive guest rooms all have sinks, and Rita Heagrey is the gracious hostess.

LAWNDALE, 5 Beach Court, Salthill, Galway, Co. Galway. Tel. 091/ 66676. 5 rms (all with bath).
$ Rates (including breakfast): IR£14.50 ($24.40) single; IR£12.50 ($21.90) per person sharing. No credit cards.
Set back on a quiet street just off Grattan Road, overlooking Galway Bay, Lawndale is the bright, welcoming home of Pat and Margaret Walsh. Three of the attractive bedrooms can sleep three people, and Margaret is glad to add a bed to make it four, if necessary.

MARLESS HOUSE, 8 Seamount, Threadneedle Rd., Salthill, Galway, Co. Galway. Tel. 091/23931. 6 rms (5 with bath).
$ Rates (including breakfast): IR£15 ($26.25) single without bath; IR£11 ($19.25) per person sharing without bath; IR£2 ($3.50) per person additional with bath. 25% reduction for children. No credit cards. **Closed:** Jan–Feb.
⭐ Mary and Tom Geraghty's lovely large, two-story Georgian house sits on Threadneedle Road, just steps from the promenade along Galway Bay. This is one of Galway's prettiest accommodations, with attractive guest rooms and the friendliest of hosts. There is central heat and good parking.

RONCALLI HOUSE, 24 Whitestrand Ave., Lower Salthill, Galway, Co. Galway. Tel. 091/64159. 6 rms (all with bath).
$ Rates (including breakfast): IR£16.50 ($28.90) single; IR£12.50 ($21.90) per person sharing. 20% reduction for children. No credit cards.
⭐ A glowing fireplace takes the chill off cool evenings at Carmel and Tim O'Halloran's two-story house overlooking Galway Bay. There's a sunny front lounge and two outdoor patios for guest use. There are two ground-floor bedrooms and four others upstairs, all with sinks and built-in wardrobes. There is central heat and good parking.

ROSS HOUSE, 14 Whitestrand Ave., Lower Salthill, Galway, Co. Galway. Tel. 091/67431. 4 rms (2 with bath).
$ Rates (including breakfast): IR£12.50 ($21.90) per person. 20% reduction for children. No credit cards.
Mrs. Sara Davy's attractive home is located beside Galway Bay in a quiet cul-de-sac. The house is centrally heated. All rooms have sink, and two have private facilities.

SAILIN, Gentian Hill, Upper Salthill, Galway, Co. Galway. Tel. 091/ 21676. 4 rms (3 with bath).
$ Rates (including breakfast): IR£16 ($28) single without bath; IR£11 ($19.25) per person sharing without bath; IR£1 ($1.75) per person additional with bath. 25% reduction for children under 10. No credit cards. **Closed:** Mid-Oct to Apr.
Parking: Enclosed car park.
⭐ Sailin ("*Saw*-leen") is next door to a bird sanctuary on the shores of Galway Bay. The modern two-story house is home to Mary and Noel McLoughlin and their three sons, and they extend an enthusiastic welcome to visitors, often joining them for bedtime cups of tea and conversation about Galway and the area. The upstairs bedrooms are bright, airy, and attractive, with built-in wardrobes. Two of the bedrooms are adjoining, making an ideal suite for families or friends traveling together. There is central heating and an enclosed car park.

A HOSTEL

GRAND HOLIDAY HOSTEL, Promenade, Salthill, Galway, Co. Galway. Tel. 091/21150. 30 rms.
$ Rates: IR£4 ($7) per person. No credit cards. **Closed:** Dec–Apr.

Formerly a hotel, this spacious hostel overlooks Galway Bay. In addition to the bright, comfortable sleeping quarters (rooms with one, two, and four beds, as well as family rooms), there's a common room and lounge with an open fire. There are free showers, laundry facilities, a restaurant, and a secure bicycle park.

READERS RECOMMEND

Ard Mhuire, Knocknacarra Road, Salthill, Galway, County Galway (tel. 091/22344). "The proprietors of Ard Mhuire, Pat and Teresa McDonagh, are extremely friendly and hospitable, and this establishment is charming and first-rate."—Judith Metcalf, Atlanta, Ga.

Ashbrook, 59 Dalysfort Road, Salthill, Galway, County Galway (tel. 091/23743). "Mrs. M. Duffy is the gracious proprietress of this immaculately clean, cheerful, and well-appointed guesthouse. It is also accessible to the main bus route to Eyre Square, the heart of the city."—Mr. and Mrs. E. Lavan, Staten Island, N.Y.

Bay View, Gentian Hill, Salthill, Galway, County Galway (tel. 091/22116). "Mrs. N. Guilfoyle presides over this delightful, clean, hospitable, and picturesque bed-and-breakfast home located on a hill overlooking Galway Bay."—James and Gwen McColm, Venice, Fla.

Osterly Lodge, 142 Lower Salthill Road, Galway, County Galway (tel. 091/23794). "In all my many years of international travel, I have never encountered a host and hostess so willing to accommodate my every need as Barbara and Pat Guiden in their cheerful, well-situated, and comfortable guesthouse. The Salthill bus from town stops directly in front of the lodge."—Raye Lee Wile-Frazier, Cambridge, Mass.

KNOCKNACARRA

LOCH LURGAN, Barna Rd., Knocknacarra, Galway, Co. Galway. Tel. 091/22450. 4 rms (2 with bath).

$ Rates (including breakfast): IR£12.50 ($21.90) per person without bath, IR£14.50 ($25.40) per person with bath. 33⅓% reduction for children. Dinner IR£9.50 ($15.20) extra. No credit cards. **Closed:** Oct–Mar.

Mrs. Christina Maloney is the hostess of this bungalow overlooking Galway Bay and the Clare hills across the bay. The house is centrally heated, and there's a garden for guests' use.

WORTH THE EXTRA MONEY

CLOONACAUNEEN CASTLE, Cloonacauneen, Claregalway, Co. Galway. Tel. 091/98265. 4 rms (all with bath).

$ Rates (including breakfast): IR£30–IR£35 ($52.50–$61.25) per person. No credit cards. **Closed:** Dec–Apr.

This 15th-century de Burgo castle, 6 miles northeast of Galway town (signposted from N17), has been converted into a charming and atmospheric small hotel by owner Sean Hanly, with the able assistance of manager Marge McKeowen. The character of the castle is still intact, with thick stone walls, the Dungeon Bar and lounge that fairly reeks of medieval times and still manages to be cozy, marble fireplaces, an elegant dining room, and bedrooms beautifully furnished, with a scattering of antique pieces.

CONNEMARA COAST HOTEL, Furbo, Co. Galway. Tel. 091/92108, or toll free 800/223-6510 in the U.S. 85 rms and suites (all with bath). TV TEL

$ Rates (including breakfast): IR£37–IR£47 ($64.75–$82.25) single; IR£67–IR£80 ($117.25–$140) double. ACC, AE, DC, MC, V.

Just 6½ miles west of Galway city via the coastal road, R336, the Connemara Coast Hotel was originally the site of Marino Cottage, home of a highly respected teacher of the Irish language and Gaelic culture who ultimately was instrumental in establishing a College of Gaelic Studies near Spiddal. Today owner Charles Sinnott has honored the respect for tradition while making the Connemara Coast Hotel an oasis of comfort bordering on luxury and an ideal base for exploration of one of Ireland's most intriguing regions. The Connemara Coast welcomes guests with a turf fire burning in the reception area. The bedrooms are nicely decorated and comfortably furnished, with tea and coffee facilities and a color television in each. Some Executive Suites even have their own turf-burning fireplaces.

Dining/Entertainment: There's a convivial, two-tier bar, where traditional folk music and a turf fire add to the ambience. The lovely two-tiered dining room overlooks a magnificent setting of private shoreline through a large window wall. Fresh seafood from local waters is featured, with delights such as lobster cooked in garlic, Irish whiskey, and cream, or breaded escalopes of salmon with cream-and-dill sauce. There are also various landlubber dishes, like Connemara lamb, steak, duckling, and chicken. Service is of as high a standard as is the food, and entertainment might be either classical piano or traditional Irish music.

Facilities: A recently added indoor leisure center includes a swimming pool, whirlpool, saunas, and steam bath.

3. WHERE TO EAT

As one of Ireland's most popular holiday spots (with natives as well as visitors), Galway is blessed with numerous exceptionally good places to eat. Pub grub is plentiful and the best budget buy, of course, but there are many moderately priced restaurants as well. In addition, the surrounding area has eateries that draw Galway residents and have gained nationwide kudos for the quality of the food, service, and ambience.

PUB GRUB

In all the pubs listed below, heaping plates of roast beef or pork or lamb plus at least two vegetables seldom cost more than IR£3.50 ($6.15), and all offer soup, sandwiches, and salad plates at well under that price. Unless otherwise noted below, food service is offered between the hours of 12:30 and 2:30pm.

DONNELLY'S OF BARNA, Coast Rd., Barna, Co. Galway. Tel. 091/ 92487.
About 5 miles west of Galway town on R336, this popular spot has won praise from locals, who quickly spread the word to visitors. The bar menu features lots of seafood, no surprise when Galway Bay is only steps away, such as a crab bake, crab claws, salmon, and mussels. There's also a vegetarian platter and an avocado-pear dish served with smoked salmon, crab, or prawns. Back of the bar, which faces the road, is an excellent seafood restaurant (see below).

MCSWIGGANS PUB AND RESTAURANT, 3 Eyre St., Wood Quay, Galway. Tel. 091/68917.

Walk into this corner pub and you'd swear it's at least 400 years old rather than its actual age of 4 years! So fantastic has the renovation of this old building been that it won an award for interior design. And no wonder—after gutting the entire insides of the building, the owners filled it with lots of dark wood, old pews from local churches, old bar objects, and antiques. Upstairs, there's an excellent restaurant, Lydon's (see below).

MALT HOUSE RESTAURANT, Olde Malte Arcade, High St., Galway. Tel. 091/67866 or 63993.

If the budget simply won't stretch for one of J. J. Coppinger's elegant dinners (see below), make a point of having a bar lunch, with marvelous seafood specialties added to the usual bar fare.

RABBITT'S, 23 Forster St., Galway. Tel. 091/62215.
Just off Eyre Square, this is Galway's oldest family-run pub. More locals than

tourists, and a place for good conversation and conviviality as well as moderately priced food.

RESTAURANTS

IN THE CITY CENTER

G. B. C. RESTAURANT AND COFFEE SHOP, 7 Williamsgate St., Galway. Tel. 091/63087.

Cuisine: TRADITIONAL/SEAFOOD/VEGETARIAN.

$ Prices: Appetizers IR£1.80–IR£3.85 ($3.15–$6.75); main courses IR£5.75–IR£10 ($10.05–$17.50); Kiddie Menu IR£2–IR£3 ($3.50–$5.25). ACC, AE, DC, MC, V.

Open: Mon–Sat noon–11pm, Sun noon–9pm.

The restaurant is upstairs from the self-service coffee shop (see "Specialty Dining," below) and is bright and pleasant, with booths along the walls, tables in the center of the large room. The extensive à la carte menu features good, solid traditional dishes of beef, pork, turkey, chicken, and seafood. Salad plates are less than the prices shown above, and wine is available by the glass, carafe, or bottle at moderate prices.

GALLEON RESTAURANT, Salthill, Galway. Tel. 091/22963.

Cuisine: SEAFOOD/BURGERS/GRILLS/TRADITIONAL/VEGETARIAN.

$ Prices: Appetizers IR£1–IR£3 ($1.75–$5.25); main courses IR£4.50–IR£8 ($7.85–$14); evening special IR£3.50 ($6.15); children's menu IR£1.30–IR£2.50 ($2.30–$4.40). ACC, AE, MC, V.

Open: Daily noon–midnight.

This small, cozy restaurant, beside the church on the main street in Salthill, is a popular spot with locals, and is one of the few late-night eating spots in Galway. There is a wide and varied menu which offers burgers, omelets, grills, steaks, fish dishes, and curries.

LYDON'S OF SHOP STREET, 5 Shop St., Galway. Tel. 091/61131.

Cuisine: TRADITIONAL/SEAFOOD/LIGHT MEALS.

$ Prices: Appetizers IR£1.50–IR£3 ($2.65–$5.25); main courses IR£4–IR£5 ($7–$8.75); daily special (three courses) IR£4 ($7); kiddie menu IR£2 ($3.50); Tourist Menu (Apr–Sept) IR£5.75 ($10.05) and IR£7.90 ($13.85). ACC, AE, DC, MC, V.

Open: Mon–Sat 9:30am–7pm.

This is an attractive, pleasant upstairs restaurant, famed for fast, friendly service and geared to budgeteers, with a touch of "Old Galway" ambience. The decor harks back to the days of Galway's thriving sea trade with Spain.

See "Pub Grub," above, for a complete description of this renovated building. The restaurant features a conservatory skylight and carries on the "old Galway" decor of the downstairs bar. As for the menu, it varies widely, from seafood to sirloin steak to escalope of pork, to grills. All main dishes come with a vegetable and potato.

MAXWELL MCNAMARA'S RESTAURANT, Williamsgate St., Galway. Tel. 091/65727.

Cuisine: SEAFOOD/STEAK/IRISH/VEGETARIAN.

$ Prices: Appetizers IR£1–IR£2 ($1.75–$3.50); main courses IR£3.95–IR£5.50 ($6.90–$9.60); special-value dinner IR£11 ($19.25). ACC, AE, DC, MC, V.

Open: Daily 10am–10pm.

There's a delightful old-fashioned look about this centrally located place just off Eyre Square that was known for many years as the Cellar Restaurant. Renovations have brought dark-wood booths, lots of brass, and old prints on the walls. The extensive menu offers light selections (hamburgers, salads, etc.), and it's fully licensed, with wine by the glass. Service is continuous, making it handy if hunger pangs strike outside regular meal hours.

NORA CRUB'S, 8 Quay St., Galway. Tel. 091/68376.

338 • GALWAY TOWN

Cuisine: TRADITIONAL/VEGETARIAN.

$ Prices: Appetizers IR£1–IR£3 ($1.75–$5.25); main courses IR£4–IR£6 ($7–$10.50). No credit cards.

Open: Summer, Mon–Sat 9am–10pm; winter, Mon–Sat 9am–6pm.

It's a pleasure just to go inside this old 16th-century stone building down in Old Galway in the docks area. There really *was* a Nora Crub who lived here, and the stone walls, arches, and cozy alcoves are just about the same as she would have known them. Wholesomeness and good home-cooking are stressed here, and the menu extends from soup (try the seafood chowder) to chicken Kiev, to beef and pork, to lasagne and salads. Service is friendly and efficient.

RABBITT'S BAR AND RESTAURANT, 23 Forster St., Galway. Tel. 091/ 66490.

Cuisine: TRADITIONAL/IRISH/VEGETARIAN.

$ Prices: Appetizers IR£1–IR£2 ($1.75–$3.50); main courses IR£4–IR£6 ($7–$10.50); bar food IR£4 ($7) and under. ACC, AE, DC, MC, V.

Open: Lunch 12:30–2:30pm; dinner 6:30–10:30pm.

Very popular with Galway locals, this is a congenial, family-run bar and restaurant, where the conversation is often quite as good as the food, which says a lot, indeed. See above for pub food. The regular lunch and dinner menu includes beef, pork, lamb, veal, chicken, and seafood.

THE ROUND TABLE RESTAURANT, 6 High St., Galway. Tel. 091/64542.

Cuisine: TRADITIONAL/IRISH/SNACKS.

$ Prices: Appetizers IR£1–IR£2 ($1.75–$3.50); main courses IR£2.50–IR£4.50 ($4.40–$7.85); snacks IR£1–IR£2 ($1.75–$3.50). No credit cards.

Open: Mon–Sat 9am–6pm.

Located in a building that dates back at least to 1586, with a 17-foot stone fireplace, stuccoed walls, and exposed ceiling beams in the back dining room, the Round Table is a great place to drop in virtually any hour of the day. Breakfast is served all day; there's a wide variety of snacks, sweet pastries, and the like; and the menu includes roasts of beef or pork or lamb, chicken, and fish. Everything's homemade and quite tasty.

SPECIALTY DINING
A COFFEEHOUSE

BEWLEY'S OF GALWAY, The Cornstore, Middle St., Galway. Tel. 091/ 65789.

Cuisine: LIGHT MEALS/SNACKS/VEGETARIAN.

$ Prices: IR£2–IR£4 ($3.50–$7). ACC, MC.

Open: Mon–Sat 9am–6pm.

This is the local branch of this famous old Dublin confectionary and coffee shop. There's a huge range of hot and cold dishes, as well as pastries that will keep your sweet tooth happy.

SELF-SERVICE

G. B. C. RESTAURANT AND COFFEE SHOP, 7 Williamsgate St., Galway. Tel. 091/63087.

Cuisine: TRADITIONAL/SALADS/SANDWICHES/BREAKFAST.

$ Prices: Mini-breakfast IR£1.75 ($3.05); Pastries and sandwiches IR£2 ($3.50); salad plates IR£3 ($5.25); hot plates IR£5 ($8.75). ACC, AE, DC, MC, V.

Open: Mon–Sat noon–11pm, Sun noon–9pm.

This popular self-service coffee shop serves an excellent mini-breakfast (egg, bacon or sausage, black pudding or tomato, brown bread, and tea or coffee), a blessing for those who can't face the traditional heavy Irish morning meal. Its extensive offerings also include excellent homemade soups, sandwiches, salads, and pastries for a light meal. (See above for the full-service restaurant.)

LYDON'S OF SHOP STREET, 5 Shop St., Galway. Tel. 091/61131.

Cuisine: BURGERS/SALADS/PASTRIES.
$ Prices: IR£1.50–IR£3 ($2.65–$5.25). ACC, AE, DC, MC, V.
Open: Mon–Sat 11am–11pm.

On the ground floor, Lydon's has its own in-store bakery, a delicatessen, and a modern self-service eatery offering a good selection of burgers, with Lydon's own sauce. Also offered is a wide selection of tempting salads, homemade pâté, and fresh-baked croissants. A good cold plate will cost around IR£2.50 ($4). There is a take-away service.

WORTH THE EXTRA MONEY

EYRE HOUSE AND PARK HOUSE RESTAURANTS AND LOUNGES, Forster St., Galway. Tel. 091/62396.
Cuisine: CONTINENTAL/IRISH.
$ Prices: Lunch IR£5.75 ($10.05); dinner IR£14.95 ($26.15). ACC, MC, V.
Open: Lunch Mon–Sat noon–3pm; dinner Mon–Sat 6–10pm.

This is a combination of two lovely restaurants, with a decor both sophisticated and warmly inviting. Lunchtime brings hordes of locals to settle in for specialties like chicken and mushroom vol-au-vent, osso buco (braised veal on the bone with garlic, white wine, onions, celery, carrots, and tomatoes), freshly caught fish, and roast rib of beef. Menus feature such dishes as roast stuffed duckling normande or escalope of veal Cordon Bleu. It is fully licensed.

MALT HOUSE RESTAURANT, Olde Malte Arcade, High St., Galway. Tel. 091/67866 or 163993.
Cuisine: SEAFOOD/CONTINENTAL.
$ Prices: Fixed-price dinner IR£17 ($29.75). Service charge 10%. ACC, AE, MC, V.
Open: Lunch Mon–Sat 12:30–2:30pm; dinner Mon–Sat 7–10pm. **Closed:** Good Friday, 1 week at Christmas.

Amid the stone walls and arches of old stone warehouses, Emer and John J. (J. J. to all and sundry) Coppinger have created an attractive restaurant, a bar area (see "Pub Grub," above), and a cozy cubbyhole lounge. The food has won all sorts of accolades, with such specialties as sirloin steak Café de Paris, peppered monkfish, scampi rolls, scallops au gratin, and veal steak St. Augustine. Fresh seafood is the house specialty. They also serve homemade ice cream, and for a special treat, order the Irish-coffee flavor. There's an excellent wine list, and a friendly, efficient staff. This popular place is packed at lunch, so come early or late.

NEARBY RESTAURANTS

KILCOLGAN

MORAN'S OF THE WEIR, Kilcolgan, Co. Galway. Tel. 091/96113.
Cuisine: SEAFOOD.
$ Prices: Oysters IR£7.50 ($13.15) per dozen; smoked salmon or crabmeat IR£5.80–IR£7.40 ($10.15–$12.95). ACC, AE, MC, V.
Open: Daily 10:30am–11pm.

About 10 miles south of Galway town on the main Galway–Limerick road (N18), keep a keen eye out for the signpost on the edge of the village that directs you down a side road to this 200-year-old thatched pub. The fifth generation of Morans are running this place, and at least a part of their success stems from the fact that oysters come straight from their own oyster beds. They're served with home-baked brown bread, as are smoked salmon, mussel soup, and other seafood items. There's food service all through normal pub hours.

CLARENBRIDGE

PADDY BURKES OYSTER INN, Clarenbridge, Co. Galway. Tel. 091/96107.

Cuisine: SEAFOOD/STEAKS.

$ **Prices:** Appetizers IR£2–IR£5 ($3.50–$8.75); main courses IR£7–IR£10 ($12.25–$17.50). ACC, AE, DC, MC, V.

Open: Daily 11am–10:30pm.

Paddy Burke's, 8 miles south of Galway town via N18, the Galway–Limerick road, is a local institution. The old pub dates back 3 centuries, and beamed ceilings, wooden benches, copper, and brass give the place a settled, comfortable feeling. It has been the hangout of such celebrities as John Huston, Paul Newman, and Burl Ives. Needless to say, oysters get star billing, and in fact, Paddy Burkes is headquarters for Galway's annual Oyster Festival. The menu also includes smoked salmon, prawn cocktail, fish chowder, and fresh cockles and mussels in garlic sauce. For non–seafood lovers, there are cold and hot platters of chicken, ham, beef, steak, and hot, homemade apple pie with fresh cream.

BARNA

Barna is about 5 miles from Salthill on the coast road to Spiddal, R336.

DONNELLY'S OF BARNA, Coast Rd., Barna, Co. Galway. Tel. 091/ 92487.

Cuisine: SEAFOOD/TRADITIONAL/VEGETARIAN.

$ **Prices:** Fixed-price dinner IR£17.50 ($30.65). ACC, MC, V.

Open: Dinner Mon–Sat 7–10pm, Sun noon–3pm.

In an old stone building that was once a stable, Donnelly's has created an attractive, light and airy eatery, with stone wall, vaulted ceiling, and an open loft overlooking the main dining room. Although steak au poivre, guinea fowl, pheasant, beef Stroganoff, escalope of veal, and vegetarian platters appear on the dinner menu, it's in the seafood department that Donnelly's really shines. Try the grilled scallops with lemon, or the Aran seafood melody mornay, or prawns in garlic cream. But before you make your choice, inquire about the "catch of the day," which is bound to be the best of that day's haul from the sea. For lunches, see "Pub Grub," above.

THE TWELVE PINS RESTAURANT, Coast Rd., Barna, Co. Galway. Tel. 091/92368 or 92485.

Cuisine: SEAFOOD/TRADITIONAL/SALADS.

$ **Prices:** Appetizers IR£1.50–IR£3 ($2.65–$5.25); main courses IR£6–IR£10 ($10.50–$17.50); lunch special IR£5 ($8.75). ACC, AE, DC, MC, V.

Open: Daily 11:30am–11:30pm. **Closed:** Good Friday, Christmas Day.

This is an attractive place for lunch or dinner, with white stucco walls, low ceilings, lots of wood, and a small lounge area with a fire lit on cool evenings. There's a daily lunch special of steak, lamb, or chicken, and salad plates of cold meats, smoked salmon, or prawns for about the same price. Dinner offers seafood specialties as well as steaks, veal, and roast duckling. It is fully licensed.

CLAREGALWAY

CLOONACAUNEEN CASTLE, Cloonacauneen, Claregalway, Co. Galway. Tel. 091/98265.

Cuisine: SEAFOOD/CONTINENTAL. **Reservations:** Essential, especially at dinner. Directions: Signposted from N17, about 6 miles NE of Galway Town.

$ **Prices:** Fixed-price meal IR£8.50 ($14.90) at lunch, IR£18.50 ($32.40) at dinner. No credit cards.

Open: Lunch Mon–Sat noon–3pm; dinner Mon–Sat 7–10:30pm.

For a full description of this atmospheric castle, see "Where to Stay," above. Needless to say, the dining room, with its lovely old marble fireplace, is the epitome of elegance. As for the menu, you'll find selections such as free-range duckling, lamb cutlets with mushroom-and-cherry sauce, scallops in white wine sauce, and fresh wild salmon.

4. WHAT TO SEE & DO

To catch the full flavor of Galway's rich and colorful history, go by the Tourist Board and pick up their booklet **"Tourist Trail of Old Galway"** (small charge), which will lead you along a signposted route through medieval streets with an informative and entertaining narrative filled with legends and anecdotes associated with places along your way.

ATTRACTIONS IN TOWN

You can't really miss **Eyre Square** (pronounce it "Air")—in the center of town, it's the site of impromptu street entertainment during the summer months. That statue of the old Irish storyteller, hat perched back and pipe in hand, is of Padraic O'Conaire, who traveled the countryside telling stories to children and committing them to paper, having begun life in New Docks in what is now the Anchor Bar. The other statue (of a standing figure) represents patriot Liam Mellows, a prominent Galway leader during the 1916 military engagements outside Dublin. John F. Kennedy addressed the people of Galway here on his presidential visit in 1963.

Other things to look for include the Civic Sword and Great Mace on display in the **Bank of Ireland** on Eyre Square. You'll want to see the **Spanish Arch** and the somewhat-cramped **Galway City Museum** just beside it. Not only is the museum filled with interesting artifacts, but its spiral staircase leads to a gallery that, in turn, leads to an open terrace with great views of the city and harbor.

On Market Street, look for two interesting **"marriage stones"** set into the walls of houses there. The stones are carved with the coats-of-arms of two families united in marriage, and these two date from the early 1600s.

Of even more interest on Market Street is the **Lynch Memorial Window.** The window claims that it was on this site that Mayor James Lynch FitzStephen carried out a harsh sentence against his own son in 1493. The story goes that the Lord Mayor's 19-year-old son, Walter, was much enamored of a lovely girl named Agnes. He was also very good friends with a young Spanish lad—good friends, that is, until Walter developed an acute case of jealousy when he thought the young Spaniard was courting Agnes. In a fit of rage he murdered his friend; then, filled with remorse, turned himself in. It was his own father who sat as magistrate and condemned the boy to death when he entered a plea of guilty. The town executioner, however, refused to perform his grisly duty, a tribute to the boy's local popularity, and the sorrowing father gave his son a last embrace and did the deed himself. From this tragic hanging—so the legend says—came the term "Lynch Law."

At the corner of Abbeygate Street and Shop Street, **Lynch's Castle** is a superb example of a medieval town house, dating back to around 1490. It's now home to a branch of the Allied Irish Bank, but look above for carved gargoyles and a lion biting off the head of an animal clutched in its claws.

At O'Brien's Bridge on Bridge Street, the **Bridge Mills** sit where milling has been going on since 1558. The mill buildings had fallen into terrible disrepair, but were rescued by one Frank Heneghan in 1988, when he began a renovation that brought back to life the old stonework and mill wheel. Today the building flourishes as home to the Millwheel Café and Coffee Shop, where you can sit outside in fine weather to watch swans on the river below. This is good browsing country—craft shops, clothing boutiques, jewelry shops, art galleries, and gift shops now inhabit much of the building's interior.

Take a stroll through Galway's version of the "Left Bank," the ✪ **High Street/Quay Street** quarter of old buildings that retain the old fireplaces, cut stones, and arches from centuries past. Craft shops, smart boutiques, excellent restaurants, and convivial pubs are located there.

FOR THE LITERARY ENTHUSIAST If you're a James Joyce fan, you'll find the girlhood home of his lady love, Nora Barnacle, at **8 Bowling Green.** It's the second house on the left as you enter the lane from Market Street.

ATTRACTIONS NEARBY

Salthill, a Galway suburb, is only a longish walk from the town center, with good bus service between the two from May to October. One of Ireland's most popular seaside resorts, it has good beaches and a broad promenade, an 18-hole golf course (see Section 6, "Sports and Recreation," below), lawn tennis, loads of restaurants, shops, pubs, discos, and some of the best accommodations in this area. Three-wheel bicycle carriages are for rent and form a traffic flow all their own along the promenade. Give the young set and yourself a break by dropping them off at the **Leisureland Amusement Park.** There's a heated indoor pool, a super waterslide, and lots of rides.

ORGANIZED TOURS

Bus Eireann runs several worthwhile day tours from Galway and Salthill: Clew Bay and Killary Harbor; the Maam Valley and Cong; Knock Shrine; Carraroe and South Connemara, etc. Some are half-day trips; others last the entire day. All are moderately priced, and you can book at the Tourist Office in Galway or Salthill, or at the railway station.

A pleasant way to see Galway and its environs is the 90-minute cruise on the River Corrib aboard the 72-passenger **Corrib Princess.** There are daily sailings from Wood Quay, and its full-length sunroof lets you enjoy the scenery no matter what the weather. You'll cruise along a traditional trade route, past historical points of interest, castles, and scenes of great natural beauty, with an interesting commentary all the way. There's full bar service, and tea and coffee. There are morning and afternoon sailings from Wood Quay daily, and the fare is IR£5 ($8.75). For exact times and to book, contact the Tourist Office, Eyre Square, Galway (tel. 091/61962, 92447, or 68903).

For an interesting **✪ walking tour of Old Galway,** just show up outside the Tourist Office Monday through Friday at 11am and a guide will lead you through 2 hours of Galway history and legend. The charge is IR£3 ($5.25), and be warned, wear comfortable walking shoes.

5. SPECIAL EVENTS

✪ RACE WEEK The Irish can come up with an instant party on an occasion no more auspicious than two friends' happening to be in the same place at the same time. And if there's a race meet, the party often turns into a gala! The folks in Galway have, in fact, perfected their party-throwing skills to such an extent that it sometimes seems the entire country shuts down to travel up this way for the 6-day Race Week in late July or early August. There's music everywhere, food stalls, private parties (to which strangers are often warmly welcomed), honest-to-goodness horse trading, and lots of activity at the track. Because so many Irish descend on the town during that week, best book way ahead if you'll be arriving during the festivities.

✪ SEPTEMBER OYSTER FESTIVAL This is the other big event in Galway, an international affair. In a colorful ceremony, the Lord Mayor of Galway gets things under way by opening and eating the first oyster of the season. After that, it's 2 solid days (usually a weekend) of eating and drinking: Oysters, salmon, prawns, and almost anything else that comes from the sea are washed down with buckets of champagne or Guinness. Oyster-openers from around the world enter competitions for opening the most oysters in the shortest period of time. The action centers around Moran's of the Weir, Paddy Burkes, and the Great Southern Hotel, and a ticket to all the scheduled partying is costly—around IR£100 ($175) for the 2 days—but since the entire town becomes a party, the general gaiety spills over into the streets and pubs at no cost at all. Again, advance booking is an absolute must. It's usually the third or fourth weekend in September, but you should check the Tourist Board's Calendar of Events.

BLESSING OF THE SEA To open the herring season in mid-August, there's a lovely ceremony on the waters of Galway Bay. Fishing boats form a procession to sail out of the harbor, led by an entire boatload of priests who petition heaven for a good and profitable season.

6. SPORTS & RECREATION

SPECTATOR SPORTS The most popular spectator sport in Galway is undoubtedly **horseracing,** especially during Race Week, but with other meets scheduled during the year. There's also **greyhound racing** at the tract at College Road off Eyre Square. For information on dates and times for both, contact the Tourist Office (tel. 63081).

RECREATION There's an excellent **golf course** at Salthill, and to arrange tee-off times, you should contact the club secretary at 091/21827 or 22169 as far in advance as possible.

 Fishing has been the very life's blood of Galway for centuries. To arrange angling (the season runs from February to September) at the Salmon Weir Bridge or other nearby waters, contact the Tourist Board (tel. 63081) or the Fishery Office, Nun's Island, Galway (tel. 62388), for information on license and booking, since rods are limited in number in some spots.

 The Tourist Office can also help in booking **sea angling,** or you can contact **Rossaveal Co-op,** Rossaveal, County Galway (tel. 091/72267 or 72119).

 For information about **tennis, badminton,** or **squash,** contact the Galway Lawn Tennis Club, Threadneedle Road, Salthill, County Galway (tel. 091/53435 or 51400).

7. SAVVY SHOPPING

SHOPPING IN TOWN
BOOKS

KENNY'S, High St. Tel. 091/62739, 61014, or 61021.

 Kenny's is widely recognized as being just about the best bookshop and art gallery in the country. First opened in the 1930s, the small bookshop has grown into a fascinating multilevel maze of rooms in ancient buildings lovingly restored by the Kenny family. There are works of Irish art, antiquarian maps and prints, old magazine issues, and rare books on Irish subjects. You'll nearly always find Mrs. Kenny behind the front counter, and at least one of her sons on hand. They'll search for a specific book, and if necessary, mail it to you in the U.S. Their own bindery will wrap a prized edition in fine, hand-tooled covers. Periodically, they issue catalogs of Irish-interest publications. Go by to browse and look for that special Irish book to carry home, but be warned—this is not an easy shop to leave! Open Monday through Saturday from 10am to 6pm.

CLOTHING & TWEEDS
PADRAIC O MAILLE'S, Dominick St. Tel. 091/62696.

✪ In 1938 the late Mr. Padraic O'Maille opened his shop, and today his sister and nephew carry on the tradition. John Ford, John Wayne, Maureen O'Hara, and Peter Ustinov have been patrons, and the business gained international recognition when O'Maille's made the costumes for *The Quiet Man*. There's a vast stock of gorgeous hand-woven tweeds by the yard to be tailored by the shop, as well as ready-made jackets, men's and ladies' suits, ladies' cashmere knits and tweed coats, ties, scarves, Irish "paddy" hats, and much more. This is also a good place to shop for Aran hand-knit sweaters (O Maille's was the first place ever to market them commercially). There's a good mail-order catalog, and major credit cards are accepted. The store is open Monday through Saturday from 9am to 6:30pm.

GIFT/SPECIALTY STORES

THE BROWNE DOORWAY LTD., 17 Eyre Sq. Tel. 091/65757.
This gift boutique has an excellent selection of crystal, china, and knitwear, and the staff are especially welcoming to Americans. Open Monday through Saturday from 10am to 6pm.

FALLERS, Williamsgate St. Tel. 091/61226.
Fallers began as a jewelry shop back in 1879 and today carries a huge stock of crystal, silver, china, porcelain, linen, jewelry, and quality souvenirs. They do an international mail-order business, and you can write for their color catalog (with prices in U.S. dollars). Open Monday through Saturday from 10am to 6pm.

GALWAY IRISH CRYSTAL, Merlin Park. Tel. 091/57311.
✪ On the outskirts of town, this factory sells beautiful crystal at one-third off prices you'd pay in shops. In the showroom it's a joy to watch master cutter John Wynne at work, Monday through Friday, creating pieces like those displayed on the shelves. Open daily from 9am to 5pm.

ROYAL TARA CHINA, Dublin Rd. Tel. 091/51301. Fax 091/57574. Telex 50027.
You can tour the factory and watch master craftspeople creating this fine bone china. There are also considerable savings on purchases here. It's located off the Dublin road at Flannery's Motel, and there's a full-service restaurant on the premises. It is open September through June, daily from 9am to 6pm; in July and August, daily from 9am to 9pm. Tours are offered Monday through Friday at 11am and 3pm, and on Saturday through Sunday by video.

CURIOSITY CORNER, Cross St.
This tiny corner shop holds a wealth of Irish-made crafts, gift items, and basketwear. Open Monday through Saturday from 10am to 6pm.

ARCHWAY CRAFT CENTRE, Victoria Place, Eyre Sq. Tel. 091/63693.
Just opposite the Tourist Office, this lovely two-story shop is chockablock with Irish craft items, including woolens and knitwear, as well as a pretty good selection of souvenirs and gifts.

SHOPPING NEARBY

ABBEY HAND CRAFTS, Clarenbridge, Co. Galway. Tel. 091/96104.
✪ This shop is some 8 miles from Galway city set back by a large car park on the road to Shannon (N18), just outside the village of Clarenbridge. The Abbey began two decades ago when the local secondary school closed down and villagers came together to help the Irish Sisters of Charity use the building to start a local knitting industry. Nowadays lay people run the Craft Shop, while the sisters teach blind people to knit and do much of the crochet and embroidery themselves. A wealth of Irish handmade items are on sale: tweeds, linens, woven bedspreads, Aran Handknit Bawneen (a specialty), blackthorn sticks, shillelaghs, handmade dolls, Waterford crystal, and Belleek porcelain. Just back of the shop is the Cottage Tea Room, where you can rest your feet and enjoy traditional Irish home-baking and tea.

CLARENBRIDGE CRYSTAL, Clarenbridge, Co. Galway. Tel. 091/96178.

This is yet another regional crystal that has sprouted from Ireland's native industry that all began in Waterford. Their showroom is at the end of the village in an old 19th-century school building. Open Monday through Saturday from 10am to 6pm.

MAIRTIN STANDUN, Galway–Spiddal Rd., Spiddal, Co. Galway. Tel. 091/83108.

In this shop, 12 miles from Galway town on R336, you can find very good bargains today. It's very much a family business, but the stocks of Aran sweaters, tweed coats and jackets, glassware, china, souvenirs, and gifts is incredibly large. There's also a currency-exchange service. In the rear of the shop is a pleasant tea room, a welcome refuge for weary shoppers. The shop is open March through December, Monday through Saturday from 9:30am to 6:30pm.

SPIDDAL CRAFT CENTRE, Spiddal, Co. Galway.

On the outskirts of this picturesque little village, this cluster of craft shops and workshops includes pottery, weaving, knitwear, jewelry, an art gallery, and a coffee shop for light snacks and lunch. Hours during the summer season are 9am to 6pm daily, but may vary during the off-season.

8. EVENING ENTERTAINMENT

THE PERFORMING ARTS

TAIBHDHEARC THEATRE, Middle St. Tel. 091/62024.

Since 1928, the Taibhdhearc (*"Thive-yark"*) Theatre has existed for the sole purpose of preserving Gaelic drama. Several nights a week during the summer months it presents a one-act play in Gaelic, with music, song, poetry, and dance both before and after the performance. Following the action is no problem, and the musical program is simply spectacular, with step dancing that will leave you breathless. This is where Siobhan McKenna began her career, and you'll see talent of much the same caliber on the stage. It's a very "Irish" entertainment, and good value-for-money, as well. You can book tickets through the Tourist Office or at the theater.

Prices: Tickets, IR£5 ($8.75).

THE DRUID THEATRE, Chapel Lane. Tel. 091/68617.

There is exceptionally good drama here. The resident professional company offers productions like *The Beggars Opera*, avant-garde plays, and Anglo-Irish classics nightly year round. There are frequent lunchtime and late-night shows, and local newspapers usually publish the schedule. Tickets can be booked by telephone or at the theater, and they should be booked as far in advance as you can manage, since the Druid has earned itself a worldwide reputation in a very short space of time, and it's extremely popular with locals as well as visitors.

Prices: Tickets, IR£5–IR£6 ($8.75–$10.50).

CULT R FOLK THEATRE, 45 Dominick St. Tel. 091/55479.

This lively company presents traditional Irish music, dance, song, and drama in traditional dress. Featured musical instruments include the bodhrán, fiddle, whistle, and harp. This is a small, intimate theater, so early booking is important, through the Tourist Office or at the theater.

Prices: Tickets, IR£5–IR£6 ($8.75–$10.50).

Open: June–Aug, Tues and Sat at 8:30pm.

A MEDIEVAL BANQUET & LITERARY EVENING AT DUNGUAIRE CASTLE

Much more intimate than the medieval banquets at Bunratty and Knappogue, this is certainly not a budget item, but it is special enough to warrant a splurge from the most devoted budgeteer. The castle is a small 16th-century keep, with banquet seating limited to 62. You'll learn its legend when you enter the reception hall and quaff a cup of mead as a young woman in medieval dress relates the story. In the upstairs banquet hall you'll dine by candlelight on such delicacies as smoked salmon, "chekyn supreme," and sumptuous desserts, accompanied by a plentiful supply of wine. When dinner is over, your costumed waiters and waitresses repair to the stage and bring to vivid life Ireland's literary heroes and heroines through their stories, plays, and poems.

Because attendance is so limited, this is one banquet you must reserve well in advance—through a travel agent before you leave home if possible, through the Galway Tourist Office, or the Tours Manager at Shannon Airport (tel. 061/61788 or 61444). The easiest way to go is to book with Bus Eireann for their tour which leaves from both Salthill Promenade and the railway station (tel. 091/62141).

The cost is IR£26 ($45.50), and the banquet is presented mid-May to September, daily at 5:45 and 9pm.

TRADITIONAL MUSIC

For the very best in traditional Irish music, check with the Tourist Board to see if your visit coincides with a Galway appearance of **Seisiun**, the troupe that tours the country during July and August. However, not to worry if you miss them—Galway is loaded with pubs that feature traditional music and sing-along nights.

CRANE BAR, Sea Rd., Galway. Tel. 091/67419.

 The upstairs ballad room in this old-style pub is often packed, and the music here is very good.

FLANAGAN'S CORNER BAR AND LOUNGE, Henry St. and William St. W., Galway. Tel. 091/63220.

This popular pub has traditional and folk music from Wednesday through Sunday nights, and they invite musicians to bring along their instruments and join in.

THE KING'S HEAD, High St., Galway. Tel. 091/66630.

Traditional music is only one of the musical forms presented at this popular pub, which has live music 7 nights a week. It's best to call ahead if you fancy a particular kind of music, since you're likely to encounter country and western on some nights; on Sunday morning, jazz usually takes over. Depending on the group performing, there may be a small cover charge.

O'CONNOR'S, Salthill, Galway. Tel. 091/46223.

O'Connor's is Galway's leading sing-along pub, with a session every night of the week.

HOTEL SACRE-COEUR, Salthill, Galway. Tel. 091/23355 or 23635.

Here, too, there's a sing-song session nightly, with no cover charge. Very popular with locals, and it usually has top-notch musical groups on the bill.

A PIANO BAR

MURRAY'S PIANO BAR, in the Hotel Salthill, Promenade, Salthill, Galway. Tel. 091/22711 or 22448.

This sophisticated piano bar sports a glass-enclosed conservatory section, where an extensive bar menu features seafood specialties from noon to 10pm daily. It's open to the main piano bar, so you can enjoy the music as you eat. The piano is frequently joined by other musical instruments, and the crowd joins in lustily to sing old favorites. It's open 7 nights a week from 9 to 11pm, and there are entrances from both the car park and the hotel entrance.

A NIGHTCLUB

C. J.'S NIGHTCLUB, in the Hotel Monterey, Salthill, Galway. Tel. 091/ 24017.

This is Galway's only nightclub/disco, and features high-tech lighting and sound effects, with dancing nightly from 10pm to 2am. Small cover charge.

9. EASY EXCURSIONS

Easily topping the list of excursions from Galway is a day trip to the **Aran Islands.** For full particulars, see Section 1, "County Galway," in Chapter 15.

Eight miles south of Galway town on N18, the little village of **Clarenbridge** is an easy drive for terrific food at Paddy Burke's Bar and Restaurant (see Section 3, "Where to Eat," above) and shopping (see Section 7, "Savvy Shopping," above).

Barna, about 5 miles west of Galway town on the coast road (R336), has one of the finest beaches on Galway Bay, the Silver Strand.

Some 12 miles west of town along the coast road (R336), **Spiddal** is a charming little village with a good beach, an excellent craft center (see Section 7, "Savvy Shopping," above), and an outstanding restaurant (see Section 3, "Where to Eat," above).

Oughterard ("*Ook*-ter-ard") is 17 miles northwest of Galway via N59, on the west banks of Lough Corrib. Needless to say, fishing is a main activity here, and there's a good golf course (tel. 091/82131 for details of play).

CHAPTER 15
COUNTIES GALWAY & MAYO

1. COUNTY GALWAY
- **WHAT'S SPECIAL ABOUT THE WESTERN REGION**

2. COUNTY MAYO

The west of Ireland. A name that conjures up an immediate image—brooding mountains, stony fields, windswept cliffs, a rugged coastline dotted with offshore islands, and air so heady that to breathe it has been compared to drinking champagne.

Counties Galway and Mayo make up Ireland's western region, and within their boundaries lie such distinct geographic divisions as Connemara, the Aran Islands, and Achill Island. For the most part, it's the scenery that stars in the western region.

1. COUNTY GALWAY

Galway's landscape in the east is made up of flat, fertile plains that reach from Lough Derg and the Shannon Valley north to County Roscommon, while to the northwest, lumpy mountains push the mainland into a great elbow bent against the Atlantic. Lough Corrib stretches its 27 miles along an invisible line that marks the change.

GORT AND CRAUGHWELL

If you're a dedicated fan of the poet William Butler Yeats (and most Yeats fans *are* dedicated), you won't want to miss a visit to Thoor Ballylee, his Co. Galway home for many summers. Lady Gregory lived and entertained her literary friends at her home in Coole Desmene nearby.

To reach the picturesque little village of Craughwell take the R347 off N18 at Ardrahan. This is the burial place of the famous 19th-century poet Anthony Raftery, but in these parts, it's better known locally as the location of the colorful Galway Blazers Hunt. It is also the home of one of the country's leading makers of Irish harps, Paddy Cafferky, Lisduff, Craughwell, Co. Galway, tel. 091/46265.

WHAT TO SEE AND DO

THOOR BALLYLEE, Gort, Co. Galway. Tel. 091/31436 or 63081.

From 1917 to 1929 Yeats spent his summers in this square, 16th-century castle keep, having bought it as a ruin for a paltry £35 and restored it to living condition. Among its chief advantages was its proximity to his dear friend, Lady Gregory at Coole Desmene. On one wall is inscribed this poignant poem:

I, the Poet William Yeats
With old millboards and seagreen slates
And smith work from the Gort forge
Restored this tower for my wife George,
And may these characters remain
When all is ruin once again.

WHAT'S SPECIAL ABOUT THE WESTERN REGION

Scenery

☐ The seaswept Aran Islands of County Galway, whose inhospitable landscape still has furnished a living to its hardy inhabitants for hundreds of years.

☐ The coastal drive from Galway to Clifden in Connemara, on roads that hug sandy little coves ringed by barren, stony hills and plains.

☐ Achill Island, in County Mayo, with its secluded sandy beaches and soaring cliffs with sheer drops to the sea.

Literary Shrines

☐ Thor Ballylee, the ancient tower near Gort in County Galway that was summer home to poet W. B. Yeats.

☐ Coole Desmene, near Gort, site of the home of Lady Gregory, patroness of Irish writers and one of the founders of the Abbey Theatre.

Film Locations

☐ Cong, in County Mayo, setting for that perennial favorite, *The Quiet Man.*

Religious Shrines

☐ Knock, in County Mayo, where Our Lady is said to have appeared in the late 1800s, a major pilgrimage point.

☐ Croagh Patrick, in County Mayo, the bleak, rocky summit on which St. Patrick is thought to have fasted for 40 days, climbed by barefoot pilgrims every July.

Fortunately, the tower has not reverted to ruins, and there's a resident staff to assist visitors, as well as sound guides that guide you through the tower and grounds. It's 4 miles northeast of Gort on the Loughrea road (N66).

Admission: IR£2.50 ($4.05) adults, 75p ($1.20) children, IR£5 ($8.10) families (parents and two children).

Open: May–Sept, daily 10am–6pm.

COOLE DESMENE, Gort, Co. Galway.

Now a national forest and wild life park, Coole Desmene was once the setting for Coole House, the stately home of Lady Gregory, one of Ireland's most influential patrons of the arts, and a founder of the Abbey Theatre. Here, she entertained and encouraged such illustrious literary figures as W. B. Yeats, George Bernard Shaw, Sean O'Casey, J. M. Synge, Oliver St. John Gogarty, and John Masefield, as well as Douglas Hyde, the first president of Ireland. The house no longer stands, its site marked only by ruined walls and stables. However, you can still see the famous "Autograph Tree," on which many of them carved their initials. There's a great atmosphere about the place that sets the imagination to work, and everyone will enjoy its peaceful beauty. It's 2 miles north of Gort and due west of N18.

Admission: Free

Open: Daily during daylight hours.

IMPRESSIONS

There's something sleeping in my breast
That wakens only in the West;
There's something in the core of me
That needs the West to set it free.
—OLIVER ST. JOHN GOGARTY,
COLLECTED POEMS, 1951

WHERE TO EAT

THE BLAZERS BAR, Main St., Craughwell, Co. Galway. Tel. 091/41674.
  Cuisine: BAR FOOD **Reservations:** Not accepted.
$ Prices: Hot lunches, less than IR£5 ($8.10); bar snacks less than IR£3 ($4.85). No credit cards.
  Open: Lunch Mon-Fri 12:30-2:30pm; bar and lounge daily, normal bar hours.

The Galway Blazers Hunt members have their headquarters and kennels just behind this attractive pub, and in winter this is the meeting place before and after hunts. Run by Teresa and Donal Raftery, the pub has a glorious mixture of rural personalities, gentlemen farmers, and visitors like yourself. If you get there at tea time, you'll be served on beautiful china from a menu of seafood, soup, and sandwiches.

THE ARAN ISLANDS

Some 30 miles offshore, where Galway Bay empties into the sea, the Aran Islands are an outpost of rugged fishermen and their families who perpetuate a heritage of self-sufficiency and culture passed from generation to generation through the centuries. The walls of pre-Christian stone forts have endured the ravages of time to remind islanders of their "Celtic Twilight" origin. Round towers, oratories, and tiny churches tell of early Christians who spoke the musical Gaelic language, as do their descendants, today's islanders. Menfolk still put out to sea in lightweight, tough little wood-and-canvas curraghs, as they have done over the ages, while their womenfolk spin and weave and knit the clothing that is so distinctly theirs.

Lying almost directly across the mouth of Galway Bay, the Aran Islands group consists of **Inishere** (Inis Oirr, "eastern island"), the smallest and nearest to the mainland (Doolin, County Clare, is 6 miles away); **Inishmaan** (Inis Mein, "middle island"), 3 miles distant from each of the other two and 3 miles long by 2 miles wide; and **Inishmore** (Inis Mor, "big island"), 7 sea miles from the Connemara coast, 5 miles long and 2½ miles wide, with the only harbor suitable for steamer docking at **Kilronan,** its main village.

Tourist Information Detailed information on the Aran Islands is available in the Tourist Office in Galway (see Chapter 14), which can also book accommodations on the islands.

GETTING THERE

By Ferry Bus Eireann operates regular service to the Aran Islands from the Galway docks, and you can book the day before at the railway station or the Tourist Office, or pay at the dockside kiosk. The round-trip fare in 1991 was IR£15 ($26.25), half that for children under 16. Inquire about their special family fares. It takes just over 2½ hours for the trip, and the water can be choppy, so if you're not a good sailor, take a motion-sickness remedy. Ferries dock only at Inishmore, but are met by curraghs at the other two islands to take off cargo.

A shorter boat trip from Rossaveal (on the coastal road past Spiddal) takes only 45 minutes and is run by Aran Ferries. The round-trip fare in 1991 was IR£13 ($22.75), half fare for children, with special family and student fares. Book at the Galway Tourist Office or call 091/68904 (091/95036 or 92447 after hours).

By Plane You can fly to Inishmore with **Aer Arann** (tel. 091/55437, 55448, or 55480), in a nine-seat, twin-engined aircraft from Caranmore Airfield on the Monivea road 4 miles out from Galway. The round-trip fare is about IR£45 ($78.75), and you can also book through the Tourist Office. Ask about their special packages that include an overnight stay on the islands. They can also arrange package deals with rail or bus connections to Galway from Dublin and almost any other part of the country.

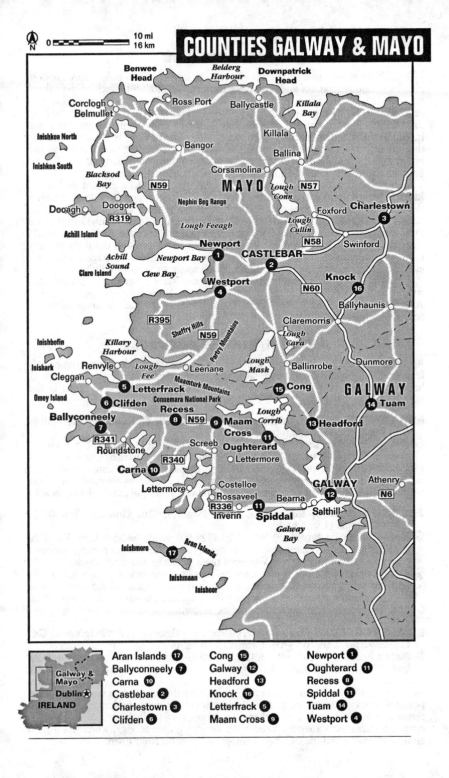

COUNTIES GALWAY & MAYO

0 [scale] 10 mi / 16 km

Benwee Head
Belderg Harbour
Downpatrick Head
Corclogh
Belmullet
Ross Port
Ballycastle
Killala Bay
Inishkea North
Killala
Inishkea South
Bangor
Ballina
Blacksod Bay
Corssmolina
N59
MAYO
Lough Conn
N57
Dooagh
Doogort
Foxford
Charlestown 3
R319
Nephin Beg Range
Achill Island
Lough Feeagh
Lough Cullin
N58
Swinford
Achill Sound
Newport 1
Newport Bay
CASTLEBAR 2
Clare Island
Clew Bay
Westport 4
Knock 16
N60
Ballyhaunis
R395
Sheffry Hills
N59
Patry Mountains
Claremorris
Lough Cara
Inishbofin
Killary Harbour
Lough Fee
Leenane
Lough Mask
Ballinrobe
Dunmore
Inishark
Renvyle
Maamturk Mountains
GALWAY
Cleggan
Letterfrack 5
Cong 15
Tuam 14
Omey Island
Clifden 6
Connemara National Park
Recess
Lough Corrib
Headford 13
Ballyconneely
7
R341
8
N59
Maam Cross 9
Roundstone
Screeb
Oughterard 11
R340
Lettermore
Carna 10
Costelloe
GALWAY 12
Athenry
Lettermore
Rossaveel
Bearna
N6
R336
Spiddal 11
Salthill
Inverin
Galway Bay
Inishmore
Aran Islands
17
Inishmaan
Inisheer

Galway & Mayo
Dublin ★
IRELAND

Aran Islands 17 · Cong 15 · Newport 1
Ballyconneely 7 · Galway 12 · Oughterard 11
Carna 10 · Headford 13 · Recess 8
Castlebar 2 · Knock 16 · Spiddal 11
Charlestown 3 · Letterfrack 5 · Tuam 14
Clifden 6 · Maam Cross 9 · Westport 4

WHAT TO SEE & DO

Life has been made easier on the islands with the introduction of electricity, modern plumbing, and regular sea and air service to the mainland. Still, much of the culture and old customs remain, and the hardy islanders are a breed apart, conditioned by generations who have braved the seas in their frail curraghs and laboriously built up the rocky soil with seaweed and sand in which to grow their meager crops. On Innishmore alone, there are said to be some 7,000 miles of stone walls, a testament to the industry of a persevering people. A wonderful introduction to these special islanders is the film *Man of Aran*, which is shown three times daily (at 3, 5:30, and 8pm) at the Village Hall in Kilronan, with a small admission charge.

When you debark at Kilronan pier on Inishmore, you'll be greeted by lines of **jaunting cars** for hire to explore the island. You'll ride through the village and down the one main road that runs the length of the island past an ancient stone ring fort, ecclesiastical ruins, and tiny hamlets to **Dun Aengus,** an 11-acre stone fort perched on a cliff some 300 feet above the sea. The jaunting-car fare runs about IR£15 ($26.25). There are **bikes** for rent as well, and if you're a **walker,** this is the country for it, with stops to chat with the people you meet on the road. Although Gaelic is the everyday language, the courteous islanders will speak to you in English.

On **Inishere** or **Inishmaan** you're much more likely to see the traditional Aran style of dress than on Inishmore. Ask any fishermen at the Kilronan pier and they'll arrange to take you over. The Tourist Board lists several good accommodations in addition to those listed here.

WHERE TO STAY ON INISHMORE

Accommodations on Inishmore are certainly more than adequate: comfortably furnished, hospitable hosts, and sweeping ocean views. What you *won't* find, however, are televisions and telephones in the rooms, as is right and fitting in this special setting.

ARD EINNE, Kilronan, Inishmore, Aran Islands, Co. Galway. Tel. 099/ 61126. 6 rms (none with bath).
$ Rates (including breakfast): IR£16 ($28) single; IR£11 ($19.25) per person sharing. Dinner IR£10 ($17.50) extra. No credit cards. **Closed:** Dec–Feb.
Mrs. Enda Gill greets you at this modern home that sits 1¼ miles from the village on an elevated site looking out to gorgeous views. All six bedrooms are nicely furnished, with sinks, and the house is convenient to fishing, a good pub, and a lovely beach.

THE CLIFF HOUSE, Inishmore, Aran Islands, Co. Galway. Tel. 099/ 61286. 6 rms (1 with bath).
$ Rates (including breakfast): IR£16.50 ($28.90) single without bath; IR£12.20 ($21.35) per person sharing without bath; IR£13.50 ($23.65) per person with bath. 33⅓% reduction for children. Weekend rates available. No credit cards.
⭐ This delightful modern bungalow perches on a site near Kilronan half a mile from town, overlooking the sea and with sweeping views of the entire island. The six guest rooms are attractively done up, and owners Michael and Olwen Gill have added an excellent restaurant (see below).

GILBERT COTTAGE, Oatquarter, Kilronan, Inishmore, Aran Islands, Co. Galway. Tel. 099/61146. 6 rms (2 with bath).
$ Rates (including breakfast): IR£10 ($17.50) per person single or double without bath, IR£15 ($26.25) per person single or double with bath. Dinner IR£10 ($17.50) extra. No credit cards.
Mr. Stephen Dirrane is your host in this lovely house that has pretty guest rooms and a peaceful, relaxing atmosphere. Mr. Dirrane spent 20 years working in New York restaurants and his meals are excellent. The house is centrally heated, which keeps it cozy and warm during winter months (an intriguing time to visit, when you'll get a glimpse of real island life). Gilbert Cottage is 1¼ miles from town.

READERS RECOMMEND

Kilmurvey House, *Inishmore, Aran Islands, County Galway (tel. 099/61218).* "*On Inishmore, I stayed at Bridget and Sonny Johnston-Hernon's manor house in Kilmurvey, and in the evenings enjoyed the company of the neighbors by a roaring fire. Bridget's meals are glorious.*"—Carol Smallenberg, Vancouver, B.C., Canada.

WHERE TO EAT ON INISHMORE

THE CLIFF HOUSE, Inishmore, Aran Islands, Co. Galway. Tel. 099/ 61286.

    Cuisine: SEAFOOD/TRADITIONAL. **Reservations:** Essential.

$ **Prices:** Dinner IR£12 ($21). No credit cards.

    Open: Dinner only, daily 7–10pm

    This small restaurant is attached to the accommodations section of Cliff House. Michael Gill specializes in wonderfully fresh seafood dishes featuring fish from local waters, and he offers a very good, moderately priced wine list. If you're there when turbot is available, don't miss Michael's turbot in mustard-and-leek sauce. Non-seafood lovers might opt for baked ham with ratatouille.

DUN AONGHUSA RESTAURANT, Kilronan, Aran Islands, Co. Galway. Tel. 099/61104.

    Cuisine: SEAFOOD/TRADITIONAL. **Reservations:** Recommended.

$ **Prices:** Lunch IR£9 ($15.75); dinner IR£12 ($21). MC, V.

    Open: June–Aug, daily 10am–10pm; Apr–May and Sept–Oct, daily noon–9pm.

    Closed: Nov–Mar.

If you gravitate toward traditional settings, you'll love this wood-and-stone restaurant with its cozy open fire. Overlooking Galway Bay, it specializes in the freshest of local seafoods, as well as mouth-watering home-baking.

CONNEMARA

This westernmost point of County Galway is a wild, thinly populated yet enchanting stretch of land between Lough Corrib and the Atlantic. As you drive the winding little roads, past blue-washed cottages, you encounter a landscape made beautiful by incredibly shifting light and shade and the starkness of rock-strewn fields and hills. Glimpses of sandy strands at the sea's edge and the tiny villages dot your route add another dimension. All in all, Connemara is an *experience* more than a place.

Tourist Information The Tourist Office in Galway (see Chapter 14) has extensive information on Connemara, as well as several helpful publications on the region.

GETTING AROUND

By Bus There's regular bus service from Galway to Clifden, as well as narrated day trips by coach. The Tourist Office in Galway can furnish details.

By Car Although Clifden, at the extreme western edge of Connemara, is only 49

IMPRESSIONS

There are few things in the world more delightful than a drive at sunset, in a bright autumn evening, among the mountains and lakes of Connemara. A friend of ours describes the air of his favourite place by saying it is like breathing champagne.
—HARRIET MARTINEAU, *LETTERS FROM IRELAND,* 1852

miles from Galway by the most direct route, those are slow, *Irish* miles. If your time is really limited you may want to drive through the heart of Connemara via N59, which takes you through Moycullen, Oughterard, and Recess to reach Clifden, returning via N59 through Letterfrack and Kylemore to Leenane, where N59 is the direct route to Westport, County Mayo, and R336 takes you back through Maam, Maam Cross, Oughterard, and Moycullen to Galway. With more time, you might follow this route through Moycullen and Oughterard as far as Maam Cross, then cut south to Screeb and west along the coast.

A much more memorable drive is the coastal road from Galway to Clifden, which will add perhaps as much as 3 hours to your travel time, but will leave pictures in your mind to be examined and reexamined for years to come. This route runs along the coast from Galway via R336 to Spiddal, Inverin, Costelloe, Carraroe, Screeb, Derryrush, Kilkieran, Carna, Glinsk, and Ballynahinch. At Ballynahinch you can join the main Galway–Clifden road for a quick run into Clifden or continue around the coastline through Roundstone, Ballyconneely, and Ballinaboy, to Clifden, returning to Galway via Letterfrack, Kylemore, Leenane Maam, Maam Cross, Oughterard, and Moycullen.

One final word: If you don't plan to return to Galway, from Leenane, you can continue northward to Westport via N59, or turn east at Maam for a drive along the shores of Lough Corrib via R345 to Cong and Castlebar in County Mayo.

WHAT TO SEE & DO

In Connemara, the serried **Twelve Bens** (sometimes called the Twelve Pins) look across a lake-filled valley at the misty peaks of the Maamturk range, and the jagged coastline is a solitary place of stark, silent beauty. This is a Gaeltacht area, where government grants make possible the survival of Gaelic as a spoken language. Among its rocky, untillable fields wander the spirits of Irishmen banished by Cromwell "to Hell or Connaught." Farther north, the long, narrow finger of Killary Harbour marks the County Mayo border.

Pleasures are simple in Connemara, most often associated with the natural rhythms of country life. Turf is cut and dried in the boglands from April through June, and especially along the coastal road you may see donkeys with loaded creels transporting the dried turf to be stacked against the winter's cold. Sheep shearing is done by hand, often within the roofless walls of ruined cottages, and if you come across sheep being herded through the fields in June and July, they're probably on their way to be shorn.

History lives here, as well. At **Ballynahinch,** a ruined castle on an island in Ballynahinch Lake is said to be the keep where the Martin clan once imprisoned their captured enemies. At **Ballinaboy,** look for the signposted memorial to Alcock and Brown, who landed near here on the first transatlantic flight in 1919—it's on a high hill between Ballinaboy and Clifden, with magnificent panoramic views.

Between **Ballyconneely and Kilkieran,** you can sometimes watch seaweed being harvested (done at the full and new moons for 4 hours only in the middle of the day). Thatchers are usually at work in September and October, and the biggest concentration of **thatched cottages** is between Ballyconneely and Roundstone (which also has a magnificent mile-long beach) and between Cleggan and the Clifden road by way of Claddaghduff. At Roundstone and Cleggan, small trawlers fish year round, with open lobster boats and currachs setting out only in summer months. Little villages all along the coast hold frequent **currach races.** Finding out the when and where of the above is a matter of keeping your eyes open—and of a well-placed inquiry over a pint at the local pub. In Roundstone, you can visit a traditional bodhrán maker (see "Savvy Shopping" below).

One thing you won't want to miss in **Clifden** is the spectacular ✪ **Sky Drive,** a cliff road that forms a 9-mile circle around a peninsula and opens up vast seascapes. It's well signposted from town. Boats are also available (through most accommodations) for **deep-sea fishing** for mackerel, blue shark, conger, cod, ling, and many other varieties. Summer evenings bring traditional music in many of Clifden's hotel bars and pubs; check with the Tourist Office or your accommodation hostess.

Letterfrack is where ✪ **Kylemore Abbey** sits in a picture-postcard setting of woodlands on the banks of Pollacappal Lough, its impressive facade reflected by the lake's mirror surface. The stone mansion dates from the 19th century, and is home to an order of teaching nuns who have established a thriving pottery industry, and welcome visitors to the shop. There's a tea room for refreshment, and you can stroll the lovely grounds.

At **Maam Cross**, lovers of *The Quiet Man* will want to stop for a look at Peacocks Restaurant's replica of the traditional Irish thatched cottage featured in that film. It's half-door, open fire, and period furnishings are reminders of rural Ireland in years gone by. Owner Theresa Keogh is an authority on that film and is delighted to chat with visitors. For more about the making of the film, see below.

About 2 miles south of **Oughterard**, you'll find the impressive ruins of **Aughnanure Castle** near the shores of Loch Corrib. It's a well-preserved example of an Irish tower house and was once a heavily fortified residence. That comes as no surprise when you learn that this was a stronghold of the battling O'Flaherty clan between the 14th and 15th centuries. The castle is open Monday through Friday from 10:30am to 6pm.

Special Events

The **Connemara Pony Show** in Clifden is held in August and buyers come from around the world to bid on the sturdy little animals; the town takes on a country-fair look, with much revelry, handcraft demonstrations, etc. Sometimes spontaneous, there are "flapper races," in which children race Connemara ponies while families gather for a great day of eating and drinking in the out-of-doors.

Clifden is also the setting for week-long sessions of the **Irish School of Landscape Painting,** founded and conducted by master painter Kenneth Webb, now assisted by his daughter, Susan. Individual instruction is given, with emphasis on techniques to catch the shimmering Connemara light shadings. You can attend for the day only or for the week, with accommodations and two meals a day thrown in. For details, contact Miss C. Cryan, Blue Door Studio, 16 Prince of Wales Terrace, Ballsbridge, Dublin 4 (tel. 01/685548).

Savvy Shopping

In Spiddal, look for the **Spiddal Craft Centre** at the western edge of the village, a delightful complex of workshops for weavers, potters, silversmiths, etc.

Mordecai Kearns, of **Roundstone Musical Instruments,** I.D.A. Craft Centre, Roundstone (tel. 095/35808), is a master craftsman, the maker of a whole range of traditional Irish instruments, including the goatskin bodhrán, which the workshop can decorate while you wait with Celtic designs or your name and/or family crest. If you're not a musician, you might want one of the attractive miniature bodhráns as a souvenir. The shop also makes tin whistles, flutes, and harps. The workshop is open daily from 8am to 7pm, and there is a good mail-order service.

✪ **Millar's Connemara Tweeds** (tel. 095/21038) has long been a Clifden landmark, with shop shelves filled with beautifully colored pure-wool lengths produced by weavers in the locality. Irish linens, glass, pottery, books of Irish interest, native food specialties, and other items complete the downstairs displays. Up the iron spiral stairs is a display of Connemara scenes depicted by Irish painters. In a stone-walled wing of the shop, you can browse through Irish fashions in a setting that includes a turf fire on the stone hearth and furnishings such as an old spinning wheel. Patchwork quilts are beautifully executed and much sought after, thus not always available. In short, this is a happy hunting ground for almost anything Irish-made. Open Monday through Saturday from 9am to 6pm.

Just outside Letterfrack, **Connemara Handcrafts** (tel. 095/41058) is one of the best craft shops in the country. Its displays feature items you'll see in few other places, as well as a good selection of Irish publications and tapes. Whether you're looking for inexpensive souvenirs, moderately priced gifts, pottery, knitwear, linens, tweeds, and clothing, or pricier works of art and jewelry, you'll find something here, and they'll gladly ship any purchases, thus saving the VAT. Upstairs, a tea room overlooks the garden, where light lunches are available in addition to tea and snacks (such as homemade buttered barm brack, the traditional Irish fruitcake). From mid-March to May, it's open Monday through Saturday from 9:30am to 6pm; in June, July, and August, Monday through Saturday from 9:30am to 7pm and on Sunday from 11am to 6pm. Closed November to mid-March.

On the Leenane–Maam Bridge road, look for the ✪ **Maam Valley Pottery and Sweater Shop,** Maam Valley (tel. 091/71109). The well-stocked shop features hand-loomed ties, hats, scarves, wool knitwear, and a host of other items, all produced within roughly a 20-mile area of the shop. The pottery workroom is open to visitors. Dublin escapees Ann and Dennis Kendrick are the helpful owner/operators. Tea and snacks are served on the premises.

In Moycullen, stop by the factory and showroom of ✪ **Celtic Crystal Ltd.** (tel. 091/85172). They specialize in the use of Celtic designs and motifs in their hand-cut crystal glassware, and are open to the public May to October, daily from 9am to 6pm.

Also in Moycullen, the **Connemara Marble Products** (tel. 091/85102) factory offers a tremendous stock of items made from polished marble, ranging from inexpensive souvenirs to moderately expensive items like jewelry, bookends, clocks, etc. Prices are better here than in shops, and they're open during the summer months, daily from 9am to 5:30pm; the rest of the year, Monday through Friday from 9am to 5:30pm. Across the road there's a tea room serving tea, coffee, and cookies.

Take a look, while you're in town, at the good buys at **Moycullen Crafts and Antiques.**

WHERE TO STAY
Spiddal

ARDMORE COUNTRY HOUSE, Greenhill, Spiddal, Co. Galway. Tel. 091/83145. 8 rms (7 with bath).

$ Rates (including breakfast): IR£16 ($28) single without bath; IR£11 ($19.25) per person sharing without bath; IR£2 ($3.50) per person additional with bath. 20% reduction for children. Discounts for stays of 3 days or more. No credit cards. **Closed:** Jan–Feb.

On the Galway Bay coastal road, just a half mile from Spiddal, Mrs. Vera Feeney's Ardmore is a modern bungalow overlooking the bay and the Aran Islands. The Cliffs of Moher are clearly visible on clear days and the panoramic view is framed by large windows in the lounge, or you can relax in the sun outside on the terrace to enjoy the landscaped gardens in proximity to the bay. The guest rooms are spacious and attractively decorated. The gracious Mrs. Feeney has thoughtfully provided washing and drying facilities to renew your travel-weary clothes. You're offered a choice of menu at breakfast that won the coveted Breakfast Award a few years back. There's central heating and good parking.

Clifden

ARD MHUIRE GUESTHOUSE, Westport Road (N59), Clifden, Co. Galway. Tel. 095/21450. 6 rms (all with bath).

$ Rates: (including breakfast) IR£15 ($26.25) per person. No credit cards accepted. **Closed:** Nov–Apr. **Parking:** Private car park.

This large, two-story Georgian house is set in attractive gardens on an elevated site overlooking the town. It's run by Jackie and Marion O'Grady (members of the family who are known for their seafood restaurant in Clifden—see below), and there's a heated swimming pool and a tennis court on the grounds.

BEN VIEW HOUSE, Bridge St., Clifden, Co. Galway. Tel. 095/21256. 6 rms (5 with bath).

$ Rates: (including breakfast) IR£13 ($22.75) per person, 25% reduction for children. No credit cards. **Open:** Year round.

This is the comfortable two-story home of Mrs. Morris, a hospitable and helpful hostess, and is now run by the third generation of the same family. The house is centrally heated and the four guest rooms are attractively decorated and comfortably furnished.

HEATHER LODGE, Westport Rd. (N59), Clifden, Co. Galway. Tel. 095/ 21331. 8 rms (4 with bath).

$ Rates (including breakfast): IR£15.50 ($27.15) single without bath; IR£11.50 ($20.15) per person double without bath; IR£1.50 ($2.65) per person additional with bath. 25% reduction for children. High tea IR£9 ($15.75) extra; dinner, IR£11 ($19.25). No credit cards. **Closed:** Nov–Easter. **Parking:** Car park.

Mrs. Frances Tiernan's Heather Lodge has magnificent views of a mountain lake and the Twelve Bens range, all framed by huge picture windows in the lounge, which also has a fireplace. The pretty modern bungalow is a short walk from town, set back from the road on a slight rise, and the eight lovely bedrooms are spacious, and there are two on the ground floor, and one has three single beds. Central heating and car park.

Maam

LECKAVREA VIEW FARMHOUSE, Maam–Cong Rd. (L101), Maam, Co. Galway. Tel. 092/48040. 6 rms (2 with bath, 4 with shower only).

$ Rates (including breakfast): IR£15.50 ($27.15) single; IR£12.50 ($21.90) per person sharing. 25% reduction for children. Weekend rates available. Dinner IR£13 ($22.75) extra. No credit cards. **Closed:** Christmas.

This large old farmhouse on the shores of Lough Corrib, 2½ miles from Maam Bridge and 32 miles from Galway town, is the comfortable home of John and Breege Gavin. Marvelous views of Lough Corrib include the little island just offshore crowned by Castle Kirk ("Hen's Castle"), once a stronghold of pirate queen Grace O'Malley. Fishing on the lough is free (the Gavins have boats for rent), and if Castle Kirk intrigues you, John will (for a small fee) row you over to the island for a bit of exploring. In consideration for her guests who've come for peace and quiet, Breege keeps the TV in a separate lounge and usually keeps a fire glowing in the main lounge.

Oughterard

KNOCKFERRY LODGE, Knockferry, Roscahill, Co. Galway. Tel. 091/ 80122. 10 rms (all with bath).

$ Rates (including breakfast): IR£18 ($31.50) per person. Reductions for 3- and 7-day stays; 25% reduction for children. Dinner IR£15 ($26.25) extra. AE, DC, MC, V.

Set in a secluded spot on the shores of Lough Corrib, just 14 miles north of Galway town, the lodge is run by Des Moran. It was originally occupied by the author of *Galway Bay*, Dr. Arthur Colohan. It was also Des's family home, to which he returned after several years in the hotel business in Europe to expand the house and establish a first-class accommodation with a superior cuisine. It is his own irrepressible personality that also added an element of fun that has attracted a loyal following of fishermen and relaxation-seekers who return again and again. There are turf fires in both of the large lounges, and there's a spacious dining room for outstanding meals (with such specialties as Corrib salmon, trout, and pike, Viennese goulash, Connemara lamb, and spiced beef, among others). A games room provides table tennis and bar billiards. Fishing boats are available for rent, and the lodge can supply tackle (no charge for fishing, except for salmon).

Guest rooms are lovely, most with lake views; one large room has four beds, sink, bidet, toilet, shower, and bath. There's central heating and plenty of parking. Des wants guests who have been here before to know that the "presence remains on the bridge"—newcomers should be sure to ask for the tall tale that goes with that statement!

Knockferry Lodge is 13 miles from Oughterard; take N59 to Moycullen and turn left onto an unclassified road (the lodge is signposted) and drive 6 miles.

LAKELAND COUNTRY HOME, Portacarron, Oughterard, Co. Galway. Tel. 091/82121 or 82146. 9 rms (5 with bath).

$ **Rates** (including breakfast): IR£12.50 ($21.90) per person sharing without bath; IR£2.50 ($4.40) per person additional with bath. IR£6 ($10.50) single supplement. IR£2 ($3.50) per person additional during special events. No credit cards. **Closed:** Mid-Oct to mid-Mar.

This lovely lakeside home of Lal and Mary Faherty is a great place for relaxing, and there are nice scenic walks nearby. The house is centrally heated as well as having turf fires, and electric blankets are supplied in the attractive bedrooms. The Fahertys have also kept families in mind by providing triple bedrooms. It's 2 miles from Oughterard.

Self-Catering

Two comfortably furnished traditional cottages, ideal for family holidays may be rented by contacting Mrs. Brenda Weir, Rookwood, Stocking Lane, Ballyboden, Dublin 16 (tel. 01/931906). One cottage is adjacent to a safe, sandy beach, with spectacular sea and mountain views; the other sits on the shore of a small lake with swans and good trout fishing. Each will sleep eight in three bedrooms, and fuel and heating are included in the weekly rate at the lake cottage. Electricity is extra. Rates are IR£275 ($445.50) per week during June, July, and August and public holidays; IR£175 ($283.50) in other months. For exact locations and booking information, contact Mrs. Weir.

Worth the Extra Money

BALLYNAHINCH CASTLE, Recess, Connemara, Co. Galway. Tel. 095/31006. Fax 095/31085. 28 rms (all with bath). Directions: 7 miles from Clifden, signposted from N59.

$ **Rates** (including breakfast): June–Sept, IR£50–IR£70 ($87.50–$122.50) single; IR£40–IR£60 ($70–$105) per person sharing. Oct–May, IR£42–IR£50 ($73.50–$87.50) single; IR£32–IR£40 ($56–$70) per person sharing. Winter break, Christmas, and fly-casting tutorial packages available. Dinner IR£20 ($35) extra. Deposit required when booking. AE, DC, MC, V.

★ If there is such a thing as casual elegance, this lovely small hotel certainly has it. Set in lush woodlands at the base of Ben Lettry in the Twelve Bens mountain range 7 miles from Clifden (signposted from N59), the impressive manor house overlooks the Owenmore River. This was the ancestral home of the O'Flaherty chieftains, and in more recent years the sporting home of an Indian maharajah. There's excellent fishing on the grounds, with boats available for rent, and miles of walking or biking paths, with bicycles for hire. Guest rooms are individually named and decorated, and some of the deluxe rooms have a fireplace. Log fires, oil paintings, and wall tapestries give a warm, comfortable air to the two beautifully furnished lounges, and the dining room overlooks the river and gardens. The Castle Pub is a favorite gathering place for residents of the locality, with traditional music on tap often during summer months.

WHERE TO EAT

Spiddal

THE BOLUISCE SEAFOOD BAR, Spiddal, Co. Galway. Tel. 091/83286. **Cuisine:** SEAFOOD/TRADITIONAL. **Reservations:** Recommended.

$ **Prices:** Lunch IR£5 ($8.75); dinner IR£13 ($22.75). Service charge 10%. MC, V. **Open:** Lunch Mon–Fri noon–2:30pm; dinner Mon–Sat 5:30–11:30pm, Sun 4–11pm. **Closed:** Jan–Feb, Good Friday, Christmas Day.

★ This is a true "Irish" restaurant, piling your plate high with generous portions at moderate prices. You can choose anything from soup right up to lobster and other delicacies. Seafood dishes are often innovative, created using fish from local waters, and non-seafood lovers, as well as vegetarians, can choose from several selections.

Clifden

O'GRADY'S SEAFOOD RESTAURANT, Market St., Clifden. Tel. 095/ 21450.
Cuisine: SEAFOOD/TRADITIONAL/VEGETARIAN. **Reservations:** Recommended.
$ Prices: Lunch IR£9 ($15.75); dinner IR£17 ($29.75). AE, DC, MC, V.
Open: Lunch daily 12:30–2:30pm; dinner daily 6–10pm. **Closed:** Mid-Jan to mid-Mar.

★ This attractive family-run restaurant has been around a long time, earning an international reputation for their excellent seafood dishes. They have their own fishing boats, so you may be sure the fish you eat is not long out of Atlantic waters. On Saturday night there are candlelight dinners, and from Halloween to Easter they feature game as well as seafood. Business lunches are served at moderate prices every day, and the Tourist Menu is offered up to 2:30pm.

Maam Cross

PEACOCKES, Maam Cross. Tel. 091/82306, 82375, or 82501.
Cuisine: SEAFOOD/TRADITIONAL/VEGETARIAN. **Reservations:** Not required.
$ Prices: Breakfast IR£4 ($7); lunch IR£5 ($8.75); dinner IR£12 ($21). No credit cards.
Open: Daily 9am–11pm.
Located at this important crossroad, Peacockes is a virtual mini-conglomerate, with a host of services for travelers. To begin with, they have built an enviable reputation for outstanding seafood at moderate prices. Depending on availability, you'll find lobster, salmon, prawns, oysters from the west of Ireland, and Lough Corrib trout on the menu, and they also feature prime steaks and a selection of vegetarian dishes. There's a well stocked craft shop, and evenings are enlivened with traditional music, as well as a disco. A rewarding stop no matter what time of day you land at Maam's Cross or vicinity.

ALONG THE CONNEMARA COAST DRIVE

Picnic spots abound in the wilds of Connemara, and country pubs often serve delicious, hearty bar food. On the coastal drive from Galway to Clifden, **Ostan Charna,** Carna, Connemara, Co. Galway, tel. 095/32255, is a small hotel on the Clifden side of this little village. It offers quite adequate and comfortable bed and breakfast accommodations for under IR£15 ($24.30) and serves good bar food at inexpensive prices, as well as the evening meal for IR£12.50 ($20.25). There's also periodic entertainment in the evenings. A good overnight stop or meal break.

EN ROUTE FROM GALWAY TO CASTLEBAR IN COUNTY MAYO

After touring Connemara and returning to Galway, there are two routes north. N17 will take you through **Tuam,** a small market town whose importance as an ecclesiastical center in years gone by is marked by **The Cross of Tuam** in the market square, and by **St. Mary's Cathedral,** rebuilt in the 1800s, but incorporating the magnificent chancel arch of its 12th-century ancestor.

The alternative route, via N84 brings you to **Headford** and historic **Ross Abbey,** some 2 miles northwest of town. The abbey was founded 1357 and fell victim to Cromwell's forces in 1656. Just north of Headford, you'll cross the County Mayo border, and at Cross, **Cong** is only a short detour west en route from Headford to Castlebar.

WHERE TO STAY

BALRICHARD FARM, Galway Rd., Headford, Co. Galway. Tel. 093/ 35421. 3 rms (none with bath).

$ Rates (including breakfast): IR£12.50 ($21.90) per person. 50% reduction for children. No credit cards. **Closed:** Dec–Feb.

Mrs. Margaret McDonagh is hostess of this lovely farmhouse less than a mile south of town on the Galway road. It is set in beautiful countryside and the house is centrally heated as well as having open turf fires. All guest rooms contain sinks.

KILMORE HOUSE, Galway Rd. (N17), Tuam, Co. Galway. Tel. 093/ 28118. 7 rms (3 with bath).

$ Rates (including breakfast): IR£14.50 ($25.40) single without bath; IR£11.50 ($20.15) per person sharing without bath; IR£2 ($3.50) per person additional with bath. 20% reduction for children; discounts for stays of more than 1 night. High tea IR£8 ($14) extra; dinner IR£13 ($22.75). No credit cards.

Josephine ("Jo") O'Connor is hostess in this lovely modern home half a mile south of Tuam. Her warm hospitality first surfaces when she brings tea and scones to guests when they arrive. She has two family rooms, and has provided a playground for children out back. Guest rooms are bright and cheerful, and Jo's substantial Irish breakfast is served in a window-walled dining room overlooking the farm and bogs beyond. Guests enjoy beautiful country walks, as well as long summer evenings sitting out on the lawn. The house is centrally heated, and there's good parking.

2. COUNTY MAYO

Near Cong, on the Plain of Southern Moytura, prehistoric battle raged between Tuatha De Danann and the Firbolgs, ending in the first defeat of the latter, who then declined in power until they were finally crushed 7 years later in Sligo. Northeast of Cong is the small village of Knock, a shrine to the many visions reported here and a place of pilgrimage for thousands of Christians. Connected to the mainland by a causeway, Achill Island, in contrast to flat eastern County Mayo, presents a mountainous face to the sea, its feet ringed by golden sandy strands.

WESTPORT & ACHILL ISLAND

If your northward route from Connemara heads directly for Westport, I suggest you leave the main road, N59, at Aasleagh and turn northwest on R335, the road that passes through stony, barren hillsides to Louisburgh and Clew Bay. At Louisburgh visit the ✪ **Granuaile Interpretive Centre,** Chapel Street (tel. 098/66195), to see mementoes of the fascinating pirate, Grace O'Malley ("Granuaile"), who roamed the waters of Clew Bay. Between Louisburgh and Westport, the drive touches the bay at several points, and on the other side of the road rises 2,510-foot-high **Croagh Patrick,** where St. Patrick is believed to have fasted for 40 days and modern-day pilgrims climb the stony paths in their bare feet in July for a 4am mass at its top.

WESTPORT

What to See and Do

WESTPORT HOUSE, Westport, Co. Mayo. Tel. 098/25141.

Westport House dates back to 1731, but it sits on the grounds of an earlier O'Malley castle, the dungeons of which are now visited by children who are happily "terrified" by the terrors that have been installed for their entertainment. The lovely old Georgian mansion house is a virtual museum of Irish memorabilia and craftsmanship, with a magnificent drawing room, a long gallery, and a grand entrance hall.

Lord and Lady Altamont and their five daughters are in residence here, and over the years they have turned their estate into a stylish visitor attraction. A full dozen shops feature quality Irish products, heraldic items, historic Irish scrolls, Irish art, fashion, gifts, and antiques. On the grounds there's a children's zoo, a playground, tea room, and boating and fishing on a lake and a river. Connemara Horse Caravans operate from the old stone stables, and there are self-catering holiday homes for rent, some right on the estate grounds. Write for a brochure detailing all these enterprises to Westport House Country Estate, Westport, Co. Mayo.

Admission: IR£5 ($8.75) adults, IR£2 ($3.50) children.
Open: Mid-May to mid-Sept, daily 2–5pm.

Where to Stay

RATH-A-ROSA, Rosbeg, Westport, Co. Mayo. Tel. 098/25348. 4 rms (3 with bath).
$ Rates (including breakfast): IR£15.50 ($27.15) single without bath; IR£12.50 ($21.90) per person sharing without bath, IR£3 ($5.25) per person additional with bath. Dinner IR£13 ($22.75) extra. No credit cards. **Closed:** Dec–Feb.

This modern farmhouse 1½ miles from Westport on the Louisburg road (R335) has magnificent views across Clew Bay to the mountains of Achill Island. Mary O'Brien, the lady of the house, is known far and wide for her cooking, using the freshest of ingredients and locally grown meats, as well as fish straight from local waters. Dinners must be booked before noon. Breakfast often features just-caught mackerel along with Mary's special mustard sauce. Husband John, a fluent Gaelic speaker, is a witty and informative conversationalist. There's central heating and never a problem with parking. With advance notice, the O'Briens are happy to arrange special-interest holidays (golfing, freshwater or deep-sea fishing, cycling, hill climbing, horseback riding).

TRAENLAUR LODGE, Louch Feeagh, Newport, Co. Mayo. Tel. 098/41358. 32 beds; self-catering facilities by special arrangement.
$ Rates: IR£5 ($8.75) for adults, IR£4 ($7) for under 18s. No credit cards.

Located 13 miles from Westport and 5 miles from Newport, in a 250-year-old fishing lodge on a famed salmon lake, this is a superior hostel for outdoors enthusiasts. Activities at the hostel or nearby include hill walking and swimming, and there are bicycles for rent. Letterkeen Forest, nature walks, and a salmon research center are nearby points of interest, as well as the 9th-century Burrishule Abbey and Rockfleet Castle. There's also traditional music at least 1 evening a week.

Where to Eat

THE ASGARD TAVERN AND RESTAURANT, The Quay, Westport. Tel. 098/25319.
Cuisine: BAR FOOD/SEAFOOD/IRISH/VEGETARIAN. **Reservations:** Not required.
$ Prices: Bar food less than IR£5 ($8.75); lunch IR£7 ($12.25); dinner IR£14 ($24.50). AE, DC, MC, V.
Open: May–Oct, bar, daily noon–8pm; restaurant, dinner only, daily 6:30–10pm. Nov–Apr, bar, Tues–Sat noon–8pm; restaurant, dinner only, Tues–Sat 6:30–10pm.

This is a delightful nautical pub where owners Mary and Michael Cadden serve award-winning seafood dishes as well as bar snacks. In the evening, you'll usually find traditional or folk music here. It's a bright, cozy place, and among the menu items not to be missed are the seafood chowder, quiche Lorraine, smoked salmon, garlic steak, and barbecued spareribs.

ACHILL ISLAND

Achill is Ireland's largest island, and its 57 square miles are connected to the mainland by a causeway that takes you into breathtakingly beautiful and unspoiled scenery. This is a wild and at the same time profoundly peaceful place, peopled by friendly, hardy natives who welcome visitors warmly. Achill has long been a favorite holiday spot for the Irish from other parts of the country, and there are good accommodations available in most of the beach villages. If time permits, I highly recommend an overnight stay on Achill, but if you can only spare a part of a day, this is one off-the-beaten-track place you really shouldn't miss.

What to See and Do

Scenery, water sports, and a lively pub scene after dark are the stars of an Achill Island stay. High cliffs overlook tiny villages of whitewashed cottages, golden beaches, and heathery boglands. The signposted **Atlantic Drive** is spectacular, and will whet your appetite to explore more of the island's well-surfaced roadways. In summer there's traditional music in many of the pubs. In late May the entire island is covered by such a profusion of rhododendrons that my bed-and-breakfast landlady smilingly told me, "Every car that leaves will be loaded with those blooms, and we won't even miss them!"

Where to Stay

ROCKMOUNT, Achill Island, Co. Mayo. Tel. 098/45272. 4 rms (2 with bath).

$ Rates (including breakfast): IR£15 ($26.25) single without bath; IR£11.50 ($20.15) per person sharing without bath; IR£2 ($3.50) per person additional with bath. 24% reduction for children. High tea IR£8 ($14) extra; dinner, IR£11 ($19.25). No credit cards.

This modern bungalow is at the eastern edge of the village and convenient to a bus stop. Mrs. Frances Masterson happily shares her knowledge of the island with guests. Guest rooms are all comfortably furnished, and during my last stay, other guests included natives who had come from other parts of the country to holiday here, making for lively Irish conversation. Central heating and off-street parking.

TEACH MWEEWILLIN, Currane, Achill, Co. Mayo. Tel. 098/45134. 4 rms (none with bath).

$ Rates (including breakfast): IR£15 ($26.25) single; IR£11.50 ($20.15) per person sharing. 50% reduction for children. Dinner IR£10 ($17.50) extra. **Closed:** Oct–Mar.

Across the sound and 5½ miles from Achill Island, this modern bungalow sits on a hill overlooking sound and island. Mrs. Margo Cannon keeps a pony for children to ride, and gladly helps guests arrange fishing, sailing, or golf. Guest rooms are attractive and nicely furnished, and there's central heating as well as good parking.

Where to Eat

AMETHYST RESTAURANT, Keel, Achill Island. Tel. 098/43104.

Cuisine: SEAFOOD/TRADITIONAL/VEGETARIAN. **Reservations:** Not required.

$ Prices: Dinner IR£12–IR£14 ($21–$24.50). No credit cards.

Open: May–Oct, dinner only, daily 7–10pm. **Closed:** Nov–Apr.

This large dining room is set on the sound in the village in an old-fashioned resort hotel run by the Irish novelist Noel Scanlon (whose books are also published in America) and his wife. It's a large, comfortable room with a fireplace at one end, a peaked, beamed ceiling, and oil paintings and prints of Achill scenes. You dine to the accompaniment of classical music. The menu is quite extensive, with seafood featured (as you might imagine in this setting), but there are other specialties such as tandoori chicken and several vegetarian selections. There's a wine license.

CONG, ASHFORD CASTLE & *THE QUIET MAN* COUNTRY

There are several good reasons to turn toward Cong—the magnificent ruins of an Augustinian abbey, Ashford Castle, and the fact that it was in this locale that most of the film classic *The Quiet Man* was filmed.

Cong is the picturesque little village where a phenomenon known as "The Rising of the Waters" takes place. The waters of Lough Mask, which go underground 3 miles to the north, come rushing to the surface here to surge through the center of town before they dissipate into several streams that empty into Lough Corrib.

WHAT TO SEE & DO

At the edge of town, the **Royal Abbey of Cong** was built by Turlough Mor O'Connor, High King of Ireland, in 1120 on the site of an earlier 7th-century St. Fechin community. Considered to be one of the finest early-Christian architectural relics in the country, it is also the final resting place of Rory O'Connor, the last High King, who was buried here in 1198.

You'll find **Ashford Castle** just outside Cong on the shores of Lough Corrib. The oldest part of the castle was built by the de Burgoes, an Anglo-Norman family, in 1228, and its keep is now a part of the impressive, slightly eccentric Ashford Castle Hotel, which also incorporates a French château-style mansion of the Oranmore and Browne families built in the early 1700s and the additions made by Sir Benjamin Guinness in the mid-1800s (undertaken as much to provide employment for famine-starved natives as to improve the property). It's a fairyland sort of concoction that makes a superb luxury hotel favored by international celebrities (President and Mrs. Reagan stayed here during their 1984 visit). No less marvelous are its grounds, with beautifully landscaped lawns sloping down to the island-dotted lake. While its rates are definitely out of reach for budgeteers, not so a stroll through its elegant public rooms or a drink in the Dungeon Bar. Not a penny charged to soak in all that luxurious beauty!

Successive generations of Americans have loved the antics of John Wayne, Maureen O'Hara, and Barry Fitzgerald as they romped through *The Quiet Man,* a film that has become a classic. So I've done a little research, and if you want to track down some of the locales, look for these. (Also, if you can get a good crack going in one of Cong's pubs, there's bound to be a local there who remembers the filming and has tales to tell.) The exterior scenes were shot on the grounds of Ashford Castle—the woodlands, the church, Squire Danaher's house, and the salmon river with its arched bridge. The main village street scenes took place near the cross in the market square of Cong, and the nearby general store was transformed into Cohan's Bar for the picture. Over in front of the abbey, that pretty house you see at the side of the bridge was the Reverend Playfair's house. Many other locales, such as John Wayne's ancestral cottage (now a ruin near Maam Bridge) were shot on the hillsides of the Maam valley in County Galway, and the village of Inishfree as seen from a distance at the very beginning of the film is actually a shot of Clifden, taken from the Sky road.

Immediately east of Cong toward Cross lies the **Plain of Moytura,** where you'll find the **Ballymagibbon Cairn.** Dating from about 3,000 B.C., the 60-foot-high, 129-yard-circumference cairn was erected to commemorate a fierce prehistoric battle between the Firbolg and de Danann tribes. It seems that the Firbolgs carried the day during the early fighting, and that first evening each presented a stone and the head of a Danann to his king, who used the stones to build the cairn in honor of the grisly tribute. On a happier note, nearby Moytura House (privately owned and not open to the public) was once the home of Sir William Wilde and his wife, Speranza, parents of Oscar Wilde.

The route north from Cong to Castlebar passes through the little town of Partry, 4 miles north of which you will find ✪ **Ballintubber Abbey.** It's the only church in the English-speaking world with a 7-century history of uninterrupted services. What makes this all the more remarkable is that mass has been said within its walls since 1216 despite years of religious suppression, two burnings, and the assault of Cromwellian troops. At times during those centuries it was necessary for supplicants to kneel before the altar in secret and under open skies when there was no roof. That it has now been completely restored is due almost solely to the devoted efforts of its pastor, Father Egan, who labored from 1963 to 1966 to push the project forward. The abbey's doors are open every day and visitors are welcome.

WHERE TO STAY

HAZEL GROVE, Drumsheel, Cong, Co. Mayo. Tel. 092/46060. 4 rms (1 with bath).

$ Rates (including breakfast): IR£14 ($24.50) single without bath; IR£12 ($21) per person sharing without bath; IR£1 ($1.75) per person additional with bath. 20%

reduction for children. Dinner IR£11 ($19.25) extra. No credit cards. **Closed:** Dec–Mar.

Mrs. Ann Coakley will welcome you warmly to her luxurious, modern bungalow with its pretty garden about half a mile from the village. The house is centrally heated, and guestrooms are nicely done up.

MRS. CARMEL LYDON, Cong, Co. Mayo. Tel. 092/46053. 6 rms (4 with bath).
$ Rates (including breakfast): IR£11.50 ($20.15) per person without bath, IR£13.50 ($23.65) per person with bath. Dinner IR£12 ($21) extra. No credit cards. **Closed:** Oct–Mar.

Mrs. Lydon's large, modern house in the village is built in the Georgian style. Set on Lough Corrib (boats available for rent) and near Ashford Castle, the house is nicely decorated throughout, with attractive and comfortable guest rooms, central heating, and good parking.

CASTLEBAR & KNOCK
CASTLEBAR

Only 11 miles northeast of Westport via N60, Castlebar is the county town. If you read *The Year of the French,* you will remember that this is where Humbert's French forces won a complete route over the English in 1798. In modern times, it is the birthplace of Ireland's top politician, Charles Haughey, and it's a good base for touring County Mayo.

Avid shoppers will want to make the short drive northeast to the little village of **Foxford,** home of the world-renowned **Foxford Woollen Mills** (tel. 094/56104). The factory shop is open Monday through Saturday from 10am to 6pm, and there are great values in rugs, blankets, and tweeds.

Where to Stay

LAKEVIEW HOUSE, Westport Rd., Castlebar, Co. Mayo. Tel. 094/ 22374. 4 rms (3 with bath).
$ Rates (including breakfast): IR£15.50 ($27.15) single without bath; IR£11.50 ($20.15) per person sharing without bath; IR£1.50 ($2.65) per person additional with bath. 20% reduction for children. No credit cards. **Closed:** Christmas. **Parking:** Paved car park.

Mary and Joe Moran's bungalow sits on spacious grounds with a large, sloping lawn out front, 2½ miles from Castlebar on the Westport road. This was Mary's family home area, and both lounge (with fireplace) and dining room look out to green fields and rolling hills. Mary bakes her own brown bread and scones and is always happy to share the recipe with guests (a frequent request). The four pretty guest rooms include one family-size room (two double beds) with private shower. Central heating.

SHALOM, Westport Rd., Castlebar, Co. Mayo. Tel. 094/21471. 3 rms (none with bath).
$ Rates (including breakfast): IR£14.50 ($25.40) single; IR£11.50 ($20.15) per person sharing. 50% reduction for children. No credit cards. **Closed:** Mid-Oct to mid-Mar.

Noreen Raftery and her husband Liam, who is a Garda, take a personal interest in their guests—as does Bruno, their gorgeous Collie dog. Conversation around the turf fire in their lounge has brought glowing letters from readers. The three nice guest rooms have sinks and built-in wardrobes, and there's one family-size room with a double and a twin bed. Central heating and good parking. Shalom is 1¼ miles from Castlebar on N60.

Where to Eat

BREAFFY HOUSE HOTEL, Castlebar. Tel. 094/22033.
Cuisine: BAR FOOD/SEAFOOD/TRADITIONAL. **Reservations:** Not required.
$ Prices: Bar food less than IR£5 ($8.75); lunch IR£6–IR£8 ($10.50–$14); dinner IR£15 ($26.25). AE, DC, MC, V.

Open: Lunch daily noon–2:30pm; dinner daily 6–9pm.

For a moderately priced meal in elegant surroundings, make it this impressive graystone edifice set in beautiful formal gardens and lawns in the town center. Its Mulberry Bar is a gracious room in the Tudor style, and a very good three-course businessman's lunch is served every day featuring the joint of the day and fresh vegetables, with poached salmon in champagne sauce, sautéed medallions of beef béarnaise, and chicken stuffed with Mozzarella cheese and garlic butter frequently among other choices.

DAVITT RESTAURANT AND LOUNGE BAR, Rush St., Castlebar. Tel. 094/22233.

Cuisine: INTERNATIONAL/IRISH/SEAFOOD/VEGETARIAN. **Reservations:** Recommended for dinner.

$ Prices: Lunch IR£5–IR£6 ($8.75–$10.50); dinner IR£14 ($24.50). AE, MC, V.

Open: Daily 12:30–11:30pm. **Closed:** Good Friday, Christmas Day.

This is an attractive bar/restaurant, with traditional leaded windows and a warm, friendly staff. Owner Raymond Kenny has a devoted local following, a testament to his fine continental creations and wonderful traditional Irish dishes. Garlic-filled chicken Kiev is terrific, and other specialties are carpetbagger steak, Mexican beef kebabs, and sole garnished with prawns and lobster sauce. Good service.

KNOCK

Twenty-five miles southeast of Castlebar, the little church in the village of Knock has become a shrine to which thousands of pilgrims come each year, for it was here, on August 17, 1879, that an apparition of Our Lady was seen at the **Church of St. John the Baptist.** After a Commission of Enquiry ruled that the apparition was genuine, Knock was officially designated a Marian Shrine. When mass pilgrimages became too much for the little church, a magnificent basilica was built on the grounds, and a highlight of the shrine's history was the visit of Pope John Paul II in 1979. Those huge crowds of pilgrims also prompted a long and eventually successful campaign for an airport to serve Knock.

On the south side of the Basilica, the **Knock Folk Museum** portrays life in the west of Ireland around the time of the apparition through exhibits that illustrate folk life, history, archeology, and religion. It's open from 9:30am to 6pm Monday through Saturday, 10am to 4pm on Sunday.

Where to Stay

RIVERSIDE, Charlestown, Co. Mayo. Tel. 094/54200. 7 rms (4 with bath)

$ Rates (including breakfast): IR£12 ($21) per person sharing, IR£1.50 ($2.60) per person extra for private bath, IR£4 ($7) single. One-third reduction for children. Dinner IR£10–IR£15 ($17.50–$26.25). No credit cards.

Open: Year round.

Mrs. Evelyn O'Hara is the delightful hostess of this attractive, century-old, family home, northeast of Knock in Charlestown at the intersection of N5 and N17. Guestrooms are quite comfortable, and Mrs. O'Hara is a friendly, helpful aid to her guests. There is also a family-run restaurant with good food at moderate prices, open from February to December, and an enclosed car park.

CHAPTER 16

COUNTIES SLIGO & LEITRIM

1. SLIGO TOWN
- **WHAT'S SPECIAL ABOUT COUNTIES SLIGO & LEITRIM**

2. YEATS COUNTRY

3. AROUND COUNTY SLIGO

4. AROUND COUNTY LEITRIM

The Northwest is not so much a place that offers things to "do" as much as it is a region to be experienced and absorbed. There are special places you won't want to miss, but mostly you'll remember the sense of tuning in to a part of your inner self that all too often has been lost in the frenetic pace at which most of us gallop through modern life.

It was this region, with some of Ireland's most wondrous landscapes of sea and mountains and far-flung vistas, that shaped the poet Yeats's life and work. His words about this part of Ireland cannot, of course, be bested, and you will find yourself recalling them again and again as you travel the Northwest.

---

1. SLIGO TOWN

Sligo (Sligeach, "Shelly Place") grew up around a ford of the River Garavogue, which rises in Lough Gill and tumbles over swift rapids as it approaches its estuary. The town's strategic position gave it early prominence as a seaport; as a religious center, it's the cathedral town of both a Catholic and a Protestant diocese. For Yeats devotees and scholars, it offers a wealth of information and memorabilia, and all visitors will find a friendly welcome and accommodations that are friendly to the budget.

ORIENTATION

ESSENTIALS   Sligo's **telephone area code** is 071. The **General Post Office** is on Wine Street, west of the bridge, open Monday through Saturday from 9am to 5:30pm.

TOURIST INFORMATION   You'll find the **Tourist Office** on Temple Street (tel. 071/61201), open in summer, daily from 9am to 6pm.

TOWN LAYOUT   Sligo sits astride the **River Garavogue,** and the **Hyde Bridge** at Stephen Street (named for Ireland's first president, Dr. Douglas Hyde) is a central point of reference. **O'Connell Street** runs south of the bridge and holds the major shopping and business district of the town. The beach resort of **Strandhill** is 5 miles to the west, **Rosses Point** is 5 miles to the north, and there are several buses a day to each from the main bus station.

   Magheraboy, where Yeats spent many childhood summers, is a short distance from town to the southwest, and **Drumcliffe Churchyard** is 5 miles north of town.

GETTING THERE

By Plane   Aer Lingus has daily flights between Sligo and Dublin. For schedules, fares, and booking, phone **Sligo Airport** at Strandhill (tel. 071/68280 or 68318).

WHAT'S SPECIAL ABOUT COUNTIES SLIGO & LEITRIM

Natural Scenery
☐ Lofty Knocknarea, where a massive, unopened cairn is reputed to be the resting place of Queen Maeve.
☐ Ben Bulben, the flat-topped mountain so beloved of the poet Yeats.
☐ The tiny Isle of Innisfree, in Lough Gill, which is featured in Yeats's poetry.

Ancient Monuments
☐ Carrowmore, south of Sligo town, which holds one of the largest concentrations of megalithic tombs in Europe.
☐ Interpretive Centre for National Monuments of the Northwest at Parke's Castle, Dromahair, County Leitrim, which presents an overview of this region's extensive array of prehistoric monuments.

Literary Shrines
☐ Grave of poet William Butler Yeats in Drumcliff graveyard.

Museums
☐ County Sligo Museum and Yeats Art Gallery, with its extensive collections of the poet's writings and paintings by his brother, Jack Yeats.

Crafts
☐ The "Sculpture Trail" to the workshops of 13 wood sculptors in the little town of Hazelwood.
☐ Woodcarver Michael Quirke's workshop on Wine Street in Sligo town, where he translates Irish legends into memorable wood sculptures.

Genealogical Center
☐ The Leitrim Heritage Centre, in Ballinamore, County Leitrim, which maintains full research facilities for those with Leitrim ancestry.

Special Events
☐ Yeats International Summer School, in Sligo town, which draws Yeats scholars from around the globe for workshops, readings, and lectures.
☐ Sligo Arts Festival, in late September or early October, a lively celebration of all the arts, as the streets come alive with music and outdoor performances.

By Train/Bus There's train service from Dublin to Sligo, with stops in Longford and Carrick-on-Shannon. Good bus connections are available from around the country. The **bus and railway station** is just above Lord Edward Street on the western edge of town. For schedule information, call 071/60066.

GETTING AROUND

By Taxi For taxi service, call 2596 or 3740; there's a taxi rank at the train station and one at Quay Street. Fares are preset to most points of interest, and cabs are not metered, so be sure to ask the fare.

On Foot Sligo town is well laid out and compact, and the best possible way to appreciate its interesting narrow streets is on foot. There are guided and self-guided walking tours available (see below), but simply rambling around the town is a real delight.

WHAT TO SEE & DO

While many visitors come to Sligo and head straight out to those spots associated with Yeats, it would be a mistake not to see the highlights of the old town itself.

THE TOP ATTRACTIONS

COUNTY SLIGO MUSEUM AND YEATS ART GALLERY, Stephen St., Sligo. Tel. 071/42212.

✪ Located in a pretty 1851 chapel, this museum holds many interesting exhibits relating to the poet W. B. Yeats, including a complete collection of his poetry written from 1889 to 1936 and an extensive collection of his prose and plays. The gallery, housed in former schoolrooms, is dedicated to his artist brother, Jack Yeats. The gallery, in fact, contains Ireland's largest collection of his drawings and paintings, as well as works by his contemporaries.

Admission: Free.

Open: Museum, June–Sept, Mon–Sat 10:30am–12:30pm and 2:30–4:30pm. Gallery, June–Sept, Tues–Sat 10:30am–12:30pm and 2:30–4:30pm. Both are open other months by arrangement with the Tourist Board.

YEATS MEMORIAL BUILDING, Hyde Bridge, Sligo. Tel. 071/42693.

This 1895 red-brick building beside Hyde Bridge is headquarters for the Sligo Yeats Society, the ultimate source of information on the poet. It also houses the **Sligo Art Gallery,** the setting for changing art exhibitions.

Admission: Free.

Open: June–Aug, Mon–Fri 2–5pm.

ARCHITECTURAL HIGHLIGHTS

Sligo's streets are literally filled with quaint old shopfronts and 19th-century buildings of architectural interest. The following are outstanding:

Town Hall, on Quay Street, which dates from 1865, is a graceful, Italian Renaissance building that legend says stands on the site of a 17th-century Cromwellian fort. At Teeling Street and Chapel Street, the **Courthouse** incorporates part of the earlier courthouse. In 1832, when cholera swept over Sligo, the building housed coffin builders. You can't miss the impressive **Pollexfen Ships** at the corner of Adelaide Street and Wine Street. The large stone building originally belonged to the largest ship owners in Sligo, who provided the sail power to transport thousands of emigrants to Canada and America in the 1860s.

On Adelaide Street, the **Cathedral of the Immaculate Conception** is a massive limestone structure of Renaissance Romanesque style. ✪ **Sligo Dominican Abbey,** on Abbey Street, is the town's only surviving medieval building, built in the mid-1400s to replace a 1250s structure destroyed by fire. **St. John's Church,** on John Street, dates from the mid-1700s and was designed by the same architect as Leinster House, the seat of the Irish government in Dublin. Its churchyard makes for interesting rambles among headstones that go as far back as the mid-1600s.

OTHER ATTRACTIONS

The local Irish Countrywoman's Association has rescued and restored ✪ **Dolly's Cottage,** in Strandhill, the last thatched house in Sligo. Dolly was a well-loved resident of the area, and now you can visit her home Monday through Friday from 3 to 5pm to see the dresser with its delft-chinawear collection, a pouch bed with its patchwork quilt, a spinning wheel, and other authentic period furnishings. Handcrafted knit, wool, and leather items are on sale, as are sheepskin rugs and pottery. During the summer months, country markets are held every Wednesday afternoon.

✪ The shop of **wood carver Michael Quirke,** Wine Street, Sligo (tel. 071/42624 or 45800), qualifies as much as a sculpture gallery as it does a commercial enterprise. Michael is a fascinating artist whose pieces include some superb representations of Ireland's mythical heroic figures, and with your browsing or purchase, he supplies more than a little storytelling about his pieces, along with expert advice on the care of the woods from which they are made. He's open Monday through Saturday from 10am to 5pm.

✪ Just 3 miles from Sligo town, the little town of Hazelwood on Halfmoon Bay is home to no fewer than 13 wood sculptors whose workshops are open to visitors. Ask at the Tourist Office for their **Sculpture Trail** guide, or simply stop by on your own.

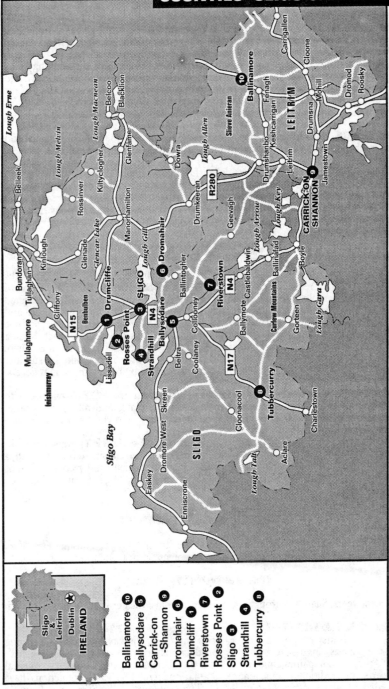

N

Lough Erne

Belleek

Bundoran
Tullaghan
Kinlough
Mullaghmore
Cliffony

Lough Melvin

Lough Macnean
Belcoo
Blacklion

Rossinver
Kiltyclogher
Glenade
Glencar Lake
Glenfarne

N15

Benbulben
Drumcliffe

1

Manorhamilton
Dowra

Lough Allen
R280
Drumkeeran

Geevagh

Ballinamore
10

Fenagh
Keshcarrigan
Drumshanbo
Leitrim

LEITRIM

Carrigallen
Cloone
Mohill
Dromod
Roosky

Drumsna
Jamestown

CARRICK-ON-SHANNON
9

Slieve Anieran

Lissadell
Rosses Point
2
Strandhill
4

Inishmurray

SLIGO
3
N4
5
Ballysodare
Beltra
Collooney
Coolaney

Lough Gill
Dromahair
6

Ballintogher

Riverstown
7
N4

Castlebaldwin
Lough Arrow
Lough Key

Boyle
Lough Gara

Ballymote
Gorteen

N17
Tubbercurry
8

Charlestown

Sligo Bay

Skreen
Dromore West
Easkey
Enniscrone

SLIGO

Cloonacool
Aclare
Lough Talt

Curlew Mountains
Ballinafad

Sligo & Leitrim
Dublin
IRELAND

ORGANIZED TOURS

WALKING TOURS   The Tourist Office has an excellent booklet that outlines a signposted **Tourist Trail** do-it-yourself walking tour (a nice souvenir, even if you go along with the guided tour described below).

To get the most out of your stay in Sligo town, join one of the walking tours conducted during July and August by young **student guides** who love the town and are intimately acquainted with all major points of interest. Tours leave the Tourist Office at 11am and last 1 hour and 15 minutes. It's perfectly in order to tip your enthusiastic young guide a minimum of IR£2 ($3.50).

BUS TOURS   Bus Eireann's day tours from Sligo include the Hills of Donegal and Glenveagh National Park, with adult fares of IR£8 ($14), half that for children.

OTHER TOURS   One of the most delightful ways I can think of to visit the beaches, Ben Bulben, Lissadell House, etc., is via horse and trap, and the **Moneygold Riding and Horse Driving Centre,** Grange, Co. Sligo (tel. 071/63337), can arrange it for you. They also have a variety of other horse-related activities, such as pony trekking, fast beach rides, and special holidays in an "organic" farmhouse and youth hostel.

SPECIAL EVENTS

For 2 weeks every August there's a glut of activity in Sligo centered around the works of William Butler Yeats. That's when the **Yeats International Summer School** presents seminars, lectures, workshops, poetry readings, and dramas for dedicated Yeats scholars. Afternoon tours are conducted, and evenings are filled with social and theatrical events. Tuition is in the IR£250 to IR£300 ($437.50 to $525) range, and the staff will help you find inexpensive accommodations. For full details, exact dates, a brochure, and an application, contact the Secretary, Yeats Society, Hyde Bridge, Sligo, County Sligo (tel. 071/42693). If you should happen into Sligo while the summer school is in session, you can attend many of the events by buying individual tickets.

FESTIVALS   The week following Easter is dedicated to the ✪ **Feiseanna,** with competitions in traditional music, dancing, singing, plays, and all sorts of other activities. It draws the Irish from all over the country, and the town is alive with festivities day and night.

In late September or early October, the **Sligo Arts Festival** is a joyous street fair, when the town comes alive with music that ranges from the classics to rock and roll, a feast of visual arts, and spectacular fireworks. For specific dates and accommodations information, contact Sligo Arts Festival, Stephen Street, Sligo, County Sligo (tel. 071/69802).

EVENING ENTERTAINMENT

In addition to current information from the Tourist Office, consult *The Sligo Champion,* which carries notices of current goings-on in town and the area.

The Performing Arts

In recent years, Sligo has brought a resurgence to live theater in the west of Ireland.

HAWKS WELL THEATRE, Temple St., Sligo. Tel. 071/61526 or 61518.
✪ As the first purpose-built theater in the West, Hawks Well places a strong emphasis on Irish playwrights, productions are performed by leading Irish theater companies, and there's the occasional evening of poetry, musical concerts, or traditional song, dance, drama, and comedy. Past productions have included *Playboy of the Western World, The Plough and the Stars,* and *Leopold Bloom: Heroic Moments.* It's a small, intimate theater with the most up-to-date

equipment and, with advance notice, facilities in the stalls for the handicapped. It's beside the Tourist Board building on Temple Street; off-street parking is available at the cathedral car park. Call to check what's playing during your visit.

Prices: Tickets less than IR£10 ($17.50).

The Pub and Music Scene

It's fairly easy to find traditional music and ballads in Sligo pubs and those nearby. However, since the "schedule" for such happenings is often a nonschedule, best check with the Tourist Office when you're there about days of the week the following are likely to have music.

McLynn's Pub, Old Market Street, Sligo (tel. 071/42088), frequently breaks out in song, almost always led by Donal McLynn, who carries on a tradition set by his late grandmother, who ran the pub for more than 30 years (the Ogham plaque by the doorway spells out "Granny" in the ancient script in her memory). The pub has the comfortable look of age, with a big hearth and lots of copper and old bar mirrors. The crowd tends to be on the young side, and you can usually count on ballads on Thursday.

Another gathering place is in Ballisodare, a few miles south of Sligo Town via N4. **The Thatch,** Ballisodare, County Sligo (tel. 071/67288), is a small cottage pub with a huge fireplace and church-pew seats in one of its two rooms, and kitchen furnishings in the other. There's usually music on Thursday.

On the bridge at Drumcliffe, the **Yeats Tavern,** Drumcliffe, County Sligo (tel. 071/63117), has nightly musical goings-on all year in a very popular, modern setting. It's out the Donegal road, about 5 miles from town.

From time to time, the **Sancta Maria Hotel,** Strandhill, County Sligo (tel. 071/68113), has a "Gaelic Night," with a lot of singing and reciting of poetry. Brush up on your own party piece and go along if you happen on one of these very special evenings (call the hotel or check with the Tourist Board—weekend nights used to be the nights for music, but it changes).

Not for music, but for a uniquely traditional Irish "local," where the crack is good and your company welcome, is **Hargedon's,** O'Connell Street, Sligo. It's more than 2 centuries old and is as authentic as they come.

WHERE TO STAY
IN & AROUND TOWN

AISLING, Cairns Hill, Sligo, Co. Sligo. Tel. 071/60704. 5 rms (3 with bath).
$ Rates (including breakfast): IR£12 ($21) per person without bath, IR£13.50 ($23.65) per person with bath. No credit cards.

Just off the Dublin–Galway road on the outskirts of town, Aisling is a centrally heated modern bungalow overlooking Benbulben and Knocknare. The five guest rooms are both attractive and comfortable—Nan and Des Faul even provide electric blankets.

RATHNASHEE, Teesan, Donegal Rd. (N15), Sligo, Co. Sligo. Tel. 071/43376. 4 rms (2 with bath).
$ Rates (including breakfast): IR£15.50 ($27.15) single without bath; IR£11.50 ($20.15) per person sharing without bath; IR£1 ($1.75) per person additional with bath. High tea IR£7.50 ($13.15) extra; dinner, IR£10.50 ($18.40). No credit cards.
Closed: Christmas.

Rathnashee (it means "Fort of the Fairies") is the home of Tess and Sean Haughey, and it's the kind of place where guests often wind up sitting around the kitchen table for long conversations in which the Haugheys share their extensive knowledge of what to see in Sligo. They also have one of the best private libraries in Sligo, and they can arrange sightseeing tours with archeologists. Tess serves traditional Irish food and homemade preserves. The centrally heated modern bungalow has nicely appointed guest rooms, and there's good parking off the road. It's 2 miles from the town center.

RENATE CENTRAL HOUSE, Upper John St., Sligo, Co. Sligo. Tel. 071/62014. 5 rms (1 with bath).

$ Rates (including breakfast): IR£16 ($28) single without bath; IR£12 ($21) per person sharing without bath; IR£1.50 ($2.65) per person additional with bath. No credit cards.

This small gabled house is surely one of the most convenient in Sligo town. Annie and Leo Hunt (he's a former mayor of Sligo) have five attractive guest rooms, plus a pretty dining room and a color TV in the drawing room. There's central heating and off-the-street parking, a great boon since Renate is near the train and bus station within easy walking distance of the town center.

ST. MARTIN'S, Cummeen, Strandhill Rd., Sligo, Co. Sligo. Tel. 071/60614. 5 rms (4 with bath). TV
$ Rates (including breakfast): IR£15.50 ($27.15) single without bath; IR£11.50 ($20.15) per person sharing without bath; IR£1.50 ($2.65) per person additional with bath. 25% reduction for children. No credit cards.
Mrs. Carmel Carr will welcome you to her attractive modern bungalow 2½ miles past the Southern Hotel on the main Strandhill road. The house is centrally heated and there is a garden for guests to use. All five guest rooms are nicely appointed, and Mrs. Carr is always happy to help guests with sightseeing advice. Good parking.

SEISNAUN, Kintogher, Sligo, Co. Sligo. Tel. 071/43938. 4 rms (1 with bath).
$ Rates (including breakfast): IR£16.50 ($28.90) single without bath; IR£11.50 ($20.15) per person sharing without bath; IR£1.50 ($2.65) per person additional with bath. 25% reduction for children. No credit cards. **Closed:** Nov–May.
Mrs. Phil Clancy is hostess of this modern luxury bungalow, which is convenient to Rosses Point, Yeats Country, and Drumcliffe. Situated in a peaceful area in town, off the Donegal road, it has beautiful views of Benbulben mountain and Yeats Country. The house is centrally heated and the food is delicious, complete with home-baking. All five attractive bedrooms are comfortably furnished, and there's central heating as well as good parking.

TREE TOPS, Cleveragh Rd., Sligo, Co. Sligo. Tel. 071/60160. 6 rms (4 with bath). TEL
$ Rates (including breakfast): IR£16 ($28) single without bath; IR£12 ($21) per person sharing without bath; IR£1.50 ($2.65) per person additional with bath. 20% reduction for children. No credit cards.
Mrs. Doreen MacEvilly is hostess of this attractive home about a 5-minute walk from the town center. About 100 yards off N4, the road to Lough Gill, Innisfree, and Holy Well, it's an ideal base for touring. The house is centrally heated and an evening meal is available. All five comfortable bedrooms are fitted with orthopedic beds, come with hairdryers, and are attractively decorated.

NEARBY ACCOMMODATIONS

GLENWOOD, Carrowmore, Sligo, Co. Sligo. Tel. 071/61449. 4 rms (2 with bath).
$ Rates (including breakfast): IR£16 ($28) single without bath; IR£12 ($21) per person sharing without bath; IR£2 ($3.50) per person additional with bath. No credit cards. **Closed:** Oct–May.

Mrs. Anna McKiernan is the hospitable hostess of the lovely, two-story house set 1¼ miles from the town center in award-winning gardens on the Sligo–Carrowmore road beside a riding school. It is convenient to Knocknarea, Yeats Country, and Strandhill, and is surrounded by megalithic tombs. The house is centrally heated and dinner is available with advance notice. The five pretty bedrooms are nicely appointed, with comfortable furnishings.

LA MER, Luffertan, Strandhill, Co. Sligo. Tel. 071/68182. 3 rms (none with bath).

$ Rates (including breakfast): IR£13.50 ($23.65) single; IR£11.50 ($20.15) per person sharing. 25% reduction for children. No credit cards. **Closed:** Oct–Apr.

Mrs. Lindsay welcomes you to this lovely modern bungalow 2 miles from Strandhill set in beautiful surroundings overlooking Ballisodare Bay. It is located on the Ballisodare-Strandhill road and the three attractive bedrooms are all nicely furnished.

SANCTA MARIA HOTEL, Strandhill, Co. Sligo. Tel. 071/68113. 9 rms (none with bath).

$ Rates (including breakfast): Apr–May, IR£10.50 ($18.40) per person single or double; June–Oct, IR£13.50 ($23.65) per person single or double. 10% reduction for children. Dinner IR£10 ($17.50) extra. No credit cards. **Closed:** Nov–Mar.

Out in Strandhill, the Sancta Maria is a small, old-fashioned country inn, with the sort of comfortable, homey air that only comes from a caring host like Brigid O'Dowd. The attention here is friendly and personal, and Brigid will happily help you plan your travels around the area, fill you in on local stories to embellish your journey, and otherwise make your stay pure pleasure. The nine guest rooms are comfortably furnished, with built-in closets and sinks, and there's central heating. There are Gaelic Nights on weekends through the summer months. The hotel is also fully licensed. All in all, it's a pleasant, relaxed "home away from home."

WORTH THE EXTRA MONEY

COOPERSHILL COUNTRY HOUSE, Riverstown, Co. Sligo. Tel. 071/65108. Fax 071/65446. 6 rms (all with bath).

$ Rates (including breakfast): IR£44 ($77) single; IR£38 ($66.50) per person sharing. Dinner IR£18 ($31.50) extra. AE, DC, MC, V. **Closed:** Nov to mid-Mar.

Coopershill is a great stone Georgian family mansion 11 miles southwest of Sligo on the Dublin road (N4), built back in 1774 amid more than 500 acres of woodlands and pastures grazed by sheep and cattle. The graciousness of its original era is reflected in the large rooms, high ceilings, and beautiful furnishings. Its owners are Brian and Lindy O'Hara. There are only six bedrooms, but all are special, with private bathrooms and most with either four-poster or canopy beds. There's fishing for pike and perch on the river that flows through the grounds (Mrs. O'Hara has a small boat available to guests), and beautiful beaches are close by.

READERS RECOMMEND

Lisadorn, Strandhill, County Sligo (tel. 071/78210). "We stayed with Lily and Paddy Diamond and were treated so grand we felt really special. They helped us with suggestions of what to see and look for along the way."—Peggy Moran, Fort Wayne, Ind.

WHERE TO EAT

IN TOWN

BEEZIES, 45 O'Connell St., Sligo. Tel. 071/45030.

Cuisine: BAR FOOD/TRADITIONAL/VEGETARIAN. **Reservations:** Not required.

$ Prices: Lunch IR£5.50 ($9.65); dinner IR£10 ($17.50). AE, MC, V.

Open: Mon–Sat 10:30am–11pm, Sun 12:30–3pm and 4–11pm. **Closed:** Good Friday, Christmas Day.

In addition to the good food dished up at Beezies, it's worth a visit, if only for a drink or a look around. The turn-of-the-century marble counters, bar partitions of Tiffany glass, and lamps with tulip-shaped shades give a real 19th-century look to the place. Bar food stars up front, and in back there's a full restaurant serving lunches and five-course dinners featuring traditional Irish ingredients.

COFFEE & CRAFTS, Market Yard, Sligo.
Cuisine: SALADS/SANDWICHES/QUICHE. **Reservations:** Not required.
$ Prices: IR£2–IR£4 ($3.50–$7). No credit cards.
Open: Mon–Sat 9am–6pm.

Recent years have seen this old market area off Temple Street near the Tourist Office in Sligo town develop into an attractive complex of shops and eateries in restored buildings. Joe Feeney, owner of Coffee & Crafts, has transformed one corner of a former fire station into this bright, cheerful restaurant with glass walls overlooking the courtyard. It's self-service, and your biggest problem as you pass along the counter is likely to be deciding when to stop—everything is homemade, from soup and sandwiches to a wide selection of salads (including vegetable, lasagne, pizza, and smoked salmon salad plates), and portions are generous.

BONNE CHERE, 45 High St., Sligo. Tel. 071/42014.
Cuisine: TRADITIONAL/SNACKS. **Reservations:** Not required.
$ Prices: Breakfast IR£4.50 ($7.90); lunch IR£6.50 ($11.40); dinner IR£14.50 ($25.40). AE, MC, V.
Open: Daily 8am–10:30pm. **Closed:** Dec 25–27.

Bonne Chère has been a favorite of Sligo families for years. Its colonial-style decor features wagon-wheel lamps and touches of brass, and the arched side booths create intimate nooks in the large room. The menu features good, plain cooking that makes full use of local produce, with fish, lamb, ham, and chicken selections. There's also a children's menu and a Tourist Menu from noon to 3pm. The extensive menu also offers soup and sandwiches, scones, and salads, and the restaurant is fully licensed.

GULLIVER'S, 23 Grattan St., Sligo. Tel. 071/42030.
Cuisine: BURGERS/SALADS/FISH/STEAKS. **Reservations:** Not required.
$ Prices: Burgers, pizza, salads IR£3.50–IR£5.55 ($6.15–$9.70); hot lunch IR£6–IR£8 ($10.50–$14); dinner IR£9–IR£14 ($15.75–$24.50); children's menu IR£2–IR£3 ($3.50–$5.25). MC, V.
Open: Daily 12:30pm–midnight.

This old-style pub/restaurant has an appealing wooden front, and there's something of the nautical about the interior, with false portholes around the walls and fish nets draped from the ceiling. The menu is huge, and I particularly like the chicken Hibernia (with a whiskey sauce). Other standouts include trout and chicken Maryland. Service is friendly and efficient, and of course it's fully licensed.

A NEARBY RESTAURANT

REVERIES, Rosses Point, Sligo, Co. Sligo. Tel. 071/77371.
Cuisine: SEAFOOD/GAME/TRADITIONAL. **Reservations:** Recommended.
$ Prices: Dinner IR£19 ($33.25). MC, V.
Open: Dinner only, Tues–Sat 7:30–10pm. **Closed:** 3 weeks in Nov, 4 days at Christmas.

Overlooking Sligo Bay, this large, modern restaurant specializes in fresh seafood, and in season, quail, pheasant, and wild duck appear on the menu. Quality steaks and beef Wellington are also featured.

PICNIC FARE & WHERE TO EAT IT

Picnic grounds are close at hand, with picnic tables scattered throughout lovely **Dooney Wood,** some 4 miles outside Sligo. Beside the car park, flat-topped Dooney

Rock is where Yeats wrote of the fiddler playing. There are also parking areas and picnic tables at **Carns,** setting of many cairns and giants' graves, a mile and a half from Sligo out the Holywell road, as well as at **Deerpark,** on the old road to Manorhamilton.

Sligo boasts two excellent delicatessens, both specializing in take-aways for meals in the open or, if your fancy so dictates, in your room.

COSGROVES OF SLIGO, 32 Market St., Sligo. Tel. 071/42809.

One of the oldest fine food shops in Ireland, Cosgroves has operated under the same family ownership for more than a century, and it still retains its charming 19th-century shopfront. The home-cooked specialties include baked ham, beef, lamb, chicken, German sausages, and poached salmon. Cheeses include Irish, English, and continental varieties, and there are fresh salads daily. An addition to the food section in recent years is the well-stocked craft shop featuring Irish pottery, watercolors, and other native crafts.

Open: Mon–Sat 9:30am–9pm.

HOOPER & PETTIT, Wine St., Sligo. Tel. 071/43022.

This small deli-cum-restaurant specializes in gourmet meals that will elevate picnicking to a new high, or you can dine right on the premises. There's also a wide selection of Irish farmhouse cheeses, cold cuts, and salads for less elegant picnics. In addition to foodstuffs, they carry a full line of Crabtree & Evelyn toiletries.

Open: Mon–Sat 9:30am–7pm. **Closed:** Bank hols.

2. YEATS COUNTRY

It was County Sligo that nurtured Yeats all his life, from boyhood stays in Magheraboy with his grandparents to the end of his life, when he was laid to rest in Drumcliffe churchyard. His imagination was fired by local legends of ancient heroes and heroines who lived out their sagas in this part of Ireland and left the countryside strewn with mementoes of their passing. Beautiful Lough Gill is where you'll find his Isle of Inisfree, and at Knocknarea's summit is the cairn where, according to legend (and Yeats), "passionate Maeve is stony-still."

WHAT TO SEE & DO

If you're rambling through Yeats Country on your own, go by the Tourist Office or a Sligo bookshop and pick up the excellent booklet **"The Yeats Country,"** which tells you which poems were written about which places. You'll also find those places associated with the great poet marked by simple signposts inscribed with the appropriate verses. One suggested route is to drive east along Lough Gill's northern shore to the **Holy Well,** a grotto where devout Catholics met during the years of the penal laws to celebrate mass in secret. Its stone altar is more than 300 years old. Look out over the lake to the southeast and the small **Lake Isle of Innisfree.** From there,

IMPRESSIONS

The Irish Literary Revivalists . . . sought in Ireland the kind of dignity and the kind of health that the industrialised world, the modern world, had lost; the Ireland they loved had an enormous West Coast and no Northeast corner.
—CONOR CRUISE O'BRIEN, *WRITERS AND POLITICS,* 1965

drive to **Glencar Lake** and leave your car to walk across the fields to Glencar Falls, where there are steps built up the left side of what Yeats called "pools among the rushes." As you return across the field, you can glimpse the little thatched cottage where Yeats called in for tea quite often as a young man.

Just before you reach Sligo's town limits, you'll see the turnoff for **Drumcliffe** to the north. This is where Yeats lies "Under bare Ben Bulben's head," and his headstone bears the epitaph he composed for himself:

Cast a cold eye
On life, on death.
Horseman, pass by!

When Yeats died in 1939 in the south of France, he was first buried in a cemetery overlooking the Mediterranean. His remains were brought home to his beloved Sligo in 1948 and placed here, as he wished, in the shadow of Benbulben. The grave is just left of the cemetery's entrance.

Drumcliffe is also where you'll find **Lissadell House** (tel. 071/63150), ancestral home of the Gore-Booth family, whose most famous member, Constance, an important figure in the 1916 uprising, spent much of her childhood. As Countess Markievicz, she became the first woman ever elected to the British House of Commons and was minister for labour in the first Irish government. It's open to the public from May to September, Monday through Saturday from 2 to 5pm, with a small admission fee.

✪ **ORGANIZED TOURS**   One of the best ways to get an overall feeling for the country is to take Bus Eireann's **Yeats Country Tour,** conducted on specific days during the summer months. It's nearly a 4-hour trip, with a very good commentary, and the low fare (about IR£5/$8.75) includes a visit to Lissadell House.

WHERE TO STAY

CASTLETOWN HOUSE, Drumcliffe, Co. Sligo. Tel. 071/63204. 3 rms (1 with shower only).
$ Rates (including breakfast): IR£15.50 ($27.15) single; IR£11.50 ($20.15) per person sharing. 20% reduction for children. High tea IR£8 ($14) extra; dinner, IR£10 ($17.50). No credit cards. **Closed:** Nov–Feb.
Mrs. Mazie Rooney's modern, centrally heated bungalow is 6 miles north of Sligo, just off N15, the main Donegal road, near W. B. Yeats's grave, and is ideal for touring Yeats Country. The three bedrooms are comfortably furnished, and there's a good restaurant nearby if you decide not to avail yourself of Mrs. Rooney's excellent home-cooked dinner.

URLAR HOUSE, Drumcliffe, Co. Sligo. Tel. 071/63110. 5 rms (2 with bath).
$ Rates (including breakfast): IR£15.50 ($27.15) single without bath; IR£12.50 ($21.90) per person sharing without bath; IR£2 ($3.50) per person additional with bath. 25% reduction for children. Dinner IR£11 ($19.25) extra. No credit cards. **Closed:** Dec–Feb.
Just a mile outside Drumcliffe on N15, the main Sligo–Bundoran road, Mrs. Healy's large, centrally heated farmhouse sits right next to Benbulben mountain. There is beautiful scenery all around the house, and the period residence is registered in Country Inns and Historical Houses of Ireland. There are five nice bedrooms, and dinner is available with advance notice.

WESTWAY, Drumcliffe, Co. Sligo. Tel. 071/63178. 3 rms (none with bath).
$ Rates (including breakfast): IR£15.50 ($27.15) single; IR£12.50 ($21.90) per person sharing. 20% reduction for children. Dinner IR£11 ($19.25) extra. No credit cards. **Closed:** Oct–Apr.

The McDonagh family's modern farm bungalow is 6 miles north of Sligo (signposted off N15) overlooking Drumcliffe Bay at the foot of Benbulben mountain. The house is centrally heated and electric blankets are supplied. There's a lovely sitting room with a log and peat fire, and the pretty bedrooms have sinks and are comfortably furnished.

3. AROUND COUNTY SLIGO

Although Sligo is a relatively small county, it encompasses an amazing variety of landscape, with mountains, lakes, and a coastline fringed with sandy beaches and low cliffs.

WHAT TO SEE & DO

All through County Sligo countless cairns, dolmens, passage graves, and other prehistoric relics bear silent witness to the lives that so engaged the poet Yeats. Scattered over the face of the county are traces of the prehistoric races who lived here during three main periods: the Late Stone Age (Neolithic, 2500–2000 B.C.), the Bronze Age (2000–500 B.C.), and the Early Iron Age (500 B.C. to A.D. 500). The Tourist Office has a marvelously detailed leaflet, **"Prehistoric Sligo,"** that tells you where to find the most important of these court cairns, portal dolmens, passage graves, ring forts, and gallery graves. In the immediate vicinity of Sligo town, you'll find **Carrowmore** (south of town near Ballysodare), a cemetery of about 65 megalithic tombs—one of the largest concentrations in Europe—in a 1-mile-long, half-mile-wide area. And at the top of **Knocknarea,** there's the great Misgaun Maeve, an unopened cairn some 200 feet in diameter and about 80 feet high that archeologists believe covers a vast passage grave, but legend insists is the burial monument to Queen Maeve.

Along the western part of the county are the **Ox Mountains;** the north holds high, flat-topped limestone hills like **Benbulben;** and for the pleasure-bent traveler, there's a fine **beach** at Strandhill, a **golf course** at Rosses Point, and good **fishing** in any number of rivers and lakes.

WHERE TO STAY

CRUCKAWN HOUSE, Ballymote–Boyle Rd., Tubbercurry, Co. Sligo. Tel. 071/85188. 5 rms (4 with bath).

$ Rates (including breakfast): IR£15.50 ($27.15) single without bath; IR£11.50 ($20.15) per person sharing without bath; IR£1.50 ($2.65) per person additional with bath. 33⅓% reduction for children. Dinner IR£11 ($19.25) extra. No credit cards. **Parking:** Paved car park.

My mail has been full of praise for Mrs. Maeve Walsh and her modern, centrally heated, two-story house just outside town. Many readers write that they have returned to Cruckawn because of Mrs. Walsh's friendliness and helpfulness. Guest rooms are nicely decorated, fitted with built-in bookshelf/ headboards, and most have good views of the Ox Mountains. There's a sun lounge, games room, and laundry facilities for guest use. Cruckawn sits on its own grounds (with a large garden) overlooking a golf course that visitors may use. Meals are superb, and there's a wine license.

WHERE TO EAT

THE TRADITIONAL RESTAURANT/LOUNGE, Teeling St., Tubbercurry, Co. Sligo. Tel. 071/85111.

Cuisine: BAR FOOD/TRADITIONAL. **Reservations:** Not required.
$ Prices: Bar food less than IR£5 ($8.75); lunch IR£6 ($10.50); dinner IR£8–IR£10 ($14–$17.50). No credit cards.
Open: Daily 10am–11:30pm.

 Service by owners Anne and Tommie Killoran is pleasant and personal in this restaurant and bar/lounge. Antiques carry out the traditional theme, and the menu is varied and dishes well prepared. There are quick snacks as well as full meals, and prices are moderate to inexpensive. From June to September, Thursday night is Irish-music night.

4. AROUND COUNTY LEITRIM

Long and narrow, County Leitrim is split down the middle by Lough Allen, an extension of the Shannon. North of the lake, tall mountains stretch to the borders of County Sligo, while to the south the countryside is dotted with lovely lakes. In Lough Scur there are remnants of prehistoric lake dwellings, called crannogs. The harbor at Carrick-on-Shannon is alive with cruisers, and there's good fishing both here and in nearby lakes.

WHAT TO SEE & DO

Dromahair (Druim Dha Eithiar, "The Ridge of the Two Air-Demons"), 12 miles east of Sligo town, is where a royal lady inadvertently set in motion the first Norman invasion of Ireland. It seems that back in the 12th century, Dervogilla, wife of Tiernan O'Rourke, eloped with the King of Leinster, who was promptly outlawed by his fellow chieftains. He went to England's Henry II for assistance, and Henry gave his permission to any of his vassals who chose to join up with the Irish king to win back his lost lands. A group of Anglo-Normans threw in with the Irish chieftain and landed near Wexford in 1169. The ruins of the lady's residence, **Breffni Castle,** are found on the riverbank adjacent to the 1626 Old Hall, built by Sir William Villiers.

There's an excellent Interpretive Centre for National Monuments of the Northwest at ✪ **Parke's Castle,** Dromahair (tel. 071/64186), a splendid example of a fortified manor house of the Cromwellian era. From June to September the Office of Public Works has daily guided tours of period rooms, as well as an audiovisual presentation on national monuments in this region. Hours are 10am to 6:30pm, and there's a tea shop for refreshment.

On the other side of the river are the ruins of the 1508 **Creevelea Abbey,** and the remains of an even-older church nearby are thought to be those of one founded by St. Patrick when he spent some time here.

If your Irish roots are in Leitrim soil, the **Leitrim Heritage Centre,** County Library, Ballinamore, County Leitrim (tel. 078/44012), stands ready to help you trace your ancestry. The center maintains a full-time professional genealogical service for the county, and if your ancestors came from this area, you can write ahead with all the details you can furnish, or call in when you come to Ireland. Fees are based on the amount of work involved, and the knowledgeable staff will let you know before any charge is made whether or not there is a high probability of success in your search. The centre is open Monday through Friday from 10am to 1pm and 2 to 5pm.

Carrick-on-Shannon (Cara Droma Ruisg, "The Weir of the Marshy Ridge") is a center for **fishing and boating** on the River Shannon. Carrick Craft (tel. 078/20236) is based here and can arrange a few days of boating on the Shannon. (See "Alternative/Specialty Travel" in Chapter 2 for details.)

The 100-acre ✪ **Lough Rynn House and Gardens,** Mohill (tel. 078/31427), was the seat of the earls of Leitrim for more than 2 centuries. From May to mid-September, the estate is open to the public for a small fee from 10am to 7pm, with guided tours to the principal historic buildings, and there are miles and miles of ornamental gardens and nature trails, as well as a picnic site and playground.

WHERE TO STAY
BED & BREAKFAST

CORBALLY LODGE, Dublin Rd. (N4), Carrick-on-Shannon, Co. Leitrim. Tel. 078/20228. 4 rms (3 with bath).
$ Rates (including breakfast): IR£15 ($26.25) single without bath; IR£12 ($21) per person sharing without bath; IR£1 ($1.75) per person additional with bath. 25% reduction for children. Dinner IR£10 ($17.50) extra. No credit cards.
Set on spacious grounds 1½ miles south of town, this pretty modern bungalow is the Rowley family home. Open turf fires are the cozy centerpiece for evening gatherings. Antiques are scattered among the tasteful furnishings, and guest rooms are both attractive and comfortable. Central heat and good parking.

GLENVIEW, Aughoo, Ballinamore, Co. Leitrim. Tel. 078/44157. 6 rms (4 with bath).
$ Rates (including breakfast): IR£15.50 ($27.15) single without bath; IR£12.50 ($21.90) per person sharing without bath; IR£2 ($3.50) per person additional with bath. 20% reduction for children. Dinner IR£12 ($21) extra. No credit cards.
Closed: Dec–Mar.
Mrs. Teresa Kennedy is the warm and hospitable hostess of this lovely modern farmhouse in peaceful rural surroundings 1¼ miles south of town. A river flows through the grounds, and there's a boat for rent for fishing. There are also a pony, donkey, and cart which are free for children. The house is centrally heated and there is an attractive TV lounge with turf and log fires. For evening entertainment, the Kennedy family will happily send you off to pubs that feature Irish music.

RIVERSDALE, Ballinamore, Co. Leitrim. Tel. 078/44122. 6 rms (2 with bath).
$ Rates (including breakfast): IR£17 ($29.75) single without bath; IR£14 ($24.50) per person sharing without bath; IR£1 ($1.75) per person additional with bath. 25% reduction for children. No credit cards. Advance reservations required Nov–Feb.
Closed: Christmas.
Violet and Raymond Thomas are hosts at Riversdale. The large farmhouse sits a mile south of town in beautiful, serene countryside on 85 acres of dairy and sheep farming. There are open fires on cool evenings to supplement central heating, and fishing right on the property, as well as an indoor swimming pool, squash court, and sauna. Dinners, under the direction of the Thomases' Ballymaloe-trained daughter, feature fresh produce, meats, and fish, and there's a wine license.

SELF-CATERING

BREFFNI HOLIDAY COTTAGES, Dromahair, Co. Leitrim. Tel. 071/64103. Fax 071/64461. 8 cottages. TV
$ Rates Oct–Mar, IR£55–IR£65 ($96.25–$113.75) per week per cottage; Apr–Sept, IR£100–IR£265 ($175–$463.75) per week per cottage. No credit cards.

These superior cottages are grouped around a courtyard in the shadow of 17th-century castle ruins on the outskirts of town. Each of the eight cottages is nicely furnished, and while each has an open fireplace for cool-night comfort, there is also central heating. The seven three-bedroom cottages, with one double and four single beds (plus a convertible couch in the living room), can accommodate six or seven comfortably, and one cottage has been adapted to the needs of the physically handicapped. Dromahair is a good base for touring the Yeats Country and most of the Northwest.

WHERE TO EAT

COUNTY HOTEL, Bridge St., Carrick-on-Shannon. Tel. 078/20042.
Cuisine: BAR FOOD/TRADITIONAL/VEGETARIAN. **Reservations:** Not required.

$ Prices: Breakfast IR£5 ($8.75); lunch IR£8 ($14); dinner IR£14 ($24.50). MC, V.
Open: Breakfast daily 8–10am; lunch daily noon–3pm; dinner daily 6–10pm.
Closed: Dec 24–25.

 This rather plain hotel dining room prides itself on using fresh, locally produced ingredients, with fish, roast beef, ham, and turkey on the menu. Service is friendly and helpful, as well as efficient.

COUNTY DONEGAL

County Donegal sits at the very top of Ireland, its jagged coastline ringed by wide strands backed by steep cliffs. Its inland mountains are cut by deep valleys, and its countryside filled with antiquities and legends. It's a county of vast uninhabited stretches, natives as rugged as the landscape in which they live, and an ancient culture kept alive in the Gaelic language. In the rhythmic patterns of Donegal speech can be heard the distinctive cadence of Ulster. From Donegal cottages come some of the world's most beautiful hand-woven woolens. Donegal tweeds are characterized by nubby textures peppered with the colors of traditional vegetable dyes, and while much is still hand-woven, the style and colors are also reproduced in machine-woven woolens.

1. DONEGAL TOWN

Where other Irish towns have a square right in the middle of town, Donegal (Dun na nGall, "the Fort of the Foreigners") has a wide triangular space they call the Diamond. It's the meeting place of three major roadways—from Derry, west Donegal, and Sligo—and it points up Donegal town's strategic location at the head of Donegal Bay and the mouth of the River Eske, a position of such importance that in ancient times the princes of Tir Chonaill (the O'Donnells) made this their chief seat. Red Hugh O'Donnell founded a Franciscan friary here in 1474, and when it was ransacked in the 1600s and the monks were sent scurrying in fear of their lives, four went to Bundrowes for safety and set about compiling the scholarly *Annals of the Four Masters,* one of Ireland's most valuable sources of early church history. In the Diamond stands a 25-foot-high obelisk, inscribed with the names of the four monks at its base. Today Donegal town, 154 miles from Dublin and 41 miles north of Sligo, is a friendly, thriving market town, famed for its woolens and as a touring base for the rest of this wildly beautiful county.

ORIENTATION

ESSENTIALS Donegal's **telephone area code** is 073. The **post office** is on Tir Conaill Street.

TOURIST INFORMATION The **Tourist Office** is on Quay Street (tel. 073/21148), open May through September with hours of 10am to 6pm. Check with the Tourist Office for what's going on when you're in Donegal.

✓ # WHAT'S SPECIAL ABOUT COUNTY DONEGAL

Ancient Monuments

☐ Grianan of Aileach, near Burt on the Inishowen Peninsula, a great circular stone cashel, once the royal seat of the O'Neills and a sacred meeting place for High Kings of Ireland.

Natural Spectacles

☐ The Inishowen Peninsula, between Lough Swilly and Lough Foyle, with some of Ireland's most impressive mountain and coastal scenery.

☐ Malin Head, the most northerly point in Ireland, at the very tip of the Inishowen Peninsula.

☐ The spectacular, 3-mile-long Barnesmore Gap is 7 miles northeast of Donegal town, cutting through wild, mountainous country that once harbored highwaymen.

☐ Lough Derg, where St. Patrick once fasted for 40 days on an island, and where pilgrims still come faithfully to observe a 3-day fast.

Parks

☐ Glenveagh National Park, near Churchill, set in the heart of the Donegal highlands, with 24,700 acres of wilderness, a castle, and magnificent gardens.

☐ Ards Forest Park, on the shores of Sheep Haven Bay between Dunfanaghy and Creeslough, Ireland's most northerly forest park, 1,200 acres of woodlands, salt marsh, sand dunes, seashore, freshwater lakes, fenland, and rock faces.

Museums

☐ Glencolumbkille Folk Village Museum, an authentic folk village, with three cottages built and furnished to bring to life three different eras from 1700 to 1900.

Shopping

☐ Donegal tweeds, much of it still hand-woven in cottages, with outstanding shops in Donegal town, Mountcharles, Kilcar, and Ardara.

☐ Irish Parian China, delicate, porcelainlike china made in Ballyshannon, Cloghore, and just across the Northern Ireland border in Belleek.

TOWN LAYOUT Small and compact, Donegal town is centered around the **Diamond,** with side streets radiating from this focal point.

GETTING AROUND

By Bus There's a bus pickup station on the Diamond for Bus Eireann buses with regular service to Derry, Dublin, Galway, Killybegs, Portnoo, and Belfast. There's no in-town bus service.

By Car My best advice for drivers is to park the car and leave it during your stay in Donegal town. Streets are narrow, and parking can be a real problem.

On Foot Every point of interest in town and on its fringes is within easy walking distance.

By Bicycle With a bike, you can ramble even farther than on foot, and **Doherty's,** on Main Street, has bicycles for rent.

WHAT TO SEE & DO

Once the chief stronghold of the O'Donnels, **Donegal Castle** is just north of the Diamond. The west tower dates from 1505, built by Red Hugh O'Donnell on the site of an earlier castle. The handsome house was built around the old tower by Sir Basil

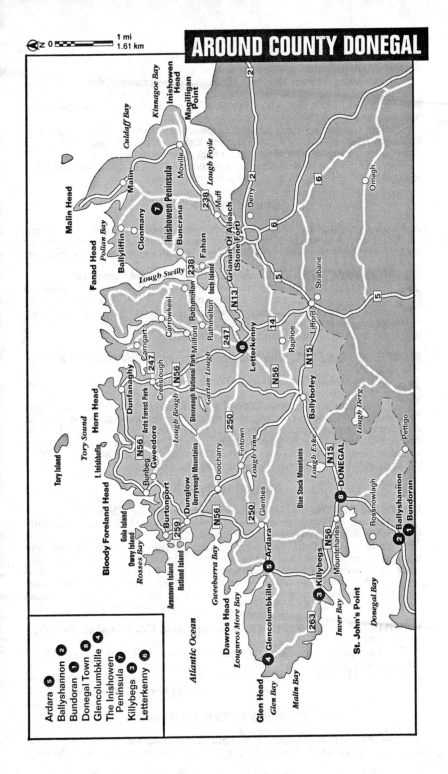

AROUND COUNTY DONEGAL

1 mi
1.61 km

Ardara **5**
Ballyshannon **2**
Bundoran **1**
Donegal Town **8**
Glencolumbkille **4**
The Inishowen Peninsula **7**
Killybegs **3**
Letterkenny **6**

Malin Head
Inishowen Head
Magilligan Point
Kinnagoe Bay
Culdaff Bay
Moville
Malin
Inishowen Peninsula **7**
Lough Foyle
Clonmany
Buncrana
Muff
Derry
2
238
Omagh
6
Fanad Head
Pollan Bay
Ballyliffin
Fahan
Grianan Of Aileach (Stone Fort)
238
Strabane
Lough Swilly
Inch Island
N13
5
5
Carrowkeel
Rathmullan
247
Rathmelton
Letterkenny **6**
Carrigart
Millford
14
Raphoe
Lifford
Tory Sound
Tory Island
Horn Head
Dunfanaghy
Ards Forest Park
247
Creeslough
N56
Glenveagh National Park
Gartan Lough
N15
Ballybofey
Lough Derg
Pettigo
Bloody Foreland Head
I. Inishbofin
N56
Bunbeg
Gweedore
Lough Beagh
Derryveagh Mountains
250
Fintown
Lough Finn
Blue Stack Mountains
Lough Eske
Gola Island
Owey Island
Rosses Bay
Dungloe
Burtonport
259
N56
Doocharry
N56
DONEGAL **8**
Rossnowlagh
Ballyshannon **2**
Bundoran **1**
Aranmore Island
Rutland Island
N56
Glenties
250
Ardara **5**
N15
Killybegs **3**
Mountcharles
N56
Gweebarra Bay
Dawros Head
Lougnros More Bay
Atlantic Ocean
Glencolumbkille **4**
263
Inver Bay
St. John's Point
Donegal Bay
Glen Head
Glen Bay
Malin Bay

Brooke in 1607 and features a mammoth Jacobean fireplace, windows, and gables. It is accessible to the public at all hours, with no admission fee.

Tip your hat to the **Four Masters Memorial** in the Diamond, then examine the large mounted anchor by the bay—it's from a French ship, perhaps one of those bringing troops to fight with Wolfe Tone in 1798, and was salvaged from the sea by fishermen in the mid-1800s.

South of town at the river's estuary, there are the interesting, but slight, ruins of **Donegal Abbey,** founded in 1474. **Lough Eske** is roughly 5 miles northeast of Donegal town, with wooded shores and a backing of mountains.

There are pleasant **river walks** along the east and west banks of the River Eske, with marvelous views of the town and surrounding area.

SAVVY SHOPPING

Although Donegal is not a spectacular shopping town, it is ideal for acquiring woolens, Donegal Parian china, and other products made in the county at competitive prices. Some shops close early on Wednesday, although this practice is disappearing.

DONEGAL CRAFT VILLAGE, Ballyshannon–Sligo Rd., Donegal.

Just outside Donegal town on the Ballyshannon–Sligo road is a group of cottagelike buildings around a courtyard. Each is the workshop of a true artisan, and you'll find pottery, woodturnings, batik wall hangings, tweeds, etc. Open Monday through Saturday from 10am to 6pm and on Sunday from 1 to 5pm (but check with the Tourist Office, as hours may vary).

MAGEE OF DONEGAL, The Diamond, Donegal. Tel. 073/21100. Fax 073/21283.

World-famous for its hand-woven Donegal tweed, Magee has set up a weaving demonstration right in the store. Woolens are hand-woven in cottages, then finished at their factory in Donegal town. Tours of the factory are organized from time to time, and you can inquire at the store for specific dates and hours. The store has a wide selection of quality clothing for men and women and a good variety of linens, knitwear, and other Irish products. The newly refurbished restaurant on the first floor specializes in home-cooking, and a satisfying lunch will run less than IR£2 ($3.50). Open Monday through Saturday from 10am to 6pm.

Shopping Nearby

GILLESPIE BROTHERS, Main St., Mountcharles, Co. Donegal.

Due west of Donegal town in the little town of Mountcharles, stop by this little white shop with red trim. Just meeting the Gillespies is a delight, but it can be profitable as well, for their tweed selections of suits and jackets, lap rugs, and blankets are exceptional (also sold by the length), and they also carry a marvelous stock of hand-crocheted dresses, capes, and blouses. Prices are about 10% below most in other shops, and from time to time there are specials with even greater reductions. The brothers are happy to mail your purchases home. Open Monday through Saturday from 9am to 6pm.

KATHLEEN'S IRISH EXPORTS, Mountcharles, Co. Donegal. Tel. 073/35344.

Don't be misled by the size of this small shop—its shelves are stocked with an amazing array of Irish-made goods. Tweeds, hand-knits, jewelry, glassware, fine chinaware, and pottery are all represented at competitive prices. There's a good mail-order service, and Kathleen Alcock will be happy to send a catalog upon request.

EVENING ENTERTAINMENT

Traditional music is on frequently at the **Talk of the Town** lounge. And Donegal has some good pubs, many of which have a "country" air about them, with the usual group of devoted regulars who'll be glad to welcome visitors. The Tourist Office can steer you to what's doing where during your visit—or better still, just ask a local.

On Saturday night June through September, the **Hyland Central Hotel,** on the Diamond, has a gala candlelight dinner and dance.

WHERE TO STAY

IN TOWN

CASTLE VIEW HOUSE, Waterloo Place, Donegal, Co. Donegal. Tel. 073/22100. 3 rms (none with bath).
$ Rates (including breakfast): IR£11 ($19.25) per person. No credit cards.
Just steps away from the town center, looking out to the castle across the river, Mrs. Tessie Timothy's bright and cheerful home is an ideal Donegal town base. Guest rooms are nicely done up, comfortable, and handy to the bathroom; all have sinks. There are two twin-bedded rooms and one family room with a double and two twin beds. There are almost always peat fires blazing in the living room and dining room, and enthusiastic readers have written that "If you stay you must have a meal," to which I must add, be sure to give Mrs. Timothy advance notice.

DRUMCLIFFE HOUSE, Coast Rd. (N56), Donegal, Co. Donegal. Tel. 073/21200. 5 rms (2 with bath).
$ Rates (including breakfast): IR£14.50 ($25.40) single without bath; IR£11 ($19.25) per person sharing without bath; IR£2.50 ($4.40) per person additional with bath. 20% reduction for children. No credit cards. **Closed:** Dec–Jan.

⭐ In a secluded woodland setting on the edge of town, this lovely old home dates back some 300 years. Both the house and its antique furnishings are interesting, and meals feature Mrs. Pearl Timony's home-baking. The attractive guest rooms all have nice views, there's good parking, and the house is centrally heated.

RIVERSIDE HOUSE, Waterloo Place, Donegal, Co. Donegal. Tel. 073/21083. 3 rms (none with bath).
$ Rates (including breakfast): IR£12.50 ($21.90) per person. 20% reduction for children. No credit cards.
This attractive home is just across the River Eske from Donegal Castle on a quiet residential terrace. The center of town is a quick walk away. Mrs. Kathleen Curristan welcomes guests here, and her comfortable guest rooms are decorated in cheerful colors. All have sinks, and there's one large family room with a double and two twin beds. Even the bathroom is bright, with matching floral wallpaper and shower curtains. The lounge frames the river and castle view through wide front windows, and its piano is often in use by guests as well as the Curristans.

NEARBY ACCOMMODATIONS

ARDEEVIN, Lough Eske, Barnesmore, Co. Donegal. Tel. 073/21790. 5 rms (4 with bath).
$ Rates (including breakfast): IR£16 ($28) single without bath; IR£11 ($19.25) per person sharing without bath; IR£1.50 ($2.65) per person additional with bath. 20% reduction for children. No credit cards. **Closed:** Nov–Mar.
Five miles outside Donegal town, this dormer bungalow sits on a rise overlooking Lough Eske and the Bluestack Mountains. The guest rooms are nicely furnished, and four have private bath with shower. Mrs. Mary McGinty is the charming hostess, and the house is centrally heated.

ATLANTIC GUEST HOUSE, Main St., Donegal, Co. Donegal. Tel. 073/21187. 12 rms (7 with bath). TV
$ Rates: IR£16 ($28) single without bath; IR£12.50 ($21.90) per person sharing without bath; IR£5 ($8.75) per person additional with bath. No credit cards.
Parking: Private car park.

Located right in the center of town, the Atlantic is presided over by Edith and Victor Browne. It's a pleasant, rambling building with comfortable guest rooms and an inviting lounge. Color TV in all rooms is a plus, and just one of the reasons this place is good value for the money. Another bonus is the adjoining restaurant (see "Where to Eat," below). The Brownes can arrange baby-sitting and the house is centrally heated.

GREEN ISLES, Beach Rd., Ballyweel, Donegal, Co. Donegal. Tel. 073/ 21343. 3 rms (none with bath).

$ **Rates:** IR£16.50 ($28.90) single; IR£11.50 ($20.15) per person sharing. 25% reduction for children. Dinner IR£11.50 ($20.15) extra. No credit cards. **Closed:** Sept–Apr. **Parking:** Private car park.

Mrs. Nora Mitchell and her family make you feel right at home in this modern bungalow 1½ miles from the town center off Killybegs Road, overlooking Donegal Bay with the Sligo Mountains in the distance. The pleasant dining room looks out to the garden against a backdrop of green hills. Guest rooms are nicely appointed and quite comfortable. The house has central heating.

WORTH THE EXTRA MONEY

HARVEY'S POINT COUNTY HOTEL, Lough Eske, Donegal, Co. Donegal. Tel. 073/22208. 20 rms (all with bath). TV TEL

$ **Rates:** IR£35 ($61.25) single; IR£54 ($94.50) double. AE, MC, V. **Closed:** Oct–May.

This lovely period house sits 4 miles from Donegal town, on the very edge of Lough Eske at the foot of the Blue Stack Mountains. Its modern, elegant decor complements this idyllic setting, and guest rooms are as nicely appointed as public rooms. There's boating on the lake, a marina, and two tennis courts. As for the restaurant (see "Where to Eat," below), the French cuisine is outstanding and dinner comes to the table to the accompaniment of soft piano music. There are also frequent musical entertainment evenings.

HYLAND CENTRAL HOTEL, The Diamond, Donegal, Co. Donegal. Tel. 073/21027. Fax 073/22295. 75 rms (all with bath). TV TEL

$ **Rates:** IR£38–IR£46 ($66.50–$80.50) single; IR£27–IR£35 ($47.25–$61.25) per person sharing. AE, MC, V. **Parking:** Private car park.

This sparkling-clean family-run hotel is that rare combination of modern facilities with an old-fashioned, homey atmosphere and a helpful, friendly staff. The dining room, overlooking the river, is lovely and serves moderately priced meals (see "Where to Eat," below). Rooms here are spacious and have a light, airy look and comfortable modern furnishings. For a gorgeous view of Donegal Bay, ask for one in the back (the view in front is of the Diamond). The recently added Leisure Complex includes a fully equipped gym, a steam room, Jacuzzi and plunge pool, indoor swimming pool, children's pool, and steam room.

WHERE TO EAT

In addition to the listings below, there are many coffeeshops around the Diamond, and most are good value.

THE ATLANTIC RESTAURANT, Main St., Donegal. Tel. 073/21080.
Cuisine: TRADITIONAL. **Reservations:** Not required.

$ **Prices:** Lunch or dinner IR£2.50–IR£4.50 ($4.40–$7.90); children's menu 90p– IR£1.50 ($1.60–$2.65). No credit cards.
Open: Daily 10am–10:30pm.

Located in the Atlantic Guest House (see "Where to Stay," above), this busy restaurant offers exceptionally good value. Chicken curry, plaice, salmon steaks, and lasagne are featured on the extensive menu, and all plates come with two vegetables and potato.

ERRIGAL RESTAURANT, Main St., Donegal. Tel. 073/21428.

Cuisine: FISH/TRADITIONAL/VEGETARIAN. **Reservations:** Not required.

$ Prices: Breakfast IR£3.50 ($6.15); lunch IR£4 ($7); dinner IR£6 ($10.50). No credit cards.

Open: Mon–Sat 9am–11pm.

Fresh fish is a specialty at this pleasant, family-run eatery, but the menu also includes such standards as chicken, ham, and beef, as well as a few vegetarian selections.

HYLAND CENTRAL HOTEL, The Diamond, Donegal. Tel. 073/21027. Fax 073/22295.

Cuisine: TRADITIONAL **Prices:** Main courses IR£5 ($8.75); mini-dinner menu IR£12 ($21); full dinner menu IR£16 ($28). AE, MC, V.

Open: Lunch daily 12:30–2:30pm; dinner daily 6–9:30pm.

The best inexpensive meals are found in this superb small hotel (see "Where to Stay," above). There's an excellent lunch special (hot meat and vegetables, and ample portions) for less than IR£5 ($8.75) served in the comfortable lounge. Evening meals are in the cream-colored dining room, which has wide windows along one wall, lots of dark-wood trim, and softly lighted, gold-framed oil paintings hung about. From June through September, there are Saturday-night candlelight dinners with dancing.

WORTH THE EXTRA MONEY

HARVEY'S POINT RESTAURANT AND BAR, Lough Eske, Donegal. Tel. 073/22208.

Cuisine: FRENCH/TRADITIONAL. **Reservations:** Recommended for dinner.

Directions: 4 miles from Donegal town.

$ Prices: Lunch IR£10 ($17.50); dinner IR£20 ($35). AE, MC, V.

Open: Apr–Dec, lunch daily 12:30–2:30pm; dinner daily 6–9:30pm.

This elegant dining room and lounge bar in the hotel on the shores of Lough Eske (see "Where to Stay," above) is the perfect setting for a romantic dinner. Local fish and beef accompanied by the freshest of Irish produce arrive at the table prepared in tempting French-style creations. Service is both friendly and efficient.

EASY EXCURSIONS

About 19 miles south of Donegal town, right on the Donegal-Sligo border, is the popular seaside resort of **Bundoran,** and **Ballyshannon,** home of Donegal Parian China, lies between the two towns. See Section 2, below, for details on both towns.

The spectacular, 3-mile-long **Barnesmore Gap** is 7 miles to the northeast, through wild, mountainous country that once harbored highwaymen. North of town, **Eglish Glen** cuts between the Bluestack Mountains and Banagher Hill, and farther along you'll find the **Grey Mare's Tail waterfall** in Sruell Glen. The good St. Patrick knew Donegal well, and he once fasted for 40 days on an island in isolated **Lough Derg,** where pilgrims still come faithfully to observe a 3-day fast.

2. AROUND COUNTY DONEGAL

Base yourself in Donegal town or Ardara to explore the splendors of southern Donegal. Heading north, the most direct route is N15 from Donegal town to **Ballybofey,** and N56 to the cathedral town of **Letterkenny,** a good base for exploring northern County Donegal. However, although this is a lovely drive, passing through **Barnesmore Gap,** you will miss a real scenic treat by passing up the longer drive around the county's coastline. If time permits, I strongly recommend that from Ardara you take the main roadway that circles the northern part of the county, N56. The route takes you to **Dungloe, Burtonport, Gweedore,** around the **Bloody Foreland, Dunfanaghy,** through **Barnes Gap** to **Letterkenny.**

A WORD ABOUT ACCOMMODATIONS IN COUNTY DONEGAL   For budget travelers, County Donegal is especially rich in hostel accommodations, ranging from simple to superior facilities: Consult the An Oige handbook for details on hostels at Killybegs and Ardara. Basic facilities are at the Red House, Carrick, and 5 miles from Dungloe there's a good hostel at Crohy Head, and good facilities at the Youth Hostel, Aranmore Island, Burtonport, with regular ferry service between Burtonport and the island. Near Glenveagh National Park, a good hostel is at Erigal, Dunlewy, Gweedore, and 4 miles from Downings there are good facilities at the Youth Hostel, Tra na Rosann, Downings. On the shores of Lough Swilly, you'll find good facilities at the Youth Hostel, Bunnaton, Glenvar; and on Tory Island (with irregular ferry service from Magheraroarty), basic facilities at the Youth Hostel.

BUNDORAN

Located on the southern shore of Donegal Bay only 22 miles north of Sligo via N15, Bundoran is 17½ miles south of Donegal town (on N15) and is one of the county's finest seaside resorts. There's a long strand for **swimming,** and an inviting promenade for invigorating seaside walks. Sea angling in the bay is excellent, and the nearby Rivers Bunduff and Bundrowes are also rewarding venues for salmon and trout **fishing.** Horseback riding can be arranged through the **Stracomer Riding School,** Bundoran (tel. 072/41787 or 41685). **Bundoran Golf Club** welcomes visitors, there are three outdoor municipal swimming pools, and during summer months there are **live music** and amateur **drama productions** in this lively town.

If time limits will prevent your driving farther north in County Donegal, Bus Eireann has excellent, inexpensive **day tours** from Bundoran to Glenveigh National Park and the Hills of Donegal; book through the bus office (tel. 072/41236) or Meehan's Travel Agency, Main Street, Bundoran (tel. 072/41351).

WHERE TO STAY

STRAND VIEW HOUSE, East End, Bundoran, Co. Donegal. Tel. 072/ 41519. 6 rms (all with bath).

$ Rates (including breakfast): IR£16 ($28) single; IR£12 ($21) per person sharing. 20% reduction for children. No credit cards. **Parking:** Private car park.

⭐ Mrs. Mary Delaney and her hospital family make you feel right at home in this centrally located, two-story house on the main Sligo–Donegal road (N15). Golfers will be interested to know that the noted golfer Christy O'Connor lived here when he was the local club's pro. The six guest rooms include three large family rooms, and all six are attractive and comfortably furnished. The house has central heating.

Worth the Extra Money

HOLYROOD HOTEL, Bundoran, Co. Donegal. Tel. 072/41232. 61 rms (all with bath). TV TEL

$ Rates: IR£26 ($45.50) single; IR£21 ($36.75) per person sharing. Breakfast IR£6.50 ($11.40) extra; dinner IR£15 ($26.25). AE, DC, MC, V.

⭐ This family-run hotel on the main Sligo–Donegal road (N15), in the town center, is as friendly and warm as the smaller bed-and-breakfast homes. Public rooms are spacious and nicely decorated, and guest rooms are especially attractive. Very good meals are served in the dining room at reasonable prices. During summer months, there's nightly entertainment in the lounge and/or bar.

WHERE TO EAT

MARLBORO HOUSE, Sea Rd., Bundoran. Tel. 072/41471.
Cuisine: BAR FOOD/SEAFOOD/TRADITIONAL. **Reservations:** Recommended for dinner.

$ Prices: Bar food IR£5–IR£8 ($8.75–$14); dinner IR£6–IR£10 ($10.50–$17.50). No credit cards.
Open: Bar food daily 12:30–6pm; dinner daily 6–10pm.

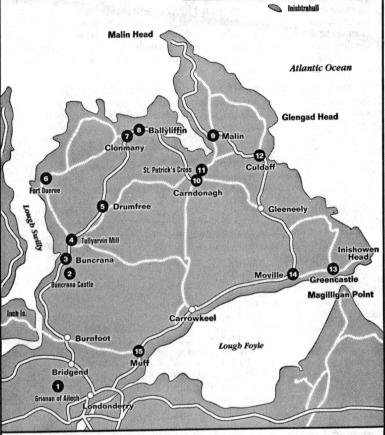

INISHOWEN PENINSULA

N

Inishtrahull

Malin Head

Atlantic Ocean

Glengad Head

8 **Ballyliffin**

7 **Clonmany**

9 **Malin**

12 **Culdaff**

11 St. Patrick's Cross

6 **Fort Dunree**

10 **Carndonagh**

Lough Swilly

5 **Drumfree**

Gleneely

4 **Tullyarvin Mill**

3 **Buncrana**

2 **Buncrana Castle**

Inishowen Head

14 Moville

13 Greencastle

Magilligan Point

Inch Is.

Carrowkeel

Lough Foyle

Burnfoot

15 **Muff**

Bridgend

1 Grianan of Ailech

Londonderry

Inishowen Peninsula

IRELAND

Ballyliffin **8**
Buncrana **3**
Buncrana Castle **2**
Carndonagh **10**
Clonmany **7**
Culdaff **12**
Drumfree **5**
Fort Drumfree **6**
Greencastle **13**
Grianan of Ailech **1**
Malin **9**
Moville **14**
Muff **15**
St. Patrick's Cross **11**
Tullyarvin Mill **4**

This lovely little restaurant/bar gives you an "at home" feeling from the moment you enter. The charming bar is very like a family living room, and the pretty dining room sports pink and white linen, with tables nicely spaced. During the day you can get salad plates and other casual dishes in the bar, and the dinner menu features dressed lamb chops with mint sauce, pork chops with mushroom sauce, beef Stroganoff, and prime sirloin steaks. There's also an extensive wine list.

STAKES RESTAURANT, Main St., Bundoran. Tel. 072/41257.
Cuisine: TRADITIONAL. **Reservations:** Not required.
$ Prices: Lunch or dinner IR£6–IR£10 ($10.50–$17.50). No credit cards.
Open: Daily noon–11pm.

This centrally located restaurant is tastefully decorated and has a cozy atmosphere. Menu items reflect local meats, fish, and vegetables prepared in traditional Irish dishes. Service is both friendly and efficient.

BALLYSHANNON

Five miles north of Bundoran on N15, Ballyshannon is the largest town in southern County Donegal. It sits on the River Erne at the point where it becomes tidal, and it is the subject of myths and legends that go back as far as 1500 B.C., when tradition has it that Ireland's first colonization actually took place on the tiny islet of Inis Saimer in the river's estuary. It is also the birthplace of the noted 19th-century poet William Allingham, who lies buried in the graveyard of **St. Anne's Church** a little north of town. St. Anne's sits high on a hill (Mullach na Shee, "Hill of the Fairies"), with fine panoramic views.

One mile northwest of town, the once-famous Cistercian **Assaroe Abbey,** founded in 1184, now lies in ruins, although its mill wheel has been restored and is driven by water from the Abbey River just as in ancient days. Some 50 yards away at the edge of the Abbey River, **Catsby Cave** is a grottolike setting where a rough-hewn altar reminds you that mass was celebrated here during the penal years when the ritual was prohibited by law.

In modern times, Ballyshannon has developed into an important tourist and shopping center. Its safe beaches along the rugged coastline provide good swimming, surfing, and other **water sports,** with the best swimming beaches at Bundoran, Creevy, and Rossnowlagh. There's good **fishing** in the sea, the Erne estuary, Assaroe Lake, and the Drowse River.

Shopping is excellent in Ballyshannon (see below), and just 4 miles to the east (on the County Fermanagh border) the little town of **Belleek** is the home of lovely handmade Belleek Parian China (see Section 2 in Chapter 23).

Evening entertainment comes in the form of traditional music in some of the town's 21 lively pubs (inquire locally about current venues, and check Sweeney's Pub; see "Where to Eat," below), and in late July or early August there's the famous **Ballyshannon Folk Festival,** when music rings through the streets day and night.

SHOPPING

CELTIC WEAVE CHINA, Cloghore, Co. Donegal. Tel. 072/51844.
Owner Tommy Daly and his family learned the art of making cobweb-light woven Parian China baskets in Belleek, then opened their own factory and showroom in this little village. Each piece is individually crafted in unique designs by Tommy and his son, Adrian, and Tommy's wife, Patricia, then hand-paints each one in delicate flower shades. The shop is 3 miles east of Ballyshannon on Belleek Road, 1 mile west of Belleek. It's open Monday through Saturday from 9am to 6pm.

DONEGAL IRISH PARIAN CHINA, Ballyshannon, Co. Donegal. Tel. 073/51826.

A relative newcomer to Irish handcrafts is the delicately beautiful Donegal Irish Parian China (much like porcelain) made in Ballyshannon. It has already made enormous impact on the homefront as well as the export scene. The Exhibition

Centre in their large, modern complex is really something of an art gallery and free tours of the factory are conducted every half hour. Look for the graceful shapes and soft green shamrock or pastel floral designs. Prices run the gamut from *very* expensive to moderate, and your purchases can be mailed home. The factory is a quarter mile from the town center on the main Ballyshannon–Bundoran road (N15). It's open Monday through Saturday from 9am to 5pm.

WHERE TO STAY

ARDEELAN MANOR, Rossnowlagh, Co. Donegal. Tel. 072/51578. 5 rms (none with bath).
$ Rates (including breakfast): IR£16 ($28) single; IR£12.50 ($21.90) per person sharing. 20% reduction for children. No credit cards. **Closed:** Sept–June.
This beautifully restored 1800 stone house is the home of Borneo-born Mrs. Fun Britton, who met her husband, Conor, when both were working in Scotland. They and their two charming young children extend warm hospitality to guests. The house is done in country style with many antique furnishings, reflecting its peaceful setting. Two of the guest rooms have sea views, while others face the garden. The Brittons can arrange baby-sitting, the house is centrally heated, and there's plenty of parking. The house is 5 miles northwest of Ballyshannon on R231.

ARDPATTON FARM HOUSE, Cavangarden, Ballyshannon, Co. Donegal. Tel. 072/51546. 5 rms (3 with bath).
$ Rates (including breakfast): IR£15.50 ($27.15) single without bath; IR£12.50 ($21.90) per person sharing without bath; IR£1.50 ($2.65) per person additional with bath. 50% reduction for children. Dinner IR£12 ($21) extra. No credit cards. **Closed:** Jan.
Mrs. Rose McCaffrey presides over this 200-year-old farmhouse 3 miles north of town on the Donegal road (N15), and she and those of her 10 children (ages 8 to 21) still living at home extend a traditional warm Irish farmhouse welcome to visitors. The house sits on 380 rural acres, and the large lounge and dining room overlook peaceful fields. The nicely furnished guest rooms are more spacious than most—one family room will, in fact, accommodate up to six people. On cool evenings there are open fires, although the house has central heating.

BRI-TER-AN, Bundoran Rd., Ballyshannon, Co. Donegal. Tel. 072/51490. 3 rms (1 with bath).
$ Rates (including breakfast): IR£16 ($28) single without bath; IR£12 ($21) per person sharing without bath; IR£1.50 ($2.65) per person additional with bath. 20% reduction for children. No credit cards. **Closed:** Jan.
Mrs. Margaret Barrett is the gracious hostess at this modern bungalow half a mile from the town center. The house is set on the shores of Donegal Bay, and as one reader wrote, "The view across the bay from the lounge is worth the price of the room." Leaving aside the view, however, the lounge is a bright, cheerful gathering point for guests, and there's a separate TV lounge. Guest rooms have built-in wardrobes, and all are close to the bath.

CAVANGARDEN HOUSE, Cavangarden, Ballyshannon, Co. Donegal. Tel. 072/51365. 6 rms (4 with bath).
$ Rates (including breakfast): IR£17.50 ($30.65) single without bath; IR£12.50 ($21.90) per person sharing without bath; IR£1.50 ($2.65) per person additional with bath. 50% reduction for children. Dinner IR£12 ($21) extra. No credit cards. **Closed:** Jan.
This lovely old Georgian home set in spacious grounds 3 miles north of town on the main Donegal road (N15) dates back to 1750 and is the home of Mrs. Agnes McCaffrey. Furnishings in the large, three-story house feature antiques, and there are turf and log fires on cool evenings, when impromptu sing-songs sometimes break out around the piano in the dining room. Guest rooms here are exceptionally spacious, and two family rooms will accommodate up to four people each.

DANBY HOUSE, Ballyshannon, Co. Donegal. Tel. 072/51138. 5 rms (all with bath).
$ Rates (including breakfast): IR£22–IR£26 ($38.50–$45.50) single; IR£14–IR£18 ($24.50–$31.50) per person sharing. AE, MC, V. **Parking:** Large car park.

Built in 1820, this gracious old house on the edge of town overlooks the Erne Estuary and a championship golf course. It's the home of owner Derry Britton, who with his wife, Chris, also operate a fully licensed gourmet restaurant (see "Where to Eat," below). Public rooms are lovely, furnished with many period pieces, as are the beautifully decorated guest rooms. The house is centrally heated.

Worth the Extra Money

SAND HOUSE HOTEL, Rossnowlagh, Co. Donegal. Tel. 072/51777, or 212/714-2323 in New York State, or toll free 800/223-6764 in the U.S. Fax 072/52100. 39 rms (all with bath). TV TEL
$ Rates (including breakfast): IR£37.50–IR£47.50 ($65.65–$83.15) single; IR£30–IR£40 ($52.50–$70) per person sharing; IR£2.50 ($4.40) per person additional for superior sea-view room; IR£5 ($8.75) per person additional for deluxe sea-view room. 50% reduction for children. $40-per-person deposit required on booking. Weekend rates available. AE, DC, MC, V. **Closed:** Nov–Feb.

With one of the most beautiful settings in the Northwest, 5 miles northwest of Ballyshannon on R231, the Sand House is a modern, first-class hotel perched among the dunes that line a 2-mile crescent beach. The entrance lounge, with its large black Kilkenny slate fireplace, is more akin to a gracious country house than a hotel lobby. Owner Mary Britton and her sons have put in chintz-covered couches and armchairs that invite friendly chats before the fire, and Georgian credenzas are filled with Belleek china and other treasures. Lovely antique pieces are sprinkled all through the hotel, the result of the Britton family hobby of haunting auctions. As for guest rooms, deluxe sea-view rooms have a small sitting area, and many of the superior sea-view rooms have antique furnishings, some with four-poster beds. Those without a sea view are also beautifully decorated and overlook a nine-hole golf course.

The Surfers Bar decor has a nautical feel, with walls done in wood in the shape of a wave breaking, while another small residents' snug bar features cases of stuffed birds. The dining room specializes in fresh seafood, as well as a nice selection of continental and Irish dishes and a good wine list. Golf is free to guests, canoes can be rented, and pony trekking is available.

WHERE TO EAT

SWEENY'S PUB AND WHITE HORSE BAR, Main St. (N15), Ballyshannon.
Cuisine: BAR FOOD. **Reservations:** Not required.
$ Prices: IR£5–IR£10 ($8.75–$17.50).
Open: Daily 10:30am–11:30pm.

Sweeny's is a delight to visit—partly because of its congenial hosts, John and Pat Sweeny, and partly because of its warm, inviting, and atmospheric interior. The first recorded sale of the premises is dated 1793, and the Sweeneys have managed to create a comfortable, semimodern environment that still retains much of the character of the old building. If you happen by on a Friday, drop in for music in the stone-arched Cellar Bar. Other times, excellent snacks, hot plates, and salads provide nourishment and a well-pulled pint provides refreshment in the bar and lounge upstairs.

Worth the Extra Money

DANBY HOUSE, Ballyshannon. Tel. 072/51138.
Cuisine: CONTINENTAL/GAME/VEGETARIAN. **Reservations:** Recommended.

$ Prices: Dinner IR£13–IR£16 ($22.75–$28). AE, MC, V.
Open: Dinner only, Mon–Sat 7–10pm.

The dining room in this lovely old home on the edge of town overlooking the Erne Estuary is quietly elegant (see "Where to Stay," above), and the menu features roast free-range duckling served "off the bone" with an orange-and-fig sauce, peppered sirloin steak with a chasseur sauce, filets of sole and wild salmon wrapped in cabbage leaves with a delicate fish sauce, and—in season—venison with a poivrade sauce and wild duck and pheasant in their own juices.

KILLYBEGS

If you can manage to get to the picturesque little harbor town of Killybegs (17 miles west of Donegal town via N56) in the late afternoon, go down to the pier to watch the **fishing fleet** come in—it's a memorable experience, with seagulls screeching overhead and half the town gathered to greet the fishermen.

Should you arrive in August, the **Killybegs International Sea Angling Festival** is great fun, with European fishing enthusiasts converging on the little town and festivities from morning to night.

Three miles south of town, **Drumanoo Head** affords splendid coastal views.

There's **traditional music** in several pubs, including the Harbour Bar, the Lone Star, the Sail Inn, and Fawlty Towers.

SAVVY SHOPPING

Eight miles west of Killybegs on the Glencolumbkille road (T72A), the village of **Kilcar** is a center of the Donegal hand-woven tweed industry, as well as for hand-embroidery and knits. Monday through Saturday from 10am to 5pm, you can stop by ✪ **Studio Donegal** in the village center, where the misty tones of Donegal tweed come in jacket, skirt, or pants lengths, as well as ready-made garments from such Irish manufacturers as Brian Boru. They also carry a good selection of local crafts. There's a hand-weaving workshop next door, and a spacious tea room serving home-baking.

You'll also be welcomed at the **Gaeltarra Eireann Factory, Connemara Fabrics,** and **Gaeltarra Snath,** all in the village center and open Monday through Friday from 10am to 5pm.

One mile west of Kilcar on the coast road, **Annmarie's Handknits** is the happy hunting ground for a good selection of knits at reasonable prices.

WHERE TO STAY

BANNAGH HOUSE, Finta Rd., Killybegs, Co. Donegal. Tel. 073/31108.
4 rms (3 with bath).
$ Rates (including breakfast): IR£15 ($26.25) single without bath; IR£11.50 ($20.15) per person sharing without bath; IR£1.50 ($2.65) per person additional with bath. No credit cards. **Closed:** Dec–Feb. **Parking:** Private car park.

✪ This lovely hilltop bungalow on the outskirts of town on the coast road has sweeping views of Killybegs harbor and fishing fleet. The home of Phyllis and Fergus (he's an ambulance driver) Melly and their five children, the centrally heated house is beautifully decorated and guest rooms are well appointed (some with harbor views). Best of all, the Melly family are as attractive and welcoming as their home.

CONKAY HOUSE, Roshine Rd., Killybegs, Co. Donegal. Tel. 073/31273.
3 rms (none with bath).
$ Rates (including breakfast): IR£13.50 ($23.65) single; IR£11 ($19.25) per person sharing. 25% reduction for children. No credit cards. **Closed:** Oct–Mar.

Mrs. McGuinness will welcome you warmly to her modern bungalow which overlooks Killybegs Bay, a short walk from the town center. The house is centrally heated and there is a garden which guests may use. The three pretty bedrooms are comfortably furnished.

LISMOLIN COUNTRY HOME, Fintra Rd., Killybegs, Co. Donegal. Tel. 073/31035. 6 rms (all with bath).

$ Rates (including breakfast): IR£16 ($28) single; IR£13 ($22.75) per person sharing. 30% reduction for children. Dinner IR£11 ($19.25) extra. No credit cards.

This is the home of Mrs. Bernie Cahill and sits half a mile from the town center right at the edge of a beautiful forest area. The modern, centrally heated bungalow is tastefully decorated, with six nice guest rooms, all with sinks as well as private shower and toilet. Turf and log fires are often lit in the lounge, even though the house has good central heating.

Worth the Extra Money

BRUCKLESS HOUSE, Bruckless, Co. Donegal. Tel. 073/37071. 5 rms (2 with bath).

$ Rates (including breakfast): IR£18 ($31.50) per person without bath, IR£20.50 ($35.90) per person with bath. Dinner IR£15 ($26.25) extra. No credit cards.
Closed: Oct–Mar.

Bruckless House dates from the late 1700s and is 3 miles east of Killybegs on N56 set in 19 acres bordering Bruckless Bay. It is now the farmhouse home of Joan and Clive Evans, who took over on their return from several years in Hong Kong. The old house retains its traditional flavor, with a cobbled farmyard, kitchen garden, and log fires. The gracious reception rooms have views of the bay, and the five comfortably fitted-out bedrooms include one double, two twins, and two singles. Horses can be booked by guests for riding, and there are two golf courses within driving distance. Coastal and deep-sea fishing can also be arranged. The Evanses serve breakfast and dinner (Joan does the cooking, with fresh garden vegetables, seafood fresh from nearby waters, and milk and cream from their dairy cow) informally around the kitchen table.

WHERE TO EAT

SAIL INN RESTAURANT AND BAR, Main St., Killybegs. Tel. 073/31130.
  Cuisine: BAR FOOD/TRADITIONAL. **Reservations:** Recommended for dinner.
$ Prices: Bar food IR£2–IR£5 ($3.50–$8.75); dinner IR£10–IR£12 ($17.50–$21). No credit cards.
  Open: Bar menu daily noon–2:30pm; dinner daily 5:30–10pm.

This popular bar and restaurant at the western end of Main Street has loads of character in the downstairs bar, where soup, sandwiches, salads, and hot plates are all well prepared. Upstairs, the cozy restaurant seats only 26, and dinner is served by candlelight. The extensive menu includes such specialties as beef Stroganoff, steak au poivre, roast duckling, and chicken Madras. There's also a good wine list at moderate prices.

GLENCOLUMBKILLE

Glencolumbkille sits at the very end of T72A, some 35 miles west of Donegal town. The drive from Killybegs to Glencolumbkille ("St. Colmcille's Glen"), through lonely mountain country with occasional glimpses of the sea, is a journey through history and a culture that has changed little since the days when (or so local legend insists) Bonnie Prince Charlie hid out in the glen. The stony hills are dotted with more than 40 cairns, dolmens, souterrains, and other relics of a past that goes back as much as 5,000 years.

THE TOP ATTRACTION

GLENCOLUMBKILLE FOLK VILLAGE MUSEUM, Glencolumbkille. Tel. 073/30017 or 30035.

⭐ This is one of the most authentic folk villages in the country, with three cottages built and furnished to bring to life three different eras stretching from 1700 to 1900. There are guided tours every hour that explain the workings of each cottage. The home of a 1720 cotter is earthen-floored, and its open hearth has no chimney; by the 1820s the cotter's home has a flagstone floor, chimney, and oil-lamp lighting (as well as, sad to relate, a tin trunk that would carry the immigrating family's treasures to "Amerikay"); and the 1920 cottage is very like many you'll have seen in your travels around today's Irish countryside. The courtyard around which the cottages are grouped holds such everyday items as a peat cart and fishing boat, with the large "famine pot," a somber reminder of famine days, when starving peasants lined up to be served a meager ration. A schoolhouse from a century ago and a country pub, or "sheebeen" (where more often than not the drink sold was illegal poteen!), complete the village. There's a cottage craft shop and tea room, where hot tea and scones are sold from June through September.

Admission: IR£1 ($1.75).
Open: Mon–Sat 10am–6pm, Sun noon–6pm.

WHERE TO STAY

CORNER HOUSE, Cashel, Glencolumbkille, Co. Donegal. Tel. 073/30021. 5 rms (4 with bath).
$ Rates (including breakfast): IR£15.50 ($27.15) single without bath; IR£11.50 ($20.15) per person sharing without bath; IR£1.50 ($2.65) per person additional with bath. 20% reduction for children. No credit cards. **Closed:** Oct–Mar.

Mrs. John Byrne presides over this nice two-story home set in the peaceful valley of Glencolumbkille 5 miles east of town on the Ardara road, and this location allows you to sink into the very special character of this remote part of Ireland. Guest rooms are quite comfortable, and sandy beaches are within easy reach, as is good fishing. The Folk Museum is less than 5 minutes away.

ARDARA

Ardara has long been a center of the home-weaving industry, and its few streets are lined with shops selling tweeds at good prices. Shoppers will have a field day, and they shouldn't miss the following factory shops, the first two of which have tea rooms on the premises: **John Molloy & Co.** (tel. 075/41133), **Kennedy's of Ardara** (tel. 075/41106), and **Cornelius Bonner & Son Ltd.** (tel. 075/41196). All are open Monday through Saturday from 10am to 6pm and all accept most credit cards. No matter where you end up buying, however, prices hereabouts are likely to be the best you'll find anywhere in the country.

I'm told that **Nancy's Pub,** on the Portnoo road in Ardara (owned by Nancy Yates's family—see below) is "very large in local character." **Peter Oliver's** is another character-laden pub, where you'll find traditional music most nights during the summer months.

WHERE TO STAY

BAY VIEW COUNTRY HOUSE, Portnoo Rd., Ardara, Co. Donegal. Tel. 075/41145. 7 rms (all with bath).
$ Rates (including breakfast): IR£16 ($28) single; IR£12 ($21) per person sharing. 20% reduction for children. Dinner IR£12 ($21) extra. No credit cards. **Closed:** Mid-Nov to Feb.

With magnificent views of Loughros Bay and the Owenea River, this centrally heated country home on the northern edge of town on the coast road has a spacious lounge with picture windows and turf fires, and a large dining room, where dinners include traditional Irish dishes as well as fresh local fish. The comfortable bedrooms all have tea-making equipment. Marian and Charles Bennett are helpful hosts, and Charles (who plays traditional music in pubs with a local group) is an active member of the Ardara Tourism Committee. There's a games room and snooker table.

GREENHAVEN, Portnoo Rd., Ardara, Co. Donegal. Tel. 075/41174. 6 rms (all with bath).

$ **Rates** (including breakfast): IR£12 ($21) per person. No credit cards. **Closed:** Nov–Feb.

Eileen and Ray Molloy are the delightful hosts at Greenhaven, at the northern edge of town on the coast road, which overlooks Loughross Bay and Slieve Tooey on the other side of the bay. There's a window-walled breakfast room open to the gorgeous view, and a large back garden. A modern extension holds the comfortable guest rooms, with lovely, puffy eiderdown quilts on all beds. The Molloys are especially helpful in pointing their guests to the things to see and do in the area (visit local weavers, etc.). Dinners many times feature fresh, locally caught seafood.

PINEWOOD, Straboy, Glenties, Co. Donegal. Tel. 075/51223. 4 rms (2 with bath).

$ **Rates** (including breakfast): IR£14.50 ($25.40) single without bath; IR£11.50 ($20.15) per person sharing without bath; IR£1 ($1.75) per person additional with bath. 33⅓% reduction for children. High tea IR£8.50 ($14.90) extra; dinner IR£10 ($17.50). No credit cards. **Closed:** Nov–Easter.

Mrs. Mary Ward is the friendly hostess of this modern bungalow located on the main Glenties–Letterkenny road 2 miles northwest of Glenties and 5 miles northwest of Ardara. It is set in lovely surroundings and the house is centrally heated, with electric blankets supplied. Mary is an excellent cook and serves wonderful meals. Her husband, Michael, is a schoolteacher and familiar with historic and scenic sites all over Ireland. The four attractive bedrooms are all nicely furnished and comfortable.

Worth the Extra Money

WOODHILL HOUSE, Ardara, Co. Donegal. Tel. 075/41112. 5 rms (4 with bath).

$ **Rates** (including breakfast): IR£21 ($36.75) single without bath; IR£16 ($28) per person sharing without bath; IR£6 ($10.50) per person additional with bath. AE, DC, MC, V.

This beautiful old country house sits on 4 acres at the edge of the village, with magnificent views of the Donegal hills. John and Nancy Yates (he's an Englishman, she's local) are the owners, and it was Nancy's grandmother for whom Nancy's Pub was named. The Yates have installed a cozy bar with peat fires, and guest rooms are beautifully done up. Both are keenly interested in their guests and are enthusiastic about this area's charms. There's central heating and good parking.

WHERE TO EAT

NESBIT ARMS HOTEL, Ardara, Co. Donegal. Tel. 075/41103.
Cuisine: TRADITIONAL/VEGETARIAN. **Reservations:** Not required.

$ **Prices:** Breakfast IR£5 ($8.75); lunch IR£7 ($12.25); dinner IR£10 ($17.50). MC, V.

Open: Breakfast 8:30–10am; lunch 12:30–2:30pm; dinner 6–9pm. **Closed:** Dec 24–25.

The dining room in this family-owned and -operated hotel serves meals featuring local produce, meat, and fish cooked in the traditional Irish manner. It's a friendly place, serving all three meals, and service is quite good.

WOODHILL HOUSE, Ardara, Co. Donegal. Tel. 075/41112.
Cuisine: TRADITIONAL. **Reservations:** Recommended.

$ Prices: Breakfast IR£5 ($8.75); dinner IR£18 ($31.50). AE, DC, MC, V.
Open: Year round.

⭐ This country house, in a scenic setting on the edge of the village (see "Where to Stay," above), specializes in dishes that feature local produce and seafood served in a beautiful dining room. Bar snacks are also available in the cozy bar.

ARDARA TO LETTERKENNY

Heading north via N56, the cliff and coastal scenery is haunting and lonely. Drive through towns and villages with sonorous names like Glenties (Na Gleannta, "The Valleys"); Dungloe, home of the famous "Mary of Dungloe" Festival; Burtonport; Gweedore, where there's always good traditional music; Bunbeg, on the alternative loop around County Donegal's fabulous Bloody Foreland; and Dunfanaghy, where you'll find **Alan Harley's Art Gallery,** which features Irish painter Tom Egginton's glowing landscape canvases and a huge stock of local crafts. This is also the takeoff point for the scenic clifftop **Horn Head Drive.**
Between Dunfanaghy and Creeslough, take time to visit ✪ **Ards Forest Park,** on the shores of Sheep Haven Bay. It's Ireland's most northerly forest park, and its 1,200 acres hold beautiful woodlands, salt marsh, sand dunes, seashore, freshwater lakes, fenland, and rock faces. Legend has it that back when time began this was the domain of Bioróg, the *bean sí* (Banshee), the fairy woman who thwarted Balor of the evil eye, god of drought and plague. Be that as it may, the park's Fairy Glen is, to this day, said to be the haunt of the Bioróg. There are traces of Ireland's earliest inhabitants in the four ring forts within the park. Nature paths are well marked, and there is informative literature available at the park entrance.
    At Creeslough, turn north again on R245 for a gorgeous drive to Carrigart. En route, some 3 miles from Creeslough, look for **Doe Castle,** the 16th-century home of the MacSweeny clan that was in residential use until 1843. At Carrigart, turn south to Milford. At Milford, R246 takes you north through beautiful scenery to Kerrykeel, where you join R247 southeast to the shores of ✪ **Lough Swilly** at historic Rathmullen. The little harbor here was the debarkation point of the tragic Flight of the Earls in 1607, and in 1798, this is where Wolfe Tone was taken prisoner. The **Flight of the Earls Interpretative Centre** (tel. 074/51178) tells the story of the earls (The O'Neill and The O'Donnell) through interesting artworks, artifacts, and wax-model exhibits. On the outskirts of town, there are interesting 15th-century **Carmelite friary ruins.** The coast road south takes you to Ramelton and on to the cathedral town of Letterkenny via N56.

WHERE TO STAY EN ROUTE

ARDEEN, Ramelton, Co. Donegal. Tel. 074/51243. 4 rms (1 with bath).
$ Rates (including breakfast): IR£16 ($28) single without bath; IR£13 ($22.75) per person sharing without bath; IR£1 ($1.75) per person additional with bath. 25% reduction for children. No credit cards. **Closed:** Nov–Easter.
Mrs. Anne Campbell is the delightful hostess of this beautiful country home furnished with antiques. It's on the outskirts of town overlooking Lough Swilly. Mrs.

IMPRESSIONS

Here is a wild. . . . country. . . . Here are gannets and seals and puffins flying and puffing and playing a quarter of a mile outside my window where there are great rocks petrified like the old Fates and destinies of Ireland, and smooth white pebbles under and around them like the souls of the dead Irish. There's a huge echo. You shout and the dead Irish answer from behind the hill. I've forced them into confessing that they're sad, grey, lost, forgotten, dead and damned forever.
—DYLAN THOMAS, Letter to Bert Trick, c. July 1935

Campbell and her family are all helpful and friendly. The house is centrally heated and the four pretty bedrooms are nicely furnished. There's a hard-surface tennis court for guests to use.

LAKE AND SEAVIEW HOUSE, Tubberkeen, Dungloe, Co. Donegal. Tel. 075/21142. 6 rms (none with bath).
$ Rates (including breakfast): IR£14.50 ($25.40) single; IR£11.50 ($20.15) per person sharing. 50% reduction for children. High tea IR£7.50 ($13.15) extra; dinner IR£11 ($19.25). No credit cards. **Closed:** Nov–Mar.

Its name tells a lot about Mrs. Caroline Ward's modernized farmhouse, which is close to both lake and sea, and the wild beauty of Glenveagh National Park is only 20 miles distant. Mrs. Ward can arrange fishing on the lake, and for swimmers (or those who just like to walk the seashore), beautiful deserted strands are right at hand. There's also a pony and a donkey to delight the younger set. The house is 1 mile west of Dungloe on N56.

Self-Catering

DONEGAL THATCHED COTTAGES on Cruit Island, c/o Conor and Mary Ward, Rosses Point, Co. Sligo. Tel. 071/77197. 8 cottages.
$ Rates: IR£120–IR£375 ($210–$656.25) per cottage per week; weekends Oct–May, IR£60–IR£95 ($105–$166.25) per cottage. Rates depend on season. No credit cards.

Ireland has many good self-catering cottages for visitors, but few in as breathtakingly beautiful a location—just offshore on an island connected to the mainland by a bridge (signposted on N56 between Burtonport and Annagry). The cottages are traditional in design (with thatch roofs and turf-burning fireplaces as well as central heat), and are set on a sheltered clifftop with spectacular seascapes of Donegal's rugged coastline, with Aranmore and Owey islands clearly visible. At the foot of the cliff is a lovely little half moon of a beach, and at the other side of the cliff, a golden strand safe for swimming goes on for miles. The fishing, boating, and swimming around here are all superb. There are good local pubs and one very good restaurant nearby. The cottages have been built and furnished with all Irish-made products, and while there's all the charm of bygone days in the decor, there are modern conveniences such as the automatic washer and dryer that are kept out of sight behind cabinet doors so as not to interfere with the traditional decor. Turf is furnished in generous quantities so you can indulge any penchant for the open hearth. Each cottage can sleep as many as seven adults comfortably, which makes the weekly rates fall easily within budget limits if you bring a full party. You can book into this very special place by contacting the owners, who will be glad to send you a brochure with full details.

Worth the Extra Money

RATHMULLAN COUNTRY HOUSE, Rathmullan, Co. Donegal. Tel. 074/58188. Fax 074/58200. 18 rms (all with bath).
$ Rates (including breakfast): IR£35–IR£45 ($61.25–$78.75) per person. Daily and weekly half-board rates available. AE, DC, MC, V. **Closed:** Jan to mid-Mar.

This lovely old house sits at the edge of town amid spacious, landscaped grounds that slope down to Lough Swilly, and in the more than 20 years that Robin and Bob Wheeler have been in residence, it has become a beloved favorite with the Irish from all over the Republic, as well as nearby Northern Ireland. The house dates back to the early 1800s, and the Wheelers have brought back a graciousness and charm that disappeared during the years of its rather checkered career. The soft glow of turf or log fires in the drawing room and library lights furnishings that combine a tasteful mixture of period and comfortably overstuffed modern pieces. The glass-enclosed Pavilion Dining Room looks out to award-winning gardens, and the cellar bar is a cozy spot for relaxed conviviality. Accommodations come in a wide range, from the large, luxuriously furnished guest rooms that look out to the lough to plainer, somewhat smaller and less expensive rooms. The Egyptian Baths Leisure Centre includes a swimming pool, sauna, and steam room. Sumptuous dinners, for which chef Bob has earned an international reputation, are quite moderately priced and feature local seafood and other products (see "Where to Eat En Route," below). Advance reservations for both accommodations and meals in this very popular place are absolutely essential.

READERS RECOMMEND

Seapoint House, Quay Road, Dungloe, County Donegal (tel. 075/21250). "Mrs. G. McKelvey welcomes you to her unpretentious home, at the water's edge of the narrow inlet, offering spacious accommodation and comfort to the weary traveler. Far from the clutches of big-city pressures, these environs offer a tranquility that is a rare commodity in today's world."—G. W. Howard, Silver Spring, Md.

WHERE TO EAT EN ROUTE

Pub grub will be your mainstay for lunches en route, and you'll find some very good cooking going under that name. As for the evening meal, it's possible to find yourself far from a large, populated town when hunger strikes, but in addition to those listed here, there are hotel dining rooms in most of the main towns (like **Arnold's Hotel,** Main Street, Dunfanaghy) that dish up quite good dinners at prices well below those in other parts of the country.

BUNBEG HOUSE, The Harbour, Bunbeg, Co. Donegal. Tel. 075/31305.
   Cuisine: SEAFOOD/TRADITIONAL/VEGETARIAN. **Reservations:** Not required.
   $ Prices: Breakfast IR£4.50 ($7.90); lunch IR£3 ($5.25); dinner IR£13 ($22.75). No credit cards.
   Open: Mar–Dec, daily 10am–10pm. **Closed:** Jan–Feb, Good Friday, Dec 24–25.

This is a charmingly informal, family-owned and -operated restaurant where you can relax before open fires and enjoy a leisurely meal. The menu features seafood from waters just outside the door and nearby rivers and lakes, and everything is home-cooked. There's also a tea room and wine bar for light refreshment.

TEACH KILLENDARRAGH, Annagry, Co. Donegal. Tel. 075/48201.
   Cuisine: SEAFOOD/TRADITIONAL/VEGETARIAN. **Reservations:** Not required.
   $ Prices: Lunch IR£6 ($10.50); dinner IR£15 ($26.25). MC, V.
   Open: Mar–Dec, daily 10am–10pm. **Closed:** Jan–Feb, Good Friday, Christmas Day.

This charming traditional-style restaurant is a delight to the eye as well as to the palate. There's a warm, welcoming atmosphere very much in keeping with Irish traditions of hospitality, and the menu offers a nice selection of local seafood, meats, and fresh produce.

Worth the Extra Money

PAVILION DINING ROOM, Rathmullan Country House, Rathmullan, Co. Donegal. Tel. 074/58188.
   Cuisine: SEAFOOD/TRADITIONAL/VEGETARIAN. **Reservations:** Essential.
   $ Prices: Breakfast IR£7 ($12.25); dinner IR£20 ($35); Sun lunch IR£10 ($17.50). AE, DC, MC, V.
   Open: Mid-Mar to Dec, breakfast Mon–Sat 8:30–9:30am; dinner Mon–Sat 7:30–8:30pm; Sun lunch 1–2pm.

This elegant glass-walled dining room looks out over well-kept lawns that slope down to the shores of Lough Swilly. The domain of award-winning owner/chef Bob Wheeler, its menu includes locally caught salmon hollandaise, roasts from Irish beef, pork, and lamb, and vegetables from their own garden. Fresh fruits from trees right on the premises go into luscious homemade pies, and if you've ever been curious about the seaweed-based Carrigeen dessert, this is the place to try it. There's a very good wine list, and service is both friendly and professional.

SHOPPING IN RAMELTON

You'll pass through Ramelton en route from Rathmullan to Letterkenny, and thanks to a reader, I can pass along this shopping tip. Just outside Ramelton on the road to Milford, there's a wonderful **craft shop** owned by Mrs. S. Browne, Black's Glen. The Aran sweaters on display were knit by Mrs. Browne and her neighbors, and she sells them at substantial savings. They're as beautiful and well crafted as you'll find anywhere. There are also a host of other interesting handcrafts in her shop.

LETTERKENNY

Letterkenny is the chief town of County Donegal and an important ecclesiastical city. If you chose the short route from Donegal town north via N15 and N56, this is an ideal base from which to make day trips to explore northern Donegal's Fanad and Rosguill peninsulas or the coastline drives outlined above. The town sits at the point where the River Swilly empties into Lough Swilly, and its main street is one of the longest in Ireland.

TOURIST INFORMATION   For information, contact the **Letterkenny Tourist Office,** Derry Road, Letterkenny, Co. Donegal (tel. 074/21160). It's open June through September, daily from 10am to 5pm; other months, Monday through Friday with shorter hours.

WHAT TO SEE & DO

You can't miss Letterkenny's most outstanding attraction—**St. Eunan's Cathedral,** near Sentry Hill on Cathedral Street, dominates the skyline and is floodlit at night. Completed in 1901, it is Gothic in style, with much Celtic carving, richly decorated ceilings, and beautiful stained-glass windows.

The **County Donegal Museum** on High Road is in the only surviving portion of an old workhouse which has only recently been converted to a museum—consult the Tourist Office for hours.

Golfers are welcomed at the 18-hole **golf course** on the outskirts of town off the Ramelton road (tel. 074/21150). There's excellent **fishing** in Lough Swilly as well as other lakes and rivers nearby. For fishing information, phone Mr. Gerry McNulty (tel. 074/24476). The **Letterkenny Leisure Centre** (tel. 074/21793) has excellent facilities, including a swimming pool, kiddies' pool, spa pool, sauna, and steam room.

Attractions Nearby

GLENVEAGH NATIONAL PARK, Churchill, Co. Donegal. Tel. 074/ 37088.

✪ This is perhaps County Donegal's premier visitor attraction. Set aside at least half a day to take in the deeply wooded reaches of the park and its impressive castle. Set in the very heart of the Donegal highlands, between the Derryveagh and Glendowan mountain ranges, the park covers almost 25,000 acres of wilderness, with the castle and its magnificent gardens set like a jewel on the edge of Lough Veagh. There's a very good audiovisual show at the Visitors Centre, and tea and scones with homemade jam are available in the castle kitchen.

The park is 18 miles northwest of Letterkenny on the Churchill road (R251); access also from N56 north to Kilmacreanan, turning left onto the Gweedore road.

Admission: IR£1 ($1.75) adults, 40p (70¢) children, 70p ($1.25) seniors.
Open: Mid-Apr to Oct, daily 10:30am–6:30pm.

GLEBE GALLERY AND ST. COLUMB'S, Churchill, Co. Donegal. Tel. 074/37071.

Some 18 miles northwest of Letterkenny on the Churchill road (R251), at the main entrance of Glenveagh National Park near Churchill Village, St. Columb's sits amid informal gardens and is the home of noted landscape and portrait painter Derek Hill, who has willed the property and the paintings to the nation. The adjacent Glebe Gallery houses his extensive art collection, and the house itself contains a wide range of antique artworks, Victoriana, and prints from China and Japan.

Admission: IR£1 ($1.75) adults, 40p (70¢) children, 70p ($1.25) seniors.

Open: June–Sept, Tues–Sat 11am–6:30pm, Sun 1–6pm.

LURGYVALE THATCHED COTTAGE, Kilmacrenan, Co. Donegal. Tel. 074/39024.

This 150-year-old cottage has been carefully restored so faithfully that it won a European Heritage Conservation Award. Visitors are welcomed with homemade scones in the kitchen, with its flagstone floor and open hearth, then given a guided tour of the homey interior. Periodic craft demonstrations include spinning, flailing, churning, and straw rope making, and on Thursday at 8:30pm, there are traditional music and dancing sessions. Outside, there's a landscaped picnic area and a nature walk through lovely wooded areas down to the Lurgy River.

Admission: IR£1 ($1.75).

Open: May–Oct, Mon–Wed and Fri–Sat 10am–7pm, Thurs 10am–12:30am, Sun 11am–7pm.

WHERE TO STAY

SEPTORA, Convent Rd., Letterkenny, Co. Donegal. Tel. 074/22330. 3 rms (2 with shower only).

$ Rates (including breakfast): IR£13.50 ($23.65) single; IR£11.50 ($20.15) per person sharing. 20% reduction for children. No credit cards. **Closed:** Nov–Feb.

Mrs. Rosleen Gill is the delightful, enthusiastic hostess here. Her attractive, centrally heated bungalow is set on a quiet cul-de-sac and has three nicely decorated bedrooms, with built-in wardrobes and sinks, two with private showers. Goose-down comforters are on each bed, and Mrs. Gill even furnishes hand tissues in all guest rooms.

Septora is right in town; to find it, turn right at the Tintai Restaurant on the road to Glenveagh National Park.

TOWN VIEW, Leck Rd., Letterkenny, Co. Donegal. Tel. 074/21570 or 25138. 4 rms (3 with bath). TV

$ Rates (including breakfast): IR£14.50 ($25.40) single without bath; IR£11.50 ($20.15) per person sharing without bath; IR£1.50 ($2.65) per person additional with bath. 20% reduction for children. No credit cards.

Vivacious May Herrity is hostess at this pretty two-story house perched on a hilltop on the outskirts of town. Panoramic views of Letterkenny are stunning, especially at night when the cathedral is spotlighted. Guest rooms, each with its own color TV, are unusually attractive, decorated, according to May, "the way I like to live myself." Those in the back of the house face peaceful green fields that resemble 18th-century landscape paintings. The pretty lounge has a huge fireplace and picture windows overlooking the town, which is where breakfast is served. Breakfast often features a selection of fresh fruits and other items, as well as the traditional full Irish menu. May is active in tourism in this area and a delightful assistant in planning your sightseeing and recreation.

To get to Town View, take the Ballybofey road (N56), cross the stone bridge at Dunnes Stores, and keep left for half a mile.

WHERE TO EAT

BOUCHER'S RESTAURANT, Main St., Letterkenny. Tel. 074/24641.
Cuisine: SEAFOOD/CONTINENTAL. **Reservations:** Recommended.

$ **Prices:** Appetizers IR£1.20–IR£4.70 ($2.10–$8.25); main courses IR£9.50–IR£12 ($16.65–$21); Early-Bird dinner IR£9.50 ($16.65). MC, V.
Open: Dinner only, Mon–Sat 6:30–10:30pm (Early-Bird dinner 6:30–8pm).

Owner Michael Bouchier-Hayes has transformed old stone stables into this gourmet restaurant through painstaking restoration that has left much of its original character intact. Dinner comes to the table by candlelight, and the Early-Bird menu (four courses with a multiple choice of appetizers and main dishes) is especially good value. For heartier meals, the à la carte menu offers a wide selection, with such specialties as grilled whole fresh black sole on the bone, fresh filet of brill à la Breval, monkfish and brill in chive sauce, Dublin Bay prawns thermidor, chicken Kiev, entrecôte au poivre, and Donegal spring lamb.

PAT'S PIZZA, Market Sq., Letterkenny. Tel. 074/21761.
Cuisine: PIZZA/SALADS/SANDWICHES.
$ **Prices:** Morning coffee and afternoon tea IR£1.05 ($1.85); à la carte items IR£1.50–IR£6 ($2.65–$10.50). MC.
Open: Mon–Wed 10am–12:30am, Thurs–Fri 10am–1am, Sat 10am–3am, Sun noon–1:15am.

This popular pizzeria has an extensive menu and you can eat on the premises or take your selections away for a picnic. Pizzas come in three sizes, with a choice of no fewer than a dozen toppings, and there are kebabs, spaghetti, chile con carne, salad plates, filled rolls, and luscious homemade desserts. The late opening hours are a bonus, as are the coffee and cappuccino made from freshly ground beans.

3. THE INISHOWEN PENINSULA

This long, broad, finger of land stretching north to the Atlantic between Lough Swilly to the west and Lough Foyle to the east is Ireland's most northerly point, and takes its name from King Niall of the Nine Hostages, a contemporary of St. Patrick in the 5th century. Along the shores of both loughs and the Atlantic Ocean long stretches of sandy beaches are backed by sheer cliffs. Inland are some of Ireland's most impressive mountains, with 2,019-foot Slieve Snacht dominating the center of the peninsula. Its history reaches back beyond recorded history, with relics of those distant days scattered across its face.

Relatively undiscovered by the majority of visitors to the country, Inishowen is a world apart, where the present-day residents revere their ancient heritage and treasure the legends and antiquities of this remote region and still observe many traditions of their ancestors. Turf is cut in the time-honored fashion and in summer months it's not unusual to see it piled beside the roads waiting to be transported to Inishowen cottages to be stacked and dried to ensure a warm winter. Traditional music and dance thrive here, and it is unlikely you will face an evening when there's not a session in a nearby pub.

Despite its completely unspoiled character, however, the peninsula provides comfortable accommodations and recreational facilities for those visitors who come for the scenic splendor and "get away from it all" peacefulness.

GETTING THERE & GETTING AROUND

By Bus There is regular bus service to Buncrana from Derry and from Letterkenny; however, service farther north is sparse to nonexistent.

By Car This is really the only way to see Inishowen properly, although stops for mountain or beach walks should figure prominently in your time schedule. The drive from Letterkenny around the peninsula to Derry is approximately 150 miles. Leaving

Letterkenny, take N13 north to the turnoff onto R238 into Burnfoot, where the **Inishowen 100 Scenic Drive** is signposted. If your Irish itinerary will take you on into the six counties of Northern Ireland, the signposts will lead you around the peninsula through its most spectacular points (with my strong recommendation for an overnight stop en route) into the province's second city, Derry (Londonderry). If you're coming from Derry, take A2 west and join R238 at Muff.

TOURIST INFORMATION

The **Tourist Office** in Letterkenny can furnish Inishowen information, as can the office in Sligo, which covers the entire Northwest. If at all possible, however, write or call ahead for more detailed brochures from the **Inishowen Community Development Group**, Chapel Street, Carndonagh, County Donegal (tel. 077/74529).

WHAT TO SEE & DO

At the little township of Burt, 3 miles south of Bridgend (10 miles south of Buncrana), look for signposts to the unclassified road that leads to a great circular stone cashel known as **Grianan of Aileach** ("Sun Palace of Aileach"), once the royal seat of the O'Neills and a sacred meeting place for High Kings of Ireland. From its 800-foot-high perch atop Greenan Mountain, there are vast panoramic views of Lough Swilly, Lough Foyle, and the distant sea. The dry-stone fort was built, as far as archeologists can determine, in about 1700 B.C., and its 76-foot diameter is enclosed by walls 13 feet thick and 17 feet high. During the Iron Age the earthen enclosures served as a temple of the sun. Virtually dismantled stone by stone in 1101 by Murrtagh O'Brien, King of Munster, it was restored in the 1870s. As you descend from this lofty antiquity, look again at **Burt Church**, which sits at the foot of the access road—its circular design follows that of the fort itself, and it is being developed as a Visitor Centre, focusing on the history, legends, and folklore of the Grianan of Aileach. There's a traditional tea room, as well as a craft shop.

A few miles farther north, **Inch Island** (reached by a bridge from the mainland), is home to the **Inishowen Heritage Centre** (tel. 077/60152). At the little resort town of **Fahan**, the old graveyard holds a flat, two-faced cross from the 7th century and two rather curious carved stones.

Buncrana, the principal town of Inishowen, is a pleasant seaside resort with 3 miles of sand beach. Along a pleasant walk and overlooking the Crana River are the ruins of **Buncrana Castle**, dating back to the late 16th century, with extensive rebuilding in 1718. This is where Wolfe Tone was taken after his capture in 1798. Close by are the ruins of **O'Doherty's Castle**. Reflecting more modern times, the **Vintage Car & Carriage Museum**, Buncrana (tel. 077/61130), has an impressive collection of classic cars, horse-drawn carriages, Victorian bicycles, motorcycles, and model cars. During summer months, it's open daily from 10am to 8pm, with a small admission charge. Half a mile north of town, **Tullyarvin Mill** (tel. 074/21160, Letterkenny Tourist Office, for details) is an imposing old restored mill being developed as a museum, information office, and genealogical facility. Buncrana has an 18-hole seaside **golf course** (tel. 074/61027) that welcomes visiting golfers. There's also good **fishing** for sea trout, salmon, and brown trout in the Crana River.

From Buncrana, signposts will lead you north to Dunree Head and **Fort Dunree**, a restored coastal defense battery stretching from the Napoleonic era to the departure of the British militia in 1938 that commands superb views of Lough Swilly. Now a museum, it also provides an audiovisual demonstration on the history of the fort and this region. There's also a good cafeteria, making this a good lunch break.

From here, your route takes you on north through the **Gap of Mamore**, some 800 feet above sea level, with spectacular views. For dedicated hill walkers, this is a good starting point for exploring the Urris Hills to the west or Mamore Hill and Raghtin to the east. Some 10 miles north of Buncrana, you encounter the village of **Clonmany**, and 2 miles east, on the face of Magheramore Hill, the huge capstone of a Bronze Age dolmen is reputed hereabouts to have been through by Ireland's legendary giant hero, which earns it the local name of "Finn McCool's Finger Stone." Just north of Clonmany, **Ballyliffin** is a delightful seaside resort with a 2-mile beach and an 18-hole golf course open to visitors. The pubs and two hotels often have Irish nights with music and dancing, and occasionally there is disco.

The prosperous town of **Carndonagh** is headquarters for the Inishowen Community Development Group (see "Tourist Information," above), and a stop by their offices on Chapel Street could reap many rewards on the rest of your journey around the peninsula. The town has been an important ecclesiastical center since the 5th century, and its most acclaimed attraction is **St. Patrick's Cross,** 11½ feet high and dating back to the 7th century. The townscape these days, however, is dominated by the striking 1945 **Church of the Sacred Heart,** which holds exceptionally fine statuary by the famous sculptor Albert Power. Nearby, the **Church of Ireland** occupies a site on which St. Patrick founded one of his churches. If you're picnicking your way around Inishowen, you'll find a picnic area in the lovely woods of oak, birch, rowan, hazel, willow, and holly on the outskirts of town on the Ballyliffin side.

From Cardonagh, drive through the village of Malin and on out to **Malin Head**—as far north as you can go on Ireland's mainland. While this northerly point lacks the spectacular clifftop heights you've seen en route, it provides marvelous panoramic views of the peninsula to the south and out to sea, and it's a good starting point for a walk to Hell's Hole, a deep cavern into which sea thunders at high tide. Besides, if you ventured down to the country's most *southerly* point in West Cork, you can now claim to have covered the length of Ireland, "From Malin Head to Mizen Head"—no small boast!

On the drive out to Malin Head, look for signposts to **Ballyhillion Beach,** a raised-beach system whose distinct shorelines clearly trace the sea's activities from some 15,000 years ago as the age of the great glaciers came to an end.

Your route now turns south, through the picturesque village of **Culdaff,** with lovely sandy beaches, to **Moville,** where a short detour through **Greencastle** (a fine beach resort named for the castle of Richard de Burgo, the Red Earl of Ulster) leads to **Inishowen Head,** site of a maritime disaster in 1588 when a number of Spanish Armada galleons sank in Kinnagoe Bay. One such vessel was located in near-perfect condition some years back, and artifacts recovered by the Derry Sub-Aqua Club are on display in Derry. With your arrival a bit farther south in **Muff,** your *Inishowen 100* Scenic Drive comes to an end.

WHERE TO STAY

BUNCRANA

KINCORA, Cahir O'Doherty Ave., Buncrana, Co. Donegal. Tel. 077/ 61174. 3 rms (none with bath).
$ Rates (including breakfast): IR£14.50 ($25.40) single; IR£11.50 ($20.15) per person sharing. No credit cards.
Mrs. McEleney is the hostess in this modern bungalow set in a flower-bordered lawn in a quiet location in town facing Lough Swilly. The three nice bedrooms are all twin-bedded, with sinks and built-in wardrobes. Breakfast is served in a bright, cheerful dining room.

Worth the Extra Money

WHITE STRAND MOTOR INN, Buncrana, Co. Donegal. Tel. 077/61059 or 61144. Fax 077/61059. 12 rms (all with bath). TV TEL
$ Rates (including breakfast): Oct–May, IR£23 ($40.25) single; IR£20 ($35) per person sharing. June and Sept, IR£25 ($43.75) single; IR£22 ($38.50) per person sharing. July–Aug, IR£28 ($49) single; IR£25 ($43.75) per person sharing. Discounts for children under 8. Golf weekends and weekly rates available. MC, V.

This sparkling-white one-story motel sits at the southern edge of town on the shores of Lough Swilly, with large windows giving its public rooms, as well as guest rooms, a light and airy look. All bedrooms come with tea/coffee makers and hairdryers. The dining room serves moderately priced meals (see "Where to Eat," below), and the dark wood and green velvet decor of the bar creates a nice setting for bar food at lunch.

CLONMANY

FOUR ARCHES, Letter, Urris, Clonmany, Co. Donegal. Tel. 077/76109. 5 rms (2 with bath).

$ Rates (including breakfast): IR£11.50 ($20.15) per person without bath, IR£12.50 ($21.90) per person with bath. No credit cards. **Closed:** Oct–Mar.

This modern, Spanish-style bungalow 4½ miles east of Clonmany is the perfect place to experience the splendor and spirit of the Inishowen countryside. There are panoramic views on all sides, and its 10 acres hold 40 sheep and three goats. This is the home of Fidelma and Michael McLaughlin and their five children, all the very essence of Irish hospitality. Fidelma's breakfasts add fruit and scrambled eggs to the traditional Irish breakfast, and guest rooms are nicely appointed, one with two double beds.

KEG O'POTEEN, Clonmany, Co. Donegal. Tel. 077/76415. 4 rms (none with bath).

$ Rates (including breakfast): IR£10 ($17.50) per person. No credit cards.

It must be said right up front that these accommodations would not suit everyone, since they're above a popular, typical village bar and lounge on the main street of the village. However, I must also tell you that I found the rooms, although somewhat plain, very comfortable, with a full bath and separate toilet within easy reach. The availability of very good bar food right downstairs was a decided plus (see "Where to Eat," below). Danny and Geraldine McCarron are the owners, and they extend a cordial welcome to guests both upstairs and down in the bar, where there's traditional music on weekends. Something a little different from the usual bed-and-breakfast, but the hospitality is the same.

BALLYLIFFIN

POLLIN HOUSE, Carndonagh Rd., Ballyliffin, Co. Donegal. Tel. 077/ 76203. 4 rms (none with bath).

$ Rates (including breakfast): IR£12.50 ($21.90) single; IR£11.50 ($20.15) per person sharing. 33⅓% reduction for children. No credit cards. **Closed:** Oct–Mar.

Mrs. Kathleen Grant's dormer bungalow sits on the northern outskirts of the village on an elevated site that affords panoramic views of the Atlantic, Malin Head, golden beaches, sand dunes, and a patchwork of fields. There's a large lounge with a bay window, and breakfast is cooked in the old manner on a traditional solid-fuel range. A hairdryer and iron are provided for guest use, and there's a "cuppa" available any time of day or night. Guest rooms are comfortably fitted out, with a bath and separate shower close by. There are two family rooms, one with a double and two twin beds, the other with two double beds and one twin. Mrs. Grant is quite active in tourism and knows Inishowen like the back of her hand—an expertise she is happy to share with guests.

Worth the Extra Money

STRAND HOTEL, Ballyliffin, Co. Donegal. Tel. 077/76107. 12 rms (all with bath). TV TEL

$ Rates (including breakfast): Oct–May, IR£26 ($45.50) single; IR£20 ($35) per person sharing. June–Sept, IR£30 ($52.50) single; IR£24 ($42) per person sharing. Weekend rates available. AE, MC, V.

This small, family hotel is a delightful stop on your tour of Inishowen. Its location in the village is ideal, and the sandy strand just outside the door has a playground for children. All public rooms are bright and cheerful, with plenty of windows to enjoy the marvelous views. Guest rooms also take advantage of the views, and furnishings are attractive and very comfortable. During the summer months there's regular live music and other entertainment.

MALIN HEAD

BARRAICIN, Malin Head, Co. Donegal. Tel. 077/70184. 3 rms (none with bath).

$ Rates (including breakfast): IR£14.50 ($25.40) single; IR£11.50 ($20.15) per person sharing. No credit cards. **Closed:** Nov–Mar.

Mrs. Maire Doyle will welcome you to her modern bungalow 3½ miles north of Malin village overlooking the sea. There are three nice guest rooms, all with sinks, and hairdryers and a tea kettle are available on request. Mrs. Doyle, who has been a moving force in Inishowen tourism development, has won much praise from our readers for her warmth and graciousness, as well as for her tremendous help in steering them to highlights of the peninsula.

WHERE TO EAT

FAHAN

Worth the Extra Money

RESTAURANT SAINT JOHN, Fahan, Co. Donegal. Tel. 077/60289.
Cuisine: CONTINENTAL/TRADITIONAL/VEGETARIAN. **Reservations:** Recommended.

$ Prices: Dinner IR£20 ($35). AE, DC, MC, V.
Open: Dinner only, Tues–Sun 6–10pm. **Closed:** Good Friday, Christmas Day.

Set back off the road on the southern outskirts of the village (signposted on R328) and surrounded by lovely old trees, this restored Georgian house has sweeping views of Lough Swilly. The menu is extensive, making full use of locally produced meats, seafood, and vegetables in sophisticated as well as traditional dishes.

BUNCRANA

WHITE STRAND MOTOR INN, Buncrana, Co. Donegal. Tel. 077/61059 or 61144.
Cuisine: BAR FOOD/SEAFOOD/TRADITIONAL. **Reservations:** Not required.
$ Prices: Bar food IR£3–IR£5 ($5.25–$8.75); fixed-price meal IR£3 ($5.25) at lunch, IR£12 ($21) at dinner. MC, V.
Open: Lunch daily 12:30–3pm; dinner daily 6:30–9:30pm.

This attractive, modern motel at the southern edge of town on Lough Swilly is a good lunch or dinner stop, even if you're not staying here (see "Where to Stay," above). While the menu is not overly adventurous, all ingredients are fresh and nicely prepared in rather traditional styles. Good value for the dollar.

CLONMANY

KEG O'POTEEN, Clonmany, Co. Donegal. Tel. 077/76415.
Cuisine: BAR FOOD.
$ Prices: IR£1.50–IR£3 ($2.65–$5.25). No credit cards.
Open: Daily noon–11pm.

It's good to know that if you're wandering the vast reaches of Inishowen mountains or coastlines at the usual dining hours, you can stop in this village bar and lounge for exceptionally good bar food at minuscule prices from noon until closing. In addition to the usual soup, sandwiches, and salads, they offer hot dishes such as stuffed roast chicken. On the main street of the village, it's a good place to meet locals, and on weekends there are traditional music sessions.

MALIN HEAD

BREE INN, Malin Head, Co. Donegal. Tel. 077/70161.
Cuisine: BAR FOOD.
$ Prices: IR£2–IR£5 ($3.50–$8.75). No credit cards.
Open: Daily 11am–11:30pm.

This lively country pub about 6 miles north of Malin village serves delicious bar food, offering fish and chips, salads, and hot dishes all through the day and evening. Behind the small bar, there's a spacious lounge, and to one side, pool and darts star in a larger room. Owners Andrew and Sarah McLaughlin have also built a large recreational center just next door (easy access for wheelchairs), where there's traditional music and other entertainment during the season.

THE MIDLANDS REGION

This chapter focuses on the seven counties of the Midlands Region, often called Lakeland—and indeed the landscape is dotted with lakes. The Rivers Shannon and Erne glide between broad banks, spreading here and there into Lough Ree and Lough Sheelin. Before or during your visit, contact the **Lakeland Regional Tourist Office, Dublin** Road, Mullingar, County Westmeath (tel. 044/48761), for literature to steer you to the treasures of the Midlands counties.

In ancient days, this region was the land of the lake dwellers, who built artificial islands called crannogs on which to raise their round huts, protected from enemy attack by the surrounding waters (see Section 1 below). At the geographical heart of the country, the great monastic community of Clonmacnois in County Offaly withstood assaults by Vikings, Normans, and Cromwell, and has left us a rich heritage of Celtic crosses and round towers.

Fishing is excellent and free in most places; hikers and walkers can tramp forest parks and lakeshores; there's golf in County Westmeath's Mullingar and Athlone; and there are miles and miles of water for dedicated boaters. For all visitors picnics are a joy in the Midlands region, with woodlands and lakeshores galore.

There must be something in the nearly flat, faintly rolling land that nurtures the creative spirit, for it has spawned such literary lights as Oliver Goldsmith, Maria Edgeworth, and the poet Patrick Kavanaugh. Musically, the region has contributed composer and songwriter Percy French, harpist O'Carolan, and tenor John McCormick.

1. COUNTY CAVAN

County Cavan's gently undulating landscape of water-splashed rolling hills rises to some 2,188 feet at its highest point at the summit of Cuilcagh Mountain right at the Northern Ireland border south of Enniskillen. Ireland's longest river, the Shannon, rises on the southern slopes of this mountain, and the River Erne flows northward from Lough Gowna through the center of the county, past Cavan town and on up into the Upper Erne, spreading its waters into myriad lakes along the way.

Americans may be surprised to learn that Edgar Allen Poe's ancestors were from the little village of Kildallon near Cavan town.

WHAT'S SPECIAL ABOUT THE MIDLANDS

Religious Sites
- ☐ The great monastic community of Clonmacnois, in County Offaly, with its Celtic crosses and round towers.

Fishing
- ☐ Lakes Sillan and Dromlona, in north-eastern County Cavan, and the Upper Erne lake/river system, in western County Cavan.
- ☐ Rivers and lakes around Clones, in western County Monaghan, about 12 miles from Monaghan town.

Forest Parks
- ☐ Killykeen Forest Park, in County Cavan, whose woodlands and wetlands include ancient crannogs, ring forts, and the ruined Lough Oughter Castle.
- ☐ Monicknew Woods, in the Slieve Bloom Mountains of County Laois, with its nature trail, forest walks, viewing points, and picnic site.
- ☐ Lough Key Forest Park, near Boyle, County Roscommon, with its interesting bog gardens.

Crafts
- ☐ Carrickmacross Lace Co-op, in Carrickmacross, County Monaghan, where delicate lacework is done by hand.

Literary Associations
- ☐ Inishkeen, County Monaghan, where poet Patrick Kavanagh was born and lies buried.
- ☐ Edgeworthstown, County Longford, home of 18th-century writer Maria Edgeworth.
- ☐ Pallas, near Abbeyshrule southeast of Longford town, birthplace of Oliver Goldsmith.
- ☐ Longford town, birthplace of poet, playwright, novelist, and essayist Padraic Colum.

Musical Associations
- ☐ Athlone, County Westmeath, birthplace of tenor John McCormack.
- ☐ Elphin, County Roscommon, birthplace of songwriter Percy French.
- ☐ Grave of the blind harper O'Carolan in Kilronan Abbey cemetery, near Lough Key in County Roscommon.

WHAT TO SEE & DO

The county's chief town, **Cavan,** sits among low green hills on the eastern edge of the Lough Oughter lake system. **Percy French,** composer of some of Ireland's best-loved ballads, including "Come Back Paddy Reilly to Ballyjamesduff" and "The Mountains of Mourne," lived at 16 Farnham Street. This is also the home of **Cavan Crystal** (tel. 049/31800 for shop and guided factory-tour hours). There's traditional music periodically at the **Well Bar & Singing Lounge** on Bridge Street, Cavan town (tel. 049/32022), and at the **Hillside Tavern** in Killeshandra.

Plan to spend some time in the 600 acres of ✪ **Killykeen Forest Park,** located between Killeshandra and Cavan town (signposted on L15). There's plenty to enjoy: fishing, swimming, boating, shady nature trails, and picnic sites, as well as a self-catering holiday village. Within its grounds you'll also find crannogs, ring forts, and the ruined **Lough Oughter Castle,** where in 1649 the great chieftain Owen Roe O'Neil died (to this day some say he was poisoned by a treacherous hand).

Four miles north of Cavan town via N3, **Butlersbridge** sits on the banks of the Annalee River, with excellent fishing. The **Derragarra Inn** pub and restaurant in Butlersbridge (see "Where to Eat," below) is a sightseeing attraction in its own right, and there's a small, but very interesting ✪ **folk museum** just across the road. Four miles north of Butlersbridge is an ideal fishing center, as it's situated midway between the Upper Lough Erne and Lough Oughter.

Some 16 miles northeast of Cavan town on R188, the little town of **Cootehill** has good fishing on Dromlona Lake, and 3 miles southeast on the Shercock road, near Cohaw village, there's a prehistoric **court cairn tomb**. It was near Shercock, at Lough Sillan, that the largest horns of the extinct giant Irish deer were found.

WHERE TO STAY

COOTEHILL

KER MARIA, Station Rd., Cootehill, Co. Cavan. Tel. 049/52293. 4 rms (none with bath).
$ Rates (including breakfast): IR£11.50 ($20.15) per person. 20% reduction for children. No credit cards.
Closed: Oct–June.
Gardens surround this pretty Georgian-style home midway between Donegal and Dublin, half a mile from Cavan town. Mrs. Teresa Colhoun is a helpful, informative hostess, and the four nice guest rooms are comfortably furnished. This house has central heating and good parking.

BALLINAGH

BAVARIA HOUSE, Ballinagh, Co. Cavan. Tel. 049/37452. 3 rms (1 with bath).
$ Rates (including breakfast): IR£16 ($28) single without bath; IR£12 ($21) per person sharing without bath; IR£1 ($1.75) per person additional with bath. Dinner IR£10 ($17.50) extra. No credit cards.
Ilse and Rolf Kiebler preside over this two-story country home with its lovely gardens. They grow their own vegetables, and can arrange golfing, fishing, and boat rentals for guests. The three guest rooms are nicely appointed, with good rural views. The Kieblers speak their native German as well as excellent English. Half a mile from Ballinagh (which is south of Cavan town via N55), the house is centrally heated, and there's good parking.

SELF-CATERING IN KILLYKEEN FOREST PARK

KILLYKEEN FOREST CHALETS, Killykeen Forest Park, Co. Cavan. Tel. 049/32541. 20 chalets.
$ Rates: IR£140–IR£230 ($245–$402.50) per chalet per week, depending on season. No credit cards.
 This is one of the prettiest sites for getting away from it all in Ireland, and the Forest Service has worked hand-in-glove with tourism people to develop a group of log-cabin units for holiday-makers. Between Killeshandra and Cavan town (signposted on L15), the beautifully wooded park also contains good fishing.

WHERE TO EAT

BUTLERSBRIDGE

DERRAGARRA INN, Butlersbridge, Co. Cavan. Tel. 049/31003.
Cuisine: BAR FOOD/TRADITIONAL. **Reservations:** Not required.
$ Prices: Bar food IR£1.50–IR£4 ($2.65–$7); four-course lunch IR£6 ($10.50); dinner IR£9 ($15.75). MC, V.
Open: Mon–Sat 10:30am–11:30pm, Sun 12:30–2pm and 4–10pm.
This award-winning pub and eatery sits 4 miles north of Cavan town by the side of the River Annalee. Its interior decor is a marvelous hodgepodge of items that range from old farm implements to exotic souvenirs owner John Clancey

collected in his years of wandering the world. In addition to bar food (steakburgers, cheese snacks, etc.), there are full dinners consisting of hors d'oeuvres, main course (such as a T-bone steak, ham, roast beef, chicken, or fish), vegetables, and dessert. Beautifully arranged salad plates with ample portions are also available.

2. COUNTY MONAGHAN

County Monaghan is the ancient territory of the powerful MacMahon clan, and today it draws hoards of fishing enthusiasts. The great Irish poet Patrick Kavanagh was born in County Monaghan, but "escaped" to live out most of his life in Dublin, where he wrote of his birthplace, "O stoney grey soil of Monaghan, / You burgled my bank of youth." Although he considered Dublin to be the place that transformed him from a "happily unhappy, ordinary countryman" into the "abnormally normal" poet, much of his poetry had to do with the place of his birth.

WHAT TO SEE & DO

Monaghan town holds the award-winning **Monaghan County Museum** (tel. 047/82928) with the medieval processional Cross of Clogher, which dates from the 14th century, as well as other artifacts from this county's rich past. Twelve miles southwest of Monaghan on N54 is a 75-foot-high **Celtic cross** in Clones and a round tower in the graveyard near the Cavan road. Two miles east of Clones, the little village of **Aughnakillagh** is the birthplace of James Connolly, hero of the 1916 rising.

Near the village of **Inishkeen** Patrick Kavanagh first saw the light of day. In the end, he was brought back to his native county, and his grave is just opposite a small stone church and the remains of an ancient round tower.

Stop by the ✪ **Carrickmacross Lace Co-op,** on Main Street (tel. 042/62506 or 62085), in the charming little town of Carrickmacross. The lace makers sketch out original designs to be worked in the sheerest lawn, appliquéed to even sheerer net. The tiny, invisible hand-stitching is done in some 20 cottages by skillful and patient women, whose numbers are dwindling every year, with few young girls willing to learn the ancient art. The world-famous Carrickmacross lace, introduced to the Monaghan area in the 1800s, has continued as a cottage industry from 1846 to this day. A Miss Reid built the first schoolhouse for the lace. Then the founding of the St. Louis Convent ensured the development of the lace and it has remained the center for the lace for many years. The toll house at the end of town is the display center run by the Carrickmacross Lace Co-op for the lace today. It is to this historic little building that the lace makers, after many patient hours of sewing their elegant lace, bring the fruits of their labor.

WHERE TO STAY
CARRICKMACROSS

ROSE-LINN-LODGE, Lurgans, Carrickmacross, Co. Monaghan. Tel. 042/61035. 3 rms (none with bath).
$ Rates (including breakfast): IR£11.50 ($20.15) per person. 20% reduction for children. No credit cards. **Closed:** Nov–Mar.
Surrounded by woods and nearby lakes, this centrally heated bungalow is about a mile from Carrickmacross. Mrs. Rosaleen Haworth has three nice guest rooms with sinks, and takes a personal interest in all her guests.

READERS RECOMMEND

Nocdale House, 9 Ard Rois Avenue, Cloughvalley, Carrickmacross, County Monaghan (tel. 042/61608). "Mrs. M. Martin was the nicest and most accommodating hostess of any we *encountered—she even did our laundry for us—and her home is modern, clean, and pretty. The breakfasts were grand affairs served overlooking a beautiful mountain view."*—E. and M. Rogers, Long Island, N.Y.

3. COUNTY OFFALY

Centrally located County Offaly's attractions cover a wide spectrum, appealing to saints and sinners alike, with the monastic ruins at Clonmacnois, one of Ireland's most impressive ecclesiastical sites, and the Tullamore Dew distillery carrying on a revered brewing tradition.

WHAT TO SEE & DO

On the banks of the Shannon, 4 miles north of Shannonbridge (on R357 near the County Galway border) ✪ **Clonmacnois** (Cluain Mic Nois, "Meadow of the Son of Nos") is where St. Ciaran founded a monastery in 548. It was plundered by Irish chieftains, Vikings, and Anglo-Normans, and finally gave up the ghost when Cromwell's forces desecrated it beyond restoration. Today you'll find among its ruins a cathedral, eight churches, two round towers, the remains of a castle, more than 200 monumental slabs, and three sculptured high crosses. There are guided tours during the summer months.

The gardens at **Birr Castle** in the town of Birr (Biorra, "Spring Wells"), 23 miles southwest of Tullamore via N52, are open to the public. The castle was a much-besieged stronghold during the 16th and 17th centuries, and was later the seat of the earls of Rosse. The third earl had an observatory in the castle, where he designed a telescope that was, for some 80 years, the largest in the world.

Seven miles north of Birr via R439, you can visit the workshop, showroom, and tea room of **Crannog Pottery**, Banagher, County Offaly (tel. 0902/51324). In the town of **Tullamore**, 60 miles west of Dublin via N6 and N52, there are conducted tours of the **Irish Mist Distillery** (tel. 0506/21399), which sits on the south bank of the Grand Canal.

WHERE TO STAY

TULLAMORE

PADRAIG VILLA, Glaskill, Screggan, Tullamore, Co. Offaly. Tel. 0506/ 55962. 6 rms (2 with bath).

$ **Rates** (including breakfast): IR£12.50 ($21.90) per person. 20% reduction for children. Dinner IR£12.50 ($21.90) extra. AE, MC, V. **Parking:** Private car park.

✪ Mrs. Bridie Casey is a charming, hospitable hostess and her modern country home, 1 mile off the Tullamore–Birr road, is surrounded by pretty gardens. You will be welcomed here with tea or coffee and home-baked cakes. Mrs. Casey also serves a lovely dinner. The house is centrally heated.

BIRR

COUNTY ARMS HOTEL, Birr, Co. Offaly. Tel. 050/20791. Fax 050/21234. 18 rms (all with bath). TV TEL

$ **Rates** (including breakfast): IR£26 ($45.50) per person. AE, DC, MC, V.

The County Arms Hotel is a graceful old (1810) Georgian house that has been transformed into a comfortable and relatively inexpensive in-town hotel. Set in a wooded lawn, with gardens to the side and back, the hotel has been owned and operated by the Loughnane family for many years, and there's an air of friendly, personal service that's sometimes hard to come by in larger establishments.

WHERE TO EAT

TULLAMORE

Worth the Extra Money

MOORHILL HOUSE, Clara Rd., Tullamore, Co. Offaly. Tel. 0506/21395 or 21527.
  Cuisine: FISH/GAME/TRADITIONAL/VEGETARIAN. **Reservations:** Recommended.
$ Prices: Dinner IR£18 ($31.50). Service charge 10%. AE, DC, MC, V.
  Open: Dinner only Tues–Sun 7–10pm.

⭐ This award-winning dining room is located in the converted stables of a lovely old country estate on the outskirts of town. Specialties are fresh fish from nearby lakes and rivers, and game dishes in season. They also offer a choice of vegetarian dishes. Dinner here is a pleasant experience as well as a superb meal.

---

4. COUNTY LAOIS

Except for the Slieve Bloom Mountains in the northwest, the landscape of County Laois is that of Ireland's central plain. Its borders enclose one of Ireland's most perfectly preserved round towers and other significant relics of Irish history.

WHAT TO SEE & DO

There's a perfectly preserved 96-foot-high, 12th-century **round tower** at Timahoe, a few miles southeast of Port Laoise via R426, as well as the ruins of a castle and an abbey.
  Port Laoise is the principal county town, and 4 miles to the east atop the 150-foot-high **Rock of Dunamase,** on the site of an ancient Celtic fortress, are ruins of the Normal castle that was a part of the dowry given to the King of Leinster's daughter when she married Strongbow as part of the power struggle that first brought English forces to Irish soil.
  Nine miles south of Port Laoise, a **Cistercian abbey** was founded by Conor O'More in 1183 at Abbeyleix. The **de Vesci demesne,** adjoining the town, holds the tomb of Malachi O'More, a Laois chieftain.
  A delightful **scenic drive** is through the deep glen of O Regan in the Slieve Bloom Mountains. At Mountmellick, north of Port Laoise via N80, take the Clonaslee road and follow signposts for "The Cut." Some 7 miles south of Clonaslee, **Monicknew Woods,** with its nature trail, forest walks, viewing points, and picnic site, are an ideal spot to stop for a little spirit renewal or for a picnic lunch.

WHERE TO STAY

NEAR PORT LAOISE

CHEZ NOUS, Kilminchy, Port Laoise, Co. Laois. Tel. 0502/21251. 3 rms (none with bath).
$ Rates (including breakfast): IR£15 ($26.25) single; IR£12.50 ($21.90) per person sharing. No credit cards.

⭐ Ms. Audrey Canavan has won raves for her warm hospitality, exceptionally good (and varied) breakfasts, and attention to detail in the decor of her home, 2 miles from town, just off the main Dublin road. Antique furnishings are displayed throughout the house, and the attractive TV lounge has oak beams and adjoins a plant-filled sunroom that opens to the patio outside. Some guest rooms have canopied beds, and all are beautifully furnished. As for breakfast, Audrey offers the traditional Irish grill or an alternative that sometimes includes fish with a side salad, both served on a nicely appointed table.

ASPEN, Rock of Dunamase, Port Laoise, Co. Laois. Tel. 0502/25405. 4 rms (2 with bath).

$ Rates (including breakfast): IR£12 ($21) per person. 20% reduction for children. No credit cards. **Closed:** Nov–Mar.

In a pretty, wooded setting on the Port Laoise–Carlow road 3½ miles from town, Mrs. Noreen Llewellyn is the gracious hostess in this spacious, centrally heated bungalow. There are lovely woodland walks just outside the door.

5. COUNTY LONGFORD

County Longford, in addition to its hunting and fishing facilities, is noteworthy for its association with such literary figures as Oliver Goldsmith, Maria Edgeworth, John Keegan Casey, and Padraic Colum.

WHAT TO SEE & DO

In **Longford town,** look for the works of leading Irish artists at the **Carroll Art Gallery,** Ulster Bank Chambers, Main Street (tel. 043/41148). Of a more recreational (convivial?) nature, ✪ **Peter Clarke's Pub,** Dublin Street, is reliably reported to pull the "best pint in Ireland." The **Longford Arms Hotel** (tel. 043/46478) has live entertainment and dancing during the summer months. Visiting golfers are welcome at the **County Longford Golf Club,** Longford (tel. 043/46310).

Five miles from Longford on the main Granard road (N55), you can visit the splendid Victorian **Carrigglas Manor** (tel. 043/45165), which dates from 1857 and displays the original contents and furniture, as well as a costume collection.

Poet **Oliver Goldsmith** was born in Pallas, near Abbeyshrule (southeast of Longford town via R393), in 1728 and spent much of his life in this county. You can trace his footsteps, guided by the "Goldsmith Country" booklet published by the Tourist Board.

County Longford was home to **Maria Edgeworth,** the 18th-century author (*Castle Rackrent*) who was an angel of mercy during the famine years. In Edgeworthstown, east of Longford town via N4, there's a small **museum** dedicated to the Edgeworth family, of whom the most notable members were Maria, English-born novelist and essayist who spent most of her life in Ireland and did much to relieve suffering during the worst famine years, and her father, an inventor and author. Both are interred in the family vault in the churchyard of St. John's Church (which also is the last resting place of Oscar Wilde's sister, Isolda). The town's **historical museum** is open during the summer months.

Padraic Colum—poet, playwright, novelist, and essayist—was a product of County Longford. Born in 1881 in the Longford Workhouse, where his father was a master, he chronicled the lives of its peasantry with an honest eye.

IMPRESSIONS

The Irish . . . were distinguished by qualities which tend to make men interesting rather than prosperous.
—T.B. MACAULAY, *HISTORY OF ENGLAND, 1849–61*

The Irish . . . always ready to react against the despotism of fact.
—HENRI MARTIN, 1865

Are not young Irish geniuses as plentiful as blackberries?
—OSCAR WILDE, quoted by Katharine Tynan, before 1900

Ballymahon, south of Longford town via R392, and its environs are central to the works of poet **John Keegan "Leo" Casey.**

WHERE TO STAY
LONGFORD TOWN

TIVOLI, Dublin Rd., Longford, Co. Longford. Tel. 043/46898. 14 rms (5 with bath).

$ Rates (including breakfast): IR£11.50 ($20.15) per person. No credit cards.

Mrs. Breege O'Donnell is a longtime favorite hostess with readers. Her large two-story home is immaculate and well appointed, and her warm friendliness makes guests feel like members of her family. The house is centrally heated.

Worth the Extra Money

CARRIGGLAS MANOR, Longford, Co. Longford. Tel. 043/45165. 5 rms (all with adjoining bath), 3 luxury apartments.

$ Rates (including breakfast): IR£35–IR£40 ($61.25–$70) per person single or double; IR£150 ($262.50) per week luxury apartments. Dinner IR£18 ($31.50) extra. No credit cards. Bookings any day except Sun and Thurs.

⭐ This magnificent Tudor Gothic mansion 3 miles from Longford town is the home of Jeffry and Tessa Lefroy. The house itself has a romantic history—its builder was Lord Chief Justice of Ireland in 1837, who counted Jane Austen among his close friends (some think he was the model for Darcy in *Pride and Prejudice*). Reception rooms are the epitome of elegance, filled with heirloom furniture, artifacts, and family portraits. As for the five guest bedrooms, the two doubles come with canopied beds, a bit more luxurious than the one twin-bedded and two single rooms. The luxury self-catering apartments are in the renovated stables. The Lefroys ask that guests not plan to arrive before 6pm the first evening.

WHERE TO EAT
ABBEYSHRULE

THE RUSTIC INN, Abbeyshrule Village, Co. Longford. Tel. 044/57424 or 57469.

Cuisine: IRISH/VEGETARIAN. **Reservations:** Not required.

$ Prices: Lunch IR£7 ($12.25); dinner IR£12 ($21). MC, V.

Open: Daily 11am–11pm. **Closed:** Good Friday, Christmas Day.

 This family-run eatery specializes in traditional Irish cuisine, and it's the very place to taste Irish stew at its best and local fish and meats prepared in time-honored fashion.

6. COUNTY ROSCOMMON

Much of County Roscommon is level plain, bogland, and river meadow, broken with low hills and island-dotted lakes. Songwriter Percy French was born near the town of Elphin, north of Roscommon town via N61, and the blind harpist O'Carolon is buried in this county.

WHAT TO SEE & DO

Roscommon town sports the ruins of **Roscommon Castle** on a hillside overlooking the town, still intact enough to set your imagination flying back to its birth era in the 13th century. A wide variety of Irish crafts are available at the **Slieve Bawn co-op handcrafts market** (tel. 078/33058) in Strokestown, north of Roscommon town via N61 and R368.

Just west of Castlerea, 19 miles northwest of Roscommon town on N60, **Clonalis House** (tel. 0907/20014) dates from the 19th century and is the home of the

O'Conor Don, chieftain of the Clan O'Conor, onetime High Kings of Ireland, traditional Kings of Connaught, and Europe's oldest family, whose descent can be traced back through 60 generations to 75 B.C. It is furnished with Sheraton pieces and a collection of artifacts that includes O'Carolan's harp, rare glass and china, paintings, and Gaelic manuscripts. There's an exhibition of horse-drawn farm machinery and carriages, plus antique lace. Afternoon tea is available, as well as a craft shop. Call ahead for opening hours.

In Boyle, 27 miles northwest of Roscommon town via N61, the ruins of a **12th-century Cistercian abbey** are impressive, and if you'd like to see the interior, look up the caretaker whose home is just next door.

Two miles east of Boyle on N4, don't miss **Lough Key Forest Park** (tel. 079/62214). It's one of the country's loveliest, and especially interesting are the **Bog Gardens,** with heathers and other small plants that grow well in peat. During the summer months there's a good, moderately priced restaurant and a shop, but this is good picnic country any time of the year, with tables provided.

Lovers of traditional Irish music may want to make a pilgrimage to Keadue village (4 miles northeast of Lough Key) where the blind harpist **Turlough O'Carolan** lies in Kilronan Abbey cemetery (just west of the village), above whose arched gateway is inscribed: WITHIN THIS CHURCHYARD LIE THE REMAINS OF CAROLAN, THE LAST OF THE IRISH BARDS WHO DEPARTED THIS LIFE 25 MARCH, 1738. R.I.P.

WHERE TO STAY

NEAR ROSCOMMON TOWN

MUNSBORO HOUSE, Sligo Rd., Roscommon, Co. Roscommon. Tel. 0903/26375. 4 rms (all with bath).
$ Rates: IR£12 ($21) per person. 20% reduction for children. AE, MC. **Closed:** Oct–Mar.

Mrs. Delia Dolan is a gracious and helpful hostess, and her home is a very attractive, three-story, Georgian house situated on 150 acres of farmland 2 miles outside Roscommon town. There is horseback riding on the farm for both adults and children. Evening meals are available with advance notice and the four lovely bedrooms all have sinks.

Worth the Extra Money

ABBEY HOTEL, Abbeytown, Galway Rd., Roscommon, Co. Roscommon. Tel. 0903/26240. Fax 0903/25305. 20 rms (all with bath). TV TEL
$ Rates (including breakfast): IR£30 ($52.50) per person. Special discounts available. AE, DC, MC, V.

Roscommon is a short detour off the main Dublin–Galway road, and rewarding not only for its own sightseeing attractions, but because the 50 miles from Roscommon to Galway go through lovely rural scenery too often missed by visitors who stick to the highways. The Abbey is a very special place to overnight on this route. Within the lovely lawns and gardens that surround this marvelous 18th-century turreted mansion, ruins of a medieval monastery bear mute witness to the history of this part of Roscommon. The Abbey is a perfect base for a stopover to explore other monastic ruins and Norman castles en route cross country.

Owners Tommy and Anya Grealy carry on a family tradition of gracious hospitality that began back in 1878 when the Grealy family opened a coaching inn. The hotel today provides all modern comforts, but retains such mementoes of the past as the curved twin staircase with its stained-glass window at the landing, whose pattern the Grealys are having duplicated in panels for the front entry and lounge. Bedrooms are of good size, with attractive decor and comfortable furnishings. The bright, window-walled dining room overlooks the back lawn and specializes in fresh Irish produce and a good wine list.

Note: If you're traveling with a party of four or more, or if you plan a stay of several days, be sure to ask about special discounts.

NEAR BOYLE

HILLSIDE HOUSE, Doon, Corrigeenroe, Boyle, Co. Roscommon. Tel. 079/66075. 6 rms (none with bath).

$ Rates (including breakfast): IR£11.50 ($20.15) per person. 25% reduction for children. Dinner IR£11 ($19.25) extra. No credit cards.

 This comfortable, slightly old-fashioned home is the domain of Mrs. Taylor. It's in a beautiful, scenic location 3½ miles from town with views of Lough Key and handy to the Forest Park. The six homey bedrooms, all with sinks, are comfortably furnished, there's central heating, and the evening meal is quite good.

READERS RECOMMEND

Abbey House, Boyle, County Roscommon (tel. 079/62385). *"Martin and Christina Mitchell's house is beautiful, on gorgeous grounds between the ruins of a Cistercian abbey—and a river. The Mitchells go out of their way to make their guests extremely comfortable."*—Mary Barber, Bradford, Mass.

WHERE TO EAT

BOYLE

LAKESHORE RESTAURANT, Lough Key Forest Park, Boyle, Co. Roscommon. Tel. 079/62214.
Cuisine: SANDWICHES/SALADS/GRILLS. **Reservations:** Not required.
$ Prices: Less than IR£5 ($8.75). No credit cards.
Open: May–Sept, daily.

 Combine sightseeing with lunching in Lough Key Forest Park, 2 miles east of Boyle via N4. Picture windows overlook the boat basin, and you can choose from light meals (salads and sandwiches) or more substantial grills. Take-aways are available, and there's a wine license.

ROYAL HOTEL, Bridge St., Boyle, Co. Roscommon. Tel. 079/62016.
Cuisine: IRISH/TRADITIONAL. **Reservations:** Not required.
$ Prices: Lunch IR£7 ($12.25); dinner IR£12 ($21). AE, DC, MC, V.
Open: Lunch daily 12:30–3pm; dinner daily 6–9pm.

This is a comfortable, family-run hotel dining room that serves a variety of good Irish-style meals, with a wide choice of standard fish, beef, pork, lamb, and chicken dishes.

7. COUNTY WESTMEATH

County Westmeath is an ideal base from which to explore the entire Midlands region, as most major attractions in nearby counties are easy day trips.

WHAT TO SEE & DO

The county town of **Mullingar** is the center of one of the country's leading beef-producing areas. It's also the home of ✪ **Canten Casey's,** an intriguing 200-year-old pub, whose interior is much the same as it was in its infancy. Mullingar was an important barracks town for the British military, and there's an interesting collection of memorabilia of those years as well as Irish Army participation in U.N. activities in the Lebanon, Cyprus, and the Congo in the **Military and Historical Museum,** Columb Barracks (tel. 044/8391).

In **Athlone** (Ath Luain, "The Ford of Luan"), 29 miles southwest of Mullingar via R390, ✪ **King John's Castle,** which dates from the 13th century and figured prominently in the famous siege of 1691, is fascinating. There's a museum within its walls, as it is currently being developed as a Visitors Centre.

Athlone is where **John McCormack,** the famous Irish tenor, was born, and his birthplace is marked by a bronze plaque in the Bawn, off Mardyke Street. You'll know this is still a musical town if you drop into **Seans Bar,** Main Street (tel. 091/92358), where Irish music breaks out nightly. Shoppers will want to go by the showroom and workshop of **Athlone Crystal,** 28 Pearse Street (tel. 0902/92867), as well as **The Treasure Chest,** 96 Sean Costello Street, Irishtown (tel. 0902/75980), which has an exceptionally fine, wide-ranging stock of Irish giftware.

From an Athlone base, no fewer than five **stately homes** and gardens are less than an hour's drive: Birr Castle is 28 miles away; Clonalis House, Castlerea, is 40 miles; Tullynally Castle, Castlepollard, is 43 miles; Emo Court is 48 miles; and Abbeyleix, Woodland Gardens, 55 miles.

Plan to stop on the outskirts of **Kilbeggan,** east of Athlone via N6, to browse around ✪ **Locke's Distillery,** once one of the largest in Europe. Residents of the town rescued the fine old stone buildings after they fell into disrepair and then installed an interesting small museum, an antique shop, and a very good tea room.

WHERE TO STAY

IN & AROUND MULLINGAR

HILLTOP, Delvin Rd., Rathconnell, Mullingar, Co. Westmeath. Tel. 044/ 48958. 5 rms (all with bath).

$ Rates (including breakfast): IR£17.50 ($30.65) single; IR£12.50 ($21.90) per person sharing. 20% reduction for children. No credit cards.

 Dympna and Sean Casey's modern split-level home is 2 miles from town in a beautiful setting overlooking Lough Sheever. Dympna is an official of the Town & Country Homes Association and warmly interested in seeing that all her guests are comfortable and get the most from their holidays. All five guest rooms are nicely furnished, and all have private toilets and showers as well as sinks.

WOODLANDS FARM, Streamstown, Co. Westmeath. Tel. 044/26414. 6 rms (none with bath).

$ Rates (including breakfast): IR£11 ($19.25) per person. 50% reduction for children. Dinner IR£11 ($19.25) extra. No credit cards. **Closed:** Nov–Feb.

One of my favorite accommodations in Ireland is this farmhouse some 10 miles from Mullingar and quite convenient to Clonmachoise. Maybe it's because serenity sets in the moment you approach the rambling two-story home by way of an avenue of aged trees which often shade grazing horses. More likely it's the warm, friendly hospitality of Mary and Willy Maxwell and their attractive children that draws me back.

The house itself is charming, with a 200-year-old section to which a wing was added about a century ago that is still called the "new" addition. Parlor windows look out onto wooded grounds, and a fire is lit most evenings when a tea tray is rolled into the gracious room, which is furnished with antiques. Breakfasts are truly special, featuring fresh milk from their own cows and Mary's home-baked bread. The house has central heating, and the six bedrooms include one cozy single. Donkeys and pet sheep are an added attraction, and guests are given the run of the farmyard and grounds.

To get here, from Mullingar take the Galway road, then the road to Athlone; at Streamstown, look for the sign near the school. If you get hopelessly lost, just stop and ask—the Maxwells are well known in the Streamstown area.

READERS RECOMMEND

Lough Owel Lodge, Cullion, Mullingar, County Westmeath (tel. 044/48714). "Owel Lake is just behind Aideen Ginnell's home 2½ miles from Mullingar on the Sligo road. My daughter is still mentioning her breakfast as the best ever."—Eileen and Carolyn Kreinsen.

Lynton, *Ballinderry, Mullingar, County Westmeath (tel. 044/40383). "Joe and Mabel Barrett have a very comfortable, modern home which caters to hunters as well as regular tourists. There is a large hunting preserve nearby. The most interesting aspect of the house is the private museum displaying old Viking swords, Finian pikes, rifles, etc., collected by the owners from the surrounding countryside."*—D. McGrath, Long Island, N.Y., and E. S. Morley, Mamaroneck, N.Y.

GETTING TO KNOW NORTHERN IRELAND

Yet another face of Ireland lies across the border that marks the six-county province of Northern Ireland. Its green fields, cliff-studded and cove-indented coastline, forest-clad mountains, and above all its hospitable inhabitants are reasons enough to cross that border. Beyond those, there are elements found only in the North that will add an extra, very special dimension to your Irish experience.

To begin with, this is where you'll find the famed Giant's Causeway—mighty Fionn MacCumhaill's rocky pathway across to Scotland. So spectacular is the Antrim coast that many of the 40,000 American visitors each year settle into this part of the area for their entire stay. Yet what a pity to miss the gentler shoreline of County Down with its romantic Mountains of Mourne sweeping down to the sea. Quiet little villages on the Ards Peninsula look across to Scotland, and the countryside is dotted with Norman castles, forest parks beckoning the hiker, plus County Fermanagh's Lough Erne and its 300 square miles of boating and fishing. There are also the fabulous Marble Arch Caves, and the Sperrin Mountains of County Tyrone.

1. GEOGRAPHY, HISTORY & POLITICS

GEOGRAPHY Northern Ireland occupies the northeast section of the Irish mainland, comprising the counties of Antrim, Armagh, Down, Fermanagh, Londonderry, and Tyrone, with a coast bordered by the North Channel and the Irish Sea. Its geographical features are outstanding: a coastline marked with towering cliffs, secluded inlets, and wide, curving strands; the mountains of Mourne and of Sperrin; the Marble Arch Caves, the most spectacular in Europe; and the extraordinary rock

WHAT'S SPECIAL ABOUT NORTHERN IRELAND

Natural Spectacles

☐ The Giant's Causeway, in County Antrim, one of the world's wonders, with its 37,000 geometric-shaped basalt columns marching off toward Scotland.

☐ The Glens of Antrim, nine green valleys, each with a distinctly different character.

☐ Marble Arch Cave, in County Fermanagh, a vast, fascinating underground fantasyland.

☐ Lough Erne, in County Fermanagh, sprinkled with islands and an important fishing and cruising center.

Historic Monuments

☐ Carrickfergus Castle, a massive fortification dating from the 12th century.

☐ The ruined Dunluce Castle, near Portrush in County Antrim, perched on the very edge of a high cliff at the edge of the sea.

Folk Parks

☐ The Ulster-American Folk Park, in County Tyrone, an outdoor museum that reflects 18th-century life of emigrants from Ulster to America.

☐ The Ulster Folk and Transport Museum, just outside Belfast, undoubtedly the best reconstruction of 18th- and 19th-century rural homes and transport in Ireland.

Religious Sites

☐ Down Cathedral, in Downpatrick, thought to be on the site of St. Patrick's first church, where he is believed to be buried.

☐ The Church of Ireland Cathedral, burial place of Brian Boru.

---

formation known as the Giant's Causeway. Lough Neagh is the largest lake in the British Isles.

HISTORY   The ancient Irish province of Ulster has its own distinctive history, and is the setting for many of Ireland's foremost legends. It has a firm claim on a good part of Saint Patrick's Irish sojourn, from his first footsteps on Irish soil to his last.

In the 17th century, after the defeat of the Irish rebellion and the "Flight of the Earls," much of the land in Ulster was confiscated by the British Crown and "planted" with Protestant settlers from Scotland. Ulster gradually took on a more industrial and Protestant character than the rest of Ireland, with industry concentrated around Belfast.

The division between the two parts of Ireland began with the idea of Home Rule, first proposed in the 19th century, but finally established by the provisions of the 1920 Government of Ireland Act, which offered Home Rule to both parts of Ireland. While the 26 counties of southern Ireland became a Free State, and later an independent Republic, Protestant Northern Ireland, fearing to be overwhelmed by a Catholic majority, elected to remain part of the United Kingdom, to which it had close industrial and commercial ties.

An environment was set up in which the Catholic minority saw itself as disenfranchised and a victim of inequities of both the present and the past. It strongly yearned for a united Ireland that would improve its status. The Protestants, who have centuries of family history firmly rooted in Ireland, are fearful of change, and must contend with a status quo not of their making.

POLITICS   In 1968 the Civil Rights movement began, only to bog down as violence

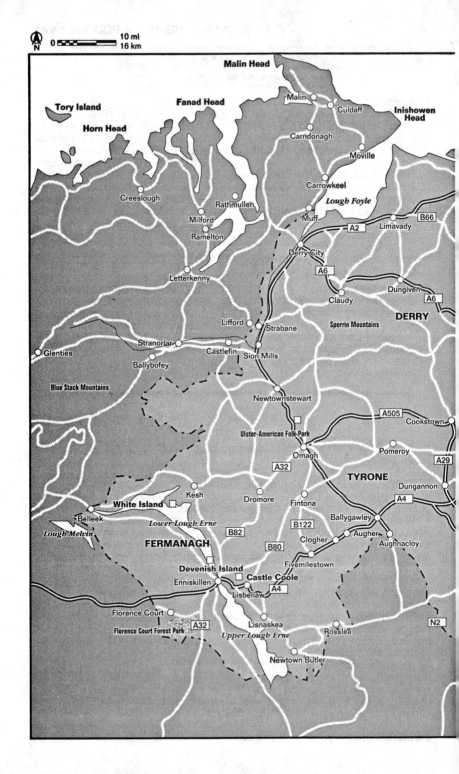

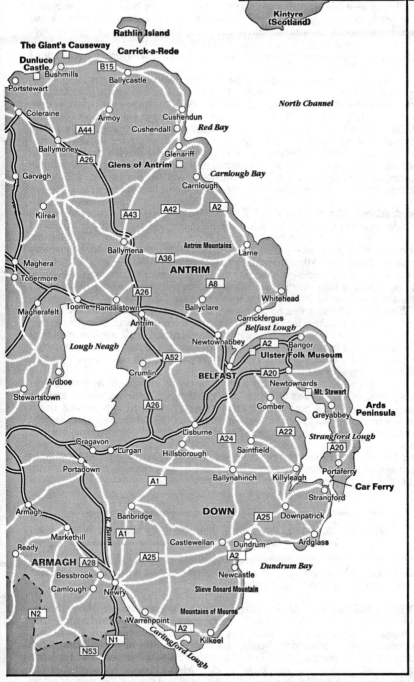

NORTHERN IRELAND

Kintyre
(Scotland)

North Channel

Rathlin Island

The Giant's Causeway   Carrick-a-Rede

Dunluce
Castle
B15   Ballycastle
Bushmills
Portstewart

Coleraine   Armoy   Cushendun   Red Bay
A44   Cushendall

Ballymoney   Glenariff
A26   Glens of Antrim

Garvagh   Carnlough Bay

Kilrea   Carnlough

A43   A42   A2

Ballymena   Antrim Mountains   Larne
Maghera   A36
Tobermore   ANTRIM   A8

A26   Whitehead
Toome Randalstown   Ballyclare
Magherafelt   Antrim   Carrickfergus
Belfast Lough
Newtownabbey   Bangor
Lough Neagh   A52   A2
Ardboe   Ulster Folk Museum
Crumlin   BELFAST   A20
Stewartstown   Newtownards
A26   Comber   Mt. Stewart   Ards
Peninsula
Greyabbey

Lisburne   Strangford Lough
Cragavon   A24   A22
Lurgan   Hillsborough   Saintfield   A20
Portadown   Portaferry
Ballynahinch   Killyleagh   Car Ferry
A1
Strangford
DOWN
Armagh   Banbridge   A25   Downpatrick
Markethill   A1   Castlewellan   Dundrum   Ardglass
Ready   A25   A2
ARMAGH   A28   Dundrum Bay
Bessbrook   Newcastle
Camlough   Newry   Slieve Donard Mountain
N2   Mountains of Mourne
Warrenpoint   A2   Kilkeel
N1   Carlingford Lough
N53

escalated and the British army was called in to keep a peace that still eludes them. In 1973 hopes were raised when a Northern Ireland Assembly held out the promise of active participation in government by the minority, only to be dashed when it was violently opposed by extreme factions of both sides. In 1974 there was an effort made to set up a power-sharing Executive, but it was too short-lived to make any headway. Today a Secretary of State for Northern Ireland is the chief administrator and reports directly to Parliament in London.

In May 1984 a report was issued by the All Ireland Forum that seemed to hold out more real hope of an eventual solution than any other development thus far. The Forum consisted of leaders from political sectors both north and south of the border, and it met nearly 100 times over the course of a full year. Its final report contained detailed, well-thought-out discussions of several acceptable compromises. In 1986 a highly controversial Anglo-Irish Agreement was signed, giving the Republic limited participation in Northern Ireland affairs. In the intervening years, it has remained in force and, with a few deviations, has seemed to walk a fairly steady path toward an eventual permanent political solution. Only time will tell if this, too, will be but another step along the long road to a free and peaceful Ireland.

What About the "Troubles"?   Every visitor to Ireland is concerned about the political situation and the "troubles" that make one hesitate to plan a trip there. As we go to press, the strife that has infected Northern Ireland since 1969 goes on, sometimes with long no-incident intervals, other times with headline-grabbing frequency. From time to time there are signs that a peaceful solution may yet be found to the problems that beleaguer the province. Talks continue between the political parties, to seek a solution that will bring peace and harmony to the region. But I cannot tell you that an end is in sight for these tragic "troubles."

What I can tell you is that up to this writing, no tourist has come to any harm (a comforting thought!), that the U.S. State Department has never issued a travel warning regarding Northern Ireland as an unsafe destination, that in all my own ramblings around Northern Ireland I have never felt endangered, and that the one guarantee I can unhesitatingly make is that the people of the province will welcome you warmly, delighted that you've come to visit.

That is not to say, of course, that you will be totally unaware of tensions. Border checkpoints, posted guards at hotels and other public gathering places, and the occasional armed road patrol you meet on country roads all indicate that this is indeed a troubled area. However, body and purse searches of the past have, happily, almost disappeared and at most checkpoints you are passed quickly through with a polite wave. Within the province, you'll see some hotels, public offices, or shopping areas fenced off with security personnel on duty. Only rarely will you be stopped when entering these areas, and even then you'll be sent through with a courteous smile after a quick look at your purse or shopping bag.

2. RELIGION, MYTH & FOLKLORE

RELIGION   About 60% of Northern Ireland's population is Protestant, because of its history of Scottish and English settlers.

MYTH & FOLKLORE   All that gorgeous scenery is not only a delight to the eye, but serves as well as a mighty spur to the imagination, for it has spawned a good many of Ireland's legends. It was in this part of Ireland that the brave Cuchulain roamed and, single-handed, guarded the border against the onslaught of Queen Maeve when she set out to capture the Brown Bull of Cooley. This was home territory for Fionn MacCumhaill (whom you may know as Finn MacCoul) and his faithful Fianna warriors. And the beautiful Deirdre o' the Sorrows played out her life's tragedy within the borders of Ulster.

If these tales of Northern Ireland's legendary heroes has set your mind soaring, let me recommend a marvelous little paperback on sale in most bookstores in Ireland: It's titled **Heroic Tales from the Ulster Cycle** and is published by O'Brien Educational Press, 20 Victoria Road, Dublin 6.

3. CULTURAL & SOCIAL LIFE

You will hear a mix of accents in the speech of the North. The soft burr of Scotland will fall on your ears, mingled with the clipped speech of England and the lilting Irish brogue. "Och, it's not a bad day at all," the Ulster men or women will remark; to which their Republican neighbors will reply, "Sure, and isn't that God's truth." It's an enchanting mix, and don't be at all surprised if you find yourself ending sentences with the distinctive lift that characterizes so much of what you hear.

Along with their speech, these descendants of Great Britain's plantation-era families have put into the mix strong elements of their cultures. Squash and cricket are sports you'll rarely find in the Republic, but they flourish above the border; the strains of traditional Irish music are interspersed with music of a distinctly British or Scottish lilt; Belfast's Opera House is as likely to play an English drawing-room comedy as an Irish classic by O'Casey or Synge. And while Orangemen parade in great numbers and with great gusto on July 12 to celebrate their beloved King Billy's victory at the Battle of the Boyne, there is no less a festive air about Catholic parades and celebrations on August 15, when the Ancient Order of Hibernian crowds take over to celebrate the Feast of the Assumption.

4. INFORMATION, ENTRY REQUIREMENTS & MONEY

INFORMATION   There are about 30 **Tourist Information offices** around the province, with helpful, friendly personnel anxious to help with any problem and make sure you see the highlights of their area.

The **Northern Ireland Tourist Board** headquarters is at River House, 48-52 High Street, Belfast (tel. 0232/246609), open Monday through Friday from 9am to 5:15pm, and from Easter to September and on public holidays, also on Saturday from 9am to 2pm. There is also an office in Dublin at 16 Nassau Street, Dublin 2 (tel. 01/679-1877).

ENTRY REQUIREMENTS   U.S. citizens need only a valid passport to enter Northern Ireland. British citizens need no passport for Northern Ireland (except as a form of identification).

MONEY   Northern Ireland uses the currency of Great Britain. As we go to press, the exchange rate against the American dollar is £1 = $1.85, and all prices quoted in these pages are based on that rate. In these uncertain days, exchange rates fluctuate with amazing frequency, so be sure to check the current situation when you travel.

Americans will be well advised to buy pounds sterling with dollars rather than Irish punts, since the dollar exchange rate is much more favorable—you can change your money at banks in the Republic before you cross the border if it's more convenient. One caution: If you're arriving in the North on a weekend or bank holiday, be sure to buy pounds sterling *before you come*. And, of course, it's always best to change your currency at a bank rather than in department stores or hotels.

In Belfast, the **Thomas Cook office,** 11 Donegal Place, Belfast 1, can also convert currency at the official rate. See the Appendix for an exchange rate table.

NORTHERN IRELAND
CALENDAR OF EVENTS

FEBRUARY

☐ **The Ulster Harp National Steeplechase,** Downpatrick, County Down. The only place to see horseracing in Northern Ireland. Late February to early March.

MARCH

☐ **Northern Ireland Spring Opera Season.** Begins in early March.
☐ **St. Patrick's Day.** Celebrated most colorfully in Downpatrick, Newry, and Cultra. March 17.
☐ **Belfast Musical Festival,** Balmoral, Belfast. Youth speech, drama, and music competitions. Early March.
☐ **Horse Plowing Match,** in Fair Head, Ballycastle. A century-old competition for farmers who plow the fields in a traditional way—no tractors.

APRIL

☐ **Belfast Civic Festival.** 15 days of concerts, competitions, and exhibitions culminating in a colorful parade for the Lord Mayor's Show. Late April or early May.
☐ **City of Belfast Spring Flower Festival,** Maysfield Leisure Centre, Belfast. Flowers and crafts star. Late April.

MAY

☐ **Belfast Marathon.** Traditional 26-mile dash. Early May.
☐ **Ballyclare Horse Fair,** in Ballyclare. You don't have to buy a horse to get a kick from the trading. Late May.
☐ **Royal Ulster Agricultural Society Show,** Balmoral, Belfast. Continuing a tradition begun in 1855, with international showjumping, sheep-shearing, goat and foxhound parades, bands, and fashion shows. Late May.

JUNE

☐ **Belfast Midsummer Jazz and Blues Festival.** Gathering of jazz musicians from around the globe. First week in June.
☐ **Black Bush Amateur Golf Tournament,** Causeway Coast. Special awards for visitors in this 4-day, four-course golf competition. Early June.
☐ **Fiddle Stone Festival,** Belleek. Fiddlers from all over Ireland gather during the 10-day Belleek Festival to play in honor of a famous 18th-century fiddle player. Late June or early July.

JULY

☐ **Enniskillen Festival,** Enniskillen. Music-making in pubs and street buskers make this town ring. Early July.
☐ **Ulster Senior Hurling Championship Final,** Casement Park, Belfast. Early July.
☐ **Battle of the Boyne Tercentenary Celebrations,** in Belfast, Londonderry, and 16 other town centers. Protestants (Orangemen) celebrate this important victory to the boom of gigantic drums and marching feet while bracing themselves for the flood of political and religious speeches that follow. July 12.
☐ **Sham Fight,** Scarva. Colorful reenactment of the Battle of the Boyne, with a joust between two horsemen garbed as William of Orange and James II. July 13.

AUGUST

☐ **Ancient Order of Hibernians Parades,** at various venues throughout the province. Feast of the Assumption celebrations with Gaelic pipers leading Hibernian processions and supplying the background music for open-air meetings. August 15.

SEPTEMBER

☐ **Belfast Folk Festival,** Belfast. A weekend of Irish folk music, dancing, and singing. Mid-September.
☐ **Dromore Horse Fair,** in Dromore, County Down. Clydesdales, Shires, and other big horse breeds star in this cavalcade of horse-drawn vehicles.

5. GETTING THERE

BY PLANE British Airways and Aer Lingus fly from the U.S. to Belfast International Airport via Shannon and Dublin airports, and other major U.S. airlines have connections through London's Heathrow and Gatwick airports.

From Great Britain, British Airways, British Midland, Dan Air, and several smaller lines operate between Belfast and London, Birmingham, Blackpool, Bristol, Cardiff, Edinburgh, Glasgow, the Isle of Man, Jersey, Leeds, Manchester, and Southampton. From Europe, KLM has regular service from Amsterdam.

BY FERRY There is quite good car-ferry service between Great Britain and Northern Island. **Sealink** (tel. 0776/2262) has frequent sailings between Stranraer and Cairnryan in Scotland to Larne (2½ hours); **P&O European Ferries** (tel. 058 12/ 276) operates frequent daily sailings between Cairnryan and Larne (2½ hours); and the **Isle of Man Steam Packet Company** (tel. 0624/72468) has regular sailings from June to September from Doublas to Belfast (4½ hours).

BY RAIL/BUS The Dublin–Belfast nonstop express train runs six times a day Monday through Saturday, and three times on Sunday. Phone the Belfast Central Station at (tel. 230310) for times and booking.

Ulsterbus (tel. 331577) operates coach service between Dublin and Belfast three times daily.

BY CAR If you're driving a rental car from the Republic, you should check to see that the insurance covers your stay above the border—and the same, of course, applies if you're going the other way. When coming from the Republic, it's always advisable to enter through one of the approved checkpoints, which are clearly marked on tourist maps. You won't have to show your passport or produce a visa.

6. GETTING AROUND

BY RAIL & BUS You can travel around the North quite easily and inexpensively using the rail and bus services. Day trips are also available to almost all sightseeing highlights. **Northern Ireland Railways (NIR)** has a 7-day, unlimited-travel Rail Runabout pass good April through October at a cost of £39 ($72.15) for adults, £19 ($35.15) for children. It's available at most railway stations. Primary rail service is from Belfast to Londonderry via Ballymena and Coleraine and Belfast to Bangor. Information on all NIR services is available at the **Travel and Information Centre** in Belfast's Central Station, or by calling 0232/230310 or 230671.

Ulsterbus service will get you almost anywhere there's no train, with departures from their stations on Victoria Street in Belfast, in the city center near the Europa Hotel (tel. 320574) and Oxford Street, near the central train station (tel. 232356).

BY CAR As in the Republic, driving is on the left. Northern Ireland has an excellent network of highways, with speed limits of 30 m.p.h. in town (unless a slower speed is posted), 60 m.p.h. on highways and country roads, and 70 m.p.h. on Northern Ireland dual carriageways (divided highways). Traffic circles are called "round-abouts," and exits are well marked.

Rental Cars The leading car-rental firms are **Avis** (tel. toll free 800/331-1212 in the U.S.), **Hertz** (tel. toll free 800/654-3131 in the U.S.), and **Europcar** (tel. toll free 800/227-7368 in the U.S.). All can be booked before your arrival or from their offices in Belfast (check the yellow pages of the Belfast telephone directory) and at Belfast International Airport.

Rules and Regulations There aren't that many, but you should know them in advance. The most important regulation concerns parking. When you see an area signposted CONTROL ZONE, it means that cars must not be left parked and unattended, even for a short time. In those areas, it is felt that cars left empty (even if locked) are a security risk, and the regulation is strictly enforced. There will usually be a parking lot close at hand with an attendant on duty.

BY TAXI There are taxi ranks at main rail and bus stations, ports, and airports. For other taxi service, check local telephone directories. Some of the black, London-style cabs are not metered, and you should agree on a fare to your destination when you start out. It's a rather common practice also to ask passengers to share a cab with other travelers if there is a long line (a money-saver, since your fare will be lower).

7. A SUGGESTED ITINERARY

The six counties of Northern Ireland are all good rambling country, and the following is by no means intended to be a rigid, not-to-be-deviated-from itinerary. It is, however, a convenient circular tour of the province that will get you to most of the highlights. My best advice is to allow at least 1 full week, 2 if time permits. As in the Republic, you're sure to discover some places not included in the outstanding sightseeing points listed in the county-by-county chapters that follow.

If you're coming from Donegal, the following route is recommended (and, of course, it can be reversed should your departure point be Belfast). From Londonderry, head east through Limavady and the Roe Valley to Coleraine and the Bann Valley. Then go on to Portrush and the Giant's Causeway. Bushmills Distillery is a short detour south from this point. Drive on through Ballycastle and enter the Antrim Coast Road, which takes you through the Nine Glens of Antrim, Larne, and Carrickfergus to Belfast. Then it's south to Downpatrick (if time permits, cut east around the Ards Peninsula) and west to Armagh, Enniskillen, and Belleek.

8. WHERE TO STAY

You'll find the same high standards for accommodations as in the Republic. The Northern Ireland Tourist Board maintains a strict inspection program. Bed-and-breakfast homes, guesthouses, farmhouses, and moderately priced hotels are in generous supply, and it is generally not necessary to book in advance—you can meander around the province pretty much at will without the worry of being stuck without a bed. The practice of charging more for rooms with private facilities varies from accommodation to accommodation, so be sure to check when you book.

A time-saving idea is to come armed with the Tourist Board's directory, **Where to Stay,** covering bed-and-breakfasts, hotels, youth hostels, self-catering, and caravan and camp sites. You can obtain a copy in advance for a small fee by writing to the Northern Ireland Tourist Board, River House, 48-52 High Street, Belfast, Northern Ireland; or British Travel Bookshop, Inc., P.O. Box 1224, Clifton, NJ 07012. It is also available at bookshops and any Tourist Office once you have arrived. The following will also be helpful: the illustrated **"Farm & Country Holidays"** booklet with about 100 listings; and **"Town & Seaside House Holidays,"** also illustrated and listing some 50 homes.

Contact the **Youth Hostel Association of Northern Ireland,** 56 Bradbury Place, Belfast BT7 1RV (tel. 0232/324733) for information about staying in hostels.

Note: During off-seasons (March to mid-June and mid-September to December), many Northern Ireland accommodations have special weekend and midweek packages. If you plan to visit during those periods, write to the Northern Ireland Tourist Board for their **"Holiday Breakaways"** booklet, which details such specials in all six counties.

9. FOOD & DRINK

The Tourist Board publishes a directory of eateries, **"Where to Eat,"** that covers all price ranges, from pub grub to posh restaurants, in all six counties.

MEALS A money-saver is the 6pm **high tea** served in many hotels and some restaurants—portions are ample, and the menu usually includes eggs, sausage, ham, or fish and chips. High tea is less expensive than the regular dinner menu (which most often goes on at 7pm). Best make reservations in the better hotel dining rooms and restaurants on weekends and holidays.

PUBS The last drinks are served at 11pm, although the doors don't close until 11:30pm. Pubs open at 11:30am every day except Sunday, when hours are 12:30 to 2:30pm and 7 to 10pm (the only remedy for a terrible thirst during other hours on Sunday is to get yourself to a licensed restaurant or a hotel bar).

10. SAVVY SHOPPING

Prices are generally lower in Northern Ireland than in the Republic for such items as Belleek, hand-woven tweeds, crystal, and many other fine products, although the price differential is fast closing.

Two shopping expeditions that can be enjoyable and profitable are those to **Belleek Pottery,** Belleek, County Fermanagh (tel. 036/565501); and **Tyrone Crystal,** Dungannon, County Tyrone (tel. 086/872-5335), but you should telephone ahead to make arrangements for your visit.

FAST **NORTHERN IRELAND**

American Express In Belfast, the American Express representative is **Hamilton Travel,** 23 Waring Street, Belfast (tel. 0232/230321).

Business Hours **Banks** are open Monday through Friday from 10am to 12:30pm and 1:30 to 3pm; closed Saturday, Sunday, and bank holidays. **Shops** are usually open Monday through Saturday from 9am to 5:30pm; closed Sunday and holidays. Most shops have one early-closing day a week, usually on Thursday.

Camera/Film   Film of most types is readily available, usually at chemist shops outside large cities. You'll find film, however, more expensive than in the United States.

Climate   See Section 2, "When to Go," in Chapter 2.

Currency   See Section 4, "Information, Entry Requirements, and Money," above.

Customs   Citizens of non-EC countries may bring in the following, if over the age of 17: 200 cigarettes, 50 cigars, and 1 liter of distilled beverages and spirits exceeding 38.5 proof, or 2 liters of other dutiable goods. Upon reentering the United States, you may bring back purchases valued up to $400 without paying Customs duties; anything in excess of that amount is assessed 10% on the next $1,000, and an average of 12% for anything above that. Antiques more than 100 years old are free with an authentication of age from the dealer. (Also see "Customs—Fast Facts" in Chapter 3.)

Driving Rules   See Section 6, "Getting Around," above.

Drug and Firearm Laws   There are strictly enforced laws prohibiting the importation of handguns or other illegal firearms, with stiff prison sentences as penalty. The importation of illegal drugs is also strictly forbidden.

Electricity   Northern Ireland's electricity is 220 volts AC, so if you bring small appliances (such as hairdryers), pack a voltage transformer and a variety of plug adapters. Electric shavers using 110 volts should be no problem, as there will be shaver points in every accommodation.

Embassies/Consulates   The **U.S. Consulate General** is at Queen's House, 14 Queen's Street, Belfast BT1 (tel. 0232/228239).

Emergencies   Dial 999 for fire, police, and ambulance.

Holidays   See Section 2, "When to Go," in Chapter 2.

Information   See Section 4, "Information, Entry Requirements, and Money," above.

Mail   United Kingdom postal rates apply, and mailboxes are painted red.

Newspapers/Magazines   The morning national newspapers are the *News Letter* and the *Irish News;* the *Belfast Telegraph* is the evening newspaper. All are published Monday through Saturday, and on Sunday most Northern Irish depend on U.K. papers, which are readily available.

Passports   See Section 4, "Information, Entry Requirements, and Money," above.

Pets   The same rules apply in Northern as in Ireland the Republic. All dogs and cats brought into the country from any country other than the U.K., the Channel Islands, and the Isle of Man must be kept in quarantine in a government-operated kennel for a period of 6 months at the owner's expense. All other animals are prohibited by the antirabies laws.

Police   The police are known as the Royal Ulster Constabulary. Except for special detachments, they are unarmed.

Radio/TV   The national radio stations are BBC Radio Ulster from Belfast, and BBC Radio Foyle, from Derry. There are a few independent regional stations as well, and good reception of the two RTE stations from the Republic and BBC Radio Scotland. Television channels are BBC Ulster Television (UTV), and most channels from both the Republic and the U.K. are received in Northern Ireland.

Safety   It is important to follow all rules (such as parking rules in Section 6, "Getting Around," above), and to cooperate with security personnel if such an occasion should arise. Whenever you are traveling in an unfamiliar city or country, stay alert. Be aware of your immediate surroundings.

Taxes   You will pay a VAT (Value-Added Tax) on almost every one of your expenses, with the exception of B&B accommodations. The percentages vary with the category of the services and purchases. See "Enjoying Ireland on a Budget," in Chapter 3 for details of recovering VAT on goods you take out of the country.

Telephones/Telegrams   See "Fast Facts" in Chapter 3.

BELFAST

In ancient times, Belfast was a fort set at a ford of the River Lagan (in Irish, Beal Feirste, "Mouth of the Sandy Ford"). A small village developed around it, and in the 17th century Protestant settlers from Scotland and parts of England moved in, while native villagers were moved out, by order of English rulers. The city grew at a steady pace until the end of the 1700s, due in large part to a thriving linen industry. In 1791 Wolfe Tone founded the United Irish Society in Belfast to bring together Protestants and Catholics who chafed under the repressive Penal Laws. In 1798 their efforts led to an uprising, one that was quickly squelched by English forces. The shipyard that was to contribute so much to the city's growth was opened in 1791, and by the time the Industrial Revolution was in full bloom during the 19th century, both shipbuilding and the linen trade welcomed newer, more modern operating methods. Both prospered, and Belfast's population grew by leaps and bounds.

The city today is a bustling, energetic center of industry, yet for the visitor it is easy to get around and holds many points of interest—most prominent of which has to be the good Queen Victoria, whose statue adorns Donegall Square and whose architectural style is in evidence all around the city.

1. ORIENTATION

ARRIVING

BY AIR   The **Belfast International Airport** (tel. 08494/22888) is in Crumlin, 19 miles northwest of the city center. There is mini-service into the city center. The **Belfast City Airport** (tel. 457745) is 4 miles to the northeast (for UK flights only).

BY TRAIN   The **Central Rail Station** (tel. 230310) is on East Bridge Street.

BY BUS   The **Ulsterbus stations** are on Great Victoria Street (tel. 320574) and Oxford Street (tel. 232356). The Great Victoria Street terminal is in the city center near the Europa Hotel.

TOURIST INFORMATION

The **Northern Ireland Tourist Board Information Office** is in River House, 48 High Street (tel. 0232/246609).

The **Irish Tourist Board** maintains a Belfast office at 53 Castle Street (tel. 327888) for information on the Republic.

The **Gay Counseling Service** maintains a telephone hotline (tel. 222023 Monday through Thursday from 7:30 to 10pm).

TOWN LAYOUT

The **city center** is fairly compact and easy to walk around. To the northwest is the **Shankill Road** area; to the west, the **Falls Road** area; south are the **Malone** and

Ballynafeigh areas; while to the east are the **Ballymacarrett, Sydenham, Bloomfield,** and **Belmont** areas.

GETTING AROUND

By Bus   Tickets for bus service within Belfast are available at the **Citybus kiosk** in Donegall Square West, Monday through Saturday from 9am to 5:30pm, and at news agents displaying the Citybus sign. Fares vary according to destination, and departures are from City Hall, Donegall Square, Wellington Place, Chichester Street, Upper Arthur Street, and Castle Street.

By Car   Arm yourself with a good city map from the Tourist Board, then be very sure to observe parking restrictions (see Section 6, "Getting Around," in Chapter 19). Your best bet is to drive to the city center and leave the car in an attended lot or garage.

By Taxi   There are taxi ranks at the Belfast International Airport, harbor ports, principal rail and bus stations, major hotels, and shopping centers, or you can call **V.I.P. Taxis** (tel. 666111). Some of the black, London-style cabs are not metered, and you should agree on a fare to your destination when you start out.

On Foot   To explore Belfast on foot, take it neighborhood by neighborhood— the city center, the university area, etc. There's good bus service to move you from one to another.

2. WHERE TO STAY

The Queen's University area is a happy hunting ground for bed-and-breakfast accommodations, and those listed outside the city are close enough to serve as a good base for exploring Belfast while enjoying the scenic countryside. The practice of charging more for rooms with private facilities varies from accommodation to accommodation, so be sure to check when you book.

IN THE CITY

BEAUMONT LODGE, 237 Stranmillis Rd., Belfast BT9 5EE. Tel. 0232/ 667965. 7 rms (1 with bath). **Bus:** 69.

$ Rates (including breakfast): £15 ($27.75) per person. Reductions for children. No credit cards.

Tucked away in lawns surrounded by green hedges, this sparkling white guesthouse has a feeling of seclusion despite its setting just off a busy road beside the New Ulster Clinic in the university area. There is good bus transportation into the city center, a convenience for nondrivers or for drivers who wish to leave their cars parked on the grounds. The ground-floor lounge is a striking, two-story room with floor-to-ceiling windows looking out to the lawn, and a classic red telephone booth, placed there by owner Valerie Kidd. The lounge has an interesting hooded fireplace, TV for guests, and tea and coffee makings (with biscuits always in supply). All bedrooms are bright and cheerful, and one of the

IMPRESSIONS

They call Belfast the Irish Liverpool. If people are for calling names, it would be better to call it the Irish London at once—the chief city of the kingdom at any rate. It looks hearty, thriving and prosperous, as if it had money in its pockets, and roast-beef for dinner: it has no pretensions to fashion, but looks mayhap better in its honest broadcloth than some people in their shabby brocade. The houses are as handsome as at Dublin, with this advantage, that the people seem to live in them.
—W. M. THACKERAY, *THE IRISH SKETCH BOOK OF 1842,* 1843

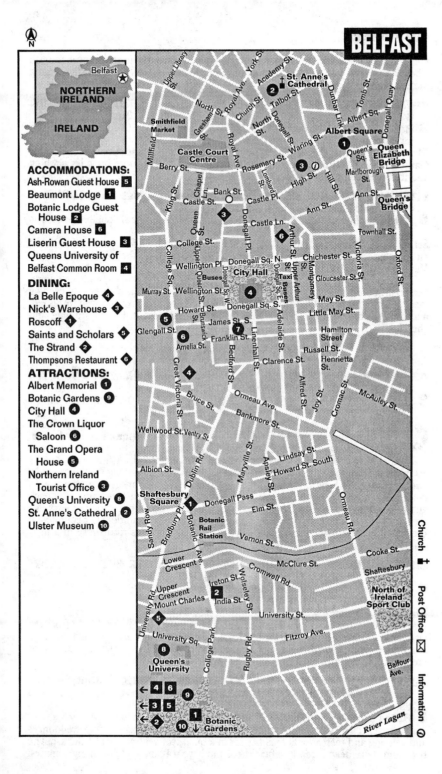

BELFAST

NORTHERN IRELAND

IRELAND

Belfast

ACCOMMODATIONS:
Ash-Rowan Guest House **5**
Beaumont Lodge **1**
Botanic Lodge Guest House **2**
Camera House **6**
Liserin Guest House **3**
Queens University of Belfast Common Room **4**

DINING:
La Belle Epoque ◆**4**
Nick's Warehouse ◆**3**
Roscoff ◆**1**
Saints and Scholars ◆**5**
The Strand ◆**2**
Thompsons Restaurant ◆**6**

ATTRACTIONS:
Albert Memorial ●**1**
Botanic Gardens ●**9**
City Hall ●**4**
The Crown Liquor Saloon ●**6**
The Grand Opera House ●**5**
Northern Ireland Tourist Office ●**3**
Queen's University ●**8**
St. Anne's Cathedral ●**2**
Ulster Museum ●**10**

Church ■+

Post Office ⊠

Information ⊙

family rooms has a private bathroom (all others share two toilets and shower rooms). There are several good restaurants nearby, but Mrs. Kidd will provide the evening meal if requested the day before.

BOTANIC LODGE GUEST HOUSE, 87 Botanic Ave., Belfast BT7 1JN. Tel. 0232/327682 or 247439. 14 rms (none with bath). TV **Bus:** 69.

$ Rates (including breakfast): £15 ($27.75) single; £28 ($51.80) double. Reductions for children. MC, V.

Mrs. Moore owns this nicely appointed guesthouse in the University–Botanic Gardens area. No-smoking rooms are available, and Mrs. Moore provides washing and ironing facilities for guests.

LISERIN GUEST HOUSE, 17 Eglantine Ave., Belfast BT9 6DW. Tel. 0232/660769. 7 rms (none with bath).

$ Rates (including breakfast): £14 ($25.90) single; £25 ($46.25) double. Reductions for children. No credit cards.

Set on a quiet street shaded by lime trees, Liserin is about a 15-minute walk into the city center, and there's good bus service at the end of the block. The brick Victorian-style town house dates back to 1892, and original woodwork, high ceilings, and spacious rooms add to its charm. Mrs. Ina Smith is the hostess, and she takes a personal interest in guests, serving evening tea and, upon request, a simple evening meal at a modest price. Guest rooms have sinks and are attractive and well furnished, and those in the back catch more sun than the ones in front, but all are light and cheerful.

WORTH THE EXTRA MONEY

ASH-ROWAN GUEST HOUSE, 12 Windsor Ave., Belfast BT9 6EE. Tel. 0232/661758. 4 rms (all with bath). TV

$ Rates (including breakfast): £28 ($51.80) single; £56 ($103.60) double. Dinner £15 ($27.75) extra. MC, V. **Parking:** Private car park.

After a career in award-winning restaurants, Evelyn and Sam Hazlett acquired this lovely late-Victorian residence and have turned it into a Grade A town house serving superb evening meals. Set back from the street in a quiet residential area between Lisburn Road and Malone Road, Ash-Rowan is only 10 minutes from the center of the city and provides private parking on the grounds. Each bedroom is beautifully decorated in individual style, and has a vanity unit, color TV, and razor points. An added feature is the dressing gown provided each guest—color-keyed to the room, no less! There's also a paperback library for the use of guests. The Hazlettes offer a choice of either a full traditional or continental breakfast, and both the cuisine and service of evening meals rival those in a first-class restaurant.

CAMERA HOUSE, 44 Wellington Park, Belfast BT9 6DP. Tel. 0232/660026 or 667856. 11 rms (all with bath). TV

$ Rates (including breakfast): £25 ($46.25) single; £35 ($63) double. No credit cards.

Miss Angela Drumm, a native of County Meath who has lived in Belfast for many years, is the hostess here. This lovely guesthouse is just a few minutes' walk from the city center. The red-brick Victorian-style house has bay windows in the guest lounge and dining room, giving a light, airy look to both. Four of the attractive guest rooms are singles, sometimes hard to find.

QUEENS UNIVERSITY OF BELFAST COMMON ROOM, 1 College Gardens, Belfast BT9 6BQ. Tel. 0232/665938. 25 rms (all with bath). **Bus:** 69.

$ Rates (including breakfast): £26 ($48) single; £40 ($74) double. MC, V.

These are excellent accommodations in a university environment. There are lounges and catering and recreational facilities set in a quiet, yet central, part of Belfast. The bedrooms have been recently refurbished, and have tea- and coffee-making facilities.

Special rates are available for long stays. Contact Mr. E. P. Black, accommodation manager.

NEARBY ACCOMMODATIONS

THE COTTAGE, 377 Comber Rd., Dundonald BT16 0XB, Co. Down. Tel. 0247/878189. 3 rms (none with bath). TEL
$ Rates (including breakfast): £14 ($25.90) single; £27 ($49.85) double. Reductions for children. No credit cards.

 Your enchantment with the Cottage is likely to begin even as you arrive, for the driveway brings you into full view of a lovely lawn and colorful flowerbeds that beckon the traveler to sit a while and enjoy such outdoor beauty. Mrs. Elizabeth Muldoon has realized every cottage-lover's dream—she has lovingly retained all the original charm of the house and at the same time has installed every modern convenience. The living room is picture-pretty, as is the rustic dining area, and bedrooms are beautifully furnished with many antiques scattered about. Decor throughout is in keeping with a traditional country home. Just a 3-mile drive east of Belfast via A20, the Cottage is one of the most inviting accommodations in the area.

GREENLEA FARM, 48 Dunover Rd., Ballywalter BT22 2LE, Co. Down. Tel. 0247/758218. 5 rms (none with bath).
$ Rates (including breakfast): £12 ($22.20) single; £22 ($40.70) double. 25% reduction for children under 12, 50% reduction for children under 8. High tea £5 ($9.25) extra; dinner, £7 ($12.95). No credit cards.

A comfortable old farmhouse that has been thoroughly modernized, Greenlea looks out from its hilltop on the Ards Peninsula and across to the misty coast of Scotland and the Isle of Man. Mrs. Evelyn McIvor is its warm, friendly hostess who teaches crafts and enjoys sharing her considerable knowledge of the area with guests. Both the lounge and dining room have picture windows that frame the spectacular view, and the dining room holds lovely antique pieces, with lots of silver and crystal on display. Recreational amenities include tennis and bowling. Mrs. McIvor has one large family room with bunk beds for two children and a double for parents, as well as accommodations for singles and doubles. Greenlea Farm is half a mile from Ballywalter, the first farm on the left on the Dunover road (about 23 miles southeast of Belfast via A2, at the top of the Ards Peninsula).

3. WHERE TO EAT

From pub grub to elegant restaurants, you'll find meals to suit your mood and your pocketbook in Belfast. Pick up a copy of "Where to Eat" to supplement the selections below.

PUB GRUB FOR LESS THAN £5 [$9.25]

You'll find good pub grub for about £5 ($9.25) from noon to 2:30pm at the following: **Crown Liquor Saloon,** 46 Great Victoria Street (tel. 249476); **Robinson's,** 36 Great Victoria Street (tel. 329812); **Beaten Docket,** 48 Great Victoria Street (tel. 242986); **The Front Page,** 106 Donegall Street (tel. 324269); **Linenhall Bar,** 9 Clarence Street (tel. 248458); **Rumpoles,** 81 Chichester Street (tel. 232840); **Botanic Inn,** 23 Malone Road, in the University area (tel. 660460); **Elbow,** 49 Dublin Road (tel. 233003); **Garrick,** 11 Montgomery Street (tel. 321984); and on the outskirts of town, **The King's Head,** Lisburn Road, Balmoral, opposite King's Hall (tel. 660455).

MEALS FOR LESS THAN £10 [$18.50]

NICK'S WAREHOUSE, 35/39 Hill St. Tel. 439690.

Cuisine: TRADITIONAL/SALADS.
$ Prices: Appetizers £2–£3 ($3.70–$5.55); salads £3–£4 ($5.55–$7.40). MC, V.
Open: Mon–Fri 11:30am–7pm.

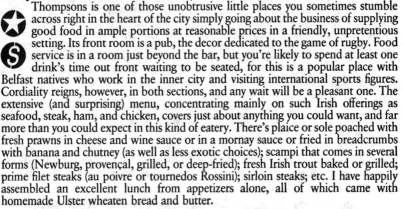

This casual restaurant and wine bar in the city center (near the Tourist Office, behind the cathedral) dishes up terrific meals for a pittance. Salads might include summer chicken and melon with yogurt-and-chive dressing and marinated herring with dill sauce, while lamb with red-currant sauce, filet of salmon with sorrel sauce, and sirloin steak with paprika and sour-cream sauce star on the main-dish menu, and vegetarians will go for the delicious nut roast. Between meal hours, this is a good place to drop in for a glass of wine and a nibble of their tomato-and-basil cheesecake.

SAINTS AND SCHOLARS, 3 University St. Tel. 325137.
Cuisine: TRADITIONAL/VEGETARIAN.
$ Prices: £4–£8 ($7.40–$14.80). No credit cards.
Open: Mon–Sat noon–11pm, Sun 5:30–10pm.

This popular eatery in the university area caters to the "scholars" in its name with a library decor downstairs, although the lively ambience does not lend itself to study. For quieter meals, opt for the upstairs dining room. In both, you'll have a choice of specialties like a cassoulet of duck, sausages, and beans, a selection of fresh fish with or without special sauces, and several vegetarian dishes.

THOMPSONS RESTAURANT, 47 Arthur St. Tel. 223762.
Cuisine: SEAFOOD/TRADITIONAL/OMELETS/SALADS/SANDWICHES.
$ Prices: Appetizers £1–£3 ($1.85–$5.55); main courses £4–£6 ($7.40–$11.10); omelets £2–£3 ($3.70–$5.55).
Open: Lunch Mon–Sat 12:15–3:15pm; dinner Mon–Sat 6–9:30pm.

Thompsons is one of those unobtrusive little places you sometimes stumble across right in the heart of the city simply going about the business of supplying good food in ample portions at reasonable prices in a friendly, unpretentious setting. Its front room is a pub, the decor dedicated to the game of rugby. Food service is in a room just beyond the bar, but you're likely to spend at least one drink's time out front waiting to be seated, for this is a popular place with Belfast natives who work in the inner city and visiting international sports figures. Cordiality reigns, however, in both sections, and any wait will be a pleasant one. The extensive (and surprising) menu, concentrating mainly on such Irish offerings as seafood, steak, ham, and chicken, covers just about anything you could want, and far more than you could expect in this kind of eatery. There's plaice or sole poached with fresh prawns in cheese and wine sauce or in a mornay sauce or fried in breadcrumbs with banana and chutney (as well as less exotic choices); scampi that comes in several forms (Newburg, provençal, grilled, or deep-fried); fresh Irish trout baked or grilled; prime filet steaks (au poivre or tournedos Rossini); sirloin steaks; etc. I have happily assembled an excellent lunch from appetizers alone, all of which came with homemade Ulster wheaten bread and butter.

MEALS FOR LESS THAN £15 [$27.75]

LA BELLE EPOQUE, 103 Great Victoria St. Tel. 223244.
Cuisine: FRENCH. **Reservations:** Recommended.
$ Prices: Dinner £15 ($27.75). DC, MC, V.
Open: Dinner only, 6pm–12:30am.

This is considered by many to be the best restaurant in Belfast. Cuisine here is of the French persuasion, with steak, pheasant, and lobster among the specialties. Reservations are recommended.

THE STRAND, 12 Stranmillis Rd. Tel. 682266.
Cuisine: TRADITIONAL. **Reservations:** Recommended.
$ Prices: Dinner £10–£15 ($18.50–$27.75). AE, DC, MC, V.

Open: Mon–Sat noon–11:30pm, Sun noon–10pm.

 Over in the university area, near the Ulster Museum and Botanic Gardens, this restaurant is popular with academics and local residents. It has won several awards for its outstanding food with dishes such as crabmeat-stuffed courgettes and chicken roulade with tomato sauce.

WORTH THE EXTRA MONEY

ROSCOFF, Lesley House, Shaftesbury Sq. Tel. 331532.
   Cuisine: SEAFOOD/TRADITIONAL. **Reservations:** Recommended.
$ Prices: Dinner £23 ($42.55). AE, DC, MC, V.
   Open: Dinner only, Mon–Thurs 7–11pm.
The 1930s are alive and well preserved in this sparkling restaurant at the foot of Great Victoria Street. Celebrities and public officials are often among its clientele, who come for such delicacies as roast monkfish, duck confit, and French pastry desserts.

4. WHAT TO SEE & DO

Make your first stop the **Northern Ireland Tourist Board Information Office** and pick up their excellent, free street map of Belfast and brochures on sightseeing highlights, city bus tours, day trips, and sports such as fishing, golf, and cruising for Belfast and for all of Northern Ireland.

ATTRACTIONS IN THE CITY

CITY HALL, Donegall Sq. Tel. 320202 ext 227.
   You can't miss this massive Portland stone building crowned with a copper dome. It was 10 years abuilding and its interior is elegant with Greek and Italian marble. The city's industrial history is traced in a large mural. If you don't recognize it otherwise, you'll know it by the bust of Queen Victoria out front (she was a guest of the city in 1846 and is much revered). A Great War Memorial sits on the west side, with a memorial sculpture to the *Titanic*, which was built in Belfast and went to the bottom in 1912.
   Admission: Free.
   Open: Guided tours, only with advance booking, Wed at 10:30am.

ALBERT MEMORIAL, High St.
   Look toward the river for the memorial—it pays tribute to Queen Victoria's consort and is affectionately known as Belfast's "leaning tower" because it is slightly less than straight.

HARBOUR OFFICE, Corporation Sq. Tel. 234422 ext 205.
   An interesting collection of stained glass, paintings, and sculptures—all dealing with Belfast's seafaring connections—is on display here. To see the collection, call the number listed above and ask for the administration officer in advance.
   Admission: Free.
   Open: By arrangement Mon–Fri 9:30am–4:30pm.

ST. ANNE'S CATHEDRAL, Lower Donegall St.
   Known locally simply as the Belfast Cathedral, St. Anne's was built between 1899 and 1904. It has a fine mosaic showing St. Patrick landing at Saul in A.D. 432, which you will find over the entrance to the Chapel of the Holy Spirit.
   Admission: Free.
   Open: Mon–Sat 10am–4:30pm, Sun at 11am services.

THE CROWN LIQUOR SALOON, Great Victoria St. Tel. 325368.

★ This marvelous old Victorian pub across from the Europa Hotel is the ultimate in casual elegance with its carved woodwork, snugs lining one wall, flickering gaslights, and painted ceramic tiles. Some "chrome and mirror" addicts got their hands on it a few years back and nearly modernized the character out of it, but the National Trust came to the rescue and it's now back to its original state.

Open: Mon-Sat 11:30am-11pm, Sun 12:30-2:30pm and 7-10pm.

THE GRAND OPERA HOUSE, Great Victoria St. Tel. 240411.

★ Try to catch a performance here. It's a marvel of rich, rococo eccentricity, with 24 gilt elephant heads separating boxes sporting canopies, Buddhas scattered about the draperies, and lots of gold and maroon. Closed from 1972 to 1981, it has been beautifully restored. It is centrally located, near the Europa Hotel and Crown Liquor Saloon.

BOTANIC GARDENS, Stranmillis Rd. Tel. 324902.

★ Cotton, banana, and coffee plants flourish in the Palm House conservatory that dates from the mid-1800s, and the Fernery is a splendid ravine in a sunken glen that you view from a balcony. The rose garden is simply spectacular. The **Ulster Museum,** with a fine collection of Irish antiquities and art, as well as treasures from the Spanish Armada shipwreck *Cirona,* is located within the garden. The entrance to the gardens is at the junction of Malone Road and University Road, adjacent to the Queen's University grounds.

Admission: Free.

Open: Gardens daily dawn-dusk; Palm House and Fernery, Mon-Fri 10am-5pm, Sat-Sun 2-5pm; Ulster Museum, Mon-Fri 10am-5pm, Sat 1-5pm, Sun 2-5pm.

ATTRACTIONS NEARBY

ULSTER FOLK AND TRANSPORT MUSEUM, Cultra Manor, Holywood, Co. Down. Tel. 428428.

★ This unique museum of folklife and transport is set on some 176 acres. The manor house holds a tea room and conference facilities, and there are interesting permanent and temporary exhibitions in the **Folk Gallery** and the **Transport Gallery** (which has a branch on Witham Street in Belfast). The open-air museum is composed of a fascinating collection of buildings of all types, rural and urban, from the 18th to the 19th century, all furnished in the style of about 1900—a microcosm of Ulster life of that period. Farms, an old church, a flax-scutching mill, schools, and many other buildings make this place well worth a visit of half a day or more.

Admission: £1.50 ($2.75) adults, 80p ($1.50) children (under 5 years old, free).

Open: May-June, Mon-Sat 11am-9pm, Sun 2-9pm; July-Sept, Mon-Sat 11am-6pm, Sun 2-6pm; Oct-Apr, Mon-Sat 11am-5pm, Sun 2-5pm. **Bus:** Ulsterbus no. 1 from Oxford Street station; it's 8 miles from Belfast on the road to Bangor.

BELFAST ZOO, Antrim Rd., Belfast. Tel. 776277.

A morning or afternoon at the Belfast Zoo is a delight. It's in a mountain park with good views of the city and the lough. A special feature is the underwater viewing of sea lions and penguins. There's also a moderately priced restaurant on the premises.

Admission: Apr-Sept, £2.50 ($4.65) adults, 80p ($1.50) children; Oct-Mar, prices are half.

Open: Apr-Sept, daily 10am-6pm; Oct-Mar, daily 10am-4:30pm. Last admission is 1-hour before closing. **Bus:** 2, 3, 4, 5, 6, or 45; it's 5 miles north of the city off Antrim Road.

TRACING YOUR ROOTS

Contact the **Irish Heritage Association,** 162A Kingsway, Dunmurry, Belfast BT17 9AD (tel. 0232/629595), for help in tracking down Irish ancestors. They'll research on a mail-order basis or provide professional help while you are in Ireland, both north and south of the border. They can also arrange personal "roots" tours for individuals or groups, and organize All-Ireland Heritage Tours and clan gatherings.

ORGANIZED TOURS

Citybus (tel. 246485) operates two Belfast tours at bargain prices. The 3½-hour ✪ **Belfast City Tour** gives you a good overview of the city's layout and visits prominent sites within the city, with a tour map giving details of major points of interest. The same-length ✪ **Parks and Gardens Tour** visits 15 parks and is accompanied by one of the City of Belfast Parks Department experts. Both tours are priced at £4 ($7.40) for adults, £2 ($3.70) for children. Call for departure times and booking.

5. SAVVY SHOPPING

Belfast city-center shops are open Monday through Saturday from 9am to 5:30pm, with late-night opening (until 8pm) on Thursday.

The pedestrian shopping area around **Donegall Square** and nearby covered arcades will satisfy the most avid shopper, with scores of boutiques selling everything from fine giftware to handcrafts to Irish linen and hand-woven woollens.

Leading department stores in this area are **Marks & Spencer** and **Debenhams,** branches of the famed London chains.

There's also good shopping in the **Botanic Avenue** and **University area.** On Friday mornings, the **Variety Market** on May Street is a lively shopping experience.

6. EVENING ENTERTAINMENT

Belfast offers a wide variety of things to do after dark, whether you fancy an elegant evening at the theater or a rousing good time on a casual basis in a singing pub. Check with the Tourist Office and in local newspapers to see what's on during your visit.

THE PERFORMING ARTS   Leading venues for opera, concerts, and musical variety shows are the **Grand Opera House,** Great Victoria Street (tel. 0232/240411), which presents everything from opera to pantomine; the **Arts Theatre,** Botanic Avenue (tel. 324936), for popular stage productions; the **Lyric Theatre,** Ridgeway Street (tel. 381081), for Irish plays, and experimental and international theater; and **Ulster Hall,** Bedford Street (tel. 323900), site of all things musical, from rock to the Ulster Orchestra.

THE PUB SCENE   Belfast's musical pubs are anything *but* hidebound traditionalists, although you'll hear some of the finest Irish music in the country here. It is, however, just one selection on a musical menu that includes folk, jazz, blues, and rock.

IMPRESSIONS

In Belfast they are of opinion that the Battle of the Boyne took place last Saturday week; actually, it happened two hundred and fifty years ago [in 1690].
—M. J. MACMANUS, *IRISH CAVALCADE*, 1939

There is a story that when incoming jets throttle back for the approach to Belfast's Aldergrove Airport, the pilots tell their passengers to put their watches back to local time—1690.
—QUOTED BY RUSSELL MILLER, *SUNDAY TIMES*, 27 April 1980

In the city center, clustered around Royal Avenue, look for: **The Front Page,** Donegall Street (tel. 324924); **Duke of York,** off Lower Donegall Street (tel. 241062); and **Kelly's Cellars,** Bank Street (tel. 324835). **The Linenhall,** Clarence Street (tel. 248458), is behind the BBC building, and on Ormeau Road you'll find the **Errigle Inn** (tel. 641410) and the **Parador Hotel** (tel. 491883).

7. EASY EXCURSIONS

You can visit many of Northern Ireland's outstanding attractions with easy day trips from a Belfast base. See Chapter 21 for Carrickfergus Castle, the Giants Causeway, and other Antrim Coast attractions within an easy drive to the north of the city. Chapter 22 highlights the top attractions of County Down to the south, most of which are a pleasant, relaxing day away from the city.

ORGANIZED TOURS Contact the **Ulsterbus Tours & Travel Centre,** 10 Glengall Street, Belfast BT12 5AH (tel. 0232/320011), for a plethora of marvelous half- and full-day excursions from Belfast listed in their "Ulsterbus Day Tours" booklet, available also from the Tourist Office. Highlights are tours to the Antrim Coast and Giant's Causeway, Nine Glens of Antrim, Bushmills Distillery and Giant's Causeway, and the Mountains of Mourne, but there are many, many more, including some into the Republic. Half-day tours cost about £6 ($11.10), and full-day tours run about £9 ($16.65) for adults (half fare for children). Every tour does not run every day, so be sure to check for current days of the week and departure times.

CHAPTER 21

COUNTIES ANTRIM & LONDONDERRY

1. COUNTY ANTRIM
2. LONDONDERRY CITY
3. AROUND COUNTY LONDONDERRY

These two counties hold some of Northern Ireland's true scenic wonders, a wealth of sightseeing attractions, and the province's second largest city.

1. COUNTY ANTRIM

County Antrim has perhaps the largest concentration of sightseeing attractions of any of the six counties. Americans will be interested to know that several **American presidents** had County Antrim roots: Andrew Jackson's parents came from Carrickfergus; Andrew Johnson's grandfather was from Larne; Chester A. Arthur's father was born near Ballymena; Grover Cleveland's grandfather was a County Antrim merchant; William McKinley's great-great-grandfather emigrated from Conagher, near Ballymoney; and Theodore Roosevelt's maternal ancestors were from Larne. Quite an impressive score for one county!

Perhaps the best way to explore County Antrim is to drive north from Belfast on A2 through Carrickfergus to Larne, where the **Antrim Coast Drive** takes you along the edge of the Glens of Antrim and on to the Giant's Causeway and Bushmills. While it's quite possible to cover the approximately 70 miles in 1 day and return to Belfast, a better plan is to take day trips into the countryside, as far north as Larne, and then to strike out on the Coast Road and plan an overnight stop. Such are the wonders of this spectacular coastline that you will want time to stop and savor each and every one.

Return to Belfast on the inland route via A26 southeast through Ballymena and Antrim town, turning east onto A52 at Nutt's Corner.

THE ANTRIM COAST DRIVE
WHAT TO SEE & DO

Northern Ireland's largest and best-preserved medieval castle dominates the waterfront in Carrickfergus. Massive **Carrickfergus Castle** dates from the late 12th and early 13th centuries, and its Great Hall is quite impressive, as are the grim dungeons. Climb to the battlements for spectacular views, and when looking out to sea, remember that it was here that Commander John Paul Jones stood offshore just below the castle in 1778 in the *Ranger* and mounted an attack on the British *Drake* that ended with his capture of the larger vessel. There's an interesting museum inside, with a small admission charge. In June, medieval banquets are held in the castle (call 096/03-63604 for reservations), and in July there's a medieval fair and crafts market. April through September it's open Monday through Saturday from 10am to 6pm and on Sunday from 2 to 6pm; other months, 4pm is closing time.

The ✪ **ancestral home of Andrew ("Old Hickory") Jackson,** U.S. president from 1829 to 1837, was just beyond the north end of Carrickfergus's seafront promenade at Boneybefore, a site now marked by a plaque. Just a few yards away, the **Andrew Jackson Centre** gives an insight into the life of his forebears. Open daily from 10am to 1pm and 2 to 5pm, plus daily from 6 to 8pm April through September.

Driving north from Carrickfergus, you'll pass through the nine ✪ **Glens of Antrim,** which open to the sea. You may want to call ahead and plan a stop to visit with **Jim McKillop,** 55 Ballymena Road, Carnlough (tel. Carnlough 885424). He was the Irish fiddle champion in 1976 and these days he makes, repairs, and sells all kinds of stringed instruments. He welcomes visitors unless, of course, there's a hooley, *fleadh,* or concert anywhere in the vicinity, when he's sure to be fiddling away.

Ten miles west of Cushendall, look for the signposted **Watertop Open Farm,** Ballyvoy, Ballycastle (tel. 02657/62576). This is a commercial hill farm in a beautiful setting that offers farm tours during July and August and, if you book in advance, pony trekking. It's a great experience for the younger set, and an eye-opener for parents who have never seen a working farm up close. There's also a farm trail, as well as a museum and tea room. Open daily from 10am to 5:30pm.

If you're an island lover, you'll want to reserve an overnight to spend on ✪ **Rathlin Island,** a rugged outpost off the Antrim coast that is Ireland's largest inhabited island. It has a fascinating history, and can be reached by boat daily from Easter through September, with departures from Ballycastle (tel. 02657/62024 to book). The mail boat makes trips on Monday, Wednesday, and Friday year round, leaving Ballycastle Harbour about 10:30am and not returning to the mainland until 9am the following day. There are marvelous cliff walks, magnificent views of Ireland's northern coast, and the fun of topping off the day at the one pub in the company of some of the 100 inhabitants. The island's only accommodation is the **Rathlin Guest House,** The Quay, Rathlin, County Antrim (tel. 02657/63917), run by Mrs. Kay McCurdy. Bed-and-breakfast rate is £10 ($18.50), with the evening meal costing £7 ($12.95).

If you're driving on the Antrim Coast Drive between May and September, stop about 5 miles northwest of Ballycastle to take a look at the **Carrick-a-Rede Rope Bridge.** The bridge has a wooden-plank walkway with rope handrails, and is strung across a 25-yard chasm to connect two clifftops separated by seas too treacherous to be crossed any other way. If you're not faint-hearted, you'll not be charged to walk over the bridge. There's a signposted roadside car park.

The ✪ **Giant's Causeway,** 8 miles east of Portrush, is much more impressive when you walk its basalt columns (there are some 37,000!) than any photograph can possibly convey. How they came to be packed so tightly together that they form a sort of bridge from the shoreline out into the sea, submerge, and then surface on the Hebrides island of Staffa, is a matter of conjecture. Scientists will tell you unequivocally that they're the result of a massive volcanic eruption about 60 million years ago, when molten lava cooled and formed into geometric shapes. But as far as the Irish are concerned, the causeway would still be above water all the way across had it not been for a ferocious tiff between the Ulster giant, Finn MacCoul, and his Scottish counterpart, Finn Gall. You see, it was the Ulsterman who built the causeway in the first place, and when he went home to rest up a bit from his labors, the wily Scotsman tripped across, club in hand, to catch his foe unawares. Now, Mrs. MacCoul was busy at the hearth with the dinner, and when Finn Gall burst into her kitchen and demanded to know if the sleeping giant were her husband, she—in a master stroke of quick thinking—assured him, "Ooh, no, sor, 'tis only ma wee babe." Well, the very thought of what the father of such a gigantic babe must be like put such a fright into the Scotsman that he hightailed it back across the water, destroying the causeway behind him to keep Finn MacCoul in Ireland where he belonged. Choose your own version, but don't miss a stop by this curiosity. It's free, and there's even a minibus (with a very small fare) down to the bottom of the cliff for those who don't care to make the short walk. You'll want time also to visit the Information Centre and craft shop, and there's a café for refreshment. The interesting audiovisual show is well worth the small admission.

Just east of Portrush, look for a rocky headland crowned by the great lump of ruined **Dunluce Castle.** Some say its name means "mermaid's fort," and they may

IMPRESSIONS

It looks like the beginning of the world, somehow: the sea looks older than in other places, the hills and rocks strange, and formed differently from other rocks and hills . . . shattered into a thousand cragged fantastical shapes; the water comes swelling into scores of little strange creeks, or goes off with a leap, roaring into those mysterious caves yonder. . . . The savage rock-sides are painted of a hundred colours. Does the sun ever shine here? When the world was moulded and fashioned out of formless chaos, this must have been the bit over—
—W. M. THACKERAY, THE IRISH SKETCH BOOK OF 1842, 1843

---

well be right—there's a deep cave that penetrates the rock on which the castle sits at the sea's edge. It's *so* close to the cliff's edge in fact, that back in 1639 a part of the castle fell away into the sea below, taking the kitchen staff with it. There are many other tales and legends surrounding Dunluce which you can read about in the official guide available at the entrance. From April through September you can visit the castle Monday through Saturday between the hours of 10am and 7pm and on Sunday from 2 to 7pm. During other months, closing time is 4pm, and it's closed all day Monday.

A short detour off the coast road will take you to the village of Bushmills and the oldest licensed distillery in the world. The ✪ **Old Bushmills Distillery** is a fascinating place, and still turning out "the wine of the country" after all these centuries. People in Northern Ireland will urge you to try Black Bush—do! To see an exhibition about its history and to see the distilling process, book for a free guided tour Monday through Thursday or Friday morning. There are sometimes schedule changes, however, so it's best to phone ahead. (tel. 02657/31521).

If you're driving on to Londonderry, continue along the coast to the pleasant little seaside resort of **Portrush.** Here, **Waterworld,** The Harbour, Portrush (tel. 0265/822001), is a terrific place to relax with or without the kids. There's a seawater aquarium, giant water slides, Jacuzzis, water cannon, kiddies' pool, and for the less energetic, a sauna, steam room, and two sunbeds. Also on the premises, the Mermaid Restaurant serves snacks, hot and cold meals, and nonalcoholic beverages. It's open in July and August Monday through Saturday from 10am to 9pm and on Sunday from noon to 9pm. Opening days vary in May, June, and September, and fees are £2.75 ($5.10) per person to the Water Play area, £3 ($5.55) for parent and toddler (under 2) to the Wet Play area.

WHERE TO STAY

Glenarm

DRUMNAGREACH LODGE, 406 Shore Rd., Glenarm BT44 0NG, Co. Antrim. Tel. 057/484529. 2 rms (none with bath).

$ Rates (including breakfast): £9 ($16.65) per person. Reductions for children. No credit cards.

This charming little house on the Coast Drive between Ballygally and Glenarm was once the gate lodge for the Drumnagreach manor house, now a first-class hotel (see "Worth the Extra Money," below). These days it's the home in which Marie Poland welcomes guests for bed-and-breakfast and provides two bright, attractive bedrooms. The hotel grill room is only a short, pleasant walk away for reasonably priced meals, and the coastal scenery along here is spectacular.

Carnlough

BETHANY CHRISTIAN GUEST HOUSE, 5 Bay Rd., Carnlough, BT44 0HQ, Co. Antrim. Tel. 0574/85667. 6 rms (all with bath).

$ Rates (including breakfast): £12 ($22.20) single, £23 ($42.55) double. Reductions for children and seniors. No credit cards.

Mrs. Mary Aiken's home on the seafront in the town center is a pleasant, homey place. Religious paintings throughout the house attest to her deep Christian faith, and as a practical measure of concern for her fellow human beings, she has provided on the ground floor one room especially suited to those who are wheelchair-bound, with a ground-level entrance from the outside and wide doors to both the bedroom and bath. There's a no-smoking rule in the lounge, dining room, and some bedrooms.

Cushendun

THE VILLA, 185 Torr Rd., Cushendun BT44 0PU, Co. Antrim. Tel. 026674/252. 3 rms (2 with bath).
$ Rates (including breakfast): £12 ($22.20) per person. Reduction for children. No credit cards. **Closed:** Nov–Mar.

 Mrs. Catharine Scally's Tudor farmhouse is within easy reach of the Glens of Antrim, and has an inviting, old-fashioned air, with stained-glass windows and antiques. The house has very comfortably furnished bedrooms with tea/coffee makers and beautiful views overlooking Cushendun. It's signposted from the Coast Drive.

At the Giant's Causeway

CAUSEWAY HOTEL, 40 Causeway Rd., Bushmills BT57 8SU, Co. Antrim. Tel. 02657/31210 or 31226. 16 rms (all with bath). TV TEL
$ Rates (including breakfast): £24 ($44.40) single, £40 ($74) double. Reduction for children. Good-value dinner, bed, and breakfast rates, as well as a mini-weekend special (2 nights dinner, bed, and breakfast). MC, V.

 This old-fashioned, country-Victorian-style hotel is the perfect place for an overnight stop to see the Giant's Causeway—it's just next door, a very short walk to the Visitors Centre. It was built in 1836 in the days when visitors arrived by jaunting car. In recent years it operated only as a bar and restaurant until Stanley Armstrong and his wife, Doreen, set about restoring it as a functioning hotel. Doreen has done most of the decorating and made exhaustive searches to find Victorian furniture in keeping with the hotel's history. An especially appealing room is the upstairs residents' lounge, with its sweeping views of the sea and causeway. Its bedrooms vary in size and decor, but all have tea/coffee makers and are comfortable and nicely done up.

Dining/Entertainment: There's a large public bar and a dining room overlooking the sea. Bar lunches, served daily from noon to 2:30pm, are less than £5 ($9.25); dining room meals, served from noon to 2:30pm and 7 to 9:30pm run £6 to £12.50 ($11.10 to $23.15).

Portballintrae

WHITE GABLES, 83 Dunluce Rd., Portballintrae, Bushmills BT57 8SJ, Co. Antrim. Tel. 02657/31611. 4 rms (all with bath).
$ Rates (including breakfast): £17.50 ($32.35) single; £31 ($57.35) double. Reduction for children. Discounts for more than 2-day stays. No credit cards. **Closed:** Nov–Feb.
Mrs. Ria Johnston is hostess of this attractive country house set in pretty countryside 2 miles from Bushmills. The house is centrally heated, there's a large guests' lounge, and washing and ironing facilities are available. Guest rooms are all very comfortable and homey, many with panoramic views of the nearby coast and all with tea/coffee makers. Mrs. Johnston is the proud winner of the 1989 Galtee All-Ireland Breakfast Award, which speaks for itself.

Portrush

A word about Portrush: Facing the sea on the eastern edge of Portrush, **Lansdowne Crescent** is a Victorian terrace with great views and value-for-dollar accommodations in a quiet resort area. Space does not permit full writeups on these exceptional guesthouses, but the following have all been inspected and have my recommendations, with rates averaging £12 to £18 ($22.20 to $33.30) single, £24 to £36 ($44.40 to $66.60) double, with discounts for families, off-season discounts for seniors, and baby-sitting services: **Alexandra,** 11 Lansdowne Crescent, Portrush BT56 8AY, County Antrim (tel. 0265/822284); **Belvedere,** 15 Lansdowne Crescent, Portrush BT56 8AY, County Antrim (tel. 0265/822771); **Clarmont,** 10 Lansdowne Crescent, Portrush BT56 8AY, County Antrim (tel. 0265/822397); and **Prospect House,** 20 Lansdowne Crescent, Portrush BT56 8AY, County Antrim (tel. 0265/822299).

ARDNAREE, 105 Dunluce Rd., White Rocks, Portrush BT56 8ND, Co. Antrim. Tel. 0265/823407. 5 rms (none with bath).
$ Rates (including breakfast): £12.50 ($23.15) single; £15 ($27.75) double. Reduction for children. No credit cards.
This chalet bungalow is on the coast road 1 mile from Portrush and 5 miles from the Giant's Causeway, overlooking the sea with the hills of Donegal in the distance. A beautiful beach is just a few minutes' walk away, and there's a good golf course in the vicinity. The centrally heated modern bungalow is the home of Mrs. Elsie Rankin, who takes a personal interest in her guests. The attractive guest rooms include two on the ground floor and one large family room, all with tea/coffee makers.

ATLANTIS, 10 Ramore Ave., Portrush BT56 8BB, Co. Antrim. Tel. 0265/82483. 14 rms (none with bath).
$ Rates (including breakfast): £13 ($24.05) single; £22 ($40.70) double. Reduction for children and seniors. No credit cards.
Just off the seafront in the eastern part of town, overlooking recreation grounds and a children's venture park, this Victorian-style town house has a large residents' lounge with a snooker table, and five of the attractive guest rooms are family-size. Some rooms on higher floors have terrific sea views. Margaret and Norman Torrens are the gracious hosts.

READERS RECOMMEND

Maddybenny Farm, 18 Maddybenny Park, Loguestown Road, Portrush BT52 3PT, County Antrim (tel. 0265/823394). "*Rosemary White won the 1989 Great Irish Breakfast Award, and her breakfast was very welcome after the daily Irish breakfast. Besides being an excellent cook, she is a delightful hostess, providing all the delights of a perfect B&B.*"—Janet Kenepp, New Holland, Penna.

Worth the Extra Money

BALLYGALLY CASTLE HOTEL, 274 Coast Rd., Ballygally BT40 2RA, Co. Antrim. Tel. 0574/83212. 29 rms (all with bath). TV TEL
$ Rates (including breakfast): £42 ($77.70) single; £60 ($111) double. Reductions for children. AE, MC, V.
Facing the beach of Ballygally Bay on Coast Drive 25 miles north of Belfast and 5 miles south of Larne, with fine views that reach as far as the Scottish coast, the castle dates from 1625. Constructed of local stone, in the Scottish style, it has remained unaltered in virtually every respect. Amazingly, modern plumbing, central heating, and other creature comforts have been added without destroying the character of this interesting old fortress. A modern extension housing hotel public rooms and additional bedrooms makes no effort to emulate the castle architecture, but the dungeon cocktail bar in the cellars of the castle is totally in keeping with its setting. All bedrooms (some in the turrets of the original building, more in the extension) are individually decorated.
   Dining/Entertainment: The dining room here has gained a widespread reputation, and inexpensive bar food is served from 12:30 to 2:15pm every day but Sunday. The dining room features moderately priced lunches those same hours, plus dinners daily from 6:30 to 9:15pm. Very popular with people in the locality are the Saturday-night dinner dances (from 7 to 11pm) and Sunday high teas (5:30 to 8:15pm).
   Facilities: There's a trout stream right on the grounds, many walks past streams and waterfalls, and less than a mile away, an 18-hole golf course. Just across the road, at the edge of the beach, the Ballygally Craft Shop offers a wide array of handcrafts at good-value prices.

THE BUSHMILLS INN, 25 Main St., Bushmills BT57 8QA, Co. Antrim. Tel. 02657/32339. Fax 02657/32048. 11 rms (all with bath). TV TEL
$ Rates (including breakfast): £38 ($70.30) single; £58 ($107.30) double. Reductions for children. AE, MC, V.

 This lovely little inn has been rescued from almost total deterioration by owners Roy Bolton and Richard Wilson, who have brought it back far beyond its beginnings as a coaching inn during the early 1800s. Its style these days is one that might be called "country elegant," with a small lobby that perfectly emulates a private drawing room. Upstairs there's a good library in the old round tower, with a whimsical concealed door. The luxury bedrooms all have pretty appointments, and two family rooms have intriguing "balcony beds" for the children—kids love them!

Dining/Entertainment: The Brasserie, a Victorian-style bar/restaurant complete with flickering gas lights, serves bar food, meals, and traditional afternoon tea daily from noon to 10pm priced at £5 to £10 ($9.25 to $18.50). The Barony Restaurant is fitted out with intimate snugs and dishes up first-class traditional meals daily from 12:30 to 2:30pm and 7 to 9:30pm; lunch runs about £7.50 ($13.85), and dinner costs about IR£14 ($25.90).

DOBBINS INN HOTEL, 6–8 High St., Carrickfergus BT38 9HE, Co. Antrim. Tel. 09603/51905. 13 rms (all with bath). TV TEL
$ Rates (including breakfast): £34 ($62.90) single; £58 ($107.30) double. Reductions for children. Weekend rates available. AE, MC, V.

If you have a secret picture of the perfect little Irish country inn, you'll be certain you've found it when you see the Dobbins Inn Hotel, with its pretty window boxes flanking the simple entrance. Inside, you're met with warm, friendly hospitality in a setting that reveals something of the history of this old building. The street on which it stands was once part of the grounds of the 16th-century Dobbins Castle, and during renovations, a great stone fireplace was uncovered in the present-day Coffee Room, as well as a short, walled-up escape passage and another passageway that connected Carrickfergus Castle to St. Nicholas Church by way of this building. Be sure to ask about "Maud," a ghostly presence said to haunt the castle/church passage. In an upstairs conference room there are framed documents also discovered during renovations.

Dining/Entertainment: The lounge bar serves snacks and light lunches from noon to 2:30pm for under £5 ($9.25), and the De Courcy restaurant has an inexpensive grill menu at lunch (same hours) and a moderately priced dinner menu from 6 to 9pm. High tea is available in the Coffee Room for £3 to £8 ($5.55 to $14.80).

DRUMNAGREACH HOTEL, Coast Rd., Glenarm BT44 0BB, Co. Antrim. Tel. 057/484651. Fax 057/841651. 16 rms (all with bath). TV TEL
$ Rates (including breakfast): £39 ($72.15) single; £55 ($101.75) double. Reductions for children. AE, MC, V.

Drumnagreach Hotel (its name means "the ridge on the marshy flat") has one of the most spectacular settings along the Antrim Coast Drive, between Ballygally and Glenarm high on a bluff overlooking the sea in front and the sweeping mountainsides of Glen Arn out back. Originally built for a linen merchant around the turn of the century, it was willed to his housekeeper in 1926, and has since seen service as a private residence, convalescent home, and hotel. Its present incarnation is that of a small hotel decorated and managed very much in the grand manner. A semi-Victorian flavor dominates the decor in the public rooms, from the reception area to the dining room, and grill room. Bedrooms are all well done up—ask for front or back locations depending on your preference for sea or country views.

Dining/Entertainment: The elegant octagonal Victorian dining room is in the conservatory style. An old-world-style grill room serves moderately priced meals in a more informal ambience. The emphasis is on traditional cuisine. Dinner in the lovely dining room runs around £16 ($29.60), grill room meals are in the £7 to £8 ($12.95 to $14.80) range, and there's an excellent Sunday carvery at £7 ($12.95).

LONDONDERRY ARMS HOTEL, 20 Harbour Rd., Carnlough BT44 0EU,

Co. Antrim. Tel. 0574/85255, 85458, or 85459. 21 rms (all with bath). TV
TEL
$ Rates (including breakfast): June–Dec, £27 ($49.95) single; £48 ($88.80) double.
Jan–May, rates are lower. Reductions for children. AE, MC, V.

This lovely old ivy-covered hotel in the town center, facing the harbor on the Coast Drive, began life back in 1854 as a coaching inn. Since 1947 the O'Neill family have been owners, and Frank (the present O'Neill manager) continues the tradition of gracious hospitality. There are beautiful antique furnishings; the tavern has a traditional decor, and the spacious lounge is warmed by a copper-hooded fireplace. Both the tavern and the lounge draw lots of locals. Guest rooms are beautifully done-up, and hand-woven Avoca bedspreads are a nice touch. Highly recommended, both for the high standards and for the O'Neills.

Dining/Entertainment: Meals are served in a dining room replete with period pieces, and if you can get a table in the front dining room, you'll have a view of the harbor as you dine. Lunch will run about £7.50 ($13.85), and dinner is about £11 ($20.35).

WHERE TO EAT

Besides the pubs and restaurants listed here, the hotels listed above in "Where to Stay" offer excellent places to dine or stop for lunch, especially the Dobbins Inn Hotel in Carrickfergus, Ballygally Castle Hotel in Ballygally, Drumnagreach Hotel near Glenarm, the Londerry Arms Hotel in Carnlough, the Causeway Hotel at the Giant's Causeway, and the Bushmills Inn in Bushmills.

Carrickfergus

COURTYARD COFFEE HOUSE, Scotch Quarter, Carrickfergus. Tel. 09603/69881.
Cuisine: SNACKS/SALADS/LIGHT MEALS/PASTRIES.
$ Prices: Less than £5 ($9.25). No credit cards.
Open: Mon–Sat 9:30am–4:30pm.

This is a good, inexpensive lunch stop as you set out on the County Antrim coastal drive. The self-service menu features light lunches such as soup, sandwiches, salad plates, quiche, and pastries, and you can eat in the light, bright indoor room or outside in the inner courtyard. It's across from the seafront on the northern end of town, just north of the town hall and library.

Portballintrae

For pub grub under £5 ($9.25), stop at the **Bayview Hotel,** Portballintrae, Bushmills (tel. 02657/31453), served Monday through Saturday from 12:30 to 2:30pm.

Portrush

The **Harbour Bar** (tel. 825044) is a good place for a before- or after-dinner libation. It sits on the wharf overlooking the boat-filled harbor, and it's mostly locals you'll find in the plain, old-style bar. Very Irish.

O'NEILL'S RESTAURANT, 36 Ballyreagh Rd., Portrush. Tel. 0265/ 822435.
Cuisine: CARVERY.
$ Prices: Full four-course meal £10 ($18.50); main course only £5 ($9.25). No credit cards.
Open: Lunch Mon–Sat 12:30–2:30pm; dinner daily 5–10pm.
This popular eatery serves an excellent carvery for moderate prices, and gives you the choice of a light or full meal.

RAMORE WINE BAR AND RESTAURANT, The Harbour, Portrush. Tel. 0265/823444.
Cuisine: SEAFOOD/TRADITIONAL/SALADS/BURGERS. **Reservations:** Recommended for dinner.

$ Prices: Salads, sandwiches, and burgers £4–£6 ($7.40–$11.10); full lunch £7 ($12.95); dinner £19 ($35.15). MC, V.

Open: Wine bar, Mon–Sat noon–2pm and 5–9pm; restaurant, dinner only, Tues–Sat 7–10pm.

 This award-winning restaurant in the town center on the waterfront offers excellent value, with full lunches of seafood, lamb cutlets with tarragon, duck breast with honey, filet or sirloin steak, and suprême of chicken, as well as less expensive burgers, sandwiches, etc. Needless to say, there's an extensive wine list, and you can order by the glass or the bottle. Downstairs, the wine bar rings with the conviviality of contented diners, while upstairs things are more restrained and elegant.

THE INLAND ROUTE

WHAT TO SEE & DO

Heading southeast on A26, look for signposts just north of Ballymoney for **Leslie Hill Historic Farm & Park,** Ballymoney, County Antrim BT53 6QL (tel. 02656/63109). This old-time working farm gives you an authentic look into the past of rural Northern Ireland. In addition to farm animals, there's a blacksmith's forge, pets corner, carriage display, horse and trap rides, and nature trails. There is also a picnic area (terrific idea) and a tea and craft shop. It's open in July and August Wednesday through Sunday from 2 to 6pm; from Easter through June and all of September, on Saturday, Sunday, and bank holidays from 2 to 6pm (closed October to Easter).

The farmhouse from which **U.S. President Chester A. Arthur's father** left for America in 1816 is at Dreen, near Cullybackey, Ballymena, and the whitewashed thatched cottage is worth a drive through beautiful countryside to meet the delightful people who maintain it for visitors like you and me. They'll greet you June through September, Monday through Saturday from 2 to 5pm. There's a small admission, but none for senior citizens and the handicapped.

In the town of **Antrim,** look for the perfectly preserved **round tower** that is 49 feet around and more than 90 feet tall.

WHERE TO STAY

BEN NEAGH HOUSE, 11 Crumlin Rd., Crumlin BT29 4AD, Co. Antrim. Tel. 08494/22271. 6 rms (none with bath).

$ Rates (including breakfast): £12.50 ($23.15) per person. Reductions for children. No credit cards.

This Georgian-style farmhouse in its parklike setting on the outskirts of town is the home of Mr. and Mrs. Peel, who make their guests feel right at home. Guest rooms are attractive and comfortable, and among the amenities are a grass tennis court and an indoor games room.

2. LONDONDERRY CITY

An aura of the ages lingers about Londonderry—in ancient times, it was known as Doire Calgach ("Calgach's Oak Wood"), later simply as Doire ("Oak Grove"). Then came St. Columba in A.D. 546 to found a monastic settlement which became Cholomcille Doire ("St. Columba's Oak Grove"). Some 10 centuries later, after years of seesaw battles to conquer it, King James succeeded in 1613 and promptly transferred it by charter to the City of London to be administered by the Honourable Irish Society, and its name became Londonderry. After all that, it's still affectionately called simply "Derry" by most of the Irish on both sides of the border.

Strong city walls 20 to 25 feet high and 14 to 37 feet wide, with seven gates, went up soon after the society took over, and despite siege after siege, those walls are still intact today.

ORIENTATION

TOURIST INFORMATION You'll find the **Northern Ireland Tourist Office** on Foyle Street (tel. 0504/267284), open Monday through Friday from 9am to 1pm and 2 to 5:15pm, and also on Saturday from 10am to 5pm June to August and 9am to 5pm September to May. The helpful staff will arrange accommodations (no charge) and walking tours, and provide sightseeing information for the city and its immediate vicinity.

The **Irish Tourist Board** is at the same address (tel. 0504/369501) providing assistance with matters south of the border.

Consult the **Women's Centre,** 7 London Street (tel. 0504/267672), Monday through Friday from 9:30am to 5pm for information and advice.

TOWN LAYOUT The **old, walled section** of modern-day Londonderry is west of the **River Foyle,** as are the main business and shopping districts, with ancient winding lanes and rows of charming Georgian and Victorian buildings. In the northeastern portion of the walls, Shipquay Gate is only two blocks from the river, and the historic old Guildhall with its turrets and tower clock is midway between river quays and this gate. Most of what you'll want to see will be within a short walk of these two points, including the bus station, Tourist Office, and inexpensive places to eat.

Surrounding the original, walled city and across **Craigavon Bridge** (south of the Guildhall), **modern Londonderry** has sprouted along the river and hillsides, covering almost 10 times the area that spawned it.

GETTING AROUND

By Bus For route and schedule information on intercity bus transportation, call 22261.

By Taxi Reliable taxi companies are **Central Taxi** (tel. 261911) and **Foyle Taxi** (tel. 263905).

By Car Unless you're exploring outlying areas, park the car and leave it—Londonderry is a great walking city, with major attractions in a compact area.

FAST FACTS

Londonderry's **telephone area code** is 0504. The **railway station** is on Duke Street, Waterside (tel. 0504/42228); the **Ulsterbus station,** on Foyle Street (tel. 0504/262261).

The main **post office** is at 3 Custom House Street, open Monday through Friday from 9am to 5:30pm and on Saturday from 9am to 12:30pm.

The **Bureau de Change,** 68 Strand Road, in the Richmond Centre (tel. 260636), changes currency Monday through Saturday from 9am to 5:30pm (to 9pm on Thursday and Friday) with no commission charge.

WHAT TO SEE & DO
ATTRACTIONS IN THE CITY

One thing you shouldn't miss in Londonderry is a walk along the ✪ **old city walls.** They are the only unbroken city walls in the British Isles, and Londonderry was the last city in Europe to build protective wall fortifications. Check with the Tourist Office about days and times of their guided walking tours along the walls (see below), and go along if you can—the narrative adds a lot to the city scene below and the landscape beyond. If you go on your own, enter at the Shipquay Gate.

Outside the walls, take time to stroll down narrow little streets such as **Albert Row** and **Nailor Row**, both lined with interesting and quaint houses and buildings.

GUILDHALL, Foyle St., Londonderry. Tel. 365151.

To get a look inside the imposing Gothic Guildhall, call the superintendent at the above number to arrange a guided tour—or better yet, try to catch one of the many concerts, plays, or exhibitions held here. The rock-faced sandstone building is quite impressive and has a somewhat-troubled history. It dates from 1890, but had to be almost completely reconstructed after a terrible fire in 1908 and again in 1972, when its interior was virtually destroyed by a bomb. Look for the window in the marble vestibule that depicts *The Relief of Derry*. The lovely stained-glass windows are the work of local artisans.

Admission: By arrangement for tour; regular admission for civic and cultural events.

Open: Tours can be booked Mon–Fri 9am–4pm.

ST. COLUMB'S CATHEDRAL, London St., Londonderry. Tel. 262746.

Built in the mid-1600s, the cathedral's basic style might be labeled "Planter's Gothic," but much of what you'll see today has been added since. One of its most important features is the memorial window showing the relief of the siege in 1689, and there's an interesting audiovisual presentation of the cathedral's role in Londonderry's history.

Admission: 50p (95¢) adults, free for children.

Open: Fri–Wed 9am–12:30pm and 2–4:30pm. **Closed:** Thurs afternoon.

O'DOHERTY TOWER, Magazine St., Londonderry.

Climb to the roof platform of this ancient tower for spectacular views of the city and its environs. It faces across to the Guildhall on the other side of the city walls and is often the venue for temporary cultural exhibitions.

Admission: 50p (95¢) adults, 25p (45¢) children.

Open: June–Sept, Tues–Sat 10am–5pm.

Walking Tours

Two-hour morning and afternoon guided walking tours within the city walls depart from the Tourist Office on Foyle Street on Monday, Wednesday, and Friday during July and August, with a £1 ($1.85) charge for adults, 50p (95¢) for children.

ATTRACTIONS NEARBY

AMELIA EARHART CENTRE, Ballyarnett/Shantallow Park, Co. Londonderry. Tel. 0504/267284.

A small cottage has been dedicated to the memory of the first woman to fly solo across the Atlantic, who landed in an adjacent field in May 1932. There's a commemorative sculpture at the landing site, and the cottage holds exhibitions centered around the famous aviatrix. It's 3 miles north of Foyle Bridge via A2.

Admission: Free.

Open: Cottage, June–Sept, Tues–Sat 2–5pm (closed Oct–May); Park, daily year round.

SHOPPING

Shopping is concentrated around the Diamond and pedestrian streets radiating from it. **Austin's,** on the Diamond (tel. 261817), is the leading department store, with an excellent, moderately priced, rooftop self-service restaurant (open late on Friday to 9pm).

The **Bookworm Community Bookshop,** 16 Bishop Street (tel. 261616), has a good selection of books of Irish interest.

EVENING ENTERTAINMENT

The **Guildhall** (see above) is the venue for concerts by the Ulster Orchestra and visiting orchestras, and for dramatic productions (including première performances of new plays by the Derry playwright Brian Friel). The theater in **St. Columb's** complex (see above) is the setting for several amateur drama productions, and the **Rialto Entertainment Centre,** Market Street (tel. 260516), presents variety concerts and plays.

The Pub Scene

Londonderry is rich in traditional Irish music, with musicians from neighboring County Donegal often coming over to join in. Check with the Tourist Office, or go by the following pubs to see when there will be music: **Phoenix Bar,** 10 Park Avenue (tel. 268978); **Gweedore Bar,** 61 Waterloo Street (tel. 263513); **Castle Bar,** 26 Waterloo Street (tel. 263118); and **Dungloe Bar,** Waterloo Street (tel. 267716). Another hangout of traditional musicians is **The Quaver,** 31 Carlisle Road, where its owner, young Doreen Rice, sells music and instruments (pick up a tin whistle for little or nothing and join in the tunes!).

To join in that most favored of all Irish pasttimes—good conversation spiced with wit—in a convivial setting, it's **The Linenhall,** 3 Market Street (tel. 371665), which also serves superb pub grub (see "Where to Eat," below).

WHERE TO STAY

Most city accommodations are well beyond the reach of budgeteers, but the Tourist Office can direct you to a few bed-and-breakfast homes in addition to those listed here.

IN TOWN

ABODE, 21 Dunnwood Park, Victoria Rd., Londonderry BT47 2NN, Co. Londonderry. Tel. 0504/44564. 5 rms (none with bath).

$ Rates (including breakfast): £9 ($16.65) single; £17 ($31.45) double. Reductions for children and seniors. No credit cards.

Mr. and Mrs. Dunn preside over this pretty bed-and-breakfast accommodation east of the River Foyle, south on Victoria Road, about 1 mile from the city center. Guest rooms are centrally heated and nicely furnished, and some are reserved for nonsmokers; all have sinks. There's private parking, a garden for guests to enjoy in fine weather, and washing and ironing facilities.

CLARENCE HOUSE, 15 Northland Rd., Londonderry BT48 7HY, Co. Londonderry. Tel. 0504/265342. 7 rms (2 with bath).

$ Rates (including breakfast): £12 ($22.20) per person. Reduction for children. High tea £10 ($18.50) extra. No credit cards.

Mrs. Eleonora Slevin has singles, doubles, twin rooms, and family rooms available in this well-kept brick town house. Guest rooms are quite comfortable, and the house and its hostess have become favorites of BBC and RTE television crews, who come back again and again. A bonus here are the facilities for washing and ironing those travel-weary duds. Baby-sitting can be arranged, and there are restaurants within easy walking distance.

FLORENCE HOUSE, 16 Northland Rd., Londonderry BT48 7JD, Co. Londonderry. Tel. 0504/268093. 5 rms (none with bath).

$ Rates (including breakfast): £11 ($20.35) per person. Reduction for children. No credit cards.

Mrs. McGinley is the hostess, and offers three doubles and two family rooms. The house has central heating, and Mrs. McGinley can arrange baby-sitting.

MRS. JOAN PYNE, 36 Great James St., Londonderry BT48 7DB, Co. Londonderry. Tel. 0504/269691. 2 rms (none with bath).
$ Rates (including breakfast): £11 ($20.35) per person. Reduction for children and seniors. No credit cards.

Nonsmokers are welcomed at this unpretentious town house. Both guest rooms are centrally heated, and Mrs. Pyne provides washing and ironing facilities. She can also arrange baby-sitting.

MRS. MARTINA HOLMES, 3 Columbia Terrace, Waterside, Londonderry BT47 1JT, Co. Londonderry. Tel. 0504/44269. 3 rms (none with bath). TV East of River Foyle in Waterside.
$ Rates (including breakfast): £10 ($18.50) per person. Reduction for children and seniors. No credit cards.

Mrs. Holmes, the hostess here, is especially happy to have families with small children. Guest rooms have sinks and are nicely furnished, the house has central heating, and baby-sitting can be arranged.

ROBIN HILL, 103 Chapel Rd., Londonderry BT47 2BC, Co. Londonderry. Tel. 0504/42776. 4 rms (none with bath).
$ Rates (including breakfast): £11 ($20.35) per person. Reduction for children. High tea £4 ($7.40) extra; dinner, £5 ($9.25). No credit cards.

You'll know that this is a special place as soon as you turn into the leafy drive around a lawn through which wild rabbits scamper. The house was built as a Presbyterian manse back in the late 1800s, and that era is mirrored in the large, bay-windowed parlor and spacious guest rooms. Malcolm Muir, father of two charming small boys, is host here and has done much of the decorating himself. Throughout, the furnishings reflect the character of the house, and front bedrooms look out to city views, while others overlook the garden. Mr. Muir cheerfully supplies a cot for children and arranges baby-sitting.

Robin Hill is east of the River Foyle. Take Spencer Road to Fountain Hill; Chapel Road is at the top of Fountain Hill, and Robin Hill is the first big house on the right (signposted).

Worth the Extra Money

WATERFOOT HOTEL, Caw Roundabout, 14 Clooney Rd., Londonderry BT47 1TB, Co. Londonderry. Tel. 0504/45500. Fax 0504/311006. 33 rms (all with bath). TV TEL
$ Rates (including breakfast): £41 ($75.85) single; £57 ($105.45) double. Reductions for children. AE, MC, V.

Set back from the highway in landscaped lawns, the restful setting of this hotel makes it hard to believe you're just a stone's throw from the city center at the eastern edge of Foyle Bridge. Its decor is softly modern, and guest rooms are spacious, attractive, and comfortably furnished, all with trouser press, hairdryer, and tea/coffee maker.

Dining/Entertainment: Tea, coffee, sandwiches, and scones are served in the lounge or foyer until 5:30pm daily at prices of 55p ($1) to £1.75 ($3.25). The nicely appointed dining room (a favorite with locals as well as guests) serves lunch daily from 12:15 to 2:30pm and dinner from 6:30 to 10:15pm Monday through Saturday, until 9:15pm on Sunday. The extensive menu is surprisingly moderate in price and includes such specialties as grilled trout in oatmeal, sirloin steak au poivre, lamb kebab, and lemon-whiskey chicken, all at prices ranging from £5.55 ($10.26) to £8 ($14.80). A nice feature is their selection of sauces (peppered, piquant, and chasseur) that can be ordered separately to dress up any dish you fancy. Specialty coffees include Irish, calypso, and royale.

NEARBY ACCOMMODATIONS

BALLYCARTON FARM, Bellarena, Limavady BT49 0HZ, Co. Londonderry. Tel. 05047/50216. 5 rms (none with bath).
$ Rates: £11 ($20.35) per person. Reduction for children. No credit cards.

Mrs. Emma Craig presides over this farmhouse which is beautifully situated on the Coast Road about 17 miles outside Londonderry, and 5 miles from Limavady, in 50 acres of mountain and coastal scenery. The comfortably furnished guest rooms have sinks and are all of ample size, many with good views. Mrs. Craig can arrange baby-sitting, and she doesn't mind travelers with dogs. The evening meal costs £10 ($18.50), and with advance booking, Mrs. Craig will prepare dinner for nonresidents.

Worth the Extra Money

WHITE HORSE INN, 68 Clooney Rd., Campsie BT47 3PA, Co. Londonderry. Tel. 0504/860606. 44 rms (all with bath). TV TEL
$ Rates (including breakfast): £40 ($74) single; £50 ($92.50) double. MC, V.

This is one of the nicest moderately priced hotels I've run across in Ireland. Its countryside setting 4 miles northeast of the city, on the Limavady road, is restful, and there's good, frequent bus service into Londonderry. The owners, Alwyn and Irish Kydd, have transformed an old inn into a modern, comfortable, and attractive hostelry. Guest rooms are spacious and well appointed, with tea/coffee makers, and there are washing and ironing facilities.

Dining/Entertainment: The Carousel Restaurant is a tasteful dining room serving all three meals daily, with specialties such as smoked Bellarena salmon. Yesterdays Grill Room is more casual, with a traditional menu of seafood, steak, chicken, and lamb, and is as popular with locals as with guests. The lunch menu is in effect from 11:30am to 7:30pm; dinner, from 7:30 to 10:30pm. There is often live music in the sophisticated bar and lounge.

WHERE TO EAT
PUB GRUB

Within the walls of the old city, ○ **The Linenhall,** 3 Market Street (tel. 371665), is a warm, convivial setting, very popular with local businessmen, for excellent pub lunches priced from £3 to £4 ($5.25 to $7.40). Affable owner Brian McCafferty has expanded the usual pub menu to include vegetarian dishes. Hours are noon to 2:30pm.

Other recommended pubs with similar hours and prices are: **The Venue,** Northland Road (tel. 266080); **The Metro Pub and Wine Bar,** 3 Bank Place (tel. 267401); and **New Monico,** 4 Custom House Street (tel. 263121).

RESTAURANTS

In addition to the restaurants listed here, see the hotel recommendations in "Where to Stay," above.

BELL'S, 59 Victoria Rd., Londonderry. Tel. 41078.
 Cuisine: CONTINENTAL/SEAFOOD. **Reservations:** Essential.
$ Prices: Fixed-price five-course dinner £12.50 ($23.15). MC, V.
 Open: Dinner only, Mon–Sat 6:30–10pm, Sun 3–9pm.
This elegant eatery is one of Londonderry's most popular, and with good reason: The kitchen uses only the freshest local products, and among the specialties are the rack of lamb and the vegetable cutlet. Service is friendly and efficient, and there's a good wine list. Bell's is east of the River Foyle, about half a mile from the city center.

JOHNNY B'S, 59 Victoria Rd., Londonderry. Tel. 41078.
 Cuisine: GRILLS/SEAFOOD/VEGETARIAN/TRADITIONAL. **Reservations:** Not necessary.
$ Prices: Lunch or dinner £3.25–£5.50 ($6–$10.15); child's plate £1.95 ($3.60). MC, V.
 Open: Lunch daily 12:30–2pm; dinner daily 5–10pm.
This downstairs restaurant is the casual, but sophisticated, moderately priced cousin to pricier Bell's, upstairs. Owner Mark Caithness has managed to imbue a smart black-and-white decor with coziness with an intimate grouping of tables. The

extensive menu includes lasagne, lamb kebab, stuffed pork filet, and a lovely vegetable bake. The steak-and-Guinness pie is also a great favorite here.

3. AROUND COUNTY LONDONDERRY

SEEING THE COUNTY

LIMAVADY   Limavady was founded back in Elizabethan times, and it gave Ireland one of its best-loved ballads, **"Londonderry Air,"** more familiarly known as **"Danny Boy."** The tune was an ancient traditional one passed from musician to musician until one Jane Ross committed it to paper after hearing it from a passing fiddler.

The town's major attraction is the nearby ✪ **Roe Valley Country Park,** 2 miles south of town via B192 (tel. 05047/62074), a terrific setting for that picnic lunch. The River Roe once turned water mills for linen production and powered Ulster's first hydroelectric plant in 1896. The old mills and the power station have been restored, and there's a museum in the old weaving shed. Activities inside the park include canoeing, rock climbing, and fishing, and there's a craft shop and café in the Visitors Centre. The park is open daily from 9am to 5pm, to 9pm June to mid-September.

If you want to picnic farther along the road, go by the **Bellarena Oak Smokers** (tel. 05047/50481), where fish are smoked by traditional methods, to buy oak-smoked fish. The smokery is open Monday through Friday from 9:30am to 4:30pm.

COLERAINE   Some 31 miles northeast of Londonderry via A37, Coleraine is the seat of the **University of Ulster.** There are concerts, theatricals, and other cultural events in its Diamond Hall and Octagon all through the year. Check for the current schedule by phoning the Cashier's Office (tel. 0265/52655).

About 8 miles northwest of Coleraine via B67, just west of Castlerock, **Magilligan Strand** stretches for 6 miles, Ireland's longest beach. The charming little seaside resort of **Portstewart** is just west of the County Antrim line on the coast road, only about 5 miles north of Coleraine. The western end of the **Antrim Coast Drive** is less than 10 miles north of town, with easy access to Bushmills, the Giant's Causeway, and Dunluce Castle. The Coleraine area is an ideal base for touring eastern County Londonderry.

WHERE TO STAY

CAMUS HOUSE, 27 Curragh Rd., Coleraine BT51 3RY, Co. Londonderry. Tel. 0265/2982. 3 rms (none with bath).

$ Rates (including breakfast): £15 ($27.75) per person. No credit cards.

✪   It's hard to say which is the more attractive, this 1685 country home 3 miles south of Coleraine (via A54) overlooking the River Bann or its owner, vivacious Mrs. Josephine King (known to all and sundry as "Joey"), who welcomes guests with tea and scones in a cozy sitting room in front of a fieldstone fireplace. The room's warmth is enhanced by lots of wood and the 125 handmade horse brasses that line the walls. Bedrooms are beautifully furnished and have sinks, spacious closets, and lamps placed strategically to give good light for reading. One family room sleeps four, one has three single beds, and one has a double bed as well as a single. In the sunny dining room, guests can tuck into a hearty Ulster breakfast fry of eggs and ham or bacon and wheaten bread accompanied by fresh fruit and juices. Joey will direct her guests to the best fishing spots on the river. It's no wonder at all that Camus House has won numerous country-house awards and gained a widespread reputation for hospitality.

KILLEAGUE HOUSE, Blackhill, Coleraine BT51 4HJ, Co. Londonderry. Tel. 0265/868229. 3 rms (1 with bath).

$ Rates (including breakfast): £14 ($25.90) single; £26 ($48) double. Reduction for children and seniors. No credit cards.

Mrs. Margaret Moore is the gracious hostess in this 1873 Georgian home on a 130-acre dairy farm 5 miles from Coleraine on A29. Guest rooms (the family room has shower and toilet) are nicely furnished. Mrs. Moore can arrange horseback riding instruction in the riding arena on the farm, as well as fishing on the river that runs through the premises.

WORTH THE EXTRA MONEY

BLACKHEATH HOUSE, 112 Killeague Rd., Coleraine BT51 4HH, Co. Londonderry. Tel. 0265/868433. 5 rms (all with bath). TV TEL
$ Rates (including breakfast): £35 ($64.75) single; £55 ($101.75) double. Dinner £16 ($29.60) extra. MC, V.

This lovely country house is set in rural surroundings 7 miles south of Coleraine. It's located near an excellent restaurant, although the hostess, Mrs. Erwin, will prepare dinner with advance notice. The house is centrally heated. A packed lunch is available should you want it, and washing and ironing facilities are there for guests to use.

READERS RECOMMEND

The Gorteen House Hotel, 187 Roe Mill Road, Limavady, Co. Londonderry (tel. 05047/63333). *"Every amenity, from good food to entertainment, is available at this mansion of yesteryear brought up-to-date by additions to both sides and back. Superior rooms make the night a comfort to be remembered."*—G. W. Howard, Silver Spring, Md.

CHAPTER 22

COUNTIES DOWN & ARMAGH

1. COUNTY DOWN
2. COUNTY ARMAGH

Counties Down and Armagh are not only filled with scenic beauty, but both have ecclesiastical roots that extend far back over the ages.

1. COUNTY DOWN

County Down is a study in scenic contrasts, from the beautiful strands that edge its coastline to the granite mass of the Mourne Mountains in the south to the Ards Peninsula in the east that juts into the sea to all but close the entrance to Strangford Lough. Aside from the attractions listed below, the county has great appeal for walkers and hill climbers. Movie buffs may be surprised to learn that actress Greer Garson was born in Castlelarne, County Down.

SEEING THE COUNTY

Leaving Belfast, the most rewarding ramble through County Down is to follow A2 through Bangor and along the Ards Peninsula to Portaferry, where a short car-ferry ride across the mouth of Stranford Lough connects to A25 into Downpatrick. From Downpatrick, a short drive southeast on B1 brings you back to A2, which carries on to Newcastle, then south around the coastline to Kilkeel. The road turns west along the shores of Carlingford Lough to Warrenport, then northwest into Newry, a major border-crossing point for the Republic. Along the coast, Bangor, Donaghadee, Newcastle, Kilkeel, and Warrenpoint are among the more important seaside resorts of County Down, and any one of them would make a good base from which to combine sightseeing with beach activities.

The ✪ **Ards Peninsula** is 23 miles of unspoiled countryside, dotted with picture-postcard villages, windmills, and ancient ring forts. Drive out to the little 19th-century village of **Kearney** and you go back through the centuries. The car-ferry that crosses from Portaferry to Strangford gives you a look straight out to sea (if, that is, you look quick enough—the crossing takes only 4 minutes). It is here, at Strangford Lough, that St. Patrick made his final entry onto Irish soil.

Near Strangford Village, **Castle Ward** is a fascinating house that's a sort of architectural hodgepodge, part pseudo-Gothic and part classical. The estate, administered by the National Trust, sits on the shores of Strangford Lough and includes formal gardens, a Victorian laundry and theater in the stableyard, and a sawmill. A tea room is open in the stableyard from April through October. The house is also open April through October from 10am to 5pm for a small admission charge; the grounds are open to the public without charge daily from dawn to sunset year round.

St. Patrick's first stone church is thought to have been erected on the site of the present-day **Down Cathedral** in Downpatrick, and a stone in the churchyard purports to be his gravestone (it's the one under a gigantic weeping willow tree), as

IMPRESSIONS

A land that floweth with milk and honey, a fertile soil truly if there be any in Europe, whether it be manured to corn or left to grass. There is timber, stone, plaster, and slate commodious for building everywhere abundant, a country full of springs, rivers, and lakes, both small and great, full of excellent fish and fowl.
—THOMAS SMITH, c. 1571

---

well as that of St. Brigid and of St. Columba. The fact that those assertions are a matter of much dispute does little to dispel the sense of the continuity of the centuries when you stand on the peaceful hillside site—certainly it would take a heart of stone not to believe that they *could* be true! To dispel doubts, stop by the **St. Patrick Heritage Centre,** The Mall, Downpatrick (tel. 0396/5218), open Tuesday through Friday from 11am to 6pm and on Saturday from 2 to 6pm.

Horse fanciers can check with the **Downpatrick Racecourse** (tel. 0396/5218), where there are about six race meets each year.

County Down has been immortalized by William Percy French for its **Mountains of Mourne** that "sweep down to the sea." One of the places you can best see that sweep is the resort town of **Newcastle,** which curves around a gorgeous bay with a wide, golden strand.

Nearby **✪ Tollymore Forest Park,** Tullybrannigan Road, Newcastle (tel. 03967/22428), is just off B180 northwest of town. It's a delightful wildlife and forestry reserve, with some magnificent Himalayan cedars and a 100-foot-tall sequoia tree in the arboretum. This is where you can walk in the foothills of the Mournes or go pony trekking or fishing. The park is open daily from 10am to dusk, and there's a small charge per car. Farther south, **Kilkeel** still has the ambience of an old-time seaside resort.

Four miles outside Newry, on the shores of Carlingford Lough, the **✪ Narrow Water Castle Art Gallery,** Narrow Water Castle, Warrenport (tel. 06937/53940), is the enthusiastic project of Maeve Hall, a former Dubliner. Devoting the ground floor of the imposing castle to art came naturally, since she has always had a deep devotion to art. The gallery is run as a nonprofit venture, with all proceeds going to a fund that will eventually create a place for an artist-in-residence. The gallery is usually open Tuesday through Saturday from 2 to 6pm, but it's best to call before you make a special trip.

The **Newry Arts Centre and Museum,** 1a Bank Parade (tel. 0693/61244), features exhibitions of ancient archeological items, folk art, and pottery, as well as touring exhibitions of interest. There's no admission charge, and it's open Monday through Friday from 11am to 4:30pm.

Bang in the middle of County Down (south of Belfast via A24), **Ballynahinch** might have been the setting for a dramatic change in the course of Irish history had not the 7,000 United Irishmen (led by a linen draper from Lisburn named Henry Munroe) been roundly defeated in their battle to take the town. The bloody battle raged the length of Ballynahinch's broad main street until, in the end, the royal forces were the victors. Munroe was executed, as was a young Presbyterian girl named Betsy Gray who had seized an old, rusty sword, mounted a horse, and joined in the fray. It was a last, desperate stand for the United Irishmen, and you might give a tip of the hat to their memory as you pass through.

WHERE TO STAY

During the summer months, many accommodations in County Down offer special-interest (fishing, golf, etc.), "Super Summer Saver," midweek, and weekend rates. For details, contact the Tourist Officer, Down District Council, Strangford Road, Downpatrick, County Down (tel. Downpatrick 4331). Remember, too, to inquire if there's an additional charge for private bath.

NEWTOWNARDS

This thriving town sits at the top of Strangford Lough 6 miles south of Bangor on A21 and makes a good base for exploring the Ards Peninsula.

BALLYCASTLE HOUSE, 20 Mountstewart Rd., Newtownards BT22 2AL, Co. Down. Tel. 0247/74357. 4 rms (2 with bath).
$ **Rates** (including breakfast): £13 ($24.05) per person. Reductions for children and seniors. No credit cards.

Mrs. Margaret Deering's home, 5 miles southeast of town on A20, is a beautiful 300-year-old farmhouse that has been elegantly refurbished. The house is centrally heated, and washing and ironing facilities are available for guests to use. Guest rooms are nicely appointed and have restful rural views.

BEECHHILL, Loughries Rd., Newtownards BT23 3RN, Co. Down. Tel. 0247/817526. 4 rms (none with bath).
$ **Rates** (including breakfast): £13 ($24.05) per person. Reduction for children. Dinner £8 ($14.80) extra. No credit cards.

Mrs. Joan McKee is the hospital hostess of this country guesthouse located in a pretty country setting 4 miles south of town on A20 (turn left at the Millisle signpost and left at Loughries school). The house is centrally heated and an evening meal is available with advance notice. There are washing and ironing facilities and one of the attractive guest bedrooms is a family room; all have sinks.

NEWCASTLE

GRASMERE, 16 Marguerite Park, Bryansford Rd., Newcastle BT33 0PE, Co. Down. Tel. 03967/22450. 3 rms (none with bath).
$ **Rates** (including breakfast): £12 ($22.20) per person. No credit cards. **Closed:** Sept–Feb.

⭐ This modern bungalow on the edge of Newcastle, off the Bryansford–Newcastle road (B180), is presided over by Mrs. Jean Hart. The two double rooms and one single all have sinks and views of the Mournes. Surrounded by green fields, Grasmere is only a 10-minute walk from the beach, and there's a golf course close by, as well as forest walks.

Worth the Extra Money

THE SLIEVE DONARD HOTEL, Downs Rd., Newcastle BT33 0AH, Co. Down. Tel. 03967/23681. Fax 03967/24830. 120 rms (all with bath).
$ **Rates** (including breakfast): £60 ($111) single; £90 ($166.50) double. Reductions for children and seniors. AE, MC, V.

⭐ At this turreted, red-brick Victorian hotel on the seafront, you look across Dundrum Bay to where the Mountains of Mourne sweep down to the sea, and then you can walk along the 4-mile curving sandy strand to their very feet. When the hotel was built, back in 1897, there were coal fires in every bathroom. These days every modern convenience is incorporated into public and guest rooms, somehow leaving intact a genteel atmosphere that evokes an era of sweeping long skirts and frock-coated gentlemen. Front rooms overlooking the sea are especially nice. Other rooms look out to the mountains or County Down Golf Course.

Dining/Entertainment: The Percy French pub and restaurant at the entrance is a whitewashed gate lodge serving food at moderate prices, and the hotel's main dining room excels in fresh seafood creations.

Note: Advance reservations are essential in summer.

KILKEEL

KILMOREY ARMS HOTEL, Greencastle St., Kilkeel BT34 4LJ, Co. Down. Tel. 06937/62220 or 62801. 12 rms (all with bath).
$ **Rates** (including breakfast): £18.50 ($34.25) single; £34 ($62.90) double. Reduction for children and seniors. MC, V.

In this pleasant seaside resort, the Kilmorey Arms is a delightful small inn, with the sort of homey atmosphere that draws Irish families back year after year. Its attractive public rooms are much favored by people in the town, and you're likely to find Miss Hopper, the friendly manager, scurrying around attending to last-minute details for a local wedding dinner or some other function. There's a nice cocktail lounge, and the flagstone-floored public bar is full of character, both from its relic-hung walls and from the faces passing the time of day at the bar (if you're just passing through Kilkeel, stop by this interesting bar for a pint).

READERS RECOMMEND

Wyncrest Guest House, 30 Main Road, Ballymartin, Kilkeel, County Down (tel. 06937/63012). *"Irene and Robert Adair work hard to make Americans feel welcome. The days we have spent in Northern Ireland have been delightful and very safe. Too bad more Americans don't visit and enjoy as we have."*—G. and P. Curten, Austin, Texas.

WHERE TO EAT
NEWTOWNARDS

The **Tudor Tavern,** 6 Georges Street (tel. 0247/815453), serves pub grub for around £3 ($5.55) Monday through Saturday from 11:30am to 11pm and on Sunday from 12:30 to 2:30pm and 7 to 10pm. For fish and chips at £2 ($3.70) and less, stop by **Scrabo Cafe,** 187 Mill Street (tel. 0247/810963), Monday through Saturday from 12:30 to 2:30pm and 8 to 11pm.

SKETTRICK ISLAND

DAFT EDDYS, Skettrick Island, Whiterock. Tel. 0238/541615.
   Cuisine: SEAFOOD/TRADITIONAL. **Reservations:** Not required.
$ **Prices:** Buffet lunch £6 ($11.10); dinner £5–£10 ($9.25–$18.50). No credit cards.
   Open: Lunch Mon–Sat 12:30–2:30pm; dinner Tues–Sat 6:30–9:30pm.

This island bar and restaurant serves an excellent hot and cold buffet lunch, with à la carte selections at dinner. Specialties are salmon, prawns, and steaks. You'll find Daft Eddys just offshore (connected by a causeway) from Killinchy on A22 halfway between Comber and Killyleagh on the western shore of Strangford Lough.

DOWNPATRICK

REA'S, 78 Market St., Downpatrick. Tel. 612017.
   Cuisine: SEAFOOD/TRADITIONAL. **Reservations:** Not required.
$ **Prices:** Lunch £3–£5 ($5.55–$9.25); dinner £10–£15 ($18.50–$27.75). No credit cards.
   Open: Lunch Mon–Sat 11:30am–3pm; dinner Mon–Sat 7–9:30pm.

This charmer is an old-style place, with two small front rooms crammed full of an eclectic collection of old objects (like the pottery bottle that was once used to hold Guinness, a marble for its stopper). Second, it always has the contented hum of a good crowd—many of them obviously regulars—enjoying good company and good food. There's a more modern dining room in back of those character-filled front rooms, and an almost-formal dining room upstairs (fireplace, gilt mirrors, etc.). Fresh seafood is the specialty here, but the menu includes beef, lamb, and other main dishes for non–fish lovers.

BALLYNAHINCH

PRIMROSE BAR, 30 Main St., Ballynahinch. Tel. 0238/36177.
   Cuisine: TRADITIONAL/SEAFOOD/SALADS. **Reservations:** Not required.

$ Prices: Appetizers £1.70–£5 ($3.15–$9.25); main courses £4–£8 ($7.40–$14.80). No credit cards.

Open: Mon–Sat 12:30–9:30pm.

The Primrose is known locally for its steak casseroles and open-face prawn sandwiches. Other offerings include fresh trout, salmon, pizza, and a variety of salads. There's always a nice fire blazing, and as a Northern Ireland friend assured me, "The crack [talk] is always good."

Their adjacent **Primrose Pop-In** serves afternoon tea, quiche, and pies Monday through Saturday from 9am to 5:30pm.

2. COUNTY ARMAGH

Armagh, Northern Ireland's smallest county, is a land of gentle hills and fertile fields, and its principal city of Armagh, in prehistoric times the seat of Ulster kings, has been Ireland's ecclesiastical capital for some 1,500 years.

SEEING THE COUNTY

With imposing edifices of both the Catholic and Protestant faiths facing each other from their respective hilltops, Armagh is Northern Ireland's most interesting cathedral town. According to a tablet on the north side of the ✪ **Church of Ireland cathedral** (restored in the 18th and 19th centuries), this is the final resting place of Brian Boru. In the Gothic-style ✪ **Roman Catholic cathedral,** which dates from the mid-1800s, you'll find the red hat of every cardinal archbishop of Armagh and medallions for each of Ireland's saints.

On the Mall in Armagh town, there's a fine small **County Museum** that holds an exceptionally good collection of prehistoric relics, historical costumes, and natural-history exhibits as well as an art gallery. It's free, and open Monday through Saturday from 10am to 1pm and 2 to 5pm. Also on the Mall is the **Royal Irish Fusiliers Regimental Museum,** housed in the Sovereign's House and open Monday through Friday from 10am to 12:30pm and 2 to 4:30pm.

About 2 miles outside Newry on the Newtownhamilton road (A25), there's an interesting 18th-century thatched manor house. **Derrymore House** (tel. Saintfield 0238/510721) is reputed to have been the setting for the Act of Union between Great Britain and Ireland. The 48-acre park is open daily, and you can go through the house by calling ahead for an appointment.

WHERE TO STAY
ARMAGH TOWN

ALTAVALLEN HOUSE, 99 Cathedral Rd., Armagh BT61 8AE, Co. Armagh. Tel. 0861/522387. 6 rms (none with bath).

$ Rates (including breakfast): £12.50 ($23.15) single; £21 ($38.85) double. Reduction for children. No credit cards.

Mrs. McRoberts' pleasant home has nicely appointed and comfortably furnished guest rooms all with sinks. She is happy to arrange baby-sitting, and in general is most helpful to her guests.

NEAR PORTADOWN

REDBRICK HOUSE, Corbrackey Lane, Portadown BT62 1PQ, Co. Down. Tel. 0762/335268. 5 rms (1 with bath).

$ Rates (including breakfast): £12 ($22.20) per person. Reduction for children. High tea £4 ($7.40) extra; dinner, £5 ($9.25). No credit cards.

  With enough advance notice, Mrs. Moreen Stephenson, the accommodating hostess here, will arrange to meet first-time visitors. At this country house 3 miles from town, guests will enjoy traditional home-cooking, and there is free laundry. The centrally heated modern bungalow counts one large family room among its nice guest rooms, all of which are on the ground floor.

WHERE TO EAT

ARMAGH TOWN

The **Cellar Lounge,** 55 Thomas Street, Armagh (tel. 0861/525147), serves good pub grub for about £3 ($5.55) Monday through Saturday from 11:30am to 11pm and on Sunday from 12:30 to 2:30pm and 7 to 10pm.

BANNISTERS, 147 Railway St., Armagh. Tel. 0861/522103.
   Cuisine: GRILLS. **Reservations:** Not required.
$ Prices: Lunch £5–£7 ($9.25–$12.95); dinner £10–£15 ($18.50–$27.75). No credit cards.
   Open: Lunch Mon–Sat noon–2pm; dinner Mon–Sat 6–9:30pm.

   This fully licensed eatery serves steaks, pork, lamb, chicken, and seafood in a relaxed, informal setting. Popular with locals as well as visitors.

PORTADOWN

There's good pub grub at **Garry's Bar,** 48 Bridge Street, Portadown (tel. 0762/334450), served Monday through Saturday from 11:30am to 11pm and on Sunday from 11:30am to 2pm and 7 to 10pm, at prices of around £3 ($5.55).

CHAPTER 23

COUNTIES TYRONE & FERMANAGH

1. COUNTY TYRONE
2. COUNTY FERMANAGH

Counties Tyrone and Fermanagh offer a veritable cornucopia of scenic beauty, from County Tyrone's mountains, gentle hills, glens, river valleys, and moorlands to County Fermanagh's fantastic lake-and-river system.

1. COUNTY TYRONE

The majestic Sperrin Mountains in the northern region near the County Derry border are County Tyrone's crowning glory. Farther south and east, the land levels out to rolling hills and level plains.

SEEING THE COUNTY

The ✪ **Sperrin Mountains** are terrific walking territory, bringing you face to face with such native inhabitants as golden plover, red grouse, and thousands of sheep, as well as friendly turf cutters getting ready for winter cold.

If you can spare half a day for this special part of Northern Ireland, take B47 from Draperstown and drive 10 miles west to the village of Sperrin, leave the car by the pub, and walk north along the road into the hills towards Sawel. After 2 miles, leave the road and make for the summit (about an hour's walk) and views of Lough Neagh, the Foyle estuary, and the Mournes. Continue west on the ridge to Dart Mountain, about half an hour away, then turn south for the 45-minute walk to the village of Cranagh, where you'll surely want to spend time in the **Sperrin Heritage Centre,** 274 Glenelly Road, Cranagh, Gortin (tel. 06626/48142). There are natural-history and gold-mining exhibits (you may want to hire a Klondike-style gold pan and try your luck), a craft shop, and a café. Another 45 minutes will bring you back to your car (with a stop at the pub if you've worked up a terrible thirst).

Three miles north of Omagh, on A5, the ✪ **Ulster-American Folk Park** (tel. 0662/3292) is an outdoor museum that has as its main theme the history of 18th- and 19th-century emigration from Ulster to North America. Life in rural Ulster and in the New World is re-created through exhibits that include the ancestral home of the Mellon family of Pittsburgh, whose forefathers were from Ulster and who endowed the folk park. There's a pioneer farm and gallery exhibitions. In summer, it's open daily from 11am to 6:30pm; in other months, Monday through Friday from 10:30am to 5pm. There's a small admission charge.

WHERE TO STAY & EAT

CRANAGH

MR. & MRS. BENNIE CONWAY, 254 Glenelly Rd., Cranagh, Plumbridge BT79 8LS, Co. Tyrone. Tel. Gortin 06626/48334. 3 rms (none with bath).

$ Rates (including breakfast): £11.50 ($21.30) per person. Reductions for children. No credit cards.

The Conways' chalet-type farmhouse sits on a 22-acre farm on B47 east of Plumbridge, 13 miles west of Draperstown, overlooking the Glenelly River and the Sperrin Mountains. Guest rooms are quite attractive and comfortable, and all have sinks and are on the ground floor. Washing and ironing facilities are available for guests, and baby-sitting can be arranged.

OMAGH

GREENMOUNT LODGE, 58 Greenmount Rd., Gortaclare, Omagh BT79 0YE, Co. Tyrone. Tel. Fintona 0662/841325. 6 rms (4 with bath).
$ Rates (including breakfast): £14 ($25.90) single; £25 ($46.25) double. Reductions for children. High tea £7 ($12.95) extra; dinner £10 ($18.50). No credit cards.

Set on a 150-acre farm 8 miles southeast of Omagh on A5, this is a large two-story farmhouse with nicely appointed guest rooms, all with sinks; four bedrooms are family rooms. Mrs. Frances Reid, the friendly hostess, is a superb cook and evening meals are a delight.

Worth the Extra Money

ROYAL ARMS HOTEL, Main St., Omagh BT78 1BA, Co. Tyrone. Tel. 0662/24363. Fax 0662/245011. 21 rms (all with bath). TV TEL
$ Rates (including breakfast): £27.50 ($50.87) single; £49.50 ($91.55) double. Reductions for children and seniors. MC, V.

Convenience, comfort, and a friendly, accommodating staff make this an ideal base. Family owned and operated, it exudes a homey warmth, and there's also an attractive lounge, a coffee shop, a hairdressing salon, and a travel agency. All 21 bedrooms are nicely appointed and comfortably furnished, with trouser press, tea/coffee maker, and hairdryer.

Dining/Entertainment: There's an old-world charm about the Tavern Lounge and the adjoining dining room, and the menu in both specializes in traditional Irish dishes (beef, lamb, chicken) and seafood. Lunch is served daily from 12:30 to 2:30pm, with pub grub in the Tavern Lounge at about £3 ($5.55) and a more extensive offering in the restaurant for £5.25 to £7 ($9.70 to $12.95). Dinner hours are 5:30 to 9:30pm Monday through Saturday, until 8:30pm on Sunday, with a choice of pub grub at £3 ($5.55) or à la carte selections at £10 to £15 ($18.50 to $27.75).

BALLYGAWLEY

THE GRANGE, 15 Grange Rd., Ballygawley BT70 2HD, Co. Tyrone. Tel. 06625/66266 or 68053. 3 rms (1 with bath).
$ Rates (including breakfast): £11 ($20.35) per person. Reduction for children. No credit cards. **Closed:** Nov–Mar.

There's loads of character in this charming little cottage near the Ballygawley roundabout and the Folk Park. It dates back to 1720, but has been thoroughly modernized, even to central heating. Mrs. Lyttle is hostess here, and her guest rooms (one is a family room with private facilities) all are nicely done up. Washing and ironing facilities are on hand, and Mrs. Lyttle welcomes small children.

2. COUNTY FERMANAGH

County Fermanagh might well be called Northern Ireland's Lake Country, although by rights it's the River Erne from which that name would derive. It winds through the center of the county, expanding into the large Upper and Lower Lough Erne, both studded with islands. In the northwest, County Fermanagh touches the shore of Lough Melvin, and in the hills to the west are nestled Upper and Lower Lough Macnean.

SEEING THE COUNTY

The **River Erne and its Upper and Lower Loughs** are tourist centers for County Fermanagh. The river and the loughs are dotted with interesting and historical islands, and a holiday cruising their waters is a very special experience. You can book a variety of watery accommodations in Enniskillen, and the **Lakeland Visitor Centre,** Shore Road, Enniskillen (tel. Enniskillen 0365/23110), publishes a detailed "Holidays Afloat and Ashore" booklet with illustrations of many of the cruisers available. To learn more about this fascinating part of Northern Ireland (some of the mountainy country around the loughs is quite mysterious and wild, and there are historic monastic ruins on many of the islands), go by the Visitor Centre and browse through the mountain of literature they can provide to help you plan an itinerary.

An experience not to be missed in this part of the province is the ☺ **waterbus cruise** that departs from the Round O pier in Enniskillen for 2-hour cruises, some of which stop at Devenish Island in Lower Lough Erne, where there's a perfect 12th-century round tower, ruined Augustinian abbey, and intricately carved 15th-century high cross. Fares are £2.50 ($4.65) for adults, £1 ($1.85) for ages under 14. For sailing times and booking, contact **Erne Tours,** 42 Meadow Lane, Sligo Road, Enniskillen.

In Enniskillen, the **Royal Inniskilling Fusiliers Regimental Museum and the County Museum** are in the Castle Keep, Castle Barracks (tel. Enniskillen 0365/325050). The castle keep dates from the 16th century, was built by the Maguires, and was remodeled in the 18th century. The Regimental Museum features battle trophies of the Dragoons and Fusiliers from the Napoleonic Wars, arms, and a host of colorful uniforms. In the County Museum, the history of the county is traced through archeological relics from the Middle Stone Age to the end of the early Christian period. It's open daily from 10am to 12:30pm and 2 to 5pm (weekends only in winter), and there's a small admission charge. Hours are subject to change, so call ahead.

On the shores of Lough Coole, about a mile and a half southeast of Enniskillen via A4, **Castle Coole** (tel. 0365/22690) is a splendid neoclassical mansion set in its own parkland. The house was completed in 1798 and has a Palladian front, fine furnishings, and exquisite plasterwork. It's open April through September, Friday through Wednesday from 2 to 6pm.

Another stately home worth a visit is ☺ **Florence Court** (tel. 0365/82497), about 8 miles southwest of Enniskillen via A4 and A32. The three-story 18th-century mansion has pavilions on each side, connected to the house by open, arched walkways. The woodland setting is as romantic as the house, with a landscaped "pleasure garden" and walled garden. Open April through September, from noon to 6pm.

Don't miss a guided tour of the ☺ **Belleek chinaware factory** (tel. 0365/65501) in the little village of Belleek right on the County Donegal border on B52. It's not only interesting, but fun—the skilled workers always welcome a bit of a chat with visitors. There are a Tourist Centre, museum, restaurant, and factory tours, offered Monday through Friday from 9am to 6pm, on Saturday from 10am to 6pm, and on Sunday from 2 to 6pm.

One of the most awesome sights in all of Europe is the **Marble Arch Caves,** Marbank Scenic Loop Road, Florencecourt, County Fermanagh (tel. 0365/828855), signposted 8 miles southwest of Enniskillen (A4 and A32). Your underground boat travels through this vast cave system, a spectacular underground world of rivers, waterfalls, lakes, lofty chambers, and winding passages. It's chilly down there, if not downright cold, so bring along a sweater, plus good walking shoes with low heels for dealing with uneven surfaces. The caves open daily at 11am (depending on the weather) from Easter to October, and closing times vary. Indeed, all these hours can vary—best call ahead to be sure the caves are open. Adults pay £3 ($5.55); children, £1.50 ($2.75); students £2 ($3.70). A family ticket is £7.50 ($13.85).

WHERE TO STAY & EAT

ENNISKILLEN

MANVILLE HOUSE, Aughnablaney, Letter, Co. Fermanagh. Tel. Kesh 03656/31668. 7 rms (3 with bath).

$ Rates (including breakfast): £15 ($27.75) per person. No credit cards.

About 12 miles from good beaches, this is the centrally heated, lakeside home of Mrs. Pearl Graham. There are marvelous views of Lough Erne and the Sligo Mountains, and there's good fishing right at hand. All the well-appointed guest rooms have good views, and Mrs. Graham very much enjoys visitors from America, greeting each with a warm welcome.

Manville House is 20 miles from Enniskillen and 9 miles west of Kesh; take A47 from Kesh and turn right at the signpost for Letter.

Worth the Extra Money

KILLYHEVLIN HOTEL, Dublin Rd., Enniskillen BT74 4AU, Co. Fermanagh. Tel. 0365/323481. Fax 0365/324726. 24 rms (all with bath), 13 self-catering chalets. TV TEL

$ Rates (including breakfast): £50 ($92.50) single; £70 ($129.50) double. Reduction for children and seniors. Weekend rates available. Self-catering chalets £220–£275 ($407–$509) per week, depending on season. MC, V.

★ This lovely hotel sits 1 mile from the town center on the shores of Lough Erne, with marvelous views of the gardens and lake. Guest rooms, which are spacious and attractively furnished, all have a window wall that opens onto a balcony. An especially good bargain is the weekend rate, which includes 2 nights' bed-and-breakfast, dinner, lounge entertainment on Saturday, and lunch on Sunday. Early booking is essential for the two-bedroom chalets.

Dining/Entertainment: The glass-walled lounge overlooks the lake, with food service from the adjoining dining room. Fresh fish and seafood are featured on the menu, as well as locally produced beef, pork, and lamb, and there's a good selection of salad plates both hot and cold. Lunch, which is served from 12:30 to 2:30pm, will run around £5 ($9.25); dinner, from 6:30 to 10pm, £10 to £15 ($18.50 to $27.75). There's live entertainment in the lounge on weekends.

BELLEEK

Self-Catering

THE CARLTON COTTAGES, Belleek, Co. Fermanagh. Tel. 0365/658181. 14 cottages.

$ Rates: £160–£335 ($296–$620) per week, depending on season. Weekend rates sometimes available. No credit cards.

These well-planned three-bedroom cottages are set in wooded grounds at the edge of the village on the banks of the River Erne. It's hard to imagine a more beautiful setting, and each cottage is fitted with twin beds, bath and shower, fully equipped kitchen, and a large lounge with an open-hearth fireplace. Patio doors open to the outside.

APPENDIX

A. GLOSSARY

COMMON GAELIC WORDS

ard height
augh (au) ford
bally or baile (balla) town, place, or farm
bearna (barna) gap between hills
boher (bo-her) road
cashel castle
carn heap of stones
carraig or corrig boulder
cahir (care) castle
cill or kill church
cnoc or knock hill
currach small keelless boat
dun (done) fort or protected house
druim or drum ridge
inis, inch, or ennis island or riverside field
lios (lis) or lis circular fort
moin or moyne (mine) bog
rath circular fort
skerry rock
slieve (sleeve) hill
teach (chock) house
tobar or tubber well
tra or tray beach
tulach, tullow, or tully small hill
uibh (iv) family or tribe
uisce (ish-ca), isk, or isky water

ARCHEOLOGICAL TERMS

Clochans ("beehives"): These remarkable stone buildings of corbel construction were erected without mortar as tiny oratories, mostly in western Ireland where wood was not a readily available building material. Through the centuries, those that have survived have remained perfectly waterproof, and they are considered outstanding examples of early construction expertise.

Court cairns: Found mostly in the northern regions of Ireland, these earliest megalithic chambered tombs derive their name from the fact that there is generally a covered gallery for burial, with one or more unroofed courts, or forecourts, for rituals.

Crannogs: These artificial islands were constructed in lakes or marshy places, and have even earlier origins than the ring forts. Look for them in the midland counties and County Clare.

Dolmens: Standing stones (usually three) surmounted by a massive capstone, they are one of the earliest forms of megalithic tombs that probably date from 3000 to 2000 B.C.

Ogham Stones: Standing stones inscribed with memorial inscriptions in Ogham script. The earliest known Irish script, it is formed of lines representing twenty letters of the Latin alphabet.

Passage graves: A legacy of Ireland's Neolithic forebears, these are great stone tombs entered through a long passageway (the one at Newgrange is 65 feet in length), with a large burial chamber. No one knows for certain exactly who was entombed in them.

Ring forts: Essentially dwelling places, these circular enclosures sometimes were built within earthen walls, sometimes behind stone walls. Within those walls was some manner of house—wood, wattle-and-daub, or stone—few of which have survived, although some 30,000 rings are spotted all over Ireland and called by a number of names—rath, lios, dun, caher, and cashel. The large number still to be found is due to the fact that this form of protected dwelling originated as early as the Bronze Age and continued to be built right up until the Norman invasion.

Stone circles: It is thought that these early Bronze Age relics served as temples of worship, as did large earthen circles.

B. CONVERSION TABLES

CURRENCY

At this writing $1 = approximately 57p (or IR£1 = $1.75), and this was the rate of exchange used to calculate dollar values of the Irish punt (rounded off).

The pound sterling in Northern Ireland has been calculated at a rate of £1 = $1.85.

These rates fluctuate and may not be the same when you travel to Ireland. Therefore the following tables should be used only as guides:

THE IRISH PUNT & THE DOLLAR

IR£	U.S.	IR£	U.S.
.50	.88	22.50	39.38
1	1.75	25	43.75
2	3.50	27.50	48.13
2.50	4.38	30	52.50
3	5.25	35	61.25
5	8.75	40	70.00
8	14.00	50	87.50
10	17.50	75	131.25
15	26.25	100	175.00
20	35.00		

THE POUND STERLING & THE DOLLAR

£	$U.S.	£	$U.S.
.50	.93	22.50	41.63
1	1.85	25	46.25
2	3.70	27.50	50.88
2.50	4.62	30	55.50
3	5.55	35	64.75
5	9.25	40	74.00
8	14.80	50	92.50
10	18.50	75	138.75
15	27.75	100	185.00
20	37.00		

METRIC SYSTEM
LENGTH

1 millimeter (mm)	=	0.04 inches (*or* less than ¹⁄₁₆ inch)
1 centimeter (cm)	=	0.39 inches (*or* just under ½ inch)
1 meter (m)	=	1.09 yards (*or* about 39 inches)
1 kilometer (km)	=	0.62 mile (*or* about ⅔ mile)

To convert kilometers to miles, multiply the number of kilometers by .62. Also use to convert kilometers per hour (kmph) to miles per hour (m.p.h.).
To convert miles to kilometers, multiply the number of miles by 1.61. Also use to convert from m.p.h. to kmph.

CAPACITY

1 liter (l)	=	33.92 ounces	=	2.1 pints	=	1.06 quarts
	=	.26 U.S. gallons				
1 Imperial gallon	=	1.2 U.S. gallons				

To convert liters to U.S. gallons, multiply the number of liters by .26.
To convert U.S. gallons to liters, multiply the number of gallons by 3.79.
To convert Imperial gallons to U.S. gallons, multiply the number of Imperial gallons by 1.2.
To convert U.S. gallons to Imperial gallons, multiply the number of U.S. gallons by .83.

WEIGHT

1 gram (g)	=	.035 ounces (*or* about a paperclip's weight)
1 kilogram (kg)	=	35.2 ounces
	=	2.2 pounds

To convert kilograms to pounds, multiply the number of kilos by 2.2.
To convert pounds to kilograms, multiply the number of pounds by .45.

AREA

$$1 \text{ hectare } (100m^2) \quad = \quad 2.47 \text{ acres}$$

To convert hectares to acres, take the number of hectares and multiply by 2.47 (for example, $20ha \times 2.47 = 49.4$ acres).
To convert acres to hectares, take the number of acres and multiply by .41 (for example, 40 acres $\times$ .41 = 16.4 ha).

TEMPERATURE

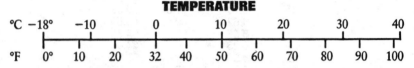

To convert degrees Celsius to degrees Fahrenheit, multiply °C by 9, divide by 5, and add 32 (example: $20°C \times 9/5 + 32 = 68°F$).
To convert degrees Fahrenheit to degrees Celsius, subtract 32 from °F, multiply by 5, then divide by 9 (example: $85°F - 32 \times 5/9 = 29.4°C$).

C. MILEAGE CHART

	Athlone	Belfast	Cork	Derry	Donegal	Dublin	Dundalk	Galway	Kilkenny	Killarney	Limerick	Portlaoise	Roscommon	Rosslare Harbour	Shannon Airport	Sligo	Waterford	Wexford	Wicklow
Athlone		141	136	130	114	78	90	58	78	144	75	46	20	130	83	73	108	117	110
Belfast	141		264	73	112	104	52	190	177	271	201	157	139	205	215	128	207	192	136
Cork	136	264		266	250	160	202	130	92	54	65	108	156	129	80	209	78	116	166
Derry	130	73	266		43	147	97	169	208	274	204	175	131	247	218	84	238	235	179
Donegal	114	112	250	43		138	98	127	192	253	184	160	94	243	176	41	222	231	171
Dublin	78	104	160	147	138		53	136	73	192	123	52	91	101	138	135	98	88	32
Dundalk	90	52	202	97	98	53		148	123	219	150	94	94	153	165	104	151	141	85
Galway	58	190	130	169	127	136	148		107	120	65	93	51	170	57	86	137	157	168
Kilkenny	78	177	92	208	192	73	123	107		123				62	85	152	30	50	77
Killarney	144	271	54	274	253	192	219	120	123		69	123	164	171	84	213	120	158	208
Limerick	75	201	65	204	184	123	150	65		69		69	94	131	15	144	80	118	141
Portlaoise	46	157	108	175	160	52	94	93		123	69		66	84	86	119	62	71	77
Roscommon	20	139	156	131	94	91	94	51		164	94	66		150	96	53	129	138	123
Rosslare Harbour	130	205	129	247	243	101	153	170	62	171	131	84	150		146	203	51	12	72
Shannon Airport	83	215	80	218	176	138	165	57	85	84	15	86	96	146		136	95	133	156
Sligo	73	128	209	84	41	135	104	86	152	213	144	119	53	203	136		182	191	162
Waterford	108	207	78	238	222	98	151	137	30	120	80	62	129	51	95	182		39	88
Wexford	117	192	116	235	231	88	141	157	50	158	118	71	138	12	133	191	39		56
Wicklow	110	136	166	179	171	32	85	168	77	208	141	77	123	72	156	162	88	56	

INDEX

GENERAL INFORMATION

IRISH REPUBLIC

NORTHERN IRELAND

DESTINATIONS

KEY TO ABBREVIATIONS: A = Apartment; B&B = Bed-and-Breakfast; CT = Cottage; D = Dormitory; F = Farmhouse; GH = Guesthouse; Hs = Hostel; Yh = Youth Hostel; * = an Author's favorite; $ = Super Special Value; W = Worth the Extra Bucks

NOW, SAVE MONEY ON ALL YOUR TRAVELS!
Join Frommer's™ Dollarwise® Travel Club

Saving money while traveling is never easy, which is why the **Dollarwise Travel Club** was formed 32 years ago to provide cost-cutting travel strategies, up-to-date travel information, and a sense of community for value-conscious travelers from all over the world.

In keeping with the money-saving concept, the annual membership fee is low—$20 for U.S. residents and $25 for residents of Canada, Mexico, and other countries—and is immediately exceeded by the value of your benefits, which include:

1. Any TWO books listed on the following pages;
2. Plus any ONE Frommer's City Guide;
3. A subscription to our quarterly newspaper, *The Dollarwise Traveler;*
4. A membership card that entitles you to purchase through the Club all Frommer's publications for 33% to 40% off their retail price.

The eight-page *Dollarwise Traveler* tells you about the latest developments in good-value travel worldwide and includes the following columns: **Hospitality Exchange** (for those offering and seeking hospitality in cities all over the world); and **Share-a-Trip** (for those looking for travel companions to share costs).

Aside from the various Frommer's Guides, the Gault Millau Guides, and the Real Guides you can also choose from our Special Editions, which include such titles as *Caribbean Hideaways* (the 100 most romantic places to stay in the Islands); and *Marilyn Wood's Wonderful Weekends* (a selection of the best mini-vacations within a 200-mile radius of New York City).

To join this Club, send the appropriate membership fee with your name and address to: Frommer's Dollarwise Travel Club, 15 Columbus Circle, New York, NY 10023. Remember to specify which single city guide and which two other guides you wish to receive in your initial package of member's benefits. Or tear out the pages, check off your choices, and send them to us with your membership fee.

FROMMER BOOKS
PRENTICE HALL TRAVEL   Date_____
15 COLUMBUS CIRCLE
NEW YORK, NY 10023

Friends: Please send me the books checked below.

FROMMER'S™ COMPREHENSIVE GUIDES
(Guides listing facilities from budget to deluxe, with emphasis on the medium-priced)

☐ Alaska $14.95	☐ Italy $19.00
☐ Australia $14.95	☐ Japan & Hong Kong $17.00
☐ Austria & Hungary $14.95	☐ Morocco $18.00
☐ Belgium, Holland & Luxembourg $14.95	☐ Nepal $18.00
☐ Bermuda & The Bahamas $17.00	☐ New England $17.00
☐ Brazil $14.95	☐ New Mexico $13.95
☐ California $18.00	☐ New York State $19.00
☐ Canada $16.00	☐ Northwest $16.95
☐ Caribbean $17.00	☐ Puerta Vallarta (avail. Feb. '92) $14.00
☐ Carolinas & Georgia $17.00	☐ Portugal, Madeira & the Azores $14.95
☐ Colorado (avail. Jan '92) $14.00	☐ Scandinavia $18.95
☐ Cruises (incl. Alaska, Carib, Mex, Hawaii,	☐ Scotland (avail. Feb. '92) $17.00
Panama, Canada & US) $16.00	☐ South Pacific $20.00
☐ Delaware, Maryland, Pennsylvania &	☐ Southeast Asia $14.95
the New Jersey Shore (avail. Jan. '92) . .$19.00	☐ Switzerland & Liechtenstein $19.00
☐ Egypt $14.95	☐ Thailand $20.00
☐ England $17.00	☐ Virginia (avail. Feb. '92) $14.00
☐ Florida $17.00	☐ Virgin Islands $13.00
☐ France $15.95	☐ USA $16.95
☐ Germany $18.00	

0891492

☐ Paris Rendez-Vous $10.95	☐ Travel Diary and Record Book. $5.95
☐ Swap and Go (Home Exchanging). $10.95	☐ Where to Stay USA (from $3 to $30 a night). $13.95

FROMMER'S TOURING GUIDES

(Color illustrated guides that include walking tours, cultural and historic sites, and practical information)

☐ Amsterdam. $10.95	☐ New York $10.95
☐ Australia $12.95	☐ Paris $8.95
☐ Brazil $10.95	☐ Rome. $10.95
☐ Egypt. $8.95	☐ Scotland. $9.95
☐ Florence. $8.95	☐ Thailand. $12.95
☐ Hong Kong $10.95	☐ Turkey $10.95
☐ London $12.95	☐ Venice $8.95

GAULT MILLAU

(The only guides that distinguish the truly superlative from the merely overrated)

☐ The Best of Chicago $15.95	☐ The Best of Los Angeles $16.95
☐ The Best of Florida $17.00	☐ The Best of New England $15.95
☐ The Best of France $16.95	☐ The Best of New Orleans. $16.95
☐ The Best of Germany $18.00	☐ The Best of New York $16.95
☐ The Best of Hawaii $16.95	☐ The Best of Paris $16.95
☐ The Best of Hong Kong $16.95	☐ The Best of San Francisco $16.95
☐ The Best of Italy. $16.95	☐ The Best of Thailand. $17.95
☐ The Best of London $16.95	☐ The Best of Toronto $17.00

☐ The Best of Washington, D.C. $16.95

THE REAL GUIDES

(Opinionated, politically aware guides for youthful budget-minded travelers)

☐ Amsterdam $9.95	☐ Mexico. $11.95
☐ Berlin. $11.95	☐ Morocco $12.95
☐ Brazil $13.95	☐ New York $9.95
☐ California & the West Coast $11.95	☐ Paris $9.95
☐ Czechoslovakia $13.95	☐ Peru. $12.95
☐ France $12.95	☐ Poland $13.95
☐ Germany $13.95	☐ Portugal $10.95
☐ Greece. $13.95	☐ San Francisco $11.95
☐ Guatemala $13.95	☐ Scandinavia $14.95
☐ Hong Kong $11.95	☐ Spain $12.95
☐ Hungary $12.95	☐ Turkey $12.95
☐ Ireland $12.95	☐ Venice $11.95
☐ Italy. $13.95	☐ Women Travel $12.95
☐ Kenya. $12.95	☐ Yugoslavia $12.95

ORDER NOW!

In U.S. include $2 shipping UPS for 1st book; $1 ea. add'l book. Outside U.S. $3 and $1, respectively.

Allow four to six weeks for delivery in U.S., longer outside U.S. We discourage rush order service, but orders arriving with shipping fees plus a $15 surcharge will be handled as rush orders.

Enclosed is my check or money order for $_____

NAME _____

ADDRESS _____

CITY _____ STATE _____ ZIP _____

0891492